BRAZIL
GUIDE

ABOUT THIS GUIDEBOOK

The hotels, restaurants, attractions, agencies, guides and other establishments and services listed in the *Brazil Guide* were selected by designated reporters in the course of 360 days of travel and research. No compensation of any kind was accepted from the establishments mentioned. Sponsors MasterCard and Unicard Unibanco exercised no control over the content of this guide.

Restaurant price categories were established by calculating the price for the most popular choice plus a 10% service fee. Hotel prices are based on the daily rate for a double occupancy room.

Addresses, telephone numbers, business hours and prices were supplied by the establishments and verified and updated by the *Guide's* researchers. However, the *Guide* cannot be responsible for any inaccuracies or changes after the publication date (February, 2005). Please note that business hours and service prices are subject to constant changes due to high and low tourist seasons and should be confirmed in advance, whenever possible.

Before traveling, visitors are advised to consult the Highway Patrol (refer to Useful Information) for information regarding road conditions and toll fees along the proposed route.

Collaborators

Alex Atala, André Corrêa do Lago, Daniel Mason, Liz Calder, Marcos Caetano, Marcos Sá Corrêa, Nelson Motta, Niède Guidon, Nirlando Beirão, Ricardo Legorreta, Sebastião Salgado, Sergio Fingermann, Thomaz Souto Corrêa and Valentino

Sponsors

2005

BEĨ
Rua Dr. Renato Paes de Barros, 717 4º andar
CEP 04530-001 Itaim-Bibi São Paulo SP
Tel.: 55 (11) 3089-8855 Fax: 55 (11) 3089-8899
bei@bei.com.br

BRAZIL
GUIDE

BEĨ

PORTUGUESE EDITION

Editors
Cristina R. Durán, Daniel Nunes,
Roberta de Lucca and the BEÏ team

Reporting Coordinator
Regner Camilo

Reporting
Alessandro Greco, Angela Nunes, Betina Moura,
Natasha Madov, Neiva Silva, Rodrigo Tramontina,
Sergio Garcia, Thiago Lotufo and the BEÏ team

Advisors
Andréa Leite de Barros, Cândido Grangeiro,
Helena Artmann, Jorge Ferreira,
José Armênio de Brito Cruz, Marcelo Ferraz,
Sergio Fingermann and Suzana Facchini Granato

Translation
Paulo César Batista Castanheira and Renato Rezende

Editing
Cláudia Cantarin and José Carlos Pegorim

Proofreading
Ana Maria Barbosa, Carmen S. da Costa,
Telma Baeza Gonçalves Dias and Vera Caputo

Cover Illustration
Daniel Caballero

Photography Coordinator
Adriano Gambarini

Maps and Illustrations
Luiz Fernando Martini

Illustrations on pages 30, 31 and 322
Yili Rojas

Illustrations on page 112
Monica Negraes

Pen and Ink Drawings
Pedro de Kastro

Illustrations on pages 55-59, 130, 131 and 148
Sírio José Braz Cançado

Index
Renato Potenza and Vivian Miwa Matsushita

Fact Checking
BEÏ team

Image Digitalization and Processing
Litokromia Pre-press

Printing
RR Donnelley

ENGLISH EDITION

Project Consultant
Ben Harder

Editors
Mark Lutes and Knight Campbell

Translation
Ibycaba Traduções

Translation Coordination
Ângela Levy

Proofreading
Marcelo Pen and Carlos Alberto Inada

Index
Knight Campbell and Renato Potenza

Dados Internacionais de Catalogação na Publicação (CIP)
(Câmara Brasileira do Livro, SP, Brasil)

Unicard Unibanco Brazil Guide / [conception,
    editorial coordination, cover, graphic design and layout BEÏ ;
    translation Ibycaba Traduções ; photography coordinator
    Adriano Gambarini ; maps and illustrations Luiz Fernando Martini]. –
    São Paulo : BEÏ Comunicação, 2005.

Vários colaboradores.
Vários ilustradores.
Título original: Guia Unicard Unibanco Brasil.
ISBN 85-86518-47-6

1. Brasil – Descrição e viagens – Guias
2. Turismo – Brasil I. Gambarini, Adriano. II. Martini, Luiz Fernando.

05-1626   CDD-918.1

Índices para catálogo sistemático:

1. Brasil : Guias turísticos   918.1

TABLE OF CONTENTS

The *Brazil Guide* was created to introduce you to the best of Brazil and at the same time provide local historical, cultural and nature information. It has been organized in the following format:

The **introduction** discusses fundamental aspects of the country: history, ethnic makeup, cuisine, folk art, visual arts, fashion and design, architecture, motion pictures, music, football, Carnival, adventure sports and environment. Articles written by professionals and renowned personalities complement the information.

The guidebook is divided in geographical regions, according to Brazil's official political boundaries. Different **destinations** or arrival points are suggested for each region. We have indicated 22 unforgettable destinations – in most cases cities equipped with airports and complete infrastructure. In some cases, however, we have suggested local destinations of great interest that are removed from the large centers. These locations can be reached by highways or roadways from the **major cities**, which are easily accessible and offer good lodging options.

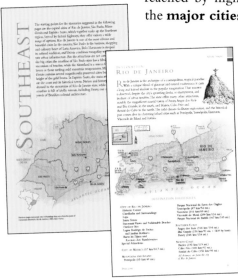

The **itineraries** for each destination are trips of a few days duration. The itineraries include short, one day excursions where we have indicated the most interesting attractions.

Maps and illustrations help you plan trips or excursions. In various cities we have indicated walking tours, directed by simple maps with point to point indications; the important cultural and architectural buildings are indicated by numbers and described in detail. However, the map numbering system, while highlighting the attractions that should be visited, does not necessarily follow a sequential route.

Sidebars with additional information about the local culture are found throughout the guidebook. Hotels, inns and restaurants that are especially pleasant or interesting have been highlighted in the sidebars indicated as **Our Recommendation**. Addresses and telephone numbers for the restaurants are found along with the description in the sidebar. Hotel telephone numbers are included in the listing at the end of the guidebook along with other complementary information.

In the section, **Hotels, Restaurants and Services**, at the end of the guidebook, color coded regional alphabetical listings of all cities are included for easy reference. The listing is not intended as a complete account of all establishments but rather to indicate those that we considered most interesting, pointing out their advantages and disadvantages.

Please note that the guide abides by the official Brazilian geographical divisions, but the itineraries were planned for practicability and touristic appeal. For example, the city of São Cristovão in Sergipe, is found under the destination of Salvador, Bahia with an itinerary beginning in the capital city of Bahia, Salvador. Likewise for the city of João Pessoa in Paraíba, with an itinerary beginning in the city of Recife.

The organized and practical layout of the *Brazil Guide* makes it a valuable travel companion, able to suggest and advise – a guidebook in the widest sense of the word.

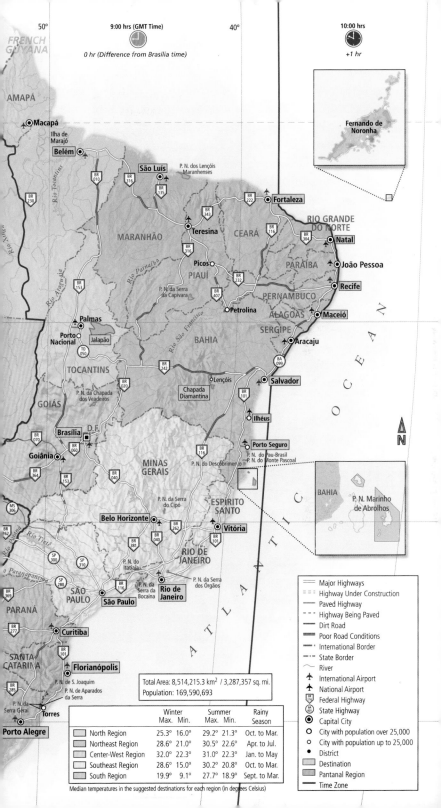

FRENCH GUYANA

AMAPÁ

50°

9:00 hrs (GMT Time)

0 hr (Difference from Brasília time)

40°

10:00 hrs

+1 hr

Fernando de Noronha

Macapá

Ilha de Marajó

Belém

Rio Tocantins

São Luís

P. N. dos Lençóis Maranhenses

BR 010

BR 316

BR 135

BR 222

Fortaleza

BR 343

RIO GRANDE DO NORTE

BR 230

MARANHÃO

Teresina

BR 316

CEARÁ

BR 116

BR 304

Natal

BR 153

Rio Parnaíba

Picos

PIAUÍ

BR 232

PARAÍBA

João Pessoa

Rio Araguaia

BR 407

P. N. da Serra da Capivara

PERNAMBUCO

Recife

Rio Xingu

Palmas

Porto Nacional

Jalapão

TO 050

BAHIA

Rio São Francisco

Petrolina

ALAGOAS

Maceió

SERGIPE

Aracaju

TOCANTINS

BR 242

BA 099

BR 020

P. N. da Chapada dos Veadeiros

Lençóis

Chapada Diamantina

BR 101

Salvador

GOIÁS

Ilhéus

O C E A N

Brasília

D.F.

BR 070

BR 060

BR 116

Porto Seguro

P. N. do Pau-Brasil
P. N. do Monte Pascoal

Goiânia

BR 364

BR 153

BR 040

P. N. do Descobrimento

MINAS GERAIS

BAHIA

P. N. Marinho de Abrolhos

MS 306

P. N. da Serra do Cipó

ESPÍRITO SANTO

BR 262

Belo Horizonte

BR 262

BR 040

Vitória

BR 101

BR 262

Rio Paraná

Rio Tietê

SP 300

SP 310

P. N. do Itatiaia

BR 381

RIO DE JANEIRO

P. N. da Serra dos Órgãos

BR 369

SP 280

SP 116

P. N. da Serra da Bocaina

Rio de Janeiro

SÃO PAULO

São Paulo

PARANÁ

BR 277

Curitiba

BR 101

SANTA CATARINA

Florianópolis

BR 285

P. N. de S. Joaquim

P. N. de Aparados da Serra

P. N. da Serra Geral

Torres

Porto Alegre

A T L A N T I C

N

Total Area: 8,514,215.3 km² / 3,287,357 sq. mi.
Population: 169,590,693

	Winter Max.	Min.	Summer Max.	Min.	Rainy Season
North Region	25.3°	16.0°	29.2°	21.3°	Oct. to Mar.
Northeast Region	28.6°	21.0°	30.5°	22.6°	Apr. to Jul.
Center-West Region	32.0°	22.3°	31.0°	22.3°	Jan. to May
Southeast Region	28.6°	15.0°	30.2°	20.8°	Oct. to Mar.
South Region	19.9°	9.1°	27.7°	18.9°	Sept. to Mar.

Median temperatures in the suggested destinations for each region (in degrees Celsius)

Major Highways
Highway Under Construction
Paved Highway
Highway Being Paved
Dirt Road
Poor Road Conditions
International Border
State Border
River
International Airport
National Airport
Federal Highway
State Highway
Capital City
City with population over 25,000
City with population up to 25,000
District
Destination
Pantanal Region
Time Zone

HISTORY

In the five hundred years that separate pre-Columbian Pindorama from modern-day Brazil, the country has evolved through colony to empire, monarchy to republic, and dictatorship to democracy. The nation's self-reinvention shows no sign of slowing.

In all the history books, the story of Brazil begins at the same point – Porto Seguro in Bahia. It was there that a fleet led by Pedro Álvares Cabral anchored on April 22, 1500. The Portuguese stayed for ten days while gathering information and exchanging gifts with the Indians. However, the discoverers found evidence of neither the spices nor the precious metals they sought and, having no idea of the size of the land they'd found, departed what they called "Santa Cruz Island".

The land that the Indians called *Pindorama* – "land of the palm trees" – was luxuriant but oriented toward subsistence. The only item that could offer economic return in trade was the pigment-containing brazilwood that covered vast areas. Within a short time, the red dye from this plentiful wood was supplying the textile industries of England and Holland. It was the Indians who logged the forests of what was now called "Land of the Santa Cruz". They exchanged it at coastal trading posts for trinkets, tools and cloth. This wood gave the new territory its lasting name. "Brazil" comes from the French *brésil*, derived from the Tuscan *verzino*, which was the name of the reddish wood from Asia previously used for dye in Europe. Within thirty years of the land's discovery, this term had supplanted other official names for the region.

The Portuguese realized that their trading posts could not maintain control of the new land, which other foreigner powers also coveted for its brazilwood. In the first decades of the 16th century, the Portuguese Crown sent Martim Afonso de Sousa to establish a colony, starting with the construction of the two villages of São Vicente and Santo André da Borda do Campo, later São Paulo. In 1494, the Tordesilhas Treaty between Portugal and Spain divided the world in two hemispheres, separated by an imaginary line, with the lands to the west being Spanish and those to the east Portuguese. The land between Brazil's coast and the boundary established by that treaty was divided from north to south in fifteen large tracts called *capitanias* and grant-

1568 map. José and Guita Mindlin Library Inventory

13

ed to noblemen called *donatários*. The system proved a fiasco. The only three to prosper were Pernambuco, Bahia and São Vicente.

THE SUGAR ECONOMY

With the failure of the hereditary system of *capitanias*, the Portuguese
Crown decided to take a new approach to their administration of the
colony. In 1549 Tomé de Sousa was appointed Governor General of
Brazil, and founded the first capital – the city of Salvador in Bahia. The
new administrator authorized the exploitation of brazilwood and established sugarcane mills. At the time, sugar was a valuable commodity in Europe, where it was sold by the gram in apothecaries.

Sugar production sustained the Portuguese administration and determined the organization of social and economic life for most of the
colony. Its legacy lasted for centuries: export-oriented economic
monoculture, based on large rural properties and dependent on African
slave labor. The sugar mill was the linchpin of this industry. The crush-
ers, ovens and other equipment for sugar production were located in
the midst of immense sugarcane fields. The sugar baron lived in the "*big
house*", while slaves resided in separate quarters. The divide between
the "*big house*" and slave quarters, and between barons and slaves,
echoed through all aspects of colonial Brazilian society.

There were, however, also some poor freemen, who formed a
group of respected, specialized workers. They lived on plantations in
the shadow of the sugar baron or settled in the towns, which were
simple administrative centers or ports that serviced trading ships.

THE NATIVE INHABITANTS

To establish the sugarcane crops, the Portuguese colonizers took
over land formerly inhabited by native Indians. Prior to the rise of
African slave labour, it was the Indians, principally the Tupi-Guarani
peoples, who cleared the land. The Tupi-Guarani around two thousand years ago had started large-scale migrations from the Amazon
basin to the South and to the North and Northeastern coastline, driving their enemies into the interior of the country. Their history is
fragmentary, having been surmised from the discovery of material remains and artifacts. The people left no written records.

Throughout Brazilian history the Portuguese, French, Dutch and
Spanish exploited disputes between different indigenous peoples. At
other times they encouraged the local native tribes to join forces to
fight off invaders. Between 1555 and 1567, the Tamoios Confedera-

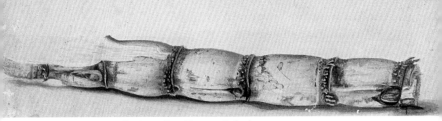

Sugarcane, Debret. Watercolor, Castro Maya Museums Collection

tion challenged Portuguese dominion over a portion of the coast that extended from Bertioga, in São Paulo, to Espírito Santo. From 1683 to 1710 the Janduís Confederation led an Indian uprising in Ceará and Rio Grande do Norte. Led by Chief Ajuricaba, the Manáos Indians from the Rio Negro, in the Amazon basin, resisted being captured as slaves during the first quarter of the 18th century. In 1767, the Guarani living in Jesuit missions, which were created to convert the natives, resisted being relocated to the Spanish side until they were defeated by Portuguese and Spanish troops.

The history of the Brazilian Indian is one of resistance – and extermination. The indigenous population was an estimated 2 to 5 million at the time of European discovery. This number has been reduced to roughly 700,000 today.

EUROPEAN INVASIONS

The Dutch were a constant threat to Portuguese dominion. First they tried to invade Bahia, where they were defeated in 1625. In 1630 they tried again, this time in Pernambuco, the world's largest sugar producer. Brazilian Holland, led by Count Maurice of Nassau, peacefully absorbed the local Portuguese inhabitants. Artists such as Frans Post and Albert Eckhout portrayed scenes of a prosperous and organized Dutch colony. When expelled in 1654, the Dutch took sugarcane seedlings with them to the Antilles. Portugal would retain the Brazilian territory, but would never again dominate the world sugar market.

The Dutch and the Indians weren't the only challenges to Portuguese dominion. English pirates prowled the South American coastline. And from the beginning, brazilwood attracted French merchants, who established trading posts on the coast in 1504, and in 1555 founded the *França Antártica* colony. In the course of Portuguese efforts to dislodge the French, Estácio de Sá founded Rio de Janeiro in 1565. The French were eventually expelled in 1567, but they returned in 1594 to Maranhão, which they left, except for the town of São Luís, in 1615. The final French attempts to invade Brazil were in 1710 and 1711.

EXPANDING THE FRONTEIRS

Brute force defined the borders of Brazil. During the first decades of occupation, Portuguese settlements stayed close to the coast. The interior was covered by dense forests and inhabited by threatening savages – and in the vivid medieval imaginations of the conquerors, perhaps even monsters and ghosts. In 1616, the Portuguese discovered the mouth of the Amazon river, where they constructed the Presépio fort, the origin of Belém. The frontier expanded to encompass territory that, by the Tordesilhas Treaty, belonged to Spain. The same process occurred in the South. Expeditions organized and funded by the Portuguese Crown (*entradas*) and by private individuals (*bandeiras*) left São Paulo and penetrated far inland in search of gold, precious stones and prospective slaves. The *bandeirantes* went as far west as the Paraguay river, where they even assaulted Jesuit missions in pursuit of Indians as slaves, and they also invaded missionary villages on Spanish territory. The Portuguese headed south from Rio de Janeiro and founded the colony of Sacramento on the opposite bank of the Prata river. During the 18th century, a series of treaties expanded the area of the colony from the original 2.5 million km² (1 million sq. mi.) to more than 8 million km² (3 million sq. mi.).

THE GOLD RUSH

Toward the end of the 17th century, *bandeirantes* discovered the first gold and precious stone deposits in Minas Gerais, Goiás and Mato Grosso. The discovery moved the colony's focus from the sugar-producing coastal regions to the newly discovered gold-mining areas, which attracted intense interest from both sides of the ocean.

A population explosion was just one consequence of the gold rush. Gold also fostered an urbanization boom and generated a flow of trade to supply the mining towns with basic necessities. The Portuguese Crown quickly implemented strategies to control the exploitation of wealth. All gold was to be sent to official foundries for weighing and casting, and one fifth of all gold was retained for the Portuguese treasury. Heavy taxation and rigid controls generated growing resentment among miners, which peaked in 1789 with the rebellion known as the *Inconfidência Mineira*. The government violently suppressed the movement and exiled most sympathizers. An unfortunate second lieutenant named Tiradentes was hanged. Only years later did the Republic recognize Tiradentes as a martyr, a symbol of the struggle for freedom.

While significant, the *Inconfidência* was by no means the first rebellion in the colony. During the 16th and 17th centuries, Portugal faced a series of local uprisings, including some among African slaves. The 18th century brought others, growing larger and developing an anti-outsider bent. Through these conflicts, a new identity emerged: the Brazilian, a person born in Brazil or who had immigrated, and no longer felt Portuguese.

BRAZIL, SEAT OF AN EMPIRE

In 1808, the Portuguese royal family took refuge in Brazil, fleeing the threat of the invasion of Lisbon by Napoleon's troops. In 1815, the colony became the official seat of the Portuguese Empire. The Royal Court's arrival transformed Rio de Janeiro, which had been Brazil's capital since 1763. Dom João VI opened Brazilian ports for trade with friendly nations – especially England – and encouraged visits by European scientists and artists. In 1816, after the fall of Napoleon, a group of French artists immigrated to Brazil. Known as the French Mission, this group included the artist Jean-Baptiste Debret and the architect Grandjean de Montigny, and they proved to have great influence on their adopted nation's visual arts.

In 1821, Dom João VI returned to Portugal, leaving his son Pedro as the prince regent. The Brazil that he departed had been changed forever from the one where he had come to stay.

Procession to kiss the hand of Dom João VI. National Library Foundation Collection

INDEPENDENCE

The conflicting economic interests of Portugal and the Brazilians drove the separatist movement that culminated in Dom Pedro's refusal to obey orders to return to Portugal. On September 7, 1822, on the banks of Ipiranga creek in São Paulo, the prince regent declared the country's independence. Proclaimed Emperor Dom Pedro I, he approved Brazil's first Constitution in 1824. In 1831 he returned to Portugal, relinquish-

Pedro I, Emperor of Brazil. National Library Foundation Collection

ing the throne to his son, who was then only five years old.

THE REIGN OF PEDRO II

In the early 1830's, Brazil was an independent empire with a child emperor. The government therefore entered a period of regency, during which successive rebellions threatened to tear the young country apart. A strategic decision to lower the age of majority for Pedro II, which allowed him to ascend to the throne in 1840, eased the crisis. The new emperor put down local rebellions and led Brazil into its largest war to date, which began in 1865 and resulted in the thorough defeat of Paraguay in 1870.

During the long reign of Pedro II, coffee became Brazil's dominant export commodity. Coffee plantations first arose in the state of Rio de Janeiro, in the region of the Paraíba Valley, and then expanded toward São Paulo. Later, plantations spread to the western regions of São Paulo state. In the beginning, the plantations relied on slave labor. By the middle of the century, however, plantation owners began to bring over European immigrants to work as farm laborers. Mass immigration of Europeans and Asians lasted until 1930 and played an important role in the development of Brazilian society and culture.

THE END OF THE EMPIRE

Starting in the 1870's, a series of political crises weakened the status of Pedro II. Controversy over proposals to abolish slavery pitted slave owners against supporters of economic modernization. The latter favored wage labor, which had already been introduced for field workers on coffee plantations. In 1871, approved on the wings of a strong popular campaign, the *Ventre Livre* (Free Womb) Law mandated that the children of slave women were born free. In 1885, the *Sexagenários* Law freed slaves over 65 years of age. In 1888, the struggle over slavery, and slavery itself, ended with Princess Isabel signing the *Áurea* Law.

The princess, however, did not enjoy the prestige that her father had, and at the time of Abolition the country was already concerned about succession. A disaffected military undermined whatever authority the government still retained. On November 15, 1889, Marshal Deodoro da Fonseca proclaimed the country a Republic, with the support of the Republican Party. The Empire bequeathed to the Republic a country of continental proportions. Though relatively unmodernized, agrarian and deep in debt, Brazil was, unlike Spanish America after its own independence, united.

The First Republic

The first Republican Constitution (1891) separated Church and State and established a centralized federal regime with a powerful president. São Paulo, the new center of economical power, dominated the political scene. Starting in 1894, politicians from São Paulo and Minas Gerais, the most populated state, alternated in administering the government. The political agreement behind this compromise was known as *café-com-leite*, or "coffee with milk", with São Paulo representing the coffee and Minas Gerais the milk. The elections excluded the illiterate, who formed the majority of the population. The country that became industrialized through revenues from coffee sales and that faced the consequences of the World War I saw the emergence of the first general strikes (1917) and military revolts.

A economic crisis in 1929 degenerated into a political crisis between the states of São Paulo and Minas Gerais. A coup d'état in 1930, which put the southern native (*gaúcho*) Getúlio Vargas in power, settled the issue. Vargas increased government intervention in the economy, centralized power and created a lasting framework of labor rights, including paid vacations, fixed working hours and a minimum wage. His legacy influences policies to the present day. In 1937, Vargas consolidated his control into a dictatorship, the *"Estado Novo"* (New State), which was overthrown by a wave of democracy in 1945.

Democratic Experimentation

For better or worse, democratic governments and regular elections followed until 1964. But economic crises and inflationary surges, the bane of the nation since the Empire, continued, with various factions manipulating nationalism and populism. In 1951, Getúlio Vargas returned to the presidency, this time by popular vote. In 1954, during an intense power struggle, he committed suicide.

Between 1956 and 1960, Juscelino Kubitschek promoted industrialization, stimulated the expansion of the country's automotive industry and constructed a new capital city, Brasília. The downside of this spurt of modernization was a deepening of the national debt and soaring inflation. Kubitschek's successor, Jânio Quadros, stepped down in 1961, and vice-president João Goulart, considered a leftist by the military, assumed the Presidency. This laid the groundwork for a 1964 coup that propelled Brazil into a long military dictatorship.

DICTATORSHIP IN BRAZIL

In twenty-one years of dictatorship, the Generals eliminated rights, suppressed political parties, imposed press censorship, battled guerrillas and tortured political prisoners. During the first few years of the regime, nevertheless, economic policies limited inflation caused by rising deficits, which brought about a surge of prosperity that modernized industrial and service sectors. The so-called "economic miracle" started to collapse in the 70's during the international oil crisis, and it gave way to an inflationary spiral marked by monetary correction and indebtedness in foreign currencies.

Toward the end of the 70's, civil society gradually resurrected itself. Under pressure, the government granted amnesty to former militants. In the industrial region of São Paulo, strikes by metal-workers helped forge a new generation of defiant leaders. Lacking political legitimacy and weakened by a serious economic recession, the military government in 1984 faced a campaign for direct presidential elections that brought millions of people into the streets. That protest, the largest popular movement in the history of the country, and a move by Congress to permit direct elections forced the military to make concessions. The subsequent indirect election in January of 1985 installed a civilian, Tancredo Neves, but he became ill just before his inauguration and died in April. In his place Vice President José Sarney, Chairman of the official party of the military regime, assumed the Presidency. Sarney nevertheless governed in relative normalcy through 1989, one year after the enactment of the new Constitution. In the midst of crises and contradictions, democracy took root in Brazil.

Protesting multitudes in the streets demanded direct presidential elections in 1984

DIRECT ELECTIONS

In 1989, in a climate of euphoria, the country finally chose its president by direct vote. The winner was Fernando Collor de Mello, who upon assuming power in 1990 began to implement an ambitious economical plan that included opening the country up to foreign investment and privatizing public companies. However, a spate of serious accusations once again brought the multitudes into the streets. Accused of corruption, Collor was impeached and removed from office in 1992, and Vice President Itamar Franco took the country's helm. Finance Minister Fernando Henrique Cardoso introduced the *Plano Real* in 1994, which finally brought an end to runaway inflation.

Buoyed by the success of the *Plano Real*, Cardoso was elected president in 1994 and reelected in 1998. The economical reforms implemented by his government included the end of government monopolies over telecommunications and oil and the privatization of state-owned companies.

In 2002 Luiz Inácio Lula da Silva, former metal worker, was elected president. To the relief of some and frustration of others, Lula did not break radically with the policies of the previous government, despite his broad base of popular support from the left

Today, as it consolidates its democratic institutions, Brazil faces great economic challenges. Perhaps the most urgent of these is to raise the average income. A mature country yet a young nation, Brazil continues to build on its history as rising to meet these challenges.

THE BRAZILIAN PEOPLE

The Brazilian population is a product of intermixing among indigenous, African and European peoples. The Portuguese language, the country's unifying factor, weaves together an ethnic and social mosaic of disparate regions and cultures.

Brazil is a nation of many faces and names, a child of the collision of Indians, Blacks and Portuguese, and subsequent waves of immigrants from every corner of the planet. It is said that a Brazilian passport is a highly sought item on the foreign black market, because any person – regardless of color or name – can pass for Brazilian. Diversity defines the country's population.

That being the case, it may seem impossible to talk about the "Brazilian people" as anything more than an abstraction. But there is unity in this heterogeneous mass.

Recognizing it requires seeing eye-to-eye with the Brazilian understanding of the word *people*. The traditional concept of people as an ethnic or national group was dear to the authoritarian tradition, and it has been used throughout the country's history to numb the perception of social inequalities and deflate political tensions. In this way, the military regime of 1964 took advantage of the nation's euphoria after Brazil's outstanding performance in the 1970 World Football Championship, presenting it as a victory for a patriotic, disciplined and courageous population. An earlier dictatorship under Getúlio Vargas instituted a farcical nativist policy that included parades of uniformed students chanting anthems in the Tupi-Guarani language.

Ironically, Brazil's long history of separatist movements has been instrumental in forging a sense of national history common to all Brazilians. For example, the leaders of the *Inconfidência Mineira*, or Minas Gerais Conspiracy, called for the creation of the "Nation of Minas". In 1798, rebellions in Salvador represented the "Bahian people"; in 1817, an uprising in Recife called for a "Pernambucan Republic". The *Farroupilhas* from Rio Grande do Sul did not

THE BRAZILIAN POPULATION ACCORDING TO THE 2000 CENSUS	
169,590,693 Inhabitants	
White	53.8%
Mulatto	39.1%
Black	6.2%
Asian	0.5%
Indigenous	0.4%

see themselves as Brazilians, but as gauchos or cowboys. The persistence of a Brazilian nation in spite of these divisive movements is a source of national pride.

This tension have presented a challenge to a long line of historians, scholars and writers. From Afonso Celso to Sérgio Buarque, from Euclides da Cunha to Jorge Amado, many have tried to define Brazil and Brazilians, scouring all this diversity in search of something that might be unique and specific to this varied and unusual population.

Gilberto Freyre, one of the most original "interpreters", suggested that intermixing was the source of Brazilian "racial democracy". But the 2000 Census, which found that 64% of poor Brazilians and 69% of indigent people are Negros, belies his romantic notion. More than half a century after Freyre, the anthropologist Darcy Ribeiro rejected the idea of racial democracy, but confirmed that Brazilians are a distinct people, with unique characteristics, originating from a confluence of races.

The concept of the Brazilian people developed gradually and only coalesced in the 19th century, with the creation of the Republic. But this people exists. Traveling across the country one discovers many cultures, each with their distinctive regional and local traits. There is an underlying unity and common culture, expressed through the Portuguese language, in a country bounded by Spanish speaking countries.

Detail of the painting *Operários*, Tarsila do Amaral. Oil on canvas, Palácio Boa Vista Collection

CUISINE

Brazil's cuisine is the best embodiment of its culture.
A wealth of traditional dishes and regional specialties
combines ingredients from across the country with influences
from throughout the world. It's only a small stretch to claim
that all the diversity and creativity of Brazilian culture can be
tasted in each bite of many dishes.

Culinary scholars insist on a distinction between gastronomy and cooking. The former, say specialists, is art; the latter is practice. Gastronomy demands a refined palate; while even the best cooking takes aim, at least in part, at the more modest goal of satisfying hunger. For those who accept this distinction, Brazil's cooking scores high marks, but in the realm of gastronomy, the country is still taking its first steps. Most of the head chefs in Brazil's leading restaurants are either foreign or follow the classical European canon. Only the younger generation has begun to examine how they can best deploy genuinely Brazilian ingredients in the kitchen and on the table.

These concepts, however, matter little to the visitor who is simply curious to taste what people cook and eat in Brazil. A trip through the country is bound to result in discovery of new flavours, aromas and combinations. Depending on one's appetite, disposition and pocketbook, the traveler may frequently go to the gastronomical temples of Rio de Janeiro and São Paulo or concentrate instead on restaurants specializing in regional cuisines throughout the country. Choose dishes from the finest European culinary traditions, or wander through street markets choosing from delicacies – such as *cupuaçu*, *cajá*, *caju* and other unusual fruits – on display.

A TASTEFUL GEOGRAPHY

More challenging than tracing the rise of the nation's culinary tradition is mapping this fragmented cuisine. Each region finds its own way to combine its natural resources and cultural influences. In the North, recipes call for freshwater fish from Amazonian rivers and seafood. These get combined with manioc – a root also known in the USA as tapioca – the staple food of the indigenous populations, now found throughout the country in different forms.

Moqueca capixaba (fish stew from Espírito Santo)

Pão de queijo (cheese bread), a symbol of Minas Gerais

In Recôncavo Baiano (the Bahia region), African influence is evident in the use of *azeite-de-dendê* (dendê palm oil), coconut milk, and hot peppers used to season dishes. Specialties include *vatapá,* in which shrimp is mixed with bread crumbs, cashews, peanuts and dendê oil, and *abará,* a purée of beans stuffed into shrimp and steamed in banana leaves.

In São Paulo and rural Minas Gerais, popular recipes such as cracklings, beef jerky, and beans mixed with manioc flour date back to the days of the muleteers and are designed to replenish the energy of travelers. The Center West region follows the same tradition, with the addition of signature recipes that take advantage of the abundance of freshwater fish.

In São Paulo and Rio de Janeiro, many codfish dishes reflect Portuguese traditions and tastes. São Paulo also dines on traditional Italian dishes, particularly pizza, as well as Japanese, Syrian and Lebanese recipes, all brought by immigrants.

Visitors heading to the South will discover in Paraná *barreado,* meat cooked in pans sealed with manioc flour, and in Santa Catarina the shrimp recipes inherited from the Azorean colonization. In the rural areas of Rio Grande do Sul, small communities preserve the 19th century culinary traditions of European immigrants, as well as the famous *churrascos* (barbecues). The country has, of course, much more to offer: sweets, preserves, breads, cookies and crackers, farmers' markets throughout the rural communities, cheeses from Minas Gerais, cold cuts from São Paulo, wines from the South, the ever-present *cachaça* (a rumlike spirit distilled from sugarcane) and *caipirinhas* (*cachaça* mixed with sugar and limes or other fruit). Cities also offer the international flavors of sandwiches and fast food. The list of dining possibilities and flavors waiting to be discovered could by itself justify a journey.

FRUITS OF THE EARTH

The *caju* (cashew apple) is the tropical version of the forbidden fruit. It has a very real legacy of danger and passion. North American poet Elizabeth Bishop suffered a severe allergic reaction to one of these fruits in 1955, during her first trip to Brazil. As fate had it, she fell in love with the Brazilian Lota Macedo Soares, who had cared for her throughout the crisis, and ended up staying in Brazil. The country subsequently served as the setting of many of her poems.

Travelers not looking to relive the poet's harrowing experience will find many other Brazilian fruits. There are those naturally associated with the tropics – bananas, coconuts, pineapples and mangos – and those of Europe ancestry that have adapted to the mild climate of Brazil's South and Southeast, including apples, strawberries, peaches and pears. Another group includes fruits native or long ago imported to Brazilian shores. Oranges, papaya, guava, passion fruit, *pitanga* (p. 29), and *jabuticaba* (p. 29) have all become part of Brazil's heritage. There are also hundreds of regional fruits that rarely make it farther than local markets. However, in the past few years, many of them have been commercialized and are becoming popular throughout the country, either fresh as frozen pulp. A short list starts with *açaí* and includes names such as guarana, *graviola* (cherimoya fruit), *cupuaçu*, bilimbi and *pequi* (souari nut). The last has a succulent pulp that hides seeds full of thorns. Perhaps it will figure in the next plot of a visitor who faces unexpected danger – and passion.

OF BEANS AND MYTHS

Any thoughts of Brazilian cuisine bring to mind its most popular dish. Elevated to the status of a national symbol, *feijoada* has a mythical origin. It is often said that the dish originated in the slave quarters, where slaves took animal parts that were not fit for the tables of the "big house" and cooked them in a pot with beans. In truth, the tradition of stewed dishes containing grains and meat comes from Portugal and other European countries. Arriving in Brazil, the Portuguese adapted their version of the stew to the ingredients that were readily available. In fact, slaves generally didn't receive so much as the tails, ears or feet that were left over from the master's table. The legend is just one more seasoning added to *feijoada*.

Açaí

Cupuaçu

Caju (cashew apple)

Cajá (yellow mombin)

Cacau (cocoa tree)

Biribá

Goiaba (guava)

Guaraná

Jabuticaba

Maracujá (passion fruit)

Palmito (heart of palm)

Pequi (souari nut)

Pitanga

The Quest for Perfect Feijoada

And so it was that *feijoada* was derived from the great Portuguese stew. I am a fanatical glutton when it comes to these two dishes. It was with the master Câmara Cascudo that I discovered the relationship between them. The Portuguese brought their stews to our country. Here they found beans cultivated by the Indians. So they started cooking beef jerky in the bean broth, adding their favorite pork cuts – sausage, back bacon, spareribs and pork loin – and so invented the almost perfect *feijoada*.

There are those who consider what is described above as perfect, just requiring the finishing touches of seasoning like garlic, bay leaf and onion. But for us, the *feijoada* fanatics, the delicacy is never complete without what the untutored call "the inferior pork cuts". As if, brave reader, the pig were not constituted entirely of prime cuts, in its serene mission to deliver itself up completely for our gluttony. According to some historians the Africans added these cuts, including the ears, feet and tail. Blessed be those who insist on the snout.

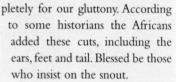

And speaking of ignorance, we bristle at the mention of the nonsense to which the misguided give the name "light *feijoada*". How is it possible, wise reader, for anyone to entertain even for an instant the idea of a "diet *feijoada*"? Of a "low-cal *feijoada*"? It's as if one could desire a "fat lettuce". Or a "succulent cauliflower".

It is impossible to have a light course of small items – a shot of *cachaça*, a sip of *caipirinha*, a little beer, some cracklings, and a few small fried sausages – unless it is just an appetizer for the hefty main course. We expect sumptuous black beans, the crock of steaming meat, the finely chopped collard greens with bits of crisp bacon, and the manioc meal, and only the last should be light. The signature pepper is essential, it must be picante enough to bring our taste buds to that final understanding between all the ingredients and give us the supreme satisfaction that is always found in good beans.

Feijoada cannot be hurried; it is not "fast". A complete *feijoada* is the one that has no time limit. An acceptable invitation for *feijoada* comes with the promise of good conversation first. The dish requires an unhurried appreciation of appetizers. We heavyweight fanatics think that it is necessary to eat a lot of pork fat cracklings as appetizers exactly because the *feijoada* is still to come. Using the same gluttonous reasoning, the fried sausage should be savoured long before the beans are served.

Nothing to do with *feijoada* can be diminutive. To eat "just a little bit" is gastronomically irresponsible. The just price is hunger and scorn.

A good *feijoada* makes time pass slowly, the hours drag on, people never feel full, the alcohol loosens up the conversation, and the palate is only satisfied when drowsiness arrives. And then one must submit to it. If there is anything better than *feijoada*, it is the post *feijoada* nap...

Never accept an invitation for a *feijoada* as if it were a normal meal. Remember that the concoction draws on three cultures: Indian, Portuguese, and African. And never forget that the incomplete *feijoada* is the worst of all. But then, on second thought, all good *feijoada* ends up being incomplete.

Thomaz Souto Corrêa,
journalist and glutton

THE BRAZILIAN MENU

The following is an abbreviated list of some typical dishes served in different regions of Brazil. However, it does not comprehensively cover the eating habits of Brazilians nor does it address more recent creations that have been incorporated into day-to-day urban life. These include the *pastel*, or deep fried pastry pocket, which is eaten in the street markets, preferably accompanied by sugarcane juice; the "*por quilo*" self-service buffet restaurants where customers pay according to the weight of the food on their plates; the "*prato feito*" (known everywhere as "PF"), a complete dish for one person that arrives on a plate filled in the kitchens of simple pubs. Equally unique are the *rodízios*, restaurants that offer all you can eat – generally meat – at a fixed price. Also absent from the list, but present everywhere in the country, is Brazil's staple dish of rice and beans, served with meat, salad and perhaps French fries. Nothing is simpler, and nothing better.

Southeast
Tutu de feijão (beans and manioc flour)
Torresmo (cracklings)
Vaca atolada (braised short ribs
in manioc paste)
Camarão ensopado com chuchu
(shrimp and chayote stew)
Cuscuz (couscous)
Quibebe (pumpkin purée)
Doce de leite (milk-based caramel dessert)
Goiabada (sweetened guava paste)

Northeast
Cuxá (dried shrimp, sesame seeds,
fish steaks, amaranth and rice)
Galinha de cabidela (stewed chicken,
tomato and onion)
Moqueca (stewed fish, tomato and onion)
Sarapatel (stewed pork liver, heart and lungs)
Caruru (okra with shrimp, cashews,
peanuts and dendê oil)
Acarajé (beans fritters fried in dendê
oil with shrimp sauce)
Arroz de hauçá (rice, beef jerky, dried shrimp,
bacon, coconut milk, dendê oil)
Bolo Souza Leão (manioc cake)
Bolo-de-rolo (roll cake)
Quindim (egg yolk and coconut based pudding)

North
Pato no tucupi (stewed duck served on
a bed of toasted manioc meal)
Tacacá (shrimp stewed in manioc broth)
Maniçoba (stewed manioc greens, beef jerky,
sausage, pork loin, tail and ears)
Pirarucu de casaca (baked fresh water fish with
banana, grapes, prunes, eggs, olives and tomato)
Frito marajoara (fried buffalo meat)
Torta de cupuaçu (cupuaçu pie)

Center West
Arroz com pequi (rice and souari nuts)
Caldo de piranha (Piranha broth)
Pamonha salgada (corn meal paste
served in corn husks like tamales)
Alfenins (sweets made from raw sugar)
Furrundum (sweet papaya purée flavored
with ginger and cinnamon)

South
Barreado (beef cooked in pans sealed
with manioc meal)
Arroz de carreteiro (rice, beef jerky,
tomato and onion)
Churrasco (Brazilian barbecue)
Caldo de Camarão (shrimp broth)
Ambrosia (milk and egg based pudding)

FOLK ART

Produced through techniques handed down from generation to generation, Brazil's handicrafts reflect the culture, ingenuity and identity of various communities. Look closely, and see their similarities and nuance contradicting as well.

They are objects handled carelessly in the course of everyday life – coffee pots, bowls, hammocks, blankets – or displayed as household or personal decorations – lace, towels and figurines. Nevertheless, handicrafts also contain history and reflect heritage and identity. While each is unique because it is handmade by one individual, all are part of a long lineage that gives them common meaning and sentimental value. Handicrafts are a form of expression as well as a set of tools for living.

Sometimes, too, they are merely tools for making a living in a world of modern economic realities: a visitor walking along the streets of any of Brazil's better-known centers for folk art will see large numbers of identical articles made specifically to appeal to the tastes of tourists.

CLAY FROM THE EARTH

Mining clay, shaping it, and firing it seem to have been almost innate in Brazil. The people of Marajó Island in the modern state of Pará were working with ceramics around three thousand years ago. The ceramic vases, urns and amphoras they created are all that remains of the Tapajônica civilization that originated west of the island, along the Amazonian tributary known as Tapajós River. Today the location is home to many stores offering replicas of the Marajoara and Tapajônica pieces. The best pieces are those that recreate originals through faithfully reproduction of traditional designs, whether the stylized and geometric forms in Marajoara, or the elaborate and embossed detailing in Tapajônica. Quality products also use dyes made from seeds, roots and fruits.

Ceramics spread far and wide early in Brazil's prehistory. Indians throughout the country still

Clay handicrafts: left, bride and groom (Pernambuco); above, a cow (Vale do Jequitinhonha, Minas Gerais)

Guarani Indian carving wood, in São Paulo

produce pieces decorated with traditional motifs. In remote areas of the Northeast, figurines molded by the followers of master Vitalino, the most famous artisan in the region, are easily found in street markets in places like Caruaru in the state of Pernambuco. Communities of women from Espírito Santo make pans known for their beauty and durability. Artisans from the Jequitinhonha Valley in Minas Gerais and Paraíba Valley in São Paulo recreate their environment through a visual repertoire of saints, traditional characters, animals and folkloric figures.

A Vast and Varied Universe

Brazilian handicrafts are very diversified. In the South you may stumble upon articles such as European embroidery and handpainted, Ukrainian eggs created by immigrants that settled in the interior of

Carranca
(gargoyle)

Paraná and Rio Grande do Sul. Along the coastline from Ceará to Santa Catarina, lacemakers continue the European tradition, brought to Brazil in the colonial days, of working cloth and thread into decorative articles. Also, along the coast, widely admired glass bottles contain landscapes created using colored sand. And in the remote interior of Brazil, along with the clay figurines, there is a cornucopia of articles made from leather, feathers, beads, seeds, stones and fibers. There, too, is a variety of indigenous basketry made from woven fibers such as bamboo, burity palm, sisal, maranta, rushes, as well as wood engravings that decorate volumes of *cordel* literature. Last but not least, a whole range of toys, bowls, figurines and decorations are carved from the same wooden material used to make *carrancas*, the grotesque figures once mounted on the bow of the ships on the São Francisco River to scare off the evil spirits that threatened the voyage.

FROM THE LAND TO THE MARKET

On the banks of the Tocantins River, in Jalapão State Park, grows a golden-hued grass. Used to make purses, bags and hats, it has moved from the landscape of the dunes and rivers to conquer the large cities of the Southeast, and it has leapt from there into fashion magazines worldwide. Buyers approve, the community works and the money circulates. However, older institutions and artisans have announced the imminent extinction of the golden grass if the region maintains the accelerated pace of production that has developed to meet demand.

Far from the savannah, on the beaches of the North coast of São Paulo, long-time inhabitants sculpt boats out of a single tree trunk, without joints, just like in the olden days. But in the past few years conflicts between organizations that support these artisans and those formed to protect the environment have been increasing. The trees used for the canoes are of valuable and rare species, and like the grass from Tocantins, they are threatened with extinction. And so, popular culture bears the weight of its own impacts.

Rag dolls in Belém, Pará

Cinco moças de Guaratinguetá, Di Cavalcanti. Oil painting, MASP Collection

VISUAL ARTS

From the beginning of its colonial period, Brazil's untamed landscapes and cultures attracted the imaginations of European artists. Over time, the country grew out of this objectification and gave rise to its own artistic tradition that drew only in part on European influences.

The first landscapes of the Americas painted by a renowned European artist are of Brazil. Maurice of Nassau brought artists Frans Post and Albert Eckhout to Brazil during the Dutch occupation of Recife (1630–1654), where they spent seven years painting scenes of the New World. Many foreign artists came to Brazil for extended stays, attracted by the country's energy and promise of adventure. They brought art forms created in the Old World, but these traditions fermented in the minds of Brazilian-born artists. By the beginning of the 20th century, the modernists coined an expression to describe what happens to art in Brazil: anthropophagy or self-consuming and self-renewing creativity.

Even the baroque style brought to Brazil by the Catholic Church was adorned with new excesses, colors, ornaments and materials in the Northeast and in Minas Gerais, where Aleijadinho wielded his talent. Portuguese art that arrived here had already absorbed the influences of the Crown's colonies in India and China. In 1808, the Portuguese Royal Court relocated to Rio de Janeiro. Intent on developing the city, King João VI invited a group of French artists to establish the Royal School of Sciences, Arts and Trades, which later became the Imperial Academy of Fine Arts.

In 1816, this French Mission arrived in Brazil – bringing with them the neoclassic style, that would serve as a model for Brazilian art and architecture throughout the following years. Members of the French Mission included the artists Nicolas Antoine Taunay and Jean-Baptiste Debret, among others. Taunay left an important series of landscapes of Rio de Janeiro and its surroundings. The vast works of Debret captured people, places, and scenes of everyday life.

In the second half of the 19th century, romanticism became deeply rooted in the country. Having finally gained independence from Portugal, the country began to construct its identity. Artists such as Pedro Américo and Victor Meireles created epic paintings of patriotic heroes and historic scenes. Almeida Júnior, born in rural São Paulo, portrayed scenes of Brazilian farm life.

In the early 1920's, São Paulo's Modern Art Week revolutionized the course of art in Brazil. Young artists, led by Oswald and Mário de Andrade, caused an uproar when they broke with the established canon. The modernists declared national art and culture anthropophagic. The top names of modernism at the time were Anita Malfatti, Di Cavalcanti, Tarsila do Amaral, Victor Brecheret and Lasar Segall. Their work reverberated through the following decades in the aesthetics of various artists such as Cândido Portinari, Ismael Nery, Flávio de Carvalho, Alfredo Volpi, Alberto da Veiga Guignard and Cícero Dias, as well as the sculptors Maria Martins, Bruno Giorgi and Alfredo Ceschiatti.

In 1951, São Paulo hosted the 1st Biennial Visual Arts Exhibition, which put Brazil on the map of the international art scene. Today, that event is considered one of the greatest of its kind. At its advent, however, abstractionism and concretism were just gaining popularity in the country, and influenced the work of Lygia Pape, Arcângelo Ianelli, Amílcar de Castro, Sergio Camargo and Lygia Clark. In the 1960's, Lygia Clark would produce an important body of work of avant-gardism and experimentialism, a field that also featured Hélio Oiticica, the creator of the famous *parangolés* – a type of fabric cape. Pop art soon incorporated the culture of the masses, often leaving the canvas behind in favor of installation pieces, using many mediums such as text, video and photography. The "happenings" emerged, events that investigated new languages and directions as well as politically engaged art. Great names of this period include Antônio Dias, Rubens Gerchman, Luis Paulo Baravelli and Wesley Duke Lee. In the 1980's, Sergio Fingermann, Leda Catunda, Daniel Senise, Leonilson, and their ilk led a comeback in the popularity of painting.

In the final years of the 20th century and the beginning of the 21st, a new artistic generation has emerged. The likes of Nuno Ramos, Vik Muniz, Adriana Varejão, Beatriz Milhazes, Waltercio Caldas and Cildo Meireles are gaining international acclaim, and their names regularly appear in the catalogues of leading museums worldwide. The sculptor Frans Krajcberg, a native of Poland who immigrated to Brazil in 1948, is also enjoying international acclaim from his works using charred trees. Academic, Baroque, contemporary – Brazil's art runs the gamut.

Figura, Ismael Nery. Oil painting, MAC Collection – USP

Ouro Preto, Guignard. Oil painting, MAC Collection – USP

Design and Fashion

Thanks to Brazil's industrial modernization and the emergence of new talents, Brazilian products are now spreading the country's styles, materials, colors and creativity around the world.

Foreigners who arrived in Brazil the early half of the 20th century, fresh out of the new European design schools, quickly recognized the valuable raw material they encountered. They eagerly applied their training to the materials, tones and forms that they discovered in Brazil. The Swiss John Graz, the Italian Lina Bo Bardi and the German Karl Heinz Bergmiller were pioneers in producing furniture with a distinctive Brazilian design. The greatest name of this era is Joaquim Tenreiro, a native of Portugal who descended from a long line of cabinet makers. Tenreiro arrived in Rio in the 1920's and criticized the "provincialism of a society that only saw value in imported items and denied its own epoch". He defended simplicity against ostentation. It was no accident that the esteemed architect Oscar Niemeyer invited Tenreiro to design the furniture for his houses. Tenreiro knew how to handle the warm climate of the country. His pieces used the diversity of Brazilian woods and reeds instead of the velvets that had been used extensively until then.

International recognition came quickly. Sergio Rodrigues received first prize in the International Furniture Competition in Cantù, Italy, in 1961 for his design of the *Mole* (soft) armchair. The 80's and 90's saw the rise of a new generation. The creative furniture of the brothers Fernando and Humberto Campana has been displayed in the New York Museum of Modern Art and is praised by foreign design magazines. Along with the Campana brothers, other noteworthy names from this period are Carlos Motta, Marcelo Ferraz, Francisco Fanucci, Claudia Moreira Salles, Maurício Azeredo, Fernando Jaeger and the team of Gerson de Oliveira and Luciana Martins. The use of Brazilian wood and an increasing awareness of environmental responsibility characterize the creations of these artists.

A similar process occurred in the fashion world. Years before, only imported items were appreciated and Brazilian fashion had to copy

Embraer executive jet, the Legacy

American and European patterns. The explosion of Brazilian models on the international runways awakened the interest of the fashion world in the country. But years before supermodel Gisele Bündchen's sensual strides conquered the runways of fashion shows, many Brazilian designers had already managed to present and sell their collections in Paris and New York. Brazilian design began to win over the international market without offering a uniform style, but rather by incorporating themes from Brazil's diversity.

Bracelet by Cecília Rodrigues

With the movement to internationalize the appeal of Brazilian styles, large investments were made to modernize the textile industry and to support Brazilian design. Brazil was the first Latin American country to establish a serious fashion calendar.

Havaianas (flip-flops) have achieved worldwide fame, and some cost a small fortune in fashionable stores in Tokyo, Milan and Paris,

The Expand ring by Antonio Bernardo

where the quintessential Brazilian brand of plastic sandals, Melissa, is also in high demand. Even high-tech projects have not been too intimidating from Brazilian designers: Embraer airplanes have gained significant worldwide market share.

The jewelry sector also received recognition. In 2000, Cecília Rodrigues was rated as one of the top fourteen jewelers in the world by Christie's. In Germany, in 2004, Antonio Bernardo received two of the most distinguished international design prizes: the Red Dot (for the ring *Expand*) and the IF Design (for the rings Expand and Ciclos). Excellence of design and the precision of technique have proven basic elements of Brazil's contribution to the world's beauty.

Havaianas
by São Paulo Alpargatas

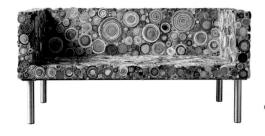

Sushi sofa by the
Campana Brothers

Iracema bench by
Claudia Moreira Salles

Girafa (giraffe). Lina Bo Bardi
stacking tables by Marcelo Ferraz
and Marcelo Suzuki

Three legged chair by
Joaquim Tenreiro

Mole (soft) armchair
by Sergio Rodrigues

Brazil Lights up the Runways

My fascination with Brazil started long before I first set foot in this enchanting country. I have always been fascinated by movies and I still have vivid images in my mind of *Flying Down To Rio*, with Fred Astaire. Entering the realm of the fashion world, one cannot think of Rio without envisioning Carmen Miranda and her incredible costumes propelled by Walt Disney World.

My first trip to Brazil was in the summer of 1962, when I was invited to the 5th Fenit (Brazilian Textile Industry Show) in São Paulo. It was a fair where six Italian couturiers were invited to show creations using Brazilian fabrics. The power of this metropolis, even then, was astounding; you could really feel the heart of the Brazilian economy throbbing.

After the São Paulo show, I took a two week vacation to visit Rio de Janeiro and Salvador. Both cities, so different from Brazil's biggest city, enchanted me with their tropical seduction. Rio de Janeiro, the *"cidade maravilhosa"* is really one of the marvels of the world, and every time I meet one of the many Brazilian friends I still have from this first trip it reminds me of the emotions of that first visit. I was staying at the Copacabana Palace Hotel and fell in love with the swing of people walking down the street – the innately gracious and harmonious moves of Brazilian beauties that have always been the greatest contingent of my catwalk shows.

Dress used by Marisa Berenson for her wedding

With its deep African roots, Salvador was a completely different picture. Its delicious food and folklore transported me to a world so different from what I had experienced until then. Years later, in 1977, I had a whole collection dedicated to Bahia and it was certainly one of my big hits. The show took place in Paris, at the Pavillon Gabriel. It started with a platform coming up from below, with thirty girls and boys all dressed in white cotton and piqué, dancing to an enthusiastic samba rhythm. Marisa Berenson chose to wear one of the finale dresses of the collection for her wedding in Los Angeles, where I was one of her best men.

The second time I went to Brazil, I was already quite famous there and I had the joy of experiencing Carnival. It was one of the most fantastic shows that I ever saw: Samba schools parading in the Avenida with their colourful and frenzied costumes. I recall two sleepless nights watching school after school passing by…

Nowadays I am in constant contact with my Brazilian friends and there are so many models gracing my shows that it is like I am always dreaming of Brazil. For many years the muse of my collections was Dalma Callado, who was awarded model of the 80's, a Paulista girl with perfect measures and a great personality. She was an inexhaustible source of inspiration. She made the finale of my shows so many times, and whatever dress she wore was guaranteed to become a bestseller of the collection.

Some years later, another beauty appeared on the catwalks: Gisele Bündchen. She is considered one of the most beautiful women in the world, and perfectly combines some very German features with a heart, a soul and a rhythm that are sensually and unmistakable Brazilian.

Bahia Tribute
Collection

Mario Testino, one of the best fashion photographers of today, and certainly a man with a fascination for Brazil, regularly returns to Europe from Brazil with planes full of beauties that embody the incredible mix of races and moods that make Brazilian men and women so special.

Sometimes during my fashion shows you can have the feeling that I work for the Brazilian Tourism Office in partnership with the Brazilian embassy: on the catwalk you see Gisele, Isabelli Fontana, Carolina Ribeiro, Raquel Zimmermann, Ana Beatriz… while in the first rows sit Brazilian friends and clients of many years.

Last but not least, Brazilian music has been part of my shows: Caetano Veloso, Gilberto Gil and Gal Costa are among my favorites, and I can never forget João Gilberto and Tom Jobim and their fabulous bossa nova.

Valentino,
Italian Fashion Designer

Pelourinho, Salvador, Bahia

Brasília, Distrito Federal

ARCHITECTURE

Brazil has a rich architectural heritage. Upon reaching Brazil,
Le Corbusier's modernism took on new forms and curves.
This was not the first instance of this phenomenon of
adaptation and interpretation.

In a famous passage in his book *Raízes do Brasil* (*Roots of Brazil*),
historian Sérgio Buarque de Holanda compared the Portuguese
and Spanish, respectively, to sowers of seeds and layers of ceramic
tiles. He noted that Portuguese cities in South America grew
haphazardly, as if from seeds scattered on the ground, whereas the
Spanish brought to the colonies the same organized and measured
urban planning that oriented their metropolitan cities back home.

Consequently, the narrow, winding streets of Brazilian cities
contrast with the perpendicular lines so common in other Latin
American cities. Brazil bears the mark of this abandonment to
chance and addiction to improvisation in its countless cul-de-
sacs, irregular intersections and labyrinthine alleyways. Through
five hundred years of history, Brazilian architects and urban planners have tried to impose, with various degrees of success, ra-
tionalism and order on this tradition of chaos. Brasília reflects
perhaps their only unequivocally triumph over the heritage of
the sowers of seeds.

However, long before the plans for Brazil's capital city left the
drawing boards of Oscar Niemeyer and Lúcio Costa, the Portuguese introduced their sense of colonial architecture. It was rapidly absorbed into the Brazilian way of doing things. An abundance
of local materials that were unknown in Europe, the lack of more
traditional Iberian materials and climatic differences encouraged
local builders to be creative and resourceful. They readily adapted
styles based loosely on models brought from the Old World.

Today this adaptation is evident in many of the country's historical centers. An excursion through Salvador, the capital city of
Bahia, for example, is a tour of a diversity of architectural styles.
There you will find churches with austere façades and luxurious
interiors, adorned with gold and Brazilian woods. This apparent
contradiction exists thanks to the historical shortage of stones used
for the Portuguese church façades, and the surfeit of quality woods.

Igreja de São Francisco de Assis, Ouro Preto, Minas Gerais

Resourceful Portuguese artisans simply carved the hardwoods using techniques that they'd previously applied to stone.

Ever since a successful revitalization project in Salvador transformed the Pelourinho area into a tourist magnet, other cities have been following suit. Many have restored long-hidden beauty to old row houses.

In the 18th century, the gold rush shifted the colony's economic center to Minas Gerais and led to magnificent, baroque constructions in cities like Ouro Preto and Tiradentes. Antônio Francisco Lisboa, an architect and sculptor known as Aleijadinho, built beautiful churches and sculpted extraordinary soapstone figures, elevating local art and architecture to a new level.

The arrival of the Portuguese royal family caused another construction boom at the beginning of the 19th century, as Rio de Janeiro replaced Lisbon as the seat of the Empire. Rio de Janeiro maintained the title of capital city after independence and during the first seventy years of the Republic, and its distinction as the center of the political, economical and cultural scenes continued to be reflected in its streets.

At the beginning of the 20th century, the city received new, wide avenues and luxurious neoclassic buildings such as the National Library, the National Museum of Fine Arts and the Municipal Theater, the last of which was inspired by the Opera House in Paris. Various architectural trends of that era, including art nouveau and art déco, distinguish the city's remarkable buildings.

Industrial growth put São Paulo on the map of modernity in the first decades of the 20th century. In the 1920's and 1930's, the works of Gregori Warchavchik and Flávio de Carvalho brought some of the country's first modernist buildings to the city of São Paulo. But it was Rio that would serve as the international launching point for this Brazilian movement. In the mid-1930's, the architect Le Corbusier helped to design the new offices of the Brazilian Ministry of Education, and the resulting building became a worldwide icon of modernism. Other architects involved in the project included a who's who of Brazil's most influential of the century: Lúcio Costa, Oscar Niemeyer, Affonso Reidy, Jorge Moreira, Carlos Leão and Ernani Vasconcelos.

Over the following two decades Brazil became a worldwide trendsetter in architecture. Modern buildings such as the Pampulha complex in Belo Horizonte, the Museum of Modern Art in Rio and the entirety of the country's new capital city, Brasília, reflect this movement. Between 1940 and 1960, Brazilian architecture presented a modern and avant-garde image to the world. Lina Bo Bardi, Vilanova Artigas, Rino Levi, Lelé and Paulo Mendes da Rocha drove this period's creative vitality. At the end of the 70's, a slump in public construction diverted innovative architectural energies toward designs for houses, stores, hotels and restaurants. Today, architects such as Aurelio Martinez Flores, Isay Weinfeld, Márcio Kogan, Roberto Loeb, Marcelo Ferraz, Severiano Porto, Roberto Montezuma, Acássio Gil Borsoi, Sylvio de Podestá, Álvaro Hardy, Flávio Kiefer, Júlio Collares, Carlos Maximiliano Fayet, James Laurence Vianna, Mauro Neves Nogueira, João Walter Toscano, Marcos Acayaba and Marcelo Moretim continue the tradition of quality in Brazilian architecture.

Lina Bo Bardi's Casa de Vidro (Glass House), São Paulo city

Modern Architecture in Brazil

During the past century, Brazil created and refined an architectural style that is one of the few globally recognized as being distinctly "national". Though comprising several separate creative impulses, which makes it difficult to define precisely, this evolving style is quintessentially Brazilian. In the 1940's, revolutionary buildings rose up around Brazil, and in the following decade, the country established itself as a global center of modern architecture. Three projects are perhaps enough to encapsulate Brazil's contribution to 20th century architecture: the Ministry of Health and Education in Rio de Janeiro (built 1936-1942), the city of Brasília (1957-1960) and the São Paulo Art Museum (1956-1968).

Ministry of Health and Education

Few could have imagined, in the 1930's, the international impact that the Ministry of Health and Education project would have on the architectural community. A glass building of that size had never before been built anywhere in the world, and it was the first time that a government had officially adopted an avant-garde design. The Ministry building, now called Gustavo Capanema Palace, and known for a time as the Ministry of Culture and Education, combined so many innovations that it was almost an experimental project. The office building, supported by tall pillars, allows pedestrians to circulate freely in its shadow, and the rest of the building structure incorporates space for public activities such as theater and exhibitions. Exposure to sunlight could be controlled by the brise-soleil. Ceramic tiles, paintings by Portinari and gardens by Burle Marx reinforce the perception that the goal was to create a complete work of art.

The project arose out of the cooperation of a group of young Brazilian architects – Affonso Reidy, Carlos Leão, Ernani Vasconcelos, Jorge Moreira and Oscar Niemeyer – under the coordination of Lúcio Costa with Le Corbusier as a consultant. Le Corbusier was so enthusiastic about the result that he counted the Ministry among his most important projects. But could Le Corbusier really claim the project as his own, or was it a creation of the Brazilians? During the following decade, the Brazilian architects demonstrated that they could create world-class modernist architecture without consulting the master.

Brasília

A British magazine once defined Brasília as both the pinnacle and the tomb of modernist ideals. On one hand, the city would swiftly become the definitive reference of 20th century urbanism. On the other, its utopian urbanism is on a scale neither attempted nor reproduced elsewhere. In Europe, the utopian urban planning of the early 20th century focused on low-income areas. In Brasília, by contrast, it was universally applied to official palaces, administrative, commercial and office buildings, and housing for various income levels. Unlike the

Ministry of Education building, Brasília does not captivate followers all over the world. But like the Ministry building, it showed that Brazil could construct on a monumental scale what Europe had done on only a limited scale.

In addition to the urban planning by Lúcio Costa, who landed the assignment by winning a national competition in 1956, Brasília is a landmark for its challenging architectural innovations. One example is the Alvorada Palace built in 1958: previously, palaces had classical columns and were designed to project solidity and formality. In Alvorada, Niemeyer created a new paradigm of monumentality that is transparent, light and almost fragile. Many criticize Brasília without understanding what it symbolizes more than any other city in the world. Brasília demonstrates that a group of Brazilians – from the President to the laborer – planned and executed the idealized form of an architectural era.

THE SÃO PAULO ART MUSEUM

Perplexed were the guests at the 1968 opening of the São Paulo Art Museum, or MASP. They encountered the finest collection of Western art south of the equator – without any form of hierarchy or emphasis. All the pieces were set out in an immense rectangular room on glass stands, with the descriptions located behind the pieces, forcing the visitor to examine the piece first without any other outside reference. That was Lina Bo Bardi's unusual approach to exhibiting the paintings.

MASP is one of the world's greatest examples of what's called brutalist architecture. Structural elements define the form of the building. Four external pillars suspend the exhibit halls and eliminate the need for internal structural elements. The ground floor, completely open, resembles a large covered public square. The main material used in the construction is exposed concrete, which creates a vivid contrast with the fragility of the exhibited artworks and eliminates the distractions of art's typical neoclassical settings. The project by Lina Bo Bardi, officially named the Assis Chateaubriand Museum after the businessman who assembled its collection, has been an inspiration to architects all over the world. A visit to MASP, in spite of some recent internal alterations, shows how Brazil absorbed and creatively recast a most diverse range of cultures.

The three examples include one instance in which Brazilians worked under the influence of a European, another in which Brazilians created their own utopian capital, and a third in which a European took inspiration from Brazil itself. Together, they demonstrate the caliber of modern Brazilian architecture, in all of its complexity and diversity.

André Corrêa do Lago,
diplomat, architectural critic, and member of the Architectural and Design Committee of
the New York Museum of Modern Art (MoMA)

CINEMA

Brazil's motion-picture industry has combined technical savvy with artistic grace, launching a renaissance that, overseas, is making cinema one of the country's best recognized areas of cultural excellence.

At the turn of this century, something new appeared in Brazil's cultural panorama: a cinematic explosion. At the beginning of the 1990's there had been only two or three feature-length movies being made each year. By 2003 the figure had leapt to forty. And the appeal of this new crop of films is not limited to domestic audiences. Cinema-goers from half the world have been moved by the raw emotion of, for example, *Central do Brasil* (*Central Station*) or *Cidade de Deus* (*City of God*), whose directors, Walter Salles and Fernando Meirelles, respectively, are developing promising international careers.

However, Brazilian cinema took time to reach the limelight. The first signs of life developed in the 1920's and 30's, with the works of Humberto Mauro and Mário Peixoto. The following decades saw the slapstick comedies of Atlântida and the melodramas of Vera Cruz, pioneering studios in terms of movie-industry professionalism. At the end of the 50's the Cinema Novo movement emerged, led by such prestigious directors as Nelson Pereira dos Santos, Ruy Guerra and Glauber Rocha, giving Brazilian productions international exposure for the first time. In 1962, Anselmo Duarte was awarded the Palme d'Or at the Cannes Festival for *O pagador de promessas* (*The Given Word*). After that came movies from directors such as Cacá Diegues, Bruno Barreto, Arnaldo Jabor, Leon Hirzman, Suzana Amaral and Hector Babenco. Despite all this talent, however, the industry almost ground to a halt at the beginning of the 90's due to the withdrawal of public financing during the Collor government.

The turnaround, triggered by a new fiscal incentive law, began in 1994. Carla Camurati's frugal production, *Carlota Joaquina, Princess of Brazil*, attracted an audience of 1.5 million with minimal advertising, as the public returned in earnest to watch Brazil on the big screen. From then on, progress was apparent in both the number of films being produced and also their quality, including their technical aspects.

Central Station: Brazilian movies return to the film festivals

If the rudimentary techniques of the Cinema Novo were part of an aesthetic and political project, the goal of the new cinema is artistic perfection. The presence of Brazilians at the Oscars is the best proof of its accomplishments. In the last ten years, four Brazilian movies have received eight Oscar nominations.

Meanwhile, *Diários de motocicleta* (*The Motorcycle Diaries*), directed by Walter Salles, shown at the official selection of the Cannes Festival, embodies Brazilian film's new internationalism. Robert Redford, an American, produced that picture; the leading roles were played by Mexican and Argentinean actors; the screenplay was written by a Puerto Rican; and it was filmed in several neighboring countries. The movie continues in the tradition of Hector Babenco's *O beijo da mulher aranha* (*Kiss of the Spider Woman*), for which William Hurt received the Oscar for best actor.

If we take critical acclaim as a measure of success, the results are equally impressive, with Brazilian productions being selected for the world's most important film festivals. Critics and public alike have applauded such movies as *O invasor* (*The Trespasser*) by Beto Brant, *Madame Satã* by Karim Aïnouz, *Amarelo manga* (*Mango Yellow*) by Cláudio Assis and *O homem que copiava* (*The Man who Copied*) by Jorge Furtado. Documentaries are also enjoying a revival. Productions such as *Janela da alma* (*Window of the Soul*) by Walter Carvalho and José Jardim, *Ônibus 174* (*Bus 174*) by José Padilha, *Nelson Freire* by João Moreira Salles and *Edifício Master* (*Master: A Building in Copacabana*) by Eduardo Coutinho have all achieved strong audience responses.

In fact, box-office success is becoming the norm. Several films, such as *O auto da compadecida* (*The Dog's Will*) and *Lisbela e o prisioneiro* (*Lisbela and the Prisoner*), both by Guel Arraes, have surpassed the 2-million-viewer mark. Hector Babenco's *Carandiru* was seen by four million. Successes have paved the way, and the subjects treated in films have subsequently diversified. Urban violence is a frequent theme, and documentaries like Caíto Ortiz's *Motoboys* (*Motoboys: Crazy Life*) portray the vibrant life of big cities. But films such as *Baile perfumado* (*Perfumed Ball*), by Lírio Ferreira and Paulo Caldas, are set in the wilderness of the *sertão*.

In recent years movie-theater multiplexes have sprung up Brazil's larger cities, setting new standards for comfort, as well as projection and sound quality. The new theaters are not only a welcome sign of the modernization of the country's film industry, but also evidence of the public's higher expectations. Nevertheless, Brazil still has only 1,600 cinemas nationwide, and all of these are concentrated in just 8% of the cities.

POPULAR MUSIC

Brazil's rich musical tradition merges influences
from all continents. Waves of innovation from foreign
shores have sculpted to national taste and, in turn, have
shaped musical tastes around the world.

I n the first years of Portuguese colonization, the Jesuits adapted religious hymns to tribal dances to help convert Indians to Chris-
tianity. This is but one example of music being used in Brazil for enticement or seduction. A few years later, Africans reached Brazil, and
their percussion instruments were incorporated into the national arsenal – *conga* drums, *cuícas* (friction drum), *ganzá* shakers
and *marimbas* (similar to a xylophone) that accompanied slaves' evening sing-alongs. Perhaps those
weary slaves were the first to recast, through music, even the most oppressive of circumstances into a festive atmosphere.

Cuíca

Enticement, seduction, lament and celebration
are the tangled roots of the tree of Brazilian Popular Music, or MPB. Its branches reflect an extensive array of styles and rhythms.

Different groups' musical styles began to merge when slave celebrations gained a degree of acceptance in the "big house". The *umbi-
gada* (navel to navel contact) and African beats took on Iberian
influences and became the *lundu* dance. The sinuous movements of
that style were often seen as lascivious, but in spite or perhaps because of this, it was welcome at the masters' balls. With the rising numbers of Africans among the Brazilian population,
the inevitable Africanization of music proceeded
in spite of critics' protestations. By the end of
the 18th century, the *lundu* was well established
in the local culture. So, too, was the *modinha*,
which are European folk songs that crossed the
ocean and got set to Brazilian themes and rhythms. The
modinha remained popular with all social classes throughout the 19th century. At the turn of the 20th century, another European
rhythm, the polka, became a national rage. The polka influenced
maxixe dance, which arose in the backyards of Rio de Janeiro's

Afoxé

peripheral ghettos.It was assimilated, with some reservations, by the elites. In 1914, Nair de Teffé, the wife of President Hermes da Fonseca, shocked conservatives at a soirée by singing the risqué *maxixe Corta-jaca*, by Chiquinha Gonzaga.The same mixture that produced *maxixe* in Rio created the *frevo* in Pernambuco. Today, the latter form is one of the most popular rhythms in Brazil and the signature music of Carnival in the Northeast.

Cavaquinho

THE BEGINNINGS OF SAMBA

In 1917, the recording of the song *Pelo telefone* by Donga marked the birth of samba, an offshoot of *maxixe*. Both musical styles originated in working class districts of Rio de Janeiro, at the parties of African immigrants who had moved here from Bahia. In the following decades, the genre matured and gained popularity. During the same period, recordings and radio became important means of mass communication. Already distinct from *maxixe* and inextricably linked to Carnival, the samba quickly swept beyond the city limits and through the social classes. By the 1930's, it was no longer the music of poor blacks in Rio but a national art form. In that short time it assumed the position that it still

Ganzá

holds today as one of the pillars of national identity. The definitive form of samba was established over the 1930's and 40's by great artists such as Sinhô, Noel Rosa, Ismael Silva, Ary Barroso, Lamartine Babo and Cartola.

BEYOND SAMBA

During the maturation of samba, Brazil's musical melting pot continued producing other styles. Donga, the creator of the first samba, played in a jazz band alongside the legendary master Pixinguinha. Pixinguinha wrote magnificent *choros*. That type of music, which became popular at the end of the 19th century among Rio's working class, features European polkas, waltzes and mazurkas by a trio playing a flute, a ukulele-like *cavaquinho* and a guitar. These *choros* later had a powerful influence on composer Heitor Villa-Lobos, who was a

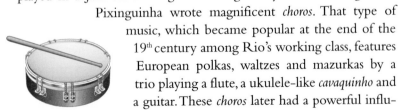

Tamborim

pioneer in the use of popular traditions in concert music. Classical music has a long history in Brazil. Classical and popular music have followed parallel paths, so at many points the two have shared influences.

Caixa

By the 1940's the musical industry discovered the traditional rhythms of the rural Northeast. For example, Dorival Caymmi incorporated the accent and themes from Bahia into the Rio samba. On the radio, the sounds of Luís Gonzaga and his accordion were at the top of the charts. Known as the "king of *baião*", after that Country and Western-like musical style, he also played *xote*, *xaxado* (folk-dances) and other sounds that were popular at country dances. By the end of the 1940's, a new and slower version of samba, known as the *samba-canção*, emerged to challenge the rural dance styles. That new form of samba created great radio idols, singers who touched legions of fans. In the post-war period, with North American influence in Brazil ascendant, the *samba-canção* bred with jazz, and bossa nova was born.

THE SOUND OF THE NEW BRAZIL

Like samba, bossa nova has a birth certificate. In 1958, the release of João Gilberto's first album marked its appearance. Young university students, gathered in apartments of Rio's upscale Zona Sul, created bossa nova to contrast with the grandiloquent and dramatic style that then dominated popular music. The new sound was intimate, with quiet vocals accompanied by innovative and sophisticated guitar rhythms. The soundtrack for modern Brazil, bossa nova shared the euphoria of industrialization and growth. Stirred into the pot with jazz and the samba were the classical approach of Tom Jobim and the lyrics of Vinicius de Moraes. In the mid-1960's, Frank Sinatra recorded bossa, opening the way for the traffic in artists and musical styles between the two countries.

Agogô

A few years after its emergence, bossa nova fragmented as a musical movement. Some factions argued for a return to the "roots", while others were captivated by the potential of electric guitars. In

Pandeiro

1964, the military dictatorship exacerbated these differences. In an environment of increasing restrictions on political liberties, television stations organized university music festivals that served to express different cultural currents. This permitted the rise of artists whose influence would carry through the century, including Chico Buarque, Caetano Veloso and Gilberto Gil. Songs of protest that challenged the censure imposed by the regime also rose up from these festivals.

In 1968, Caetano, Gil and Tom Zé launched tropicalism, a movement that explicitly proclaimed the anthropophagic character – the assimilation and transformation of foreign influences – of Brazilian music. Tropicalism discussed the concepts of good and bad taste, of national and foreign. It mixed the influences of the Beatles, the traits of music considered tacky, and the great popular Brazilian tradition. The bands Mutantes and Secos e Molhados brought this potent brew of influences to the masses. At the same time, American easy-listening and commercial rock became Brazil's Jovem Guarda or New Guard. Artists such as Roberto and Erasmo Carlos popularized that youth movement. In the 1970's, in another development, Paulinho da Viola renovated and revitalized classic samba. At the same time, composers and vocalists such as Milton Nascimento and Elis Regina made names for themselves.

Berimbau

THE "ANTHROPOPHAGIC" TRADITION

The movement of absorption and re-creation of international musical influences continued throughout the last years of the 20th century. In the 1980's, Brazilian rock reached the hit parade, finally achieving success in one of the few areas where foreign music had always outdone its homegrown competition.

Emerging Brazilian "rock stars" included Cazuza and Lobão, and bands such as Legião Urbana, Paralamas do

Flute

Sucesso and Titãs. Yet international influences continue to arrive and take on a local flavor. In Maranhão, dancers turned reggae into a romantic ballroom style. In Rio, the funk beat of Miami Bass acquired a strong dose of eroticism, while in São Paulo, the rap lyrics of Racionais MCs became a channel for protest against violence and racism.

In Recife, the heirs of Chico Science mixed the traditional *maracatu* (a Brazilian dance of African origin) with electronic rhythms and punk in a movement known as the *mangue* beat. In Brazil's rural interior, traditional *caipira* or "country" music has survived the success of its commercial offshoot, the "romantic" *sertanejo* music. Electronica fuses with samba in the music of Marcelo D2, and with bossa nova with Bebel Gilberto. Meanwhile, Marisa Monte continues the tradition of Brazilian Popular Music, but brings it closer to international pop. Los Hermanos from Rio mix rock with the *samba-canção*. Moving between the old and the new, the vulgar and the sophisticated, Brazilian music continues to reinvent itself – and to redefine international expectations – every day.

Atabaque

To Hear the Masters

The Reserva Técnica Musical do Instituto Moreira Salles (Rua Marquês de São Vicente, 476, Gávea, Rio de Janeiro, tel. 21/3284-7474) maintains much of the tradition of Popular Brazilian Music, or MPB. The Institute is home to the Centro Petrobras de Referência da Música Brasileira which holds roughly 13,000 recordings made between 1902 and 1964, including those of Noel Rosa and Chiquinha Gonzaga. Researcher Humberto Fransceschi painstakingly obtained, restored and catalogued the collection, starting with 78 rpm records, over a fifty year period. Visitors can learn about and listen to the recordings at no charge at the Institute's access terminals, and research rooms are open to the public. There are also occasional lectures and exhibitions. The collection may be accessed at the website www.ims.com.br.

BRAZILIAN MUSIC

When people talk or think of Brazil, before even the classic images of the sun, the beaches, the suntanned girls, or Carnival, or football, the first thing that comes to mind is the sound, the rhythm. It could be a swinging samba or a cool and elegant bossa nova. Music may well be Brazil's greatest contribution to beauty and joy in the world. Brazilian music has become our finest, most widely consumed and most desired export product – with the exception, of course, of Gisele Bündchen. Above all else, it has such an intense and intimate place in Brazilians' lives that one can tell the history of modern Brazil through nothing more than the history of its popular music. Melodies and lyrics throughout time have witnessed every crisis, each moment in the past, and shows precisely how the Brazilian nation felt at the time. So, popular music tells a story about the feelings of Brazilians.

An analysis of the rich and glorious history of our music, the most powerful cultural production we have, combines the miseries and downfalls of our social and political tradition, and can help any foreigner, and ourselves, to better understand us. Popular music has a presence and importance in the daily lives of Brazilians that is matched in few countries.

Music, like football, both demands and gives pride, talent and national passion: the passion to dribble and sidestep, the love of dance and of joy. We can acknowledge that we are politically, socially and scientifically underdeveloped. But the music we produce is very modern, globalized, competitive, diversified and increasingly respected and in demand in the most demanding markets. Like no other form of national expression, Brazilian popular music tells the story of our dreams and passions, our fears and frustrations. It embodies our imagination. Heard by rich and poor, young and old, men and women of all races, it talks, it sings about all of them. Americans know this well: it is impossible to understand the United States without movies and popular music. In Brazilian culture, movies are less culturally prominent than the *novelas*, or nighttime soap operas. So, the quality art of Brazil's musicians and lyricists, their popular music, assumes the task of registering our feelings, of capturing important moments, and of recording our personal and collective history.

Since the explosion of bossa nova in the 1960's, popular music has become Brazil's greatest contribution to international pop culture. Bossa's strong and contagious beats, and its soft melodies and sweet words, inspired musicians, writers and filmmakers, and became the imagined sound track for the lives of millions of people. It receives respect and fosters friendship everywhere that music is loved.

Everyone knows, well, on second thought they likely don't know, that we have very talented writers. There are a few translations of Jorge Amado, Machado de Assis and Guimarães Rosa, but one cannot speak of a "Brazilian literature". We have world-class poets such as João Cabral de Melo Neto and Carlos

Drummond de Andrade, but they write in Portuguese and there isn't anything that you could call a "Brazilian poetry".

Celebrated movies like *Central do Brasil* (*Central Station*) or *Deus e o Diabo na Terra do Sol* (*Black God, White Devil*) are expressions of the talent of Walter Salles Jr. and Glauber Rocha, but unlike the Iranians we do not have anything that could be called "Brazilian cinema".

Of course, besides the physical beauty of our young men and women, we have a number of great athletes. They play not only football but also volleyball, tennis, Formula 1, yachting and Olympic gymnastics. Still, we are far from being a world power in sports.

We have been blessed with the occasional first-rate actress, like Fernanda Montenegro and Marília Pêra, and an extraordinary playwright or two, including Nelson Rodrigues. But we cannot talk about a "Brazilian theatre".

However, in any place in the world, when the subject is music, we feel like the French talking about wine or an American talking about business. The music of Antonio Carlos Jobim and João Gilberto not only enchanted the world but also influenced American jazz and inspired geniuses such as Miles Davis and Stevie Wonder. Since bossa nova, the sounds of Sergio Mendes, Caetano Veloso, Milton Nascimento, Gilberto Gil, Hermeto Paschoal, Ivan Lins and more recently Marisa Monte, Daniela Mercury, Bebel Gilberto and many others continue to bring happiness, elegance and sophistication to international pop music. Brazilian beats make people dream and dance. Above all else, with its diversity of rhythms, beats, styles, and endless recombinations, Brazilian Popular Music expresses the country's ethnic and cultural diversity, the richness of our melting pot, and shows the best that we have to offer as people and as artists. Welcome to the *Brazilian Melting Pop*.

BASIC ALBUM COLLECTION

Chega de Saudade – João Gilberto
O Amor, o Sorriso
e a Flor – João Gilberto
Terra Brasilis – Antonio Carlos Jobim
A Tábua de Esmeraldas – Jorge Ben
Minas – Milton Nascimento
Tropicália – Caetano Veloso, Gilberto Gil, Os Mutantes, Tom Zé
Acabou Chorare – Novos Baianos
Maria Fumaça – Banda Black Rio
Amoroso – João Gilberto
Gal Canta Caymmi – Gal Costa

Brasil – João Gilberto, Caetano Veloso, Gilberto Gil e Maria Bethania
Falso Brilhante – Elis Regina
Tim Maia Disco Club – Tim Maia
Charme do Mundo – Marina Lima
O Último Romântico – Lulu Santos
MM – Marisa Monte
Ao Vivo – Cássia Eller
Orchestra Klaxon – Max de Castro
Tribalistas – Arnaldo Antunes, Carlinhos Brown, Marisa Monte
À Procura da Batida Perfeita – Marcelo D2

Nelson Motta,
writer, journalist and music producer

FOOTBALL

In Brazil, football is more than just a popular sport. It was key in forging the national identity, and it still plays a crucial role in the country's economy, culture and social life.

A passion for football, or what North Americans call soccer, is not exclusive to Brazilians. Many other nationalities exhibit the same enthusiasm, and even fanaticism, of the fans who flock to stadiums in São Paulo or Rio de Janeiro. But for Brazilians, football is more than just a sport or a game. It is part of the identity, an expression of the culture, a metaphor for the potential of the people and nation.

According to the CBF (Brazilian Football Confederation) there are 800 professional clubs in Brazil, 13,000 amateur ones and over 300 stadiums. It is estimated that more than 30 million people play the game, and it supports a $32-billion a year business. Brazilian Portuguese has even absorbed several idioms from football jargon. Even people who have never been to a match use such familiar expressions as "*pendurar a chuteira*" (literally "to hang up one's boots", to retire), "*pisar na bola*" ("step on the ball", to make a mistake) or "*tirar o time de campo*" ("withdraw the team from the field", to beg off or quit).

Football provides an effective conversational ice-breaker. If you find yourself among strangers in a bar or a taxi, or at a party, you can easily start a conversation by commenting on the performance of a player or a team.

However, the game's greatest attribute is something else – it is a truly democratic sport. Social background is of no importance and it can be played by anyone, regardless of their physique; you don't have to have an athletic build or be of a particular height to dominate the ball. For children from underprivileged backgrounds, the sport has become a dream ticket to fame and fortune, but very few actually make it – according to the CBF, the vast majority of professional players only earn around R$500 a month. But in the end, what really matters is that football allows Brazilians to dream. Life in Brazil is hard, sometimes very hard, but all it takes is a little boy and a ball to conjure up the possibility of triumph and glory.

Pelé and Tostão during the final game of the 1970 World Cup against Italy

BRAZILIAN FOOTBALL

If a recently arrived visitor were to make a list of the five greatest tragedies in Brazil's history – tragedies being understood as events so traumatic that people gather in the streets to sit on the curb and cry on each other's shoulders – he would discover that no less than three of them have to do with sports. The first occurred in 1950 at Rio's Maracanã Stadium; just weeks after it opened, when the Brazilians fell to Uruguay in the final of the 1950 World Cup. The event subsequently became known as the *Maracanazo* (the Maracanã fiasco). Second was the elimination of the unforgettable 1982 team of Zico, Sócrates, Júnior, Cerezo and Falcão in the quarter-finals of the World Cup against Italy, an episode that became known as the *tragédia do Sarriá* (the Sarriá tragedy). And third, the tragic death of Ayrton Senna on the Tamburello curve of the Ímola grand-prix circuit on Labor Day in 1994. (Only two national tragedies are political: the suicide of the so-called "people's president", Getúlio Vargas, in 1954, and the death of Tancredo Neves, the first civilian president after more than twenty years of military rule, just a few days before his inauguration in 1985.)

If the same visitor were also to list the country's five most glorious moments, the result would be even more oriented toward sports. The achievements that fill every Brazilian with pride are not represented by any of the several stars on our flag, but by those five little stars embroidered above the crest of the national football team, representing the country's World Cup victories in the 1958, 1962, 1970, 1994 and 2002. At first glance, this might appear somewhat insubstantial, to say the least, but in a world where football is increasingly becoming a symbol for the unity of peoples and the identity of nations, and where FIFA (the sport's governing body) has more members than the UN, the perspective is a little different. Many Europeans would willingly trade their respective countries' military and scientific exploits for the right to display those five stars on the shirts of their national sides.

After this brief survey of Brazil's triumphs and failures, our visitor would certainly conclude that the country lacks great generals, revolutionary leaders, space-travel pioneers and almost every other type of traditional heroic figure. Our Alamo was the Sarriá, our Waterloo the *Maracanazo* and our great heroes are not historical giants like Henry V, Lincoln or Gagarin. Nevertheless, even though they have won no wars, led no revolutions and never journeyed through space, Brazil's heroes are just as famous as those of the great nations. The country's distinctly unmilitary idols need only one name each: Didi, Garrincha, Tostão, Gérson, Romário and Ronaldo. Surnames, military ranks, and noble titles are superfluous. Only one title exists as an exception to that rule, and it too belongs to a football hero: *o Rei* (the King), conferred on Pelé in recognition of his peerless footballing genius, became a title accepted nearly worldwide without the need to fire a single shot.

A visit to a football stadium offers valuable insight into local customs. This experience is imperative. To return home from Brazil without having been to a game is as serious a cultural omission as going to Athens and not visiting the Parthenon. Brazil's stadiums fall short of European and North American ones in terms of comfort and safety, but with a few simple precautions you can enjoy an unforgettable experience and, at the same time, capture the true essence of the Brazilian character. And there is a wide choice, from the simple Vila Belmiro in Santos, the home ground of Pelé, the greatest of them all, to the majestic Maracanã in Rio and Morumbi in São Paulo, not to mention Brinco de Ouro da Princesa and Moisés Lucarelli, the grounds of Campinas arch-rivals Guarani and Ponte Preta, both with a 30,000 capacity and a mere 300 meters (328 yards) apart. The Estádio Zerão, in the city of Macapá in the Amazon region, is located exactly on the equator, so the line at midfield also divides the world. Nowhere else can people attend a game where one goal is in the northern hemisphere and the other in the southern hemisphere.

Brazilians will put up with people who change their vocation, their political party, their religion and even their sex, but they will not, under any circumstances, tolerate a fan who switches teams. So, as a visitor, think very carefully about which side you intend to support to avoid being branded as a turncoat later. Keep in mind, every Brazilian has a favorite team, and turning your back on theirs is a sin almost as mortal as suggesting that Maradona was better than Pelé. (Warning: maintaining that Maradona was better than Garrincha is also considered a serious breach of good manners.)

Taking these few precautions, visitors will discover that everything about Brazilian football is pure delight. The game is slower here, and best players have time to show off their skills, relishing their domination of the ball with a series of swerves, feints and dribbles. The rhythmic play of the ball dictates the tone of the game. The fans are spirited but extremely demanding – referee, players and authorities are routinely booed. As Nelson Rodrigues, one of the country's acclaimed sports columnists, once wrote: "Brazilians don't even respect a minute of silence". It is no coincidence that Rodrigues was also the country's best playwright, because here drama and football are inseparable. Football imitates art; art imitates life; life imitates football. And so, regardless of politics, the economic situation, or international crises, as long as the Brazilian shirt is yellow, that yellow that turns gold with the sweat of the players, and emblazoned with the stars of the country's footballing triumphs, Brazil will be a united, peaceful and happy nation.

Marcos Caetano,
sports columnist

CARNIVAL

A festival of European origins, Carnival has been transformed over the centuries by Brazil's Negro population. Today, it's the most magnificent mass celebration in the world.

Other countries celebrate Carnival, but Brazil is the country of Carnival. Throughout the country, the four-day spectacle lures frolicking masses to the streets, attracts legions of tourists, and drives the economy. It's fair to criticize the commercialization and the prices of admission tickets and costumes, and to dismiss the naïve idea that social hierarchies temporarily disappear. Nevertheless, for most Brazilians, Carnival is a ritual celebration of life, full of untamed, authentic energy that transcends the demands of the market, the ogling tourists and the television broadcasters.

FROM *ENTRUDO* TO PARADES

The Portuguese precursor to Carnival was called *entrudo*. These pre-Lent festivities, which arrived in Brazil in the 16th century, consisted of pranks involving invasions of homes and play fighting in the streets using mud, flour, egg and water as ammunition. Those traditions persisted but changed gradually over centuries. "*Limõezinhos de cheiro*", small wax balls filled with perfumed water, replaced the dirty water once thrown at passers-by. In 1840, a hotel in Rio de Janeiro introduced the country to the word *Carnival* when it organized a Carnival Ball inspired by the elite costume balls of Venice. But the *entrudo* didn't disappear. In 1850 the architect Grandjean de Montigny, a member of the French Mission, died of respiratory complications from a cold that he caught in Rio after receiving a "soaking". During the Carnival of 1907, the daughters of President Afonso Pena drove along the avenue in a convertible. That began the tradition of the "*corso*", a procession of decorated cars that attracted multitudes who gathered along the streets.

While the rich paraded down the streets in cars and enjoyed themselves at the balls to the sound of polkas, the people in the suburbs of Rio de Janeiro transformed the *entrudo*. They organized groups that paraded in the streets and played the novel rhythms of

Olinda Carnival: festival in the streets

At the parades in Marquês de Sapucaí in Rio de Janeiro, thousands dance the samba until the break of day

sambas and *marchinhas* (Carnival songs). These groups, called *ranchos*, *cordões* and *blocos*, were the beginnings of the samba schools.

In 1932 the first competitive parade between the samba schools was held in Rio de Janeiro. The municipal administration, recognizing its potential appeal to tourists, began to support the parades in 1935. (It was also at this time that Carnival became one with the *jogo do bicho*, an illegal lottery that involves animal symbols and is akin to the numbers game in Harlem.) To the present day it is one of the largest financial sponsors of the samba schools. The professionalization of the festival had continued throughout the century, particularly in the 1960's with the introduction of television.

Carnival, Carnivals

Rio de Janeiro's innovations of balls, parades and floats spread to other Brazilian cities, where the *entrudo* got replaced with the new Rio trend. However, each region added its traditions and music, creating in the festival the regional variations that persist to this day. Today, São Paulo and most other large cities reproduce the Rio Carnival with minor adaptations, while smaller rural towns, as well as Recife and Olinda in the state of Pernambuco, and Salvador in Bahia, forgo the celebration.

In Rio the parades have become so large that they have been assigned a special stadium, the Sambódromo, since 1984. The compe-

tition between samba schools attracts celebrities and tourists from all over the world. It is an expensive extravaganza, organized by professionals. The music used today is a narrative samba that interprets the theme of the school's parade. The *marchinhas* persist in the dance parties and in the *blocos* that still pass through the city.

In Pernambuco, Carnival is a street festival. Here, *frevo* emerged from the combination of European traditions and African rhythms. Along with this music, the Carnival in Pernambuco also maintains various local traditions, including dances called *maracatus*, which slaves created to display religious and historical symbols and set to percussion instruments, *caboclinhos,* and *ursos*. In Salvador, the *trios elétricos*, which are trucks equipped with sound systems and stages for bands to perform on, dominate the festivities. Created in the 1950's, the *trios* lead multitudes of people through the city streets, playing everything from *frevo* to *axé*, a musical style popular since the early 1980's. Recife, Salvador and various other Brazilian cities also organize off-season Carnivals, called *micaretas*. Although they lack the long tradition of Carnival, they give visitors a taste of the real thing – and generate welcome income for residents.

A European tradition infused with African flavors, Carnival has survived as part spontaneous celebration, part tourist-driven spectacle. A festival for all classes, it is the strongest proof of the Brazilian gift for joy and happiness.

ADVENTURE AND ECOTRAVEL

Opportunities for ecotourism and adventure exist all over Brazil. Some areas welcome guests with fully modern services, while others offer more rudimentary facilities in the midst of magnificent and nearly untouched wilderness.

Adventure tourism and adventure sports aren't entirely one, according to specialists, but there's plenty of room for both in Brazil. Adventure sports such as mountain biking and rafting demand training, discipline and a high level of physical fitness. Adventure tourism broadly refers to both these demanding sports and other adventure-related activities, such as rappelling and snorkeling, which can be undertaken with a minimum of preparation. Rappelling can be done in various situations, and snorkeling is a leisure activity that does not require previous training.

Since nature and adventure sports go hand in hand, it's easy to see why Brazil has become an important ecotourism destination. The country's size and its diverse landscapes make it irresistible both for those seeking to peacefully contemplate beauty and for those looking for thrills, excitement and the "adrenaline" that adventurers talk about so much. The natural richness and abundance is unparalleled – and unfortunately not always matched by organization and infrastructure, even in officially designated Conservation Areas such as national parks, environmentally protected areas and privately owned reserves. The traveler is therefore best off thoroughly investigating his or her destination in advance, through tourist information centers, travel agencies, sports magazines and experienced tourists and adventurers – as well as, of course, this volume.

A COUNTRY OF INFINITE POSSIBILITIES

Which destinations should be recommended to an ecotourist willing to brave Brazil? There's almost nowhere one can go wrong. One place to start might be the city of Brotas, in the center of São Paulo state, with its many rivers and a unique geological structure that is the source of some 30 waterfalls. Thanks to these unique natural features, the city has become one of the most popular and well estab-

Canyoning, in Bahia

lished centers of adventure tourism in Brazil, with a range of sports including rafting, *bóia cross* (going down a river on an inflatable inner tube), rappelling, horseback riding, trekking, mountain biking and canopy tree climbing. If the adventurer wants to combine sports with big-city attractions, the best place to head to is Rio de Janeiro, which has managed a rare feat: preserving a magnificent forest reserve – Parque Nacional da Tijuca – in the heart of the large city. The reserve is well designed to address the needs of visitors, and myriad trails leading to waterfalls and caves, as well as to Pedra Bonita, a popular jump point for hang gliding. Mountain climbers can climb Pão de Açúcar and many of the city's other landmark mountains.

Chapada Diamantina, an oasis of crystal clear waters and gentle hills in the backlands of Bahia, offers opportunities for mountain climbing, trekking, biking and snorkeling. Caves, lagoons, rivers and waterfalls compose a landscape that many describe as the most beautiful in Brazil.

In the state of Mato Grosso do Sul, in the Central West region, is another favorite destination – the town of Bonito – a paradise for hiking, snorkeling, diving and rafting. The nearby Pantanal offers many options for trails and horseback riding in one of the country's largest ecological sanctuaries. The region is also one of the country's most popular locations for sport fishing.

Jalapão, in Tocantins, offers one of Brazil's best locations for rafting in an almost untouched region, perfect for those willing to trade comfort for the pleasure of being surrounded by wild nature. Far to the south, Florianópolis, in the state of Santa Catarina, combines trails and coastline that is ideal for surfing and diving.

Countless opportunities for water sports line Brazil's vast coastline. There are the favorite diving destinations such as Fernando de Noronha in Pernambuco, Abrolhos in Bahia, Arraial do Cabo in Rio de Janeiro, and Bombinhas in Santa Catarina. For sailing the best areas include Ilhabela in São Paulo, Angra dos Reis in Rio de Janeiro, Jericoacoara in Ceará, and Imbituba in Santa Catarina.

This list hardly scratches the surface of what the country has to offer the adventurous traveler. There are also the mountain ranges in the south, the mountains and high peaks in the southeast, the wild beaches in the Northeast, and the rich and lush Amazon Rainforest. A wide range of amazing possibilities await those seeking adventure or tranquility, physically demanding challenges or serene and timeless beauty.

Sailing

Diving

Paragliding

Motocross

Surfing

Rock climbing

Flora and Fauna

The huge expanse of Brazilian territory offers a diversity of environments. Each ecosystem is a universe: travel through them and experience the sense of enchantment and wonder that must have enveloped Brazil's first visitors.

Throughout the 19th century, many European researchers crisscrossed Brazil to inventory its riches. Coming from France, England, Germany and the Netherlands, these naturalists – a term describing botanists, zoologists, geologists and other natural history experts – not only catalogued an host of Brazilian animal and plant species, but also classified the territory itself for the first time, broadly delineating what scientists would eventually call ecosystems. Currently, IBAMA (Brazilian Institute of the Environment and Renewable Natural Resources) distinguishes seven broad ecological regions in the country – a classification that does not differ greatly from that proposed by the pioneering studies of the naturalists.

The Amazon Rainforest

When considering Brazilian plants and animals, it is impossible to not mention the immense green patch that spreads over the northwestern part of the country. Brazil contains roughly 3.5 million km² (1.35 million sq. mi.) of the Amazon's total 7 million square kilometers (2.7 million sq. mi.). The Amazon River and its tributaries form a complex network of waterways that sustain an incredible biodiversity.

The variety of forest environments accounts for this diversity. There are regions of aquatic forests (*igapó*) that are constantly flooded, meadows that are periodically flooded and upland forests that are spared direct contact with running water. Patches of savannah landscapes and a type of dry scrub vegetation called *campinarana* by the locals are nestled in the heart of the forest. Each area has distinct animal and plant life. There is a considerable variety, including tree species like mahogany (threatened by illegal logging), cabbage-bark, cedar, palm, Brazil nut, silk-cotton, sapodillas, *pau-mulato*, mauriti palms, Guiana chestnut and Brazilian spiny club palms. There is also an immense variety of herbs and grasses, as well as the Amazon's sig-

A tree toad in a bromeliad, Atlantic Rainforest

Royal water lily, Amazon region

nature flower, the royal water lily that floats on rivers and inlets displaying flowers on top of large circular leaves. The list of birds includes macaws, toucans, woodpeckers, hoatzins, wrens (the *uirapuru*, whose song, according to legend, is so sweet that other birds stop to listen), cock-of-the-rocks and manakins. Reptiles include Brazilian land turtles, turtles, lizards, anacondas, boa constrictors, bushmasters and dozens of other snake species. The list of mammals includes bats, grisons, coatis and anteaters, as well as the whitelipped peccary, the three-toed sloth, the spotted cavy and the Brazilian tapir. There are various primate species such as ouakari monkeys, capuchin monkeys and howling monkeys. The cat family includes jaguars and cougars. There are also roughly 3,000 species of fish swimming in the rivers, as well as aquatic mammals like manatees and Amazon porpoises.

THE CERRADO (SAVANNAH)

The Cerrado has a distinct landscape: large tracts of level land scattered with sparse vegetation and gnarled tree trunks with thick bark. The savannah's dry winters leave the fields yellowish and the trees bare. In the summer, the green returns along with the rain.

A dense forest of tall trees flourishes along the riverbanks which divide the plateau. Outlining the marshes, long lines of mauriti palms form pathways – and throughout centuries, these palm trees guided muleteers, indicating from afar the location of water for the cattle. The Brazilian savannah has 10,000 plant species. Trees found here include tecomas, golden spoon fruit trees, rosewoods and copals, as well as shrubs such as vellozia. Flowers include strawflowers; fruit trees include souari nuts, the fruit of which is used extensively in local cuisine.

These ecosystems are also the habitat of hundreds of different animal species. Among the birds are ostriches, crested seriemas, owls, macaws, parrots and parakeets. In the fields roam animals such as anteaters, deer, armadillos, jaguars, cougars, bush dogs and maned wolves. There are also snakes like the boa constrictor, the Brazilian dragon aroid and the tropical rattlesnake, as well as lizards and a large number of insects that are far from being completely identified.

THE PANTANAL

The waterways flowing down from the Andes and the central Brazilian plateau join with those from the Paraguay basin to form the Pantanal. This large region of lowlands in the hearts of the states of Mato Grosso and Mato Grosso do Sul extends to the west toward Bolivia and Paraguay, covering an area of 250,000 km² (96,500 sq. mi.) – larger than the United Kingdom. It is a vast system made up of more than 100 rivers. It is a universe unto itself, split into two seasons: the rainy season that the locals call winter that extends from November to March and is characterized by extensive flooding. The dry season or summer runs from April to October, when the water levels

Black beaked toucan, Amazon region

Macaw, Amazon Rainforest

Brazilian tapir, Amazon Rainforest

Hairy saki monkey, Amazon Rainforest

Subauma tree, Amazon Rainforest

Capybaras, Pantanal

Caranda palm trees, Pantanal

Margay tiger cat, Southern Pampas

SPECIES OF THE AMAZON RAINFOREST, THE PANTANAL, THE SAVANNAH, THE SEMI-ARID SCRUBLANDS AND THE SOUTHERN PLAINS

Quipá cactus, Semi-arid Scrublands

Hairy six-banded armadillo, Semi-arid Scrublands

Brazilian guinea pig, Semi-arid Scrublands

The great anteater, Savannah

Black-collared hawk, Pantanal

Maned wolf, Savannah

Mauriti palm trees, Savannah

TRANSITION AREAS
Amazon/Semiarid Scrublands
Amazon/Savannah
Savannah/Semiarid Scrublands

BIOMAS
Amazon Rainforest
Caatinga (Semiarid Scrublands)
Cerrado (Savannah)
Atlantic Rainforest
Pantanal
Southern Plains
Coastal Region

slowly drop and leave behind a nutritious loam that enables the proliferation of life on the lowlands. The floodplain becomes an expanse of grassland with a few scattered trees, ideal for cattle grazing. It is not a coincidence that cattle ranching is one of the pillars of the Pantanal economy.

This unique environment is a meeting point for plants and animals from many different regions. This is what distinguishes the Pantanal — not the existence of exclusive species, but the huge numbers and variety of species. Plants and animals typically found in the Amazon, the Savannah and the central plateau are also found here.

Bird species include red and blue macaws, toucans, hummingbirds, spoonbilled ducks, hawks, jabiru storks, kingfishers and cormorants. Mammals include capybaras, jaguars, anteaters, deer, otters and Brazilian otters. The region also has an abundance of anacondas, boa constrictors, adder snakes, alligators and lizards such as the teju lizard and iguanas, as well as frogs and toads of all sizes and colors. The Pantanal waters contain more than 200 different species of fish (including dourados, speckled catfish and piranhas) that attract fishermen from all over the world. Fishing is prohibited during the spawning season, when the schools of fish swim upstream to lay their eggs. The vegetation of the Pantanal varies in accordance with its own ecological niches. There are palm trees from the Savannah and others such as yellow and purple tecomas. The dry hilltops are home to cacti, as well as bromeliads.

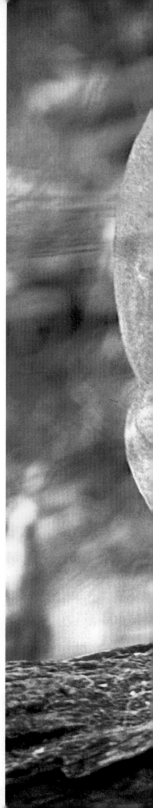

Cougar, Semi-arid Scrublands

Brazilwood tree, Atlantic Rainforest

The other extreme of the Pantanal has rich aquatic vegetation that is fundamental for the development of animal life in the rivers. These plants often group together and form floating green "islands" on the rivers. In the hidden waters of the Pantanal, it is even possible to find the quintessentially Amazonian royal water lily.

THE CAATINGA (SEMI-ARID SCRUBLANDS)

Life can actually thrive in the parched vastness of the Caatinga. There are roughly 700,000 km² (270,000 sq. mi.) identified by rugged ground and a hot, dry climate.

The semi-arid climate of the Caatinga is characterized by two seasons: the rainy summer season and the dry winter season. During the drought, the rivers dry up, the plants shed their leaves and the soil cracks. When rain starts to fall, green foliage spreads once again.

In the Caatinga, regions dotted with shrubs, cacti and thorny plants alternate with sparse forests consisting of small trees and bushes. There, visitors will find cacti like the Peru cereus (whose flower, according to the locals, is a sign of the rainy season), the xique-xique cactus, the palm cactus and the floral wreath cactus. There are also shrubs and trees such as the castorbean plant, aveloz, acacia, piassava palm, angico, tecoma and nettlespurge. Some regions boast fruit trees such as the yellow mombin and cashew, as well as the hardwoods brauna, the tonka-bean tree and the Chinese date tree. The region's animals include bats, cavies, three-banded armadillos, brockets and lizards, as well as snakes like the tropical rattle snake, the false coral snake and the boa constrictor. The most common birds are caiques, doves, picazuro pigeons (known as the *asa-branca*, it is the symbol of the *sertão* or backlands of the Northeast, thanks to the song by Luís Gonzaga of the same name) and the laughing hawk, a small hawk whose call is considered an omen of doom.

THE ATLANTIC RAINFOREST

When the Portuguese arrived in Brazil, the Atlantic Rainforest covered more than 1 million square kilometers (400 thousand sq. mi.). Today, only 7 percent of this area remains. Even so, it is still one of the world's most diversified ecosystems.

Extending from the states of Rio Grande do Norte to Rio Grande do Sul, the rainforest covers coastal and inland areas in a strip of land of varying width (on average 200 kilometers, or 124 mil.). In the Northeast it is a narrow strip along the coast, widening in the south of Bahia and continuing southward in an irregular pattern until it reaches Paraná and Santa Catarina where it extends far inland. Moisture carried by the winds blowing off the ocean is a common factor among all regions.

The forest, fragmented by human devastation, contains an immense biodiversity. As well as huge variety of invertebrate fauna (many still unknown) and fish, amphibians, snakes and other reptiles, there are 25 species of primates, many exclusive to the regions. These include the golden lion tamarin in the south of Bahia, the saki monkey in the regions between Espírito Santo and Minas Gerais and the spider monkey in the Southeastern region. Throughout the entire forest, there are large cats like the margay tiger cat, the leopard and the jaguar. The forest is also home to anteaters, hairy six-banded armadillos and three-toed sloths. Birds include the Brazilian tanager that inhabits the coastal region and the seven-colored tanager that lives in Alagoas and Pernambuco. Toucans, white herons and parrots are also found throughout the forest. Typical plant species are ferns, bromeliads and orchids, as well as flowering trees such as the manaca rain tree, princess flower and the ringworm shrub. The forest also boasts palm trees – such as the one from which açaí (p. 28) is extracted –, silverleaf pumpwood trees, pink shower trees, Paraná pines, sibipirunas and albarco jequitibas that can reach a height of 50 meters (164 feet). The brazilwood tree that gave Brazil its name, now almost extinct, is also native to the Atlantic Rainforest.

THE SOUTHERN PAMPAS

The Southern part of the country contains a large area of open plains. Vegetation is thicker between Santa Catarina and Rio Grande do Sul, especially in the more mountainous areas. Heading further south, the land becomes flatter and more homogenous, forming an immense green carpet called the Pampas that extends beyond the border of Rio Grande do Sul to Uruguay and Argentina. The grassy plains are dotted with fig, trumpet and other trees. Typical animals include the Pampas fox (or grison), the Pampas cat, deers, jaguars and raccoons. Closer to the coast, the fields encounter wetland ecosystems with aquatic plants like water lilies and rushes. The area is inhabited by mammals such as rice rats, capybaras and gophers, reptiles such as the broad-nosed cayman and birds such as the great white shouldered tanager, the black-necked swan and teal ducks from Patagonia. The region also hosts many fish, including the cichlid.

COASTAL LOWLANDS

Brazil's long coastline features a wide array of natural formations: sea cliffs, beaches, dunes, remote rocky stretches, coastal lowlands and forests. But the mangrove swamps deserve special attention. These swamps are found from Amapá to Santa Catarina in bays and estuaries where the rivers flow into the ocean. The currents of water deposit sediment and organic material on the loamy bottom where the mangroves trees grow.

These trees vary in height. Their roots protrude from the ground and coexist with the swamp animal life: shrimp, crabs, oysters and mussels, as well as salt-water fish like snook fish, catfish and mullet. Sea otters, coatis, raccoons also reside in the lowlands; birds like the scarlet ibis, bittern and heron also seek out the habitat to reproduce.

For many years, the mangrove swamps – dark areas full of mud and insects – were associated with unhealthiness and backwardness, and as a result, many were filled in or used as garbage dumps. Their importance to the equilibrium of marine life was only recognized a few decades ago, and today many of them are legally protected. Despite many recurring problems such as pollution, smuggling and deforestation, the country has matured, and the swamps still offer the same sensation of enchantment and wonder that the ancient explorers experienced.

Mangrove swamp, Coastal Lowlands

SPECIES OF THE ATLANTIC RAINFOREST AND COASTAL LOWLANDS

Scarlet ibis, Coastal Lowlands

Marine land crab, Coastal Lowlands

Bromeliads, Atlantic Rainforest

Fungi, Atlantic Rainforest

Snout beetle, Atlantic Rainforest

Yellow tecoma, Atlantic Rainforest

Orchids, Atlantic Rainforest

Woolly spider monkey, Atlantic Rainforest

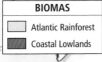

BIOMAS	
	Atlantic Rainforest
	Coastal Lowlands

A Portuguese Primer

Brazilian Portuguese may use familiar characters, but that fact belies its foreignness. A little practice with the language will help you request directions and will ease other attempt to communicate.

Many letters are pronounced in ways that seem strange or counterintuitive to native English speakers. For example, double r's and r's that begin words sound like an h. In addition, vowels crowned like (ã) or followed by an n or m are nasal, a sound difficult for many foreigners to make. (To say "São", sound out the first three-and-a-half letters of *sound*.) When not nasal, vowels sound like:

a: "ah" or "uh"
e: "e" as in *Meg*, or almost silent
i: "ee"
o: "au" as in *caught*, "o" as in *or*, or "ou" as in *you*
u: by itself, "ou", but "w" when followed by another vowel

Portuguese consonants are even trickier, because pronunciation may depend on which other letters appear nearby. For example, real (the unit of currency), sounds rather like "hey-ow". A few of the most confusing ones are:

ç: "s"
ch: "sh"
di or **de** (at the end of a word): often "jee"
h: silent
j: "zh", like the "z" in *azure*
l (at the end of a word when following an o or a): often "o" or "ow"
lh: "li" as in *million*
nh: "ni" as in *onion*
q: k as in *kiss*
r: a short rolled r
r (at the beginning of a word) or **rr:** h as in *how*
s: "s", "sh", "z", or "zh", depending on neighboring letters
te or **ti:** often "ch" as in check

Communication

0: zero	6: seis	30: trinta
1: um	7: sete	40: quarenta
2: dois	8: oito	50: cinqüenta
3: três	9: nove	100: cem
4: quatro	10: dez	500: quinhentos
5: cinco	20: vinte	1000: mil

I: Eu
I am: Eu sou
You are: Você é
Hello/Goodbye: Oi, Olá/Tchau
Please/Thank you:
   Por favor/Obrigado (male);
   obrigada (female)
Yes/No: Sim/Não
I am a foreigner:
   Sou estrangeiro
I'm sick/hurt:
   Estou doente/com dor
Help me, please:
   Me ajuda, por favor.
How much (is it)?: Quanto (é)?
What's your name?:
   Qual é o seu nome?
My name is: Meu nome é...
When...? Quando...?
Straight ahead: Siga em frente
Today/Tomorrow: Hoje/Amanhã
Where is...?: Onde fica...?

a hotel/inn: um hotel/pousada
a hospital: hospital
a doctor: um médico
a bank: o banco
the embassy: a embaixada
I'd like...: Eu gostaria...
a room: um quarto
a bathroom: um banheiro
a guide: um guia
Food/drink: comida/bebida
Beer, draft: cerveja/chope
Bread: pão
Chicken: frango
Egg: ovo
Fish: peixe
Pork: carne de porco
Steak: bife
Water: água
Close: perto
Far: longe
Left: esquerda
Right: direita

COMMON TERMS

Baiano: a native of Bahia
Caatinga: Semi-arid scrublands
Cachaça: a spirit distilled from
   sugarcane (also called *pinga*)
Caipirinha: *cachaça*, lime
   or other fruit, sugar and ice
Carioca: a native of Rio
Chope: draft beer
Churrasco: Brazilian barbacue
Dendê: a nut oil
Feijoada: beans stewed with
   sun-dried meat, smoked pork,
   sausages, and spices (p. 30)
Forró: a traditional Brazilian
   music and dance style
   with syncopated rhythms
Gaúcho: a native of
   Rio Grande do Sul
Ibama: Brazilian Institute
   of Environmental and Renewable

Natural Resources
Igreja: church
Ilha: island
Jardim: garden
Lagoa: lagoon
Largo: plaza
**Mandioca, also called aipim or
macaxeira (manioc):** an edible root
   that can be steamed, fried (like
   french fries), pounded into flour
   (*farofa*) or meal (*tapioca*)
Mercado: market
Paulista: a native of São Paulo
Pousada: a simple inn, usually cosy
   and homey
Praça: square
Praia: beach
Rua: street
Serra: hill
Vale: valley

SOUTHEAST

The starting points for the itineraries suggested in the following pages are the capital cities of Rio de Janeiro, São Paulo, Minas Gerais and Espírito Santo, which together make up the Southeast region. Served by federal highways, they offer visitors a wide range of options. Rio de Janeiro is one of the most vibrant and beautiful cities in the country, São Paulo is the business, shopping and culinary heart of Latin America, Belo Horizonte is steeped in cultural tradition, and Vitória combines tranquility with first-rate urban infrastructure. But the attractions are not confined to the big cities: the coastline of São Paulo state has a fabulous succession of beaches, while the hinterland is a mecca for sports lovers or those seeking mild mountain temperatures. Minas Gerais contains several magnificently preserved cities built at the height of the gold boom. In Espírito Santo, the main attractions are the coast and its historical towns. Nature and history also abound in the mountains of Rio de Janeiro state, while the Rio coastline is full of idyllic retreats, including Paraty, one of the jewels of Brazilian colonial architecture.

DESTINATION
RIO DE JANEIRO

Rio de Janeiro is the archetype of a cosmopolitan, tropical paradise.
With a unique blend of glamour and natural exuberance, it casts
a long and haloed shadow in the popular imagination. That renown
is deserved, despite the city's sprawling *favelas*, or shantytowns, and
its share of urban troubles. The state offers many other attractions,
notably the magnificent coastal towns of Paraty, Angra dos Reis
and Ilha Grande, in the south, and Búzios, Cabo Frio and
Arraial do Cabo to the north. The mild climate facilitates exploration, and the historical
past comes alive in charming inland cities such as Petrópolis, Teresópolis, Vassouras,
Visconde de Maúa and Itatiaia.

DESTINATION HIGHLIGHTS

CITY OF RIO DE JANEIRO
  Historic Center
  Cinelândia and Surroundings
  Lapa
  Santa Teresa
  Panoramic Views and Fashionable Beaches
  Outdoor Rio
  Lagoa Rodrigo de Freitas
    and Jardim Botânico
  Barra da Tijuca and
    Recreio dos Bandeirantes
Special Attractions

CITY OF NITERÓI (17 km/10.5 mi.)

MOUNTAINS AND INLAND
  Petrópolis (65 km/40 mi.)

Parque Nacional da Serra dos Órgãos
Teresópolis (87 km/54 mi.)
Vassouras (111 km/69 mi.)
Visconde de Maúa (200 km/124 mi.)
Parque Nacional do Itatiaia (167 km/103 mi.)

SOUTHERN COAST
  Angra dos Reis (168 km/104 mi.)
  Ilha Grande (150 km/93 mi. + 1h30 by boat)
  Paraty (248 km/154 mi.)

NORTH COAST
  Búzios (192 km/119 mi.)
  Cabo Frio (148 km/92 mi.)
  Arraial do Cabo (158 km/98 mi.)
  *All distances are from the city
  of Rio de Janeiro*

CITY OF RIO DE JANEIRO

HISTORIC CENTER

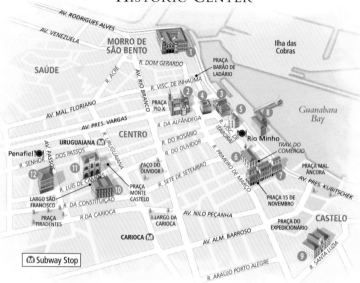

MORRO DE SÃO BENTO
SAÚDE
AV. RODRIGUES ALVES
AV. VENEZUELA
R. DOM GERARDO
PRAÇA BARÃO DE LADÁRIO
Ilha das Cobras
R. ACRE
R. RIO BRANCO
R. VISC. DE INHAÚMA
AV. MAL. FLORIANO
PRAÇA PIO X
AV. PRES. VARGAS
R. DA ALFÂNDEGA
Guanabara Bay
CENTRO
R. DO ROSÁRIO
Rio Minho
R. DO OUVIDOR
TRAV. DO COMÉRCIO
URUGUAIANA
Penafiel
R. SENHOR DOS PASSOS
R. URUGUAIANA
PAÇO DO OUVIDOR
R. SETE DE SETEMBRO
R. PRIMEIRO DE MARÇO
R. VISC. DE ITABORAÍ
PRAÇA MAL. ÂNCORA
AV. PRES. KUBITSCHEK
R. LUÍS DE CAMÕES
PRAÇA MONTE CASTELO
LARGO SÃO FRANCISCO
R. DA CONSTITUIÇÃO
PRAÇA 15 DE NOVEMBRO
PRAÇA TIRADENTES
R. DA CARIOCA
LARGO DA CARIOCA
AV. NILO PEÇANHA
PRAÇA DO EXPEDICIONÁRIO
CASTELO
CARIOCA
AV. ALM. BARROSO
R. SANTA LUZIA
R. ARAÚJO PORTO ALEGRE
Ⓜ Subway Stop

1 - Igreja do Mosteiro de São Bento
2 - Igreja Nossa Senhora da Candelária
3 - Casa França–Brasil
4 - Centro Cultural Banco do Brasil (CCBB)
5 - Centro Cultural Correios
6 - Igreja Nossa Senhora da Lapa
    dos Mercadores

7 - Paço Imperial
8 - Espaço Cultural da Marinha
9 - Igreja Nossa Senhora do Bonsucesso
10 - Igreja de São Francisco de Paula
11 - Real Gabinete Português de Leitura
12 - Centro de Arte Hélio Oiticica

This walking tour is designed for weekdays during normal business hours when most churches are open, the area is well policed, taxis are easily found and the streets are busy – which provides an opportunity to watch the comings and goings of the *cariocas* (Rio residents). On weekends, however, there are important attractions, such as religious services and events at the cultural centers, although there is less of a police presence and the streets are not so bustling.

❶ IGREJA DO MOSTEIRO DE SÃO BENTO

This monastery church was built by the Benedictines in the 17th century.

Baroque exuberance of the monastery church

Nossa Senhora da Candelária: a majestic downtown presence

A masterpiece of baroque architecture, its sober façade hides the exuberance of the interior's wooden *talhas* (ornamental carvings) covered in gold leaf. The eight magnificent side altars are decorated with sacred sculptures from the 17th and 18th centuries, and the soft lighting used to preserve the artworks helps to create a muted atmosphere. The cloisters are rarely open to the public, but exceptions are made on Palm Sunday and Corpus Christi. Every Sunday at 10am, people gather to hear the monks sing Gregorian chants. It is advisable to arrive in plenty of time.
Rua D. Gerardo, 68, Centro, tel. (21) 2291-7122. Open daily from 8-11am and 2:30-6pm.

❷ Igreja Nossa Senhora da Candelária

The Candelária church stands next to several cultural centers at one end of Avenida Presidente Vargas, which crosses the downtown area. Built between 1775 and 1898, its interior is decorated with marble of various colors and the pulpits have bronze stairs. Note the beautiful doors, also in bronze, engraved by the Portuguese artist Antonio Teixeira Lopes (1866-1942). *Praça Pio X, Centro, tel. (21) 2233-2324. Mon-Fri, 8am-4pm; Sat, 8am-noon; Sun, 9am-1pm.*

❸ Casa França–Brasil

This house was designed by Grandjean de Montigny, an architect who introduced the French neoclassicist style after his 1816 arrival in Brazil with the French Mission. Casa França–Brasil was inaugurated in 1820 as a business center; later, it was used as a customs house and a storehouse for bank archives. It became the seat of the Jury Court between 1956 and 1978, when it was restored. It now functions as a cultural center. Although it has no permanent collection of its own, the house holds important art exhibitions throughout the year. It is also worth seeing the 24 Doric columns bordering the area beneath the huge central dome's crowning skylight, as well as a bookstore, a café and a movie theater that holds screenings during the day.

Rua Visconde de Itaboraí, 78, Centro, tel: (21) 2253-5366. Tue-Sun, noon-8pm.

❹ CENTRO CULTURAL BANCO DO BRASIL (CCBB)

This building has been a cultural center since 1989 and hosts the city's most widely respected arts program. Equipped with exhibition and video rooms, a theater, cinema, library, bookstore and restaurant, it also serves as a meeting place during leisure hours – and something interesting is always going on, so there's no need to check the program before visiting. One of Grandjean de Montigny's disciples designed the building, which was built in 1880 as a commercial center.
Rua Primeiro de Março, 66, Centro, tel. (21) 3808-2020. Tue-Sun, 10am-9pm.

❺ CENTRO CULTURAL CORREIOS

The eclectically styled building hosts free art shows in 10 exhibition halls and contains a 200-seat auditorium showing films, plays and concerts of Brazilian music, plus a small video theater. A cultural center since 1993, it was initially built as a shipping company's training school between 1921 and 1922. The elevator that carries three passengers plus the operator is a relic from the latter year. Eventually, the building housed part of the Post Office administrative apparatus. Currently, a small art gallery, an attractive cafeteria and a post office are located at the ground level. Open-air events and film festivals are held in the neighboring **praça dos Correios**.
Rua Visconde de Itaboraí, 20, Centro, tel. (21) 2503-8770. Tue-Sun, noon-7pm.

❻ IGREJA NOSSA SENHORA DA LAPA DOS MERCADORES

After leaving the Centro Cultural Correios, follow the narrow Rua Visconde de Itaboraí in the direction of the restaurant Cais do Oriente to this tiny building, considered by many to be the most charming church in the city. Built by merchants in 1750 as a public oratory, it was thoroughly renovated in the 19th century. In 1893, during the Revolta da Armada, a navy

Paço Imperial – from royal residence to cultural center

POPULAR DOWNTOWN HANGOUTS

Bars and restaurants, especially those with a Portuguese influence, are scattered throughout the narrow and historic streets of downtown Rio. In the traditional and pleasant **Rio Minho**, visitors can eat savory snacks at the bar while admiring the ceramic tiles. Open since 1884, the restaurant quickly became renowned for its dishes such as the seafood soup Leão Veloso, and its famous regulars (*Rua do Ouvidor, 10, tel. 21/2509-2338. Mon-Fri, 11am-4pm*).

Lunch at **Penafiel**, with its homey atmosphere and Portuguese cuisine – not to mention its enormous portions – should not be missed. Try the fish and squid risotto, the *mocotó* (calfs' feet Portuguese style), the stewed tripe and the salt-cod with rice and broccoli. The interior of the building has been declared a Cultural Heritage of Rio (*Rua Senhor dos Passos, 121, tel. 21/2224-6870. Mon-Fri, 11am-3:30pm*).

Bar Luiz is a compulsory stop for a well-chilled draft beer. Open since 1886 and located on Rua da Carioca since 1927, the restaurant offers German food, wurst and a wide variety of cold cuts and cooked meats. The walls are decorated with photographs of bygone Rio. Bar Luiz is one of the stops in the Cinelândia and Surroundings itinerary suggested on page 96 (*Rua da Carioca, 39, tel. 21/2262-6900. Mon-Sat, 11am-11:30pm; Sun noon-6pm*).

insurrection against the government, a cannon ball aimed at the Palácio do Itamaraty hit the belfry and knocked down a marble statue of the Virgin Mary. Both the cannon ball and the sacred sculpture, which escaped unscathed, are displayed in the sacristy. The Rua do Ouvidor, a historic street lined by charming antique streetlamps, is an attraction itself.
Rua do Ouvidor, 35, Centro, tel. (21) 2509-2339. Mon-Fri, 8am-2pm.

❼ PAÇO IMPERIAL
When members of the royal family arrived in Brazil in 1808, they stayed in the **Paço Imperial**. The building was constructed in 1743 as the governor's residence and seat of government, and it became the scene of historic events such as the signing of the *Lei Áurea* (literally the "Golden Law"), which abolished slavery. Today, the site is a cultural center offering a contemporary arts program and equipped with a cinema, café and restaurant. The **Paço Imperial** is right behind the **Arco do Teles**, a small passageway connecting the **Travessa do**

Comércio with the spacious **Praça Quinze de Novembro**. (To get to the Arco do Teles, after leaving the Igreja Nossa Senhora da Lapa dos Mercadores, turn right at the Travessa do Comércio, and go straight ahead past the colonial houses converted into bars.) To the left of the building, near the sea, you can see the **Chafariz do Mestre Valentim**, a 1789 pyramid-shaped fountain carved in granite and marble. Just behind it, on the shoreline, a ferryboat station that links Rio de Janeiro to Niterói, Ilha do Governador and Paquetá. Praça Quinze de Novembro, formerly the Cais Pharoux (Pharoux docks) was, for centuries, the gateway for visitors arriving in the city by sea (*Praça Quinze de Novembro, 48, Centro, tel: 21/2533-4470. Tue-Sun, noon-6pm*). Crossing over to the bustling Rua Primeiro de Março two churches are situated side by side. Many historians consider the **Igreja de Nossa Senhora do Carmo, former Sé**, the city's cathedral until 1977, to be the best-preserved example of the baroque style in Rio (*Rua Sete de Setembro, 15, Centro, tel. 21/2242-7766. Mon-Fri,*

Igreja da Ordem Terceira do Monte do Carmo: a truly impressive sight

7am-5pm. Closed on Sat and Sun). Next to it is the **Igreja da Ordem Terceira de Nossa Senhora do Monte do Carmo**, which was built in several stages between 1755 and 1768 in the baroque and rococo styles. The representation of the *Via-Crúcis* (Stations of the Cross) is particularly worth seeing (*Rua Primeiro de Março, Centro, tel. 21/2242-4828. Mon-Fri, 8am-3:30pm. Closed on Sat and Sun).*

❽ Espaço Cultural da Marinha
The destroyer Bauru and the submarine Riachuelo, both now converted into museum vessels, are especially worth a visit – as is the small galley used by the royal family. From here, travelers can take a guided tour to **Ilha Fiscal**, where the last grand imperial ball was held just a few days before the institution of the Republic.
Avenida Alfredo Agache, Centro, tel. (21) 2104-6025. Tue-Sun, noon-5pm. Tours to Ilha Fiscal: Thu-Sun, 1-4pm. Tours of Guanabara Bay: Thu-Sun, 1:15-3:15pm.

❾ Igreja Nossa Senhora do Bonsucesso
Originally built as a chapel in 1567 – two years after the official foundation of the city, when the Portuguese ousted the French – this church has been subjected to several renovations. Its present façade dates back to the 19th century. The church houses the crucifix and the *bandeira da misericórdia* (the "flag of mercy" used during processions of condemned prisoners) that accompanied the conspirator Tiradentes on his way to the gallows. It also contains the pulpit, altar and tablets from the Jesuit School that once crowned the Morro do Castelo and was demolished in 1922. Constructed in the 17th century, the tablets are the oldest in Rio and the only ones painted in the Mannerist style, a Portuguese architectural style of the 16th and 17th centuries. The building is connected to the Santa Casa da Misericórdia.
Largo da Misericórdia, Centro, tel. (21) 2220-3001. Mon-Fri, 7am-3:30pm. Closed on Sat and Sun.

⑩ IGREJA DE SÃO FRANCISCO DE PAULA

Built in the 18th century, this church is poorly preserved and surrounded by street vendors, giving it a unprepossessing appearance. But it is still worth a visit because of the richness of its interior, especially the fine wooden *intaglio* carvings from the early 19th century (but still in the baroque style), Mestre Valentim's decoration in the main chapel, Antonio de Pádua Castro's carvings and Vítor Meireles' paintings.

Largo de São Francisco, Centro, tel. (21) 2509-0067. Mon-Fri, 9am-1pm.

⑪ REAL GABINETE PORTUGUÊS DE LEITURA

Built in the Manueline style and inaugurated in 1837, the library houses more than 350,000 volumes, the most spectacular collection of Portuguese literature outside Portugal. The beautiful and imposing 400-square-meter reading room, with its 23-meter-high ceiling, is a truly awesome sight, decorated with ornamental metalwork and golden medieval motifs. A stained-glass skylight that covers the whole room, and the reading tables are made of carved jacaranda wood. Among other unusual finds is a copy of the 1572 first edition of Camões' *Os lusíadas*. Except for the rare books, the collection is open to the public.

Rua Luís de Camões, 30, Centro, tel. (21) 2221-3138. Mon-Fri, 9am-6pm.

⑫ CENTRO DE ARTE HÉLIO OITICICA

This building houses the collection of Hélio Oiticica (1937-1980), one of the most radical Brazilian artists of the 1960's and 70's. Oiticica is renowned for his *parangolés*, multi-colored works of art that can be worn like capes, and the collection includes pieces from different phases of his career. Six galleries all stage temporary exhibitions; their catalogues can be seen in the library of the Modern Museum of Art in New York.

Rua Luís de Camões, 68, Centro, tel. (21) 2242-1012. Tue-Fri, 11am-7pm; Sat, Sun and holidays, 11am-5pm.

Relics from the colonial past in the Real Gabinete Português de Leitura

CINELÂNDIA AND SURROUNDINGS

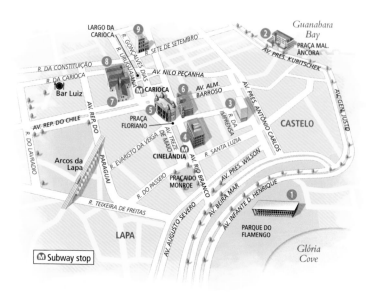

1 - Museu de Arte Moderna
2 - Museu Histórico Nacional
3 - Palácio Gustavo Capanema
4 - Biblioteca Nacional
5 - Theatro Municipal

6 - Museu Nacional de Belas-Artes
7 - Igreja e Convento de Santo Antônio
8 - Igreja da Ordem Terceira
   de São Francisco da Penitência
9 - Confeitaria Colombo

Cinelândia became a meeting place for politicians, artists and intellectuals at the beginning of the 20th century, in the area around the then-recently inaugurated Avenida Central (later renamed Avenida Rio Branco). It was here that the city's first movie theaters opened, although most have been converted into churches. Nevertheless, the area is still one of the most important hubs of *carioca* cultural life: the **Theatro Municipal**, the **Biblioteca Nacional**, the **Museu de Belas-Artes** and the recently refurbished movie theater **Cine Odeon** BR are all located here. The complex was built during the reform carried out by Mayor Pereira Passos in the early 20th century. Start the tour near the **Museu de Arte**

Moderna in the **Aterro do Flamengo**, located by the sea.

1 MUSEU DE ARTE MODERNA
This museum was opened in 1958 and remains one of the country's most extraordinary examples of 20th century architecture. It is the crowning achievement of the *carioca* architect Affonso Reidy, and Roberto Burle Marx designed its gardens. Held up by a series of V-like supports (see photograph opposite), the huge horizontal structure seems to float above the **Aterro do Flamengo**, also designed by Reidy. The open structure allows visitors to walk straight from the gardens to the sea without taking a detour around the building. In 1978, fire devastated the collection and the

museum was closed to the public for more than a decade. Today, it houses 11,000 pieces of Brazilian and international modern and contemporary art, including the Gilberto Chateaubriand Collection of early Brazilian modernists. Tarsila do Amaral's *Urutu*, Jackson Pollock's *Number 16* and Antonio Manuel's installation *O fantasma* are all here. The museum also hosts Fashion Rio, the *carioca* fashion week. Make the most of the visit and explore the **Aterro do Flamengo**, Burle Marx's most important landscaping project. The park also contains a vast leisure and sports area. On Sundays and holidays, it is closed to traffic.
Avenida Infante Dom Henrique, 85, Parque do Flamengo, tel. (21) 2240-4944. Tue-Fri, noon-6pm; Sat, Sun and holidays, noon-7pm.

❷ MUSEU HISTÓRICO NACIONAL
The museum is located on the site of the **Fortaleza de Santiago**, a fortress built in 1603, and the **Prisão do Calabouço**, a prision built in 1693. It houses a collection of 287,000 pieces from the Colonial period, although only a few are on display at any given time. The coaches and the coin collection (the largest in Latin America) are particularly worth seeing.
Praça Marechal Âncora, Centro, tel. (21) 2250-9260. Tue-Fri, 10am-5:30pm; Sat, Sun and holidays, 2pm-7pm.

❸ PALÁCIO GUSTAVO CAPANEMA
The palace – a global architectural icon and the first major modernist building in the world – was built between 1936 and 1942. Le Corbusier consulted on the undertaking, which was designed and executed by a brilliant team of architects including Lúcio Costa, Oscar Niemeyer and Affonso Reidy. It stands on 10-meter-high piles, allowing free circulation from the street. It is closed to the public because the government still

Museu de Arte Moderna: a landmark of the artistic avant-garde in the 1950's and 60's

The supports of the Palácio Gustavo Capanema building, one of the first examples of modernist architecture

uses the building, which was once the federal Ministry of Education, but it is still worth visiting for the beautiful gardens by Burle Marx, tile panels by Cândido Portinari and the sculptures by Bruno Giorgi.
Rua da Imprensa, 16, Centro, tel. (21) 2220-1490. Mon-Fri, 9am-5pm.

❹ BIBLIOTECA NACIONAL
The majestic staircase leading to the National Library's first floor impresses visitors immediately. But the building's chief attraction is its collection of more than 3 million volumes, including some very rare items such as letters from the imperial family, two 1572 copies of the first edition of *Os lusíadas* and two copies of the Moguncia Bible from Meinz, Germany, printed on vellum in 1462. The guided tour takes place from Monday to Friday at 11am, 1pm and 4pm, and lasts between 30 and 40 minutes.
Avenida Rio Branco, 219, Cinelândia, tel.

(21) 2262-8255. Mon-Fri, 9am-8pm; Sat 9am-3pm.

❺ THEATRO MUNICIPAL
Although the cultural season lasts from March to December, this building is well worth a visit even in the off-season for the architecture inspired by the Paris Opera, its marble staircases and onyx handrails, Rodolfo Bernardelli's sculptures and Eliseu Visconti's paintings. The charming 2,400-seat theater was opened in 1909 and built sideways to align it with the then-recently opened Avenida Rio Branco to provide a view of the Guanabara Bay and the Arcos da Lapa – today covered by the city's skyscrapers. Guided tours leave every hour, Monday to Friday, from 10am till 5pm. On Sundays, at 11am, there is a program of concerts entitled Domingo no Municipal (Sunday at the Municipal Theater).
Praça Floriano, Cinelândia, tel. (21) 2262-3935. Mon-Fri, 10am-5pm.

⑥ MUSEU NACIONAL DE BELAS-ARTES

Constructed because of Dom João VI's initiative to house the European masterpieces brought by the French Mission in 1816, the former Royal Academy of Fine Arts has a beautiful collection of approximately 5,000 Brazilian 19th century artworks. The collection is mainly drawings; highlights include *Batalha dos Guararapes* by Vítor Meireles, *Juventude* by Eliseu Visconti and *São Tomé das Letras* by Nicolau Facchinetti. The original pictures showing major events in national history familiar to all Brazilian children from schoolbook illustrations are all here in living color. The entire collection comprises more than 16,000 works by artists such as Frans Post, Cândido Portinari, Anita Malfatti, Lasar Segall and Auguste Rodin.
Avenida Rio Branco, 199, Cinelândia, tel. (21) 2240-0068. Tue-Fri, 10am-6pm; Sat, Sun and holidays, 2pm-6pm.

⑦ IGREJA E CONVENTO DE SANTO ANTÔNIO

Close to the bustle of the Largo da Carioca, the Igreja e Convento de Santo Antônio are located on the remains of a hill named after the saint.

The church, built between 1608 and 1620, contains treasures like the *arcaz*, the sacristy's large wood cabinet made in 1749 by Manuel Setúbal, and tiles and panels depicting scenes from the life of Saint Anthony. The convent was built later, in the second half of the 18th century. The collection was declared a historical heritage in 1938.
Largo da Carioca, Centro, tel. (21) 2262-0129. Mon-Fri, 8am-6:30pm; Sat, 9am-11am; Sun, 10am-11am.

⑧ IGREJA DA ORDEM TERCEIRA DE SÃO FRANCISCO DA PENITÊNCIA

This building is located on the same hill as the Igreja e Convento de Santo Antônio; together they provide a dazzling example of colonial architecture in downtown Rio. In fact, this particular church has few rivals when it comes to the colonial style, and the opulence of its golden ornamental carvings provides a feast for the eyes. Reopened to the public in 2000 after 12 years of restoration, the 1657 church was a forerunner of Brazilian baroque, anticipating the fully developed style in Minas. Take time to admire the sacred art, altars and carved images covered with gold leaf. Most works are by the Portuguese wood carver Manuel de Brito; Francisco

---

FROM THE FRENCH MISSION TO URBAN RENEWAL

The seeds of Brazilian artistic production in the European mold were brought by French Mission, which arrived in March of 1816. Dom João VI prompted the mission with the object of creating an academy for the systematic teaching of arts and crafts. The scholar Joaquim Lebreton, head of the Mission, brought a small collection of paintings that eventually gave rise to the present collection at the Museu Nacional de Belas-Artes, the construction of which was part of a drastic urban overhaul at the beginning of the 20th century. Dilapidated row houses and slums were demolished to make way for the Avenida Central (later Avenida Rio Branco), which cut through the area between the docks and Flamengo beach and changed the city's entire look. Cinelândia was built at this time, as was the eclectic group of buildings with Neoclassical flourishes, which included the Museu Nacional de Belas-Artes itself as well as the Theatro Municipal and the Biblioteca Nacional.

Aerial view of the Igreja da Penitência

high image of Nossa Senhora Imaculada Conceição, dating from the 18th century. And if visitors have any questions, caretaker Maria Desidéria will be happy to answer them. *Largo da Carioca, 5, Centro, tel. (21) 2262-0197. Tue-Fri, 9am-noon and 1-4pm.*

⑨ CONFEITARIA COLOMBO
This most traditional of Rio's gastronomic temples opened in 1894. Frequented by generations of politicians, artists and bohemians, it seems to be suspended in time: everything is original, from the huge imported Belgian mirrors and the stained-glass windows to the decorated floor and marble fittings. It is an excellent stop for coffee and a snack before continuing to stroll around the city or for late-afternoon tea. Try the famous *leques* (gaufrette wafers), served on their own or with ice-cream. The confectioner also has a smaller, less ornate branch at the Forte de Copacabana.
Rua Gonçalves Dias, 32, Centro, tel. (21) 2232-2300. Mon-Fri, 9:30am-8pm; Sat, 9:30am-5pm. Closed Sun.

Xavier de Brito, a sculptor and teacher of Aleijadinho; and Caetano Costa Coelho, painter of the magnificent illusionist painting of the Glorification of Saint Francis on the 114-foot-high ceiling over the main aisle. Also, don't miss the almost six-and-a-half-foot-

A visit to the charming Confeitaria Colombo will take you back in time

Arcos da Lapa, with a streetcar heading to Santa Teresa. In the background, the Igreja de Santa Teresa

LAPA

The birthplace of *carioca* roguery, Lapa was first settled in the 18th century. It is named after the 1751 Church of Nossa Senhora do Carmo da Lapa do Desterro. The area is full of historical corners just waiting to be rediscovered. One is the **Passeio Público**, an expanse of lawns and trees lying between Lapa and Cinelândia, planned by Mestre Valentim during the 18th century and offered as a gift from the Viceroy Luís de Vasconcelos to his mistress (*Rua do Passeio, Centro; open daily from 9am-5pm*). Another is the Armazém Romão, a warehouse built in 1896 and now converted into the **Sala de Concertos Cecília Meirelles**, an 835-seat concert hall (*Largo da Lapa, 47, tel. 21/2224-4291. Box office: Mon-Fri, 1pm-6pm, Sat and Sun, 1pm-6pm, when there are performances*). The poet Manuel Bandeira and the composer Antonio Maria lived in Lapa, and the artist Cândido Portinari maintained his studio here. The area was also frequented by bohemians such as Noel Rosa and Madame Satã in the 1930's. In the 50's and 60's, it was the musical heart of Rio, and its cafés, restaurants and snack-bars were meeting places for the artists and intellectuals. These establishments were replaced by others that maintained Lapa's reputation as a bohemian redoubt. Travelers will find the famous **Circo Voador** (*Rua dos Arcos, tel. 21/2533-5873/0354*), which caused a furor in the 80's when it housed the first shows by famous rock groups like Barão Vermelho (with Cazuza), Blitz, Legião Urbana and Kid Abelha, as well as performances by renowned artists like Regina Casé and Luís Fernando Guimarães. Closed throughout the 90's, it was reopened to the public in 2004 following a restoration. Behind it there is the **Fundição Progresso**, a huge cultural center that houses shows, circus performances and a cine-club (*Rua dos Arcos, 24, tel. 21/2220-5070*).

NIGHTLIFE IN LAPA

Old-time *sambistas*, well-dressed youngsters, body-piercing devotees, university students, foreign tourists, businesspeople, transvestites and prostitutes make the **Arcos da Lapa** area a lively cross-cultural mix at night. The vibrant bars that now occupy Lapa's small, old houses – especially on Avenidas Mem de Sá, Gomes Freire and Rua do Lavradio, which is famous for its antique shops – sway to the rhythm of *chorinho*, MPB and samba shows, sometimes two or three a night. Chilled draft beer, happily dancing couples and the architecture of the bars themselves give the area a bohemian atmosphere. One of the most famous bars is the traditional **Carioca da Gema** *(Avenida Mem de Sá, 79, tel 21/2221-0043. Mon-Thu, 6pm-1am; Fri, 6pm-3am; Sat, 9pm-2am).* Another is the musician-owned **Comuna do Semente**, right beneath the Arcos *(Rua Joaquim Silva, 138, tel. 21/2509-3591. Thu, from 9pm; Sun, from 11pm).* In front of the **Rio Scenarium** show-house (see the box) is the **Mangue Seco**, which specializes in *cachaça*, Brazil's sugar-cane spirit, and mixes live music, seafood and sidewalk tables *(Rua do Lavradio, 23, tel. 21/3852-1947. Mon, 11m-3pm; Tue-Sat, 11am till the last customer leaves).* A good suggestion for dinner is the **Nova Capela**, a traditional restaurant that is open almost all night and is a favorite after-hours hangout for musicians and journalists *(Avenida Mem de Sá, 96, tel. 21/2252-6228. Open daily, 11am-4am).*

OUR RECOMMENDATION

🍽 The high point of Lapa nightlife is the **Rio Scenarium**, a beautiful three-story house decorated with antiques where couples and even the most inhibited of tourists dance to live popular music. During a 15-day season, 106 musicians play here. And during the day, some of the hundreds of objects – a complete old pharmacy, a bust of Getúlio Vargas, sofas, bookcases, etc. – are rented out as scenery for movies, plays or TV programs, so the furnishings are in a constant state of flux. A quaint old elevator leads to the upper stories. There is also an annex with a cabaret and exhibition hall *(Rua do Lavradio, 20, tel. 21/3852-5516. Tue-Sat, from 7pm on).*

Chorinho music and ice-cold draft beer give the Lapa bars a bohemian atmosphere

View of the historic Largo das Neves from inside the Santa Saideira bar

SANTA TERESA

The Santa Teresa district, known as the *carioca* Montmartre and located on top of a hill, is steeped in the bohemian atmosphere generated by artists who installed their studios here, such as José Bechara, Marcos Chaves and Raul Mourão. Take the streetcar up the central region's lanes to the steep, narrow streets lined with beautiful old houses and manicured gardens. During the day, the streetcar jolts its way between the City Center and Santa Teresa along the **Aqueduto da Carioca**, a 270-meter-long (886 feet) aqueduct with 42 white arches. Better known as the **Arcos da Lapa**, the aqueduct was built in 1750 to supply the city with fresh water from the Carioca River. *Streetcar station: Rua Lélio Gama (Petrobras building, close to the Aqueduto da Carioca, near the Catedral Metropolitana), Centro, tel. 21/2240-5709. Open daily from 6am-11pm. Departures every 15 minutes.*

FOOD AND DRINK

Santa Teresa boasts numerous small bars and restaurants on and around the Largo dos Guimarães and Largo das Neves where travelers can eat lunch or enjoy an extended night out. Good suggestions include **Bar do Arnaudo**, a restaurant serving food in the Northeast style beloved by the locals (*Rua Almirante Alexandrino, 316-B, tel. 21/2252-7246. Mon-Fri, noon-10pm; Sat-Sun., noon-8pm*). Sample the draft beer at the **Adega do Pimenta** (*Rua Almirante Alexandrino, 296, tel. 21/2224-7554. Mon-Fri, noon-10pm; Sat-Sun,*

LOCAL PERSONALITY

The Bahia-born sculptor Zé Andrade is famous for his clay dolls of more than 70 well-known Brazilians, including Vinicius de Moraes, Toquinho, Tom Jobim, Cartola, Carlos Drummond de Andrade, Ary Barroso and, more recently, President Lula. His work is displayed in Travessa bookstores, Toca do Vinicius in Ipanema and the Biblioteca Nacional. Travelers can also visit his studio by appointment (*Rua Leopoldo Fróes, 83-A, Santa Teresa, tel. 21/2242-1415*).

OUR RECOMMENDATION

🍽 With its breathtaking view of the city and its greenery, outdoor tables, superb Brazilian food, tasteful décor and attentive service, **Aprazível** is the perfect restaurant for lunch or dinner. Try the baked fresh hearts of palm and, as a main course, the *pescada amarela* (acoupa weakfish, a tropical fish from Maranhão), served with orange sauce, coconut rice and baked plantains *(Rua Aprazível, 62, tel. 21/2508-9174).*

The patisserie **Alda Maria Doces Portugueses** uses about 560 eggs a day to offer Brazilians a traditional taste of Portugal. Visitors can find *pastéis de nata* (custard tarts), *ovos moles, toucinho do céu* and *fios de ovos* (convent sweets), as well as cakes and preserves *(Rua Almirante Alexandrino, 1.116, tel. 21/2232-1320).*

noon-8pm). Another excellent choice is the simple, no-frills **Sobrenatural**, which specializes in fresh seafood caught by the owners' two boats *(Rua Almirante Alexandrino, 432, tel. 21/2224-1003. Open daily from noon)*.

MUSEU CHÁCARA DO CÉU

This museum houses the collection of Raimundo Castro Maya (1894-1968), an industrialist and patron of the arts. Works on display include paintings by Picasso, Dali and Miró, as well as Brazilian artists such as Portinari, Di Cavalcanti and Iberê Camargo. Visit Portinari's *Dom Quixote*, a series of 21 colored-pencil drawings inspired by Cervantes' book. Debret's watercolors and drawings are the highlights of the Coleção Brasiliana, which includes paintings and engravings as well as 19th century travelers' maps. The museum also contains paintings by Matisse and Taunay. The Pará-born architect Wladimir Alves de Souza designed the current building in 1954 as Castro Maya's home. Burle Marx's gardens are an additional attraction. The parking lot affords a beautiful view of Guanabara Bay.
Rua Murtinho Nobre, 93, Santa Teresa, tel. (21) 2507-1932 or 2224-8981. Wed-Mon, noon-5pm.

PARQUE DAS RUÍNAS

This park is on the grounds of a neoclassical mansion, which, at the

Museu Chácara do Céu: breathtaking collection, gardens and view

beginning of the 20th century, was the home of Laurinda Santos Lobo – a society hostess nicknamed the "Lady Marshal of Elegance" by the famous columnist João do Rio. It offers a unique view from the top of the hill. The gardens are open to visitors, but the mansion's ruins are not. A cultural center offers sporadic shows, plays and exhibitions.

Rua Murtinho Nobre, 169, Santa Teresa, tel. (21) 2252-1039. Tue-Sun, 8am-8pm.

IGREJA NOSSA SENHORA DA GLÓRIA DO OUTEIRO

Built on top of a hill with a view of Guanabara Bay probably in the first half of the 18th century, this was one of the royal family's favorite churches and a popular subject for foreign artists. The aisle and the high altar are decorated with ceramic tiles made between 1735 and 1740, and the adjacent museum contains a collection of about 1,000 objects *(Tue-Fri, 9am-5pm; Sat and Sun, 9am-1pm).* A small funicular is one way to reach the church.

Praça Nossa Senhora da Glória do Outeiro, 135, Glória, tel. (21) 2557-4600. Mon-Fri, 9am-5pm.

Igreja Nossa Senhora da Glória do Outeiro and (above) a detail from its decorative tile-work

PANORAMIC VIEWS AND FASHIONABLE BEACHES

← São Paulo

GUADALUPE

COSTA BARROS

ACARI

VILA MILITAR

DEODORO TURIAÇU

MARECHAL HERMES

CASCADURA

JARDIM SULACAP

ÁGUA SANTA

ABOLIÇÃO

SERRA DO NOGUEIRA

TAQUARA

JACAREZINHO

Projac

JACAREPAGUÁ

CIDADE DE DEUS

FREGUESIA

SERRA DOS PRETOS FORROS

MÉIER

BENFICA

Autódromo Nelson Piquet

GARDÊNIA AZUL

LINHA AMARELA

ANIL

Morro da Panela

GRAJAÚ

SERRA DOS TRÊS RIOS

The access roads to the Parque Nacional da Tijuca offer panoramic views of various parts of Rio

ANDARAÍ

Lagoa da Tijuca

AV. DAS AMÉRICAS

Pedra da Gávea
842 m/2762.5 ft.

Pedra Bonita
696 m/2283.5 ft.

ALTO DA BOA VISTA

Floresta da Tijuca

USINA

MUDA

ESTRADA DAS FURNAS

Panoramic view of the Pedra da Gávea and São Conrado beach; paragliding and hang-gliding take-off point

Mesa do Imperador
483 m/1582.7 ft.

Estrada das Paineiras

Parque Nacional da Tijuca

Marina Barra Grande

ESTRADA DA CANOA

Morro do Cochrane

ESTRADA DA VISTA CHINESA

BARRA DA TIJUCA

Vista Chinesa
413 m/1355 ft.

From the Estrada da Canoa, you can see São Conrado and part of the coast towards Guaratiba

JOÁ

Cabo da Gávea

Ponta do Mourisco

Praia de São Conrado

Favela da Rocinha

From the Vista Chinesa and the Mesa do Imperador there is a panoramic view of the forest and the built-up area around the Lagoa Rodrigo de Freitas. Access via the Estrada Dona Castorinha in the Jardim Botânico

JARDIM BOTÂNICO

Jardim Botânico

SÃO CONRADO

Morro Dois Irmãos

GÁVEA

Jóquei Clube Brasileiro

AV. BORGES DE MEDEIRO

Lagoa Rodrigo de Freitas

Ilha do Meio

Gruta da Imprensa

VIDIGAL

AV. NIEMEYER

LEBLON

AV. DELFIM MOREIRA

Waters

This map shows Rio's best vantage points and its most fashionable beaches – Leme, Copacabana, Ipanema and Leblon. The meeting points for the various "tribes" – tourists, young people, old people and children – are the 12 Postos de Salvamento (lifeguard stations), dotted along the shore from Leme (Posto 1) to Leblon (Posto 12) at intervals of a kilometer or less. Along this 10 km stretch, beachgoers play beach football, volleyball, footvolley, gymnastics and beach tennis, and go rollerskating, surfing, biking, running and jogging.

Cabo Dois Irmãos

12

Mothers and babies

11

Praia do Leblon

Volleyball

10

Praia de Ipanema

IPANEMA

AV. VIEIRA SOUTO

9

Football, footvolley and volleyball

Gay me

8

Body-boarding

7

Ilha das Palmas

Ilha Comprida

Ilha Cagarra

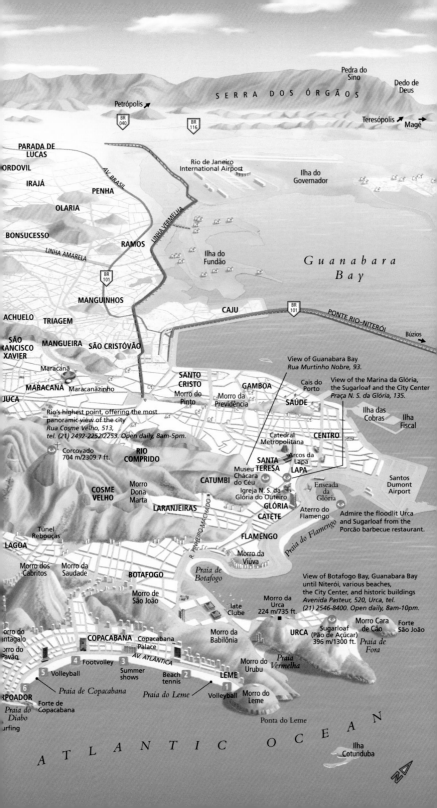

SERRA DOS ÓRGÃOS

Pedra do Sino

Dedo de Deus

Petrópolis ↗

Teresópolis ↗ Magé →

BR 040

BR 116

PARADA DE LUCAS

ORDOVIL

IRAJÁ

PENHA

OLARIA

BONSUCESSO

RAMOS

Rio de Janeiro International Airport

Ilha do Governador

AV. BRASIL

LINHA VERMELHA

LINHA AMARELA

Ilha do Fundão

Guanabara Bay

BR 101

MANGUINHOS

ACHUELO

TRIAGEM

SÃO FRANCISCO XAVIER

MANGUEIRA

SÃO CRISTÓVÃO

CAJU

BR 101

PONTE RIO–NITERÓI

Búzios →

Maracanã

MARACANÃ   Maracanãzinho

JUCA

Rio's highest point, offering the most panoramic view of the city
Rua Cosme Velho, 513,
tel. (21) 2492-2252/2253. Open daily, 8am-5pm.

Corcovado
704 m/2309.7 ft.

RIO COMPRIDO

SANTO CRISTO

Morro do Pinto

GAMBOA

Morro da Previdência

Cais do Porto

SAÚDE

View of Guanabara Bay
Rua Murtinho Nobre, 93.

View of the Marina da Glória,
the Sugarloaf and the City Center
Praça N. S. da Glória, 135.

Ilha das Cobras

Ilha Fiscal

Catedral Metropolitana

CENTRO

COSME VELHO

Morro Dona Marta

CATUMBI

Museu Chácara do Céu

SANTA TERESA

Arcos da Lapa

LAPA

Santos Dumont Airport

LARANJEIRAS

R. PINHEIRO MACHADO

Igreja N. S. da Glória do Outeiro

GLÓRIA

Enseada da Glória

Túnel Rebouças

CATETE

Aterro do Flamengo

Admire the floodlit Urca and Sugarloaf from the Porção barbecue restaurant.

LAGOA

FLAMENGO

Praia do Flamengo

Morro dos Cabritos

Morro da Saudade

BOTAFOGO

Morro da Viúva

Praia de Botafogo

Morro de São João

Iate Clube

Morro da Urca
224 m/735 ft.

View of Botafogo Bay, Guanabara Bay
until Niterói, various beaches,
the City Center, and historic buildings
Avenida Pasteur, 520, Urca, tel.
(21) 2546-8400. Open daily, 8am-10pm.

orro do antagalo

orro do Pavão

COPACABANA

Copacabana Palace

Morro da Babilônia

URCA

Sugarloaf
(Pão de Açúcar)
396 m/1300 ft.

Morro Cara de Cão

Forte São João

Praia de Fora

AV. ATLÂNTICA

4 Footvolley

3 Summer shows

Morro do Urubu

Praia Vermelha

5 Volleyball

2 Beach tennis

LEME

6

RPOADOR

Praia de Copacabana

Praia do Leme

1 Volleyball

Morro do Leme

Praia do Diabo

Forte de Copacabana

Ponta do Leme

urfing

ATLANTIC OCEAN

Ilha Cotunduba

Aerial view of Avenida Atlântica, along the country's most crowded seafront

COPACABANA

The 4-km stretch of seafront between Leme and the Forte de Copacabana is where the *carioca* spirit exists at its least inhibited. One of the most populated districts in the city, Copacabana vibrates day and night – the kiosks, sidewalk and bikeways are always crowded and there are frequent games of volleyball and football. It's also a favorite spot for energetic seniors, who take regular walks and hold exercise sessions here. Since urban decay set in and replaced the middle-class community with evidence of prostitution, the district has lost some of its allure. But it is still the site of the glamorous **Copacabana Palace**. It also hosts one of the world's biggest New Year's celebrations, and thousands of people, both locals and tourists, dress up in white and gather to watch the spectacular fireworks show.

WHERE TO EAT
There is no problem finding somewhere to eat in Copacabana.

Numerous eateries – ranging from tiny *botecos* (bars) to sumptuous restaurants – are scattered along the seafront and the neighboring streets. Don't miss the **Alfaia** and the **A Marisqueira**. The Alfaia, a small and cozy establishment, is famed for its substantial portions of *bacalhau* (salt cod) *à patuscada* (*Rua Inhangá, 30, loja B, tel. 21/2236-1222. Mon-Sat, noon-midnight; Sun, noon-11pm*). *Codfish* is also the main attraction at the Marisqueira, especially the *bacalhau à Mario Soares*, not to mention the savory seafood *caldeirada* (stew) (*Rua Barata Ribeiro, 232, tel. 21/2236-2062. Mon-Sun, 11am-midnight*). Another noteworthy spot is the oceanfront **Cais da Ribeira**, which offers delicious Portuguese cuisine and a spectacular view (*Avenida Atlântica, 2964, tel. 21/2548-6332. Daily, noon-3pm and 7:30-11:30pm*). **Le Pré Catelan** features chef Roland Villard's irresistible menu, one of the best in the city, which rotates every fifteen days (*Avenida Atlântica, 4240, tel. 21/2525-1160. Daily, 7:30pm-11:30pm*). Finally, there is **Shirley**, a small, simple restaurant one block from the seafront, which has been offering excellent Spanish cuisine for the last fifty years. Try the *camarão* (shrimp) *ao lulu* and the *polvo* (octopus) *à espanhola* (*Rua Gustavo Sampaio, 610, Leme, tel. 21/2542-1797. Daily, noon-1am*).

COPACABANA PALACE

The Guinle family built this magnificent and elegant symbol of Rio in 1923. It was Copacabana's first building, and it's played an important role in making the district famous worldwide. The charming hotel has hosted presidents, kings and Hollywood stars in its 225 suites. It was the scenario for the 1933 movie *Flying Down to Rio*, in which Fred Astaire and Ginger Rogers danced together for the first time. Ava Gardner swam in its swimming pool. The playboy Jorginho Guinle, who dated such Hollywood divas as Marilyn Monroe and Rita Hayworth, was born here and made it a point to die here, in 2004. Declared a historic monument, the "Copa" is rich in history and grandeur. Enjoy an afternoon reading by the pool, perhaps with a slice of pie and coffee from the **Pérgola**. The "Copa" also houses **Cipriani**, one of Rio's most exclusive restaurants, run well under the hand of chef Francesco Carli. *Av. Atlântica, 1702, Copacabana, tel. (21) 2548-7070.*

FORTE DE COPACABANA

The fort was built at the beginning of the 20th century on the site of the old Igreja Nossa Senhora de Copacabana, after which the district was named. Its most famous episode took place in July 1922, when a group of 18 leaders of the so-called Lieutenants' Revolt (known as "The 18 of the Fort") marched out to do battle with loyalist troops on Avenida Atlântica. The fort houses the **Museu Histórico do Exército**, or Army History Museum. It also contains the famous **Confeitaria Colombo**, where you can have breakfast or take afternoon tea at parasol-covered tables and enjoy a breathtaking view of Copacabana beach. There's also a stunning view of the open sea visible from the extreme tip of the fort. *Praça Coronel Eugênio Franco, 1, Posto 6, Copacabana, tel. (21) 2287-3781. Tue-Sun, 10am-5pm.*

The black-and-white Portuguese stone mosaic of a trademark Copacabana sidewalk

Cajá

Guabiroba

Avocado

Graviola

Mangaba

In most cities, the décor, the reputation of the chef and, above all, the quality of the ingredients are key determinants of a restaurant's ranking. These rules do not apply in Rio. *Cariocas* do not much care for dressing up, after a day at the beach, to go out to dinner. So they tend to favor small, homely places, where the food is unsophisticated but delicious (and comes in huge portions). At such establishments, one can sit at the table wearing shorts and a pair of flip-flops, or even shirtless, without getting disapproving looks from the waiter. This network of *botecos*, juice bars and ice-cream parlors has a name all its own: *baixa gastronomia* (simple fare). To enjoy it to its full extent, take off your tie or exchange your high-heeled shoes for something more comfortable. The **Mil Frutas** ice-cream parlor (*Rua Garcia d'Ávila, 134, loja A, Ipanema, tel. 21/2521-1384. daily, 10:30am-12:30am*) offers a wide variety of Brazilian fruit sherbets (*mangaba*, Surinam cherry, banana) and delicious guava paste with cheese. The bars are the focal points of Rio's social life, where profession, social class and family name are left at the door in exchange for good conversation and cold beer. Some bars have virtually become institutions, such as **Jobi**, where you can drink draft beer into the small hours (*Rua Ataulfo de Paiva, 1166, Leblon, tel.*

21/2274-0547. Open daily from 9am-4am). In the same district, **Bracarense** (*Rua José Linhares, 85-B, Leblon, tel. 21/2229-3549. Mon-Sat, 7am-midnight; Sun, 7am-10pm*) is a famous tourist attraction, with *petiscos* (snacks) like the *bobozinhos* and *bolinhos de camarão com catupiry* (shrimp rolls with cream cheese). If the place is packed, however, come back another day; only people who know the waiters can get a table at times like these. **Devassa** (*Avenida General San Martin, 1241, Leblon, tel. 21/2540-6087. Mon-Fri, from 5:20pm; Sat and Sun, from 2pm*), with its home-brewed draft beer, is another bar that has been adopted by the *cariocas*. The same is true of **Belmonte**, which has branch outlets in Leblon, Ipanema and Flamengo (*Praia do Flamengo, 300, tel. 21/2552-3349. Open daily, 7:30am-3am*). Another traditional bar is **Cervantes** (*Avenida Prado Junior, 335B, Copacabana, tel. 21/2275-6147. Tue-Thu, noon-4am; Fri and Sat, noon-5:30am; Sun, noon-4am*), which offers draft beer and sandwiches. The juice-bars are another city institution. **Balada Sumos** (*Avenida Ataulfo de Paiva, 620, loja B, Leblon, tel. 21/2239-2699. Sun-Thu, 7am-2am; Fri and Sat, 7am-3am*) serves dozens of fruit juices and unusual mixes and is particularly worth visiting. Another good option is the traditional **Polis Sucos** (*Rua Maria Quitéria, 70 A, tel. 21/2247-2518. Daily, 8am-midnight*).

Pitanga

Papaya

Persimmon

Coconut

Serigüela

The Arpoador rocks, between the vibrant Copacabana and Ipanema beaches

IPANEMA AND LEBLON

The city's most upscale stretch of seafront was the first to hear the opening chords of "Garota de Ipanema" ("The Girl from Ipanema"). Tom Jobim and Vinicius de Moraes song immortalized the district. With something to please all styles, tastes and budgets, it stretches from Arpoador to Leblon. There, it is separated by the Jardim de Alah canal, which links the Lagoa Rodrigo de Freitas with the sea. The six kilometers of Ipanema and Leblon beaches are busy day and night. Vitality spills along the bustling sidewalk and bikeways, and inspires the collective bursts of applause at sunset around Posto 9, the children's volleyball schools run by famous players, the games of ladies' footvolley and the football matches. There is even a place for mothers and babies only, called **Baixo Bebê**, which has a nursery room and a playground right in front of Rua Venâncio Flores, in Leblon.

WHERE TO EAT

Countless bars and restaurants for every taste, as well as a host of small shops and arcades selling local and international brands, are scattered along the seafront Avenidas Vieira Souto and Delfim Moreira. Similar establishments run up Ruas Prudente de Moraes, Visconde de Pirajá and Barão da Torre. Diners can choose among meat, pasta, seafood or Portuguese cuisine. For those wanting a touch of sophistication, we suggest dinner at the traditional and highly respected **Antiquarius**, whose menu goes well beyond *bacalhau*. The duck rice and the *açorda* (baked crab, shrimp and mussels) are musts. After your meal, visit the antique shop on the mezzanine floor (*Rua Aristides Espínola, 19, Leblon, tel. 21/2294-1049. Daily, noon-2am*). **Margutta** is the place for lovers of seafood and Italian cuisine (*Avenida Henrique Dummont, 62, Ipanema, tel. 21/2259-3718. Mon-Fri, 5pm-midnight; Sat, Sun and holidays, noon-1am*), while the traditional **Porcão** in Ipanema is for

Movie Theaters
1 Espaço Leblon de Cinema
2 Leblon
3 Estação Ipanema
4 Cineclube Laura Alvim

Bookstores
1 Letras & Expressões Leblon
2 Argumento
3 Livraria da Travessa
4 Travessinha
5 Letras & Expressões
6 Toca do Vinicius

those who can't survive without meat (*Rua Barão da Torre, 218, tel. 21/2522-0999. Daily, noon-midnight*). If it's pizza you're after, try always-crowded **Capricciosa** (*Rua Vinicius de Moraes, 134, tel. 21/2523-3394. Daily, 6pm-2am*).

BEACHWEAR
With a large number of important fashion outlets, Ipanema is renowned for its incomparable beachwear, which is exported to all corners of the globe. The stores are concentrated in the rectangle bounded by **Barão da Torre**, **Garcia d'Ávila**, **Visconde de Pirajá** and **Aníbal de Mendonça** streets. And you can visit them all on foot, strolling around the attractive, elegant and bustling streets, lined with almond trees and dotted with newspaper stands and flower kiosks. The **Galeria Ipanema 2000** (*Rua Visconde de Pirajá, 547*) sells bikinis at **Salinas** (*Loja 204, tel. 21/2274-0644. Mon-Fri, 9am-7pm; Sat 9:30am-3pm*). Or sample the colorful and charming dresses and T-shirts at **Totem** (*Loja 212, tel. 21/2540-0661. Mon-Fri, 10am-7:30pm; Sat, 10am-4pm*). Close by is **British Colony**, with clothes by Máxime Perelmuter, one of

the most praised young *carioca* stylists (*Rua Visconde de Pirajá, 550, loja 111A, Top Center, tel. 21/2274-1693. Mon-Fri, 9am-8pm; Sat, 9am-5pm*). Also not far away is **Fórum**, another famous youth brand (*Rua Barão da Torre, 455, Ipanema, tel. 21/ 2521-7415. Mon-Fri, 10am-8pm; Sat, 10am-4pm*). The **Antonio Bernardo** jewelry store, which sells pieces by the renowned Brazilian jewelry designer, is another highlight (*Rua Garcia d'Ávila, 121, Ipanema, tel. 21/2512-7204. Mon-Fri, 10am-8pm; Sat, 10am-5pm*). Jeweler **H. Stern**'s main store offers tours where one can see jewelry cut and polished from Brazilian gems and hear the process explained in most major languages. A free shuttle service

---

TOCA DO VINICIUS

A charming record shop that doubles as a bookstore, museum and cultural center, the **Espaço Cultural Toca do Vinicius** specializes in MPB, bossa nova, samba and *choro* records and books. On Sundays, there are shows and lectures on the sidewalk in front, sometimes accompanied by an enormous piano.
Rua Vinicius de Moraes, 129, Ipanema, tel. (21) 2247-5227.

Art Galleries
1. Anita Schwartz Galeria
2. Galeria de Arte Ipanema
3. Galeria Jean Boghici
4. Bolsa de Arte
5. Silvia Cintra Galeria de Arte
6. Laura Marsiaj Arte Contemporânea
7. Athena Galeria de Arte
8. Márcia Barrozo do Amaral Galeria de Arte
9. Maurício Pontual Galeria de Arte

gets the tourists under reservation (*Rua Garcia d'Ávila, 113, Ipanema, tel. 21/2274-8897; for groups, 2106-0000, ext. 1465. Mon-Fri, 8:30am-6:30pm; Sat, 8:30am-2pm*).

FEIRA HIPPIE

Every Sunday from 8am till sunset, for more than 35 years, the **Praça General Osório** has hosted the traditional **Feira Hippie de Ipanema** (Handicraft Market). Here, one block from the seafront, 600 exhibitors sell costume jewelry, handicrafts and clothes.

BOOKSTORES

Rio's South Zone, which houses the city's most upscale neighborhoods, has more to offer than beaches, boutiques and arcades, although it has plenty of those. It also has numerous quality café bookstores, where you can not only check out the latest titles, but also enjoy a coffee, a draft beer or even a light meal. The biggest of four **Livraria da Travessa** stores (*Rua Visconde de Pirajá, 572, Ipanema, tel. 21/3205-9002. Mon-Sat, 9am-midnight, Sun, 11am-midnight*) has an

Charming bookstores, like Travessa, draw together Rio's bohemians and intellectuals

excellent collection of books on Rio, stacked on shelves that remind one of a library. A visitor could spend a whole afternoon here rummaging through the merchandise, which also includes CDs and DVDs. The restaurant **B!**, on the mezzanine floor, serves light dishes and snacks. The bookstore chain's smallest and most charming branch, nicknamed **Travessinha** (*Rua Visconde de Pirajá, 462, Ipanema, tel. 21/2287-5157. Mon-Fri, 10am-7pm; Sat, 10am-4pm; closed on Sundays*), also deserves a visit. The **Café Severino** in the **Argumento** bookstore (*Rua Dias Ferreira, 417, tel. 21/2239-5294*) stays open until midnight. While on the subject of coffee, the cappuccino at the **Café Ubaldo**, in the Ipanema branch of **Letras & Expressões**, is justly renowned. This three-floor store, which contains a bar and a huge collection of magazines, is a rendezvous point for insomniac intellectuals, especially on Friday and Saturday nights (*Rua Visconde de Pirajá, 276, Ipanema, tel. 21/2521-6110. Mon-Thur and Sun, 8am-midnight;*

Fri and Sat, 8am-2am). At the Leblon branch (*Avenida Ataulfo de Paiva, 1292, tel. 21/2511-5085*), the menu is the same, only the name of the place is different: **Café Antônio Torres**.

MOVIE THEATERS

Two movie theaters in Ipanema and another two in Leblon offer a pleasant choice after a day in the sun. The **Cineclube Laura Alvim**, on the Ipanema seafront, has three small auditoriums (*Avenida Vieira Souto, 176, tel. 21/2267-1647*) and the **Estação Ipanema** has another two (*Rua Visconde de Pirajá, 605, tel. 21/3221-9221*). Three blocks from Leblon beach, there is the **Espaço Leblon de Cinema** (*Rua Conde Bernadotte, 21, loja 10, tel. 21/2511-8857*). The **Leblon**, the biggest of them all, with two spacious auditoriums, completes the circuit (*Avenida Ataulfo de Paiva, 391, tel. 21/3221-9292*).

ART GALLERIES

It's hardly surprising that the arts have

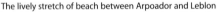

The lively stretch of beach between Arpoador and Leblon

Sunday, height of summer: *cariocas* at play fill the seafront pedestrian mall and road

blossomed in Rio, given the abundance of natural, human and architectural inspiration. A tour of the art circuit should begin with those galleries specializing in contemporary Brazilian art. Two good spots are neighbors: **Laura Marsiaj Arte Contemporânea**, which exhibits works by artists such as Hildebrando de Castro and Rosângela Rennó (*Rua Teixeira de Melo, 31C, Ipanema, tel. 21/2513-2074. Tue-Fri, 10am-7pm; Sat, noon-6pm*) and **Silvia Cintra Galeria de Artes** (*Rua Teixeira de Mello, 53, loja D, Ipanema, tel. 21/2267-9401. Mon- Fri, 10am-7pm; Sat, noon-4pm*), with works by Antônio Dias and Daniel Senise. At the Copacabana Palace, the **Bolsa de Arte**, an appraisal and authentication house, holds auctions that set the standard for the Brazilian art market. All works go on display on the Bolsa's two floors five days prior to each sale, of which there are about four a year (*Rua Prudente de Moraes, 326, Ipanema, tel. 21/2522-1544. Mon-Fri, 11am-7pm*). The long experience of dealer Jean Boghici, head of the **Galeria Jean**

Boghici, guarantees the excellence and variety of the work on offer, from Portinari to Wesley Duke Lee (*Rua Joana Angélica, 180, Ipanema, tel. 21/2522-4660 and 2547-1972. Mon-Fri, 2-8pm; Sat 2-6pm*). Another highlight is the traditional **Marcia Barrozo do Amaral Galeria de Arte**, with works by Frans Krajcberg, Anna Letycia and Sued (*Avenida Atlântica, 4240, basement, Loja 129, Shopping Cassino Atlântico, Copacabana, tel. 21/2521-5195. Mon-Fri, 10am-6pm; Sat, noon-6pm*). The neighboring **Athena Galeria de Arte**, owned by Liecil Oliveira (*Avenida Atlântica, 4240, ground floor, Loja 120, Shopping Cassino Atlântico, Copacabana, tel. 21/2523-8621 and 3813-2222. Mon-Fri, 3-8pm*) specializes in modern artists like Di Cavalcanti, Segall and Tarsila. There are also many excellent galleries in the areas of Botafogo, Laranjeiras, Leblon, Gávea and Jardim Botânico. **Lurixs Arte Contemporânea** mixes works by acclaimed and lesser-known artists (*Rua Paulo Barreto, 77, Botafogo, tel. 21/2541-4935. Mon-Fri, 10am-7pm*). It also has a

Aerial view of Leblon and Ipanema

collection of photographs. **Pé de Boi** specializes in signed national handicrafts from almost every Brazilian state. Its impressive collection ranges through dolls from the Vale do Jequitinhonha, in Minas Gerais, to Marajoara pottery, from the Amazon (*Rua Ipiranga, 55, Laranjeiras, tel. 21/2285-4395/5833. Mon-Fri, 9am-7pm; Sat 9am-1pm*). The long-established **Anita Schwartz Galeria** has two addresses – the easiest one to find being in Leblon (*Avenida Ataulfo de Paiva, 270, loja 301A, Rio Design Leblon, tel. 21/2274-3873. Mon-Fri, 10am-10pm; Sat, 10am-8pm*). The tiny **Mínima Galeria Bistrô** can be relied upon for high-quality temporary exhibitions (*Rua Marquês de São Vicente, 189, Gávea, tel. 21/2512-4616. Tue-Sat, 7pm-midnight*). Meanwhile, **Galeria Anna Maria Niemeyer**, owned by the daughter of architect Oscar Niemeyer, is famous for its collection of paintings, sculpture and drawings (*Rua Marquês de São Vicente, 52, loja 205, Shopping da Gávea, tel. 21/2239-9144. Mon-Fri, 10am-9pm; Sat,*

10am-6pm). The charming **H.A.P. Galeria**, owned by Heloisa Amaral Peixoto, alternates exhibitions of its collection with solo shows by contemporary Brazilian artists (*Rua Abreu Fialho, 11, Jardim Botânico, tel. 21/3874-2830/2726. Mon-Fri, 11am-7pm; Sat, 2pm-8pm*). The **Cavalariças**, close by in the Parque Lage, is worth visiting to see the artists who use the structure of the old building as a basis for their creations. It is next to the **Escola de Artes Visuais do Parque Lage**, where art students can been seen hard at work (*Rua Jardim Botânico, 414, tel. 21/2538-1091/1879. Mon-Thu, 9am-9pm; Fri, 9am-7pm; Sat, 2pm-5pm*).

GAY RENDEZVOUSES

Some visitors may remember old fashion-magazine photos of bronzed athletes wearing nothing but *tangas* by Mario Testino. Most of them were taken here, between Postos 8 and 9, in front of Rua Farme de Amoedo, Rio's most important gathering spot for gay men and recommended by all GLS itineraries worldwide. After the beach, the groups meet at the bars on Farme, in the block between the Ruas Visconde de Pirajá and Barão da Torre. One of the most popular is **Bofetada** (*Rua Farme de Amoedo, 87A, Ipanema, tel. 21/2227-1675. Daily, 8am until the last customer leaves*). The bar and nightclub **Dama de Ferro** isn't far in the direction of Lagoa Rodrigo de Freitas (*Rua Vinicius de Moraes, 288, Ipanema, tel. 21/2247-2330. Wed-Sat, 11pm until the last customer stumbles out*). Another nightclub, more traditional, is **Le Boy**, in Copacabana (*Rua Raul Pompéia, 102, Posto 6, Copacabana, tel. 21/2513-4993. Tue-Sun, from 11pm on*). The **Fundição Progresso**, in Lapa, has infamous GLS parties (*Rua dos Arcos, 24, tel. 21/2220-5070. Daily, from 9pm*). Travelers should call before showing up.

OUTDOOR RIO

TRAILS

Cariocas love to walk, and they take full advantage of the city's geography and landscape. Aside from the stunning trails in the heart of the Floresta da Tijuca, one of the most attractive is the **Pista Cláudio Coutinho**, neighboring the Urca and Sugarloaf mountains, which makes a headlong plunge into nature. Other important trails include **Pedra do Conde**, **Pico da Tijuca**, **Tijuca-mirim**, **Bico-do-papagaio**, the mountains of the **Parque Nacional da Tijuca** and **Pedra da Gávea**. Make sure you hire an experienced guide.
Local Tour Operator: Trilhas do Rio Ecoturismo & Aventura, tel. (21) 2424-5455 or 9207-1360.
www.trilhasdorio.com.br

MARATHONS

There are two important events in Rio for lovers of street running. The lively **Rio de Janeiro International Half Marathon**, which takes place in the second half of the year on dates that vary, brings together 12,000 competitors in a race of just over 21 kilometers (13 mi.). The course stretches from São Conrado beach along the shore to finish at the Largo do Machado, beyond Flamengo beach (*call 11/3714-0506 for further information*). The **Rio de Janeiro Marathon**, covering just over 42 kilometers (26 mi.), attracts about 3,000 contestants yearly, and takes place on the last Sunday in June. It starts at Praça do Pontal do Recreio and runs along the waterfront to the Aterro do Flamengo before reaching the finishing line on Rua Cruz Lima (*dial 21/2223-2773 for more info*).

HELICOPTER FLIGHTS

A helicopter ride over Rio quickly reveals why the metropolis is known as the Marvelous City. The view from the helicopter is unrivaled, and people who take this tour swear they will never again climb up to the Christo

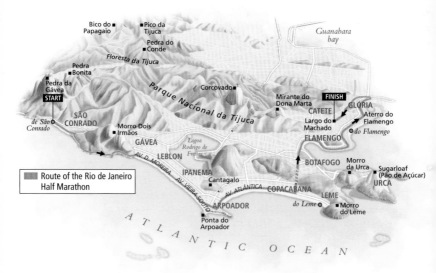

Redentor – the city's highest panoramic viewpoint. The most important heliports are in **Lagoa, Morro da Urca** and **Morro Dona Marta**. With a minimum of twenty passengers, night flights are possible. *Local Tour Operator: Helsight, tel. (21) 2511-2141.*

CLIMBING

Rio is a major center for urban climbing. A wealth of different routes, of varying degrees of difficulty, offers impressive views and are thickly surrounded by nature. **Sugarloaf Mountain** alone offers more than forty such routes, and if the hike up is enough, it's not even necessary to make the return trip. A cable car stands at the summit to wing people back down. Another option is to scale **Corcovado mountain** via k2 and enjoy the breathtaking view from the summit.

Other climbs include **Pedra da Gávea, Morro Dois Irmãos, Cantagalo** and the mountains on the other side of Guanabara Bay.
Local Tour Operator: Centro de Escalada Limite Vertical, tel. (21) 2527-4938 or 9343-8972. www.escaladarj.com.br

PARAGLIDING AND HANG GLIDING

On Saturdays and Sundays, the **Pepino beach**, in São Conrado, is the perfect landing strip for paragliders and hang gliders, creating a stunning aerial show of color. At the **Pedra Bonita runway**, overlooking the beach, novices can hire fliers licensed by the Brazilian Hang Gliding Association (ABVL). A professional will accompany you on tandem paragliding or hanggliding flights (instructor and tourist), including filming and photos.
Local Tour Operator: ABVL, Bruno Menescal, tel. (21) 3322-0266 or 9962-7119.

Climbing the Corcovado, with the Sugarloaf in the background

Amid sprawl, Lagoa Rodrigo de Freitas offers *cariocas* a sanctuary for water sports

LAGOA RODRIGO DE FREITAS AND JARDIM BOTÂNICO

Walking, running, biking or roller-skating on the 7.4 km (4.6 mi) bikeway around **Lagoa Rodrigo de Freitas** is one of the great pleasures Rio has to offer. At night, live music shows pop up in the kiosks around the shore of the lagoon. The best tend to be in the **Parque dos Patins** (roller-skating arena) and the **Corte do Cantagalo.** You need to be patient to get a table in summer, but it is well worth the sacrifice. Sports clubs where you can practice waterskiing, tennis and rowing also dot the lakeshore.

FUNDAÇÃO EVA KLABIN RAPAPORT

The sisters Eva (1903-1991) and Ema Klabin (1907-1994) inherited their art collection, and the collecting bug, from their father, a paper-pulp tycoon. Eva's collection is displayed in her former home, a house in the Norman style characteristic of the early 1930's. There are more than a thousand items, including ancient Egyptian and Greek artworks, Flemish and Renaissance paintings and British pictures from the 18th century. Don't miss the *Portrait of Nicolaus Padavinus,* by Tintoretto, the earthenware by Andrea della Robbis and the Roman glass collection from the 2nd to 5th centuries.

Avenida Epitácio Pessoa, 2480, Lagoa, tel. (21) 2523-3471. Wed-Sun, 2pm-6pm, by appointment only.

JARDIM BOTÂNICO (BOTANICAL GARDEN)

The more than 8,000 plant species make this one of the ten most important botanical gardens in the world. Dom João VI created the 137 hectare (350 acre) area soon after he brought the Portuguese royal family to Brazil in 1808. UNESCO declared it a Biosphere Reserve in 1992. The major attractions, aside from the grandeur of the imperial palms (*Roystonea oleracea*), are the **Museu Botânico** (Botanical Museum) and the **Orquidário** (Orchid House). The latter houses approximately 1,000 exotic species. You can also buy seedlings close to the gardens at Avenida Pacheco Leão, 2040. Take time to visit the cottages in the old workmen's village. Some are now used as studios by

Palm-lined avenue in the Botanical Gardens

Table, which is reputably where Dom Pedro II took his family for picnics.
Ruâ Jardim Botânico, 1008, tel. (21) 2294-6012. Open daily, 8am-5pm.

FAVELA DA ROCINHA
Rocinha is a shantytown, but with one of the most beautiful views in Rio, it has also become a tourist attraction. Having been urbanized, it is now seeking official recognition as a district of the city. In fact, it is a self-contained town where more than 100,000 inhabitants support numerous shops, a bank, a hotel, and even a cable-TV station that reports on issues of local interest. However, this does not mean you can visit it alone. Take a guided tour – this is unquestionably the safest way to visit the hill, which occasionally witnesses violent confrontations between police and drug-dealers. Make sure you get information on the local situation before booking your tour.
Local Tour Operator: Favela Tour (www.favelatour.com.br), tel. (21) 3322-2727 or 9989-0074.

PLANETARIUM
Considered the most modern in Latin America, the planetarium contains two domes, one of which is 23 meters (75.4 feet) in diameter and houses the Universarium

such contemporary artists as Gabriela Machado, Adriana Varejão and Beatriz Milhares. Continue by taxi up the Estrada Dona Castorina past IMPA (Instituto Nacional de Matemática Pura e Aplicada, or National Institute of Pure and Applied Mathematics), an important scientific research center. You'll find spectacular views at the **Vista Chinesa**, a beautiful Chinese-style pavilion, and the **Mesa do Imperador**, or Emperor's

Pleasant bikeway close to the lagoa Rodrigo de Freitas

The exuberant greenery of the Floresta da Tijuca, close to the City Center

VIII projector, capable of projecting 9,000 star-like points of light. The other, with a diameter of 12.5 meters (41 feet), contains the Spacemaster projector, equipped with mechanisms that simulate the movement of the heavens and project the night sky (with 6,500 stars) in any latitude. And in here, you don't have to deal with pollution, clouds or extraneous light that might interfere with clarity. After the visit, electronic-music lovers can visit the 00 (that's "Zero Zero" to you), a restaurant and bar with DJs inside the Planetarium, which serves contemporary cuisine (*tel. 21/2540-8041*).
Avenida Padre Leonel Franca, 240, Gávea, tel. (21) 2274-0046. Tue-Thu (star-gazing only), 6:30-8:30pm; Sat, Sun and holidays (dome sessions only), 4-5:30pm (children) and 7pm (adults).

Floresta da Tijuca

During the 19th century, the slopes of the **Tijuca massif** were gradually deforested as trees were felled to provide fuel for the brick kilns and sugar mills. Land was also cleared to permit the expansion of the coffee plantations. The result was an ecological disaster that almost left the city without water. In 1861, Dom Pedro II ordered a reforestation program, making this 3,300-hectare site Brazil's first example of government intervention for the sake of conservation. As time went by, nature recovered her footing, and today one of the largest urban forests in the world grows here. It is once again home to a rich and diversified flora and fauna. Marmosets, coatis, armadillos, anteaters and countless bird species thrive among the yellow trumpet trees, *angicos* and *jequitibás*. Trails lead to the heart of the forest, as well as viewing points and 43 crystal-clear waterfalls. In summer, the pools below are perfect for cooling off. Some easier routes start at the **Largo do Bom Retiro**, the park's central point, but others are only for the highly fit. Complete information is available at the Visitors' Center. One historical point of interest is the **Capela Mayrink**, a chapel built in 1850. It was restored in the 1940's, when three panels painted by Cândido Portinari were installed. For people who'd rather not walk, some operators offer tours in open vehicles.
Praça Afonso Viseu, Tijuca, tel. (21) 2492-2253. Open daily, 8am-6pm.
Tour Operator: Jeep Tour, tel. (21) 3890-9273.

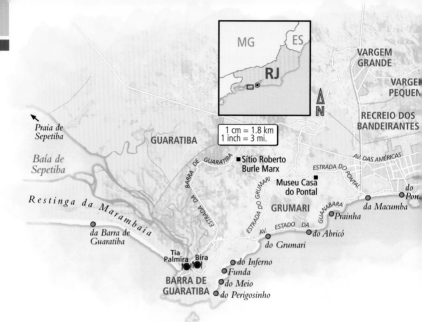

BARRA DA TIJUCA AND RECREIO DOS BANDEIRANTES

Fifty years ago, while Ipanema was inspiring bossa nova, the **Barra da Tijuca** was nothing more than a vast tract of sand. Following the construction of the Joá viaduct in the 1970's, however, *cariocas* were able to reach the dangerous waves of the Barra, the pollution-free waters of Grumari beach and the charm of the tiny Prainha. Then the district began to grow. There are no traditional bakeries, juice bars or corner *botequins* in Barra da Tijuca. In fact, there are hardly any corners. Streets serve only to separate one condominium from another, and apartment buildings and shopping centers run up against natural scenery. This is why the place is called the Brazilian Miami. You can either love or hate such ostentation, but you cannot remain indifferent to it.

BARRA DA TIJUCA BEACHES
There are basically five beaches on the coast of Rio's West Zone: **Barra da Tijuca**, Recreio dos Bandeirantes, **Macumba**, **Prainha** and **Grumari**. Strong winds make **Prainha** and

Macumba paradises for surfers but discourage casual swimmers. **Grumari** is known for its crystal-clear waters, while the 15-kilometer-long **Barra beach** is the city's biggest and busiest, with kiosks and bikeway. The most famous spot is **Pepê beach**, frequented by artists, football stars such as Romário and Ronaldinho, fitness fanatics, wind-surfers and kite-surfers. Brazil's first surfing school is on Barra, at Posto 4, right in front of the Sheraton Barra. It's headed by Rico de Souza, a two-time Brazilian champion and at one time world vice-champion. With bilingual instructors, it has classes for everyone from executives to children (*21/2438-1821 and www.ricosurf.com.br*). **Recreio beach** is long and ideal for surfing, biking and walking. The neighboring Grumari and Prainha are farther out, towards the south, which is why they are so clean. Both are environmentally protected areas, cradled by hills and sandbank vegetation. **Abricó**, a tiny strip of sand and a continuation of Grumari, is officially a nudists' beach. There are no bus-routes to the area, but that doesn't keep away the

weekend crowds. On weekdays they are largely deserted, except for the surfers. Down the coast, in order, are the **Inferno**, **Funda**, **Meio**, **Perigosinho**, **Barra de Guaratiba**, **Pedra de Guaratiba** and **Sepetiba** beaches.

CASA DO PONTAL AND SÍTIO BURLE MARX

The Casa do Pontal houses the largest collection of popular art in Rio and is located on a bucolic 12 sq. km (4.63 sq. mi.) site in the Recreio dos Bandeirantes. An 8,000-piece collection, which includes contributions from some 200 popular artists, portrays aspects of everyday Brazilian life. The French designer Jacques Van de Beuque, who died in 2000, amassed the collection, which his son and widow now oversee (*Estrada do Pontal, 3295, tel. 21/2490-3278. Tue-Sun, 9:30am-5pm*). To complete your tour, continue to the **Sítio Roberto Burle Marx**, 5 km (3.1 mi.) from the Casa do Pontal (*Estrada da Barra de Guaratiba, 2019, tel. 21/2410-1412*). It is open to the public by appointment only (*Tue-Sat, 9:30am-1:30pm; Sun, 9:30am*). The estate, with an area of approximately 3.65 sq. km (1.4 sq. mi.), contains around 3,500 plant species from Brazil and abroad. The landscape designer began collecting them during childhood, and they are organized by the *paulista* Harri Lorenzi. Burle Marx spent his last years here, where he died in 1994 at the age of 84.

BARRA DE GUARATIBA

A meal at **Tia Palmira** is enough to justify the trip out here (*Caminho do Souza, 18, tel. 21/2410-8169. Tue-Fri, 11:30am-5pm; Sat, Sun and holidays, 11:30am-6pm*) and **Bira** (*Estrada da Vendinha, 48, tel. 21/2410-8304. Thu-Fri, noon-6pm; Sat, Sun and holidays, noon-8pm*). Bira is Palmira's nephew and competitor. While the décor may be basic, the food is far from it. Both are excellent options for seafood and Bahian cuisine. The **Restinga da Marambaia** is the area's natural attraction. If there are no traffic jams, this beach with calm waters and muddy sand is less than an hour's drive from Copacabana.

CIDADE DA MÚSICA

Work began in 2003 on this square, designed by the urbanist Lúcio Costa at the junction of Avenida das Américas and Avenida Ayrton Senna (known as the Cebolão). Construction will transform the place into a musical center named after the media baron Roberto Marinho, who died that year. The project is headed by Frenchman Christian de Portzamparc, who was responsible for the Cité de La Musique in Paris and is a winner of the Pritzker Prize, the architectural equivalent of a Nobel. The cultural complex with boat-shaped buildings will have the largest concert hall in Latin America. In addition to serving as the seat of the Brazilian Symphonic Orchestra, it will be equipped with movie theaters, shops and restaurants.

Events and Sights

Carnival

In terms of sheer size, not to mention significance, few popular festivals compare to the *carioca* Carnival. The joyful energy of the thousands of revelers, the pounding beats of the music, and the sophistication of the floats are guaranteed to invoke admiration in even the most austere of spectators. Officially, Carnival lasts for four days, but the rehearsals of the samba schools and *blocos* (parades) give the city a festive atmosphere well in advance. Tickets for these rehearsals are cheap, but they don't offer much in the way of comfort or service. Exceptions are the **Mangueira** and **Salgueiro** *quadras*, or samba school headquarters. Warm beer, suffocating heat and long lines outside

the restrooms – this is the price you pay to experience the tingle in your spine as the deafening beat of the drums announces the beginning of the rehearsal. It is impossible to avoid being moved, in both senses of the word, by the power of the *bateria*. The *bandas* and *blocos de rua* (informal parades), whose rehearsals are free and in the open air, are an excellent evening alternative after a day at the beach. Popular ones include **Carmelitas**, **Banda de Ipanema** and **Escravos da Mauá**. Others, like **Simpatia é Quase Amor**, **Suvaco do Cristo** and **Monobloco**, usually rehearse in enclosed areas, and admission requires tickets. If you wish to take part in a samba school parade, prepare months ahead. The closer it gets to Carnival, the

Sambódromo

Oscar Niemeyer used a paper towel in a bar to sketch the original idea for Sambódromo. The work was completed in 120 days, in time for the 1984 Carnival parade.
R. Marquês de Sapucaí, Praça Onze, Cidade Nova.

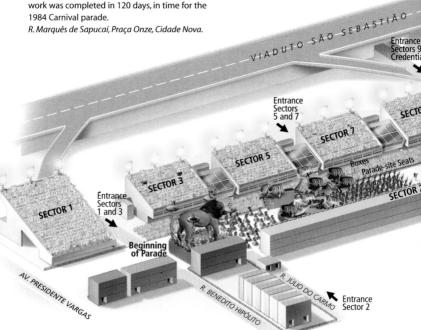

more expensive the costumes become. Two tips: inquire about the costume you can expect to wear, as some of them are extremely hot; also find out exactly when the school's group is scheduled to enter the avenue. If you only intend to watch the spectacle, buy tickets well in advance. Otherwise, you'll be at the mercy of ticket-scalpers.

REHEARSALS AT MANGUEIRA AND SALGUEIRO

From October onwards, two of the most sought-after rehearsals take place in the *quadras* of Mangueira and Salgueiro, each a ten-minute ride from the Center. They offer good facilities, with parking lots and box seats. The **Palácio do Samba**, at the base of Mangueira Hill, is an usually egalitarian place that attracts locals, young people from all over the city and plenty of Brazilians and foreigners tourists. On Saturdays, as of January, the *quadra* is hotly-disputed. So get there by 10pm, before it really gets going. If you want a table, call to make a reservation. The **Salgueiro** *quadra*, in the Tijuca district, attracts a generally younger crowd and the flirting is constant. The neighboring *quadras* of **Portela** and **Império Serrano** are located farther away from the Center, but also in the North Zone, in Madureira.

Local Tour Operator: Carioca Tropical Tour Operator, tel. (21) 2547-6327/2256-6273.

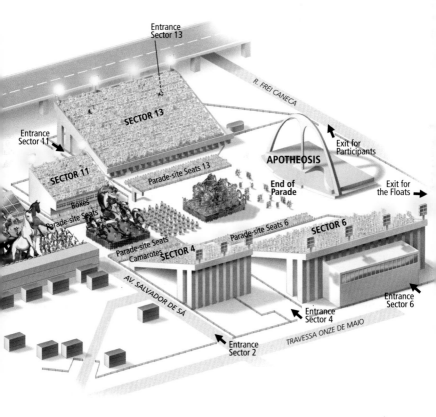

MARACANÃ

First-time visitors are invariably awed by the Maracanã, the country's largest football stadium. Built to host the 1950 World Cup, it was the site of Brazil's ultimate loss in the final to Uruguay. Its capacity has since been reduced to 80,000, but it has lost none of its grandeur and majesty. Take the guided tour and see special viewing areas, changing rooms and the tunnel leading onto the pitch itself. The **Museu dos Esportes Mané Garrincha**, in the hall of the stadium, contains a collection of football memorabilia, including photographs, players' uniforms and the ball Pelé used to score his 100th goal. If you have time to see a match in a full stadium, you'll know a truly electrifying experience.

Rua Professor Eurico Rabelo and Avenida Maracanã, tel. (21) 2568-9962. Portão 18. Open daily, 9am-5pm.

MUSEU NACIONAL DA QUINTA DA BOA VISTA

After the arrival of Dom João VI in Brazil, this palace became the official residence of the royal (and later imperial) family. A museum since 1892, it houses an enormous collection of rare treasures, including Egyptian sarcophagi and mummies, the skeletons of prehistoric animals, and indigenous weaponry, to name but a few. Unfortunately, the area around it is dangerous, despite the presence of security guards in the park.

Quinta da Boa Vista, São Cristóvão, tel. (21) 2568-1149. Tue-Sun, 10am-4pm.

MUSEU DO AÇUDE

This sophisticated museum is located on a vast 15 sq. km (6 sq. mi.) site in the heart of the Floresta de Tijuca. Cradled in the magnificent greenery of the forest, it contains a beautiful, open-air art collection. Visitors can stroll among works by such important contemporary Brazilian artists as Hélio Oiticica, Lygia Pape, Iole de Freitas and Nuno Ramos. Inside the Neocolonial mansion, which belonged to art collector Raimundo Castro Maya, there are Portuguese tiled panels from the 18th and 19th centuries and items of furniture in Portuguese-Brazilian styles. Particularly worth visiting is Castro Maya's Asian art collection, which includes iron statues and pottery. A cultural event on the last Sunday of every month features MPB shows.

Estrada do Açude, 764, Alto da Boa Vista, tel. (21) 2492-2119/5219. Thu-Sun, 11am-5pm.

CASA NIEMEYER (CASA DAS CANOAS)

Oscar Niemeyer built this house as his family residence at the beginning of the 1950's. A fine example of Brazilian modern architecture, its sinuous lines blend perfectly with the lushness of the surroundings.

Estrada das Canoas, 2310, São Conrado, tel. (21) 3322-358. Tue-Fri, 2-5pm; Sat, and Sun, 9am-noon.

CORCOVADO

Even Christ the Redeemer wanted to live in Rio, *Cariocas* can proudly claim. At the summit of Corcovado, He enjoys the highest and most encompassing view of the city, and so do the travelers who visit him. From the summit, one can see the cable car on the Sugarloaf. However, you need the patience of the faithful to get there. The city government closed the access road to private cars and the route is now monopolized by a small mafia of taxis and vans. To avoid this,

Museu do Açude: art and sophistication amid the forest

take the train from Cosme Velho station, which leaves every half hour. The brief trip offers a spectacular view of the South Zone, the beaches and Lagoa Rodrigo de Freitas. A curve just clear of the forest offers a series of magnificent views from unique angles. At the summit itself, you can climb 220 steps to the belvedere or opt for the escalators or elevator.
Rua Cosme Velho, 513, Cosme Velho, tel. (21) 2492-2252/2253. Open daily, 9am-7pm.

INSTITUTO MOREIRA SALLES (IMS)
Architect Olavo Redig de Campos designed the splendid building that houses the Instituto Moreira Salles, while Burle Marx laid out its spacious gardens to straddle a small stream. Marx was also responsible for the beautiful tiled panel behind the fountain. While the setting alone would be worth the visit, the house is also an important cultural center, with a movie theater, exhibition rooms, a café, an art shop, a studio and extensive photography and music collections. The Institute's Musical Reserve preserves and promotes MPB and is one of Brazil's most important record collections, with at least 13,000 old recordings.
Rua Marquês de São Vicente, 476, Gávea, tel. (21) 3284-7400. Tue-Sun, 1-8pm.

PALÁCIO DO CATETE
Built in the 19th century as the presidential residence, back when Rio was the country's capital, this exquisitely decorated palace now houses the Museu da República (Museum of the Republic), which contains a collection of Republican-era artifacts such as furniture, paintings and sculptures. There is also a cultural center. On the third floor, the Getúlio Vargas exhibition shows the room where that statesman shot himself in 1954. It has been perfectly preserved, down to the pajamas he was wearing at the time are displayed, complete with the fatal bullet-hole.
Rua do Catete, 153, Catete, tel. (21) 2558-6350. Tue, Thu, Fri, noon-5pm; Wed, 2-5pm; Sat, Sun and holidays, 2-6pm.

MUSEU CARMEN MIRANDA
Carmen Miranda fans can't miss the guided tour of her collection of costumes, ornaments and other possessions. The museum is in the Aterro do Flamengo, in a pavilion designed by Affonso Reidy, the same architect responsible for the Museu de Arte Moderna. Book a visit by telephone.
Avenida Rui Barbosa, in front of Parque Brigadeiro Eduardo Gomes, 560, Flamengo, tel. (21) 2299-5586. Tue-Fri, 10am-5pm; Sat and Sun, noon-5pm.

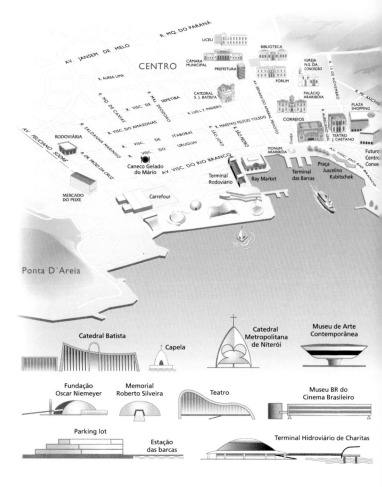

Niterói will be the site of a large building complex designed by Oscar Niemeyer.

CITY OF NITERÓI

The city of Niterói, 17 km (11 mi.) from Rio, is accessible by either a 20-minute ferry ride from Praça Quinze de Novembro or a trip across the Rio–Niterói bridge. Niterói's **Museu de Arte Contemporânea** is perhaps the only museum where the eyes of visitors are drawn away from the exhibits to the windows – the view of Guanabara Bay is spectacular. Designed by Oscar Niemeyer and opened in 1996, the

building has rapidly become a city landmark and an architectural icon. The panorama window encircling the ring-shaped building reveals a new "work of art" at every step, including a unique view of the Sugarloaf. The MAC holds paintings by Daniel Senise and contains the João Sattamini Collection, with works from scores of important Brazilian artists, mostly from the 1980's (*Mirante da Boa Viagem, tel. 21/2620-*

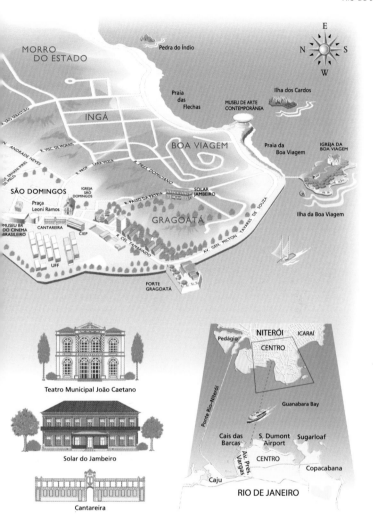

Teatro Municipal João Caetano

Solar do Jambeiro

Cantareira

2400. *Tue-Sun 11am-6pm*). Finish your tour with a draft beer and *bolinhos de bacalhau* (fried codfish balls) at **Caneco Gelado do Mário**, a bar in downtown Niterói (*Rua Visconde do Uruguai, 288, loja 5, tel. 21/2620-6787. Mon-Fri, 9am-10pm; Sat, 9am-7pm. Closed Sun*).

CAMINHO NIEMEYER
The MAC is the first of the nine buildings which, together with the already-open Praça Juscelino Kubitschek, will make up the so-called

Niemeyer Route complex. The route will make Niterói the city with the second-most buildings designed by the architect, after Brasília. The other buildings will include: the Fundação Oscar Niemeyer, which will house his own collection and an art school; Niterói's metropolitan cathedral; a Baptist cathedral; the Memorial Roberto Silveira; a new ferry station; the Museu BR do Cinema Brasileiro; a theater and a chapel. Most are expected to open by the end of 2005.

MOUNTAINS AND INLAND

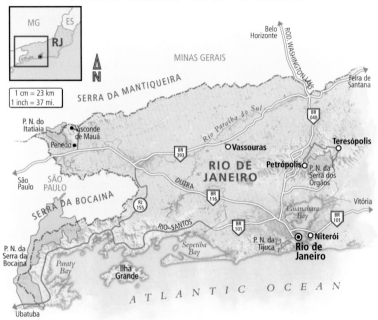

PETRÓPOLIS

With a mild climate and mountains covered in the lush vegetation of the Atlantic Rainforest, Petrópolis became the Brazilian imperial family's favorite summer resort in the 19th century. The family had remarkably good taste. Today, celebrities and commoners alike enjoy the beauty of this city nestled 800 meters (2,600 feet) above sea level in the Serra dos Órgãos. The mountain range lies 65 km (40 mi) from Rio via the BR-040. The emperor Dom Pedro I acquired a plot of land here to build a summer palace, and Dom Pedro II ultimately fulfilled his father's idea when he founded Petrópolis in 1843. The engineer Júlio Frederico Koeler pioneered the style of many of the German immigrants' houses, and one of the city's most beautiful streets is

named after him. Petrópolis retained its glamour even after the proclamation of the Republic – witness the kitsch splendor of the **Palácio Quitandinha**, where a casino operated in the 1940's. In more recent years, several excellent restaurants have opened in the region, earning it the nickname "Gourmet Valley".

CATEDRAL DE SÃO PEDRO DE ALCÂNTARA
This imposing cathedral, in the French Neogothic style, dates from 1939. The 70-meter (230-foot) steeple houses five bronze bells which were cast in Germany and weigh nine tonnes. To the right of the central aisle, constructed in marble, onyx and bronze, the **Capela Imperial** houses a mausoleum

containing the remains of Dom Pedro II, Dona Teresa Cristina, Princess Isabel and Count D'Eu. The altar contains relics from Saints Magnus, Aurelia and Tecla, all brought from Rome, while poems written by Dom Pedro II during his exile have been inscribed on the stained-glass windows.

Rua São Pedro de Alcântara, 60, tel. (24) 2242-4300. Tue-Sun, 8am-noon and 2pm-6pm.

MUSEU IMPERIAL

This pink, Neoclassical palace offers a glimpse of everyday life in the imperial family. Their former summer residence is exquisitely decorated, from the white Carrara and black Belgian marble of the entrance to the dining-hall's mahogany furniture. Highlight include the jacaranda hardwood of the music room where Dom Pedro II held soirées and recitals, the Princesses Isabel and Leopoldina's room, the paintings and objects of the Emperor's study, and the decor of Empress Teresa Cristina's drawing-room. The collection of artifacts on view contains jewelry, crowns, paintings and personal effects. Visitors must wear felt slippers when touring the museum. Designed by the French landscape artist Jean Baptiste Binot, the gardens sport imposing imperial palms and one hundred species of exotic plants and trees such as the Portuguese cypress. All this is the setting for the Son et Lumière show, a choreographed play of light and shadow on the building's façade.

Rua da Imperatriz, 220, tel. (24) 2237-8000. Tue-Sun, 11am-5:30pm. Shows: Thu-Sat, 8pm.

PALÁCIO RIO NEGRO

Built in 1889, shortly before the proclamation of the Republic, this Neoclassical building was named after its first owner, the wealthy coffee baron Barão do Rio Negro. It served as the seat of the Rio de Janeiro state government between 1894 and 1902, when Petrópolis was the state capital. It's also been Brazil's official

The Museu Imperial, showing the daily life of the Brazilian royal family

The imposing Catedral de São Pedro de Alcântara

presidential summer residence since 1903, although it is not frequently occupied. The furnishings reflects the taste of the many presidents who have stayed here. Getúlio Vargas converted the wine cellar into a Roman-style bath-house and Juscelino Kubitschek had built-in closets installed.
Avenida Koeler, 255, tel. (24) 2246-9380. Mon, noon-5pm; Wed-Sun, 9:30am-5pm.

CASA DA PRINCESA ISABEL
This pink Neoclassical building was the home of Princess Isabel and her husband Count D'Eu until 1889. Now it's the headquarters for the real-estate firm Cia. Imobiliária Petrópolis, and the antiquities dealership Antiquário da Princesa. Both companies belong to descendants of the imperial family. The property firm owns the original map of the sub-divisions that gave rise to the city.

Avenida Koeler, 42, Centro, tel. (24) 2242-4706.

PALÁCIO DE CRISTAL
The metal and glass components of the Palácio de Cristal (Crystal Palace) were manufactured in 1879 in Saint-Saveur-les-Arras, France. This type of building was popular in Europe after the Industrial Revolution. Princess Isabel funded its construction for the Petrópolis Horticultural Association, which her husband Count D'Eu ran. In 1888, four years after it opened, the princess held a spectacular party here. At that memorable event, she granted freedom to several slaves, almost as a prelude to her signing the Lei Áurea, the law that officially abolished slavery in Brazil. Today the Palace houses occasional exhibitions as well as plays and concerts. On Saturdays, at 6pm, there are shows of *chorinho*, MPB and classical music. To check the program, call the city's tourism service *(0800-241516).*
Rua Alfredo Pachá, tel. (24) 2247-3721. Tue-Sun, 9am-5:30pm.

CASA DE SANTOS DUMONT
Santos Dumont, who surprised the

WHO WAS THE FIRST TO FLY?
This controversy spans many decades. When the world learned that Brazilian Alberto Santos Dumont had flown a heavier-than-air machine in 1906, the American brothers Wilbur and Orville Wright claimed they had accomplished the same feat three years earlier. But Dumont's flight on the 14 Bis around the Eiffel Tower in Paris was recorded and photographed, while the Wright brothers' flight had no witnesses. Only in 1908 were the Wrights seen piloting their Flyer in the United States and France. However, Americans still assume that their citizens were the first to fly, and few are even aware of Dumont's feat.

world in 1906 when he made the world's first observed heavier-than-air powered flight in the 14 Bis, designed this fine three-story house in 1918 and lived there periodically. There are several curiosities popular with children, such as the alcohol-heated shower and the fact that the first step of the staircase is constructed in such a way that you have to start climbing with your right foot. On top of the house, Dumont, an amateur astronomer, installed a telescope. *Rua do Encanto, 22, tel. (24) 2247-3158. Tue-Sun, 9:30am-5pm.*

PALÁCIO QUITANDINHA

This impressive building once contained the largest casino in Latin America, but it operated as such for only two years, as gambling was banned in Brazil in 1946. Today, it is a convention center. From the outside it appears to be an austere Norman palace, but the interior resembles the set of a 1940's Hollywood melodrama, with garish pink, red, green and turquoise walls designed by then-famous interior designer Dorothy Draper. Celebrities such as Marlene Dietrich, Lana Turner and Orson Welles visited. Everything is on the grand scale: the dome of the **Salão Mauá** is 30 meters (100 ft) high and 50 meters (165 ft) in diameter. The mechanized theater has

three revolving stages and seats 2,000, while the entire building can hold 10,000. In the lake, which is shaped like Brazil itself, there is a lighthouse on the spot corresponding to the Ilha de Marajó. *Avenida Joaquim Rolla, 2, Quitandinha, tel. (24) 2237-1012. Tue-Sun, 9am-5pm.*

THE SURROUNDING AREA

The Petrópolis region is known for the variety and quality of its cuisine, which attracts gourmets from all over. Many undoubtedly wish they could spend the rest of their lives here, perhaps settling in at one of the charming, fireplace-equipped inns. To indulge the taste-buds, take the Estrada da União–Indústria from the town center to **Correas**, **Araras** and **Itaipava**. In Correas, visit the **Pousada da Alcobaça**, a Norman-style riverside inn with charming gardens, a small waterfall and a garden which supplies the kitchen of the in-house restaurant (*Rua Agostinho Goulão, 298, Correas, tel. 24/2221-1240*). In Araras, one of the most-visited restaurants is **Locanda Della Mimosa**, run by chef Danilo Braga, who has won several awards for his homemade, must-have Italian pasta dishes (*Alameda das Mimosas, 30, Vale Florido, off km 72 on the BR-040, tel. 24/2233-5405*). Wine lovers will delight in **Fazenda das Videiras**, a European-style inn whose cellar is stocked with some of the finest wines in the world (*Estrada Paulo Meira, 6,000, via Est. Araras–Vale das Videiras, tel. 24/2225-8090*). In Itaipava, which has a pulsating nightlife, don't miss the **Castelo do Barão de Itaipava**, a Renaissance-style building constructed in the 1920's by Lúcio Costa, the modernist urban planner responsible for Brasília, and his partner Fernando Valentim.

Parque Nacional da Serra dos Órgãos

Created in 1939, this national park extends over almost 12,000 hectares of mountainous country and encompasses Petrópolis, Guapimirim, Magé and Teresópolis. Most of it is clad in the typical vegetation of the Atlantic Rainforest, but the higher parts are covered with the scrub-like vegetation of the highlands. The peak **Dedo de Deus**, at 1,692 meters (5,550 feet), is its best known landmark, although the highest point is the **Pedra do Sino**, at 2,263 meters (7,425 feet). The park is a paradise for adventure-sports lovers, and the trails afford spectacular views. On clear days, one can see Rio de Janeiro and can catch glimpses of Guanabara Bay through the foliage. There are two ways in – from Petrópolis (*Estrada do Bonfim, km 18*) or Teresópolis, where the park's headquarters is (*Avenida Rotariana, tel. 21/2642-1070*). It is open to the public from Tuesday through Sunday, between 8am and 5pm, for short trips. At other times, only climbers who have bought tickets in advance can enter. The best period for hiking is from May to October, while river-bathing is most tolerable between November and February. However, beware of the summer storms, as headwater levels tend to rise extremely rapidly and hurtle downwards, abruptly increasing river currents and creating flashfloods that sweep away everything in their path. The Soberbo, the park's major river, offers wonderful waterfalls for bathing and is the terminus for the most accessible trails. The easiest ones, like **Primavera** and **Mozart Catão**, take less than an hour. The route takes less than two hours to the **Véu de Noiva** waterfall, located in Bonfim, a canyoning and rappelling spot. The 2,232 meter (7,323 feet) hike to the top of **Pedra do Açu** takes five and a half hours on average, but the resulting view of Guanabara Bay is well worth the climb. The most challenging yet interesting trek is the four-day hike across the mountains on the 42 km (26 mi.) trail from Petrópolis to Teresópolis, or vice versa. The services of a qualified guide are well worth the expense. The Mundo do Mato travel agency (*tel. 21/2742-0811*) can help locate hostels and guides licensed by Embratur, the Brazilian Tourism Agency.

The mountain landscape invites either adventure or relaxation

TERESÓPOLIS

Teresópolis was named after Dona Teresa, Dom Pedro II's wife, who near the end of the 19th century fell under the spell of the region's natural beauty and its mountain climate. While nearby Petrópolis recalls the glorious days of empire, with its palaces and historic collections, Teresópolis, 87 kilometers (54 mi.) from Rio on the BR-040 and then BR-116, is better known for its nature and as a base for highland excursions. It is the highest town in the state of Rio de Janeiro, nestling in the Serra dos Órgãos at 910 meters (3,000 feet) above sea level and surrounded by a breathtaking landscape of mountains, rivers and waterfalls, not to mention a rich diversity of flora and fauna. It also houses the headquarters of the **Parque Nacional da Serra dos Órgãos**, with a camping site, rock pools and trails leading to the peaks. Teresópolis remained virtually untouched for many years. The natural bulwark of the soaring mountains and dense vegetation helped deter potential explorers. The **Dedo de Deus**, an icon in local mountaineering circles, is in the park and was first climbed by Brazilians in 1912. There are no palaces in Teresópolis; instead you will find farms, such as the one that belonged to George March. A Portuguese of English descent, he raised cattle, horses and mules and grew vegetables to supply the state capital. Other *cariocas* followed him and founded a small village, in which they offered lodging to merchants from Minas Gerais en route to the port of Estrela, in Guanabara Bay, via Petrópolis. Tourism really began to take off in 1908, when the railway came through and hotels, inns and restaurants started to go up in its wake. The town became a favorite

mountain destination after the road to Rio was opened in 1959. In addition to natural beauty, the place offers local handicrafts in wood, wicker and leather, the woolen clothing and the delicious homemade sweets.

OUR RECOMMENDATION

🍽 Be prepared for a banquet at **Dona Irene**, a Russian restaurant worthy of the tzars! The portions are enormous, accompanied by plenty of homemade vodka and tales recounted by the owners, José Hibello and Maria Emília. Try the *varenik*, a type of ravioli made with potatoes, scaloppini, herbs and crispy onions. Reservations required (*Travessa Luiz Meirelles, 1800, tel 21/2742-2901*).

🏨 The **Hotel e Fazenda Rosa dos Ventos** is located in a private 100-hectare park in the middle of the mountains. Its ample leisure facilities make it almost a resort on its own. It is the only Brazilian hotel belonging to the Relais & Chateaux chain, a brand known for charm and comfort.

Additional information begins on page 462.

The Dedo de Deus dares climbers

VASSOURAS

In the middle of the 19th century, Vassouras, in the Paraíba Valley, 111 km (69 mi.) from Rio via the BR-116 and then the RJ-127, was the country's top coffee-producing region. Coffee was the main source of wealth during the imperial era, and successful growers rapidly became rich. They built magnificent mansions and plant imperial palms and fig trees along the town's streets. They also built imposing manors on their plantations, with dozens of rooms, and imported furnishings from Europe to decorate their estates. Within a few decades, however, the soil became impoverished, and the abolition of slavery led inevitably to the economic decline of the labor-intensive plantations. The town has not grown since, which has at least facilitated the preservation of its heritage.

HISTORICAL CENTER
The largest buildings are grouped around the Praça Barão de Campo Belo. The **Matriz Nossa Senhora da Conceição**, a Neoclassical church built in 1846, is noteworthy. The **Prefeitura** (City Hall) occupies an 1849 mansion, and the **Casa da Cultura** is an 1844 building. Don't miss the beautiful stone fountain. The colonial-style **Casa da Hera** museum, dating from 1830, has a rich collection of 19th-century crystal, silverware, porcelain, candlesticks, lamps, clothing and furniture. *Tel. (24) 2471-2342.*

IMPERIAL ESTATES
Fifteen estates from the imperial era have been preserved and opened to visitors. It's wise to book a trip organized by one of the hotels, as some of them are only open by appointment. Most offer an afternoon snack or the so-called "colonial tea", which comes with sweets and breads. One of the oldest estates is **Cachoeira Grande**, dating from 1825, which belonged to the Barão de Vassouras. It displays, among other things, a chair that belonged to Dom Pedro II, an 1830 piano, a phonograph and peacocks in the garden. Ask to see the family's antique car collection in advance; some of them date back to 1910. *Tel. (24) 2471-1264.*

Drawing-room in the Casa da Hera, a typical coffee-baron mansion

Charming hotels and restaurants create romantic settings amidst a wealth of waterfalls

VISCONDE DE MAUÁ

A hippie enclave in the 1970's and 80's, Visconde de Mauá chills out 200 kilometers (125 mi.) from Rio. It still retains some of the charm of those rebel years, but it avoids the shortcomings of many alternative communities. With some of the most charming hotels in the region and excellent restaurants, it is one of the state's most romantic and picturesque destinations. Coming from Rio, take the Presidente Dutra Highway to km 304, in Resende, and then the RJ-163; from São Paulo, 305 kilometers (190 mi.) away, take the Presidente Dutra Highway to km 311. Low winter temperatures, especially in July, are perfect for a romantic evening and a glass of wine by the fireplace. Most inns cater for couples, serving noon until breakfast and not permitting guests to bring children. From December through March, the summer temperatures are mild, making conditions ideal at the many nearby waterfalls, with its crisp cold natural pools. Located on the border of Rio de Janeiro state and Minas Gerais to the north, the place actually consists of three villages: **Visconde de Mauá** itself, **Maromba** and **Maringá**, the most attractive. An array of handicraft shops, left over from prior decades, operate out of small, standardized wooden cottages in the center of Maringá. That downtown is also full of young couples strolling hand in hand. A 40-minute drive along the bumpy and winding RJ-163 will take you from President Dutra Highway to Visconde de Mauá. A word of caution: when it rains the road is subject to landslides, so phone some of the village's inns to check on conditions before you set out, and drive slowly to ensure a safe journey while enjoying the view.

Visconde de Mauá was named after Baron, later Viscount, de Mauá (1813-1889), a banker and industrialist who owned most of the land in the region. At the end of the 19th century, with government support, his son established a European colony here and divided the land into more than two hundred lots. Visconde de Mauá's modern economy is based on tourism.

VALE DO ACANTILADO

Visconde de Mauá has an abundance of beautiful scenery and waterfalls. Traversing the trail to the 20-meter (66-foot) **Acantilado waterfall** takes about an hour and a half (one-way). The waterfall is the highest in the region, and the valley's main attraction, but the trail also passes another eight stunning cataracts. You can admire the photogenic Acantilado waterfall, nestled in the mountain, from the start and the magnificent view helps encourages tired feet upward and onward. Less energetic visitors will still appreciate the first three waterfalls, which offer wonderful bathing just ten minutes from the parking lot. The valley is located on a private property, and you have to pay an entrance fee.

Estrada Mauá–Mirantão, km 3, tel. (24) 9264-5146/(12) 3931-1303.

VIEW FROM PEDRA SELADA

Many tourists, sports enthusiasts and adventure seekers visit Visconde de Mauá with the sole intent of climbing the **Pedra Selada** peak. The 1.7 kilometers (1.1 mi) hike to the summit takes about two and a half hours and has some very steep stretches through dense vegetation. But all the effort is worthwhile – the view of the Paraíba Valley from the summit is breathtaking.

The Visconde de Mauá mountains are full of waterfalls

The Conjunto das Prateleiras, in Itatiaia, Brazil's first national park

Parque Nacional do Itatiaia

This was Brazil's first national park, created in 1937. Situated on the border of Minas Gerais, São Paulo and Rio de Janeiro states, 167 kilometers (104 mi.) from Rio and 265 kilometers (165 mi.) from São Paulo, it comprises 30,000 hectares of stunning scenic beauty. The lower-lying part, which can be reached through **Itatiaia** (Presidente Dutra Highway, off km 316), is clad in the dense vegetation of the Atlantic Rainforest. There are several inns and numerous waterfalls, including the 40-meter **Véu de Noiva**, which splashes into a natural pool. The rugged, rocky landscape of the highlands, accessible from the same highway, off km 330, is a different story, however. The name Itatiaia, which means "spiky rocks", refers to its two most famous peaks: **Agulhas Negras** and **Prateleiras**. In the lower part, guides are essential if you want to climb or go on extensive treks in the region. Before leaving the park, stop at the **Mirante do Último Adeus**, a magnificent vantage point 2 kilometers (1.3 mi.) from the lower entrance.

Eating Out in Penedo

Although most hotels in Itatiaia offer full board, it might be worth having a meal out in **Penedo**. This former Finnish colony is 12 kilometers (7.5 mi.) from the town center. **Koskenkorva** (*tel. 24/3351-2532*) serves excellent Finnish cuisine and is located in a lush green area. **Rei das Trutas**, a simpler restaurant, specializes in trout dishes (*tel. 24/3351-1387*), while **Zur Sonne**, in the Alambari mountains, 15 kilometers (9.5 mi.) from Penedo, 4 kilometers (2.5 mi.) of which are unpaved, serves carefully prepared German food. The owner chats pleasantly with customers (*tel. 24/3391-7108*).

Our Recommendation

Hotel Donati, a cozy hotel located in the park's preservation area, has natural and heated pools, a sauna and an inviting lounge in the main house, as well as several comfortable individual chalets. Have a drink in the basement-bar, which serves fondue in the winter.

Additional information begins on page 462.

SOUTHERN COAST

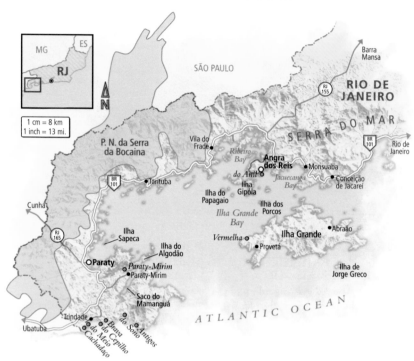

ANGRA DOS REIS

The bay of Angra dos Reis owes its beauty to the sea, and it's one of the most beautiful destinations in the Southeast. Magnificent, crystal-clear waters, dozens of beaches and enough islands and islets that it would take exactly a year to visit each for a day. The bay, which means the Bay of Kings, was named after Epiphany Day, or the Day of the Three Kings. It was on that day, January 6, in 1502, that it was discovered.

Sea excursions, whether long and short, offer time for swimming and snorkeling. The Associação dos Barqueiros (*tel. 24/3365-3165*), in the town center, rents out boats of varying size (and cost) for trips. But virtually all the hotels offer a boat service and some even include it in their rates. The schooner trip to the **islands of Cataguases, Botinas, Gipóia** and **Francisco** is particularly recommended.

Angra is located 168 kilometers (105 mi.) south of Rio, on the BR-101. On approach from this direction, the small town center may look disappointing, the beaches are not nearly as attractive as the ones farther along. The best thing to do is head straight for one of the region's resorts. Five-star hotels and charming inns offer beautiful views, secluded beaches and modern amenities.

Many Brazilian celebrities have

summer houses in or around Angra, and it's a popular place for many to usher in each New Year. One of the highlights of New Year's Day is a flotilla of brightly-decorated boats. **Anil Beach** in Angra is also the departure point for trips to nearby Ilha Grande (see page 145), famed for its natural beauty.

GIPÓIA

The region's second largest island, **Gipóia** is renowned for its magnificent beaches and its inviting snorkeling spots. It's just a 30-minute boat-trip from the Santa Luzia docks in the center of Angra. If you like bustle, head for **Jurubaíba** beach or **Praia do Dentista**, where floating bars deliver snacks and drinks to the boats that crowd the area. **Juruba** Beach, sheltered by hills, a rocky shoreline and native vegetation, is more peaceful and secluded. It can only be reached by canoe. Fishermen cast nets and set up traps. A small but beautiful beach is **Norte**, with its fine white sand.

Almost-deserted **Sururu** has golden sands and strong waves that crash against the reefs. **Oeste** beach is wilder, with warm, shallow waters.

DIVING SITES

Angra's calm, crystal-clear waters, its good visibility for most of the year, and its average temperature of 23°C (73.4°F), make it ideal for diving. Off the islands of **Búzios** and **Cobras**, there are *parcéis*, or rock pathways, at between 4 and 12 meters (13 and 40 ft). The waters off the rocky shore of **Brandão**, **Josefa**, **Redonda** and **Papagaio** islands are recommended for

Ideal spot for sports like sailing and jet skiing

sponges, coral and colorful fish. The sea bed off **Laje Zatim** and the **Imboassica** and **Queimadas** (**Grande** and **Pequena**) **islands** is very similar, while the waters off the **Botinas** and **dos Porcos** islands are so abundant in fish and so clear that you can see enormous schools, even from the boat. Off **Laje Preta**, however, where the sea is between 4 and 12 meters (13 and 40 ft) deep, the water becomes darker farther from the shore.

WRECK DIVING

The wreck of the Panamanian freighter *Pinguino*, which sank in **Sítio Forte inlet** in 1967, makes a great diving site. At a depth of 15 to 20 meters (50 to 60 feet), divers can explore its hold, engine-room and captain's cabin. In **Araçatiba inlet**, near the Vermelha beach on Ilha Grande, rests the *California*, a Brazilian vessel that sank in 1866. In **Laje Matariz**, there is a helicopter 7 meters (22 feet) down, and the water is so transparent that on clear days even snorkelers can make it out. Off one of the bay's headlands is the wreck of the *Bezerra de Menezes*, a steam-driven freighter that sank in 1860.

Angra dos Reis: clear waters, white sands and thick vegetation

Ilha Grande: 106 magnificent – and mostly deserted – beaches

ILHA GRANDE

Ilha Grande is the largest island in the region and belongs to the municipality of Angra dos Reis. It's 150 kilometers (93 mi.) from Rio and one and a half hours by boat from the mainland. The island has more than a hundred beaches, some of them reachable as a one-day excursion. The splendid **Lopes Mendes**, one such beach, has strong waves that make it ideal for surfing. But Ilha Grande is so beautiful and majestic, and has such a wealth of good hotels, that it's worth scheduling several days to explore its trails, visit its hidden beaches and scuba dive off its shores. Its 192 sq. km (74 sq. mi.) are clad in lush vegetation and are part of the Tamoios APA (Environmental Protection Area). It is also under the protection of three other conservation areas: the Parque Estadual Marinho do Aventureiro (a state park), the Parque Estadual da Ilha Grande and the Reserva Biológica da Praia do Sul. Since cars

are forbidden, the natural surroundings remain largely untouched in spite of the increasing presence of people. Nearly all restaurants, shops and travel agencies that offer excursions are concentrated in the small **Vila do Abraão**, where arriving boats make landfall. The best hotels, however, are scattered elsewhere around the island and a bit more difficult to reach. In the village, there are lively *forró* parties on weekends, where tourists and locals meet to have fun. *Forró* is a typical rhythm from northeastern Brazil. The **Saco do Céu**, one of the island's most charming spots, is a small inlet, with calm waters, where boats dock during the night. On clear evenings, the flat sea becomes mirror-like and reflects the stars – an unforgettable sight.

TREKKING ON THE ISLAND
At least 16 trails, running the gamut

of difficulty, lead to peaks, the **Acaiá grotto**, and the many waterfalls, beaches and mussel-breeding farms. The most interesting one is quite demanding and requires a whole week. It rings the island and features camping sites along the way. The 990 meter (0.6 mi.) hike to the top of the **Pico do Papagaio** affords a worthwhile view. The best times of the year for trekking are from May to July and from October to November, when temperatures are mild and rainfall is low. Although the trails are well signposted, it is advisable to hire a guide as some of them can be dangerous. A good agency in the area is Sudoeste sw Turismo (*tel. 24/3361-5516*).

BOAT TRIPS

The schooner excursion to **Freguesia de Santana** offers a marvelous view of the Angra coast. The **Igreja de Santana**, a church in Freguesia dating from 1796, is considered the area's most important historic structure. In addition to the beautiful beaches, the excursion visits snorkeling spots in the **Lagoa Azul**. The small lagoon, enclosed by tiny islets, is full of brightly-colored tropical fish. Boat trips also pass through **Saco do Céu** and **Japariz**, where the sea is calm and ideal for jet-skiing in an area close to the mangrove swamps. Another interesting trip is to **Palmas**, with a one-hour hike to **Lopes Mendes** and a stop at **Morcego** island and **Abraãozinho**. If the boat is capable and the weather cooperative, add on an excursion to the open sea. Rent a seaworthy vessel at the Associação de Barqueiros de Ilha Grande, whose boats are safe, registered with the Port Authority and piloted by qualified boatmen (*tel. 24/3361-5920*).

Boats at anchor in Provetá, Ilha Grande

Colonial Paraty holds prominent cultural and food-related events

PARATY

Paraty is one of the most charming sites on the Southeast coast and a gateway to the past. Founded in the mid-17th century, it received the status of UNESCO World Heritage Site in 1966. The historical center, where cars are prohibited, preserves numerous architectural treasures from the 18th century. The streets are paved with the original and irregular rough cobblestones, and at high tide become canals that allow in and easily drain the sea. The small colonial center abounds with artistic life. On every corner someone plays music, makes arts and crafts or performs a puppet show. An intense cultural program fills the calendar, featuring events of gastronomic, musical and folkloric nature, the last including the beautiful Festa do Divino. In mid-2003, it hosted the first FLIP, an annual international literary festival promoted by British publisher – and contributor to this volume – Liz Calder. Calder loves the town and has a home here. Paraty is also synonymous with

cachaça, the local sugar-cane spirit, thanks to the premium brands turned out by the neighboring *alambiques* (distilleries). The Serra da Bocaina mountains surround the town, and its dozens of small islands dot its bay. Numerous beautiful beaches, some nearly deserted, and excellent snorkeling spots border the ocean. Located at the foot of the mountains, the town is also a starting point for trekking tours in the highlands and visits to the many waterfalls. Paraty lies 248 kilometers (154.1 mi.) from Rio and 350 kilometers (217.5 mi.) from São Paulo on the BR-101.

HISTORICAL CENTER

Set aside an afternoon for strolling around the narrow streets of Paraty's colonial center. The **Casa da Cultura** (*Rua Dona Geraldá, 177, tel. 24/3371-2325*) occupies a magnificent mansion built in 1754 and holds a good permanent exhibition on local history and culture, as well as periodic cultural events. On the same street is the

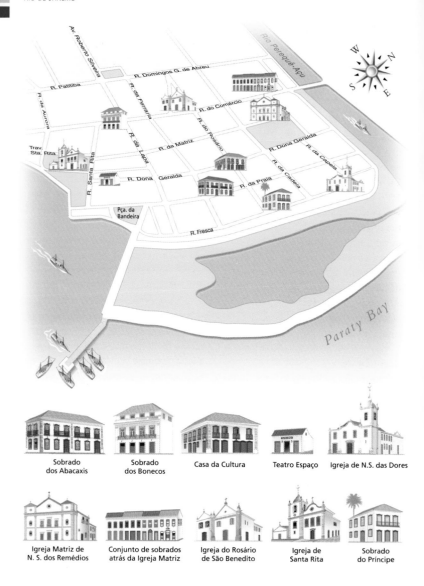

Sobrado
dos Abacaxis

Sobrado
dos Bonecos

Casa da Cultura

Teatro Espaço

Igreja de N.S. das Dores

Igreja Matriz de
N. S. dos Remédios

Conjunto de sobrados
atrás da Igreja Matriz

Igreja do Rosário
de São Benedito

Igreja de
Santa Rita

Sobrado
do Príncipe

Teatro Espaço, home of the renowned, traditional Puppet Theater. The churches are an attraction in themselves. The **Igreja da Santa Rita**, in the Largo de Santa Rita, is the oldest, dating from 1722, and it houses the **Museu de Arte Sacra**, a museum of religious art. The 1725 **Igreja do Rosário**, in the Largo do

Rosário, was the slaves' church. It is correspondingly decorated in a simple manner, except for the gold leaf on the altars, which was added in the early 20th century. The **Igreja Matriz de Nossa Senhora dos Remédios** is also worth a visit. Construction began in 1787, but it took almost 100 years to finish the church. The ambitious project was just too expensive. Right in front, in the Praça da Matriz, a fair displays many of Paraty's arts-and-crafts. The fair is open daily and always offers music and puppet shows. The **Igreja de Nossa Senhora das Dores** sits on Rua Fresca, a street appropriately named after the fresh sea breeze that wafts over it. Also known as the **Capelinha**, this church was built in 1800 in typical 18th century style and was used by the aristocracy during the imperial era. Note the delicate tracery of the balconies and the crystal chandelier over the choir stalls. Finally, admire the architecture of the **Sobrados dos Bonecos, dos Abacaxis** and **do Príncipe** – the last belongs to the Orleans e Bragança royal family.

BOAT TRIPS

Schooners, small fishing boats and trawlers are all available for hire at the quay. Various routes stops at three or four beaches and permit diving, amidst spectacular scenery, off **Algodão** and **Sapeca** islands. The stunning **Saco do Mamanguá**, a green bay flanked by steep cliffs, is an unforgettable destination that's reachable by boat from the **Paraty-mirim** beach.

A TRIP TO CUNHA

A winding, narrow, unpaved and bumpy road, which narrows to single lane at the sharp curves, leads to the historic town of **Cunha**. The site offers breathtaking views of the bay and the beauty of the forest, but only 4-wheel-drive utility vehicles can safely reach it during the rainy season. For additional information on **Cunha**, see this guide's São Paulo section.

SURFING AND DIVING IN TRINDADE

Trindade is a memorable destination just 25 kilometers from Paraty, and 7 kilometers (4.3 mi.) from the Rio–Santos highway on a paved and well-signposted road. The former fishing village and one-time hippie enclave thrives on tourism. The dirt roads are packed on holidays, but it never loses its rustic charm, even during the high season. There are beaches excellent for surfing, such as **Cepilho** and **Brava**, and others with calm waters and rock pools, like **do Meio** and **Cachadaço**. The last has a huge natural stone pool, ideal for diving and fish watching, and is only a 20-minute walk from **Meio** beach. A boat that can be hired at the beach takes just 5 minutes to go between them. Adventurous visitors head to the more distant beaches of **do Sono** (a one-hour walk from Vila Oratório) and **Antigos** (an additional 40-minute walk from do Sono). They are seaside paradises untouched by tourism.

The colonial Sobrado dos Abacaxis

A LITERARY PARADISE

Paraty took hold of my imagination long before I ever went there. During my 20's I lived in São Paulo for four years. This was in the 60's, and Brazil and its enchanting music, art, literature and film held me in thrall. We and our friends partied all night and danced to the music of the young Chico Buarque and Gilberto Gil. It was "heaven itself".

Every so often people would mention a mysterious place on the coast between São Paulo and Rio, a place that could be reached only by sea or mule. Artists, bohemians, and gays, so I was told, lived blissfully alongside the local fishermen in this secret place of wonderful architecture and natural beauty. Paraty – the very name was romantic, and I longed to go. But it was never possible at that time.

In 1992 I finally made it there. By then, a road had been built, and Paraty had become a national monument and a favourite holiday place for *paulistas*. It was Carnival, and Paraty's historical centre was gearing up for a party – everyone milling around in the colourful streets filled with dancing, music and children in fancy dress.

The town was just as I had imagined it. Intimate, gay, sometimes melancholy, throbbing with street life at times, quiet as a grave at others. Tucked into that narrow strip of flat land between the protecting mountains and the calm sea, it looks out from its prime spot in the bowl of the bay, decorated by the most ravishing rain forest. It welcomes visitors to share its bounty. And it sighs with relief when they all go away again… Its unique charm is a confluence of this unrivalled natural beauty and the grace of its 18th century colonial buildings, funded first by gold from Minas Gerais and then by coffee.

As I reminisce, I have in front of me a postcard that I sent my husband Louis Baum in London during that trip in 1992. The card shows the classic view of Paraty: the Santa Rita church and the quays taken from the sea, and on it I wrote: "Here is where we are going to live. Start packing now!" How ever did I know?

In 1999 we returned to this side of the bay to look at a property that was for sale. It was terribly neglected and overgrown, and the land that dropped steeply down to the sea had just a small house on it. Protected by the island of Araujo, its steep banks have been softened by terracing, zigzagging pathways and Mauro Munhoz' inspired architecture. Munhoz is a visionary architect from São Paulo who has worked for many years on a project to reclaim the Paraty waterfront, which has become silted up.

How, then, did Paraty acquire a literary festival – and an international one at that? From way back when we first met Mauro, we have dreamed of ways to bring Paraty's riches to the attention of more people. Not all people, of course – just those in the know. For much of the year there is a tranquility about the place that is precious to the people who live there. In the holidays it fills up with visitors, and the shops and restaurants and *pousadas* (inns) do their business.

We wondered, "What might help the town to prosper during the off-season?" The beauty and intimacy of the 18ᵗʰ century historic center, the existence of so many *pousadas*, well over 100, and of so many charming bars, restaurants, shops and art galleries, all make it an ideal location for festivals, and Paraty is blessed with many of these, both religious and cultural. But since Louis and I are both book people, we began to wonder if a literary festival had any possibility here. A strong motivating factor was our belief that the riches of Brazil's art and literature – not to mention its natural beauty – are not sufficiently appreciated in the rest of the world: how better to raise their international profile than by inviting leading international writers to meet their Brazilian counterparts in such a beautiful and intimate setting?

The first FLIP (Festa Literária Internacional de Paraty), in 2003, was an amazing success. I say amazing because none of us expected such a huge response, from the media, from the authors, from the people of Paraty, and from the public. More than 6,000 people visited Paraty for the four days of the festival. We were able to bring to Paraty the Federal Minister of Culture, Gilberto Gil, on his first visit to the town. We were able to bring Chico Buarque and Adriana Calcanhoto, international literary stars like Don DeLillo, Julian Barnes and Hanif Kureishi, one of the world's leading historians, Eric Hobsbawm, and several leading Brazilian writers.

The success of the literary festival demonstrates a way forward for the town. For all its beauty – *because* of its beauty – Paraty is at a crossroads. Unlike nearby Angra dos Reis, which offers a stark and depressing warning to all beauty resorts with dreams of growing, Paraty has preserved its isolation to a degree. But since the building of the Rio–Santos road and the development of international transport and communications, its tourism has increased. This has brought great benefits to the town, but also dangers. Traditional communities in some outlying settlements are losing inhabitants to the town. And the subtle ties that have held the town and its surroundings together, and made it the jewel it is, are being threatened. Yes, Paraty needs more tourists, but they should be tourists who are sensitive not only to its beauty but also to the fragility of that beauty.

Paraty also, we believe, needs state and federal support for its infrastructure, to enable it to cope with growing numbers of tourists without damage to the natural and urban environment. Should that be allowed to occur, the very things that make Paraty one of the world's most beautiful coastal towns would be under threat.

Liz Calder, director of Bloomsbury Publishing and president of Festa Literária Internacional de Paraty

NORTHERN COAST

Urban sophistication in a fishing-village set

BÚZIOS

Búzios is an idyllic, 8-kilometer (5-mi.) peninsula surrounded by clear green waters. It is also a global village, whose streets and sands visitors from all over the world throng. In the 1950's it was a secluded *carioca* beach retreat that was extremely difficult to get to. In the following decade, however, actress Brigitte Bardot discovered it and her attentions helped transform it into a fashionable international tourist destination. Today, it has first-class infrastructure, with comfortable accommodation, cozy bars, sophisticated restaurants, elegant stores and even a movie theater named after the French actress. With more than two hundred hotels and inns, it has lost much of the fishing-village atmosphere and glamour of fifty years ago, but its services are the perfect pairing for the informality of the beaches. The peninsula is 192 kilometers (120 mi.) east of Rio on the BR-101 highway and then the RJ-124 and RJ-106. A visit to **Barra de São João** makes for an enjoyable day trip. It is a small village 30 kilometers (18.6 mi.) from Búzios. Once the home of Brazilian poet Casimiro de Abreu, who celebrated it in his verses, some of the town's houses have lined the clear waters of the picturesque, mangrove-lined São João river since the 17th century.

RUA DAS PEDRAS

The heart of Búzios is the so-called Street of Stones, actually a 400-meter (quarter-mile) stretch of Avenida Bento Ribeiro Dantas that bisects the town. It was named after its rough-cut paving stones, which act as a deterrent to drivers and an

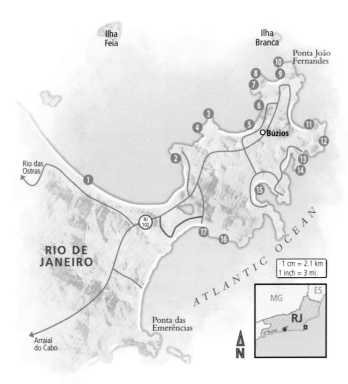

Ilha Feia

Ilha Branca

Ponta João Fernandes

Rio das Ostras

Búzios

RJ 102

RIO DE JANEIRO

1 cm = 2.1 km
1 inch = 3 mi.

ATLANTIC OCEAN

MG

ES

RJ

Ponta das Emerências

Arraial do Cabo

N

encouragement to pedestrians. Here, amid famous designer boutiques, sophisticated restaurants and night clubs, ice-cream parlors, *crêperies* and street artists, a gregarious visitor can mingle with people from all regions and walks of life. Things begin to heat up at sunset.

THE BEACHES

Armação dos Búzios, a sinuous peninsula dotted with beautiful bays, has beaches for every taste – with or without waves, deep or shallow, cold or mild, crowded or deserted. A sailor's paradise, the town has four yacht clubs and annually hosts more than a dozen events and competitions, such as the Búzios Sailing Week. Multiple boats depart from **Armação**

beach each hour, and most serve *caipirinhas*, fruit, mineral water and soft drinks on board.

❶ MANGUINHOS
Its calm waters and constant winds make it ideal for windsurfing, as is the neighboring **Formosa** bay. It faces **Feia** Island, a perfect scuba-diving spot.

❷ TARTARUGA
Noted for its rock pools, unspoiled vegetation and multicolored pebbles. Divers can also enjoy the coral reefs.

❸ PRAIA DOS AMORES
Deserted, untouched and with calm waters, it is perfect for swimming. Nudity can be practiced, albeit

informally. Accessible by sea or by scrambling along the rocky coastline.

④ Praia das Virgens
Another deserted beach. Also accessible along the rocks or by sea from the **Amores** beach, but only at low tide. Be sure to keep an eye on the tides.

⑤ Praia do Canto and da Armação
Dotted with colonial houses and fishing boats, both of these beaches are unfit for bathing. Equipped with an anchorage, **Armação** beach, quite close to **Canto** beach, also has a statue of the actress Brigitte Bardot.

⑥ Praia dos Ossos
This small but well-known inlet has calm blue waters and is the setting for many international sailing and windsurfing competitions. Renting a schooner and glass-bottomed boat, to observe marine life, is possible. A flight of stairs leads to the **Igreja de Sant'Ana**, a church dating from 1740 and named after Búzios's patron saint.

⑦ Azeda
Accessible only on foot from the Ossos beach, it offers delightful scenery. The sea is calm, making it ideal for diving.

⑧ Azedinha
Like Azeda, it is listed as an environmental reserve and is also excellent for diving. It has a breathtaking bay with green waters.

⑨ João Fernandes
Crowded and vibrant, with many rocky outcrops. There are many kiosks serving lobster and local fish.

⑩ João Fernandinho
Almost deserted, despite its beautiful rock pools. Accessible from João

Fernandes beach. Both beaches are good for fishing and diving.

⑪ Brava
Large and dotted with viewing-points, Brava's huge waves make it a surfers' paradise. Beware of the currents in the vicinity of Laje do Criminoso.

⑫ Olho-de-Boi
So deserted that nudity is common. Accessible on foot from Brava beach.

⑬ Forno
A tiny, enchanting inlet with calm waters, moderate winds and several rock pools. Ideal for divers and those seeking solitude.

⑭ Foca
Accessible from the sea or via a trail, this beach has a narrow strip of sand and heavy breakers.

⑮ Ferradura
A placid bay dotted with kiosks and beach houses; perfect for diving and sailing, and for couples with small children. From here you can reach the **Ponta da Lagoinha**, which has a stunning sunset.

⑯ Ferradurinha
A sandy beach with calm, crystal-clear waters and a natural rock pool. Accessible by car from Portal da Ferradura, or on foot from Geribá. Ideal for diving.

⑰ Geribá
A fashionable beach 4 kilometers (2.5 mi.) long and extremely popular with the younger generation. You have to pay for the privilege of sitting in the shade of a parasol, but the beach's many bars and restaurants will pamper you if you do. There are powerful breakers in certain stretches.

Cold waters and white sands surrounded by gentle dunes

CABO FRIO

Much more crowded than Búzios, this is the biggest and most developed town in the Região dos Lagos. It lies two hours and 148 kilometers (91.9 mi.) by car from Rio de Janeiro on the BR-101, and then the RJ-124 and RJ-140. Cabo Frio has cold, crystal-clear waters, abundant sun, and a year-long temperate climate. The constant, northeasterly wind has sculpted fine white sand into dunes. If you want to tour the dunes, do so during the day, when it is safest. The town is one of Brazil's major salt producers, hence the windmills.

RUA DOS BIQUÍNIS

With 200 shops, **Gamboa** is known as "bikini street". During summer, more than 3,500 people visit it daily to buy everything they need for the beach – shorts, t-shirts, sarongs, sandals, and, of course, bikinis. In fact, you can acquire a complete summer wardrobe here.

BEACHES

The most famous and crowded beach in Cabo Frio is **Forte** beach, where the fortress of São Mateus was built in 1620 in the town center. Frequent music shows spring up on the esplanade. In summer, it's almost impossible to find a spot to sunbathe, but it is a fine beach for sailors and surfers. Walk along it to eventually reach the dunes, but take care, as **Dama Branca**, the highest one, is not safe. Also along here is **Foguete** beach, which is full of summer houses. Powerful breakers make Foguete ideal for surfing and also good for fishing. Carry on northwards to reach **Brava** beach, which is popular with surfers due to its powerful waves. Further on in the same direction, there is **Conchas** beach, a good fishing spot where you can also hire horses. From there, you reach **Peró** beach, which has spectacular dunes. You can eat and drink there at shorefront kiosks.

Arraial do Cabo

Known as a scuba-diving capital, Arraial do Cabo's main attraction is the sea. The town itself, surrounded by hills and resembling a fishing village, has white dunes, sandbanks, lagoons, unspoiled beaches and beautiful headlands. From the **Pontal do Atalaia**, one such headland, you can admire a glorious coastal sunset. Originally the land of the indigenous *tupinambás* and of the finest *pau-brasil* (brazilwood, after which the country was named), Arraial is part of colonial history. It was the scene of Dutch timber smuggling, piracy and dozens of shipwrecks – there are said to be at least 88 in the area. Today, though, it is quieter than its more fashionable neighbors.

The waters of Arraial: ideal for scuba diving

At **Grande** beach, stretching as far as the horizon in the direction of **Saquarema** beach, there is drift-net and you can indulge in a late-afternoon drink and a bite to eat in one of the bars or kiosks. For the more energetic travellers, there is scuba diving and a number of trails to explore, such as the one to the old lighthouse. The boat trips are also unforgettable, especially the one to the **Azul** grotto, which stops at the **Pontal do Atalaia**. To reach Arraial from Rio city, take the BR-101, then the RJ-124, RJ-106 and RJ-140. It is 158 kilometers (99 mi.) by car.

Ilha de Cabo Frio

The island of Cabo Frio, close to Arraial do Cabo and a 40-minute boat trip from Anjos beach, is magnificent walking country, but visitors need the Navy's permission to spend the day here. The tiny **Forte** beach, with its typical sandbank vegetation, cold, blue crystal-clear waters, and fine white sand, was declared the most perfect beach in the country by Brazilian National Institute of Space Research. (Who knew that planetary scientists were such experts on beaches?) From do Forte beach, the traveller can see breathtaking views as the **Racha de Nossa Senhora** (a rock formation), the hill on the Pontal do Atalaia headland, **Porcos** island and **Prainha**. There is also a one-and-a-half-hour trail to the new lighthouse, the ruins of the old one, built in 1833, and the lighthouse keeper's home at the peak of the headland, from where

you can see the entire Região dos Lagos. The thick fog, that led to the closure of the old lighthouse, lends a mysterious atmosphere to the place. The waters around the island, excellent for diving, have good visibility and contain some 60 species of fish and coral. Very different from Brazil's other scuba-diving areas due to its unique geographical characteristics, Arraial do Cabo was declared the capital city of this sport. The coastal currents change direction here, veering from north-south to west-east and forcing the deep waters flowing from the Antarctic up to the surface. As a result, the area is exceptionally rich in marine species.

① SACO DO CHERNE
Its coral-covered seabed make it ideal for shallow diving.

② TEIXEIRINHA
At Ponta da Jararaca, visitors can find abundant marine life encrusting great blocks of rocks. The Teixeirinha, a ship which sank in 1923, can be seen scattered into chunks at various depths.

③ PORCOS (OFF EASTERN SHORE)
Not for inexperienced divers; depths can reach up to 40 meters (130 feet) close to the rocks.

④ PORCOS (OFF SOUTH SHORE)
A 15-meter (50 foot) dive features lots of sea fans (known as gorgónias), sea horses and, occasionally, turtles.

⑤ CARDEIROS
Shallow diving, from 6 to 10 meters (20 to 33 feet), in quiet seas; green sponges, sea horses and pink coral.

⑥ MARAMUTÁ AND ⑦ PEDRA VERMELHA
Once favorite spots for diving schools to "baptize" learners; however, Ibama, Brazil's environmental agency, has prohibited diving in the area, now solely given over to research.

⑧ ANEQUIM
Forests of sea fans plus the wreck of the *Wizard*, which sank in 1839; depths here are between 10 and 15 meters (33 and 50 feet).

⑨ PONTA LESTE
Exceptionally rich in marine life – rays, turtles, barracuda, yellowtail and mackerel, to name but few.

⑩ CAMARINHA
For experienced divers only, and even then only when the sea is calm and visibility is high. For safety, never dive alone.

⑪ GRUTA AZUL
A long-established tourist destination, the walls of this underwater grotto turn shades of blue that depend on the strength of incoming sunlight. Do not dive in its underwater cave unless the sea is calm and visibility is excellent.

⑫ HARLINGER
The seabed off Atalaia Headland is strewn with the 1906 wreck of the Dutch ship *Harlingers*. The 18 to 25 meter (60 to 80 feet) dive in the open sea requires extreme caution.

⑬ DONA PAULA
The Brazilian Navy warship *Dona Paula* foundered here in 1827 while pursuing an Argentinean corsair. It offers a dive of between 5 and 15 meters (16 and 50 feet).

Crystal-clear waters and a profusion of underwater life make the cape a diver's paradise

DESTINATION
SÃO PAULO

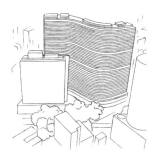

São Paulo is Brazil's wealthiest and most populous city and, with 17 million souls in its urban embrace, the largest metropolis in the Western Hemisphere, save Mexico's capital. The place looks and lives like the big city it is. It throbs to the liveliest nightlife in the country, it contemplates the most diverse cultural and artistic offerings, and it is always racing to take advantage of an extraordinary array of dining and shopping opportunities. Stunning modernist architecture makes it the most brightly gleaming gem in the crown of São Paulo state, but there are other, more natural jewels beyond the glass-and-concrete forest of the capital. Magnificent coastline, pleasant mountain towns and wild hinterlands invite beach goers and intrepid adventurers alike to journey afield.

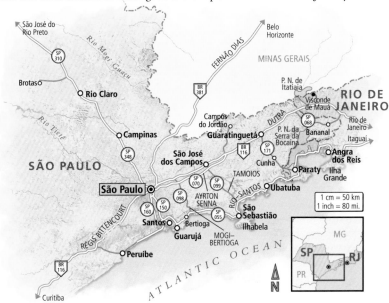

DESTINATION HIGHLIGHTS

CITY OF SÃO PAULO
  Historic Center
  Mercado Municipal
  Liberdade
  Higienópolis
  Avenida Paulista
  Jardins
  Gabriel Monteiro da Silva
    and Surroundings
  Parque do Ibirapuera
  Vila Madalena
  Special Attractions

BROTAS (245 km/152 mi.)

THE COAST
  Juréia (153 km/95 mi.)
  Santos (85 km/53 mi.)
  Guarujá (87 km/54 mi.)
  São Sebastião
    (214 km/133 mi.)
  Ilhabela (224 km/139 mi.)
  Ubatuba (235 km/146 mi.)

MOUNTAINS AND COUNTRYSIDE
  Campos do Jordão
    (167 km/104 mi.)
  Cunha (222 km/138 mi.)
  São Luís do Paraitinga
    (171 km/106 mi.)
  Parque Nacional da Serra
    da Bocaina (295 km/183 mi.)

All distances are from the city of São Paulo

CITY OF SÃO PAULO
HISTORIC CENTER

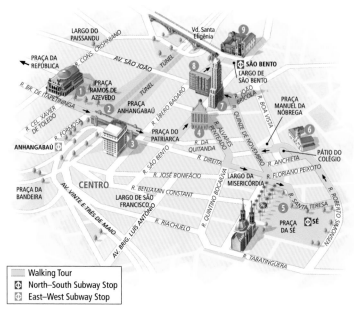

Walking Tour
🚇 North–South Subway Stop
🚇 East–West Subway Stop

1 - Teatro Municipal
2 - Viaduto do Chá
3 - Palácio do Anhagabaú

4 - Centro Cultural Banco do Brasil
5 - Praça da Sé and surrounding area
6 - Pátio do Colégio

7 - Prédio do Banespa
8 - Edifício Martinelli
9 - Largo São Bento

Though four and a half centuries old, this massive metropolis has yet to slow down. A stroll through the downtown of the third-largest city in the world is accompanied by the buzz of activity surrounding the constant remodeling and restoration projects. Officially, the city center is divided into the old and the new areas, separated by the Vale do Anhangabaú. The borders of the **Centro Velho** (the old center), located on the right side of the valley, are defined by the Pátio do Colégio, Catedral da Sé and the Mosteiro de São Bento, while the **Centro Novo** (the new center), on the left, is bounded by the Praça da

República and Avenidas Ipiranga, São João and São Luiz.

1 TEATRO MUNICIPAL
Opened in 1911, this eclectically-styled 1464-seat theater was designed by Francisco Ramos de Azevedo's after the Paris Opera House. It is the home of several municipal music and dance companies, including two orchestras (a full-scale symphony orchestra and a smaller one dedicated to experimental music), a string quartet, two choral groups and a ballet company. Theater companies also occasionally perform. There are weekly recitals of vespers on

Mondays at 6pm and concerts every Wednesday at 12:30pm. Both are free and seating is on a first-come-first-served basis. There are also free guided tours (*Tue and Thu, noon-1pm and 1pm-2pm, tel. 11/223-3715*). In 1922, the theater was the scene of the so-called Modern Art Week, a seminal event in Brazilian cultural history, when a group of artists and intellectuals, led by Mário de Andrade, Oswald de Andrade, Di Cavalcanti, Anita Malfatti and Villa-Lobos, broke once and for all with the stuffy academic airs that permeated the national arts at that time.
Praça Ramos de Azevedo, tel.(11) 222-8698. Box Office: daily, 10am-7pm.

❷ VIADUTO DO CHÁ

São Paulo's first viaduct, overlooking the Vale do Anhangabaú, was built in 1892. Named after the large tea plantation that occupied the area at the time (*chá* is "tea" in Portuguese), it was subsequently rebuilt and widened in 1938 to accommodate the needs of the rapidly expanding city.

❸ PALÁCIO DO ANHANGABAÚ

This building was designed by the Italian architect Marcello Piacentini to the specifications of Count Matarazzo. It housed the offices of Matarazzo's industrial empire in the 1940's. Originally named after him, it was re-baptized when it became the headquarters of the São Paulo city government. It is closed to the public, but visitors can still admire the façade.
Viaduto do Chá, 15, tel. (11) 3113-8000.

❹ CENTRO CULTURAL BANCO DO BRASIL

Over one hundred years ago, Banco do Brasil opened its first São Paulo location to safeguard the city's money. Now it has applied itself to a far greater treasure: the São Paulo cultural center opened in 2001 to showcase the arts. Its diverse program includes the visual arts, films, plays and meetings with artists. Art exhibitions are held in the former bank vaults in the basement and the building is also equipped with a video-room, theater, auditorium, restaurant, confectionery store, coffee shop and bookstore. Notice the enamel mosaic flooring, the fresco paintings, and the original windows. Guided tours by appointment (*tel. 11/3113-3649. Mon-Fri, 9am-6pm*).
Rua Álvares Penteado, 112, tel. (11) 3113-3651.

❺ PRAÇA DA SÉ AND SURROUNDING AREA

The Praça da Sé, which marks the exact center of the city, is the traditional location for popular demonstrations. To stroll through it is to walk through the city's tumultuous history. It was in this square that demonstrators gathered in the mid-80's to demand direct elections and, in 1992, to force the

---

TAXIS

Using taxis is imperative if you want to explore this huge, sprawling city. It's safest to get one at one of the many stands or call one of the specialized taxi firms (*Ligue Táxi, tel. 11/3866-3030 or 3873-2000; Coopertax, tel. 11/6195-6000; or Rádio-Táxi Vermelho e Branco, tel. 11/3146-4000, the most expensive of the three*). It is a good idea to note some reference points on your proposed route to orient the drivers, who are frequently only familiar with their own area. Also, make sure they know the destination and, if not, insist that they check a map. No need to tip.

São Paulo's Manhattan: the Prédio do Banespa, a miniature Empire State Building, with the Edifício Martinelli

impeachment of president Collor. Thousands of people pass through here every day, but take care – more than a few are petty thieves. Facing the square and worth a quick visit is the Catedral Metropolitana, a mixture of neogothic and byzantine styles. It opened in 1954 and got restored in 2001 under the direction of Paulo Bastos. The cathedral can seat 8,000 and its attractions include the Italian organ, the stain-glass windows and the 61-bell carillon (*tel. 11/3107-6832. Mon and Wed-Sat, 9:30am-11:30am and 1pm-4:30pm; Sun, 3pm-5pm*). The **Conjunto Cultural da Caixa** is located next to the cathedral and close to Sé subway station. This 1939 art-déco building holds periodic art and photography exhibitions. The **Museu da Caixa**, on the fourth floor, has a display of antique bank furniture and a collection of past Brazilian currencies. Both are open to the public and free of charge (*Praça da Sé, 111, tel. 11/3107-0498, Tue-Sun, 9am-9pm*).

⑥ PÁTIO DO COLÉGIO

This historic site takes its name from a Jesuit school built by the Indians when São Paulo was a village. All that remains of the original building, however, is a single wattle-and-daub wall. The **Museu Anchieta** now occupies the site and houses a collection of religious artifacts and items belonging to the first *paulistas*, or people from São Paulo state. It also has a library, chapel and coffee shop (*tel. 11/3105-6899, ext. 118/119. Tue-Sun, 9am-3pm*). *Praça Pátio do Colégio.*

⑦ PRÉDIO DO BANESPA

A small-scale replica of New York's Empire State Building, the 1947 Altino Arantes (or Banespa) Building is 161 meters (528 feet) high, making it one of the tallest buildings in São Paulo. Since it also stands on the highest part of the central area, the observation deck on the 35th floor affords a panoramic view of the city. There

are four telescopes with a range of 40 kilometers (25 mi.) and viewing is best on clear days in the late morning hours. To visit the building you have to join one of the free guided tours (*tel. 11/3249-7405. Mon-Fri, 10am-5pm*).
Rua João Brícola, 24, tel. (11) 3249-7180.

⑧ EDIFÍCIO MARTINELLI
Built in the 1920's by the Italian businessman Giuseppe Martinelli, this 30-story, 130-meter-high (426 feet) building was São Paulo's first skyscraper of this scale. The Martinelli building combines several then-popular European architectural styles. It was refurbished in the 70's and declared a historical heritage site in 1992. It is now a government office building. The terrace offers a view of the Parque Dom Pedro, the Serra da Cantareira Mountains and the transmission towers on the high-rise buildings of Avenida Paulista. Visits to the terrace are free, but groups

have to book in advance (*tel. 11/3104-2477. Mon-Wed and Fri, 9am-11am and 2pm-5pm; Sat and Sun, 9am-11am*).
Avenida São João, 35, tel. (11) 3104-3693.

⑨ LARGO SÃO BENTO
The São Bento Plaza is the site of the **São Bento school**, **monastery** and **basilica**. The basilica was originally constructed by Benedictine monks in 1598 and rebuilt between 1910 and 1922 (*Mon-Wed and Fri, 6am-6pm; Thu, 2pm-6pm; Sat and Sun, 6am-noon and 4pm-6pm*). Authentic Gregorian chants make masses an interesting attraction (*Mon-Fri, 7am; Sat, 6am; Sun, 10am*). But even more essential is a visit to the monastery shop, to sample the delicacies made by the monks (*Mon-Fri, 7am-6pm; Sun, after the 10 o'clock morning mass*). People wait in line for the São Bento bread (made from a kind of manioc), the Santa Escolástica apple-and-nut cake and the Monges banana-and-plum cake.
Largo São Bento, tel. (11) 228-3633.

BEXIGA, THE ITALIAN DISTRICT

The Bexiga district – also written as Bixiga due to the popular pronunciation – arose in the late 19th century. At that time, thousands of Italian immigrants in search of factory work arrived and settled this area of the rapidly industrializing city. In the early 1980's, the centrally located district became "the" spot for artists and bohemians, who supported many local bars and night clubs. Now, both the Italians and the bohemians have dispersed, giving the place a somewhat forlorn look, although it still contains vestiges of both communities

and is definitely worth a visit. One should try the dozens of Italian restaurants and pizzerias. The **Capuano**, in 1907, was the first to open and is still in business (*Rua Conselheiro Carrão, 416, tel. 11/288-1460*). The equally traditional **Speranza**, which opened in 1958 (*Rua Treze de Maio, 1004, tel. 11/288-8502*), serves excellent pizza and sausage bread. The narrow, old-fashioned bakeries, famous for their bread, attract discriminating customers from the city's wealthiest neighborhoods and supply many upscale supermarkets. Don't miss the opportunity

to visit three of the best – **Basilicata** (*Rua Treze de Maio, 614, tel. 11/289-3111*), **São Domingos** (*Rua São Domingos, 330, tel. 11/3104-7600*) and **14 de Julho** (*Rua Catorze de Julho, 90/92, tel. 11/3106-4795*). Many of the city's leading theaters are also located in Bexiga, such as **Abril Theater**, which presents great musicals (*Avenida Brigadeiro Luís Antônio, 411, tel. 11/6846-6060*), the traditional **Sérgio Cardoso Theater** (*Rua Rui Barbosa, 153, tel. 11/288-0136*), and the tiny, historical **Ruth Escobar Theater** (*Rua dos Ingleses, 209, tel. 11/289-2358*).

The wavy Copan, designed by Niemeyer, with the Edifício Itália on the left

EDIFÍCIO ITÁLIA

The 42-story Edifício Itália is one of the tallest buildings in São Paulo, at 165 meters (541 feet). Designed by Adolf Franz Heep, it has the highest observation point in the city and a correspondingly spectacular view. From the Terraço Itália restaurant on the top two floors, you can admire the Edifício Copan and the São Paulo sunset. Winter is the best time to enjoy the latter, preferably at the end of a rainy day, when the sky is clear and there is good visibility. The restaurant opened in 1967, two years after the building itself was finished, and it has three dining areas and a bar. Be warned: there is a mandatory minimum charge (*Lunch: Mon-Fri, noon-3pm; Sat and Sun, noon-4pm. Dinner: Mon-Thu, 7pm-midnight; Fri and Sat, 7pm-1am; Sun, 7pm-11pm. Dinner and dancing to a live orchestra: Tue-Sat, 9pm-2am*). *Avenida Ipiranga, 344, tel. (11) 3257-6566.*

EDIFÍCIO COPAN

Designed by Oscar Niemeyer, the building opened in 1966, fifteen years

OUR RECOMMENDATION

One of the highlights of the downtown area is a small, 65-year-old bar named **Bar Léo**. Sit at one of the tables, or at the crowded counter if you can find a spot, and try some *bolinhos de bacalhau* (fried codfish balls), accompanied by a draft beer that many consider the best in town. Warning – it is invariably jam-packed during happy hour (*Rua Aurora, 100, tel. 11/221-0247*).

after the plans were first drawn. It's the greatest example of modernist architecture in São Paulo. Its signature features are the serpentine structure and the horizontal lines of the brise soleil. The building has 38 stories, 1160 apartments divided into six blocks, with studios and luxury apartments, and 72 stores on the ground floor. The Copan is one of the largest reinforced-concrete structures in the country with approximately 400 kg of concrete per cubic meter (25 lbs/cubic foot), a height of 115 meters (377 feet) and an area of 120,000 sq. mi. (29.5 acres). *Avenida Ipiranga, 200.*

SALA SÃO PAULO

Once the great hall of the Júlio Prestes railway station, itself built between 1926 and 1938, the building was comprehensively restored and renovated, reopening in 1999 as an ultramodern concert hall, home of the São Paulo State Symphony Orchestra. The charming construction and impeccable acoustics of the 1501-seat main auditorium, designed by the architect Nelson Dupré and built on the site of the station's interior garden, not only make it the best location in the city for symphonic and chamber music, but one of the best in the world. The ceiling is equipped with 15 adjustable acoustic panels designed to ensure perfect sound quality. Depending on their position, the panels reveal or hide a pair of stained glass windows displaying the coat of arms of the former Sorocabana Railway. Guided tours (*Mon-Fri, 12:30pm and 4:30pm; Sat, 2pm; Sun, 1pm*) include a visit to the auditorium, whose ivory-wood seats and panels do not distort the acoustics, and the **Estação das Artes** with its collection of stained-glass windows depicting the history of the railway and coffee era. Tours by appointment only (*tel. 11/3351-8286 and 3337-5414*). There is a matinee performance at 11am every Sunday featuring either popular or classical music. The concert hall also has a restaurant and snack bar.

Praça Júlio Prestes, tel. (11) 3337-5414. Box Office: Mon-Fri, 10am-6pm; Sat, 10am-4pm; Sun (on concert days), 9am-4pm. The box office closes two hours prior to each concert.

The Sala São Paulo, located in a refurbished railway station, has Brazil's best acoustic chamber

Edifício Viadutos, designed by Artacho Jurado

styles. The recreation room on the 27th floor is finished with purple tiles and a profusion of glass, offering one of the best views of São Paulo's skyline. Unfortunately, you have to know someone to see it; the building is not open to the public.
Praça General Craveiro Lopes, 19.

PINACOTECA DO ESTADO
Some of the country's best visual art exhibitions are held at the Pinacoteca do Estado (São Paulo State Art Gallery). Ramos de Azevedo designed the neoclassical building and had it constructed in 1896. Between 1993 and 1998, it was subjected to an ambitious and award-winning restoration overseen by Paulo Mendes da Rocha. The gallery houses some 6,000 items, including 400 sculptures, of which 1,200 are on display at any one time. The collection includes works by 19th and 20th century painters and also sculptures by Rodin, Maillol and Brecheret. Another highlight is the permanent exhibition *Vistas do Brasil – Coleção Brasiliana* which features 19th century Brazilian landscape painting. In recent years, the Pinacoteca has been the venue for

EDIFÍCIO VIADUTOS
This enormous residential building was inaugurated in 1955, when the city center was still considered a prime location. It was designed by the self-taught architect João Artacho Jurado and reveals his eclectic vision through the combination of modernist, art-déco and art-nouveau

PIZZA, A SÃO PAULO INSTITUTION

Whether you are visiting the city on business or for pleasure, you cannot leave without sampling one of São Paulo's great institutions, pizza – probably the greatest legacy of the strong Italian influence on local cuisine and customs. Whether your preference is for thick or thin crust, double cheese or just a little, a stuffed border or plain, it's the favorite Sunday-night choice and most districts offer a delivery service. The older pizzerias were located in the areas where the first Italian immigrants settled. Some still defiantly remain in the city center and in other somewhat-rundown neighborhoods, turning out the traditional recipes from bygone days. Others, however, have moved to better locations and adapted to ever-changing tastes and fashions. To find authentic São Paulo pizza, look for a pizzeria that adapts the recipes without changing the original spirit and uses only the very best of ingredients for the sauce and the dough. Three excellent suggestions are: **Braz** (*Rua Vupabussu, 271, Pinheiros, tel. 11/3037-7975*), **Camelo** (*Rua Pamplona, 1873, Jardins, tel. 11/3887-8764*) and **Castelões** (*Rua Jairo Góes, 126, Brás, tel. 11/229-0542*).

highly-praised exhibitions by Alberto Eckhout, Iberê Camargo and Miguel Barceló, among others. Free guided tours by appointment (*tel. 11/3227-1655*). The Pinacoteca also has an auditorium, restaurant, cafeteria and library (*Praça da Luz, 2, tel. 11/3229-9844. Tue-Sun, 10am-5:30pm*). In Largo General Osório, alongside the Estação Júlio Prestes and the Sala São Paulo, is the **Estação Pinacoteca**, which used to be headquarters of the Department of Social and Political Order, the agency responsible for political repression during the military dictatorship. The building was restored under the direction of architect Haron Cohen and is now used for the Pinacoteca's temporary exhibitions. On the ground floor is the **Memorial da Liberdade**, where you can visit the cells where the political prisoners were held. The **Parque da Luz**, in the surrounding area, is maintained by the Pinacoteca. The park was the city's first botanical garden and was a popular location for family outings during the 19th and 20th centuries.

ESTAÇÃO DA LUZ

Luz Station was originally built to transport coffee from the inland plantations to the port of Santos on the state's southern coast. It is a fine example of early 20th century European architecture and still retains some of its coffee-driven history. It was recently remodeled as a hub for the city's rail and subway network and it will also house a museum dedicated to the study of the Portuguese language. Warning: the station and its vicinity are not safe; exercise extreme caution if you intend to visit.
Praça da Luz.

MUSEU DE ARTE SACRA

This museum houses around 4,000 examples of religious sculpture, gold and silverware, tablets, altars, furniture and paintings. One of the country's most important collections of sacred art, it includes works by Antônio Francisco Lisboa, better known as Aleijadinho (*Nossa Senhora das Dores*), Francisco Xavier de Brito (*Santa Madalena*), brother Agostinho da Piedade and Manuel da Costa Ataíde. Another feature is the **Museu dos Presépios**, which contains 190 nativity scenes from Brazil and abroad. The highlights include the Presépio Napolitano, a reproduction of an ancient Italian village, and the 9,000-item currency collection, especially the coins from the colonial era. Guided tours by appointment.
Avenida Tiradentes, 676, tel. (11) 3326-1373/3326-5393. Tue-Sun and holidays, 11am-7pm.

Pinacoteca: Great exhibitions in a great exhibit space

MERCADO MUNICIPAL

The Municipal Market, known affectionately as the *Mercadão* or "huge market", opened in 1933. The towering roof is dotted with skylights and glass tiles that provide natural lighting. There are also 55 stain-glass windows imported from Germany. Originally, the market was supplied with fruit and vegetables that arrived by boat from local farms via the Tamanduateí river. Currently it employs about 1,600 people and some 300 stands. These sell 350 tons of produce to about 14,000 customers per day. One can spend a pleasant afternoon

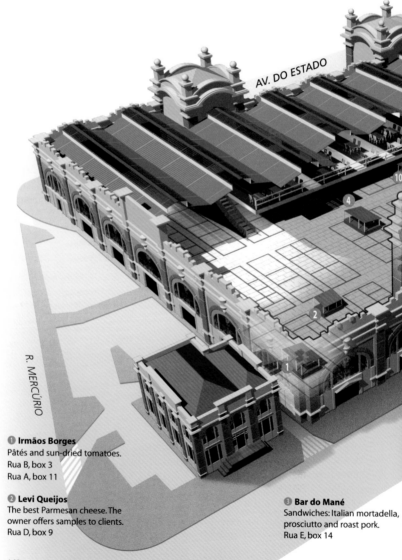

AV. DO ESTADO

R. MERCÚRIO

❶ Irmãos Borges
Pâtés and sun-dried tomatoes.
Rua B, box 3
Rua A, box 11

❷ Levi Queijos
The best Parmesan cheese. The owner offers samples to clients.
Rua D, box 9

❸ Bar do Mané
Sandwiches: Italian mortadella, prosciutto and roast pork.
Rua E, box 14

strolling through the hall amid spices and fruit from all over the world, the tobacco stands, and the huge variety of seafood, meat and fish. Two particular attractions are the Hocca Bar, famous for its codfish *pastel* (a kind of deep-fried pastry), and the Bar do Mané, renowned for its Italian mortadella, prosciutto and roast pork sandwiches. The market is much more than a glorified grocery store, it is a neighborhood institution. Many families have long worked here, and today sons and grandsons continue their predecessors' traditions.

Rua Cantareira, 306, Parque Dom Pedro II, tel. (11) 3228-0673. Tue-Sat, 8am-7pm; Sun, 8am-1pm.

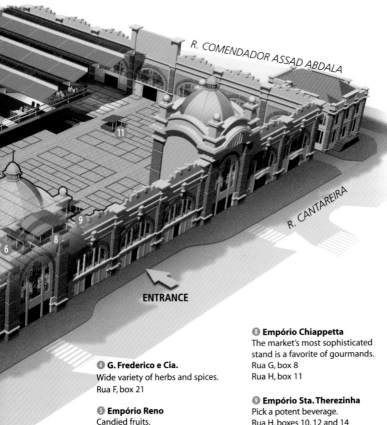

ENTRANCE

❹ **G. Frederico e Cia.**
Wide variety of herbs and spices.
Rua F, box 21

❺ **Empório Reno**
Candied fruits.
Rua F, box 12

❻ **Hocca Bar**
The best codfish pastel.
Rua G, box 7

❼ **Empório Raga**
Codfish, pine nuts and pecorino cheese.
Rua G, box 11

❽ **Empório Chiappetta**
The market's most sophisticated stand is a favorite of gourmands.
Rua G, box 8
Rua H, box 11

❾ **Empório Sta. Therezinha**
Pick a potent beverage.
Rua H, boxes 10, 12 and 14

❿ **Banca do Juca**
Specializes in tropical fruits.
Rua H, box 24

⓫ **Geração Saúde**
Coconut water, sugar-cane juice and chili peppers.
Rua L, box 30

LIBERDADE

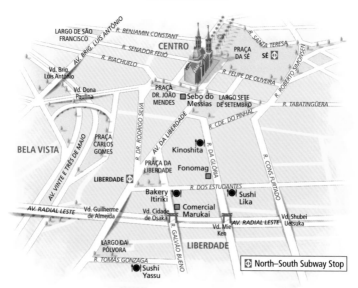

The streets of this district, in particular **Galvão Bueno** and **Glória**, are chock-a-block with Japanese and Chinese restaurants, stores selling imported goods, small markets and mini-malls. The traditional Sunday market in **Praça da Liberdade** offers a perfect introduction to the area with its food-stands where you can find Japanese yakisoba noodles, tempura-fried delectables and *pastéis* interspersed with arts and crafts stalls. Three of the best Japanese eateries are: **Kinoshita**, with a superb sampler menu that you have to order specially (*Rua da Glória, 168, tel. 11/3105-4903*); **Sushi Yassu**, with its exotic dishes and authentic sushi and sashimi (*Rua Tomás Gonzaga, 98, tel. 11/3209-6622*); and **Sushi Lika**, which serves up a delicious salmon teppan (*Rua dos Estudantes, 152, tel. 11/3207-7435. Mon-Sat, 11:30am-2:30pm and 6:30pm-12:30am*). **Comercial Marukai** offers a wide selection of Asian food products and imported

articles (*Rua Galvão Bueno, 34, tel. 11/3341-3350. Daily, 8am-8pm*). Another highlight is the spacious and cheerful **Bakery Itiriki**, which offers an ample range of Japanese and Brazilian bread and a buffet (*Rua dos Estudantes, 24, tel. 11/3277-4939. Daily, 8am-7:30pm*). If you are looking for Japanese comic books or origami, head straight for **Fonomag** (*Rua da Glória, 242, tel. 11/3104-3329. Mon-Fri, 8:30am-6:30pm; Sat, 8:30am-5pm*). The surrounding area is also full of surprises. If you walk to **Praça João Mendes**, you will find several second-hand bookstores selling many hard-to-find volumes on philosophy, literature and the arts, not to mention DVDs. The famous **Sebo do Messias** has four outlets, the largest of which is behind the Catedral da Sé (*Praça João Mendes, 166, tel. 11/3104-7111. Mon-Fri, 9am-7pm; Sat, 9am-5pm*). There are also some good second-hand bookstores close to **Praça Carlos Gomes**.

HIGIENÓPOLIS

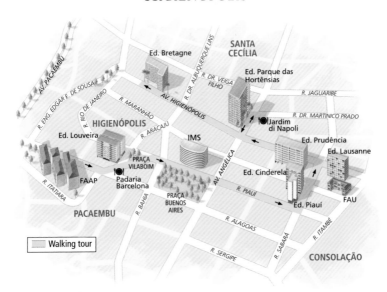

Higienópolis, the first area of São Paulo to be modernized with urban infrastructure and public sanitation facilities, is one of the city's most distinct districts. Its name (literally "City Hygiene") is tied to its elevated position, which protected it from the floods and epidemics that plagued other areas of the city through the end of the 19th century. A few mansions from this era still survive, but most have been demolished to make way for apartment buildings. Over the years, Higienópolis has absorbed new architectural styles, but without losing the unique elegance. *Wallpaper* magazine once reported that it has one of the world's largest single concentrations of modernist-style residential buildings. If you want to explore its tree-lined streets and parks, there's nothing better than a walking tour. Start at the traditional bakery **Padaria Barcelona**, on Rua Armando Penteado, 33, at the corner with Rua Alagoas, and be sure to check out their range of pastries and breads. Directly across the street is **Faap (Armando Álvares Penteado Foundation)**, which houses a theater, museum and university. Continue along the street until you come to the tiny but charming **Praça Villaboim**, taking advantage of the opportunity to visit the busy stores and restaurants along the way. Cross the *praça* and you will see the **Condomínio Louveira** (*Rua Piauí, 1081*), an exquisite building designed by Vilanova Artigas, built in the 1940's and declared a cultural heritage site in 1992. Returning to **Praça Villaboim** and turning down the side street, you will come to **Praça Buenos Aires**, a spacious park established many years ago and a favorite of the locals.

INSTITUTO MOREIRA SALLES (IMS)

Located near Praça Buenos Aires, the IMS is a cultural center that holds art and photography exhibitions, courses, workshops, conferences and meetings with writers. Check the event schedule during your visit to the city.

Adolf Franz Heep's Edificio Lausanne is one of many modernist buildings in Higienópolis

Rua Piauí, 844, 1ª floor, tel. (11) 3825-2560. Tue-Fri, 1pm-7pm; Sat and Sun, 1pm-6pm.

MID-20th CENTURY MODERNIST RESIDENTIAL BUILDINGS

In Higienópolis, admire some of the luxurious buildings designed by the controversial architect João Artacho Jurado. They combine modernism with references to Hollywood, such as the tiles in pink, blue and lilac – the predominant colors in the melodramas of the 1940's and 50's. Jurado's first project in the neighborhood was the 1949 **Edificio Piauí** (*Rua Piauí, 428, at the corner with rua Sabará*). In the same block, the **Edificio Cinderela**, dating from 1956, displays a combination of granite, marble and ceramic tiles (*Rua Maranhão, 163, at the corner with rua Sabará*). To the left on Avenida Higienópolis stand two buildings designed by other famous modernist architects: the **Prudência**, by Rino Levi and Roberto Cerqueira César,

with landscaping by Burle Marx; and the **Lausanne**, by Adolf Franz Heep. The Prudência (*Avenida Higienópolis, 265*) was built between 1944 and 1948. One of São Paulo's first condominiums, it is now a listed building. The elegant Lausanne (*Avenida Higienópolis, 101*) is distinguished for its innovative metallic brise soleils and use of color on the façade. When you reach Avenida Angélica, turn right and you will see another Jurado building, the huge **Edificio Parque das Hortênsias**, built in 1957 and surrounded by extensive gardens (*Avenida Angélica, 1106*). Returning to Avenida Higienópolis, in front of the Colégio Sion, is Artacho's masterpiece, the massive **Bretagne** (*Avenida Higienópolis, 938*). Here Jurado used a mixture of brightly-colored ceramic tiles for the exterior finishing, created several communal areas, including a bar, and installed serpentine coverings over the winter roof-garden.

FACULDADE DE ARQUITETURA E URBANISMO DA USP

Built in 1902 as the home of Conde Antônio Álvares Penteado and designed by Carlos Ekman, this was the city's first true art-nouveau building. Declared a cultural heritage site, it is now used by the University of São Paulo for post-graduate courses in architecture and urban planning. Entry is restricted, but the exterior alone is worth a visit.
Rua Maranhão, 88, tel. 11/3091-4796.

MUSEU DE ARTE BRASILEIRA

This museum is located inside the Faap building. The extensive collection of modernist works and the first-class international exhibitions, all of which are free, make it one of the best art venues in the city. The 1961 building houses around 2,500 works by Brazilian artists, including oil paintings, prints and sculpture. Of particular interest is the Flávio de Carvalho collection, comprising paintings, drawings, photographs, architectural designs and reproductions of clothing designed and worn by the modern artist. Also deserving of attention are the works of Heinz Khün, which make up the largest collection in the museum, and those of Arcângelo Ianelli and Clóvis Graciano.
Rua Alagoas, 903, Pacaembu, tel. 11/3662-7198. Tue-Fri, 10am-9pm; Sat, Sun and holidays, 1pm-6pm.

ESTÁDIO DO PACAEMBU

Built in 1940 to seat 45,000, the art-déco Paulo Machado de Carvalho stadium, better known as Pacaembu, was one of the first stadiums built in São Paulo. Highlights of the guided tour include a display of historical photographs along with visits to the playing field, the sports center, the great hall and the radio and TV broadcasting booths. Schedule tours in advance *(tel. 11/3661-9111, ext. 113 and 114. Mon-Fri, 9am-4pm).*
Praça Charles Miller.

PASTÉIS AND CALDO DE CANA

Street markets, extremely popular all over in Brazil, are everywhere in São Paulo. The one in Praça Charles Miller across from the Pacaembu Stadium is among the best. The doughy, fantastically deep-fried *pastéis*, best accompanied by a glass of classic *caldo de cana* (sugarcane juice), are appreciated by even the most demanding of the city's gourmets *(Praça Charles Miller. Tue, Thu, Fri and Sat, 5am-1pm).*

Estádio do Pacaembu provides an art deco setting for football games and rock concerts

AVENIDA PAULISTA

1 - Instituto Itaú Cultural
2 - FIESP
3 - MASP
4 - Conjunto Nacional

São Paulo's symbol of prosperity, Avenida Paulista, is one of Brazil's major financial conduits. For more than a century, banks, office buildings, stores, cultural centers, movie theaters and a few residential buildings have lined the 3 kilometers (2 mi.) long avenue between the Paraíso and Consolação districts. It is also a venue for protests and popular public events such as the New Year's Eve party, the São Silvestre Marathon, the Gay Pride Parade and most football championship victory celebrations. At the beginning of the 20th century, it had a completely different aspect: a series of extensive gardens and mansions built by the coffee barons. Between 1940 and 1970, most of these mansions were demolished as the avenue began its transformation into a financial center. One of the few survivors is the **Casa das Rosas**, designed by Ramos de Azevedo, and situated at number 37. It was converted into a cultural center in 1991 and now houses the library of the Brazilian poet Haroldo de Campos.

❶ INSTITUTO ITAÚ CULTURAL
All of the institute's programs – videos, films, documentaries, meetings with writers and shows – are free of charge. It also houses the **Museu da Moeda**, with its collection of coins and banknotes, and a cultural information center with publications, books and CD-ROMs. Check the daily schedule. *Avenida Paulista, 149, Paraíso, tel. (11) 2168-1776. Tue-Fri, 10am-9pm; Sat, Sun and holidays, 11am-7pm.*

❷ FIESP

The São Paulo State Industry Federation is the state's most important industrial association and is housed in a building designed by Roberto Cerqueira César and Luís Roberto Carvalho Franco. There are cultural centers on the ground floor, refurbished by Paulo Mendes da Rocha, with an art gallery, library and theater. Check the schedule for events (*tel. 11/3146-7405*). The **Galeria do Sesi** is currently one of the city's most important art venues.
Avenida Paulista, 1313, Cerqueira César, tel. 11/3549-4499.

❸ MUSEU DE ARTE DE SÃO PAULO

MASP, as it's called, contains the most valuable collection of paintings in Latin America. It originally opened in 1947 at Rua Sete de Abril, 230, with the support of media baron Assis Chateaubriand and Italian art critic Pietro Maria Bardi. The current building was designed by Lina Bo Bardi and constructed in 1968. The box-like structure is supported by four pillars, creating a 74 meters (243 feet) span. The 5500-piece collection includes paintings by Van Gogh, Cézanne, Monet, Manet, Renoir, Velázquez, Goya, Rembrandt, Botticelli and Rafael, as well as a collection of bronze sculptures by Edgar Degas. There is also a collection of paintings portraying scenes of Brazilian life by national and foreign artists including Post, Debret, Di Cavalcanti and Portinari. Guided tours by appointment (*tel. 11/3283-2585. Tue-Fri, 11am, 1:15pm, 1:30pm and 3:15pm*). A restaurant is in the basement (*tel. 11/3253-2829. Mon-Fri, noon-3pm; Sat and Sun, noon-4:30pm*). On Sundays there is a traditional antique fair at ground level. The **Parque Trianon**, a haven of greenery amid the concrete of the avenue, is directly across the street from the museum.

Avenida Paulista, 1578, Bela Vista, tel. (11) 251-5644. Tue-Sun, 11am-6pm. Ticket window closes at 5pm.

❹ CONJUNTO NACIONAL

The city's first multi-purpose building complex, designed by architect David Libeskind in 1958, the Conjunto Nacional contains residences, offices, movie theaters, restaurants, shops (including bookstores), art exhibitions and a

---

LET'S GO SHOPPING

The **Cultura** and **Fnac** bookstores, both of which stock at least 100,000 titles, deserve at least one lengthy visit between them. Livraria Cultura (*Avenida Paulista, 2073, Cerqueira César, tel. 11/3170-4033. Mon-Fri. 9am-10pm; Sat, 9am-8pm*) has four stores in the Conjunto Nacional, with 20,000 art books and an extensive collection of English-language publications, as well as another branch in the Shopping Villa-Lobos mall in the Pinheiros region. A series of debates with intellectuals, called the Café Filosófico, is of particular interest – they are always scheduled for 7:30pm, although the day varies, so check the schedule first. Fnac has approximately 60,000 CDs and at least 7,000 DVDs, plus a cafeteria. It also sponsors events such as mini-shows by local artists, workshops and book signings (*Avenida Paulista, 901, Cerqueira César, tel. 11/2123-2000. Daily, 10am-10pm*).

MASP: the greatest art collection in Latin America

GAY PRIDE

The **Gay Parade** has become a permanent fixture on the city's calendar, and the event has gained international stature. In its 8th year, in 2004, it attracted more participants than the older gay parades in San Francisco and New York. More than 1.5 million Brazilians and foreign tourists followed some 20 *trios elétricos* (trucks fitted with sound systems and stages for bands to perform on) along Avenida Paulista. The largest congregation formed in front of MASP. The parade, which takes place in June, is the main event of the GLBT (Gays, Lesbians, Bisexuals and Transvestites) Pride Month, and all the bars, restaurants and nightclubs on the gay circuit do a brisk business. Additional information can be obtained at the Associação do Orgulho GLBT de São Paulo (*tel. 11/3362-2361*). Throughout the rest of the year, the main GLS meeting points include the Saturday arts and crafts sale at Praça Benedito Calixto, in Pinheiros, and the various gay bars and dance clubs in the Jardins district close to the intersection of Rua Consolação and Alameda Franca.

fitness center. Around 25,000 people pass through it every day (*daily, 8am-10pm*).
Avenida Paulista, 2073, Cerqueira César, tel. (11) 3179-0656.

FILM FESTIVALS ALL YEAR ROUND

There are 230 movie theaters in São Paulo. Three districts alone (Jardins, Paulista and Consolação) have dozens of top-quality ones offering a wide variety of options. A few that deserve mention are **Cinesesc**, **Cinearte**, **Espaço Unibanco de Cinema**, **Unibanco Arteplex**, located in the Frei Caneca mall, the **HSBC Belas Artes** and the **Museu da Imagem e do Som (MIS)**, in Jardim Europa. In addition to their regular programming, they also host several film festivals throughout the year. These include the São Paulo International Documentary Film Festival called **It's All True**, which takes place at the end of March and beginning of April at Cinesesc and others. In July, the international animated film festival known as **Anima Mundi** takes place, followed in August by the **São Paulo International Short Film Festival** at the MIS, which presents a selection of Brazilian and foreign short films. The main annual event, however, is undoubtedly the **São Paulo International Film Festival**, which takes place in October or beginning of November and gives a comprehensive picture of the latest in international cinema, as well as some retrospectives. The features are shown at Cinearte, Unibanco Arteplex, Cineclube DirecTV, Sala Cinemateca and other cinemas throughout the city. In November, the city hosts **Mix Brasil – Festival of Sexual Diversity**, whose sex-positive themes have a strong gay bias. These films can be seen at the Centro Cultural Banco do Brasil, Espaço Unibanco, Centro Cultural São Paulo and MIS among others. Finally, there is the **International One Minute Film Festival**, which takes place in either June or November, which presents sixty such films at the Centro Cultural Banco do Brasil, as well as other venues in the city. Check the local newspapers for dates, times and locations.

JARDINS

In Brazil's shopping and dining capital, the Jardins or Garden District (including the Cerqueira César area) boasts the city's best restaurants and stores. The heart of the district is the bustling **Rua Oscar Freire**, which may remind visitors of New York's Madison Avenue, albeit on a much smaller scale. If you plan to go shopping or eat out, there are almost too many options. Here you can buy the most famous Brazilian designer labels such as Fórum, Ellus, Triton, Zoomp, Clube Chocolate, Alexandre Herchcovitch, Maria Bonita, as well as renowned international names such as Armani, Louis Vuitton, Tiffany, Versace and Bulgari. There is also a fine selection of restaurants, whose wide variety of atmospheres, menus and chefs guarantee the best gourmet options in São Paulo. Those deserving special mention include **Antiquarius**, which offers excellent Portuguese cuisine in a sophisticated setting (*Alameda Lorena, 1884, tel. 11/3082-3015*); **Fasano**, with its irresistibly authentic Italian cuisine (*Rua Vitório Fasano, 88, tel. 11/3896-4077*); **Gero** (*Rua Haddock Lobo, 1629, tel. 11/3064-0005*); the traditional **Massimo** (*Alameda Santos, 1826, tel. 11/3284-0311*); **D.O.M.**, with its contemporary creativity (*Rua Barão de Capanema, 549, tel. 11/3088-0761*); and the fabulous **Figueira Rubaiyat**, with its Mediterranean cuisine (*Rua Haddock Lobo, 1738, tel. 11/3063-3888*). **Spot** (*Alameda Ministro Rocha Azevedo, 72, tel. 11/3284-6131*) is more casual than the others in the district and offers a simple but contemporary menu. It is located closer to Avenida Paulista and has been one of the most fashionable places to be seen for more than ten years, a popular hangout for artists and celebrities. One block from Oscar Freire, is the **Galeria dos Pães** (*Rua Estados Unidos, 1645, tel. 11/3064-5900*), a combination of bakery, grocery store and restaurant, which is open 24 hours a day and serves as a meeting place for the local night owls.

OUR RECOMMENDATION

Hotel Fasano, with its elegant decor reminiscent of the 1940's, offers 64 comfortable suites, business and fitness centers, a spa and a shuttle service to and from the city's airports. Attractions include the Baretto lounge with live jazz; the Fasano restaurant headed by chef Salvatore Loi; and Nonno Ruggero (named after the Fasano clan's grandfather), a breakfast room that also functions as a *trattoria* for lunch and dinner. Located between Ruas Oscar Freire and Estados Unidos, some of the rooms offer a magnificent view of the city.

Additional information begins on page 462.

Hotel Fasano: luxury in the Garden District

A COSMOPOLITAN AND GLOBALIZED CITY

Jardins is a magical place where the people of São Paulo share not only the trappings of luxury living but the everyday assurance that they are living in a cosmopolitan metropolis. An island of luxury bounded by the so-called *Quadrilátero*, an area that expands outwards from the intersection of Ruas Oscar Freire and Haddock Lobo, Jardins is a shopper's paradise reminiscent of Avenue Montaigne in Paris, Sloane Street in London, or upper Madison Avenue in New York.

Although its precise borders are tough to define, one thing is certain: this dense urban enclave runs from the ridge of Avenida Paulista, once lined with the mansions of the coffee barons and industrial magnates and now forming the great capital's skyline, and slopes down towards an area that up until the 1940's was nothing more than a mangrove swamp, periodically polluted by the flooding of the Pinheiros river.

Today Jardins is a golden quarter where the women carry Vuitton purses and prepare for life's hardships in fitness centers. But there was nothing in the district's early history that heralded its future incarnation as Brazil's Beverly Hills. Describing São Paulo in her memoirs *Anarquistas, Graças a Deus (Anarchists, Thank God)*, the writer Zélia Gattai contrasted the wealthy pedigree of Paulista with the area below Alameda Santos. That ghetto's funeral processions and delivery trucks were prohibited on the millionaires' boulevard, and its buildings, two-story semi-detached houses, were on a much simpler scale.

The construction of an oasis of wealth began in the 1920's with Jardim América, Brazil's first example of urban development. The British real-estate company, Cia City, sold the concept of housing surrounded by lush trees and circular streets reserved for local traffic only. So the area cultivated the mystique that would eventually attract MASP and the Clube Paulistano, as well as the elite of the affluent community.

Driven by its appetite for self-consuming trends, the commercial heart of São Paulo deserted the city center and entrenched itself on Rua Augusta during the 1960's. Soon it became the new retail and nightlife center, where an automobile was an indispensable accessory to any romantic dalliance. While the young rebels of the 70's raced along Augusta at dragster speeds, exemplifying the legend of the city that never stops, the Conjunto Nacional marked the new frontier for the rich and fashionable. Just as years before the Jardins storefronts had been emblazoned with the names of local fashions like Bibba, Paraphernalia, Spinelli, Old England and Hi-Fi, today the cosmopolitan world of high fashion reveals its fascination with globalization, displaying Armani, Versace, Boss, Cartier, Tiffany, Montblanc, Hermès, Ferragamo, Dior and Baccarat. All within walking distance, although certainly not within the reach of the average pocketbook.

Nirlando Beirão,
a journalist from Minas Gerais who has resigned himself
to living in São Paulo, except for the occasional escape

GABRIEL MONTEIRO DA SILVA AND SURROUNDINGS

The stores along Alameda Gabriel Monteiro da Silva, in Jardim Europa, is where the top Brazilian designers display their wares and nine of them are particularly worth a visit. **Etel Interiores** features the furniture of Carlos Motta, Claudia Moreira Salles and the owner Etel Carmona, all made from ecologically certified wood (*#1834, tel. 11/3064-1266. Mon-Fri, 9am-6:30pm; Sat, 10am-2pm*).
Conceito: Firma Casa focuses on "conceptual" products, ranging from tea cups to clothing designed by the Campana brothers (*#1522, tel. 11/3068-0380. Mon-Fri, 10am-8pm; Sat, 10am-6pm*). **Firma Casa** offers items such as the *Banquete* sofa and the *Favela* chair, also by the Campana brothers, and the *Cadê* chair, by Gerson de Oliveira and Luciana Martins (*#1487, tel. 11/3068-0377. Mon-Fri, 9am-7pm; Sat, 10am-2pm*). **La Lampe** specializes in lighting fixtures and table lamps (*#1258, tel. 11/3082-4055. Mon-Fri, 9am-7pm; Sat, 10am-2pm*). **D-Pot** features reissues of Sérgio Rodrigues' furniture designs, such as the Mole armchair (*#1250, tel. 11/3086-0692. Mon-Fri, 10am-7pm; Sat, 10am-3pm*). **House Garden** specializes in outdoor furniture (*#1218, tel. 11/3081-7999. Mon-Fri, 10am-7pm; Sat, 10am-2pm*). **Ornare** offers closets and bookcases (*#1101, tel. 11/3061-1713. Mon–Fri, 10am-8pm; Sat, 10am-4pm*). **Tecer**, a representative of the Italian Cappellini brand, sells stylish carpets (*#785, tel. 11/3064-6050. Mon-Fri, 10am-7pm; Sat, 10am-2pm*). And **Benedixt** features glassware by Jacqueline Terpins and ceramics by Caroline Harari (*#663, tel. 11/3088-1045. Mon-Fri, 9:30am-7:30pm; Sat, 10am-3pm*).

MUSEU BRASILEIRO DA ESCULTURA

This sculpture museum opened in 1995 in a building designed by Paulo Mendes da Rocha. It holds occasional exhibitions and workshops, as well as recitals, conferences and symposia. On Saturdays there is an arts and crafts fair and on Sundays an antique one.
Rua Alemanha, 221, Jardim Europa, tel. (11) 3081-8611. Tue-Sun, 10am-7pm.

MUSEU DA CASA BRASILEIRA

This museum specializes in design and architecture. It opened in the 1940's and its collection includes items that mark the evolution of Brazilian furniture from the 17th to the end of the 20th century. The Crespi Prado collection deserves special attention, with works by Victor Brecheret, among others. The museum also holds musical presentations and lectures. There is an outdoor restaurant.
Avenida Brigadeiro Faria Lima, 2705, Jardim Paulistano, tel. (11) 3032-3727. Tue-Sun, 10am-6pm.

SHOPPING IGUATEMI

Opened in 1966, it was Latin America's first mall. There are 330 outlets, including renowned Brazilian and international designer labels, department stores, restaurants and movie theaters.
Avenida Brigadeiro Faria Lima, 2232, Jardim Paulistano, tel. (11) 3816-6116. Mon-Sat, 10am-10pm; Sun, 11am-10pm.

OUR RECOMMENDATION

🍽 *Chef* **Jun Sakamoto** heads this select restaurant that carries his name. Indulge yourself with harumaki and with sushi and sashimi made from carefully selected fish. If you manage to find a seat at the popular-counter, sample the impromptu creations. Dinner only, reservations required (*Rua Lisboa, 55, Pinheiros, tel. 11/3088-6019*).

PARQUE DO IBIRAPUERA

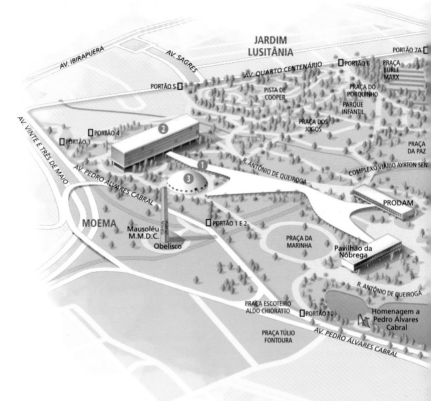

1 - Museu de Arte Moderna
2 - Pavilhão da Bienal
3 - Oca

Open since 1954, Ibirapuera is the city's largest and most popular park. The architectural project was Oscar Niemeyer's and the landscaping by Roberto Burle Marx. In the midst of its eight pavilions, three lakes, and many streets and lawns are the **Museu de Arte Moderna**, the **Pavilhão da Bienal** and the **Oca** (check the exhibition schedule for these galleries). The park is also a favorite spot for outdoor shows and sports tournaments and is full of runners on weekday mornings. Stop and admire the *Monumento às Bandeiras* at the entrance to the park, designed by Victor Brecheret as a tribute to the São Paulo's *bandeirantes* (pioneer explorers).
Avenida Pedro Álvares Cabral, Ibirapuera, tel. (11) 5574-5177. Daily, 5am-midnight.

❶ MUSEU DE ARTE MODERNA
The museum's collection of around 3,700 works includes sculptures,

sided concrete canopy, designed by Oscar Niemeyer, constructed in 1953 and remodeled in the 1980's under the direction of Lina Bo Bardi. National and international exhibitions are held in the building as well as choral music, films and plays, round-table discussions, lectures and book launches. In addition to the two exhibition areas there is an auditorium, studio, store and restaurant. Don't miss the *Aranha*, sculpture by Louise Bourgeois.

Parque do Ibirapuera, portão 3, Ibirapuera, tel. (11) 5549-9688. Tue, Wed and Fri, noon-6pm; Thu, noon-10pm; Sat, Sun and holidays, 10am-6pm.

❷ PAVILHÃO DA BIENAL
Oscar Niemeyer designed this structure for the city's 1962 Biennial Visual Arts Exhibition. Every two years since, usually between October and December, the three floors of the Pavilhão Ciccillo Matarazzo (its official name) display works by hundreds of Brazilian and foreign

paintings and prints by modern and contemporary Brazilian artists such as Amílcar de Castro, Hélio Oiticica, Leda Catunda, Leonilson and Volpi. Latin America's first modern art museum, it originally opened in 1948 in a temporary facility, before being transferred in 1968 to its current, permanent location. That is in a pavilion under the Ibirapuera *marquise*, or open-

FASHION CAPITAL

Gisele Bündchen began her career in São Paulo, the country's fashion capital and a magnet for svelte, would-be models. Twice a year, the Pavilhão da Bienal in Ibirapuera Park hosts the glamorous **São Paulo Fashion Week**, the largest such event in Latin America and a perennial tourist attraction. Here around 100,000 journalists, buyers and beautiful people gather to inspect the latest fashion trends. There are at least 40 shows with dozens of models during the week-long event that require a special stage set, as well as such temporary accessories as a restaurant, bookstore and bar. Attendance is by invitation only, and said invitations are eagerly sought.

The interior of the Oca: Oscar Niemeyer's revolutionary building hosts important exhibitions

artists, including sculptors, painters and photographers, with a special emphasis on new talents. It also hosts events such as the Bienal de Arquitetura, the São Paulo Fashion Week, as well as the International Animated Film Festival. Nearby is the **Museu Afro-Brasil** (Pavilhão Manuel da Nóbrega).
Parque do Ibirapuera, 10, tel. (11) 5579-0593.

❸ OCA

Oca's official name is the Pavilhão Lucas Nogueira Garcez, but everyone in São Paulo calls it Oca after the similarly-shaped indigenous dwellings. The huge white dome, designed by Oscar Niemeyer and opened in 1951, is an excellent arts venue. It has hosted such exhibitions as a Picasso retrospective; *The Warriors of Xi'an* and *The Treasures of the Forbidden City*, dealing with imperial China; and *The Rediscovery of Brazil*, all of which attracted

> ### THE PARK BY NIGHT
>
> At dusk, head for the bar in the **Skye** restaurant on the top floor of the **Hotel Unique**, order a drink and enjoy the stunning view of Ibirapuera Park and the buildings in the Jardins district. The bar opens onto a giant terrace with a beach-like atmosphere and cushioned wooden chairs to better admire the scenery. The lights are dimmed so that neighboring buildings provide most of the illumination (*Avenida Brigadeiro Luís Antônio, 4700, tel. 11/3055-4702*).

thousands to Ibirapuera park. As it happens, the building is worth visiting in itself. On the ground floor, note the curving ramps leading to the four floors and the absence of columns. As you walk up (or down) the ramps, pay attention to the sinuous nature of the construction, softly illuminated by natural light entering the porthole-like openings lining the base.
Avenida Pedro Álvares Cabral, Ibirapuera, tel. (11) 5549-0449. Tue-Fri,

9am-9pm; Sat, Sun and holidays, 10am-9pm. Ticket office closes at 8pm.

VILA OLÍMPIA

A place of non-stop action, where new restaurants, nightclubs and bars open every week. This is Vila Olímpia, an extension of Itaim heading towards Vila Funchal close to the Ibirapuera district, which contains a great concentration of night-spots in São Paulo. Here, clubs pumping out techno music until dawn live cheek-by-jowl with show-houses, bistros, pubs and romantic bars. Most of the clientele is made up of the young, wealthy elite known as *mauricinhos* (preppies), and their female counterparts, *patricinhas*. The list of places to go is almost endless and it is impossible to recommend the most fashionable ones – the "in" place today may be "out" tomorrow and end up closing the following week. Better, therefore, to check the weekend newspapers and weekly magazines. But Vila Olímpia also offers options for the older crowd. Three of the city's best Argentinean restaurants are located here, offering excellent meat rigorously cut and prepared in the Argentine tradition. The so-called *triângulo portenho* comprises **Rincón de Buenos Aires** (*Rua Santa Justina, 99, tel. 11/3849-0096*), **Bárbaro** (*Rua Dr. Sodré, 241, tel. 11/3845-7743*) and the charming **348 Parrilla Porteña** (*Rua Comendador Miguel Calfat, 348, tel. 11/3849-5839*). On same street as the Bárbaro is the Italian restaurant **Totó**, named after the famous Italian comedian. It serves traditional pasta in a simple setting, but boasts one of the best *caipirinhas* in town (*Rua Dr. Sodré, 77, tel. 11/3841-9067*). Since Vila Olímpia is very close to Ibirapuera Park, the bakeries and bars are always full of young people and sports enthusiasts. **Bread and Co.** is a bakery and snack-bar as popular for breakfast on weekends as it is for sandwiches and quick meals in the afternoon (*Rua Lourenço de Almeida, 470, tel. 11/3842-5156*).

DASLU, A SYNONYM FOR ELEGANCE AND COMFORT

Daslu is not only the largest designer-label store in São Paulo, it is also a nationwide synonym for luxury and exclusiveness. Located in the Vila Nova Conceição district, close to Ibirapuera and Vila Olímpia, it occupies three neighboring addresses. The women's department (*Rua Domingos Leme, 284, tel. 11/3841-4000*) extends through a series of interconnected buildings. The merchandise, in the elegant showrooms that feature accessories, clothing, shoes and purses, is organized according to color. Another building (*Rua João Lourenço, 536*) houses Daslu Man (*tel. 11/3841-3000*) and Daslu House (*tel. 11/3841-3010*), which sells china, crystal and silverware, as well as top-quality linen and towels. Finally there are the childrens, teens and infants' department (*Rua João Lourenço, 512, tel. 11/3841-3019*). Each house is dotted with exclusive areas called corners, featuring specific products (or makes), such as accessories, jewelry, wine, lingerie, magazines, stationery and even luxury real estate. Most of the saleswomen are themselves customers or the daughters of customers, ensuring both attentive service and the exclusivity that clients have come to appreciate. Daslu also offers personal service by appointment (*tel. 11/3848-1710*), fittings either at the store or the clients home, and a delivery service to drop the purchases off at customers' homes or offices. The store is open daily except Sunday (*Mon, Wed, Thu and Fri, 10am-8pm; Tue, 10am-10pm; Sat, 10am-6pm*). However, it will be moving to a new location in May, 2005, so keep an eye on their website www.daslu.com.br.

VILA MADALENA

Vila Madalena's vitality comes from its wealth of artists' studios, coffee shops, restaurants, bars, taverns, art galleries and bookstores. The best way to see the district is on foot on Saturday morning, beginning on Rua Harmonia:

🍽 **Deliparis** (*Rua Harmonia, 484, tel. 11/3816-5911*). An incomparable breakfast featuring almond croissants.

❶ **Satiko** (*Rua Harmonia, 478, tel. 11/3032-4905*). Clothing created by the architects Satiko and Isabel Mascaro and accessories by selected designers.

❷ **Marcenaria Trancoso** (*Rua Harmonia, 233, tel. 11/3032-3505*). Furniture and other items made from Brazilian wood.

❸ **Marcenaria Baraúna** (*Rua Harmonia, 87, tel. 11/3813-3972*). Handcrafted wooden articles.

🍽 **Sacolão** (*Rua Medeiros de Albuquerque, 352*), featuring small places to eat such as **Sushi do Sacolão** (*tel. 11/3813-5482*), **Kafaraka – Empório Árabe** (*Tel. 11/3819-2876*) and **Acarajé da Keka.**

❹ **Ateliê Carlos Motta** (*Rua Aspicuelta, 121, tel. 11/3815-9228*). Furniture.

❺ **Fábrica Livros e Brinquedos** (*Rua Aspicuelta, 135, tel. 11/3813-0889*). Books and toys.

🍽 **Feijoada da Lana** (*Rua Aspicuelta, 421, tel. 11/3814-9191*). One of the city's best *feijoada* (a dish of black beans and pork).

❻ **Galeria Gravura Brasileira** (*Rua Fradique Coutinho, 953, tel. 11/3097-0301*). Etchings.

❼ **Ateliê Piratininga** (*Rua Fradique Coutinho, 934, tel. 11/3816-6891*). Works by several visual artists.

❽ **Livraria da Vila** (*Rua Fradique Coutinho, 915, tel. 11/3814-5811*). Bookstore.

❾ **Livraria Fnac** (*Rua Pedroso de Morais, 858, tel. 11/4501-3000*). Bookstore.

❿ **Cemitério São Paulo** (*Rua Cardeal Arcoverde, 1250, tel. 11/3032-5986*). The cemetery has sculptures by Italian artisans from the 1940's and 50's (best take a taxi to this one).

⓫ **Praça Benedito Calixto.** Every Saturday the square holds a popular antique fair. There are also several excellent design stores, including **Cor do Sol** (*Praça Benedito Calixto, 50, tel. 11/3062-8272*), **L'Oeil** (*Praça Benedito Calixto, 182, tel. 11/3088-3143*), and **Benedixt** (*Praça Benedito Calixto, 103, tel. 11/3062-6551*).

⓬ **Amoa Konoya** (*Rua João Moura, 1002, tel. 11/3061-0639*). Arts and crafts and indigenous artifacts.

Sergio Fingermann,
artist and Vila Madalena resident

SPECIAL ATTRACTIONS

THEATRES

São Paulo has more than 100 theatres. A few of them are located in the region of the traditional **Rua Nestor Pestana**. The **Teatro Cultura Artística**, with its two auditoriums and combined seating capacity of 1,500, hosts national and international shows as well as classical and jazz concerts, photography exhibitions, drama courses and classical and popular music lessons. Subscriptions are sold at the beginning of the year but some extra tickets usually go on sale 15 days prior to each event. Note the huge glass-mosaic fresco by Di Cavalcanti adorning the building's façade (*Rua Nestor Pestana, 196, Consolação, tel. 11/3256-0223). Box Office: noon-7pm; advance sales and show days: noon-9pm).* The **Teatro Sérgio Cardoso** also has two auditoriums, with a combined seating capacity of 1,000, and four rehearsal halls that are used by local drama groups. National productions are extremely popular and usually sell out (*Rua Rui Barbosa, 153, Bela Vista, tel. 11/3288-0136. Wed-Sun, 3pm-9pm*). The original **Teatro Oficina** was designed by Joaquim Guedes and has been declared a historical heritage site. Partially destroyed by fire, it was rebuilt by Flávio Império and later restored by the architects Lina Bo Bardi and Edson Elito. It opened in the 1960's, accompanied by the foundation of the avant-garde theater company of the same name, still directed by José Celso Martinez Corrêa. It is a round theater with a seating capacity of 350 (*Rua Jaceguai, 520, Bela Vista, tel. 11/3160-2818. Tue-Sat, 11:30am-6pm*).

SESC POMPÉIA

This cultural and sports center has occupied a former drum factory since 1982. The project headed by Lina Bo Bardi preserved the old warehouses, converting them for use as a library, restaurant and theater in the round, and transformed the mezzanine into reading and games rooms. The main attractions include art and thematic exhibitions on specific aspects of history, the environment and popular culture, plus frequent, and extremely popular, presentations of Brazilian popular music, rock and alternative music. Check the program schedule. *Rua Clélia, 93, Pompéia, tel. (11) 3871-7700. Tue-Fri, 10am-8pm; Sun, 9am-5pm.*

SHOWS AND CONCERTS

By the end of the 1990's, São Paulo's concert halls had attained high standards and esteem, with a series of shows all year round. The **DirecTv Music Hall**, formerly the Palace, has a 3,000 seating capacity and presents Brazilian artists with various styles, from MPB to rock (*Avenida dos Jamaris,*

Teatro Oficina: José Celso's productions take the stage

Fundação Maria Luísa e Oscar Americano: afternoon tea and an art collection in a green oasis

213, Moema, tel. 11/6846-6040. Box office: Mon-Sun, noon-8pm or until the start of the show). The **Teatro Alfa**, which seats 1,212, specializes in major dance spectaculars, concerts and opera. The main auditorium is decorated in Brazilian walnut, whose shock-absorbent qualities make it ideal for ballet (*Rua Bento Branco de Andrade Filho, 722, Santo Amaro, tel. 11/5693-4000. Box office: Mon-Sat, 11am-7pm; Sun, 11am-5pm; on show days, 11am until the start of the show).* The 7,000-seat **Credicard Hall** is known for its mega-shows and musicals. Since it opened in 1999, it has hosted such diverse performers as the Imperial Circus of China and Lou Reed, as well as numerous Brazilian artists (*Avenida das Nações Unidas, 17955, Santo Amaro, tel. 11/6846-6010. Box office: Mon-Sun, noon-8pm or until the start of the show).* **Sesc Vila Mariana** is renowned for its extensive and varied program,

including samba, Brazilian and international pop, dance and drama (*Rua Pelotas, 141, Vila Mariana, tel. 11/5080-3000. Box office: Tue-Fri, 9am-9:30 pm; Sat, 10am-9:30pm; Sun, 10am-6pm).* The 400-seat **Bourbon Street**, inspired by the clubs in New Orleans, is *the* place for jazz, blues and soul. B.B. King christened the venue, and artists such as Billy Paul, Nina Simone and Dianne Schuur have all performed here. On Sundays the program includes salsa, meringue, mambo and Brazilian music (*Rua dos Chanés, 127, Moema, tel. 11/5095-6100. Tue-Sun, from 9pm).*

FUNDAÇÃO MARIA LUÍSA E OSCAR AMERICANO

Spending an afternoon at this charming place, designed by architect Osvaldo Bratke and surrounded by woods, is one of the most pleasurable activities in the city. It houses the Americano family's paintings,

sculpture, furniture, china and silverware. The permanent collection concentrates on certain aspects of Brazilian history, particularly the colonial era, which is shown in tapestry, chinaware, eight paintings by the Dutchman Frans Post and other articles. The collection also highlights the imperial period, including a bust of Dom Pedro II by Zéphyrin Ferrez and a bust of Empress Teresa Cristina by Rodolfo Bernardelli, as well as the masters of the 20th century, including paintings by such artists as Guignard, Di Cavalcanti and Portinari and sculptures by Brecheret and Bruno Giorgi. To end your tour, stop by the Salão de Chá, a tea-room renowned for its quality food and service. On Sundays, classical concerts are held in the 107-seat auditorium.
Avenida Morumbi, 4077, Morumbi, tel. (11) 3742-0077. Gallery: Tue-Fri, 11am-4pm; Sat and Sun, 10am-5pm. Grounds and tea-room: Tue-Sun, 11:30am-6pm.

MUSEU DE ARTE CONTEMPORÂNEA DA USP

The University of São Paulo Museum of Contemporary Art is on a somewhat secluded spot in the grounds of the Cidade Universitária, the interesting university campus. It opened in 1963 and houses 8,000 works by such artists as Giorgio de Chirico, Max Bill, Kandinsky, Paul Klee, Maria Martins, Matisse, Miró, Modigliani, Braque, Henry Moore, Tarsila do Amaral, Di Cavalcanti, Volpi, Brecheret, Flávio de Carvalho, Manabu Mabe and Umberto Boccioni. A series of exhibitions by invited artists or displaying parts of the permanent collection are scheduled throughout the year.

WHERE TO PLAY GOLF

The elegant **São Paulo Golf Club** has an 18-hole course that is largely flat (*Praça D. Francisco de Souza, 540, Santo Amaro, tel. 11/5521-9255. Tue-Sat, 8am-5pm*). The **São Fernando Golf Club** has a challenging 18-hole course that is rated for professional players. Most of the country's main championship tournaments are held here (*Estrada Fernando Nobre, 4000, Cotia, tel. 11/4612-2544. Tue-Fri, 8am-5pm; Sat, Sun and holidays, 7am-5pm*). Both are private and visitors must be accompanied by a club member. For those with no such connections, we suggest the **São Francisco Golf Club**, where the only entry requirement is to pay the green fees. It is a 9-hole course and, although it doesn't compare with the other two, there are some attractive lakes, and even some alligators! (*Avenida Martin Luther King, 1527, Osasco, tel. 11/3681-8752; Tue-Sun, 7am-6pm*). All three offer club rentals.

Guided tours by appointment (*tel. 11/3091-3328*).
Rua da Reitoria, 160, Cidade Universitária, tel. (11) 3091-3039. Tue-Fri, 10am-7pm; Sat, Sun and holidays, 10am-4pm.

MUSEU LASAR SEGALL

The museum is located in the former home and studio of the painter Lasar Segall, one of the first modernist domiciles in Brazil, designed by Gregori Warchavchik. It contains around 3,000 of the artist's works, including the famous painting *Navio de emigrantes*, a landmark in Brazilian modernism, but also holds exhibitions by other artists. In addition, there is the **Cine Segall**, which offers a good line-up of films (*Tue-Sun, 5pm-8pm*), a library and courses in engraving, photography and creative-writing. Guided tours by appointment (*tel. 11/5574-7322*). Take a look at other modernist houses on Rua Berta.

The Museu do Ipiranga retells Brazil's history on the site where the nation declared independence

Rua Berta, 111, Vila Mariana, tel. (11) 5574-7322. Tue-Sat, 2pm-7pm; Sun, 2pm-6pm.

MUSEU DO IPIRANGA
This huge neo-renaissance-style palace, whose Baroque gardens take after Versailles, opened in 1890 on the site where Dom Pedro I declared Brazil independent of Portugal. The huge, 125,000-piece collection ranges from the 16th to the mid-20th century. It includes sculptures, paintings, documents and weapons, as well as smaller items such as medals and cufflinks. The great hall features the famous painting *Independência ou morte*, by Pedro Américo, and the Imperial Chapel contains the remains of Empress Leopoldina and Dom Pedro I.
Parque da Independência, Ipiranga, tel. (11) 6165-8000. Tue-Sun, 9am-5pm.

MEMORIAL DA AMÉRICA LATINA
Oscar Niemeyer's Latin America Memorial building opened in 1989 to promote Latin American culture. The Pavilhão da Criatividade Popular Darcy Ribeiro contains articles from the Andean cultures, as well as Brazilian folk art and a miniature model of Latin America, while the Victor Civita Latin American library has 30,000 volumes, as well as a publication archive and a video, audio and record library. Other highlights include the Auditório Simón Bolívar, used for events and conferences; the Salão de Atos, with paintings by Latin American artists, including Cândido Portinari's *Tiradentes* (1948); and the Galeria Marta Traba, where temporary exhibitions are held. At the Praça Cívica, one can admire Niemeyer's sculpture, *Grande Mão*. Guided tours by appointment (*tel. 11/3823-4667/4746/4747*).
Avenida Auro Soares de Moura Andrade, 664, Barra Funda, tel. (11) 3823-4600.

MORUMBI AND
MUSEU DO SÃO PAULO
The Cícero Pompeu de Toledo

Stadium, popularly known as Morumbi and the home of São Paulo F.C., opened in 1960 with 80,000 capacity. Guided tour visit dressing rooms, the playing field, and the VIP area, terminating in the two-floor Memorial Hall, which relates the football club's history through trophies, a photographic mural, display panels, historical archives and the Cine Tricolor, a 50-seat movie theater. Tours by appointment only. The Memorial (*Mon-Fri, 9am-4pm; Sat, noon-4pm, tel. 11/3749-8037*) is closed on match days.
Praça Roberto Gomes Pedrosa, Porta 17, Morumbi, tel. (11) 3749-8019/8020.

WHERE TO PLAY TENNIS

The twelve-court **Unisys Arena** is the largest and most modern tennis complex in Latin America. There are six indoor courts, five of which are clay and one fast acrylic (*Marginal Pinheiros, 16.741, Morumbi, tel. 11/3759-3177. Mon-Fri, 6am-midnight; Sat and Sun, 8am-6pm*). **Vertical Tennis**, housed in a very tall building, has six indoor courts, three textured acrylic and three clay. You can watch matches from the restaurant (*rua Gomes de Carvalho, 127, Vila Olímpia, tel. 11/3845-0066. Mon-Fri, 7am-11pm; Sat, 8am-6pm; Sun, 9am-4pm*). **Play Tennis** offers eleven outdoor courts, three clay and eight synthetic (*avenida Giovanni Gronchi, 3,399, Morumbi, tel. 11/3744-7075. Mon-Fri, 6:30am-midnight; Sat, 8am-8pm; Sun, 8am-6pm*).

ZOOLÓGICO DE SÃO PAULO

There are approximately 3,800 animals in the São Paulo Zoo, making it the largest in the country and one of the biggest in the world. Founded in 1958, it is located in the Parque Estadual das Fontes do Ipiranga, an enclave of Atlantic Rainforest inside the city. Here you can see the largest collection of Brazilian fauna: 102 mammal species, 216 bird species, 95 reptile species, 15 amphibian species and 16 invertebrate species. These include such exotic creatures as howler monkeys, red-breasted toucans and tegu lizards. There are guided tours at all hours. Nighttime tours are extremely popular and should be booked in advance (*tel. 11/5073-0811, ext. 2081*). Special attractions include the serpent house, the giant enclosure containing an entire ant colony and an environmental studies school.
Avenida Miguel Stéfano, 4241, Água Funda, tel. (11) 5073-0811. Tue-Sun and holidays, 9am-5pm.

HOPI HARI

The largest theme park in Latin America, Hopi Hari can accommodate some 23,000 visitors. Located in the municipality of Vinhedo, 79 kilometers (49 mi.) from São Paulo, it offers around 40 different attractions, divided into five sections according to age group. Highlights of the tour include a 55-meter-high (180 feet) hang-gliding simulator, the looping roller-coaster and the 69.5-meter-high (228 feet) elevator that free-falls at a speed of up to 94 km/h (58 mph). The park has several cafeterias, restaurants and ice-cream parlors. You can purchase a Hopi Hari passport that gives you free access to all the attractions, or special entrance tickets for adults that are just accompanying their children. The park website (www.hopihari.com.br) gives information on departure locations and schedules of private bus companies that have pick-up points throughout the city and state of São Paulo.
Rodovia dos Bandeirantes, km 72.5, Vinhedo, tel. 0300-7895566 or (11) 3058-2207. Opening hours vary.

BROTAS

Every holiday, hundreds of adrenaline-filled young people, keen to take on nature's challenges, invade this ecotourism mecca. Their zest for flirting enlives the normally peaceful atmosphere of this quiet inland town, which lies 245 kilometers (152 mi.) from São Paulo via the Bandeirantes highway. Protected native forest and rivers that emerge from the Itaqueri plateau and pour down the São Pedro mountains make the region ideal for adventurous water sports such as rafting and cascading. In fact, every year the place comes up with some new sporting activity to attract more participants. One of the latest is canopy climbing, which involves a sort of aerial trail above the treetops, complete with suspended platforms, pulleys and zip-cords. But even the more sedentary can enjoy themselves here. Exquisite waterfalls that are easy to reach, and the two main avenues, Mário Pinotti and Rodolpho Guimarães, provide plenty of options for entertainment and shopping. Brotas has numerous quality hotels and inns, and about a dozen agencies offering tours in the region. It's important to book in advance for holiday periods.

WHITEWATER RAFTING

Climb into a small inflatable with five other people, don a helmet and life-jacket and then plunge down rapids, negotiating waterfalls and dodging rocks. It may sound somewhat frightening, if not downright dangerous, but after 90 minutes of adrenaline-fueled enjoyment, some of it literally in the water, you will almost certainly find yourself lining up for another go. Rafting requires no physical training and can be done by almost everyone, from friends of the same age to entire families. Parents are as likely to enroll their children and teenagers are to drag in their somewhat reluctant parents. Keep in mind that falling overboard is par for the course.

Tour Operator: Mata'dentro Ecoturismo e Aventura, tel. (14) 3653-5656.

Waterfalls and whitewater define Brotas

OUR RECOMMENDATION

🍽 Decorated with motifs of the chili pepper that gives it its name, the **Malagueta** is the most pleasant restaurant in Brotas. The food is simple but delicious, featuring excellent grilled meat and home-made pasta. A large window displays the efficient and well-equipped kitchen, while the atmosphere and lighting inside are subdued. The menu is bilingual and the owner, who speaks both English and French, attends foreign guests personally (*Avenida Mário Pinotti, 243, tel. 14/3653-5491*).

THE COAST

Juréia: a virtually untouched Atlantic Rainforest reserve, just two hours from São Paulo

JURÉIA

Peruíbe, accessible via the Anchieta or Imigrantes highways to Guarujá and then the SP-055, is the gateway to this wilderness paradise 153 kilometers (95 mi.) from São Paulo. To reach Juréia itself, pass through the center of Peruíbe and head for Guaraú district, a six-kilometer (3.7-mi.) trip over a hill on a road that's narrow and winding, but also paved and well signposted. Guaraú has precarious infrastructure, with dirt tracks that are impassable when it rains and frequent landslides on the Vau Una Guaraú road. All this is offset by the tranquil beach and mountain atmosphere. The **Estação Ecológica Juréia-Itatins** comprises 80,000 hectares (197,684 acres) of Atlantic Rainforest, but only 5% of this area is open to visitors. The region harbors various ecosystems, including some animal species in danger of extinction. Travel agencies offer interesting trekking, jeep and canoeing excursions, but hiring a guide is not mandatory. A three-hour roundtrip by canoe up the Guaraú river rewards the hardy with exotic scenery and the delight of taking a dip in the **Secreta** waterfall. Guides will point out and identify plant and animal species and share entertaining local legends.
Tour Operator: Eco Adventure, tel. (13) 3457-9170/9390.

OUR RECOMMENDATION

Remo, the friendly German owner of the **Waldhaus Hotel**, knows every inch of Juréia. His wife, Ana Paula, will regale you with tips about the place and its attractions, including a 20-minute trail to a scenic lookout point that begins close to the inn. The rooms may be modest, but the view is dazzling. With advance arrangements, Remo can also be hired as a tour guide to take guests to locations such as Ilhabela and Florianópolis.

Additional information begins on page 462.

SANTOS

Santos is located 85 kilometers (53 mi.) from São Paulo on the Anchieta or Imigrantes highways. It was founded in 1546 as one of Brazil's first settlements, and several 16th century buildings remain standing. The city reached its heyday during the coffee boom, but continued to grow as a result of its port, Brazil's largest, and it boasts excellent ocean-side infrastructure. It also offers a lively nightlife, beautiful scenery and a variety of outdoor activities. However, the urban beaches lack the charm of their famous gardens. To take advantage of the sun, one option is to head to **Guarujá**, five minutes by ferry from the Ponta da Praia district, and spend the day there.

HISTORICAL CENTER

The **Bonde Turístico**, a guided streetcar tour of the main attractions (*Praça Mauá. Tue-Sun, 11am-5pm*), is the way to begin. In fifteen minutes you will be back at your starting point and ready to visit all the sites again on foot. Start at the **Paço Municipal** (City Hall) in Praça Mauá and then head to the **Igreja do Carmo** in Praça Barão do Rio Branco. This church, a historical and cultural heritage site, was built in 1599 and has an attached chapel dating from 1760. The altars in the church are covered in gold leaf, and those in the chapel are elaborately carved in wood. As you leave, turn left and follow Rua Quinze de Novembro for three blocks until reaching the **Bolsa Oficial do Café**, a sumptuous coffee-trading exchange inaugurated in 1922 and now a museum (*Rua Quinze de Novembro, 95, tel. 13/3219-5585. Tue-Sat, 9am-5pm; Sun, 10am-5pm*). In addition to the original furniture, it contains paintings and stained-glass windows by Benedito Calixto, and a cafeteria. Continue along the broad sidewalk on Rua Quinze de Novembro, turn right on Rua do Comércio and admire the **Casa da Frontaria Azulejada**, a

The Bolsa do Café: belle-époque splendor in Santos's Historical Center

striking two-story house built in 1865. The façade is covered with Portuguese ceramic tiles. Continuing along for two more blocks you will come to Largo Marquês de Monte Alegre and the **Igreja Santo Antônio do Valongo**. Built in 1691, the baroque-style church features tiled panels and a series of beautiful fresco paintings. In the same plaza is the recently refurbished **Estação São Paulo Railway**, which was inaugurated in 1867 in the English style.

THE BEACH GARDENS AND THE LEANING BUILDINGS

Just under 5.4 kilometers (3 mi.) long and covering an area of 218,800 m^2 (54 acres), the **Jardim da Praia** has around 1,700 trees, mainly palms and tropical almonds, and 77 types of flower. From the bars on the **Píer de Santos** in the Ponta da Praia district you can see the **Fortaleza da Barra de Santos**, an old fort protecting the harbor entry, and the ships entering and leaving the port. The nearby **Museu de Pesca** (*Avenida Bartolomeu de Gusmão, 192. Wed-Sun, 10am-6pm*) is a fishing museum containing a 23-meter (75 foot), 7-tonne whale skeleton, as well as stuffed and mounted squid and sharks. Note the famous **leaning buildings** on the ocean-front avenue, especially those between canals 3 and 4. There are roughly 90 of them, with up to 20 floors each, all built between 1940 and 1960. At Avenida Conselheiro Nébias, the garden has a large **marquise**, or open-sided concrete covering, designed by João Artacho Jurado. That architect was also responsible for some of the 1950's buildings on the shoreline. Almost directly in front is the **Pinacoteca Benedito Calixto** (*Avenida Bartolomeu de Gusmão, 15. Tue-Sun, 2pm-7pm*). This art-nouveau house dating from 1900 is one of the last remaining residences of the coffee barons. Now an art museum, it contains paintings by Calixto and also hosts periodic exhibitions. Don't miss the magnificent gardens. The **Morro de José Menino**, the last hill before you reach the town of São Vicente, is a popular hang-gliding spot.

MIRANTE DE OSCAR NIEMEYER

Following the shoreline to São Vicente, you will come to the Mirante dos 500 Anos, an observation deck designed by Oscar Niemeyer as part of Brazil's 500th anniversary celebrations. Located on top of the **Porchat** island (*Alameda Paulo Gonçalves*), it offers a wonderful view of Santos and São Vicente.

VILA BELMIRO

Football fans should absolutely seek out the unforgettable experience of watching a game in the Vila Belmiro stadium, where the great Pelé's career blossomed. Upon arriving in the city, find out when Santos is next playing at home. Before the game, visit the Memorial das Conquistas, which narrates the club's history through posters, photographs, films and trophies. *Rua Princesa Isabel, 77, tel. (13) 3257-4000. Mon, 1pm-7pm; Tue-Sun, 9am-7pm.*

DIVING AT THE LAJE DE SANTOS

The Laje dos Santos is 45 kilometers (28 mi.) off the coast and takes about an hour and a half to reach by boat from São Vicente. Some say that the 500-meter (1640 foot) long rocky islet resembles a sperm whale, sculpted by hand. It is forbidden to approach the rock, but the underwater visibility of up to 20 meters guarantees divers an unforgettable experience that brings them face to face with sea turtles, dolphins and a huge variety of fish. The entire trip lasts around seven hours. *Tour Operator: Agência Cachalote: tel. (13) 3239-7213.*

Pitangueiras in Guarujá: a bustling urban beach with ample facilities

GUARUJÁ

A place of status in the 1970's, Guarujá is 87 kilometers (54 mi.) from São Paulo and has excellent infrastructure. Although most of the stunning beaches are invariably packed, there are still a few less accessible ones where you can find peace and quiet. Two of the best are **Iporanga** and **São Pedro**, located in gated communities north of the popular **Enseada** and **Pitangueiras** beaches. Both communities regulate the number of incoming cars, causing traffic jams on weekends and holidays. Iporanga is very calm and has a large waterfall forming a rock pool, while São Pedro is a so-called *praia de tombo*, with an abrupt drop just offshore that makes it perfect for surfing. All facilities there are restricted to local home owners, so be prepared to manage without food and drink stands. Three other popular surfing spots are the **Preta**, **Camburi** and **Branca** beaches, which can only be reached by trekking or by boat.

ACQUA MUNDO – AN ENJOYABLE LEARNING EXPERIENCE

Those fond of marine life should visit the Acqua Mundo. It is one of the largest aquariums in Latin America, covering approximately 3,000 m^2 (32,000 sq. ft), and it has a correspondingly huge variety of fresh and salt-water fish, including sharks and rays. Snakes, turtles, penguins and even alligators are all housed in replicas of their natural habitats. In addition, the guides are highly informative and offer instructive tours of the 35 tanks. The hourly feeding of the penguins, sharks or fish are showy events announced over the P.A. system. The guides give a lecture and entertain the visitors during feedings. An aquarium tour, lasting about three hours, is especially recommended for families with children.
Avenida Miguel Stéfano, 2001, tel. (13) 3351-8867. Closed Mon. Please call to check the hours as they vary with the season.

SÃO SEBASTIÃO

Maresias, Camburi, Camburizinho, Baleia, Paúba and **Juquei** lead the list of the north coast's most fashionable beaches, and all are in São Sebastião, which lies 214 kilometers (133 mi.) from São Paulo of via the SP-098 (Mogi–Bertioga) and SP-055 or BR-101 highways (Rio–Santos). The enjoyable scenic drive along the BR-101 cuts through the Atlantic Rainforest. Young people seeking high waves and romance launch weekend invasions on some of these beaches. At peak times, especially between December and March and during holidays, it seems as if all of São Paulo city has descended down the mountains, and many fashionable bars, designer stores and restaurants open branches on the shoreline. Along a car-accessible stretch of around 100 kilometers (62 mi.), São Sebastião offers beaches for all tastes – calm ones for families; wilder ones, with powerful waves, for water-sports enthusiasts; crowded ones and semi-deserted ones. Driving along the stretches of road between beaches requires extreme care, especially at night. Cars commonly exceed the speed limit and overtake at dangerous speeds even on blind curves.

There is more to São Sebastião than beautiful beaches and impulsive teenagers. The city, founded at the end of the 17th century, has a well-preserved historical center that's been recognized as a historical and cultural heritage site since 1970. Reminders of the past can be found on every corner. Cannons that once protected the colonial village from frequent attacks by French and English pirates now stand in peaceful repose in the gardens lining the main street's broad sidewalks.

Mountains, Atlantic Rainforest and ocean sprinkled with isolated islands

SÃO SEBASTIÃO SHORELINE

❶ Barra do Una

In the left corner, the Una river flows into the ocean and a long sand bar separates fresh from salt water. This large beach and its calm waters attract families and groups of friends.

❷ Juqueí

Families frequently go to this expansive beach, which offers calm waters, white sands, and good hotels and services.

❸ Barra do Saí

This long, crescent-shaped beach with calm water and white sands has a wonderful rock pool in its right-hand corner. It has a peaceful family atmosphere, but gets packed on weekends.

❹ Baleia

The waters here are calmer than those of the neighboring beaches, and the facilities are more rudimentary. Long, straight and ideal for walks. Reachable by car from Camburi or via the Rio–Santos highway (SP-055).

❺ Camburi and Camburizinho

The white sands of Camburi, a meeting point for surfers, are always busy. Set off behind a small hill, **Camburizinho** is a little calmer. A dirt road parallel to the ocean is dotted with hotels, bars, restaurants and dance clubs.

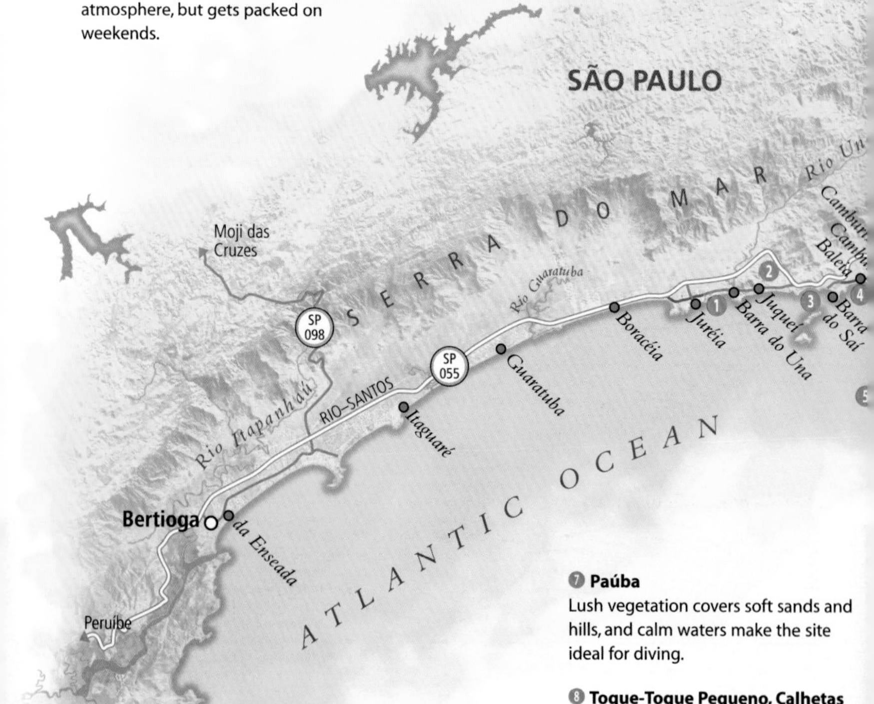

❼ Paúba

Lush vegetation covers soft sands and hills, and calm waters make the site ideal for diving.

❽ Toque-Toque Pequeno, Calhetas and **Toque-Toque Grande**

These beaches lack tourist facilities, but the three small neighbors are nevertheless worth a visit. **Toque-Toque Grande** and **Toque-Toque Pequeno** both have a stunning view of Toque-Toque island, while the tiny but beautiful **Calhetas** is a bit harder to reach.

❻ Maresias

This meeting point for surfers and celebrities is a venue for surfing competitions, festivals and shows. An always-festive atmosphere pervades its 5 kilometers (3 mi.) of white sands, but its popularity also means traffic jams and almost endless lines.

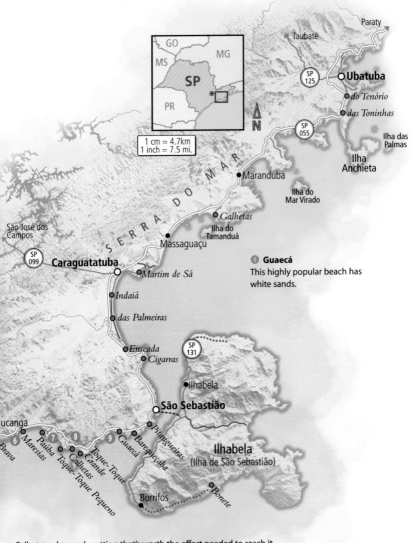

Paraty

Taubaté

SP 125

Ubatuba

do Tenório

das Toninhas

Ilha das
Palmas

SP 055

Ilha
Anchieta

1 cm = 4.7km
1 inch = 7.5 mi.

Marunduba

Ilha do
Mar Virado

São José dos
Campos

Galhetas

Ilha do
Tamanduá

Massaguaçu

⑨ **Guaecá**
This highly popular beach has
white sands.

SP 099

Caraguatatuba

Martim de Sá

Indaiá

das Palmeiras

Enseada
Cigarras

SP 131

Ilhabela

São Sebastião

ucanga

⑥ ⑦ ⑧ ⑨
Maresias *Paúba* *Toque-Toque* *Guaecá*
Toque-Toque Pequeno *Calhetas* *Grande* *Barequeçaba*
Brava

Pitangueiras

Ilhabela
(Ilha de São Sebastião)

Borrifos

Bonete

Calhetas: a heavenly setting that's worth the effort needed to reach it

Toque-Toque Grande: a deserted, peaceful beach

ISLAND BOAT TOURS

The islands' amazing scenery makes it worth venturing offshore, in spite of the headaches of planning an excursion. The tour includes **As Ilhas**, two islands joined by a sand bar, the **Ilha dos Gatos**, the **Ilha das Couves** and the **Montão de Trigo**. Stops for diving and swimming punctuate the day. Although São Sebastião has good hotels and restaurants, other tourist services are somewhat less available. Arranging a decent boat trip in the nearby islands with adequate professional service can be a trying process. Such tours are weather-dependent, requiring very calm seas, and require enough bodies on board to justify scheduling the trip. Low demand can result in cancellations.

Tour Operator: Marina Canoa, Avenida Magno Passos Bittencourt, 325, tel. (12) 3867-1699.

OUR RECOMMENDATION

🍽 **Manacá**, hidden away on a little street by Camburizinho beach and surrounded by nature, is one of the area's most pleasant restaurants. The three kiosks built on stilts at the edge of the water offer an intimate atmosphere. The menu, which emphasizes fish, is delicious and comes with the prized rarity of a decent international wine list. The menu also changes frequently thanks to the creativity of *chef* Edinho Engel which commands the *cuisine*. Reservations are recommended, especially for weekends and holidays, since the few tables are in high demand (*Rua Manacá, 102, tel. 12/3865-1566*).

🏨 The most charming hotel on the north coast is also in Camburizinho. The Thai-themed **Villa Bebek** has a pool that resembles a bend in a river – 3 to 4 meters (10-13 feet) wide and 30 meters (98 feet) long. Along this "river" stands a village of 22 cabins, in turn surrounded by a wonderful garden. Each uniquely decorated cabin has a verandah. The staff, also dressed in Thai style, are well-trained and exceptionally courteous.

Additional information begins on page 462.

ILHABELA

Many a visitor has fallen in love with the beaches and relaxed atmosphere of Ilhabela, which is 15 minutes by ferryboat from the center of São Sebastião or 224 kilometers (139 mi.) from São Paulo via the BR-101. The island's west side, which faces the mainland, has several calm and easily accessible beaches. Also on the west shore is the **Vila**, a forever-crowded village with stores and restaurants. Beaches on the east side of the island face the wilder waters of the open sea. These can only be reached by boat, by hiking overland or by four-wheel-drive vehicle, because other cars can only get as far as Jabaquara on the north side and Sepituba on the south side. Excellent sailing conditions have earned Ilhabela the moniker the "sailing capital". The best spots include **Ponta das Canas** on the north coast and off the **Pinto**, **Armação** and **Feiticeira** beaches. A car is necessary for getting from one beach to another and reaching restaurants. The island's other attractions include dozens of waterfalls and typical Atlantic Rainforest vegetation. Two words of caution: enormous lines for the ferry on weekends and holidays can delay the crossing for hours; also the island is a paradise for mosquitoes as well as people, so stock up on repellent.

INTERNATIONAL SAILING WEEK

Each July, hundreds of competitors and thousands of visitors gather at Ilhabela

OUR RECOMMENDATION

🍽 The exquisite **Free Port Café**, decorated to resemble the inside of a ship, is one of Vila's best attractions. Try the coffee with ice-cream or whipped cream, accompanied by delicious cakes and live piano music. You can also buy perfume, eye glasses and purses (*Rua Dr. Carvalho, 112, tel. 12/3896-5577/2237*).

🏨 Located on Viana beach, 2.5 kilometers (1.5 mi.) from the Vila, the European-style **Porto Pacuíba** inn is one of the most charming on Ilhabela. The owners speak German and English and offer attentive service.

Additional information begins on page 462.

Competitors from all over the world participate in the International Sailing Week each July

for the International Sailing Week, one of the world's most important sailing competitions. Renting a boat is the best way to see the action up close (*BL3 Escola de Iatismo, Avenida Perimetral Norte, 5013, Praia de Armação, tel. 12/3896-1271; or Maremar Turismo, Rua Princesa Isabel, 90, Perequê, tel. 12/3896-1418/2443/3679*). The local government and the Yacht Club de Ilhabela offer sailing courses (*tel. 11/5502-6720*).

THE EAST COAST:
BOATS, JEEPS AND TRAILS

The most extraordinary beaches, which are on the east side of the island, can only be reached by boat or four-wheel-drive vehicle, or by trekking along difficult trails. For example, the trail to the compact **Bonete** beach, whose sleepy fishing-village atmosphere is enlivened by the exuberance of the surfers, is 15 kilometers (9 mi.) long. It takes roughly four hours of hiking through the midst of the forest to get there. Weather permitting, boat is the best way to go. However, the ocean in this area can get rough and the various tour operators in Vila that offer trips cancel them when the weather is bad. In this case the best option is to go by jeep. **Castelhanos** Bay is ideal for surfing, popular with sports enthusiasts and extremely crowded during the high season. Here also, boats provide the best transport, although the bay can also be reached by jeep. A schooner to **Fome** beach at the north end of the island offers the shortest and least expensive voyage, which is generally immune to bad weather. If fortune smiles on you, frolicking dolphins may accompany the vessel. There are stops for diving and to enjoy some of the beaches along the way.

WRECKS

More than twenty wrecks lie around the island, providing a major attraction for divers. Turbulent seas, however, frequently kick up debris and reduce visibility. The **Fome**, **Jabaquara** and **Poço** beaches are good spots for snorkeling and watching fish.

The tranquil Feiticeira beach, at the south end of the island, is easy to reach

Domingas Dias: one of the eighty beaches in Ubatuba, surrounded by the Serra do Mar

Ubatuba

Ubatuba, 235 kilometers (146 mi.) from São Paulo and accessible via the Ayrton Senna (SP-070) and the Tamoios (SP-099), is one of the most beautiful areas of São Paulo state. The beaches are cradled by hills, which are themselves carpeted with Atlantic Rainforest, creating a landscape that is unique along the entire Brazilian coast. Beaches include the popular **Grande** and **Itamambuca**, with strong waves that attract surfers, calmer and less crowded ones such as **Lázaro**, and even some practically deserted ones, like **Figueira**, whose isolation and lack of services appeal to more adventurous visitors. In addition to swimming in the ocean, visitors trek along the trails in the **Parque Estadual da Serra do Mar**, which encompasses 87% of the municipal area, enjoy boat trips and scuba dive. Since the Ubatuba coastline is extensive, 100 kilometers (62 mi.), with more than 80 beaches, a car is indispensable if you want to fully explore the region. Good hotels are scattered up and down the coast, but the best restaurants are in the town itself. A word of warning: the region is a popular spot for summer vacations (December to March) and long weekends. The quality of service declines noticeably at these times, and traffic jams and long lines become the norm.

Southern Beaches
Around 15 kilometers (9 mi.) south of the center of Ubatuba is tiny **Sununga** beach, with strong waves that delight

---

A Breathtaking View

At the scenic lookout points of **Saco da Ribeira**, **Enseada**, **Toninhas** and **Félix** beaches on the Rio–Santos highway, you can safely park your car and enjoy the fantastic view. Green hills and the blue ocean, dotted with islands, frame the scalloped shoreline of white beaches.

---

the younger crowd. Also here is the legendary **Gruta que Chora** (Crying Grotto). Loud sounds actually cause water to spill down the walls. Just beside it is **Lázaro** beach, whose calm waters attract families during the high season. To the right, a narrow path between two high walls leads to **Domingas Dias**, a small and tranquil cove with soft sands. Access by car is difficult due to the presence of a gated community.

CENTRAL BEACHES

Itaguá, between the esplanade and the shoreline, offers the best mountain view in the city, particularly at daybreak. However, the water here is unsuitable for swimming. Good services make **Toninhas** particularly popular with families, and dolphins can occasionally be spotted in the distance. **Tenório** has calm waters, while **Vermelha**'s strong waves are a magnet for surfers.

NORTHERN BEACHES

Itamambuca, 12 kilometers (7.5 mi.) from the town center, is the venue for year-round surfing competitions thanks to its perfect waves. You can also surf and dive at **Félix**, which also offers an amazing view of the northern coastline, with the mountains ending practically on top of the water. Roughly 18 kilometers (11 mi.) from downtown Ubatuba is the idyllic Prumirim beach and the nearby **Prumirim** waterfall, accessible from the Rio–Santos highway. To reach the **Puruba** beach you must cross a river; this sand bar leading to the ocean is void of houses, here, only nature rules.

BOAT TRIPS AND TRAILS

Brave the wilds of Ubatuba by schooner. One trip goes to **Prumirim** island. The boat departs from the Saco da Ribeira beach and follows the coastline, offering an amazing view of the region. There are also excursions to **Anchieta** island, the second largest island off the São Paulo coast, which also gives you a magnificent view of Ubatuba. The island also offers scenic trails, but you must be accompanied by an authorized tour guide (ask the *Associação de Monitores de Ubatuba, tel. 12/9142-3692,* or local travel agencies). And don't miss the **Sul** beach – a twenty-minute hike up a steep trail takes you to this perfect diving beach.

Tour Operator: Mykonos Turismo, Itaguá Beach: Avenida Leovigildo D. Vieira, 1052, tel. (12) 3832-2042; and Saco da Ribeira Beach: Rua Flamenguinho, 17, tel. (12) 3842-0329.

PICINGUABA: TRAILS AND WATERFALLS

Almost all of the Ubatuba region is located within the **Parque Estadual da Serra do Mar**. Controls in the greater part of the park are somewhat lax, but the **Núcleo Picinguaba**, the only section of the conservation area that extends to the ocean, encompassing beaches, mangrove swamps, rocky coastline and typical sandbar vegetation, is extremely well-organized. Entry is monitored and there are guided tours along the trails to beautiful waterfalls and deserted beaches. Visits should be scheduled in advance.

Rodovia Rio–Santos, BR-101, km 8, tel. (12) 3832-9011. Daily 9am-5pm.

OUR RECOMMENDATION

🍽 The refined menu and creativity of owner Vanice, the beautiful beach-side garden and the simple decor make the **Terra Papagalli** restaurant at Itaguá beach an excellent choice for a fish or seafood lunch or dinner. Try the grilled squid and Provençal-style octopus (*Rua Xavantes, 537, Itaguá, tel. (12) 3832-1488*).

MOUNTAINS AND COUNTRYSIDE

The Brazilian pine tree is native to Campos do Jordão; in the background, the Pedra do Baú

CAMPOS DO JORDÃO

Campos do Jordão, 167 kilometers (104 mi.) from São Paulo via the Ayrton Senna highway (SP-070), is the state's most popular destination in the winter months of June and July. The cold climate, Alpine-village-style buildings and the excellent musical attractions of the Winter Festival draw hordes of tourists to this town in the Serra da Mantiqueira. The younger set, indifferent to long lines, squeezes into fashionable bars. In the off-season, however, Campos do Jordão is something else. Excellent food, quality service and a profusion of adventure tourism options, set in beautiful mountain scenery, makes the two-and-a-half-hour drive from São Paulo worth every second. At **Pedra do Baú** you can hike and go rock climbing. Hire a guide for the more difficult climbing areas (*information: 12/3971-1470*). During the day, visit the official winter home of the state governor at the **Palácio Boa Vista**, which contains works by Tarsila do Amaral, Cândido

Portinari and Di Cavalcanti (*Avenida Ademar de Barros, 3001, tel. 12/3662-1122. Wed-Sun, 10am-noon and 2pm-5pm*). Rounding out the local attractions, the tree nursery offers pleasant trails through a Brazilian pine forest (*Avenida Pedro Paulo, 12 kilometers (7.5 mi.) from the town center. Tue-Sun, 8am-5pm; also open Mondays in July*).

A DAY AS A BREWER

Founded hardly five years ago, the **Baden Baden** microbrewery has already become a local tradition. The brewery is open for guided tours, although they must be scheduled in advance. These include tastings and a quick course in beer-making, during which visitors make their own brew and take 50 bottles home, all with personalized labels. You can sample its draft beer on sidewalk tables at the restaurant of the same name in downtown Campos do Jordão. *Cervejaria Baden Baden: Rua Mateus da Costa Pinto, 1653, tel. (12) 3664-2004.*

CUNHA

Cunha lies 222 kilometers (138 mi.) from São Paulo on the Presidente Dutra highway (BR-116) and then the SP-171, a single-lane paved road in good condition. It's famous for trails leading to magnificent waterfalls and the **Pedra da Macela**, from where you can see the Paraty coastline. Throughout the day the benches in the square and the windows of the two-story houses are full of local residents chatting or watching the world go by. Strangers are regarded with curious eyes, but you will always find a friendly face willing to share information and perhaps even offer a tour of the town.

ORIENTAL POTTERY

In the mid-1970's, a group of Japanese potters relocated to Cunha and began to produce ceramics in the traditional Oriental manner. The clay is shaped, painted, glazed and finally fired in upward-sloping woodfired kilns called *noborigama*. Their glazed surfaces make the resulting pieces surprisingly strong. There are still five artisans using this technique, and they hold "kiln openings" several times a year. These events, where the public can watch as the artisans remove finished pieces from the firing chamber, functions as a small-scale exhibition (*Mieko Ukeseni and Mário Konishi; tel. 12/3111-1468*). The **Atelier do Antigo Matadouro** offers pottery courses and lectures (*tel. 12/3111-1628*).

PEDRA DA MACELA

The magnificent view from the Serra da Bocaina, with the Paraty coastline in the background, is worth the rigorous 2 kilometers (1.25 mi.) hike up the steep slope to the Pedra da Macela. Initial access is via the Paraty–Cunha highway, off km 65, where you continue for another 5 kilometers (3 mi.) of dirt road until you reach an entrance. Park here and start the upward climb. Some particularly adventurous visitors choose to camp out at the top.

SÃO LUÍS DO PARAITINGA

If you visit Cunha, don't miss São Luís do Paraitinga, 171 kilometers (106 mi.) from São Paulo and around 80 kilometers (50 mi.) from Cunha itself. The majority of its 18th and 19th century mansions and churches are still intact and the town is renowned for encouraging and preserving the cultural traditions of the Paraíba Valley and the surrounding area. During Carnival, when the history of São Luís gets retold through traditional Carnival songs called *marchinhas*, tourists line the steep, narrow streets to watch the parade of enormous *papier-mâché* dolls. This is Carnival nearly as it appeared long ago. The **Festa do Divino Espírito Santo** between May and June is another traditional folklore festival, with exhibitions involving horseback riding and the African-derived *moçambique* and *congo* dances. São Luís's infrastructure, while modest, evokes an era now forgotten. The atmosphere is an additional attraction for the nostalgic. For adventure-lovers, there are rafting trips on the Paraibuna river.

PARQUE NACIONAL DA SERRA DA BOCAINA

The Serra da Bocaina National Park is set in the Atlantic Rainforest 295 kilometers (183 mi.) from São Paulo via the Presidente Dutra highway (BR-116) and then the SP-068. Its several waterfalls and rich diversity of fauna, ranging from jaguars to woolly spider monkeys, make it perfect for adventure-lovers. Modest inns guarantee seclusion, offering a moment of peaceful relaxation in the midst of nature for those with nerves wracked from negotiating the bone-jangling access road. To reach the entrance, take the 27 kilometers (17 mi.) Bocaina dirt road that begins at São José do Barreiro. When it rains, only four-wheel-drive vehicles can make it through. Even in the dry season, conventional cars suffer. Renting an appropriate vehicle in São José do Barreiro is advised. Located halfway between the cities of São Paulo and Rio de Janeiro, the park encompasses the entire Serra da Bocaina mountain range. There is a spectacular trail through the middle of the forest down to the Paraty coastline. Authorization is automatic for day trips to the waterfalls close by the entry-point, but advance permission is needed to spend the night camping or exploring part of the **Trilha do Ouro**. Contact the Ibama administration office at the park entrance (*tel. 12/3117-1225*). But be warned: logistical support is negligible and it is even difficult to get a good meal in São José do Barreiro. For information on the **Parque Nacional do Itatiaia** see the section **Destination Rio de Janeiro**.

THREE DAYS IN THE FOREST

Along the Trilha do Ouro, or gold trail, smugglers spirited away a portion of the gold mined during the 18th century. Some stretches of the original road have been maintained, and it can now be covered in a three-day walking tour, although a guide is required. Waterfalls line the route close to the entrance of the park in São José do Barreiro. The **Veado**, with a 100-meter (328 foot) double cascade, is one of the most beautiful along the way. Local residents offer simple accommodations and meals in small houses, for those that do not want to camp. The tour ends at the **Mambucaba** beach in Angra dos Reis. To avoid surprises, ask about return transportation to São José do Barreiro when arranging the tour with a guide (*information: tel. 12/3117-1365*).

BANANAL

Another starting-point for exploring the Serra da Bocaina is Bananal, 348 kilometers (216 mi.) from São Paulo. Like the other towns in the region,

Trails decorated with waterfalls

it flourished at the beginning of the coffee era, but the plantations quickly drained the land of nutrients and sent the area into rapid decline. The Brazilian writer Monteiro Lobato referred to them as ghost towns. Since then, Bananal's economy has recovered thanks to history-oriented tourism, and a walk along the mansion-lined streets is a glorious experience. Note the **Igreja da Matriz**, a church dating from 1811, and the **Pharmacia Popular**. The latter, Brazil's oldest pharmacy, looks exactly as it did when it opened in 1830, down to the measuring instruments and bottles on the shelves.

Coffee Estates

Around Bananal, a number of estates help tell the history of the coffee barons. The **Fazenda dos Coqueiros**, dating from 1855, contains period furniture, as well as a collection of implements used to torture slaves. The highly professional guided tours know their history and tell stories well (*Rodovia dos Tropeiros, 5 kilometers/3 mi. from Bananal, tel.*

12/3116-1358). The **Fazenda Resgate**, once the most prosperous estate in the region, has a series of beautiful murals by the Spanish artist Vilaronga. Visits must be scheduled in advance (*SP-064, km 324, 10 kilometers/6 mi. from the town center, tel. 12/3116-2007*). **Pau d'Alho**, another important plantation in the neighboring municipality of São José do Barreiro, dates from 1817 and earned the designation of historical heritage site in 1968. On the guided tour, you can see the slave quarters, the main homestead and the water wheel used to shell the coffee beans (*Rodovia dos Tropeiros, km 265, tel. 12/3117-1310*).

Our Recommendation

🍽 The kitchen of the **Dona Licéia** restaurant in the Fazenda Caxambu, in Arapeí, 20 kilometers (12 mi.) from Bananal, is located right in the middle of the dining room so you watch hostess Licéia as she goes about her business. The daily specials always seem to hit the right tone. Try the orange glazed duck and country chicken (*Rodovia dos Tropeiros, SP-068, tel. 12/3116-1412*).

Fazenda Resgate was the most prosperous estate in Bananal during the coffee era

DESTINATION
BELO HORIZONTE

Founded in 1897, Belo Horizonte was the first planned city of Brazil. Its highlights include modernist architecture, such as the sprawling Pampulha building complex designed by Oscar Niemeyer and commissioned by mayor Juscelino Kubitschek, who later became president of Brazil. The city has a rich cultural and artistic life, and excellent cuisine: it's the homeland of *pão de queijo* (cheese bread), *goiabada* (guava paste), *tutu à mineira* (bean purée with pork sausage, manioc flour and seasoning), and the Minas white cheese dessert. Belo Horizonte is also the point of departure for the beautiful historic towns of Minas Gerais, founded during the gold rush in the late 17th and early 18th centuries. Sabará, Ouro Preto, Congonhas, Mariana, Tiradentes, São João Del Rei and Diamantina feature plenty of churches generously decorated with gold leaf (above, right), as well as saints sculpted by Aleijadinho, Brazil's most important baroque artist. The large number of towns scattered through the mountains, and their rich historic heritage, make Minas one of the most charming destinations in Brazil.

DESTINATION HIGHLIGHTS

BELO HORIZONTE
Pampulha
Attractions
Trails of Minas

SABARÁ (25 km/15 mi.)
Parque Natural do Caraça

OURO PRETO (99 km/62 mi.)
Historic Center
The Mines

MARIANA (107 km/66 mi.)

CONGONHAS (82 km/51 mi.)

TIRADENTES (215 km/134 mi.)

SÃO JOÃO DEL REI
(185 km/115 mi.)

DIAMANTINA (285 km/177 mi.)

ESTRADA REAL (The Royal Trail)

*All distances are from
Belo Horizonte*

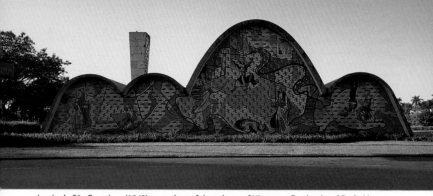
Igreja de São Francisco (1943), a product of the talents of Niemeyer, Portinari and Burle Marx

BELO HORIZONTE

PAMPULHA

The principal landmark of Belo Horizonte is the Pampulha complex, built in 1940, whose buildings and landscape cover an 18-km-long band around an artificial lake. The complex includes the Igreja de São Francisco de Assis, the Museu de Arte, the Casa do Baile, and the Yacht Club, in addition to the Mineirão and Mineirinho stadiums and the Zoobotanical Foundation.

IGREJA DE SÃO FRANCISCO
This innovative church broke with the baroque architectural tradition in Minas Gerais. It was only in 1959, more than fifteen years after its inauguration, that the Catholic Church recognized it as their place of worship. In an impressive collaboration, Niemeyer designed this church's undulating lines; Burle Marx laid out the spectacular landscape; Portinari decorated the interior with valuable art, such as the fourteen canvases of the Via Crucis; and Alfredo Ceschiatti sculpted the baptistery with its baptismal font. The exterior wall behind the nave is decorated with tiles by Portinari and relates the story of

Saint Francis. The arches along the lateral walls are covered by abstract mosaics by Paulo Werneck.
Avenida Otacílio Negrão de Lima, Pampulha, tel. (31) 3441-1198. Mon-Sun, 8am-6pm.

MUSEU DE ARTE DA PAMPULHA
This museum, also known as the Palácio de Cristal, was originally intended by Oscar Niemeyer to be a casino. It now has a library and a collection of over one thousand contemporary artworks. Unfortunately, it is closed to the public except during important temporary exhibits.
Avenida Otacílio Negrão de Lima, 16585, Pampulha, tel. (31) 3443-4533. Tue-Sun, 9am-7pm.

CASA DO BAILE
The Casa do Baile (Ballroom) is distinguished by its sinuous lines. Built in 1943, today it doubles as a cultural center and a heritage site.
Avenida Otacílio Negrão de Lima, 751, Pampulha, tel. (31) 3227-7443. Tue-Sun, 9am-7pm.

ATTRACTIONS

The main attraction of Belo Horizonte's 8,000 bars is the famous *cachaça* (sugarcane-based spirit) of Minas. Many of these bars are located on Praça da Savassi, where on Saturdays the art exhibits and live music draw large crowds. The best *chope* (draft beer) in town in served at **Albanos'** bar. In the evening, the Seis Pistas area and the districts of Santo Antônio and Santa Lúcia offer the romantic **Oficina d'Idéias** (*Rua Congonhas, 539, Santo Antônio, tel. 31/3342-3232. Tue-Sun, 7pm-3am*) and the **Utópica Marcenaria** (*Avenida Raja Gabaglia, 4700, Santa Lúcia, tel. 31/3296-2868. Thu-Sat, 9pm-3am; Sun, 7pm-2:30am*), a combination of architecture studio, bar and cultural center with great live music such as samba, MPB (Brazilian popular music) and *forró* (dance music from the northeast of Brazil). The glass façade offers a beautiful view of the city by night. Popular meeting points are **Avenida Afonso Pena** and the **Praça da Liberdade**, a track and field training site and a common spot for demonstrations. On this square sits the eclectic state government building, a stylistic contrast to Niemeyer's Edifício Niemeyer, which has eight stories but appears to have fifteen. On Sundays, the **Feira de Artes e Artesanatos**, the largest arts and crafts fair in Latin America, is held on Avenida Afonso Pena. The **Palácio das Artes**, located within the Parque Municipal, attracts lovers of movies and the arts.

OUR RECOMMENDATION

🍽 The best cheese bread in town is made by the **Boca do Forno** chain, with thirteen shops (*Avenida André Cavalcanti, 571, tel. 31/3334-6377*). **Xapuri** has modernized the traditional cuisine of Minas. Their *galinha ao molho pardo* (chicken stewed in its blood with herbs) is a must (*Rua Mandacaru, 260, tel. 31/3496-6455*). **Quintal** has superb meat options such as kid goat ribs and smoked chops. Reservations advised (*Rua Sebastião Antônio Carlos, 350, tel. 31/3443-5559*). With its 500 label wine list, **Taste Vin** is a must. Reservations required (*Rua Curitiba, 2,105, tel. 31/3292-5423*).

Additional information begins on page 462.

Companhia Primeiro Ato: a contemporary dance show from Minas Gerais

A symbol of Minas Gerais's culture, the Mercado Central has stands, stores and even a chapel

MERCADO CENTRAL

Open since 1929, this central market has more than 400 stalls selling medicinal herbs, pots and pans, china, and the famous *cachaça* from Minas, with prices ranging from R$2.50 to R$200. People meet in the bars to sample appetizers like *jiló* (a type of eggplant) fried with onions and iced beer.

Avenida Augusto de Lima, 744, Centro, tel. (31) 3274-9434. Mon-Sat, 7am-6pm; Sundays and holidays, 7am-1pm.

CULTURAL PERFORMANCES

Home to the most prestigious dance companies and music groups of Brazil's contemporary scene, Belo Horizonte's performing arts scene is breaking down barriers. The dance company **Corpo** is the best known Brazilian troupe abroad. Created 25 years ago by the Pederneiras brothers, it has made a name for itself by combining popular language and Brazilian music with classical ballet steps. Another company, **Primeiro Ato,** is also taking a fresh approach to ballet by combining dance and theatre. Since 1978 the music group **Uakti** has been building an avant-garde repertoire using instruments made by the musicians themselves. **Giramundo** has dedicated itself to puppet theater since the 1970's. Its headquarters is a combination of museum, theater and school and is open to visitors (*Rua Monte Carmelo, 222, Floresta, tel. 31/3446-0686*).

THE CUISINE OF MINAS

Even when the dishes are prepared with the most modern equipment, Minas' flavorful cuisine maintains the essence of traditional recipes cooked slowly over a wood stove and served to miners and mule drivers. Influenced by Portuguese and African cooking, traditional dishes include: *galinha ao molho pardo* (chicken stewed in its blood with herbs), *leitão à punuruca* (roast suckling pig with crispy skin), *feijão tropeiro* (beans cooked with olive oil, garlic, onion, parsley and chives, thickened with manioc flour), *torresmo* (cracklings), collard greens, and simmered *ora-pro-nóbis* (spinach-like leaves). Minas is also the land of milk, café au lait, and different types of pastries and bread (with cheese, of course), *broas* (corn bread) and biscuits such as *sequilhos* and *brevidades*. And to end a typically *mineiro* meal, try one or two of the myriad of sweets made with milk, pumpkin, guava or coconut, or *ambrosia* (milk pudding with spices), rice pudding and fruit preserves, all with Minas white cheese.

TRAILS OF MINAS

Mountains, mining sites and no access restrictions provide plenty of options for sports and nature lovers. Trails near Belo Horizonte range from easy to very difficult, and you can take them by motorcycle (most popular), bicycle, four-wheel drive vehicle, or simply on foot. **São Sebastião das Águas Claras**, known as **Macacos**, is a departure point for motorcycle and bike rides. You should leave early to best explore this complex network of trails. We suggest that tourists join a group of *treieiros* on the trails, as these adventurers are known. The principal meeting point is Posto Fernanda, a gas station located on the road from Belo Horizonte to Nova Lima, roughly 1 kilometers past the BH Mall. Adventurers also meet at the **Bar do Engenho** and the **Bar do Marcinho**, in Macacos. Four-wheel drive enthusiasts can choose the trails near **Sabará**, which is a city 25 kilometers (15 mi.) from Belo Horizonte. Many agencies in the region organize outings, and tourists can even follow the guide from the comfort of their own vehicles. The excursions are in the midst of woods, rivers and waterfalls, and the panoramic view from the mountain tops is wonderful.

Local Tour Operator: Caminho das Pedras Expedições e Acessórios, Avenida Raja Gabaglia, 3601, tel. (31) 3293-8608.

The trails of Minas offer adventure and beautiful sights

SABARÁ

Founded in 1674 when its rivers ran golden, Sabará was one of the first villages established during the gold rush, and is 25 kilometers (15 mi.) east of Belo Horizonte on the BR-262. Sabará is nestled in a stunning valley at the confluence of two rivers, **Velhas** and **Sabará**, after which the city was named. Matching the natural attractions in the surrounding area are the historic buildings downtown. **Igreja Nossa Senhora do Ó**, from the 18th century, is the main landmark. Its austere polygonal façade, made of mud reinforced by interlocking horizontal and vertical sticks, blends into the simplicity of the square it faces. Unlike its plain exterior, the church's interior is lavishly decorated in red, gold and blue, as in the seven panels with gold-leaf oriental motifs. Scholars claim that these panels were made by craftsmen from the Portuguese oriental colonies. Leonardo Ferreira, the church's caretaker, tells this and other stories. For additional information, call the **Matriz** (mother church) at *(31) 3671-1724. Largo Nossa Senhora do Ó, Siderúrgica. Tue-Sun, 9am-noon and 1:30pm-5:30pm.*

PARQUE NATURAL DO CARAÇA

Continuing on the BR-262 that leads to Sabará, you'll reach the **Caraça** massif, 1,297 meters (4,255 feet) above sea level, in the municipality of Catas Altas. This 11,000-hectare (27,000-acre)

Neo-gothic Igreja do Caraça

ecological reserve is in the shape of a huge face (*cara*, in Portuguese) and was therefore named Caraça (literally, *big face*). It has a shrine in a seminary founded in 1820 by missionaries, with one of the first neo-gothic churches in Brazil. The buildings were immortalized in a painting by Rugendas. A wild-maned wolf comes every night to be fed by the priests. Sit on the church's veranda, enjoy the tea offered by the priests, and ready your camera to record this ritual. The Caraça trails lead to two waterfalls that form pools: **Cascatinha**, with four small falls, and the spectacular **Cascatona**, over 100 meters (328 feet) high with rust-colored water. You may stay at the old and damp seminary, but if you want a little more comfort, it's best to head to **Hotel Quadrado**, in **Santa Bárbara**, a nearby town. On the way, you'll see **Catas Altas**, a small and well preserved town from the gold rush days. Have lunch at the excellent **Histórias Taberna** restaurant. *Additional information begins on page 462.*

OURO PRETO

HISTORIC CENTER

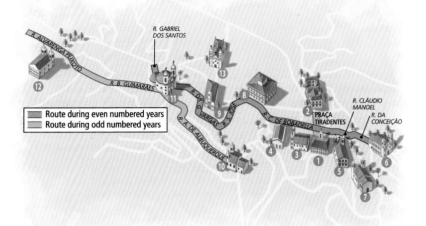

R. GABRIEL DOS SANTOS

R. ALVARENGA PEIXOTO

R. B. GUIMARÃES

R. DE G. VARGAS

R. S. JOSÉ

R. A. DE ALBUQUERQUE

R. C. DE ROBADELLA

R. CLÁUDIO MANOEL

PRAÇA TIRADENTES

R. DA CONCEIÇÃO

Route during even numbered years
Route during odd numbered years

1 - Museu da Inconfidência
2 - Museu da Mineralogia and Escola de Minas
3 - Igreja de Nossa Senhora do Carmo
4 - Teatro Municipal Casa da Ópera
5 - Igreja de São Francisco de Assis
6 - Matriz de Nossa Senhora da Conceição de Antônio Dias
7 - Capela do Padre Faria
8 - Casa dos Contos
9 - Igreja de São José
10 - Igreja de Nossa Senhora do Pilar
11 - Igreja Nossa Senhora do Rosário
12 - Igreja do Bom Jesus de Matosinhos
13 - Igreja São Francisco de Paula

Protected by mountains, Ouro Preto – the first capital of Minas Gerais, formerly known as Vila Rica – embodies the history of Brazil's gold rush era from the 17th to 18th century. Explorers and religious orders wisely filled the town with cobblestone streets, austere houses and small churches with richly decorated interiors. The result in terms of architecture is an impressive harmony. Two geniuses of Brazilian arts, architect and sculptor Antônio Francisco Lisboa, or Aleijadinho, born in Ouro Preto; and painter Mestre Ataíde, born in Mariana, poured their creativity and spirit into making Ouro Preto a unique town. It was here, 99 kilometers (62 mi.) from Belo Horizonte, that the first independence movement arose, the *Inconfidência Mineira*. Years went by, gold mines were exhausted, and the town fell into oblivion. The lack of wealth prevented change and preserved Ouro Preto; it's now listed on Unesco's World Heritage List. However, the establishment of industries in the surrounding area, population growth and increased traffic now threaten the harmony inherited from the past. Contributing to the activity, and luring university students from far corners, is its exciting street carnival. Trace history left in the alleys and streets; note that the two-staged itinerary suggested below requires climbing and descending the steep streets. Also, remember to check the visiting hours of the attractions.

❶ MUSEU DA INCONFIDÊNCIA
The old city hall and jail (1785–1855) with neoclassical touches, is now a museum holding the mortal remains of the twelve rebels, a collection of religious art and copies of Aleijadinho's works.
Praça Tiradentes, 139, Centro, tel. (31) 3551-1121. Tue-Sun, noon-5:30pm.

❷ MUSEU DE MINERALOGIA AND ESCOLA DE MINAS (PALÁCIO DOS GOVERNADORES)
This building was erected in 1741 and served as the Governors' house until 1898. When Belo Horizonte became the state capital, it became home to the School of Mining, and today houses the Museum of Science and Technology and the Museum of Mineralogy. The internal fountain was designed by Aleijadinho. The view from the Girândola point, behind the building, is magnificent.
Praça Tiradentes, 20, Centro, tel (31) 3559-1597. Tue-Sun, noon-5pm.

❸ IGREJA DE NOSSA SENHORA DO CARMO
Aleijadinho's last works are in this charming church, in the sacristy and on the altars of Nossa Senhora da Piedade (Our Lady of Mercy) and of the "Bound Christ." The church was built in 1766 and is the only church in the region which has Portuguese tiles from the 18th century. It also introduced the rococo style to Minas Gerais. The painting in the sacristy is by Mestre Ataíde. In the novice house beside the church is the grandiose **Museu do Oratório**, with 300 pieces of religious art from the 17th to 20th centuries and 160 splendid *oratórios* (small altars or cabinets containing carvings of saints) ranging from 3 centimeters (1 in.) to 3.2 meters (10.5 feet) in height. It also houses the so-called itinerant *oratórios*, which were carried on the back of mules for protection during muleteers' journeys, and the more refined *oratórios* which attested to the wealth of the church's congregation.
Rua Brig. Musqueira, Centro, tel. (31) 3551-2601. Church open from Tue-Sat, noon-4:45pm; Sun, 9:45am-11am and 1pm-4:45pm. Museum, tel. (31) 3551-5539. Daily, 9am-5:30pm.

Igreja de Nossa Senhora do Carmo: the monastery contains the lavishly decorated Museu do Oratório

The multicolored baroque work by Mestre Ataíde on the ceiling of the Igreja de São Francisco de Assis

**4 TEATRO MUNICIPAL
CASA DA ÓPERA**
Built in 1769, this theatre and opera
house is in the shape of a lyre and has
perfect acoustics. It's the oldest theatre
in operation in Brazil. You can visit it
during the day, and in the evenings
there are concerts and shows, especially
during the Winter Festival in July.
*Rua Brig. Musqueira, Centro, tel (31)
3559-3224. Daily, noon-5:30pm.*

5 IGREJA DE SÃO FRANCISCO DE ASSIS
This church, built in 1776, is
Aleijadinho's masterpiece and the
highest expression of the rococo style. It
has some oddly military features, such as
cylindrical towers that look like
watchtowers, and roofs that resemble
helmets adorned with spears. The Cross
of Lorena, with two arms flanked by
balls of fire, is especially impressive.
Inside, Aleijadinho created sculptures for
the pulpits, wood panels, a soapstone-
sculpted door, the main chapel's altars,
and the fountain of the sacristy. Mestre
Ataíde painted the ceiling, which
appears higher due to the arrangement
of the columns and parapets.
Information at the Museu Aleijadinho
(tel. 31/3551-4661).
*Largo de Coimbra, Centro. Tue-Sun,
8:30am-11:50am and 1:30pm-5pm.*

**6 MATRIZ DE NOSSA SENHORA
DA CONCEIÇÃO DE ANTÔNIO DIAS**
This façade is very similar to the Pilar
church, but the 1727 church
distinguishes itself on the inside. The
eight altars, four on each side, are
lavishly decorated, and the church
contains the graves of Aleijadinho and
his father, Manuel Francisco Lisboa,
who is believed to have adorned the
nave. Don't miss the **Museu
Aleijadinho**, located in the sacristy;
the basement; and the chambers. The
museum has priceless pieces such as a
soapstone bust of São Francisco de
Paula (Saint Francis of Paola), whose
eyes appear lifelike.
*Praça Antônio Dias, Antônio Dias.
Church: tel. (31) 3551-3282.
Tue-Sat, 8:30am-11:45 am and 1:30pm-
4:45pm. Sun, noon-4:45pm.
Museum: tel. (31) 3551-4661.*

⑦ CAPELA DO PADRE FARIA

Built in the mid-18th century at the initiative of Father João de Faria, this chapel, also known as **Igreja Nossa Senhora do Rosário dos Brancos**, is a small gem. Well preserved, it's important historically (making the creation of the city) and architecturally, since it is the only remaining example of the first buildings in the Ouro Preto mountains. Notice the cross with three arms in the church plaza, the scenes from the life of Mary on the side panels and the gilded wood carvings on the three tablets.
Rua Nossa Senhora do Parto, Padre Faria.

⑧ CASA DOS CONTOS

Between 1724 and 1735 this building served as the Mint, where gold was weighed and cast. It was also where the rebels (the *inconfidentes*) were imprisoned. One of them, the poet Cláudio Manuel da Costa, died here in 1789. As was usual, the lower part of the building served as slave quarters. This is one of the best preserved houses in Ouro Preto. It contains an exhibit of 18th and 19th century

The opulent pulpit of the Pilar church

furniture and operates as a library and research center for the gold rush era.
Rua São José, 12, Centro, tel. (31) 3551-1444. Tue to Sat, 12:30-5:30pm. Sun and holidays, 9am-3pm.

⑨ IGREJA DE SÃO JOSÉ

Construction of this church, which replaced the original chapel dating from 1730, began around 1752 and was only completed in 1811. Aleijadinho, who served as Judge of the Brotherhood, designed the chapel altar and the tower. Notice the soapstone banister around the central tower. The building is currently being renovated.
Rua Teixeira Amaral, no fixed hours.

⑩ IGREJA DE NOSSA SENHORA DO PILAR

This building was completed in 1731 as a replacement for the original main church, constructed between 1700 and 1707 of mud and wood reinforcements. It is considered the pinnacle of baroque opulence and dramatic quality. Its austere façade is a sharp contrast to the lavish interior, decorated with 434 kilograms (956 lb) of gold and 400 kilograms (880 lb) of silver. Francisco Xavier de Brito, one of Aleijadinho's mentors, is believed to have designed the main altar. Visit the **Museu de Arte Sacra** in the basement.
Praça Monsenhor João Castilho Barbosa, Pilar, tel. (31) 3551-4735. Tue-Sun, 9am-10:45am and noon-4:45pm.

⑪ IGREJA NOSSA SENHORA DO ROSÁRIO

The unusual circular shape and three oval sections is similar to northern European churches. Constructed in 1785, it replaced the original chapel built in 1709. Information: (31) 3551-4735.
Largo do Rosário, Rosário. Tue-Sun, noon-4:45pm.

Ouro Preto, with the Museu da Inconfidência in the upper right

⑫ Igreja do Bom Jesus de Matosinhos

Built in the second half of the 18th century, this church's magnificent soapstone portal was made by Aleijadinho. Mestre Ataíde is believed to have painted the interior. Information: (31) 3551-4735.
Rua Alvarenga, Cabeças. Mon-Sat, 1pm-4:45pm.

⑬ Igreja São Francisco de Paula

This is the newest church in Ouro Preto. Its construction started in 1804 and took more than 80 years. Aleijadinho is credited with the sculpture of Saint Francis of Paola. On the top floor, life-size sculptures represent the Last Supper. The church offers a breathtaking panoramic view of the town.

Rua Henrique Adeodato, São Cristóvão. Tue-Sat, 9am-11:15am. Sun, 1:30pm-4:40pm.

Religious Processions

Just like other historic towns, Ouro Preto maintains its traditional processions. The most impressive are during the Holy Week, which ends on Easter Sunday, when the town is decorated for the procession of angels, brotherhoods and Biblical figures. Everyone goes out to cover the streets with flowers and sawdust. Colorful rugs and flags are hung from the windows. In even-numbered years the procession leaves from Igreja Nossa Senhora do Pilar and heads towards the plaza of Igreja Bom Jesus de Matosinhos, whereas in odd-numbered years it starts in Nossa Senhora da Conceição de Antônio Dias and heads towards Nossa Senhora do Rosário.

The Mines

There is no more gold, but the empty mines remain and are open to visitors. The most famous one is the **Chico Rei** mine, excavated in the 18th century. It belonged to a slave who had been a king in Africa who was able to buy his own freedom and the mine that bears his name (*Rua D. Silvério, 108, Antônio Dias, tel.*

31/3551-1749. Daily, 8am–5pm). He built the **Igreja Santa Efigênia dos Pretos** (*Rua Santa Efigênia, 396, Alto da Cruz, tel. 31/3551-5047. Tue-Sun, 8:30am-4:30pm*), which has plenty of early baroque wood carvings. Above the entrance, on the façade, is a work by Aleijadinho. The view of the town is magnificent.

OURO PRETO, MY FANTASY LAND

Many years ago I visited Brazil as a typical tourist and I realized what a great country it is. However, I left with the impression that there was a hazy line that separated the country I knew from the real Brazil. I designed a house in Barra do Una and was involved in the construction of a fascinating complex in the state of São Paulo, and had the privilege of meeting some extraordinary Brazilians who honored me with their friendship. Through them I'm getting to know the country and, of course, Ouro Preto was one of the first places I went to.

Some towns have a "soul" that embraces and wins us over, and makes us part of them. From the day I arrived in Ouro Preto I realized that it was one of these towns. The topography and vegetation are powerful and the town respects both in an impressive manner. The streets follow the natural contour of the land and the buildings adapt to the terrain in such a way that their walls and roofs create an urban sculpture. The churches, located in strategic points, become icons within the landscape but do not overpower the scenery. Colors and textures add a final touch to this fascinating town.

Walking along the streets, sitting in the squares and churches I pondered the true values of life, dreamed of romantic and mysterious stories, and created an imaginary world, something that our contemporary lifestyle no longer allows us to do.

The colonial and baroque architecture of Ouro Preto deserves special mention. Almost completely unknown abroad, it is undoubtedly one of the most interesting styles in the Americas. The churches designed by Aleijadinho, with their exceptional proportions, are remarkable. One of their unique features is the contrast between the large flat surfaces and the elaborate stonework, as well as the incredible sculptures integrated into the façades, plazas and staircases. This concept has almost been forgotten by modern architecture, and it should continue to be contemplated by architects. The same can be said of the symmetry of the scale and design of the exteriors and interiors of these churches; their luxurious details emphasize their spirituality. This type of architecture teaches us many concepts and invites us to consider and appreciate its excellence.

I was fortunate enough to be in Ouro Preto during the Holy Week and watch the incredible ceremonies and processions that carried me back in time. These ceremonies, with their local color, demonstrate the spirituality of this very special town.

The people who live here are elegant, peaceful and humane, and have a complement lifestyle. Hotels, restaurants and public areas reflect this way of life, and make the town a consistent and fascinating place. For those who appreciate beauty, elegance and a deeply emotional way of life, Ouro Preto is a mandatory destination.

Ricardo Legorreta,
Mexican architect

MARIANA

Mariana's beautiful churches and manors appoint it yet another gem of baroque architecture. It was the first capital city of Minas Gerais and birthplace of painter Manuel da Costa Ataíde (Mestre Ataíde), who decorated the churches of many of the historic towns. His Biblical figures and angels have mulatto features, like his own. Mariana is located 15 kilometers (10 mi.) east of Ouro Preto on BR-356.

MINA DE OURO DA PASSAGEM
This mine, which operated until 1985, is located 4 kilometers (2.5 mi.) before the entrance to Mariana, from the direction of Ouro Preto. A small trolley car pulled by a cable descends to a depth of 120 meters (394 feet). *Rua Eugênio E. Rapallo, 192, Passagem de Mariana, tel. (31) 3557-5000. Mon and Tue, 9am-5pm; Wed-Sun, 9am-5:30pm.*

CATEDRAL BASILICA DA SÉ
This church has twelve gold altars, Bohemian crystal chandeliers, paintings by native son Ataíde, and a German Arp-Schnitiger organ donated by Dom João v. The organ was built in 1701, has over 1,000 pipes and still has a heavenly sound. Listen on Fridays at 11am and Sundays at 12:15pm. *Praça Cláudio Manoel, Centro, tel. (31) 3557-1216. Tue-Sun, 7am-6pm.*

IGREJA SÃO FRANCISCO DE ASSIS
Aleijadinho designed this church's carved stone entrance, featuring a soapstone medallion and additional carvings around the altar. Mestre Ataíde, buried in the church, painted the ceiling panels of the central aisle and sacristy. Beside this church is the **Igreja de Nossa Senhora do Carmo**, with cylindrical towers inspired by Aleijadinho. For additional information call the Catedral Basílica da Sé, *tel. (31) 3557-1216. Praça Minas Gerais (formerly the pelourinho, where the slaves were punished), Centro. Tue-Sun, 9am-5pm.*

São Francisco de Assis (left) and Nossa Senhora do Carmo churches, both in baroque style

CONGONHAS

Also founded during the gold rush, Congonhas has maintained little of its old splendor. Unlike other preserved historic towns, Congonhas resumed its growth in the 1950s with iron ore mining. The harmony of the old town was disrupted with the construction of newer buildings and the demolition of several mansions. Fortunately one major landmark of the 18th century remained to attest to the glory of the old days: the **Basílica do Bom Jesus de Matosinhos**, built between 1757 and 1761. A calm, leisurely visit to the church is like a stroll through heaven. Twelve prophets welcome visitors in the church plaza, and over 66 life-size images representing scenes of the Passion of the Christ, carved by Aleijadinho, decorate the six chapels that line the path leading to the church. The multi-colored finish was completed by Ataíde. A room at the back of the church houses a spectacular collection of votive offerings, given to the present day as a payment for promises made.

MESTRE ALEIJADINHO

Aleijadinho was born in Vila Rica in 1730 to Manuel Francisco Lisboa, a Portuguese construction foreman, and his slave Isabel. The famous artist learned his father's trade at an early age. Afflicted with leprosy in 1777, he still managed to create the works of Congonhas between 1796 and 1805 with the help of his disciples. These treasures languished in obscurity, lost in the mountains of Minas, until in 1919 modernists like Mário de Andrade and Manuel Bandeira drew Brazilians' attention to them.

The creation of the prophets
Specialists in the work of Aleijadinho believe that the sculptures of the prophets were carved by Aleijadinho with the collaboration of his disciples. The most perfect sculpture is of Daniel, and stands out for its austere beauty; art historians think it was made by the master himself.

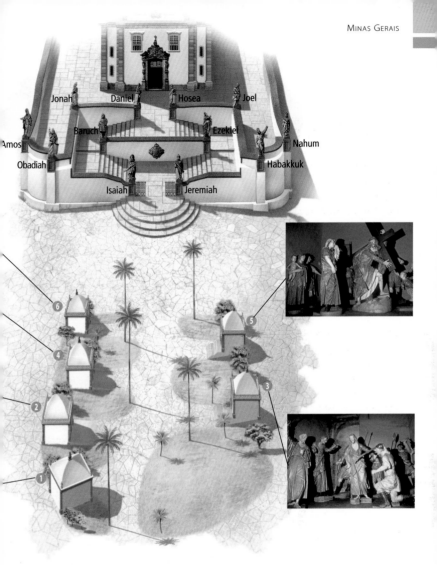

Jonah Daniel Hosea Joel

Baruch Ezekiel

Amos Nahum

Obadiah Habakkuk

Isaiah Jeremiah

❶ The Last Supper
Fifteen figures represent Jesus, the twelve apostles and two servants. The eight figures behind the table are sculpted from the waist up.

❷ Agony in the Garden
Jesus prays in the Garden of Gethsemane while the apostles Peter, James and John sleep.

❸ Arrest of Jesus
The scene of Judas' kiss of betrayal is composed of eight figures. The figures of Jesus, Saint Peter and Judas are believed to have been sculpted by Aleijadinho, whereas his disciples are credited for the soldiers.

❹ Scourging and the Crown of Thorns
The two scenes are in the same chapel. In the first, soldiers who look like puppets surround Jesus, tied to a column. In the second, seven grotesque soldiers, holding the crown of thorns, surround Jesus.

❺ Jesus on the Road to Calvary
Fifteen figures portray the most emotional moments of the Passion: Jesus carrying the cross to the top of Mount Calvary. He stops and tells his followers not to cry for him.

❻ The Crucifixion
The scene, with ten figures, portrays Jesus nailed to the cross between two thieves.

TIRADENTES

The stone-paved street and colonial mansions frame the Matriz de Santo Antônio

Although it lacks the rich architecture landmarks which abound in Ouro Preto, Tiradentes has plenty of colorful, harmonious colonial houses. The town appears to have been frozen in time, and attracts tourists seeking both peace and quiet and cultural events. The town was named after Joaquim José da Silva Xavier, better known by his nickname Tiradentes (literally "toothpuller"), who was a leader of the independence movement called the *Inconfidência Mineira*. He was born on Pombal farm, located between Tiradentes and nearby São João Del Rei. The town, nestled between the Mortes river and the São José mountains, was practically forgotten between the end of the mining period and the 1970's, when businessmen in Rio helped restore the beautiful old houses. Soon the locals pitched in, and Tiradentes soon became a refuge for artists and intellectuals from Rio and São Paulo.

MATRIZ DE SANTO ANTÔNIO
Unlike other towns in the state, Tiradentes most important church is dedicated to Saint Anthony, not Saint Francis. Half a ton of gold was used to decorate its interior, evidenced by the gilded flower garlands on the elegant altars and the chancel. Another highlight is the Portuguese organ, imported in 1788, with the exterior casing, designed in Brazil, covered in rococo carvings and paintings. A stone staircase leads to the plaza and to a soapstone sundial made by local craftsmen in 1785. The façade and entrance, from 1732, were designed by Aleijadinho.
Rua da Câmara, Centro. Casa Paroquial (Parish House), tel. (31) 3355-1238. Daily, 9am-5pm.

IGREJA NOSSA SENHORA DO ROSÁRIO DOS PRETOS
Built by and for slaves in 1708, this church is decorated with a stonework arch, paintings on the ceiling and images of black saints in the two side

altars. For more information on the church call the Casa Paroquial (*tel. 32/3355-1238*).
Praça Padre Lourival. Tue-Sun, 9am-noon and 2pm-5pm.

Chafariz de São José
Built in 1749, this blue soapstone fountain features an oratory with an image of São José de Botas. Three faces, representing Love, Fortune and Health, spout drinking water from the Mãe d'Água woods, at the foot of the São José mountains (guided tours can be arranged). The 6 kilometers (3.7 mi.) trail to the top is easy. The restaurant Canto do Chafariz, close to the fountain, offers great regional cuisine.
Rua do Chafariz, Centro.

Culture and Gourmet Food
In January Tiradentes hosts a film festival that attracts artists and intellectuals. In June, the town's streets and alleys fill up with bikes and their owners for the Harley Davidson reunion. In August, during the 10-day International Culture and Gourmet Festival, chefs from Brazil and abroad tempt taste buds. Visitors will enjoy dishes and drinks in addition to musical and theater presentations, exhibits and cooking courses.

Arts and Crafts
In Tiradentes, silver and brass are used to make jewelry, drinking cups, candlesticks and vases. Stores display pieces made from iron, wood, clay, and cloth that tell the history of the people of Minas, the *mineiros*. Visit **Zé Damas'** **Studio** (*Rua do Chafariz, 130*) and buy the town's trademark wooden troughs, pots and stones painted with colorful houses. Another famous local craftsman is **Vantuil Onofre**.

The simple and typical crafts of Tiradentes

He makes his iron flowers into candelabra, lamps and key rings. His shop is difficult to find, so phone in advance to ask for directions (*tel. 32/3355-1866*).

Bichinho
Bichinho is a small village near Tiradentes where fine handicrafts can

Our Recommendation

🍽 On the oldest street of Tiradentes, the **Tragaluz** restaurant serves the traditional cuisine of Minas with contemporary touches (*Rua Direita, 52, tel. 32/3355-1424*). **Virada do Largo** offers superb traditional cuisine that can be eaten near the wood stove (*Rua do Moinho, 11, tel. 32/3355-1111*).

🏨 The owners of **Solar da Ponte**, Anna Maria and John Parsons, renovated an 18th century manor to create this traditional inn. Anna, a specialist in baroque art, has beautifully decorated the 18 rooms with colonial furniture to match the town's historic atmosphere.

Additional information begins on page 462.

The well-preserved colonial houses in Tiradentes: the city attracts cultural tourism

be found on every corner. Most articles are sold in the Tiradentes shops, but it's worth visiting the village to watch craftsmen work and buy directly from them. The most interesting studio is **Oficina de Agosto**, run by Antonio Carlos Bech, aka Toti, who owns a shop with the same name in his native city of São Paulo. He trains youth to become professional craftsmen, provided that they attend school. Many of his former students have opened their own studios. The **Igreja Nossa Senhora da Penha de França**, from 1737, is located in the village.

NEARBY TOWNS (PRADOS AND RESENDE COSTA)

The large Julião family has become a tourist attraction in **Prados**, near Tiradentes. The nine brothers and their children are spread throughout the town sculpting wooden lions, capuchin monkeys, and turtles. To find them, go to the main square and ask one of the loitering boys to guide you through the village. The

region's handicraft tradition is maintained in neighboring **Resende Costa**, where the women support the village with their woven handicrafts. This is an excellent opportunity to buy rugs, bedspreads, decorator blankets, tablecloths, and a myriad of colorful pieces available in the shops on the main street leading into the town.

STEAM LOCOMOTIVE TOUR TO SÃO JOÃO DEL REI

This charming train, called "*Maria Fumaça*", was inaugurated by Dom Pedro II in 1881, and takes passengers to nearby São João Del Rei. The 12-kilometer (7.5-mi.) ride takes 35 minutes. The winding route passes through areas of Atlantic Rainforest in the **São José** mountains, an environmental preservation area since 1990. Along the route you can also see stretches of the **Mortes** river. In April and May the landscape is spotted with small and colorful wildflowers.
Estação Ferroviária (Train Station). Fri-Sun, and holidays, departs 1pm and 5pm.

São João Del Rei

The bells of the town's thirteen churches ring differently to announce weddings, funerals and masses. The sound echoes between the colonial buildings and the cobblestone streets. From the Cristo Redentor monument, on Alto da Bela Vista, you can look down on this town, which in 1709 was the setting for a battle between fighters from the state of São Paulo and the Portuguese.

Churches

Don't miss the **Catedral Nossa Senhora do Pilar** from 1721, the only one with gilded carvings on the altars (*Rua Getúlio Vargas, tel. 31/3371-2568*), and the octagonal towers of the **Igreja Nossa Senhora do Carmo** (*Largo do Carmo, tel. 32/3371-7996*), built in 1733. The igreja **Nossa Senhora do Rosário**, on the Largo do Rosário, built in 1719, is one of the oldest. The most important church is the **Igreja São Francisco de Assis** (*Praça Frei Orlando*). Aleijadinho designed and created the carvings on the ornamental façade in 1774. Notice the effect of the golden highlights on the white background in the main chapel and the Baccarat crystal chandelier in the shape of the Portuguese Crown. On the arch of the main door look for the face of Jesus formed by angels' heads. There are no fixed visiting hours, so it's best to call ahead.

The Capital of *Rocambole*

Every small shop in Lagoa Dourada, on BR-383 between Belo Horizonte and São João Del Rei, claims to make the most authentic and best *rocambole* of Minas Gerais. See for yourself and try one, two, or as many as you can of this roll cake filled with guava jam, chocolate or caramel.

Museu Ferroviário

The first locomotive with a luxury cabin, eleven trains with Baldwin steam engines and freight cars can be seen in this railway museum, which also features a collection of mechanical parts and photos.
Avenida Hermílio Alves, 366, Centro, tel. (32) 3371-8485. Tue-Sun, 9am-11am and 1pm-5pm.

Museu do Estanho (Tin Museum)

John Somers is a large producer of the artifacts seen here and has the most traditional factory in São João Del Rei, where he moved in the 1960's. The museum has objects from all over Brazil and Europe. The collection features objects taken from two ships which sank off the Brazilian coast in 1648 and 1668.
Avenida Leite de Castro, 1150, Fábricas, tel. (32) 3371-8000. Mon-Fri, 9am-6pm. Sun, 9am-4pm.

Igreja São Francisco de Assis

DIAMANTINA

In the 18th century Diamantina was one of the final destinations of the *bandeirantes*, the explorers who braved the Brazilian interior, on the route created by the Portuguese Crown for diamond mining. Diamantina is now a World Heritage Site and is the best preserved and most tranquil historical towns of Minas, although it is not as rich as Ouro Preto. It is at the edge of the *sertão*, the semi-arid backlands of the Northeast, 100 kilometers (62 mi.) away from the São Francisco and Jequitinhonha river valleys. The town is on an irregular plateau, nestled at the edge of the Espinhaço mountains. The top of Diamantina reveals **Itambé** peak, at 2,002 meters (6,568 feet).

ORIGINAL STREETS AND MUSIC
Some streets of the historic center still have the original rough stone pavement, and cars do not exceed 30 km/hr (18 mi./hr). For proof, visit the alley **Beco do Mota**, immortalized in a song by Milton Nascimento. Nearby, on Rua da Quitanda, musicians play on the balconies and from the windows of the houses. This event, called *Vesperata*, takes place two Saturdays per month, from March to October. Former President Juscelino Kubitschek, born in Diamantina, was a big fan of these serenades. To honor him, the town organizes a Serenade Day, on September 12th, his birthday. "A serenade in Diamantina is more beautiful than an evening with minstrels in Naples," he used to say.

NOSSA SENHORA DO CARMO AND OTHER RELIGIOUS BUILDINGS
The most opulent church in town is the Igreja Nossa Senhora do Carmo (*Rua do Carmo, Centro, Tue-Sat, 9am-noon and 2pm-6pm*), which houses a 600-pipe organ adorned with gold. It is said that the steeple was placed at the back of the church because the slave Chica da Silva, who always got her way after she became the mistress of João Fernandes de Oliveira, a contractor to the Portuguese Crown, disliked the chime of bells. Visit also the **Igreja Nossa Senhora do**

Igreja Nossa Senhora do Carmo: the tower was built at the back of the church

Rosário (*Largo do Rosário, Tue-Sat, 9am-noon and 2pm-6pm; Sun, 9am-noon*), whose walls are inclined. Beyond the town center awaits the neo-gothic **Basílica do Sagrado Coração de Jesus**, erected at the end of the 19th century, with its French stain glass windows (*Praça do Sagrado Coração de Jesus*). The **Catedral Metropolitana**, in the Praça da Matriz, was built in the 1930's but looks, unlike the rest of the town, as if it's from a much early period.

PASSADIÇO DA GLÓRIA

This walkway links two buildings from the 18th and 19th centuries. The first was the home of Diamantina's first bishop, João Antonio dos Santos; the other belonged to the Nossa Senhora das Dores Catholic School. The suspended and covered walkway that connects the two buildings was reportedly built by the nuns in 1876 to ensure the privacy of their pupils. An exhibit of stones is located there.
Rua da Glória, 298, Centro, tel. (38) 3531-1394. Tue-Sun, 1pm-6pm.

SLAVES' ROUTE

Passing through white quartz rocks and the savannah, the route between the Tijuco and Medanha villages was traveled in the 18th century by slaves carrying out bags of diamonds and bringing in supplies. Part of this route has been restored and is accessible to tourists. It's close to **Cruzeiro**, an area with a view of Diamantina and the sunset.

SÃO GONÇALO DO RIO DAS PEDRAS AND MILHO VERDE

Two small villages 40 kilometers (25 mi.) south of Diamantina are worth visiting. **São Gonçalo do Rio das Pedras**, a former mining village with

The charming colonial houses of Diamantina

less than three thousand inhabitants, is perched on a rocky bluff, surrounded by mountains and waterfalls. **Milho Verde** is a hippie community, ideal for hiking and bathing under waterfalls. Caution: the dirt road is in very bad shape. Be careful not to get stuck in the mud on rainy days or bogged down in the sand in the dry season.

OUR RECOMMENDATION

🍽 In the **O Garimpeiro** restaurant we recommend the *xinxim da Chica* (chicken, okra, onions and seasonings), *ora-pro-nóbis* (spinach-like leaves) with steak, *feijão tropeiro* (beans cooked with olive oil, garlic, onion, parsley and chives, thickened with manioc flour), and fern sprouts with pork loin (*Avenida da Saudade, 265, tel. 38/3531-1044*). **Raimundo Sem Braço** is in a wood hut, but the homemade food and barbecue are extraordinary (*Rua José Anacleto Alves, 18, BR-367, exit to Belo Horizonte, tel. 38/3531-2284*).

🛏 Designed by Oscar Niemeyer, the **Hotel Tijuco** still has the same atmosphere of the 1950's and contrasts beautifully with the surrounding colonial houses. The view of the town from the rooms' balconies is unforgettable.

Additional information begins on page 462.

ESTRADA REAL

MG
GO
BA
ES
SP
RJ

1 cm = 84 km
1 inch = 133 mi.

Diamantina

MINAS GERAIS

Belo Horizonte

Mariana
Ouro Preto

Congonhas

Prados
Tiradentes
São João Del Rei

Diamond Route
Old Route
New Route

Juiz de Fora

RIO DE JANEIRO

Petrópolis

SÃO PAULO
Paraty

Rio de Janeiro

ATLANTIC OCEAN

Take the **Estrada Real** (Royal Trail) and travel three hundred years back in time. Start in Paraty, Rio de Janeiro or Rio's historic center and head towards Ouro Preto, continuing on to Diamantina. The road was used to transport gold, and crosses mountains, broad plateaus, meadows, creeks and the *cerrado*. When carrying the Portuguese flag to the far corners of Brazil in the 17th century, the "Old Route" was formed by connecting Paraty to the gold mines of Minas. To return, the expeditions departed from Ouro Preto, crossed the Mantiqueira mountains and reached a ravine which led down to Paraty. From there they continued to Rio, then shipped their load to Portugal. The trip took three months. It worked this way until Garcia Rodrigues, companion of the famous *bandeirante* (explorer) Fernão Dias Paes, devised

a shorter route directly to Rio de Janeiro. In 1698 he obtained a permit from the Portuguese Crown to build the "New Route," and began the construction in the beginning of the 18th century. In a little while the Estrada Real became the only route for official gold shipments, and the ten-day trip required the Crown's authorization. At present the **Instituto Estrada Real** (the Royal Road Institute), through a partnership with the state government, is reconstructing the entire route. The Old and New Routes together total 1,400 kilometers (870 mi.) and cross 177 cities starting from the São Paulo coast or the old center of Rio de Janeiro, and reveal a wealth of colonial and baroque architecture and natural beauty. From the heart of Minas Gerais, the Old Route heads from Diamantina to Ouro Preto, where it splits in two directions. One passes through São João Del Rei and Tiradentes, crosses the esoteric São Tomé das Letras, and then Caxambu and São Lourenço in the "Medicinal Waters Circuit," across the Paraíba Valley, through the cities of Guaratinguetá and Cunha, then down to the port of Paraty. The other crosses Barbacena, Juiz de Fora, Itaipava and Petrópolis and ends in Rio de Janeiro. These routes allow tourists to discover the purest Minas Gerais, as embodied in the towns built during the gold rush, and the *sertão* that was immortalized in the writings of Guimarães Rosa. Visit www.estradareal.org.br to schedule your visit.

DESTINATION
VITÓRIA

The coast of the state of Espírito Santo offers a wide variety of attractions. Urban beaches with a full range of leisure activities await in Vitória and Vila Velha, semi-deserted beaches nestle among sand dunes in Itaúnas, and small bays in Guarapari feature black sands that are famed for their medicinal properties. Further inland, in the tranquility of the mountains only 50 kilometers from Vitória, there are opportunities for adventure sports in the waterfalls and rapids, quality hotels, the chance to visit the awesome Pedra Azul, and some of the most thrilling whitewater rafting in Brazil. The state also has reserves of the Atlantic Rainforest and contains a key destination for religious pilgrims, in the municipality of Anchieta.

DESTINATION HIGHLIGHTS

VITÓRIA
Historic Center
The Beaches

VILA VELHA (3 km/1.8 mi.)

SERRA CAPIXABA
(50 km/31 mi.)
Domingos Martins

GUARAPARI (58 km/36 mi.)
Anchieta

ITAÚNAS (270 km/168 mi.)

All distances are from Vitória

View from Vitória Bay of the Terceira Bridge that links Vitória to Vila Velha

VITÓRIA

Originally 34 islands, with the one known as Vitória being the largest, the city has coalesced as landfills and bridges have linked the archipelago. In the city center, some buildings have been designated heritage sites and opened to visitors. The mangroves that ring the island complete the natural setting and can be admired via a boat tour. Vitória is also a haven for water sports – especially ocean fishing – and the city holds the world record for blue marlin sport fishing. Despite its long coast, proximity to the ports sometimes makes its beaches unfit for swimming. Visitors often get disoriented by the many bridges along the coast and in the city center, and getting around requires a car or taxi.

Local Tour Operator: Fomatur, tel. (27) 3200-3155; Vitória Receptive, tel. (27) 3325-3637.

HISTORIC CENTER

The walking tour starts in front of the **Vitória port** (*Avenida Jerônimo Monteiro*), next to **Palácio Anchieta**, where one can see the **Escadaria Bárbara Lindemberg** (1912) in front of the Palace. This stairway, as well as many others in the city, links the Cidade Baixa (Lower City) to Cidade Alta (Upper City). Built by the Jesuits in the 16th century, the palace is presently the seat of the State Government. Behind it is the tomb of **Anchieta**, which is open to visitors (*tel. 27/321-350, Tue-Sun, noon-5pm*). Walk straight ahead along Ruas Comandante Duarte or São Gonçalo to reach **Igreja de São Gonçalo** (built between 1707 and 1715). Then continue along Rua Carneiro Araújo to the 16th-century **Capela de Santa Luzia**, from where you can see part of Vitória bay. Leading away from the Chapel is Rua José Marcelino, with its beautiful pair of recently restored, two-story houses. These homes are the last architectural vestiges of the 19th century. The one on the right has trellised balconies with Moorish influences, and the one on the left has a mansard roof. On this same street is the **catedral Metropolitana**

(1920-70), a neo-Gothic cathedral with stately windows. After walking around the square in front of the cathedral, go down the **São Diogo** stairway – the oldest in the city, dating back to the 18th century – and walk towards **Teatro Carlos Gomes** (1927). Inspired by the Scala from Milan, it is located in **Praça Costa Pereira**, at the center of the city.

THE BEACHES

The city's best beaches are on the islands **Frade** and **Boi**. On Frade island, the best beach is **Castanheiras**, which is ideal for diving. On Boi island, the small **Direita** and **Esquerda** (literally, Right and Left beaches) offer clear water and command a view of Vila Velha. In Vitória itself, the beaches have white soft sand and are dotted with kiosks, sports areas and museums. From north to south, the first beach is **Camburi**, which is busy night and day and has dozens of kiosks offering snacks and live music. **Canto** is ideal for water sports, thanks to the presence of the Yacht Club. Next to it, there is the **Praça dos Namorados** (Sweethearts square), where a crafts market takes place every weekend, and the **Praça da Ciência**, a sort of open-air museum (*tel. 27/3345-0882. Tue-Sun, 9am-6pm*). **Curva da Jurema** beach, on **Suá** Bay, is ideal for jet-skiing and sailing. At night, the bay is the gathering point for young people, with shows and events during the summer.

PRAIA DE MANGUINHOS

The **Manguinhos** beach in Jacaraípe, 30 kilometers (18.6 mi.) from Vitória (on the Rodovia do Sol – is a superb one-day tour. At lunch, enjoy the seafood dishes at the **Estação Primeira da Manguinhos**. The service is slow, but it is worth waiting (*Avenida Atapuã, corner of Piaquira, tel. 27/3243-2687*). In the afternoon, go to **Casa de Pedra** (*Rua Nossa Senhora de Lourdes, on the way to Nova Almeida, daily, 8am-6pm*), a gallery and studio where the artist Neusso Farias displays sculpture and furniture. Twelve kilometers ahead is Nova Almeida, home to the **Igreja Seiscentista dos Reis Magos** and the oil painting *Adoration of the Three Wise Men*, one of Brazil's oldest pieces of religious art (*Praça dos Reis Magos, tel. 27/3253-1842. Wed-Mon, 9am-6pm*).

FISHING AND WATER SPORTS

The coast between Vitória and Guarapari is one of the three best places in the world to fish for billfish like blue marlin from October to March and white marlin in November. (The other points are Canavieiras, in Bahia, and the coast of Guatemala.) In January and February, Vitória hosts the International Ocean Fishing Championship.

Other water sports events are the Regatta Eldorado Brasilis, one of the largest in the world, held during the last two weeks of January, and the Vitória Nautishow, a boat and

---

RUA DAS PANELEIRAS

To see the production of pots in which traditional Espírito Santo (called *capixaba*) stews are served, visit the Associação das Paneleiras de Goiabeiras (*Rua das Paneleiras, 55, Goiabeiras, tel. 27/3327-0519*). In a shed at the edge of a mangrove, the clay is prepared and shaped into pots that will be baked on the embers of an open fire. The black color comes from tannins extracted from the mangrove trees.

---

equipment show. Tour operators will arrange boats, crew and equipment.
Tour Operator: Dolphin Pesca Oceânica, tel. (27) 3345-9455; Iate Clube do Espírito Santo, tel. (27) 3225-0422.

MANGROVE ROUTE

A beautiful schooner tour departs from **Cais do Hidroavião** (*Avenida Dario Lourenço de Souza, Santo Antônio*). From there, the boat sails northwest, passing along an unspoiled environment, protected by **Estação Ecológica Ilha do Lameirão**, a marine fauna and flora nursery. During a two-hour trip, tourists can visit the 892 hectares (2,204 acres) of one of the largest urban mangroves in the world. The tour will also visit ilhas **da Pólvora, do Cal** and **das Caieiras**, the **Santo Antônio** district and its sanctuary, the mouth of the Jucu and Santa Maria rivers, as well as the Canal dos Escravos.
Tour Operator: Agência Náutica Cores do Mar, tel. (27) 3222-3810. Departures daily, 10am and 3pm (Dec. to Feb.); Fri-Sun (March to Nov.), or book in advance.

The Ponta da Fruta, in Vila Velha: a favorite family beach with calm waters

Convento da Penha, built over rocks: pilgrimages here started in the 16th century

VILA VELHA

Vila Velha's historic buildings, like the **Convento da Penha**, are few but significant. There are environmental protection areas, but they have little infrastructure for tourists. In terms of beaches, however, Vila Velha boasts greater variety than Vitória: **Costa** and **Itapuã**, within the city, are very crowded during the summer; **Barra do Jucu** and **Ponta da Fruta** beaches, to the south, are long and quiet.

CONVENTO DA PENHA AND SURROUNDINGS

Perched atop a 154 meter (505 foot) hill, the convent commands a beautiful view of Vitória bay and Terceira Ponte. Founded in 1558, the convent has exquisite wood carvings and valuable works like the 16th century *Nossa Senhora das Alegrias,* one of the oldest paintings in the Americas. It also contains four paintings by Benedito Calixto and a 1569 sculpture of the saint in the main altar (*entrance on Rua Vasco Coutinho, tel. 27/3329-0420. Daily, 5:30am-4:45pm*). To get there, leave your car in the parking lot and climb the stone stairway.

On the foot of the convent hill, at **Parque da Prainha**, stroll along the lane lined by imperial palms and admire **Igreja Nossa Senhora do Rosário**. The church, founded in 1551, is the oldest in the state and opens only during services (*Rua Almirante Tamandaré, tel. 27/3239-3113. Sun, 8am and 5:30pm, first Friday of the month, 7pm*). Also visit the **Forte de São Francisco Xavier**, originally built by the local administrator of the *capitania* in the 16th century (*Parque da Prainha, Mon-Fri, 9am-noon and 2-5pm; Sat and Sun, 9am-noon*).

LINHARES ECOLOGICAL RESERVE

A walk in the **Reserva Natural da Vale do Rio Doce** in Linhares, 137 kilometers (85 mi.) north of Vitória, is a plunge into the Atlantic Rainforest. Ninety percent of the 22,000 hectares (54,363 acres) forest area is untouched, and it houses 43 reptile species, 102 mammal species, 1,500 butterfly species and 400 bird species. (Around 5 percent of all bird species on the planet live here.) The visit can take half a day or several days, and the reserve maintains a hotel room for multiple-day visitors. Highlights are the scientific collections, including an herbarium, a wood library and an area to study insects, but only part of these collections is open to the public (*BR-101, km 120, Linhares, tel. 27/3371-9797. Tue-Sun, 7:30am-4pm. Reservation required*).

Serra Capixaba

Parque da Pedra Azul: cozy inns are scattered along the foot of the rocky wall

Domingos Martins

Relax in cozy inns and colonial coffeehouses, admire the landscape or head off for adventure along forest trails in the Serra Capixaba. In the mountain range of Espírito Santo, which is covered by the Atlantic Rainforest, temperatures can drop to 0°C (32°F) in winter. Tours begin in the city of Domingos Martins and its Italian-influenced districts of **Paraju** and **Aracê**, just 50 kilometers (31 mi.) from Vitória and reachable via BR-262. In the city, see the 1866 Lutheran church and walk along streets filled with restaurants and shops. Book a visit to the **Reserva Kautsky**, which hosts 100,000 orchid species (*tel. 27/3268-1209. Mon-Fri, 7-10am and 2-5pm*).

Parque da Pedra Azul
The trails are the main attractions of this Aracê district park, at km 89 of highway BR-262. One goes to the foot of Pedra Azul, which affords a vertiginous view of the 500-meter (1,640 foot) rocky massif, which looks greenish-blue because of lichens. The more difficult trail leads to rock pools. *Highway BR-262, km 89, Aracê, tel. (27) 3248-1156. Schedule tours in advance.*

Adventure in the Mountains
Options for canyoning and rappelling include the **Galo waterfall** (70 meters, 229 feet), the railway track (50 meters, 164 feet) and the **Biriricas rock** (40 meters, 131 feet). Guests can also go whitewater rafting on the **Jucu** river, cross an old coffee plantation at the **Reserva Breemnkamp**, climb the **Campinho rock** with a view of Vitória and Vila Velha and walk along **Capela**, a dirt road surrounded by orchids in the **Reserva Kautsky**. *Tour Operator: Emoções Radicais, tel. (27) 3268-2165.*

GUARAPARI

Driving along Rodovia do Sol, visitors will reach Guarapari (58 kilometers 36 mi. from Vitória) and Anchieta (89 kilometers, 55 mi. from Vitória), the two trendiest sea resorts in the south of the state, with good restaurants, hotels and tours. Guarapari has areas for scuba diving and well-protected nature areas in the **Parque Estadual Paulo César Vinha**. Although a wall of buildings lines the shore, the green sea and golden sands of the **Areia Preta**, **Castanheiras**, **Namorados** and up to **Fonte** are a beautiful sight. These beaches, together with **Morro**, provide an active social life, with many shows and competitions. At night, the hot spot is **Meaípe**. Many beaches north of the city center escaped the skyscrapers and noise, including **Três Praias** and **Setibas** beaches: **Setiba**, **Setiba Pina** and **Setibão**. To the south, there are peaceful **Peracanga**, **Bacutia** and **Enseada dos Padres** beaches, surrounded by private low-rise condominiums. A schooner tour provides a view of the entire Guarapari coast.

Tour Operator: Monte Santo, tel. (27) 3261-3356.

DIVING IN GUARAPARI

You can go scuba diving alone in **Pacotes**, **Escalvada** and **Rasas** beaches as well as in the **Três Ilhas** archipelago, amidst submerged ledges and the century old shipwreck Beluccia. The Croatian freighter Victory 8B is also worth exploring. The greatest visibility is from the second week of January to the end of March.

Tour Operator: Acquasub, tel. (27) 3325-0036.

PARQUE PAULO CÉSAR VINHA

A two-kilometer (1.2-mi.) trail leads to **Setiba** beach. During the walk, hikers will see lagoons and dunes, lizards and butterflies. A warning: the beach has powerful breakers. Another 800 meters (2,624 feet) ahead is **Lagoa de Caraís**, a lagoon with dark but very clean waters. The freezing temperature of the water and the awe-inspiring view are worth the walk.

Rodovia do Sol, km 38, Setiba, tel. (27) 3367-0002. Daily, 8:30am-4:30pm.

Vitória is one of the three best places in the world to find billfish, like the blue marlin

ANCHIETA

The **Ubu** and **Parati** beaches north of town are well preserved and receive very few visitors. The center and south beaches are more built-up and crowded in the summer, especially Iriri, 5 kilometers from the city center. Next to the shore, there is a beautiful and well preserved sandbank area, as well as a mangrove area and extensive, beautiful lagoons along the Rodovia do Sol and **Beneventes** river. Boat tours sailing upstream are not frequent (*arrange the tour at the fishing village, tel. 28/3536-1554/1044*). A tip: bring insect repellent.

SANCTUARY AND MUSEUM

The Santuário and Museu de Anchieta is the region's highlight. The former Jesuit building from the 16th century, which will be of great interest to architecture and history buffs, contains a collection of religious and personal items of the Jesuit José de Anchieta, including a piece of his tibia. Recent archeological excavations, part of the restoration of the building, have revealed its many uses over the years. *Praça da Matriz, tel. (28) 3536-1103. Daily, 9am-5pm.*

FOLLOWING THE STEPS OF THE JESUIT

Since 1999, during four days in June – the month of the death of Anchieta, whom Pope John Paul II beatified in 1980 – hundreds of people make a 100–kilometer (62–mi.) pilgrimage following the path of the Jesuit's 16th-century voyage. Warm up to the pilgrimage of Anchieta in the summer, with an 18-kilometer (11–mi.) walk to Aquecimento dos Passos de Anchieta between **Convento da Penha** and **Barra do Jucu**, in Vila Velha.
Tour Operator: Associação Brasileira dos Amigos dos Passos de Anchieta, tel. (27) 3227-2661/9928-4684.

Anchieta sanctuary, where the Jesuit priest spent his last days

In the north of Espírito Santo, an extraordinary setting: sky, dunes and vegetation

ITAÚNAS

Itaúnas, 270 kilometers (168 mi.) north of Vitória, is an unassuming place with sand streets, modest houses, inns and restaurants. Reaching the village requires a 23-kilometer dirt road off ES-421, and cars might get stuck in heavy rains. And don't forget to fuel up before heading in, because Itaúnas has no gas station. But difficulties are forgotten as soon as visitors meet the local inhabitants. There are many folklore festivities (mainly during January) and hikes in **Parque Estadual de Itaúnas**, including the **Itaúnas** and **Riacho Doce** beaches surrounded by dunes. At night, the suggestion is *forró (music and dancing)*. Try to see the opening of nests of sea turtles (January through March), monitored by Projeto Tamar (*tel. 27/3762-5196/3761-1267*). If luck holds, tourists will be able to see turtles hatching at night and admire the dense clusters of stars in the sky. To complete the experience, watch dawn break over the dunes – another spectacular show.

PARQUE ESTADUAL DE ITAÚNAS
After crossing the bridge over the Itaúnas river at the end of the village, visitors arrive in Itaúnas State Park, almost 3,700 hectares (9,142 acres) of dunes, beaches, mangroves, sandbanks, Atlantic Rainforest, river and marsh. But be physically prepared to visit it all, and don't miss the horseback tour along Itaúnas beach, crossing the dunes and sandbank trails to the deserted **Riacho Doce** beach, near the border with Bahia. Enjoy the sunset on the tranquil **Itaúnas river** or its tributary **Angelim** in a canoe or kayak tour. The trails show the beauty of the local flora and the ruins of the former village of Itaúnas, buried in the dunes in the 1970's. A dune buggy tour will lead to a labyrinth of trees (but beware, signage is poor) until the beautiful bluffs at **Costa Dourada** beach in the state of Bahia. *Tour Operator: Casinha de Aventuras, tel. (27) 3762-5081.*

NORTHEAST

The northeast region of Brazil is made up of the states of Bahia, Paraíba, Sergipe, Alagoas, Rio Grande do Norte, Pernambuco, Ceará, Piauí and Maranhão. The map below highlights suggested departure points for recommended itineraries. Federal highways connect the coastal capital cities and traverse spectacular landscapes where sophisticated hotels and restaurants are intermingled with simple rustic inns and wilderness areas. In the interior of Bahia, Lençóis is the destination for discovering the Chapada Diamantina, whose historic cities are surrounded by waterfalls, caves and canyons. The northeast, however, has much more to offer than beautiful scenery. The arid and storied inland region, called the *sertão*, contains a vibrant, unique and varied culture with great popular festivals, extraordinary arts and crafts, remarkable architecture and a rich culinary heritage. This region is the cradle of much of Brazil's dynamic cultural heritage.

DESTINATION
SALVADOR

A fro-Brazilians account for the majority of the population and proudly maintain their traditions and religious rites. Accompanied by the drums of the bands Olodum and Timbalada, the capital of Bahia, with approximately 2.5 millions residents, is the center of Afro-Brazilian culture and the site of Brazil's largest street carnival. Salvador was founded in 1549, and was Brazil's first federal capital city. The hundreds of baroque churches fascinate architects and visitors of all faiths. Many foreigners come to study the city, only to fall in love with it and convert their subject into a permanent home. The French anthropologist and photographer Pierre Verger researched the rich Afro-Brazilian culture in depth and portrayed it in fantastic photographs. New inns, hotels and first class restaurants bring professionalism to a region whose tourist services have traditionally been better known for their friendly informality than for efficiency. Use Salvador as a base to explore the attractions of the southern coast, such as Morro de São Paulo, and the beaches to the north, like Praia do Forte and Mangue Seco. The rich colonial city of São Cristóvão is north in the state of Sergipe.

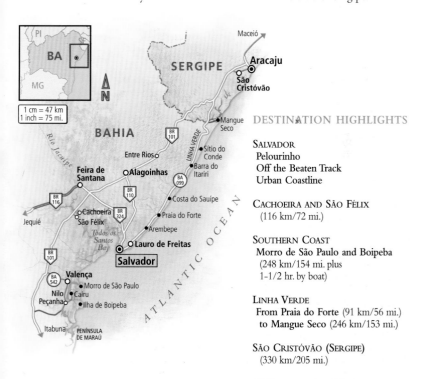

DESTINATION HIGHLIGHTS

SALVADOR
Pelourinho
Off the Beaten Track
Urban Coastline

CACHOEIRA AND SÃO FÉLIX
(116 km/72 mi.)

SOUTHERN COAST
Morro de São Paulo and Boipeba
(248 km/154 mi. plus
1-1/2 hr. by boat)

LINHA VERDE
From Praia do Forte (91 km/56 mi.)
to Mangue Seco (246 km/153 mi.)

SÃO CRISTÓVÃO (SERGIPE)
(330 km/205 mi.)

All distances are from Salvador

SALVADOR

PELOURINHO

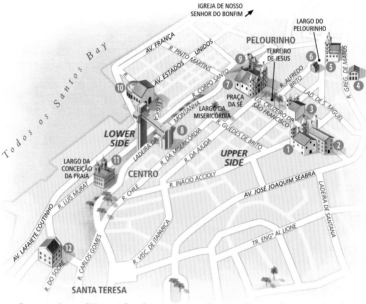

CIDADE ALTA (UPPER SIDE)

1 - Convento and Igreja de São Francisco
2 - Ordem Terceira de São Francisco
3 - Ordem Terceira de São Domingos de Gusmão
4 - Museu Abelardo Rodrigues
5 - Igreja Nossa Senhora do Rosário dos Pretos
6 - Fundação Casa de Jorge Amado
7 - Catedral Basílica

CIDADE BAIXA (LOWER SIDE)

8 - Elevador Lacerda
9 - Plano Inclinado Gonçalves
10 - Mercado Modelo
11 - Igreja Nossa Senhora da Conceição da Praia
12 - Museu de Arte Sacra da Bahia

Part of Brazil's history lies in the uneven stone streets and multicolored houses located in the Historical Center of **Cidade Alta** (Upper Side). Start your excursion here and continue to **Cidade Baixa** (Lower Side), via the **Elevador Lacerda** and the **Plano Inclinado Gonçalves**. Pelourinho's importance stems from the fact that it is a Portuguese urban landscape in the tropics. It is made up of more than a thousand 16th to 19th century mansions and was declared a World Heritage Site by UNESCO in 1985. Three hundred years ago it was the home of sugar barons, wealthy traders and government authorities. At the end of the 19th century, the area entered a period of decline and the buildings were transformed into tenements and shelters for prostitutes and criminals. A restoration program was started in 1992, and although the area is still not completely safe – keep a close eye on purses, wallets, and cameras – it has become one of the most popular tourist attractions in the country. One absent relic of its past is the *pelourinho* (pillory), the wooden post where slaves and criminals were tied and publicly whipped.

① CONVENTO AND IGREJA DE SÃO FRANCISCO

The Igreja de São Francisco is the most lavishly decorated church in Salvador, one of the best examples of the Portuguese baroque in the world and one of the most beautiful Franciscan temples in the Americas. Reportedly 800 kilograms (1764 lb.) of gold leaf lines the altar, the blue ceramic tiles that decorate the convent and the church, and the black rosewood carvings. The convent's courtyard has 37 panels inspired by the paintings of the Flamenco painter, Otto van Veen, and bears Latin inscriptions from the works of the poet Horatio. The interior of the church features ceramic tile art that portrays scenes of Francisco de Assisi's life created by the Portuguese ceramic tile artist Bartolomeu de Jesus.

Largo Cruzeiro de São Francisco, tel. (71) 322-6430. Mon-Sat, 8am-5:30pm; Sun, 8am-noon and 3pm-4:30pm.

② ORDEM TERCEIRA DE SÃO FRANCISCO

Even though the lighting is poor and the badly cracked building is in desperate need of a restoration, this church's magnificent façade alone is worth the visit. The carved limestone church features sandstone cornerstones and is Brazil's only example of the Spanish American plateresque baroque style with rich silver decorations. The church also contains one of the largest ceramic tile collections outside Portugal, and a good portion of them portrays scenes of life and landscapes that were destroyed by the Lisbon earthquake of the 1755. One panel, located in the cloister, portrays José de Portugal and Maria Ana de Bourbon's wedding procession.

Rua Inácio Accioly, Centro Histórico, tel. (71) 321-6968. Mon-Sun, 8am-5pm.

③ ORDEM TERCEIRA DE SÃO DOMINGOS DE GUSMÃO

The ceiling of this damp and poorly maintained church reveals its main

Igrejas Nossa Senhora do Rosário dos Pretos (left) and Santíssimo Sacramento rise above rows of houses

Ceramic tiles in the courtyard contrast with the austere façade of the Convento de São Francisco

attraction, a baroque trompe l'oeil painting created in 1781 by José Joaquim da Rocha, who also left works in the Nossa Senhora da Conceição da Praia and Nossa Senhora do Rosário dos Pretos churches. The scene here was painted on the wooden ceiling of the nave and is an allegory of Saint Domingos entering heaven. The artist also created panels for the great hall. The church's interior is finished with neoclassical carvings and the façade is rococo style.
Terreiro de Jesus, Centro Histórico, tel. (71) 242-4185. Mon-Fri, 8am-noon and 2pm-6pm; Sun, 8:30am-10am.

④ MUSEU ABELARDO RODRIGUES
This sacred art collection of Abelardo Rodrigues, a native of the state of Pernambuco and a cousin of the playwright Nelson Rodrigues, is one of the largest in Brazil. There are more than 800 works in wood, soapstone and clay originating from Europe, the Far East and South America. The pieces are on display in the Solar do Ferrão, a 17th century building that at one time was a Jesuit Seminary.
Rua Gregório de Matos, 45, Centro Histórico, tel. (71) 321-6155, ext. 296. Tue-Sat, 1pm-6pm.

⑤ IGREJA NOSSA SENHORA DO ROSÁRIO DOS PRETOS
Passers-by on Tuesday evenings may think that the priest lent out the church for an Olodum concert. Don't be fooled, it's just a Bahian syncretic mass. Every Tuesday at 6pm, the parishioners of the Nossa Senhora do Rosário dos Pretos pray to the sound of conga drums, tambourins and bells while singing African hymns. The church was built by slaves in their spare time, which is why it took almost 100 years. One of the first Negro brotherhoods in Brazil also began here.
Largo do Pelourinho, Centro Histórico, tel. (71) 241-5781. Mon-Sat, 9am-8pm; Sun, 9am-2pm.

⑥ FUNDAÇÃO CASA DE JORGE AMADO
From the novel *O País do Carnaval* to *Gabriela Cravo e Canela, Dona Flor e Seus Dois Maridos* and *Capitães de Areia*, and finally *O Milagre dos Pássaros*, this house bears witness to more than seventy years of the literary life of Jorge Amado, and holds the history of the more than thirty books that he wrote, now translated into 49 different languages. The house contains photographs, documents, videos

and objects related to the life of one of Brazil's greatest authors, who died in 2001 at the age of 88.

Largo do Pelourinho, Centro Histórico, tel. (71) 321-0122. Mon-Sat 9am-6pm.

❼ CATEDRAL BASÍLICA

The first chapel on this site was built in 1604. The cathedral that stands today, built between 1657 and 1672, is actually the fourth church and is the last remaining portion of the Colégio de Jesus complex, where Father Antonio Vieira delivered his sermons and the poet Gregório de Matos studied. The façade is finished with Portuguese limestone and is a combination of the traditional Portuguese twin tower style and the new Jesuit volute style façade with spiral decorations. Highlights of the interior include the sacristy, the different eras of altar pieces, and the caisson ceiling in the nave decorated with geometric designs instead of the usual painted panels.

Terreiro de Jesus, Centro Histórico, tel. (71) 321-4573. Daily, 8:30am-11:30am and 1:30pm-5:30pm.

❽ ELEVADOR LACERDA AND
❾ PLANO INCLINADO GONÇALVES

In the 17th century the Jesuits created a transport link between Cidade Alta (Upper Side) and Cidade Baixa (Lower Side). Known as the "priests' hoist," it was used to transport construction materials to the Colégio dos Jesuítas (Jesuits' school). Today, this funicular railway makes about 200 trips each day providing transportation for more than 200,000 passengers a month. The Elevador Lacerda is 74 meters (243 feet) high and connects the Praça Visconde de Cairu, in the lower side, to the Praça Tomé de Souza, in the upper side. If you are in Pelourinho, take the funicular train down to the Lower Side, as it offers a better view, and start your tour of the Cidade Baixa. The elevator is named after the designer, engineer Antônio de Lacerda. The Plano Inclinado Gonçalves, named after a Jesuit priest who came to Brazil in the 16th century, connects Praça Ramos de Queiroz, located in Cidade Alta, to Rua Francisco Gonçalves in Cidade Baixa.

The sacristy of the Catedral Basílica where Vieira delivered his sermons and Gregório de Matos studied

Ordem Terceira de São Francisco

⑩ MERCADO MODELO

This market, one of Salvador's most popular tourist attractions, is the traditional center for sale of handicrafts and products from the region. It has seen better days and some of the stalls now sell mass-produced trinkets, but the site is worth visiting. The market is located in the former Customs Building at the base of the Elevador Lacerda and surrounded by the Todos os Santos Bay.

Praça Visconde de Cairu, 250, Comércio, tel. (71) 241-2893, Mon-Sat, 9am-7pm; Sun, 9am-2pm.

⑪ IGREJA NOSSA SENHORA DA CONCEIÇÃO DA PRAIA

Spacious and illuminated by natural light, this is believed to be Salvador's first church. Originally built in 1549 as a chapel, under the direction of Governor General Tomé de Sousa, it was rebuilt in 1736, using Portuguese limestone. Following the architecture of the city of Alentejo, Portugal, it features a monumental neoclassical façade. The original design included two nonsymmetrical towers.

Largo da Conceição da Praia, Comércio, tel. (71) 242-0545. Open Mon 7am-11:30am; Tue-Sun, 7am-11:30am and 3pm-5pm.

⑫ MUSEU DE ARTE SACRA DA BAHIA

This museum holds Brazil's main collections of religious art, and is located in the former Convento de Santa Tereza from the 17th century. The highlights of the collection are the ivory statues. The windows at the back of the convent offer a magnificent view of the Todos os Santos Bay along with a mango tree in the backyard that is loaded with fruit between November and March. Avoid the Ladeira da Preguiça because of the risk of being mugged – take the Largo Dois de Julho instead.

Rua do Sodré, 276, Centro Histórico, tel. (71) 243-6511, Mon-Fri, 11:30am-5:30pm.

IGREJA DE NOSSO SENHOR DO BONFIM

The Basílica Nosso Senhor do Bonfim stands out from the rest of the city's Catholic churches, and that's quite a feat. According to a song by Dorival Caymmi, there is one godly edifice here for each day of the year, and it's not much of an exaggeration. Nosso Senhor is a popular place of worship and a symbol of the syncretism of Bahia's culture. The sculpture of Nosso Senhor do Bonfim was brought to Bahia in 1745 from Portugal and was placed in the Capela da Penha. In 1754, the neoclassical style church was inaugurated, decorated with Portuguese ceramic tiles, mosaics and fresco painting, and the saint was transferred from the chapel with great pomp and ceremony. In Bahia's syncretic tradition, the Senhor do Bonfim is seen as Oxalá, the African god of creation. Inside the church, the *ex voto* room is proof of the church's place in the hearts of all social classes. Outside, people sell ribbons named after the saint; tie one to your wrist and make wishes come true (*Praça do Senhor do Bonfim*).

CAPOEIRA

"A Capoeira that is good doesn't fall
And if one day he falls, he falls gracefully
Capoeira sent me
To say that it has arrived
It has arrived to fight
The Berimbau confirmed it
There is going to be a fight for love
Sadness, comrade."

Berimbau,
Baden Powell and Vinicius de Moraes

Capoeira is a combination of *ginga* (a rhythmic dance step) and guile. It combines martial arts, dance and rituals from different places in Africa. The mixture was created in Brazil, probably in Salvador, in the 19th century during the slave era, although it was also developed in Recife and Rio de Janeiro. Made up of a series of movements, it is a skirmish accompanied by the sound of instruments and songs. The songs are litanies or tales of woe, in four verses that may be sermons or warnings. They can be prayers, thanks, challenges or homages. Regardless, the *berimbau* (a single string percussion instrument) is a faithful companion, and sometimes is accompanied by caxixi basket rattes, congo drums, tambourines and guiros. However, without a *berimbau* there is no capoeira, as it sets the rhythm of the fight through a series of different beats.

The German painter Rugendas, from the Langsdorff expedition, painted two canvases on the subject in his 1834 book *Viagem Pitoresca ao Brasil (Picturesque Trip to Brazil)*. He observed that "the Negros have another warrior game that is much more violent called *capuëra*, in which two opponents throw themselves at each other, trying to knock the other over with head butts to the chest." In other words, it was a very different and much more violent capoeira than this one. Since slaves created the capoeira in part to teach martial arts, authorities began to be repress it in 1814 and in 1890 completely forbade it by law.

It was only in 1930, under Getúlio Vargas, that it could be practiced freely once again. Schools emerged after slavery, which had driven capoeira underground. In Salvador, Maestro Bimba inaugurated his school in 1930; in 1941 Maestro Pastinha followed suit. They are the "grandfathers" of all practitioners of capoeira. Manoel dos Reis Machado, known as Bimba, was born in 1900. Initiated into capoeira at age twelve, he became a feared fighter which earned him the nickname "Three Blows", supposedly the quantity that any opponent could take. Bimba created his own personal style, the regional technique of Bahia, later known as *capoeira regional*. This style incorporated new moves and techniques that did not exist in the traditional capoeira, as practiced by Vicente Ferreira Pastinha, known as Maestro Pastinha. Maestro Bimba's school is run by his students (*Rua das Laranjeiras, 1, Pelourinho, tel. 71/3492-319. Daily*). Visitors may watch shows held at 6pm daily or take lessons.

Cidade Baixa: Elevador Lacerda (left) and Igreja de Nossa Senhora da Conceição da Praia

FEIRA DE SÃO JOAQUIM

Salvador has approximately forty street markets that are organized by the municipal government, but none of them compare to the Feira de São Joaquim in terms of originality and fun. Everything is sold here: live chickens, dried shrimp, fruit and vegetables, medicinal herbs, spices, dendê palm oil, and African religious articles. Seven thousand vendors hawk everything at bargain prices and the narrow alleys accumulate garbage and form a maze similar to African markets.

Avenida Oscar Pontes, Calçada, tel. (71) 314-6096. Mon-Sat, 6am-8pm; Sun, 6am-2pm.

FORTE DO MONTE SERRAT

This is one of the most remarkable military constructions in Brazil. Its symmetrical lines form an irregular polygon with large circular towers that protected the northern limits of the colonial city. Built between 1583 and 1587, the fort was restored between 1591 and 1602 to provide the city with more protection from attacks. Nevertheless, it was overthrown by the Dutch in 1624

SHOPPING OPTIONS

Instituto Mauá – Sells products ranging from clay pots and lace towels to handicrafts of wood and leather and musical instruments. Of special interest are the ceramics from Maragogipinho, a small village located 113 kilometers (70 mi.) from Salvador.
Porto da Barra, 2, Barra, tel. (71) 267-7400.

Coisas da Terra – Specializes in arts and crafts. The products are well-designed and sophisticated.
Rua Gregório de Matos, 19, Pelourinho, tel. (71) 322-9322.

Didara – Carries clothing inspired by Afro-Brazilian culture created by the designer Goya Lopes, as well as fabrics, pillows, dresses, bed spreads and other decorative items for the home.

Rua Gregório de Matos, 20, Centro Histórico, tel. (71) 321-9428.

Galeria Pierre Verger – Has a permanent photographic exhibition. Also sells books, T-shirts and posters derived from the works of the French anthropologist and photographer Pierre Verger, who made Bahia his home.
Rua da Misericórdia, 9, Centro Histórico, tel (71) 321-2341.

and in 1638. It offers a spectacular view of the mouth of the Todos os Santos Bay, with Salvador on one side and Itaparica on the other. *Rua Boa Viagem, Ponta de Humaitá, tel. (71) 313-7339. Daily, 9am-5pm.*

SOLAR DO UNHÃO

This is a remarkable architectural complex made up of warehouses; the beautiful Nossa Senhora de Monte Serrat chapel; an outdoor sculpture park; and the Museu de Arte Moderna, a mansion displaying works by Cândido Portinari, Tarsila do Amaral and Carybé, among others. Constructed in the 17th century, the complex was the home of Justice Pedro de Unhão Castelo Branco. Later it was transformed into a trade center. The warehouses and pier were constructed in the 19th century for the site to be used as a sugar warehouse, distillery and snuff factory. During the 1960's, the complex was restored by architect Lina Bo Bardi, who also designed the Museu de Arte de São Paulo (MASP). The chapel features a magnificent Brazilian baroque altar by Friar Agostinho da Piedade,

with images of the Patron Saint Monte Serrat and São Pedro Arrependido. The best time to visit is at sundown, for one of the most magnificent views of the sunset in the city, comparable only with the view from the lookout at the Ladeira da Misericórdia, right behind City Hall. *Avenida do Contorno, Contorno, tel. (71) 329-0660. Tue-Sun, 1pm-7pm.*

OUR RECOMMENDATION

Located on the shore, the **Yemanjá** restaurant serves Bahia's best delicacies. *Moquecas* (a fish or seafood based stew with tomato, onion, coconut milk and dendê oil) are the main attraction. A city tradition, it has been attracting tourists and businessmen for many years (*Avenida Otávio Mangabeira, 4655, tel. 71/461-9008*).

The **Paraiso Tropical** is far from sophisticated, but the food is excellent and much lighter than the Bahian cuisine. The *dendê* oil is extracted from the fruit and instead of coconut milk they use fresh coconut pulp. The restaurant is located on the veranda of a ranchhouse and offers seafood dishes prepared with *maturi*, the nut from a green cashew apple. For dessert try the exotic fruits picked from the trees located on the ranch (*Rua Edgar Loureiro, 98-B, tel. 71/384-7464*).

Forte do Monte Serrat: a spectacular view of the mouth of Todos os Santos Bay

CHASING THE TRIO ELÉTRICO

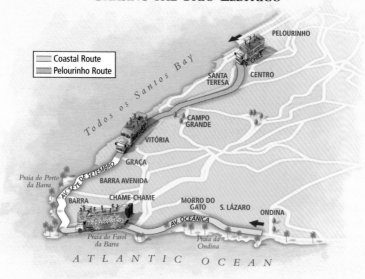

Like a current that carries one to paradise, the *trios elétricos* – transport trucks with sound systems and stages for live bands – sweep along everyone in Salvador during Carnival. The trucks travel three official routes, leading the way for more than two million dancing revelers. The route called Osmar starts in Campo Grande and ends at Praça Castro Alves, in downtown Salvador; the Dodô route runs from the Farol da Barra to Ondina on the shoreline; and the Batatinha route runs through Pelourinho.

The Osmar route, the oldest one, is where the traditional parades start early in the morning. The Dodô route, where the VIP boxes are located, starts festivities in the late afternoon and continues until dawn. There are two ways to participate in these two circuits: buy an *abadá* (a kit with a T-shirt and identification bracelet) from one of the groups and dance in the secured roped-off area; or avoid payment, dance outside the ropes, but run the risk of being mugged.

The trios were invented in 1950. The musicians Adolfo Antônio Nascimento, Dodô, and Osmar Álvares de Macedo, Osmar, rented an old red 1929 Ford, installed two speakers and went on a tour of the downtown area with their instruments on the Sunday morning of Carnival weekend, playing *frevo* music and attracting a group of followers. The "electric duo" became a trio in the following Carnival.

Up until 1950, the Carnival in Bahia was much calmer, with the traditional parade and Carnival balls held at clubs. It was the presentation of Clube Carnavalesco Vassourinhas, from Recife, that introduced the delirious crowds to *frevo* street dancing. The locals loved it and Dodô and Osmar were inspired to take their amplifiers and play *frevo* music the following month.

Starting in the 1980's, the *trios elétricos* introduced *axé* music, a combination of pop music, *frevo*, African groups and *afoxés*. In Salvador alone, there are seventy different official and independent groups.

HEAT RELIEF

Salvador's average temperature in the summer can exceed 30°C (86°F). For relief from the heat there is nothing better than ice-cream. Three shops in Salvador stand out for their tradition, quality and exotic flavors. **Le Glacier Laporte** (*Largo do Cruzeiro de São Francisco, 21, Centro Histórico, tel. 71/266-3649*), run by French ice-cream maker Georges Laporte, makes homemade sherbets from fruit, mineral water, milk and sugar. There are no preservatives, artificial coloring, or texture enhancers. The forty different varieties include flavors such as *jaca* (jack fruit), *tamarindo* (tamarind), *umbu* (Brazilian plum), *graviola* (cherimoya) and *cajá* (yellow mombin). **Cubana** (*Rua Alfredo Brito, 12, Centro Histórico, tel. 71/321-6162*) is the oldest ice-cream parlor in town. Opened in 1930, it offers generous portions of both traditional and exotic flavors, such as chocolate, strawberry and *cupuaçu* (an Amazon fruit). The most traditional and

Olodum rehearsal: the beat of the drums...

...infects Pelourinho with euphoria

popular ice cream parlor is the **Sorveteria da Ribeira** (*Praça General Osório, 87, Ribeira, tel. 71/316-5451*) opened in 1931, one year after the Cubana. It offers a selection of fifty homemade flavors including tapioca and coconut.

TRY A BAHIAN CIGAR

Besides the distinct impact of the African culture, the great music, and colonial and baroque architecture, Bahia shares another characteristic with Cuba. The state is the largest cigar manufacturer in the country. Production is concentrated in the region of the Recôncavo Baiano, in cities such as Cruz das Almas, São Felix and São Gonçalo dos Campos. Three producers stand out: **Menendez & Amerino**, from the family that manufactured the legendary Montecristo and H. Upmann cigars in Cuba;

Dannemann, founded by the German Gerhard Dannemann in the second half of the 19th century; and **Le Cigar**, created by Arend Becker, a native of Bahia who has worked in the tobacco exporting sector for over 35 years. One of the best cigars from Bahia is called Dona Flor, after the novel by Jorge Amado. Some experts say that the Bahia cigar quality is equal to those in Cuba, but try and convince Fidel Castro of that... In Cuba, the longer cigars are more popular and the tobacco is strong and sweet. In Bahia, the

cigars are a medium size and the tobacco is softer, with a slightly spicy flavor. A significant difference is that Cuban cigars are made by men; but the cigars from Bahia are handmade by women who learned the craft from their mothers and grandmothers. To sample or buy the cigars visit **Corona** tobacco shop (*Avenida Otávio Mangabeira, 6000, Aeroclube Plaza Show, tel. 71/461-0549*) or **Rosa do Prado Cigar Shop**, which only sells cigars from Bahia (*Rua Inácio Accioly, 5, Centro Histórico, tel. 71/322-1258*).

Exu

Ogum

Xangô

Logunedé

Iemanjá

BAHIAN SYNCRETISM

Bahian syncretism is a combination of African Candomblé and Christian rituals. In order to get around their masters' prohibition of African religions, the slaves "disguised" their gods as Catholic saints in order to worship them. In the *terreiros* (African temples) the saints were *orixás*, or African divinities. The Igreja de Nosso Senhor do Bonfim is one example where once a year the parishioners unite to honor both African and Christian gods.

Candomblé draws on magical rituals and assumes supernatural powers. The *orixás* have their roots in the ancestors of the African clans, deified around five thousand years ago. They are believed to have the power to manipulate forces of nature.

In Brazil, only a few of the more than two hundred African *orixás* are worshipped. One of the most important is Exu, the intermediary between men and gods, and the guardian of crossroads. Other *orixás* are Xangô, of fire and thunder; Iemanjá, of seas and oceans; and Iansã, of wind and lightning, and owner of souls of the dead.

The services take place at the *terreiros*. There live the *ialorixá* or *mãe-de-santo* (priestess), the woman of the house, and the *babalorixá* (high priest); the other residents are the *iaôs* or *ekedes*.

There are approximately two thousand *terreiros* in Salvador. The most famous ones are **Ilê Axé Iyá Nassô Oká, Ilê Axé Opô Afonjá** and **Ilê Axé Iyá Omi Yamassê**. The first, the Casa Branca, was opened in 1830 and is the oldest in the country (*Avenida Vasco da Gama, 463, tel. 71/334-5694*). The second was founded in 1910 and has been designated a heritage site (*Rua Direita de São Gonçalo do Retiro, 557, tel. 71/384-6800 and 385-3159*). The last one, located in the Federação district, is the Terreiro do Gantois (*Alto do Gantois, 23, tel. 71/331-9231*), and was run for 64 years by Mãe Menininha (1894-1986). She promoted the values of Candomblé and gained the admiration of figures such as Jorge Amado, Pierre Verger and Carybé.

The ritual washing of the steps of the Igreja de Nosso Senhor do Bonfim (Jesus Christ, who corresponds to the Oxalá divinity) represents the merging of the two religions. The washing ceremony is held annually in January on the second Sunday following the Festa de Reis (January 6). The 8-kilometer (5-mi.) procession to the hill of Bonfim starts at 10am in front of the Igreja de Nossa Senhora da Conceição da Praia, in Cidade Baixa. From there, five hundred women dressed in traditional African attire depart for the church. They pour water and sprinkle lavender on the first ten steps and wash, singing hymns in African languages.

Buruku

Iansã

Obá

Ossaim

Oxóssi

OFF THE BEATEN TRACK

Two important museums are located a little outside the Historical Center. The **Museu Carlos Costa Pinto** is located on the main street of the Vitória district, an upper class neighborhood on the way to Pelourinho, coming from Rio Vermelho. The other is the **Museu do Mosteiro de São Bento**, located at the end of Rua Sete de Setembro.

MOSTEIRO DE SÃO BENTO

Founded in 1582, this monastery has a museum that displays more than 280 examples of Brazilian sacred art. The exhibit is renewed from time to time with pieces from the complete collection of 2,000 works. There are paintings, porcelain items, crystal ware, gold ornaments, furniture and vestments. Part of the exhibition shows the differences between crucifixes made over the centuries. The monastery still maintains a cloister regime and houses 34 monks. Monday through Saturday at 7am, and Sundays at 10am, there is mass with Gregorian chants at the Igreja de São Sebastião da Bahia, next to the monastery. After visiting the museum and the church, ask to visit the library. It has more than 100,000 rare books with titles from the 16th century, written in Latin, that describe morals and conduct.
Largo de São Bento, Centro, tel. (71) 2106-5200. Mon-Fri 9am-11:30am and 1pm-4:30pm.

MUSEU CARLOS COSTA PINTO

This museum, located in a rare American colonial style house, was inaugurated in 1969 and specializes in decorative art. It contains a collection of at least 3,000 decorative items from the 17th to the 20th centuries, displayed according to theme. The silverware collection, mostly from Portugal and Brazil, is the largest. Two rooms that deserve a longer visit are those displaying the Baccarat crystal chandeliers and the jewelry and accessories. There is also a beautiful garden at the entrance, and a pleasant coffee shop at the back.
Avenida Sete de Setembro, 2490, tel. (71) 336-6081. Daily, except Tue, 2pm-6:45pm.

Women from Bahia during the January step washing celebration at the Igreja de Nosso Senhor do Bonfim. The neoclassic construction, from 1754, is a hallmark of religious syncretism in Bahia

Urban Coastline

Forte de Santo Antônio da Bahia and Farol da Barra

Salvador originated in Barra, where the navigator Américo Vespúcio caught his first glimpse of Todos os Santos Bay, and the Portuguese claimed the new land for the Crown. The fort was built 34 years after discovery. Initially it was only a trench of compacted earth, loose sand and mud reinforced with sticks. The lighthouse was added to the structure in 1698, the first in the Americas. It is still used today and is a city landmark, but unfortunately it is not open to the public. The fort is also the site of the **Museu Náutico**, containing material about different types of ships and objects from the *Sacramento* galleon, a Portuguese ship that sunk in the Rio Vermelho region in 1668.

Praça Almirante Tamandaré, tel. (71) 264-3296. Tue-Sun, 8am-7pm (closed during year-end holidays).

Beaches and Lagoa do Abaeté

The city's shoreline has more than ten beaches. In the urban area, the highlight is the small **Barra**. However, the most beautiful (and least polluted) are located north of Salvador, approximately 40 minutes from downtown. The fashionable Barra stretch is divided between the calm **Porto** and **Farol**, with high surfing waves and a mystical twilight. The white sand of **Itapuã**, located 27 kilometers (17 mi.) from downtown and close to the multicolored lighthouse, has been immortalized in many songs. Close by is the **Lagoa do Abaeté**, made famous by the lyrics of Dorival Caymmi's songs, with its dark waters surrounded by delicate white dunes. The next beach, **Stella Maris**, has many coconut trees, a green ocean with strong waves, and food kiosks. Located 3 kilometers (2 mi.) away is the beautiful **Flamengo**, which has maintained its wilderness state because there is no road running along it. The **Aleluia** area has good waves for surfing.

Farol de Itapuã, a beach immortalized in the songs of Caymmi, Toquinho and Vinicius

TASTEFUL CREATIONS

The specialties of Bahia are shrouded in both mystery and a multiplicity of influences. Africans introduced items such as okra, dendê oil, yams and a vast array of exotic delicacies to Brazilian colonial cooking. Their innovations have wafted down to us through generations of improvisation and revision. Ary Barroso describes the food offered today by *baianas*, or Bahian women, as a selection of *vatapá* (shrimp mixed with bread crumbs, peanuts, cashews, and dendê oil), *caruru* (okra, with shrimp, peanuts, cashews and dendê oil), *mungunzá* (white hominy corn, coconut milk, sweetened condensed milk, cinnamon or cloves) and *umbu* (Brazilian plum).

Slave cuisine survived in Brazil thanks to the adaptations made by Candomblé. The African women who worked in the master's kitchen combined the food of the *orixás* with the ingredients they had on hand, modifying the recipes to suit their master's tastes. *Amalá*, for instance, an exotic delicacy prepared with whole okra, was not well-liked by the Portuguese. So the slaves chopped the okra and mixed it with dry shrimps, peanuts and cashews. Thus was invented *caruru*, one of Bahia's most famous dishes. *Ipetê*, the food of Oxum, became *bobó de camarão* (shrimp, manioc, coconut milk, cashews and dendê oil), and *acará*, the food for the gods Xangô and Iansã, was transformed into *acarajé*. *Acarajé*, a symbol of local cuisine, is a small deep-fried bun made from cowpeas and stuffed with dried shrimp mixed with bread crumbs, peanuts, cashews, fried in dendê oil and seasoned with hot pepper sauce. In Salvador, women sell this delicacy on practically every street corner, but the most famous are Dinha, Regina and Cira, the "holy trinity" of *acarajé*. Dinha and Regina work close to each other at Largo de Santana, in the Rio Vermelho district. Cira also has a kiosk close by at Largo da Mariquita, but her main post is in Itapuã, on Rua Aristides Milton. You can order a complete *acarajé* (with *vatapá*, dry shrimp and salad) or with just *vatapá*. When asked about pepper, ask for "*quente*" if you like it hot, or decline with "*não*".

Abará is a variation of *acarajé* made from cow peas and dendê oil and stuffed with dried shrimp, then rolled in banana leaves and steamed. The places that sell this delicacy are very popular. The most famous is Olga kiosk, near Casa de Cultura do Benin, in the Historical Center. The kiosk has been there for more than 40 years and is currently run by Olga's daughters Elisabeth and Jacira. Want to know how to make it? Don't bother asking the guardians of the delicacy. They won't reveal the recipe to anyone except their own daughters. "At home, when we prepare the *abarás*, we lock the kitchen door and don't let anyone in," says Elisabeth.

Cachoeira and São Félix

One of the most beautiful cities in Bahia is Cachoeira, on the banks of Paraguaçu River, 116 kilometers (72 mi.) west of Salvador in the Recôncavo Baiano. At the Praça da Aclamação, you can hire a guide for a walking tour of the historical buildings, alleys and hills. In this square, Nega sells delicious *abarás* and *acarajés*. In the city's restaurants, try the *maniçoba*, an Indian dish that is prepared with the same ingredients as *feijoada*, but uses manioc leaves instead of beans. The town's former wealth from sugar cane and tobacco exports gave Cachoeira its fine colonial architecture. From this golden era remain the buildings that now house the **Museu do Iphan** (1723), the **Museu Hansen Bahia** (1830), **City Hall and Jail** (1698-1712) and the four two-story houses of the **Irmandade da Boa Morte** from the 18th century, renovated in 1995. In addition to the architecture, Cachoeira is also known for the artisans' studios that create wood-carvings, ceramics and wood engravings. Visit the studios of

Louco Filho, **Dory**, **Fory**, **Mimo** (*all on Rua Treze de Maio)*, **Davi Rodrigues** (*Rua J. J. Seabra, 68*) and **Doidão** (*Rua Ana Nery*).

On the other side of the river, crossing over the 1885 Dom Pedro II bridge, is the charming town of **São Félix**. It has colonial buildings such as the **Fábrica de Charutos** (Cigar Factory) and the **Centro Cultural Dannemann**, where you can tour the cigar factory. This Cultural Center offers workshops and exhibitions (*Rua Salvador Pinto, 29, tel. 75/425-2208. Tue-Sat, 8am-5pm; Sun, 1pm-5pm, except the factory*). The largest event of Cachoeira takes place during the first two weeks of August. This is the **Festa da Irmandade da Boa Morte**, organized by a group of women descended from slaves. The festival has become part of worldwide Afro tourism, attracting charter flights from the United States and Africa. Cachoeira has yet another gem, the **Igreja Ordem Terceira do Carmo**. Built in 1691, this church has baroque and rococo details (*Praça da Aclamação*).

The view of São Felix from Cachoeira, in Recôncavo Baiano

SOUTHERN COAST

The cozy Primeira Praia, in Morro de São Paulo, seen from the observation deck at the lighthouse

MORRO DE SÃO PAULO AND BOIPEBA

Morro de São Paulo, 248 kilometers (142 mi.) south of Salvador, has trees left from the Atlantic Rainforest, lowlands, dunes, mangrove swamps, and beautiful beaches with reefs and crystal clear pools. It is one of the villages on **Tinharé** island, which together with **Boipeba** island, **Cairu** island and 23 other smaller islands form the only Brazilian archipelago municipality, known as **Cairu**. Cars are prohibited. Only some four-wheel drives and tractors are used to access the more remote locations, and there are no streets, just alleys. The village of Morro de São Paulo is a study in contrasts – rustic yet sophisticated, with restaurants, bars, inns and boutiques offering name-brand products. Tourism is cosmopolitan and egalitarian. You can meet top models, movie stars, hippies and backpackers. The diversity is also present in its architecture, with everything from simple beach houses

and cabins to grand colonial buildings. Small planes arrive here from Salvador, as do boats of every shape and size coming from the Mercado Modelo pier. Coming from Itaparica, another water transportation alternative is via Valença, a coastal city located south of Salvador.

THE HISTORY OF THE VILLAGE

The best time to begin this tour is around 4pm, finishing in time for seeing sunset. Start at **Fonte Grande**, dating from 1746. Go down to Praça Aureliano Lima and admire the façade of the 19th century **Casarão** (mansion), which operates as an inn. To the right is **Igreja Nossa Senhora da Luz**, built between 1811 and 1845. Near Praça Amendoeira is a hundred-year old tree and the **Portaló**, where troops for the fort disembarked. Follow the fort's wall, with its many observation points, until you reach

Rustic Boipeba island's Cueira and Tassimirim beaches are turtle nesting areas

Forte da Ponta dos Fachos or **Fortaleza Tapirandu,** constructed in 1630. This is a great spot to watch the sunset and the dolphins. From there a trail up a steep hill leads to the **Farol** (lighthouse), from 1845, which even today guides ships. The path is not well-marked but the panoramic view of the beaches makes the trip worthwhile. Adventurous types may try the Morro *tirolesa* (flying fox) with a drop of 68 meters (226 feet). If you prefer peace and quiet, return to Portaló, sit at one of the tables at the **Passárgada** lookout and sip on fruit juice in the twilight.

THE BEACHES

The varied numbering of the beaches at Morro reveals only their order from north to south. **Primeira Praia** (first beach) is the smallest, 500 meters (1640 feet) long with soft white sand. **Segunda** (second) has natural pools at low tide. A trendy beach, it is the venue for nighttime beach parties. **Terceira** (third) is quiet and lined with inns; the beach almost disappears at high tide. **Quarta** (fourth) is also quiet, with beautiful pools, crystal clear water and sophisticated inns. **Quinta** (fifth), also called **Encanto,** can only be reached by a tractor from Terceira, or via a trail that crosses two coastal mangrove swamps and two streams. Further to the south is **Garapuá**, with pools and a fishing village. At the tip of the island is the deserted **Pontal**, with 17 kilometers (11 mi.) of coconut groves. The latter two are accessible by boat, tractor or tour agency jeeps. On the mainland side of the north tip, facing Valença, is the **Gamboa** beach,

OUR RECOMMENDATION

At high tide, the ocean almost reaches the pool of **Porto do Zimbo Small Resort,** located on the Quarta Praia. Gardens and walkways covered with *piaçava* grass link the public areas. The apartments are comfortable and well-equipped and have verandas. Half of them have whirlpool bathtubs. Employees welcome the guests on the runway or at the wharf and a transport to the villa is provided at various times.

Additional information begins on page 462.

accessible only by boat, or during low tide by a trail that crosses a medicinal mud bath site.

INLAND MORRO
This area of the Atlantic Rainforest has a nature reserve for various species of crab such as the blue crab, and in the southern part many miles of sand, coastal lowlands, marshes and mangrove swamps. The region can only be reached by four wheel drive vehicles, tractors or horse.

ILHA DE CAIRU BY BOAT
Boat tours depart from Terceira Praia, the Morro wharf or the Gamboa wharf. Destinations include the **Coroa Grande** sand bar, the almost deserted **Ponta do Curral** beach, or the sleepy village of **Galeão**. In **Canavieiras** there is a tilapia fish farm, fresh oysters and a smokehouse for shrimp. When you reach the island and its mangrove swamps, take the historical tour. At the **Convento de Santo Antônio**, built in 1554, ask one of the Franciscan friars to take you to the cells and patios that are decorated with Portuguese ceramic tiles. Afterwards, relax in the clear pools at **Garapuá** beach.

ILHA DE BOIPEBA
More rustic and primitive, this island has trees, mangrove swamps, and beaches with pristine blue water that can be admired from the trails on foot or horseback. Tour agencies offer day excursions by boat and jeep that depart from Gamboa or Terceira. Turtles lay their eggs in the **Cueira** and **Tassimirim** beaches. The reefs here have plenty of lobsters and seafood, and Guida, a local fisherman, serves up fresh appetizers for visitors. Using an improvised wood stove, he grills delicious lobsters caught the night before. Tassimirim is already called the most beautiful beach in Brazil. **Moreré** is just as beautiful, has warm clear water and coral pools forming natural aquariums. **Castelhanos** point, located at the southernmost tip of Boipeba, is the gravesite for the ship Madre de Dios that sank in the early years of Brazil's history.

LINHA VERDE

Mangue Seco's sand dunes and coconut groves are almost untouched

FROM PRAIA DO FORTE TO MANGUE SECO

Linha Verde was the first ecological highway constructed in the country. Located north of Salvador, it is 142 kilometers (89 mi.) long and extends from Praia do Forte to Mangue Seco. With few curves and good asphalt, it was built based on environmental impact studies, avoiding the coastline to minimize damage to the ecosystem. It runs through five municipalities, with exits to beautiful beaches interspersed with rivers, sand dunes, coconut groves and mangrove swamps.

AREMPEBE

Located 24 kilometers (15 mi.) north of Salvador, this beach became the hangout for hippies in 1970. The alternative community remains to the present day, where the population of no more than fifty people live in thatch-roofed cabins with no electricity or sewage systems. Caetano, Gil, Polanski, Janis Joplin and Mick Jagger have all visited Arempebe. At the entrance to the

village is a **Projeto** TAMAR operation, dedicated to protecting sea turtles. To the south, the **Arembepe** and **Piruí** beaches are protected by a barrier reef, but there are good waves for surfing. To the north, you can take the road to **Barra do Jacuípe**, an old fishing village that is now largely beach houses. The key attraction is the mouth of the **Jacuípe** river which winds through the mangrove swamps on its way to the ocean.

ITACIMIRIM

In 1984 Amyr Klink crossed the Atlantic Ocean alone in a rowboat to

OUR RECOMMENDATION

🍽️ The **Mar Aberto** restaurant is located in the center of Arembepe, in an airy house with a terrace by the sand. A good option is *casquinha de siri* (sea crab) for an appetizer, *peixe à escabeche* (marinated fish) or lobster for the main course and chocolate mousse for dessert (*Largo de São Francisco, 43, tel. 71/624-1257*).

visit this magnificent beach, 50 kilometers (32 mi.) north of Salvador. You can bring the family along and enjoy how the calm sea, located close to the mouth of the **Ipojuca** river, forms pools at low tide. **Espera** is located on a stretch of open sea with low waves.

PRAIA DO FORTE

Respect for nature, and everything professionally run and well-organized: welcome to Praia do Forte, located 55 kilometers (35 mi.) from Salvador. The person responsible for this is Klaus Peters, a São Paulo businessman of German descent who owns practically all the land on this beach, including the **Praia do Forte Eco Resort**. The ecological atmosphere is further enhanced by neighboring **Projeto Tamar** and the whale-focused **Instituto Baleia Jubarte**. No cars are allowed in the picturesque village of colorful houses, inns and restaurants. The 12 kilometers (8 mi.) long beach is lined with coconut trees and has calm water and reefs that form pools.

CASTELO GARCIA D'ÁVILA

This castle is one of the oldest stone buildings in Brazil and an example of Portuguese military residential architecture. Ten generations of the Garcia D'Ávila family has lived there. The first arrived in the country in 1549 with the mission of Governor General Tomé de Sousa. The castle was constructed between 1551 and 1624. It has a well-preserved chapel that is dedicated to Nossa Senhora da Conceição.

Access via 2.5 kilometers (1.5 mi.) of dirt road, on the road into Praia do Forte; tel. (71) 676-1073. Daily (in the summer) 9am-6pm. During low season, closed Mon.

IMBASSAÍ

This 6 kilometers (4 mi.) beach is bordered by sand dunes and the rusty colored, warm waters of the **Imbassaí** river that runs parallel to the ocean. Food kiosks between the ocean and the river offer drinks and appetizers. The village of **Santo Antônio** is located 5 km (3 mi.) north, accessible from the beach.

Garcia D'Ávila Castle: one of Brazil's oldest stone buildings

Barra do Rio Sauípe: concentration of five-star hotels for comfort lovers

MASSARANDUPIÓ

The 8 kilometers (5 mi.) of bumpy dirt road filled with potholes is all worthwhile when you see this magnificent beach. Park the car 200 meters (656 feet) from the sand, where there is a spectacular view of the coastal lowland vegetation. The deserted beach is protected by sand dunes and coconut trees. At the extreme right side of the beach, approximately 2 kilometers (1.25 mi.) from the entrance, is a nudist area; unaccompanied men are not allowed.

SÍTIO DO CONDE

Sítio do Conde lacks great natural attractions and urban development, but it is the base point to visit the surrounding beaches. It is easy to reach and most of the inns and restaurants are located here. Just to the south on the Linha Verde highway, before reaching the exit to the Sítio, is **Barra do Itariri**, which can also be reached from the Sítio exit; its 19 kilometers (12 mi.) of dirt road are in terrible shape, and impassible when it rains. The beach is quiet, with fine white sand, dunes and coconut trees. Heading north from Sítio, after 16 kilometers (10 mi.) of dirt road in poor condition with beautiful scenery, is the **Siribinha** fishing village with some small inns and two restaurants. Be careful: the beach slopes off steeply and some places have a strong undertow. Two rowboat excursions offered by the locals are worthwhile. One goes to the mouth of the **Itapicuru** river and the other to the **Cavalo Ruço** lagoon.

OUR RECOMMENDATION

A good option for those who enjoy grand hotels, resorts and comfort is the **Costa do Sauípe**. The amenities include a golf course, water sports, horseback riding and tennis courts that are spread over the 72 hectare (178 acre) complex. The resort offers a shuttle service to the attractions on the grounds as well as bicycle rentals. Costa do Sauípe, located 76 kilometers (48 mi.) from Salvador, has large-chain hotels as well as some smaller inns. It is the most complete and sophisticated tourist destination in the region. If you don't want to stay at the complex, the hotels offer a daily rate for the use of their pools, beach and leisure facilities.

Additional information begins on page 462.

BARRA DO ITARIRI FAIR

The serene **Barra do Itariri** is transformed into a noisy, colorful market every Sunday. From 7am to 1pm vendors sell meat, fruit such as plantain bananas and jack fruit, and various spices (coriander, habanera peppers, etc.) in an old warehouse provided by the local government. It is worth a visit if only to see the locals from nearby villages arriving by donkey.

MANGUE SECO

This village was the setting for a TV drama and movie based on Jorge Amado's novel *Tieta do Agreste*. It's received well-deserved publicity as the last stop on the Linha Verde, separated from Sergipe by the Real river. Located between the ocean and the river, Mangue Seco is a peaceful village with sand dunes and a beach with gently rolling waters. The village is only accessible by water. Four passenger boats are available in Pontal, in the state of Sergipe. The crossing takes 15 minutes.

PROJETO TAMAR

Through the 1970's, recipes using turtle meat were listed in many classic cookbooks. Threatened by extinction, turtles are now protected by law. Killing a turtle is a non-bailable environmental crime. Founded in 1980, the well-known Projeto Tamar carries out work to preserve the species. A joint project with participation from Ibama (Brazilian Institute of Environmental and Renewable Natural Resources), it monitors more than 1,000 kilometers (600 mi.) of beaches. There are currently 20 bases in eight states. The base located at Praia do Forte is the national headquarters for the project and offers talks and night excursions to see the turtles burying their eggs in the sand. Eggs are laid between September and March, during which the baby turtles hatch and make their way to the ocean. Tourists are allowed to come and bear witness at the end of the day. *Praia do Forte, tel. (71) 676-1045. Daily, 9am-5:30pm.*

Igreja e Convento de São Francisco, site of the São Cristóvão Sacred Art Museum on the Upper Side

SÃO CRISTÓVÃO

One of Brazil's oldest cities, São Cristóvão was founded in 1590 and is located 85 kilometers (53 mi.) north of Mangue Seco, Bahia, and 23 kilometers (15 mi.) south of Aracaju in the state of Sergipe. It was the capital city of Sergipe until 1855 when the capital was transferred to Aracaju. The town is divided into the Cidade Alta (Upper Side) where the historical center is located, and Cidade Baixa (Lower Side) where the port and industries are located. In 1939 it was declared a World Heritage Site. The main attractions include the **Museu de Arte Sacra**, located on the Praça de São Francisco, and the **Igreja da Matriz**, located in the Praça da Matriz. The Museu de Arte Sacra contains a collection of more than five hundred pieces from the 17th to 19th centuries. Most of them are multicolored wooden sculptures of saints. The museum opened in 1974 and is located in the old Franciscan convent built between 1658 and 1726. There is a neoclassic chapel dedicated to St. Francis. Its ceiling was painted by a student of the painter Teófilo de Jesus, from Bahia. There is a guided tour. Another attraction on the Praça da Matriz is a restored mansion from the end of the 17th century and currently houses the **Solar de Parati** restaurant. Decorated with period furniture, it offers excellent dishes such as sun-dried beef with manioc purée and manioc meal. Located next door is the **Casa da Queijada**, where Givalda operates her mother's thirty-year-old business and guards the secret recipe for her *queijadinha* (dessert made of cheese and coconut).

OUR RECOMMENDATION

One downside of São Cristóvão is the lack of good hotels. But the neighboring city Aracaju, located thirty minutes away by highway BR-101 or highway SE-04, provides options such as **Celi Praia Hotel**, facing the Praia de Atalaia. It offers executive services, and is a favorite of artists and politicians. It has 93 rooms with a pleasant breeze on the veranda, a pool, sauna, massage service and cyber cafe.

Additional information begins on page 462.

DESTINATION
ILHÉUS

The grace and beauty of the Bahia coastline between Barra Grande and Canavieiras inspired the Brazilian writer Jorge Amado's best novels. His character Gabriela lived in Ilhéus, where neoclassical houses harken back to the rich history of the cocoa trade. The 1980's brought Brazil's first modern resort to the region, in Comandatuba, offering excellent infrastructure. Today the region boasts a number of comfortable hotels and charming inns. Canavieiras offers blue marlin fishing and a wide variety of seafood. In Itacaré, sports fans may enjoy rafting, mountain biking, trekking and rappelling. Or venture to virtually unexplored territory in Barra Grande through excursions to the islands in Camamu bay and the Península de Maraú, or the coral lined ocean at Taipus de Fora beach.

DESTINATION HIGHLIGHTS

ILHÉUS
   Historic Center
   Canavieiras

ITACARÉ (66 km/41 mi.)

PENÍNSULA DE MARAÚ AND CAMAMU BAY
   Adventure Sports

All distances are from Ilhéus

ILHÉUS

HISTORIC CENTER

1 - Vesúvio Bar
2 - Teatro Municipal
3 - Casa de Cultura Jorge Amado
4 - Casa dos Artistas
5 - Associação Comercial

6 - Palácio Paranaguá
7 - Rua Antônio Lavigne
8 - Igreja Museu São Jorge
9 - Palacete de Misael Tavares
10 - Casa de Tonico Bastos

11 - Catedral de São Sebastião
12 - Ilheos Hotel
13 - Old Port
14 - Bataclan nightclub

A short city-tour reveals the life of writer Jorge Amado and scenes from his famous novel *Gabriela*. Start at the **Vesúvio Bar**, a home away from home. During Jorge Amado's youth, effervescent cultural life centered at the **Teatro Municipal** (built in 1932). Culture continues as what is now **Casa de Cultura Jorge Amado**, built in the 1920's by Amado's father; this is where Amado wrote his first novel *O País do Carnaval* (*Land of Carnival*). The **Casa dos Artistas** (constructed at the end of the 19th century), the **Associação Comercial** (1932) and the **Palácio Paranaguá** (1907) attest to the affluence of the golden age of cocoa. The tour should include **Rua Antônio Lavigne**, paved with stones imported from England for the wedding of the daughter of Misael Tavares, one of the most powerful political bosses from *Gabriela*. The street ends at the **Igreja Museu São Jorge** (1556). Refined paintings face down from the ceiling at **Palacete de Misael Tavares** (1914). From **Casa de Tonico Bastos**, a womanizer in the novel, return to the **Catedral de São Sebastião** (1931). Take a final sweep through the **Ilheos Hotel**, the **Old Port** and the **Bataclan nightclub**.

Chalana Excursion

Founded in 1532, at one time Ilhéus boasted eight large sugar mills. The **Capela de Sant'Ana do Rio do Engenho**, accessible by *chalana* (a small flat-bottomed boat), is the remnants of one of the mills. A four-hour tour covers downtown Ilhéus, the old port and views of the Pontal bay shoreline from the Engenho's river, as well as the mangrove swamp and the beautiful confluence of the Engenho (or Santana), Cachoeira and Fundão rivers, at a place known as **Coroa Grande**. The mill displays an iron boiler, big crusher and other pieces that have survived the passing of time. **Horto Havaí**, a private reserve, serves lunch. *Tour Operator: NV Turismo, tel. (73) 634-4001.*

Cocoa Plantations

The old cocoa plantations are reminders of the wealth and opulence of the late 19th and early 20th centuries, when Ilhéus was the largest cocoa producer in the world. Two good examples are **Fazenda Primavera** (*Rodovia Ilhéus–Itabuna, km 24, tel. 73/613-7817 or 231-3996*) and **Fazenda Yrerê** (*Rodovia Ilhéus–Itabuna, km 12, tel. 73/656-5054*). Tours by appointment only. Because cocoa trees require shade in order to grow, growers cleared only the understory, leaving the Atlantic Rainforest with high quality hardwood trees. The tour explains the cocoa production process, including harvesting methods, how to break the fruit open and the drying process under the *barcaças*, mobile roofs that protect the cocoa beans. Taste the bitter chocolate flavor of cocoa nuts and try the fruit's tasty juice.

Southern Coast

Once the playground of only the wealthy, the **Milionários'** beach still offers many conveniences, including showers, beach tents and inns. The powerful waves on the neighboring beach, **Cururupe**, make it dangerous for swimming. The beaches in the **Olivença** district are popular with surfers, with waves at **Cai N'Água, Batuba** and **Back Door** that can reach 2.5 meters (8 feet). In Olivença you can also enjoy the iron-rich medicinal waters at the **Balneário Tororomba**, where the best places are the Canabrava Resort and the Tororomba Ecoresort. Non-resort guests pay a day rate. The **Canabrava** beach is calmer and quieter. Heading south, the road follows the mountain and is farther from the beach, making it difficult to reach the vast coconut groves at the practically deserted **Acuípe** and **Itapororoca** beaches.

Ecoparque do Una

Sample the Atlantic Rainforest's rich biodiversity at Una Ecological Park, 45 kilometers (28 mi.) south of Ilhéus, in the municipality of Una. The 383 hectares (946 acres) of virgin forest include huge century-old trees and two hundred bird species, including species unique to the park. The park has two trails, the beginner level **trilha das Passarelas**, 2 kilometers (1.25 mi.); and the more advanced **Juarana**, 5 kilometers (3 mi.). If you're lucky you may catch a glimpse of animals such as the golden lion tamarin, the park's emblem. *Access via the Ilhéus–Canavieiras highway, km 45, tel. (73) 633-1121. Tue-Sun, 8am-5pm (excursions start at 9am). Reservations required.*

Everyday life: searching for crabs in the mangrove swamp

Canavieiras

The mangrove swamps and Atlantic rainforest that spread over seven marine islands and four river islands comprise the Canavieiras region, located 13 kilometers (70 mi.) south of Ilhéus via highway BA-001. It provides homes for a wide variety of shellfish, earning the nickname "crab capital". There is no shortage of beaches along the 17 kilometers (11 mi.) of golden sand and turquoise waters. Many bars are on **Atalaia** island's beautiful **Costa** beach, accessible from the town by a bridge. From there, you can reach the quieter **Barra do Albino** beach. To the north is the **Barra Velha** beach, virtually deserted because access depends on a dirt road and ferryboat crossing. In the direction of Belmonte there is **Atalaia**'s fishing village and the deserted **Sul**'s mangrove swamps. Downtown Canavieiras houses hot nightlife, the beautiful historical site

Governador Paulo Souto, and well-maintained neoclassical style mansions from the 18th and 19th centuries. In addition, Canavieiras is an excellent place for river fishing and blue-marlin fishing, attracting fishermen the world over from November to March.

Tour Operator: Artmarina, tel. (73) 284-1262.

Our Recommendation

Brazil's first resort, the **Transamérica** on the Ilha de Comandatuba, north of Canavieiras, is still the best option. The hotel occupies almost the entire island, controls the channel access and has 21 kilometers (13 mi.) of beaches lined by coconut trees. Non-resort guests may visit both the island and the village of fishermen and craftspeople. The hotel offers kayaks to ocean cruisers; swimming, a golf course, stores, a L'Occitane spa, five restaurants, six bars, a disco and a cyber cafe keep the guests entertained.

Additional information begins on page 462.

ITACARÉ

The long shoreline of Itacaré, located 66 kilometers (41 mi.) north of Ilhéus, via highway BA-001, is punctuated by hills and rugged coastline with beautifully preserved vegetation. The locals divide the fifteen beaches into three groups. First are the **Pontal, Coroinha** and **Concha** located close to the turbulent **Contas** river. Next are the urban beaches reachable by short scenic trails, such as **Resende, Tiririca, Costa** and **Ribeira**. Finally, eight more remote beaches extend to the border with Ilhéus. Some can only be reached by trails that cross mangrove swamps and waterfalls, so check with the tour operators. In addition, ferryboats deliver riders to the beautiful **Península de Maraú**. Itacaré offers other great attractions such as *capoeira* presentations, puppet theatre and *forró* dancing at night. *Tour Operators: Caminho da Terra, tel. (73) 251-3053/251-3060; Itacaré Ecoturismo, tel. (73) 251-2224; Eco Trip Itacaré, tel. (73) 251-2191; Papa Terra Extreme, tel. (73) 251-2137/251-2045.*

RIO DE CONTAS

Don't miss an excursion up **Contas** river in a canoe used by local fishermen – check at the wharf or with tour operators for more information. The highlight is entering the narrow canals that lead into the mangrove swamps. The monotony of the dark muddy world is broken by the parades of hundreds of colorful red and yellow crabs along the shoreline, close enough for pictures. Along the way, try the homemade dishes at the Restaurante do Miguel, on Manguinhos island.

OUR RECOMMENDATION

🍽 The **Dedo de Moça** restaurant, in the central region of Itacaré, has a rustic atmosphere decorated with colorful light fixtures, sofas and an outdoor patio. Enjoy the *bobó de camarão* (shrimp mixed with manioc meal, coconut and dendê oil) and fish with cashews. Prepare your palate for food with the excellent selection of wines and *cachaças* (sugarcane spirit) *(Rua Plínio Soares, 26, tel. 73/251-3372).*

Engenhoca river, south of Itacaré: good for surfing, accessible by a trail from km 12 of the road to Ilhéus

PENÍNSULA DE MARAÚ AND CAMAMU BAY

The unique geography of the Península de Maraú and Camamu Bay offers islands, beaches facing the open sea and the bay, lagoons, sand dunes, rivers and mangrove swamps. At over 40 kilometers (25 mi.) of land, the peninsula forms Brazil's third largest bay, after Salvador's Todos os Santos bay and Rio de Janeiro's Guanabara bay. Easy but slow, reach **Camamu** by car on highway BA-001, then switch to a 30 minute speed boat cruise or a 90-minute row boat excursion to the peninsula. Departure times vary. Another way to reach the peninsula is via **Itacaré**, by ferryboat and car, preferably a four-wheel drive vehicle, along highway BR-030. The useful village of **Barra Grande** rents all-terrain vehicles, motorcycles or bicycles for full-day trips. Visit picturesque villages such as **Taipus de Dentro, Saquaira** and **Maraú**, or rent a boat and enjoy the bay at your leisure.

Tour Operator: Camamu Adventure, tel. (73) 255-2138; Naturemar, tel. (73) 255-2343; Sollarium Taipus Ecoturismo, tel. (73) 258-6151/258-6191.

OUR RECOMMENDATION

The **Kiaroa Beach Resort**, located at Três Coqueiros beach, 3 kilometers (2 mi.) from Barra Grande, offers 32 exclusive rooms and bungalows overlooking the ocean. Many of the bungalows have private swimming pools right outside the door. Shells decorate the bathrooms and local artists have designed the furniture. Amenities include DVD players and 29" TVs. It also has a private runway with regular flights from Salvador.

Additional information begins on page 462.

❶ Ponta do Mutá
A short walk from Barra Grande. A lighthouse marks the entrance of the bay. View coconut trees and rocks breaking through the surface of the water.

❷ Praia de Taipus de Fora
Almost deserted, it is worth a long stop to enjoy the beach's warm waters. The coral pools are excellent for snorkeling.

❸ Lagoa Azul
Close to Taipus de Fora beach, the 22°C (72°F) water of this lagoon is good for swimming.

❹ Lagoa do Cassange
The 6 kilometers (3.75 mi.) of blue water are as smooth as glass.

❺ Morro do Farol
The soft dunes are a challenge for four-wheel drive vehicles and hiker's legs, but the reward is a 360° panoramic view of the peninsula.

❻ Ilha da Pedra Furada
One of the most interesting islands. At low tide a magical sandbank materializes, providing a path to the hollow arch that lends the name.

❼ Ilha do Goió
The islet has an eclectic geography: the front is sand and the back is a mangrove swamp full of crabs.

❽ Ilha do Campinho
Great for a late afternoon swim, it is connected to the peninsula by a bridge. A friendly Italian couple serves specialties from Italy at Matataúba's restaurant.

❾ Ilha do Sapinho
Local resident Jorge will catch fresh lobsters and crabs straight out of his pond for you to enjoy. Order the Bebida da Confusão, a drink seasoned with fresh allspice leaves.

❿ Vila de Cajaíba
The village features boatyards where schooners are built by hand. At the wharf, look for Zezito, known for his miniature boats.

⓫ Cachoeira do Tremembé
A fan-shaped 5 meters (16 feet) high waterfall refreshes the passengers from inside the boat.

⓬ Coroa Vermelha
At night, restore energies at this offshore sandbar. Luaus are held here to mark the start of the full moon cycle.

Ituberá

BA 001

BA 001

Tapuia

Jequié

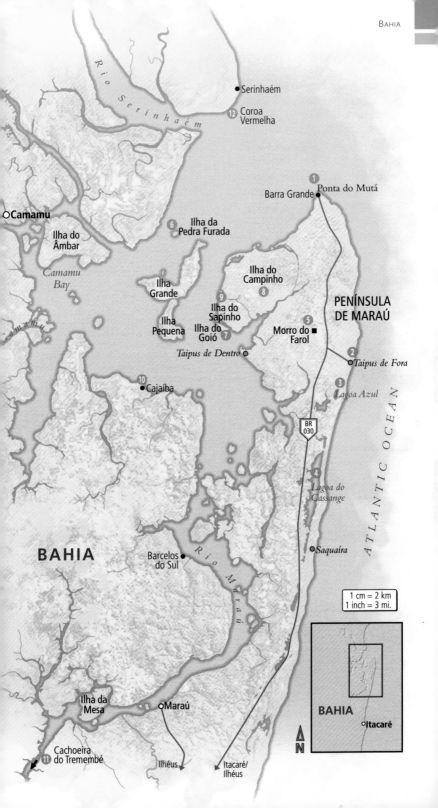

Serinhaém

12 Coroa
Vermelha

Rio Serinhaém

1 Barra Grande · Ponta do Mutá

○ Camamu

Ilha do
Âmbar

6 Ilha da
Pedra Furada

Camamu
Bay

Ilha do
Campinho

Ilha
Grande

9 Ilha do
Sapinho

8

PENÍNSULA
DE MARAÚ

Ilha
Pequena

Ilha do
Goió

7

5 Morro do
Farol ■

Camamu

Taipus de Dentro ○

2 ○ Taipus de Fora

10 Cajaíba

3 Lagoa Azul

BR
030

4

Lagoa do
Cassange

ATLANTIC OCEAN

BAHIA

Barcelos
do Sul ●

Rio Maraú

○ Saquaíra

1 cm = 2 km
1 inch = 3 mi.

Ilha da
Mesa

○ Maraú

BAHIA

○ Itacaré

11 Cachoeira
do Tremembé

Ilhéus

Itacaré/
Ilhéus

N

ADVENTURE SPORTS

With its hot temperatures and warm waters all year round, Itacaré stands out in the northeast because of its trails, waterfalls and opportunities for adventure sports, similar to the coastal regions of São Paulo and Santa Catarina. The region offers levels 2 to 4 of white water rapids, unusual even in the south and southeastern regions of Brazil, where the sport is more popular. One of the most difficult routes is on the Contas river, down a stretch in the Taboquinhas region with waterfalls and white water, 28 kilometers (17 mi.) from the town of Itacaré and accessible only by four-wheel drive vehicles.

Or relax and float down the **Taboquinhas** or Tijuípe rivers in inflatable rubber kayaks. Different mountain biking tours are available and equipment can be rented from agencies. The best biking trails are **Jeribucaçu** and **Prainha**, as well as the 66–kilometer (41-mi.) bike path along the Itacaré–Ilhéus

highway that has stretches through the mountains. The 40-meter (131-foot) **Azevedo** waterfall is a good location for rappelling, accessible from 40-minute long intermediate level hiking trail. Another rappel option is the 18-meter (60-foot) **Noré** waterfall in Taboquinhas, suitable for beginners. *Tour Operator: Caminho da Terra, tel. (73) 251-3053/3060; Itacaré Ecoturismo, tel. (73) 251-2224; Bahia Alegria, tel. (73) 575-1690 and 8802-5033; Ativa Rafting, tel. (73) 696-2219.*

SHOPPING OPTIONS

Fern stems, bunches of *açaí*, moon flower vines, and coconut fiber make up part of the materials list used by Lenilton Morais and his family to produce the lighting fixtures and wall and table lamps that have become famous even in Europe. Prices range from R$30 to R$250, and larger pieces may be shipped.
Artluz, Praça Santos Dumont, 55, Centro, tel. (73) 251-3168.

Whitewater rafting in Itacaré region's spectacular rapids

DESTINATION
PORTO SEGURO

L earn about Brazil from ground up at Porto
Seguro, located 700 kilometers (435 mi.) south
of Salvador. One hundred beaches are framed by the
Atlantic Rainforest and cliffs ranging in color from
white to red. The landscape hasn't changed much
since Cabral's fleet saw it and Caminha described it
in his letter to the King of Portugal. Indian
traditions and the restaurants, resorts, and quality
inns of Arraial D'Ajuda, Trancoso and Caraíva now
dominate with charm and sophistication. Further
south, Cumuruxatiba is the current tourist magnet,
combining simplicity with the modern equipment
required for boat or jeep excursions. Spectacular
coral reefs and humpback whales await divers at Parque Nacional Marinho de
Abrolhos, close to the pleasant historical city of Caravelas.

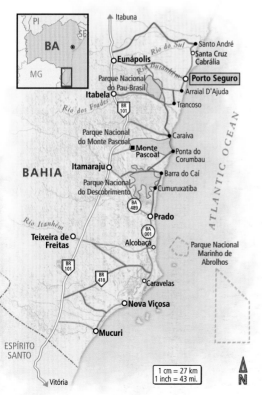

DESTINATION HIGHLIGHTS

PORTO SEGURO
  Historic Center
  The Coastline

ARRAIAL D'AJUDA (4 km/
  2.5 mi.)
  TRANCOSO (25 km/15.5 mi.)
  CARAÍVA (65 km/40 mi.)

PONTA DO CORUMBAU
(189 km/117 mi.)
  CUMURUXATIBA
  (236 km/147 mi.)

CARAVELAS (210 km/131 mi.)

All distances are from Porto Seguro

PORTO SEGURO

HISTORIC CENTER

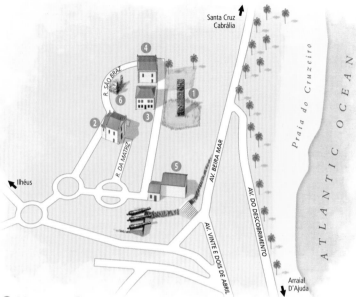

Santa Cruz
Cabrália

R. SÃO BRAZ

R. DA MATRIZ

Ilhéus

AV. BEIRA MAR

AV. DO DESCOBRIMENTO

AV. VINTE E DOIS DE ABRIL

Praia do Cruzeiro

ATLANTIC OCEAN

Arraial
D'Ajuda

① MARCO DA POSSE
A marble monument marking
Portugal's possession of Brazil
engraved with the royal seal of the
Portuguese Crown and the cross of
the Order of Christ, brought from
Portugal by the Gonçalo Coelho
expedition, in 1503.

**② IGREJA DE NOSSA
SENHORA DA PENA**
Built in 1535, this church holds
Brazil's first religious statue, of Saint
Francis of Assisi.

③ MUSEU DO DESCOBRIMENTO
The former site of the **House of
Representatives** and the **Jail**, and a
great example of 18th century
architecture.

④ IGREJA DA MISERICÓRDIA
Built in 1526. Features a remarkable
image of Christ on the cross.

⑤ IGREJA DE SÃO BENEDITO
Built by the Jesuits, probably in 1549.
Enjoy the breeze and the magnificent
view of the coast.

**⑥ RUINS OF THE COLÉGIO
DOS JESUÍTAS**
The Jesuit school was created in 1551.
Today there are native dance and *capoeira*
presentations held on the site in front of
the ruins.

**MEMORIAL DA EPOPÉIA
DO DESCOBRIMENTO**
Some distance from historical center, on
the Curuípe beach, this Epic Discovery
Memorial has a replica of Cabral's
flagship. The tour through the interior
of the ship shows how risky the grand
colonial expeditions really were.
*BR-367, km 63, Curuípe beach, tel. (73)
268-2586. Daily, 8:30am-6pm (during the
high season); Mon-Sat 8:30am-noon;
1:30am-5pm.*

Colonial houses in Porto Seguro; construction started in the 16th century

THE COASTLINE

The beach kiosks that made *lambada* such a hit in the 1980's are still all the rage, but the soundtrack today includes *axé* and *forró*. Check them out if you like lots of action, crowded beaches and the convenience of seaside services. **Taperapuã** beach has many hotels and kiosks that are always crowded. There are shows day and night, dance lessons, exercise classes, restaurants, as well as water sports, helicopter flights and paragliding. In the center of town, **Cruzeiro**'s coral reefs mix with the dark waters of the Burunharém river, but is not suitable for swimming. The nearby **Curuípe** (with clear coral pools at low tide), **Itacimirim** and **Mundaí** beaches are more serene. The **Rio dos Mangues** beach offers a quiet mangrove area and pools where the river is dammed by the reefs, but also the popular Barramares kiosk. The last two beaches, **Ponta Grande**, with crystal clear waters and reefs, and **Mutá**, are long and nearly deserted. **Coroa Vermelha**, in Santa Cruz Cabrália, is a pleasant bay with shallow waters, reefs and a few kiosks. In the surrounding area there are many people selling arts and crafts made from brazilwood by the Pataxó indians. There is also a cross marking the first mass held in the country.

SANTO ANDRÉ AND THE PARQUE ECOLÓGICO DO SANTUÁRIO

The small district of Santo André, 30 kilometers (19 mi.) north of Porto Seguro, is a ten-minute ferryboat ride from Santa Cruz Cabrália and the point of departure for a drive to explore the roughly 50 kilometers (31 mi.) of wilderness beaches, and the villages along the road leading to historical Belmonte. It is a pleasant day excursion, but hotels await for overnight visits. The **Parque Ecológico do Santuário** preserves 450 hectares (1,112 acres) of the Atlantic Rainforest and offers trails, a suspension bridge, flying foxes, river swimming, *chalana* (a small flat-bottomed boat) excursions, fishing (releasing what you catch) and a pony farm for children. Belmonte, the last stop, has many mansions from the cocoa era. Check the ferryboat schedule for the return trip.

Parque Ecológico do Santuário: access via highway BA-001, km 39.5, Santo Antônio, 12 kilometers (8 mi.) from the ferry, tel. (73) 671-5052. Daily, 8am-5pm.

Cliffs follow Bahia's southern coast

ARRAIAL D'AJUDA, TRANCOSO AND CARAÍVA

The three villages south of Porto Seguro, Arraial D'Ajuda, Trancoso and Caraíva, all offer excellent beaches, some nearly deserted and others crowded, as well as scenic landscape that can be explored by hiking, horseback, bicycle, four-wheel drive or boat. **Arraial** has more action, including luaus and raves in the middle of the forest. The place is so lit up at night that it looks like an outdoor shopping mall decorated for Christmas, complete with plenty of stores. **Trancoso** is simultaneously sophisticated and simple – you can have an expensive breakfast barefoot on the beach, or dinner at a rustic wooden table covered with a fine tablecloth. **Caraíva**, separated by the river, is pure rusticity, with no cars or electricity, and narrow sand streets. However, they have lively *forró* dances, organized in a different place every night to preserve general peacefulness.

VILLAGE VITALITY

Linked to Porto Seguro by a ten-minute ferryboat ride, the village of Arraial was once a calm place. Today, the narrow streets attract crowds who come to wander between designer-label boutiques, shops selling local handicrafts, and bars and restaurants. Sooner or later, visitors gravitate toward the beaches, then feast on a wide variety of gourmet food, from Thai to traditional Brazilian dishes from Minas Gerais. The beautiful little church **Nossa Senhora D'Ajuda** from 1549 and the nearby houses are reminders of when Arraial was a peaceful Jesuit village.

ARRAIAL BEACHES
The beaches **Apaga-Fogo** and **Araçaípe**, although next to the ferry landing, have peaceful stretches near Arraial D'Ajuda Ecoresort and the reefs. What distinguishes **D'Ajuda** and **Coqueiros** is **Paradise Water Park**, with a water slide, wave pool and manmade river. **Mucugê** waves and lively kiosks are ideal for surfing. **Parracho**, famous for parties, offers rentals for windsurfing and kayaking. **Pitinga**, closer to Trancoso, attracts the rich and famous to its sophisticated inns and restaurants, high waves, reefs and seaside bluffs.

LAIDBACK SOPHISTICATION

Laid back yet lively, Trancoso is 25 kilometers (16 mi.) from Porto Seguro, and a ten-minute ferry ride from Arraial D'Ajuda. The town has maintained the shape of Jesuit villages. **Igreja São João Batista**, built in 1656, is located on top of a cliff with the large square known as **Quadrado** flanked by small colorful houses. This square is where the action is, with its concentration of inns, bars, restaurants and studios. The cultural traditions are also centered there, with *capoeira*, Christian festivals as well as pagan activities like luaus, *forrós* and reggae nights. Brazilian singers and other celebrities play an active role in the community: Gal Costa's house has become a charming inn and Elba Ramalho owns a tourist agency.

TRANCOSO BEACHES

The cliffs along the almost deserted **Taípe** rise to 45 meters (148 feet) and guide tourists to Arraial. **Nativos**, deserted and closer to town, is a nude beach. **Coqueiros**, the departure point for boat excursions, has the Barraca do Jonas, a kiosk serving seafood. From this beach you can visit heavenly places such as **Rio Verde** (also known as **Pedra Grande**), **Itapororoca**, **Itaquena** and **Barra do Rio dos Frades** by boat, horseback or on foot.

ADVENTURE IN THE OUTSKIRTS

The area surrounding Trancoso offers adventures like horseback riding, bicycling, schooner and motorboat excursions and touring on all terrain vehicles. You can also go snorkeling at the coral reefs of Itaquena, Itapororoca, Pedra Grande and Espelho or go down the Trancoso river in a kayak.

Tour Operators: Bikes: Natural Cicloturismo e Aventura, tel. (73) 668-1955/8804-5557. Off-road: Latitude 16 Expedições, tel. (73) 668-2260/8803-0016. Horseback riding: Solomar e Nique, tel. (73) 668-1637. Motorboats: Jarbá Lancha, tel. (73) 668-1479. ATV: Bahia Alegria, tel. (73) 575-1690/8802-5033. Kayaks, motorboats and schooners: Trancoso Receptivo, tel. (73) 668-1333.

Quadrado in Trancoso retains the character of its colonial past

TRANQUIL WILDERNESS BEACHES

Rustic and hard to reach, **Caraíva** blends natural beauty with the customs of friendly people. Ideal for those seeking peace and quiet, the only access is by boat from Trancoso. If you are traveling by car, park at the end of highway BA-001 (reached from highway BR-367). Cross the Caraíva river by canoe if there is no chance of rain. The village has no streets, just sand trails, and electricity is provided by generators that are turned off at 10pm.

CARAÍVA BEACHES

Spend sunny days on wild and enchanting beaches such as **Barra Velha**, **Caraíva** (in the town), **Juacema** and **Satu**, with its fresh water lake and a lookout point on the cliff. At night, enjoy live bands and *forró* dances at Ouriço and Pelé. The **Reserva Indígena de Barra Velha** is open for visits and is home to the last remaining Pataxó indians. Also located in Caraíva is **Monte Pascoal**, sighted by Cabral upon his "discovery" of Brazil.

ESPELHO AND CURUÍPE BEACHES

At dawn during high tide, the calm sea reflects blue sky and looks like an enormous mirror (*espelho* in Portuguese). Low tide exposes the reefs, with its pools holding colorful fish. **Curuípe** and a fishing village are located to the left on the bay, and can be reached on foot. It is an enchanting place. The inns hang hammocks under the trees and place sofas and cushions on the sand. Access is controlled by the gated community Outeiro das Brisas, or by boat from Trancoso or Caraíva.

OUR RECOMMENDATION

The **Restaurante do Baiano** is a treat. Baiano, the owner, creates all the dishes, welcomes the clients, provides chaise longues and serves typical seafood dishes or new discoveries from his travels. Since the service is slow, you might want to order ahead of time then go and enjoy the beach (*Praia do Espelho, 22 kilometers (14 mi.) from downtown, tel. 73/668-5020*).

Espelho beach at low tide: crystal clear waters and natural pools

PONTA DO CORUMBAU AND CUMURUXATIBA

PONTA DO CORUMBAU

With deserted stretches towards the south, this long beach offers a fishing village with a few restaurants on the northern end. Nearby, the clear Corumbau river meets the ocean, zigzagging through the white sand. On the other side of the river is **Barra Velha** and the **Pataxó Indian Reserve**; its inhabitants sell handicrafts in Corumbau. Cross the land from Cumuru to Ponta do Corumbau by car, or have a guide take you along trails.
Tour Operator: Aquamar, Cumuruxatiba beach, tel. (73) 573-1360.

Lighthouse at Ponta do Corumbau

VILLAGE OF LEISURE

Cumuruxatiba, or Cumuru as the locals call it, is a tiny village with dirt roads accessible from Porto Seguro via highways BR-101 and BA-489. The beaches are spectacular and sometimes deserted, with cliffs, coconut groves, rivers and various leisure options that include reef snorkeling, horseback riding along the cliffs, jeep tours and boat excursions to see the humpback whales. You can also drive through Fazenda Guaíra and take a hiking trail to the mouth of the Japara river. There are boat excursions north to **Ponta do Corumbau**, one of the most beautiful and wild points on the Brazilian coastline, with clear waters and the option of scuba diving. The inns located there are comfortable and exclusive, though they do not have electricity or telephones.

WHALE WATCHING

The *baleias jubarte* (humpback whales) reach a length of 18 meters (59 feet) and usually appear between July and November. The boat excursion, about an hour from land, includes a presentation by biologists. The boat remains in the area for roughly two hours and is equipped with a hydrophone so that passengers can listen to the whale calls. During whale-watching season, it is so common to see whales that the company reimburses part of the excursion fee if there are no sightings during your tour.
Tour Operator: Aquamar, Cumuruxatiba beach, tel. (73) 573-1360.

DIVING ON THE REEFS

For those who like scuba diving, the Cumuru region offers many little-explored coral reefs. At **Barreira Branca** and **Alto Caí** the coral reefs form an underwater labyrinth. You can go snorkeling at the **Corais do Pataxo** and also **Recife da Coroa**, a sandbar that can be reached by canoe.
Tour Operator: Aquamar, Cumuruxatiba beach, tel. (73) 573-1360.

OUR RECOMMENDATION

🍽 The **Restaurante do Hermes** was formerly a beach kiosk that was transformed into a restaurant with glassed-in dining rooms and a pleasant deck. The house specialty is the generous fish and seafood trays. Geraldo, one of the owners, runs the kitchen and roams dining areas, making sure the customers are happy with their food (*Avenida Beira-Mar, Cumuruxatiba, tel. 73/573-1155*).

Aerial view of the Abrolhos archipelago: diving reveals vast and colorful schools of fish

CARAVELAS

Caravelas is a small town with narrow streets that serves as the departure point for **Parque Nacional Marinho de Abrolhos**, located 67 kilometers (42 mi.) from the coast. It also provides access to the diving area **Parcel das Paredes**, as well as other destinations for spear fishing. Reach the Pataxó indian community at **Monte Pascoal** with a 2-hour boat ride plus a drive and a hike over a trail. Caravelas is 210 kilometers (130 mi.) from Porto Seguro.

ABROLHOS

According to the local legend, *Abrolhos* comes from the Portuguese expression "*abra os olhos*" (keep your eyes peeled), credited to the navigator Américo Vespúcio in 1503. It's no fisherman's yarn or local politician's brag – the truth is that Abrolhos is dazzling. Its enormous variety of colored and designed coral reefs are the most beautiful in the South Atlantic, and frame the setting for sea turtles and humpback whales. The park encompasses the **Recifes das Timbebas**, in front of **Alcobaça**, and five islands: **Redonda**, **Guarita**, **Sueste**, **Siriba** (the only island where tourists can go on shore, as long as they are accompanied by a guide from the Ibama environmental agency) and **Santa Bárbara**, which has a Navy lighthouse. Going ashore on Siriba, you can get a close look at boobies and frigate birds. The waters are crystal clear and in the May to September dry season you can see for up to 20 meters (65 feet). Scuba diving and free diving are allowed at night. The water temperature is about 24°C (75°F) all year round. Only authorized boats are allowed in the region. One-day excursions are from 7:30am to 5pm; two-day trips are also available. The trip to the location takes 2.5 hours on an ocean cruiser or 6 to 7 hours by sailboat. For longer stays rent a sailboat or catamaran for diving and stay at the houseboat hotel.

Tour Operators:
Abrolhos Turismo, tel. (73) 297-1149;
Abrolhos Embarcações, tel. (73) 297-1172;
Iate Clube Abrolhos, tel. (73) 297-1173;
Paradise Abrolhos, tel. (73) 297-1352.

DESTINATION
CHAPADA DIAMANTINA

L ocated in the heart of Bahia, Chapada Diamantina offers spectacular caves, waterfalls, canyons and rivers with eddies and water gushing like outdoor whirlpool tubs. Everyone agrees it's magical and fascinating, and all visitors want to return. The Parque Nacional da Chapada Diamantina attracts families, foreigners, adventurers, and outdoor sports enthusiasts, though it is a challenge in itself to reach the 152,000 hectare (375,559 acre) park by the potholed highway BR-242. There are regular flights to the Lençóis airport from Salvador, Recife and São Paulo. The departure points for the attractions are the base cities of Lençóis, Palmeiras, Andaraí, the district of Xique-Xique do Igatu and Mucugê. Prepare for long walks and many options for trekking, snorkeling, mountain biking, rappelling and bungee-jumping.

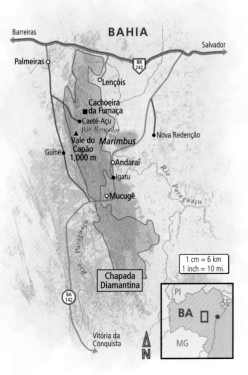

DESTINATION HIGHLIGHTS

CHAPADA DIAMANTINA
Lençóis, Palmeiras (86 km/53 mi.)
Caeté-Açu (74 km/46 mi.)
Andaraí (101 km/157 mi.)
Xique-Xique do Igatu
  (114 km/71 mi.)

All distances are from Lençóis

Chapada Diamantina, an adventurer's paradise, with Morro do Camelo in the background

Lençóis, Palmeiras and Caeté-Açu

The town of Lençóis is the door to the Chapada. It is quiet during the day but activity picks up at 5pm when jeeps and vans return from excursions. Lençóis dates back to the 18th and 19th centuries when the town was a bustling center for mining, especially for diamonds.

The town retains its stone streets and the colonial houses of the Praças **das Nagôs** and **Horácio de Matos**, the **Igreja do Rosário** and the **Igreja de Nossa Senhora dos Passos**. More rustic and 86 kilometers (53 mi.) from Lençóis, **Palmeiras** and the **Caeté-Açu** district, also known as Capão, offer accommodation options and guides for those wanting to explore the **Vale do Capão** mountains. Nestled here are the **Fumaça** waterfalls, the highest in Brazil at 340 meters (1,115 feet), and one of Chapada's main attractions.

Morro do Pai Inácio

A 30-minute hike will take you to the top of Morro do Pai Inácio, where 1,170 metets (3,839 feet) above sea level permits an exquisite 360° view of the mountains and valleys of the Chapada. The hill is 22 kilometers (14 mi.) from Lençóis on highway BR-242 heading to Seabra. Don't miss the chance to stop at the **Mucugezinho** river,

---

Exploring Tips

The Chapada is extensive and poorly marked. Explore with the help of agencies and tour guides in the base cities, such as the Associações dos Condutores de Visitantes (tourist guide associations). Agencies provide transportation; you're self-sufficient with free-lance guides. One day excursions include swimming in the rivers and waterfalls. There are also guides that specialize in longer hikes, excursions and adventure sports.

20 kilometers (13 mi.) from Lençóis, just off highway BR-242.

RONCADOR, REMANSO AND MARIMBUS

When you reach **Roncador** river you will feel like you are at an outdoor spa, but without the radical diets. The tour is done in stages. First take a four-wheel drive vehicle to the village of **Remanso**, a former refuge for runaway slaves. From there, canoe down the **Santo Antônio** river to the **Roncador** with a local guide. This involves around two hours of floating by royal water lilies, water-ferns and large lakes, and glimpsing **Marimbus**, a small swampy area that can be seen better from Andaraí. A fifteen-minute hike leads to the wonderful river whirlpools. Then return to the four-wheel drive for the 18-kilometer (11 mi.) journey over a bumpy road back to Lençóis.

Tour Operator: Marimbus Ecoturismo, tel. (75) 334-1718/1292

SUPER RADICAL ADVENTURES

Guides are essential for a more extreme contact with Chapada's lush nature.

Rappelling and/or canyoning: visit Cachoeira do Mosquito, with two falls of 35 meters (115 feet) and 50 meters (164 feet); Morro do Camelo, 250 meters (820 feet); Morro do Pai Inácio, 150 meters (492 feet); Gruta do Lapão, a 55 meters (180 feet) cave; also offers a bungee-jump. Other locations are further away and the excursions include transportation: Gruta dos Brejões, 123 meters (400 feet); and Brejões mountains, 170 meters (558 feet); Morro do Chapéu, 350 kilometers (218 mi.) from Lençóis; Cachoeira do Buracão with a height of 100 meters (328 feet) in Ibicoara, 230 kilometers (143 mi.) from Lençóis. *Tour Operator: Lençóis: Nativos da Chapada, tel. (75) 334-1647/1314; Andrenalina, tel (75) 334-1689.* **Hot Air Balloon Panoramic Flight** (morro do Pai Inácio). *Lençóis: Nativos da Chapada, tel. (75) 334-1647/1314.*

IRAQUARA: THE CITY OF CAVES

A sign at the junction of highways BR-242 and BA-432, leading to Iraquara, announces *Cidade das Grutas* or "City of Caves". The area, roughly 82 kilometers (51 mi.) north of Lençóis, has dozens of caves and grottos. **Torrinha** is considered one of the most complete in Brazil in terms of formations sprouting from the ceiling, floor and walls of the caves. There you will also see extremely rare aragonite mineral flowers. **Lapa Doce** has spectacular rock formations, a wide tunnel 40 meters (131 feet) high, and a maze of huge galleries. **Lapa do Sol** displays interesting prehistoric rock drawings. An underground river of crystalline waters starts at the entrance of **Pratinha**, so the only way in is by swimming. Local guides take visitors into the first 170 meters (558 feet) of the cave. The water is up to 14 meters (46 feet) deep and it is possible to see some fish. Other caves include **Mané Ioiô** and **Fumaça**. Access via highway BA-142, at km 17.

Tour Operator: José Carlos, from the Ibirapitanga Inn, tel. (75) 335-2196.

A flowerlike Aragonite formation

Prehistoric rock drawings inside Lapa do Sol

SERRANO AND SURROUNDING AREA

Enjoy a sunny morning or afternoon at the waterfalls. Begin walking in the center of **Lençóis**. Less than 3 kilometers (2 mi.) away, relax in whirlpools in the pink rocks of **Lençóis** river, shaped by water erosion. Another 2-kilometers (1.25-mi.) walk leads to **Cachoeirinha**, a waterfall with crystal clear waters, and to **Primavera** waterfall with a height of 6 meters (20 feet). The next swimming hole is a twenty-minute walk away at **Poço Halley**. From there a short trail leads to the **Salão das Areias Coloridas**, with colored sands. In the afternoon go sliding down the natural waterslide at **Ribeirão do Meio**, an hour's walk

from Poço Halley. One more stop is the magnificent **Sossego waterfall** where the water falls over the pink rock walls. Getting there involves a 6-kilometers (3.75-mi.) walk along a trail and another 2-kilometers (1.25-mi.) of hiking over rocks in the river.

CACHOEIRA DA FUMAÇA

This excursion leaves you breathless twice – first during the 2,5 hour hike up to the top of the mountain, and then when you see the 340-meters (1,116-foot) abyss into which the water plunges, only to dissipate like smoke before reaching the bottom (hence the name *fumaça*, meaning "smoke"). Above the waterfall, you can lie on a rock ledge and inch towards the edge of the precipice to admire the deep gorge. Fumaça is located in the Capão district, in Palmeiras, 86 km (53 mi.) from Lençóis.

ANDARAÍ AND XIQUE-XIQUE DO IGATU

Andaraí, reached by highways BR-242 and BA-142, has better roads and is closer to Salvador. It offers waterfalls, caves and a mountainous landscape, and is the base for various excursions, including **Poço Encantado** and **Marimbus**. Founded at the height of the mining era in 1845, it once supported a large wealthy population. The attractive village and stone house ruins of Xique-Xique do Igatu, now home to 400, appear to be frozen in time, earning it the nickname "ghost town". Alongside the ruins is the outdoor **Arte & Memória** gallery (*Rua Luís dos Santos, tel. 75/335-2510. Tue-Sun, noon-7pm*) with exhibits by local artists; and the **Memorial do Garimpeiro**, with a display of mining tools. A stone road runs 7 kilometers (4 mi.) into the village. Half a day is enough time to see the village.

POÇO ENCANTADO AND POÇO AZUL

The dazzling color effects in the photo on this page are from **Poço Encantado**. It is located in Itaité, 40 kilometers (25 mi.) from Andaraí. The best times to see this phenomenon are between April and September, from 9am to 1pm, and between December and February, from 10pm to 2am by moonlight. The water is so transparent that it seems the rocks located at the bottom of the pond, 61 meters (200 feet) deep, are just beneath the surface. Float in the pool or snorkel at **Poço Azul**, similar but smaller and shallower. It's 67 kilometers (42 mi.) from Andaraí at the km 17 exit off highway BA-142; although longest, this route is best for passenger cars. The best time to visit is between February and October, from noon to 3pm. Visits to either require a local guide and proper equipment.

MARIMBUS: THE CHAPADA SWAMP

For close contact with the beauty of local flora and fauna, go to **Marimbus**, the swamp area known as the **Pantanal da Chapada** located between Lençóis and Andaraí. Weave a canoe through a series of interconnected lagoons fed from ten different rivers and crystal clear springs; these form a large marsh area during the rainy season between May and October. Royal water lilies and native plants such as beakrushes are visited by different types of birds and alligators. Hire a local guide and rent a boat from the camp site and snackbar located on highway BA-142, at km 45.5.

Poço Encantado: an impressive visual effect

MUCUGÊ

Relax in temperate Mucugê, 150 kilometers (93 mi.) from Lençóis and perched at 1,000 meters (3,280 feet), granting an average annual temperature of 19°C (66°F). The well-preserved 19th century buildings in the downtown area earned it historical heritage status. Some examples include the **Igreja Matriz de Santa Isabel, Igreja de Santo Antônio** and the **Byzantine cemetery**. There are also many easy trails leading to countless waterfalls.

WEST SIDE WATERFALLS

The west side of Chapada has a profusion of waterfalls. Those near Andaraí include **Garapa**, with its large pink sandstone pool, requiring an 8-kilometer (5-mi.) drive, 3.5 kilometers (2 mi.) over dirt road, then a 30-minute walk along a trail; **Ramalho**, with 100-meter (328-foot) waterfall, reached by an 8-kilometers (5-mi.) intermediate level hiking trail; and **Donana**, on highway BA-142 heading to Mucugê, a 600-meter (3/8-mi.) walk from Andaraí, that leads to the **Paraguaçu** canyon. Perch on a rock surrounded by gushing water in Xique-Xique do Igatu at **Pombas**, 4 kilometers (2.5 mi.) from the center; a little further ahead is **Taramba**, good for swimming. From Mucugê there is **Sandália Bordada**, a 1-kilometer (5/8-mi.) drive; **Piabinha**, a 4-kilometer (2.5-mi.) drive; **Tiburtino**, a 4-kilometer (2.5-mi.) drive plus a 2-kilometer (1.25-mi.) hike; **Andorinhas**, a 4-kilometer (2.5-mi.) drive plus a 4-kilometer (2.5-mi.) hike; **Funis**, a 5-kilometer (3-mi.) hike; **Sibéria**, a 3-kilometer (2-mi.) drive plus a 8-kilometer (5-mi.) hike; and **Cardoso**, a 7-kilometer (4.25-mi.) hike, all with great volumes of water. A huge pool for swimming awaits at **Mar de Espanha**, after a 3-kilometer (2-mi.) drive plus 5-kilometer (3-mi.) hike. In Ibicoara, **Buracão**, a 1.5 hour hike along an intermediate level trail leads to a beautiful waterfall 85 meters (279 feet) high.

RAMPA DO CAIM

This marvelous 2.5–hour hiking trail provides a view similar to the long hikes through the Paty valley. Depart from Igatu heading towards the Carbonado canyon, with a view of the Paraguaçu canyon, and directly across from the Paty river canyon with an altitude of 480 meters (1575 feet). Pure vertigo.

Tour Operator: Sincorá, tel. (75) 335-2210.

The remarkable cemetery in the midst of greenery and rocks

DESTINATION
MACEIÓ

Green sea, plenty of sun, and sensational beaches – these typical northeastern ingredients have a special flavor in Alagoas. Outside of capital city Maceió, the resorts and developed beachfronts give way to stretches of wild coastline with charming inns. The 230 kilometers (143 mi.) coastline is presented here as four itineraries, ranging from the urban beaches of Maceió, the incomparable Gunga beach, and the historical town of Penedo on the banks of the São Francisco river. Northwards are the deserted beaches of Barra de Santo Antônio, the stunning Rota Ecológica (Ecological Route) and the rock pools of Maragogi, bordering the state of Pernambuco.

DESTINATION HIGHLIGHTS

MACEIÓ
  The Beaches
  The Streets of Maceió

PENEDO (168 km/104 mi.)
  Mouth of the São Francisco River

NORTHERN COAST
  From Barra de Santo Antônio
  (56km/35 mi.) to Morro (63 km/40 mi.)

ECOLOGICAL ROUTE
  From Barra do Camaragibe
  (98 km/61 mi.) to
  Japaratinga (110 km/69 mi.)

MARAGOGI (141 km/88 mi.)

All distances are from Maceió

MACEIÓ

THE BEACHES

The Alagoan capital, nicknamed "Water Paradise", runs along a narrow strip of land between the Mundaú lagoon and the Atlantic Ocean.
As if it were not enough water, Maceió also has another beautiful lagoon, Manguaba. Its 800,000 inhabitants enjoy the comforts of a big city and a charming urban coastline: from **Pontal da Barra** at the entrance of the city, to **Cruz das Almas**, the gateway to the north coast, nature blends in with the bustling city and its active nightlife. Kick off your visit at the beaches, and visit the Historical Center later.

PAJUÇARA

This is the most popular beach in Maceió, with beautiful rock pools and many hotels. The bucolic scene of the *jangadas* (traditional wooden boats of this region) heading for the rock pools contrasts with the crowds attracted by its warm shallow waters. The neighboring **Ponta Verde** has a delightful beachfront promenade which attracts beachgoers between the Ponta Verde and Maceió Mar hotels.

JATIÚCA

One of the oldest resorts in Brazil is named after this beach, known for its calm and crystalline waters. The powerful breakers at neighboring **Cruz das Almas** are wonderful for surfing. Between them, **Antas** lagoon

OUR RECOMMENDATION

🍽 The restaurant **Wanchako** specializes in *Nikkei*, a fusion of Peruvian and Japanese cuisine. The highlight is *ceviche*, fish and other seafood marinated in lemon *(Rua São Francisco de Assis, 93, tel. 82/327-8701).*

🏨 Each floor of the **Ritz Lagoa da Anta**, in Maceió, has its own distinctive style. Romance is in the air on the Bali Floor; the faded lights of the corridors and the rooms are inspired by Indonesia. The Design Floor's clean, more modern style caters to businessmen.

Additional information begins on page 462.

Ponta Verde: lighthouse, clear waters and a lively beachfront promenade

is the favorite of windsurfers and sailing sports fans.

NORTH OF THE CITY

Close to Maceió, many beaches deserve a visit. One of them is **Garça Torta**, 13 kilometers (8 mi.) from the capital on highway AL-101. This sloping beach with strong waves has maintained its luxuriant vegetation. **Ipioca**, 9 kilometers (5.5 mi.) from there, with hardpacked sand, stretches across both calm and heavy seas. There are few signs on the road, so pay close attention to the marked distances so as not to miss the entrances. **Paripueira**, 32 kilometers (20 mi.) from the capital, marks the start of the longest reef barrier in Brazil, running up all the way to Porto de Galinhas in the state of Pernambuco. At low tide, it is possible to walk 1 kilometer (0.62 mi.) in knee-deep water.

TO THE SOUTH, BARRA DE SÃO MIGUEL AND GUNGA

Barra de São Miguel, 33 kilometers (21 mi.) south of Maceió, is a village of simple houses and dirt roads, flanked by **Roteiro** lagoon. There are two beaches:

Barra de São Miguel, a surfers' paradise; and **Niquim**, a favorite of families with children, because a coral reef protects the broad beach from waves. For more beautiful landscapes, proceed past the sign indicating the entrance to the municipality, continuing along highway AL-101 (if coming from Maceió). Continue for almost 1 kilometer (0.6 mi.), past the entrance to the beach farm, then park. A lookout provides an excellent view of the white-sands of the **Ponta do Gunga** and Roteiro lagoon. On the other side there is a sloping beach with constant breakers – not even the many kiosks interfere with the view. For peace and quiet framed by palm trees, continue straight ahead, seek a calm spot and enjoy the landscape.

HOW TO GET TO GUNGA

Gunga means "big boss". Coincidence or not, to cross the farm and reach **Ponta do Gunga** by car, you must obtain a permit from the local boss, which is the **Hotel Enseada** in **Pajuçara**. From the docks of Barra de São Miguel, *jangadeiros* (local boat operators) charge a small fee for the 10-minute crossing.

THE STREETS OF MACEIÓ

JARAGUÁ DISTRICT

Since 1995, a successful revitalization project restored life and beauty to this centuries-old port district, located next to Pajuçara and the center. Among the restored buildings are neoclassical manors, the marble-staired **Associação Comercial** and the **Museu da Imagem e do Som**. The district of Jaraguá started to develop in the 16th century, when ships harbored to load brazilwood. Later, they exported sugar, and then tobacco, coconut and leather. In the second half of the 19th century, the port expanded its trade and became an important business center, with beautiful two-story houses, and spacious fabric, hat and shoe stores. After a time, the district entered a period of decline, and became home to run-down bars and brothels. In the last few years, it is reenergized as an important daytime commercial center, converting to a bustling nightlife with crowded bars, nightclubs and music houses.

PONTAL DA BARRA

Pontal da Barra is a district on the shore of **Mundaú** lagoon, on the way out of the city heading south. Fishermen's wives make lace and sell their work in front of their own houses, along the main paved road. They offer Maceió's traditional *renda filé (filé* lace), *renda de labyrinto* (high quality embroidered lace), *renda de bilro (bilro* lace) and the *renascença* (*renascença* lace), one of the most elaborate. From Pontal da Barra boats leave on four-hour excursions along the Mundaú lagoon and its channels, reaching **Barra Nova**. Departures at 9am and 1:30pm.

WHERE TO SHOP

Armazém Sebrae occupies an old ware-house in Jaraguá, and is one of the best places in town to buy genuine Alagoan handicrafts. There is a good variety of lace, bedcovers, carpets, pieces of furniture and decoration objects produced in many regions of the state.
Avenida da Paz, 878, tel. (82) 223-8200. Mon-Wed, 10am-7pm; Thu-Sat, 10am-10pm.

Lace is a highlight of Alagoas handicrafts

Jaguará district is the beating heart of Maceió's commerce and nightlife

ATELIER VIVER DE ARTE

The artists mix academic art and traditional handicrafts, and the result is original creativity. Occupying a pleasant 1960's-era house in the Farol district, the atelier is run by the sisters Rosa Maria Piatti and Ana Maia. Rosa works with wood and ceramics, and Ana creates lamps hand-painted on Italian paper, and goatskin and canvas bags. The pieces have won awards in arts and design fairs abroad.
Rua Manoel Maia Nobre, 257, tel. (82) 223-5257. Mon-Fri, 8-noon and 2pm-6pm.

TAPIOQUEIRAS

Just as Salvador has its famous *baiana* women selling *acarajé*, Maceió has dozens of *tapioqueiras*. Tapioca, a very thin pastry of manioc flour starch, is a legacy of the Brazilian indians, enjoyed since colonial times. In the Alagoan capital, this exotic delicacy is prepared with many different fillings – from the traditional ground coconut with cheese to fried banana with *brigadeiro* (a chocolate dessert made with condensed milk), and can serve as a meal. *Tapioqueiras* come to the seafront, between Jatiúca, Ponta Verde and Pajuçara, starting at 5pm. Most of the tapioca is standard; but the tapioca "Da Irmã" in Ponta Verde excels both in care of preparation and friendly service.

OUR RECOMMENDATION

🍽 Curiously, one of the best places to have lunch or dinner in Maceió is **Divina Gula**, serving the typical food of Minas Gerais. The most popular restaurant in town, it serves a good *cachaça* (*Rua Engenheiro Paulo Brandão Nogueira, 85, tel. 82/235-1016*).

🏨 A resort in disguise, the **Jatiúca Resort** is located inside the city, on one of the best beaches of Maceió. The front gate leads to the wide oceanfront promenade; the gardens exit opens to the clear green sea.

Additional information begins on page 462.

PENEDO

One of the oldest and historically most important cities of Alagoas, Penedo, built on a large rock outcropping for which it's named, contributes a rich collection of colonial buildings. Located on the São Francisco river, 168 kilometers (104 mi.) from Maceió, it is reached from highways AL-101 South and AL-225. It has cobblestone streets and many magnificent churches, including **Nossa Senhora dos Anjos** and **Nossa Senhora da Corrente**. The baroque architecture of the churches and constructions bear witness to the colonizers and Franciscan missionaries. A good starting point to explore the city is **Fundação Casa do Penedo** (*Rua João Pessoa, 126, Centro Histórico, tel. 82/551-3371 or 551-5443*), which contains crafts and objects and documents related to the history of the old settlement. The Nossa Senhora dos Anjos church and convent are close by, on Rua Sete de Setembro. Inaugurated in 1786, after one hundred years of construction, it has a chapel dedicated to the Ordem Terceira de São Francisco. The ceiling, painted by the Portuguese artist Libório Lázaro Leal, portrays Nossa Senhora dos Anjos, who seems to be always looking at her observer. Visit the convent kitchen and see its huge conical chimney. In the low part of the city, near the river, stands the 1756 **Igreja de Nossa Senhora da Corrente**. Its baroque altar is lavishly decorated in gold leaf, and the floor is made of mosaics brought from England and Portugal. One highlight is the original tile work brought from Lisbon portraying the life of Mary.

OUR RECOMMENDATION

🍽 Even though it's not Pantanal, good alligator meat is still served up, with coconut sauce, at **Forte da Rocheira**, on the banks of the São Francisco river. The restaurant has a simple ambience, and a beautiful view of the river (*Rua da Rocheira, 2, tel. 82/551-3273*).

Penedo, a gem on the São Francisco river. The pink house (right) contains a beautiful historical museum

Where the river meets the sea, the beauty of "Velho Chico"

MOUTH OF THE SÃO FRANCISCO RIVER

The São Francisco river, dubbed the "river of national integration," flows through five states (Minas, Bahia, Sergipe, Alagoas and Pernambuco) and five hundred municipalities. It begins at 1,428 meters (4,685 feet) in Minas Gerais, in the highlands of the Canastra mountain range on the Zagaia plateau. It passes through savannahs, forests, pastures, caves and archeological sites; it has rapids and waterfalls, and supplies water to many towns. Finally, after having covered 2,660 kilometers (1,615 mi.), it flows into the sea on the boundary between the states of Sergipe and Alagoas. The river was "discovered" by the Genovese navigator, Américo Vespúcio, on October 4th, 1,501, Saint Francis Day. It is also affectionately known as "Velho Chico" (Old Chico), since *Chico* is the diminutive of Francisco. In colonial times, it was the route of Portuguese expeditions to explore the Brazilian hinterland in search of gold. A strategic water resource for regional development of the country, scientists claim that if it were not for its waters, the region would be a desert. One good way to see this important river is by a 2.5-hour tour departing from Piaçabuçu wharf, 30 kilometers (19 mi.) from Penedo, descending 13 kilometers (8 mi.) to the river mouth. During the excursion, swim in a lagoon and walk to the point where the São Francisco meets the sea.

Visit **Pixaim**, a village with a former *quilombo* (community formed by run-away slaves); or make a three-day tour up the river to a region with canyons. The excursions, with daily departures at 7am, can be booked at the agency Mercator, located at the wharf (*Praça Prefeito Ronulfo Victor de Araújo, 184, tel. 82/552-1137*). You can also hire a boat at the Beira Rio bar, known as Alô Alô (*Avenida Amadeu Lobo, 192, tel. 82/552-1837*).

NORTHERN COAST

Carro Quebrado: white sand, green sea, pools and cliffs

FROM BARRA DE SANTO ANTÔNIO TO MORRO

The best stretch of fantastic and wild beaches on the coast of Alagoas starts at **Barra de Santo Antônio**; a river with the same name runs through the town. Don't miss **Tabuba**, with rock pools, south of the village and accessed by highway AL-101.

ILHA DA CROA

To get to the best beaches north of Barra go to this peninsula (it's not really an "island"), five minutes away by ferry boat. Guides are only needed for the Ecological Route, which includes a drive to **Morro** beach; we recommend Val and Almir, experts of the area. Be forewarned: there are many aggressive guides.

CARRO QUEBRADO

The name of this beach, 6 kilometers (4 mi.) from the city center, means broken car, and it got its name from a car that got stuck and remained here for a long time. Coming from Croa,

you might just wish for the same luck as the driver of that vehicle had. Carro Quebrado has white sands, green warm waters, rock pools and cliffs. Three fishermen kiosks serve seafood.

DESERTED BEACHES

Ilha da Croa and Carro Quebrado are slowly becoming popular among tourists. However, Alagoas's north coast offers much more to those that are searching for tranquility and virgin nature. To the left of Carro Quebrado are marvelous deserted beaches that can be reached on foot by physically-fit adventurers; beware of tide variations. The beaches **Pedra do Cebola**, **Ponta do Gamela** and **Morro** are there, protected by cliffs, coconut palm trees and a coral barrier in the sea. Hire a recommended guide. The road crosses a sugar cane plantation and the access is through farms with restricted entrance.

Ecological Route

From Barra do Camaragibe to Japaratinga

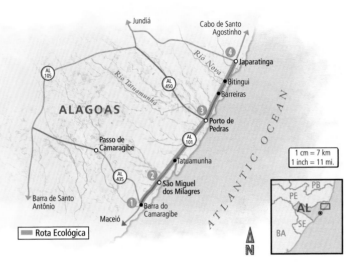

Jundiá

Cabo de Santo Agostinho

Rio Nova

④ Japaratinga

AL 105

Rio Tatuamunhá

AL 450

● Bitingui

● Barreiras

ALAGOAS

③

○ Porto de Pedras

Passo de Camaragibe

AL 101

ATLANTIC OCEAN

② ● Tatuamunhá

1 cm = 7 km
1 inch = 11 mi.

AL 435

○ São Miguel dos Milagres

Barra de Santo Antônio

①

● Barra do Camaragibe

Maceió

▬ Rota Ecológica

N

PB
PE
AL
SE
BA

Enjoy it while it lasts: magnificent beaches, picturesque villages with extremely friendly inhabitants and charming and comfortable inns. This is a quiet and peaceful region with well-protected, relatively undiscovered nature. Officially it is part of the coral reef itinerary, but local inhabitants call it the **Rota Ecológica**, which doesn't do justice to the astonishing landscape with fourteen beaches on the 40 kilometers (25 mi.) of coastline between **Barra do Camaragibe** and **Japaratinga**. There are two ways to get there: by paved highway AL-435 (alternating new and potholed stretches), going from **São Luís do Quitunde** down to Barra do Camaragibe, or by a dirt road from Barra de Santo Antônio to **Morro** beach – here there are no signs, so hire a local guide. If you come from

Coconut forest near Ponta do Gunga, with its sloping, white-sand beach

Barra do Camaragibe: gateway to a region of tranquility and nature

Pernambuco, just stay on the narrow road along the coast after Japaratinga. The Ecological Route is protected under the environment protection area Costa dos Corais, extending 135 kilometers (84 mi.) from Formoso river (next to Porto de Galinhas) in the state of Pernambuco, to Meirim river (Paripueira), in Alagoas.

OUR RECOMMENDATION

Stay at **Pousada do Toque**, in São Miguel dos Milagres, 85 kilometers (53 mi.) from Maceió. Nilo, from Espírito Santo, and his *alagoana* wife Gilda, provide impeccable service. He's in charge of the kitchen, she oversees the presentation. To boot, the couple pampers you by serving breakfast any time of day.

Stand on a 300 m² (3228 sq. ft) deck offering a panoramic ocean view at the **Pousada do Alto** in Japaratinga, elevation 120 meters (394 feet). The dining room has glass walls and the ten rooms are decorated with a good mix of antique and modern pieces.

Additional information begins on page 462.

❶ BARRA DO CAMARAGIBE
Three beautiful beaches are a great introduction to the least explored – and for many, the most beautiful – stretch of coastline of the state of Alagoas. **Marceneiro** is a long and deserted beach, with a calm sea; **Barra** beach has a fishing village, next to the mouth of Camaragibe river. You can cross the river by canoe to visit the almost untouched **Morro** beach, protected by cliffs and vegetation, with calm, crystal-clear waters.

❷ SÃO MIGUEL DOS MILAGRES
Stop to enjoy the beautiful **Toque** beach and a charming inn with the same name (see box). There are some 8 kilometers (5 mi.) of fine and hard sand, and a sea dotted with rock pools. It is worth tipping locals to get the right directions.

❸ PORTO DE PEDRAS
Just beyond São Miguel is Porto de Pedras, a little village with colonial buildings and coconut plantations. It

is located between the mangrove-spread **Manguaba** and **Tatuamunha** rivers. Nearby beaches include **Laje**, **Tatuamunha** and **Patacho**.

❹ JAPARATINGA

Even today, the natural beauty of Japaratinga – which started as a small fishing village in the 18th century – seems undisturbed. Cross the Manguaba river by ferryboat, from **Porto de Pedras**. Before arriving at the village, pass two of its most beautiful beaches, **Boqueirão** and **Barreiras do Boqueirão**. Lined with coconut trees, both beaches have cliffs and a sea with mild waves. In Barreiras do Boqueirão there are bars, some shops and two pleasant fresh water fountains.

COSTA DOS CORAIS MARINE UNIVERSE

This is the largest marine conservation area in Brazil, with more than 413,000 hectares, stretching 135 kilometers (84 mi.) along the Brazilian coast. The coastline includes thirteen municipalities in the states of Alagoas and Pernambuco, and more than 200,000 residents make a living from fishing and farming. Costa dos Corais was established in 1997 to protect coral reefs, beaches, mangroves, and endangered marine species listed by Ibama, such as the *peixe-boi* (manatee). One of these is Nina, a female manatee that lives in the mangrove of Porto das Pedras, and one of the last manatees in this stretch of the coast of Alagoas. (According to studies, today there are only four hundred manatees living between the states of Alagoas and Maranhão.) Gentle and docile, the *peixe-boi* was unfortunately easy prey for fisher-men who were attracted by their fat, meat and leathery skin. The females give birth to a calf only every three years, after a gestation period of thirteen months. The mother then nurses her calves for two years.

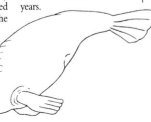

MARAGOGI

The state's second most popular destination, after Maceió, Maragogi's main attractions are its *galés* (see below) and 22 kilometers (14 mi.) of coastline. The town is reached by highway AL-101 North. The main inns, hotels and restaurants are located along the seafront avenue. **São Bento** is a bucolic fishing village where women sell home-made *sequilhos*, a type of cookie. It is located south of the bridge over the Salgado river, on the border with the municipality of Japaratinga. To the north of Maragogi, almost on the border with Pernambuco, is **Ponta do Mangue**, a peaceful beach, with a narrow strip of sand, *jangadas* and unobtrusive houses. The sea is warm and calm.

GALÉS

Galés are coral reefs located 6 kilometers (4 mi.) off the coast, which form pools of crystal clear water at low tide covering over 5,000 m²

(54,000 sq. ft). There are two small boats selling food, and the area is well preserved and diversified. You can take a two-hour tour by catamaran or motorboat. Ponto de Embarque, at the entrance to Maragogi, is a good place to hire a boat.

OUR RECOMMENDATION

🍽 **Restaurante do Mano** has been at the same beachfront location for more than thirty years, offering well-prepared meals served in generous portions. It sets the standard for seafood restaurants in Maragogi (*Rua Semião Ribeiro de Albuquerque, 606, Praia de São Bento, tel. 82/296-7106*).

🏨 The resort **Club Hotel Salinas do Maragogi** has a rustic air, and the Maragogi river runs through its grounds. It has plenty of greenery, swimming pools and sports facilities. Its family-oriented environment attracts both those who prefer peace and quiet, as well as visitors seeking activity.

Additional information begins on page 462.

Jangadas and *galés* along a 22 kilometers (14 mi.) coastline

DESTINATION
RECIFE

Pernambuco throbs to the infectious rhythms of *frevo*, *maracatu*, *forró* and the new mangue beat. The state is home to two Carnivals, in Recife and Olinda, which are different from each other and also from those elsewhere in the country. The city was the stage for Dutch invasions and independence movements, and it has a remarkable heritage and a rich culture that includes handicrafts from Bezerros e Caruaru and *literatura de cordel* – small booklets containing poems or short stories are hung in the stores by a string. The state has a long and diverse coastline, along with one of the most incredible ecological sanctuaries in the country: the archipelago of Fernando de Noronha. Finally, Pernambuco is the starting point to explore the Capivara mountain range in the state of Piauí, as well as João Pessoa and Campina Grande in the state of Paraíba.

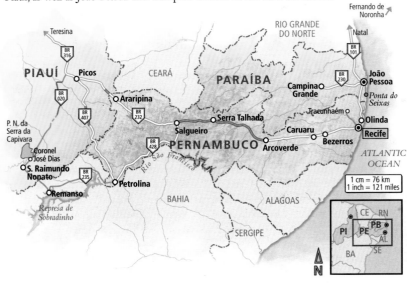

DESTINATION HIGHLIGHTS

RECIFE
  Historic Center
  Santo Antônio and São José
  Off the Beaten Track

SOUTHERN COAST

OLINDA (7 km/4.25 mi.)
  Igarassu

FERNANDO DE NORONHA (545 km/339 mi.)

TRACUNHAÉM (63 km/39 mi.)

CARUARU (134 km/83 mi.)

BEZERROS (107 km/67 mi.)

SERRA DA CAPIVARA, in Piauí (1,155 km/693 mi.)

JOÃO PESSOA, in Paraíba (120 km/75 mi.)

All distances are from Recife

Recife

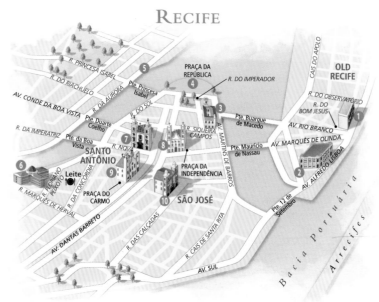

Old Recife

1 - Sinagoga Kahal Zur Israel
2 - Pólo Alfândega

Santo Antônio and São José

3 - Capela Dourada
4 - Praça da República
5 - Rua da Aurora
6 - Casa da Cultura
7 - Nossa Senhora da
    Conceição dos Militares

8 - Matriz de Santo Antônio
9 - Basílica de Nossa Senhora
    do Carmo
10 - Pátio do Terço and Pátio São Pedro

Founded in the 16th century, Recife was transformed when the Dutch seized control of the city (1630-1654) and brought along with them city planners, scientists and painters. The architectural legacy from the colonial period mixes with modern buildings along the shoreline. Water is a dominant theme: the city was built where the Capibaribe and Beberibe rivers empty into the ocean. A total of 39 bridges cross the many canals and form a tropical Venice. The local custom of hearty meals tempts the taste buds with fruits and delicacies such as *bolo-de-rolo* (jelly roll cake), *fruta-pão* (fruit bread) and *cajá* (yellow mombin fruit).

Historic Center

Recife Antigo (Old Recife), located on one island, and Santo Antônio and São José, on another, embody the historical essence of this city of approximately 1.5 million. Both islands have forts, colonial mansions, museums and churches. The tour starts with a visit to the synagogue and the surrounding area. Then cross either the Buarque de Macedo bridge or the Maurício de Nassau bridge to reach the districts named after two saints, Antônio and José.

① Sinagoga Kahal Zur Israel

The Dutch granted freedom of worship to Jews. As a result, many Jewish people emigrated from Europe to Recife, where they built the first synagogue in the

Americas in 1641. With the revival of the Portuguese regime and the coming of the Inquisition, they were forced to leave the country. Some went to North America and settled in New Amsterdam, today New York. At the synagogue you will be able to learn more about this history and see parts of the original building. Next to the synagogue, the Espaço Cultural Paranambuco sells handicrafts (*Rua do Bom Jesus, 215*). If you happen to be there at dusk visit the 42 meters (138 feet) high Torre Malakoff, dating from 1855 (*Praça Arsenal da Marinha*). From the top of the tower you can see Old Recife, Marco Zero (the center point of the city), the port and the Teatro Santa Isabel.
Rua do Bom Jesus, 197, Recife Antigo, tel. (81) 3224-2128. Tue-Fri, 9am-4:30pm; Sat and Sun, 3pm-6:30pm.

② PÓLO ALFÂNDEGA

This site is a combination shopping mall and cultural center formed by the old Customs House building from 1732, and the Chanteclair building from 19th century. The first, Paço da Alfândega, with 7,000 square meters (75,000 sq. ft), currently contains 45 designer stores including Fause Haten and Alexandre Herchcovitch. The ground floor features the mega bookstore Livraria Cultura. The third floor has the restaurants Melograno, whose chef is Luciano Boseggia, and Assucar, with the chef César Santos, as well as a nightclub. To the left of the building is Igreja Madre de Deus.

VANGUARD AND TRADITION

Recife is the capital of the state that introduced Luís Gonzaga's *forró*, Capiba's classical *frevos*, Chico Science & Nação Zumbi's mangue beat and the music of Mundo Livre S.A. and Otto. In addition, Pernambuco inspired the paintings of Cícero Dias, the sociology of Gilberto Freyre, the poetic lyricism of Manuel Bandeira and the incisive poems of João Cabral de Melo Neto. It is currently generating the feverish verbal provocations of playwright Ariano Suassuna, who was born in the state of Paraíba but, as did writer Clarice Lispector for some years, adopted Recife as his home.

Recife, the tropical Venice: 39 bridges cross the many canals

SANTO ANTÔNIO AND SÃO JOSÉ

❸ CAPELA DOURADA

The "Golden Chapel," built in 1697, is Recife's best example of baroque expression. The interior contains an abundance of gold that is displayed in the gilded carvings; there are also paintings on the caisson ceiling panels and rosewood woodwork. It is part of the complex formed by **Convento de Santo Antônio**, the **Igreja da Ordem Terceira**, the old **Hospital dos Terceiros Franciscanos** and the **Museu Franciscano de Arte Sacra**. *Rua do Imperador, Santo Antônio, tel. (81) 3224-0530. Mon-Fri, 8-11:30am and 2-5pm; Sat, 8-11:30am.*

❹ PRAÇA DA REPÚBLICA

The most important architectural complex in the Santo Antônio district is located on this square, which has a century-old Baobab Tree. The tree is recognized as a historical heritage monument. Nearby is the **Palácio do Governo**, a neoclassical building from 1841. The official name is Palácio do Campo das Princesas (the Princesses' Garden Palace), a tribute to the daughters of Emperor Dom Pedro II. Beside it is the imposing **Teatro Santa Isabel**, inaugurated in 1850, and at one time the site of important political debates. To the left is the lavishly decorated **Palácio da Justiça**, with stained glass windows, marble flooring and Baccarat crystal chandeliers.

❺ RUA DA AURORA

Located on the left bank of the Capibaribe river and facing the east, this street receives the first rays of sunshine. This is the best time to admire the colorful façades of its colonial mansions. Start at **Rua da Imperatriz** and go up to **Avenida Norte**, in Boa Vista. From **Praça da República**, it may be reached by crossing the **Princesa Isabel** bridge. The region used to be a marsh that

Neoclassic houses along Rua da Aurora, on the banks of the Capibaribe river

Teatro Santa Isabel, the traditional stage for political and cultural life, has been carefully restored

was filled in for the construction of the first neoclassical buildings in 1807. Highlights are the **Ginásio Pernambucano** and the building of **Secretaria da Segurança Pública** (Secretariat of Public Security), the former residence of the Count of Boa Vista.

6 CASA DA CULTURA

This cultural center and market is in the former City Jail, which closed in 1973. It contains a little of everything, from Alto do Moura ceramics to hammocks from Tacaratu. One of the 156 cells was maintained in its original state and can be visited, but the others are now stores. The building is divided into north, south, east and west wings. On the ground floor, cell 120 of the east wing, is home to **Geração 65**, an interesting bookshop with excellent books about the state of Pernambuco.
Rua Floriano Peixoto, Santo Antônio, tel. (81) 3224-2850. Mon-Fri, 9am–7pm; Sat, 9am-6pm; Sun, 9am-2pm.

7 NOSSA SENHORA DA CONCEIÇÃO DOS MILITARES

This church was built in 1710 by a fraternity whose members were officials, sergeants and military soldiers from the Firing Squad and Cavalry. The chapel, the high altar, the altarpiece and the central arch are decorated with exquisite gilded carvings. The rococo-style ceiling is decorated with camellias, volutes and flowers and features a painting of a pregnant Virgin Mary, surrounded by angels. The ceiling of the choir area portrays another imposing painting of the first battle of Guararapes.
Rua Nova, 309, Santo Antônio, tel. (81) 3224-3106. Mon-Fri, 7am-5pm.

8 MATRIZ DE SANTO ANTÔNIO

The Divine Sacrament Fraternity built this church between 1753 and 1790. It features crystal chandeliers and panels by the sacred art painter Sebastião Tavares.
Praça da Independência, Santo Antônio, tel. (81) 3224-5076/9494. Daily, 7am-noon and 2pm-6pm.

**⑨ BASÍLICA DE NOSSA
SENHORA DO CARMO**
One of the most beautiful and
impressive churches in the city. Located
on the site of the former Palácio da
Boa Vista, the construction of this well-
illuminated and airy church began in
1687 under the direction of then
Governor Maurício de Nassau, and was
donated to the Carmelites by Emperor
Dom Pedro II. Concluded in 1767, it
has traces from the Baroque transition
stage, when the lateral chapels were
replaced by a single nave flanked by
corridors. Frei Caneca, a 19th century
revolutionary leader, was ordained
priest at the attached convent.
*Praça do Carmo, Santo Antônio, tel. (81)
3224-3341. Mon-Fri, 7am-6pm; Sat,
7am-noon.*

**⑩ PÁTIO DO TERÇO
AND PÁTIO SÃO PEDRO**
Located in the São José district, these
courtyards have played an important
historical and cultural role. They were
created in the 18th century with the
construction of the **Igreja São Pedro**
dos Clérigos and **Igreja Nossa
Senhora do Terço** in the 18th century.
Igreja São Pedro features a carved
rosewood portal with raised panels
flanked by Corinthian columns. The
courtyard has become a refuge for
bohemians. On Tuesdays, the **Projeto
Terça-Feira Negra** stage organizes
outdoor shows there. Slaves built the
Igreja do Terço on the ground where
visitors arriving in Recife thanked the
Virgin Mary by saying the rosary.
Every Monday of Carnival the **Noite
dos Tambores Silenciosos** (Night of
the Silent Drums) ceremony is held in
the courtyard in tribute to the African
slaves killed during the slavery era. At
midnight the drums are silenced and
the lights turned off.

OUR RECOMMENDATION

🍽 **Leite**, a restaurant opened in 1882 in the
Santo Antônio district, is recognized as one
of Brazil's oldest restaurants. They serve two
wonderful desserts: the *cartola* (rennet cheese
and banana topped with sugar and cinnamon) and chestnut mousse (*Praça Joaquim
Nabuco, 147, tel. 81/3224-7977*).

Detail of Mercado Municipal de São José, built in 1875 using French iron. The market offers medicinal
herbs, groceries and handicrafts

CARNIVAL AND THE FRENZY OF FREVO

Carnival in Recife does not have Salvador's *trios elétricos* or Rio de Janeiro's huge, expensive floats. But what it lacks in terms of glitz it makes up for in originality and variety. In Recife, Carnival is a street party that unites *frevo* clubs, carnival groups, folkloric characters such as *caboclinhos*, *maracatus*, bear costumes, African drum schools and samba schools. The festival starts on Saturday morning with the parade of Galo da Madrugada (literally, "early morning rooster"). Up to one million revelers follow behind, starting at the Cinco Pontas fort heading to the Guararapes and Dantas Barreto avenues in downtown. It then continues to Recife Antigo and the districts of Santo Antônio and São José, where it divides into eight different corners that cover an area of 12 sq. km (4.6 sq. mi.).

In the corner called Todos os Ritmos, in the Pátio São Pedro, a little of each rhythm can be heard, including *coco*, *afoxé*, samba and *maracatu*. The Afro corner, in the Pátio do Terço, celebrates black culture with shows by the Afro groups. On the Monday of Carnival the Noite dos Tambores Silenciosos celebration attracts thousands of people. The Mangue corner on Avenida Cais da Alfândega, holds a vanguard position with the Rec Beat festival, featuring shows by national and international bands combining regional and modern music.

The Pernambuco Carnival has something that no other Carnival has: *frevo*, which was created at the end of the 19th century and involves dancers performing a fast-paced choreography with fancy footwork and maneuvers with colorful umbrellas.

In the morning, the *frevo* groups go out in the streets and play music with a slow, rhythmic tempo. As the hours pass by the rhythm picks up, the percussion instruments join in, and it begins to resembles *maracatu*, another rhythm intimately linked to the state's culture. Maracatu has its roots in an older, 18th century dance that likely came from the "Rei do Congo" tradition brought to Brazil by the Portuguese. The roots of *maracatu* are religious and it contains mystical elements similar to Candomblé. The costumes are of African and white kings, Indians, slaves and the traditional dresses of the women from Bahia. There are various styles of *maracatu*. The people from Recife aren't exaggerating when they call the throbbing performance of Carnival the "Center of all Rhythms".

Francisco Brennand's studio: an outdoor museum in Pernambuco's capital city

OFF THE BEATEN TRACK

OFICINA DE CERÂMICA FRANCISCO BRENNAND

A museum and studio constructed in a wide strip of the Atlantic Rainforest contains the sculptures of the award-winning artist Francisco Brennand, which include phallic and mythical figures. Some of the sculptures are displayed on the lawn and the rest are exhibited in a 15,000 m² (3.7 acre) warehouse that once housed the family's brick and tile factory. Many of Brennand's murals are displayed throughout the city. He also designed the 32-meter (105-foot) obelisk also known as the Coluna de Cristal located at the port.

Access via Avenida Caxangá, km 16, Várzea, tel. (81) 3271-2466. Mon-Thu, 8am-5pm; Fri, 8am-4pm.

INSTITUTO RICARDO BRENNAND

It looks like a medieval castle and houses a museum, art gallery and a library. The museum contains a collection of 3,000 weapons. The art gallery displays Ricardo Brennand's personal collection of paintings by Frans Post, the first European artist to paint South American landscapes, and paintings by traveling artists who visited Brazil in the 19th century. The library has more than 20,000 books from the 16th to 20th centuries.

Alameda Antônio Brennand, Várzea, tel. (81) 2121-0352; Tue-Sun, 1-5pm.

MUSEU DO HOMEM DO NORDESTE

An excellent place to learn more about the state of Pernambuco. This museum is owned by the Joaquim Nabuco Foundation and is divided in three sectors that show the history of the Northeastern culture. The **Açúcar** (sugar) sector addresses historical and technological aspects of sugarcane plantations. The **Oh de Casa!** (home) sector contains objects from regional buildings, and the **Antropologia** (anthropology) sector contains items pertaining to expressions of folklore, religion and handicrafts from the state. The museum is under renovation until August 2005.

Avenida Dezessete de Agosto, 2187, Casa Forte, tel. (81) 3441-5500. Tue, Wed and Fri, 11am-5pm; Thu, 8am-5pm; Sat and Sun, 1-5pm.

FUNDAÇÃO GILBERTO FREYRE

A history that covers 87 years (1900-1987), more than 70 books published in Brazil, including the classic *Casa-Grande e Senzala* (*The Masters and the Slaves*), and hundreds of articles. All the literary works of the renowned sociologist Gilberto Freyre, one of Brazil's greatest intellects, is assembled in his home the **Vivenda Santo Antônio**. The 19th century manor features the almost intact original decoration as well as personal items and a 40,000 book library.

Rua Dois Irmãos, 320, Apipucos, tel. (81) 3441-1733. Mon-Fri, 9am-5pm.

MUSEU DO ESTADO DE PERNAMBUCO

This 19th century estate belonged to the family of the Baron of Beberibe and contains more than 12,000 pieces, including 17th and 18th century furniture, Chinese and English porcelain and paintings by the artist Telles Junior from Pernambuco. At the annex at the back, the **Espaço Cícero Dias** is dedicated to exhibitions and regional painters.

Avenida Rui Barbosa, 960, Graças, tel. (81) 3427-9322/3427-0766. Tue-Fri, 10am-5pm; Sat and Sun, 2-5:10pm.

BOA VIAGEM BEACH

Warning: since many surfers have been attacked by sharks in the past few years, some precautions are in order to enjoy Boa Viagem, one of the city's landmarks. Do not go out beyond the coral reefs and don't even think about surfing. The best liveliest area is in front of the Acaiaca building, between Ruas Félix de Brito and Antônio Falcão.

OUR RECOMMENDATION

🍽 A modern atmosphere and contemporary cuisine made from fresh ingredients: this is the secret of **Wiella Bistrô**, a cozy restaurant in Boa Viagem (*Avenida Eng. Domingos Ferreira, 1274, tel. 81/3463-3108*).

Forte Frederick Hendrik, Frans Post. Oil on canvas, from the Instituto Ricardo Brennand

SOUTHERN COAST

Cabo de Santo Agostinho was a a point of reference for the first European ships that arrived in the country, and in the 17th century its fort resisted the Dutch invasion. Its calm waters, rocky outcroppings and hills mix with fashionable beaches such as **Calhetas**, **Gaibu** and **Pedra do Xaréu**. The main beaches are Muro Alto, Cupê, Vila and Maracaípe. In the southern part of Pernambuco, Carneiros beach, in Tamandaré, is an obligatory stop for those traveling along the Maceió–Recife route. **Porto de Galinhas**, an isolated fishing village until the 1970's, was invaded by tourists in the 1990's, and hotels, restaurants, bars and shops sprang up. It is said that the name, which means "chicken port" in Portuguese, originated in the 19th century. After the slave trade was banned in 1850, African slaves were identified as "Angolan chickens" to mislead the authorities. The main beaches are **Muro Alto**, **Cupê**, **Vila** and **Maracaípe**. In the southern part of Pernambuco, **Carneiros Beach**, in **Tamandaré**, is an essential stop for those traveling along the Maceió–Recife route.

DUNE BUGGY EXCURSIONS

The Dune Buggy Association (*tel. 81/3552-1930*) offers various excursions. The most popular is the "point to point", which in 2.5 hours takes you from Muro Alto beach to Maracaípe and can be extended to Serrambi, south of Porto de Galinhas.

ATELIÊ CARCARÁ

The artist Gilberto Rodrigues do Nascimento, also known as Carcará, was born in the state of Piauí, but has become a symbol of Porto de Galinhas. His gigantic chickens, made out of coconut tree trunks and roots, adorn the entrance and at least 26 street corners of the village. His large studio, in Quadra H, lote 7 (*tel. 81/9136-6688*), employs six artisans and is open to the public.

1 Pedra do Xaréu
The shoreline is framed by rocks and a calm, blue ocean. Access is a bit of a challenge – from Calhetas beach go 9 kilometers (6 mi.), continuing on the dirt road after the pavement ends, head in the direction opposite that to Paiva beach.

2 Gaibu
With summer houses and fishermen's homes, this is one of the most developed and popular beaches in Cabo de Santo Agostinho. It is 3-kilometer (2-mi.) long, with coconut trees, kiosks, soft sand and calm sea.

3 Calhetas
The 200-meter (700-foot) beach on a small bay is dotted by seaside rocks, and has clear waters and lush vegetation. On weekends it is crowded with tourist excursions. Bar do Artur serves a wide variety of dishes and appetizers.

4 Muro Alto
This tranquil beach is named after the coral reefs that form a 2-kilometer (1.25-mi.) pool. Ideal for water sports and sailing.

5 Cupê
A beautiful landscape with coconut trees and ocean water that alternates between blue and green. The left end of the beach has calmer waters. A strong undertow from March to December makes swimming not advisable along the other stretches of the beach.

6 Vila
This beach is in the center of Porto de Galinhas, and is the departure point for the *jangada* (boat) excursions to the reef pools. Always crowded in the summer, it is a trendy hangout.

7 Maracaípe
Open sea and waves of up to 2.5 meters (8 feet) all year round attract surfers. The beach has many bars and restaurants, and the right bank of the river offers an unforgettable view of the sunset. Daily boat excursions from 8am to 5pm to visit a mangrove swamp, where seahorses are protected by the Hippocampus project.

Recife

**Cabo de
Santo Agostinho**

Rio Pirapama

BR
101

PE
028

PE
060

Escada

Maceió

PE
060

Ipojuca

Rio Ipojuca

PE
038

① Pedra do Xaréu

② Gaibu

Gaibu ③ Calhetas

Cabo de
Santo Agostinho

Porto de Suape

cm = 2.5 km
inch = 4 mi.

RN

PB

PE

AL

SE

N

Nossa Senhora do Ó

④ Muro Alto

⑤ do Cupê

Porto de Galinhas

Porto de Galinhas

⑥ da Vila

Maracaípe

⑦

Ponta de
Serrambi

Rio Sirinhaém

Sirinhaém

ERNAMBUCO

A T L A N T I C   O C E A N

PE
060

Formoso

⑧ de Carneiros

Tamandaré

PE
076

Tamandaré

Maragogi

⑧ **Carneiros**
This beach has crystal, light clear blue
water. One part faces the open sea and
the other part is protected by coral reefs.
Coconut trees and the mouth of the
Formoso river complete the scenery. Reach
the beach from the Farol Inn, or if you're
up to it, walk the 6 kilometers (4 mi.)
from Tamandaré.

OLINDA

"Linda" means "pretty" in Portuguese; it is said that the name of this town came from an exclamation made by Duarte Coelho, the grantee of Pernambuco, when he went up to a hilltop overlooking the site and said "Oh! Linda!" Visitors tend to agree with him. Founded in 1537, it was the capital of Pernambuco for years until the capital was moved to Recife, 7 kilometers (4 mi.) away by highway PE-01. The churches, museums and streets take the visitor back in time to a quaint Brazilian colonial town which can be explored by a walking tour through the Historical Center, a Unesco cultural heritage site.

CONVENTO DE SÃO FRANCISCO
Constructed in 1585, this is Brazil's first Franciscan convent. One of the most interesting features is the **Chapter House**, the room where the priests met for discussions. The small room is decorated with blue, yellow and white Portuguese ceramic tiles and has a caisson ceiling with paintings that portray the Sacred Family.
Rua de São Francisco, 280, Centro Histórico, tel. (81) 3429-0517. Mon-Fri, 7-11:30am and 2-5pm; Sat, 7am-noon.

IGREJA NOSSA SENHORA DA GRAÇA AND SEMINÁRIO DE OLINDA
Father Antônio Vieira, author of the famous *Sermons*, taught rhetoric in this seminary during the first half of the 17th century and helped transform the Royal College of Olinda known into the "Coimbra of South America," after the prestigious university in Portugal. The church, built by Duarte Coelho in 1550, was destroyed in a fire set by the Dutch and restored in 1660.

OUR RECOMMENDATION
🍽 Shrimp and squash are a marriage made in heaven, so vow to visit the restaurant **Oficina do Sabor**, where that's the main dish, in a pitanga sauce (*Rua do Amparo, 335, tel. 81/3429-3331*).

Historical center of Olinda, founded in 1537, with the city of Recife in the background

Rua Bispo Coutinho, Centro Histórico, tel. (81) 3429-0627. Mon-Fri, 2:30pm-4:30pm.

IGREJA DE NOSSA SENHORA DA MISERICÓRDIA

The interior of this church features baroque carvings in Dom João v style, a beautiful pulpit with the House of Austria's coat of arms, a baptismal font in Portuguese stonework, and the medallions on the ceiling portraying the life of the Virgin Mary. The plaza at the front of the church, which offers a remarkable view of Olinda, is the site where Captain André Temudo and many men from Pernambuco lost their lives resisting the Dutch invasion in 1630.

Rua Bispo Coutinho, Centro Histórico, tel. (81) 3429-2922. Daily, 6-11am and 2-6pm.

MOSTEIRO DE SÃO BENTO

The high altar is the main attraction of this monastery. It is 13.6 meters (45 feet) high, 7.9 meters (26 feet) wide and 4.5 meters deep, and weighs around 12 tons. It was made of gilded wood between 1783 and 1786, under the direction of Abbot Miguel Arcanjo da Anunciação, and features carved garlands, flowers, shells and angels. Despite being classified as one of the finest examples of rococo art, it also hints at the balance of neoclassical lines. Damaged by termites, it was restored and displayed in 2001 at the Guggenheim Museum in New York, in 2001.

Rua de São Bento, Centro Histórico, tel. (81) 3429-3288. Daily, 8-11:30am and 2-5pm.

RUA DO AMPARO

One of the oldest streets in Olinda, this culture-rich corridor is lined having with inns, restaurants, museums and art studios. One could easily spend half a day wandering along it. At #45 is the studio of Silvio Botelho (*tel. 81/3439-2443*), known as the **Casa dos Bonecos Gigantes** (the house of giant puppets), where he creates the famous giant puppets for the Olinda Carnival. Nearby, at #59, is the collection of at least 700 of these puppets at **Museu do Mamulengo** (*tel. 81/3439-3495*). That collection is a traditional part of folk theater in the Northeast, where the puppets dance, sing, and talk to the audience as they whack each other. A good place to see a show is **Teatro Só-Riso**, on Rua Treze de Maio (*tel. 81/3429-2934*). At #91, they sell an "aphrodisiac" drink called *pau-do-índio*, that is said to contains 32 different herbs, honey and *cachaça*. The bohemian bar **Bodega de Véio** awaits at #212, the end of the street.

CONTEMPLATIVE LEISURE

This simple town offers four lookout points that are ideal for contemplation. The most inviting views are from the courtyards of the **Seminário de Olinda** and the Largo da **Igreja da Sé**. From the former site you can admire the towers of century-old churches, with the Atlantic Ocean in the background.

DRESSED IN YELLOW

Olinda's non-official tourist guides invent elaborate stories to lure tourists. Avoid them. Look for the *guias-mirins* (junior guides) that are city employees. They wear yellow uniforms and are usually found at the tourist information center (*Praça do Carmo, 100, tel. 81/3305-1048 and 3429-9153*). The English service is free of charge, and they are well-informed.

Igreja and Mosteiro de São Bento: built in the 16th century, it is the second oldest church in Brazil

Further to the south you can see the port, the city of Recife, the Ponta D'el Chifre beach and a stretch of the Beberibe river. The latter offers a picturesque view of the roofs of the old colonial houses surrounded by fruit and palm trees spread throughout the backyards of Olinda. Two other lookout points are the Ribeira lookout and the **Largo da Misericórdia**.

STUDIOS

In addition to religious and historical buildings, steep streets and quaint houses, Olinda also is home to many studios of important artists, who began to move to the city in the 1960's. One is **Gilvan Samico**, considered Brazil's greatest wood engraver, who works out of his home. There are more than 70 studios spread throughout the city, and a dozen of them on Rua do Amparo alone. Other leading studios are those of **Iza do Amparo**, **J. Calazans** and **Teresa Costa Rêgo**. The watercolor painter **Guita Charifker** lives nearby (*Rua Saldanha Marinho, 206, tel. 81/3429-1758*). The famous magical realist painter **João Câmara** from Paraíba is also worth a visit (*Rua de São Francisco, 157, tel. 81/3429-2845*).

IGARASSU

One of the first sites of Portuguese occupation of Brazil, this charming historical city has irregular streets and buildings from the 16th, 17th, and 18th centuries. It's 30 kilometers (19 mi.) north of Recife on highway BR-101. A good one-day tour, it's worth the trip just to see **Igreja Matriz de São Cosme e Damião**, built in 1535 of *taipa* (clay reinforced by wood), and considered to be Brazil's oldest standing church, even though only the four walls remain. In 1634, the church was damaged by the Dutch invaders. It was rebuilt after 1654 with stones and lime, in the mannerist style, with straight lines and a triangular pediment. The eponymous saints Cosmas and Damian were credited with the miracle of 1685, when the residents escaped unscathed from the yellow fever that devastated the neighboring cities of Recife, Olinda, Itamaracá and Goiânia. The old Igarassu sugar mills are also worth visiting. One of the best to visit is **Monjope**, built in 1756. The main homestead, slave quarters, the chapel and the *cachaça* sugarcane distillery remain intact. One of the natural beauties of Igarassu is located offshore, on the **Coroa do Avião** island, where there is a research center for migratory birds.

CARNIVAL ON THE STREETS OF OLINDA

At least five hundred Carnival groups invade the steep streets of Olinda during the six-day festival that starts on Friday and ends on Ash Wednesday. The festivities take place in the Historical Center, an area dominated by the Carnival groups, musical groups, folkloric characters, African drum schools and samba schools parade. It is one of the most authentic carnivals in the country, preserving Pernambuco's folkloric traditions and accompanied by *frevo* music minus Salvador's *trios elétricos*, the roving trucks with bands performing on them, that are used in Salvador.

A feature attraction is the giant puppets made from cloth and paper mâché, some over 3 meters (10 feet) high. The most famous is the **Homem da Meia-Noite** (Midnight Man) who has been parading since 1932 and hosts the official start of Carnival on Saturday at midnight. The

Mulher do Meio-Dia (Midday-Woman), his companion, was created in 1967. Anyone wishing to attract a *bloco* (group of revelers) outside of the official program just has to go through the streets playing a trumpet, and soon they will be joined by at least half a dozen followers. The group A Corda, for example, started out with just one reveler carrying a thick rope at 4am yelling "wake-up, wake-up!" Today it has dozens of people who go from house to house waking up people to join the party.

On Monday **Mestre Salustiano**, one of the greatest authorities of popular culture in Pernambuco, organizes the spectacular *maracatus* presentation. There are 90 *maracatus* or Carnival dance groups in **Cidade Tabajara**, a district of Olinda. The all-day presentation starts at the **Casa da Rabeca**, Mestre Salú's studio, and proceeds to the **Espaço Cultural Ilumiara**.

Gigantic puppets exemplify the Olinda street carnival

FERNANDO DE NORONHA

```
1 cm = 1.2 km
1 inch = 2 mi.
```

Ilha da Rata
Ilha do Meio
Ilha de São José
Ilha Sela Gineta
Ilha Rasa
Mar de Dentro
Museu do Tubarão
de Santo Antônio do Cachorro
do Meio
Enseada da Caieira
da Conceição
Ilha Dois Irmãos
do Boldró
do Americano
do Bode
Quixaba
Cacimba do Padre
Dos Porcos Bay
Do Sancho Bay
Vila dos Remédios
Vila do Trinta
Airport
START
da Atalaia
BR 363
Mirante dos Golfinhos
Dos Golfinhos Bay
Mirante do VOR
Sueste Bay
END
Mirante da Viração
do Leão
Mar de Fora
Mirante do Farol
Ponta das Caracas
Mirante do Capim-Açu
Ponta do Capim-Açu

···· Capim–Açu Trail

Located four degrees south of the Equator and 545 kilometers (339 mi.) from Recife, this archipelago has 21 protected islands. They've become an ecological sanctuary for birds and marine animals such as turtles and dolphins. In 1988, part of the area was made into a National Park, which prohibits fishing and spear fishing. Visitors to the island must pay an environmental conservation tax, an amount that varies according to the length of stay. There are two daily flights to the archipelago from Recife, and two from Natal (*Nordeste-Varig, 0300/7887-000; Trip-Linhas Aéreas, 0300/7898-747*). Between October and February, ocean liners depart from different locations throughout the country and anchor here (*see www.naviosecruzeiros.tur.br*). Fernando de Noronha is one hour ahead of Brasília standard time. The dry season is between September and March. In the other months of the year, sun alternates with heavy rains. In September and October, with some luck, tourists may see whales.

ISLAND SURVIVAL GUIDE
Fernando de Noronha harbors one post office, one bank and one road. Both establishments are located in **Vila dos Remédios**, the main urban center. The road, BR-363, is the shortest federal road in the country; it's only 6.8 kilometers (4 mi.) connecting the port to the Southeastern bay. The best way to tour the island is to rent a dune buggy. One rental agency is Locbugue (*tel. 81/3619-1490*). Alternatives are to rent motorcycles or bicycles, take a taxi or use the bus that passes every half hour. If time is not an issue, you can do the same as the locals and hitchhike.

BEACHES
The main island of Noronha covers

Aerial view of Fernando de Noronha: an ecological sanctuary for birds and marine animals

17 km² (7 sq. mi.) and has
16 beaches with free access. Eleven of
them are located on the side facing
the mainland, the "Mar de Dentro"
where the water is calm. The others
face the open sea on the Atlantic
side, called the "Mar de Fora". Four
beaches that deserve special mention
are **Atalaia**, **Leão**, **Porcos bay**, and
Sancho. Make sure you bring a
mask, snorkel and flippers.

ATALAIA

Try to remember the clearest waters
you have ever seen; then consider
that this beach has even clearer
water. It is a pool with a white sand
bottom filled with small colorful
fish. IBAMA limits access to 25 people
at a time, for 20 minutes and only at
low tide.

LEÃO

Usually deserted despite being one of
the island's largest beaches, this has
rough waters and a delightful pool at
each end. Sea turtles lay their eggs

here from January to June. Because of
this, visits are prohibited after 6pm.

BAÍA DOS PORCOS

Baía dos Porcos ("Bay of Pigs") is
said have been named by Americans
because of the beach's similarity to
the infamous Bay of Pigs in Cuba,
which they invaded in 1961 in an
attempt to overthrow Fidel Castro's
government. But the original may in
fact be independent of that U.S.
military catastrophe: locals claim that
a pig fell from hill above to the
beach, giving the bay its name. In
any case, the 70 meters long beach,
dominated by rocks with a small
stretch of sand and emerald-green
waters, doesn't look anything like a
pigsty. There is a remarkable view of
the Dois Irmãos hill with a backdrop
of sheer rock wall and vegetation.
Use a diving mask to explore a
dozen small pools.

SANCHO

Many believe that this is Noronha's

most beautiful beach. Come and find out why. Seeing is believing, so take the trail that starts at the Golfinhos lookout point. Admire the full view of the infinite green ocean and waves gently rolling over the soft golden sand. The scene is completed with lush vegetation surrounding the sheer rock walls. To reach the sand you must go down a staircase embedded in a rock crevice, then another dozen steps down to the beach.

BOAT AND KAYAK EXCURSIONS TO "MAR DE DENTRO"

Seeing a beach from the perspective of the ocean is like watching a classical concert from the choir. Noronha upgrades the quality to the level of a Bernstein or a Karajan piece. Along with the spectacular beauty of the beaches, you can see dolphins up close in the **Golfinhos** Bay. Try to take the boat in the morning. The 3-hour tour departs from the port and passes the 11 beaches on the mainland side with

a stop for diving at **Sancho** Bay. Reservations can be made at Abatur (*tel. 81/3619-1360*). The kayak excursion heads to **Dois Irmãos** hill. Leave at 8am in a double kayak, with a guide and motorboat escort.
Tour Operator: Remos da Ilha, tel. (81) 3619-1914.

TRAILS

The English naturalist Charles Darwin stepped ashore on Fernando de Noronha in February, 1832, to investigate the island and collected data for his research. But you don't need to be a scientist to explore unknown places here. You just need to walk down any trail. The main trail, **Capim-Açu**, is about 6 kilometers (4 mi.) long. Requirements for the excursion include an IBAMA-authorized guide, a minimum of physical fitness and an adventurous spirit. As you walk, you can watch birds and see trees such as the *mulungu*. The four lookout points (Vor, Viração, Farol

Dolphins spend the morning frolicking

and Capim-Açu) offer remarkable and unusual views of the island. Guides may be contracted at the **Centro de Visitantes** (*Alameda Boldró*) after 8pm.

DIVING

There are 19 points where free style and scuba diving are allowed. Twelve of them are located on the mainland side. Depending on the time of the year, visibility can reach up to 50 meters (164 feet), and the average water temperature is 26°C (79°F). There are batoid fish, sharks, moray eels, trumpetfish, turtles and barracudas. *Tour Operator: Águas Claras, tel. (81) 3619-1225; Atlantis, tel. (81) 3619-1371; Noronha Divers, tel. (81) 3619-1112.*

GOLFINHOS BAY LOOKOUT POINT

The best time to see dolphins is between 5:30 and 7:30am. It is worth getting up early because at sunrise you can see schools of more than 100. They spend most of the morning in the bay, frolicking and resting, and at the end of the day, they head out into the ocean to feed.

PROJETO TAMAR

Every night, at 9pm, members of the Projeto Tamar give fascinating free lectures at Centro de Visitantes (*tel. 81/3619-1171*) on a rotating list of ecological topics like the lives of dolphins and turtles. There are various themes and change daily, and include dolphins and turtles.

TV GOLFINHO

The one-of-a-kind *Jornal da Ilha*, the local TV news, is produced by TV Golfinho (the local Globo broadcaster). It airs weekdays, before the 7pm soap opera (aired at around

Diving locations lure beginners and experts

7:50pm). Tune in for 15 minutes of local "news", produced by one reporter, one camera and one anchorwoman. Don't miss it – if nothing else it is a novelty.

OUR RECOMMENDATION

🍽️ An alternative emerges for those who do not want to be restricted to the restaurants at the inns or are looking for a change of pace. Iraci Silva has been running the kitchen of **Ekologiku's** restaurant since 1990. She skillfully prepares traditional fish and seafood recipes. During high season the place is always crowded, so arrive early and enjoy the shrimp or lobster *moqueca* (*Estrada Velha do Sueste, tel. 81/3619-1807*).

TRACUNHAÉM

Clay handicrafts: a tradition and standard of quality in the country

Thanks to the skills of its residents, Tracunhaém is one of Brazil's major centers for ceramic arts. The town of 13,000 people is located in the Zona da Mata, or forest region, 63 kilometers (40 mi.) from Recife via highways BR-408 and BR-090. Almost half the population works with either sugarcane or clay. This tradition is a legacy from the Tupi indians, who made pipes out of the local clay. Roughly 300 artisans produce household items, figures and sacred statues. A visit to their studios is an enjoyable walk through the city. Some of the main studios include **Zezinho de Tracunhaém**, who has been working with clay for more than 40 years,

making religious items such as statues of Saint Francis and Saint Anthony. Four of his 13 children are artisans (*Avenida Desembargador Carlos Vaz, 110, tel. 81/3646-1215*). The charisma and simplicity of **Mestre Maria Amélia** make this elderly lady one of the dearest and most respected persons in the city. She learned to work with clay at a very young age from her father, who owned a ceramic factory. As a child she made little animals and progressed to exquisitely crafted religious statues (*Praça Costa Azevedo, 76, tel. 81/3646-1778*). **Mestre Nuca**, one of the oldest artisans in the village, is very well known for his lions with curly manes (*Rua Manuel Pereira de Moraes, 118, tel. 81/3646-1448*). **Zé Dahora** produces household items such as pots, plates and bowls (*Rua do Rosário, 14, tel. 81/3646-1277*). The **Centro de Produção Artesanal**, in a warehouse, contains the studios and works of about 50 local artisans (*Praça Costa Azevedo*).

CARUARU

Caruaru is located in the heart of the arid landscape between the Zona da Mata and the Sertão, or backlands of the Northeast, 134 kilometers (83 mi.) from Recife on highway BR-232. It is recognized worldwide for clay handicrafts and is the heart of the traditional rural Northeast rhythm, *forró*. The city is home to the **Feira de Caruaru**, considered the largest local market in the Northeast. It is held daily at **Parque Dezoito de Maio**, in a 20,000 sq. mi. (5 acre) area in the town center, and sells everything from handicrafts, fruits, vegetables, meat, and electronics to herbs. The **Museu do Cordel**, in the costume jewelry section, has hundreds of cordel poetry and literature booklets and woodcut prints for sale, but it is closed on Sundays. Another market is **Feira da Sulanca**, held on Monday morning, where useful household products attract customers from neighboring villages. **Alto do Moura** district is located 7 kilometers (4.2 mi.) away and is famous for the ceramics made by **Mestre Vitalino**. Other

important artisans living there are **Zé Caboclo**, **Mestre Galdino** and **Manuel Eudócio**. Unesco considers the area a major center for representational art works in South America. On the main street, **Rua Mestre Vitalino**, the studios are open for visits. There is also a collection of the artist's works at the **Memorial Mestre Galdino**, with a collection of the artist's works (closed on Mondays), and the **Casa-Museu Mestre Vitalino**, the artist's last home before his death (*open daily*). Try to catch the **Festa de São João**, which competes with the festival held in Campina Grande, in the neighboring state of Paraíba, to attract the largest crowds. It is held at the **Parque de Eventos**, lasts 30 days and attracts draws as many as 100,000 people per night to watch the shows by popular Brazilian performers and regional *forró* groups. In this same park, the **Museu do Forró** tells the story of *forró* music and the **Museu do Barro**, of regional handicrafts (*Praça Cel. José de Vasconcelos, 100, tel. 81/3722-2021*).

Casa-Museu Mestre Vitalino contains personal belongings and works by the artisan

A Journey into the Backlands

My first introduction to the Brazilian backlands known as the *sertão* was literary: a tattered, used copy of Mario Vargas Llosa's *War at the End of the World*, and then, five minutes after its last page its inspiration: the classic *Os Sertões* (*Rebellion in the Backlands*) by Euclides da Cunha. Perhaps a fitting introduction. Although few travelers physically visit the *sertão*, there is hardly a Brazilian who has not dreamed of it, read *Grandes Sertões: Veredas* (*The Devil to Pay in the Backlands*), seen or read *Vidas Secas* (*Barren Lives*), watched *Deus e o Diabo na Terra do Sol* (*Black God White Devil*). Indeed, I continue to be struck by the role of the *sertão* in the Brazilian imagination. I was surprised, then, on my first visit to Brazil, to learn how few Brazil: visit the *sertão*, a pity, as during my travels, I have found few places that are as remarkable.

The *sertão's* beauty lies not in its immediate attractions. It has natural beauty, in the canyons of the Rio São Francisco, and the rich thornscrub ecosystem called caatinga in the Raso de Catarina, the Serra do Araripe, or the Borborema mountains. It has unique food, from a surprisingly good stew of viscera called *sarapatel* to the ubiquitous sun-dried beef known as *carne-de-sol*. It is the birthplace of music like *forró* and *xaxado*. And yet, the greatest beauty of the *sertão* lies in something less palpable, a spirit of the place, of history, of the people who live there.

It is impossible to travel anywhere in the *sertão*, and not be reminded that so many of Brazil's great stories come from here. One can visit Canudos or Monte Santo and pass through the towns that grace the pages of *Os Sertões*, meet old men and women whose grandparents or even parents were alive at the time of Antônio Conselheiro. Although the town of Canudos has been moved and the Rio Vasa Barris dammed, when the water in the dam is low enough, the churches towers can still be seen, and the days of the revolt easily remembered.

One can follow the footsteps of Lampião, starting in his birthplace outside of Serra Talhada, recently turned into a fascinating and picturesque museum by a dedicated researcher who leads tours to the site. Or the site of his first great robbery, in Casa Branca, Alagoas, or Mossoró, Natal, where he made a miscalculated attack and was turned back. Or one can hire a fishing boat to Angicos, Sergipe, a painted town which clings to the Rio São Francisco, and take the same path along which, nearly

65 years ago, *volantes* flying columns of the police slipped silently downstream to attack the band of *cangaceiros* camped in the shade and silence of a dry river bed, and with rain of bullets began the end of the long rule of *cangaço* banditry.

In Juazeiro do Norte, one can see the true faith of backlanders who have traveled for days to pay homage to Padre Cícero Romero.

Besides the famous historical sites of the *sertão* are others, which continue to live. Not two hours from Recife lies Caruaru, where a raucous free market explodes once a week with crowds that have come from the neighboring towns. There, watchmakers and traditional healers set up shop alongside of mountains of fruit and bags of rice, children dance before heavy speakers blasting the newest *forró* from bands with names like The Cat's Tail (Rabo do Gato), or Snake's Armpit (Sovaco da Cobra), and salesmen hawk copies of popular poems called *literatura de cordel* ("string literature"; it is often sold dangling from string like pieces of laundry) with names like *Caruaru Today and Yesterday* (*Caruaru Hoje e Ontem*), and *The Girl who Turned into a Snake* (*A Moça que Virou uma Cobra*). The fair runs all week, and is worth visiting any day, although it is on Saturday that one really sees the true role that it plays in the life of the *sertão*.

Other sites in the *sertão* are similarly famous: the pilgrimages of Juazeiro, the waters of the Rio São Francisco, the moutains of the Serra do Araripe. And there are other, less famous, but equally fascinating spots: the Catimbau National Park near Boique, Pernambuco, the workshop of the great cordel illustrator, J. Borges, in Bezerros, Pernambuco, the religious colony of Santa Brigada, outside Paulo Affonso, Bahia.

In the *sertão*, I often found myself alone. But the loneliness of the place is softened by the kindness of its inhabitants. Indeed it is hard to go for a walk, without being offered a wicker chair and a cup of coffee. The great histories of popular saints and bandits are surrounded by thousands of other stories, shared by the old folk who lived through the droughts and continue to work in the fields.

My two favorite spots in the *sertão* are the towns of Triunfo, in central Pernambuco, and Piranhas, Alagoas. A small town perched in the Borborema mountains, Triunfo is blessed with cool weather, beautiful walks to local waterfalls, a fine museum on the history of the *cangaço*, cobbled streets, and some of the kindest people I have ever met. It is part of Pernambuco's "cold circuit" (*circuito do frio*), a series of mountain-top cities which have festivals celebrating the cold of winter. It is close to Serra Talhada, from which Lampião's birthplace can be visited, as well as other sites of historical interest such as Princesa Isabel, Paraíba, where the independent República Princesa was once declared.

Piranhas lies in a steep valley along the banks of the São Francisco. Its houses wear a rainbow's array of colors, a flowering against the backdrop of unscarred Caatinga. Restaurants line the river. There is a museum in the railway station. It has two lovely little hotels; otherwise visitors can stay across the river at the Xingo resort. Trips are easy to arrange into the canyons above the Xingo dam, or downstream, to Angicos, Sergipe, where Lampião spent his final night.

If the living history or the kindness of the backlanders is not enough to get one to visit the *sertão*, there is a final reason. While the days can be hot and dry and the shuttered windows of the little towns leave the streets silent, as soon as the sun begins its descent, a tremendous change takes over the *sertão*. There is nothing like this light, which turns the Caatinga an exquisite yellow, and drapes the whitewashed walls gold. Then, from the shuttered houses, children swarm into the streets to play, teenagers gather around music, old men set up on the porch steps in rocking chairs. A single evening makes the long journey worthwhile.

Daniel Mason,
American physician and writer, author of The Piano Tuner

BEZERROS

Bezerros is located 24 kilometers (15 mi.) east of Caruaru by highway BR-232, and is proud of its title as the "xylography capital". Xylography or woodcut printing is a technique that originated in China for transferring images onto paper using engraved wooden blocks. No one really knows how the technique was introduced to the Northeast but some believe that it dates back to the time of the Dutch invasions. The popularity of xylography is associated to the cordel booklets that usually portray scenes from everyday rural life, such as the markets, outlaws, festivals and drought. The pioneer was Mestre Noza from Pernambuco. In the 1960's, Bezerros became one of the main xylography centers in the country and its most prominent artist is José Francisco Borges, known as **J. Borges** (*BR-232, km 100, tel. 81/3728-0364*). Today, many artists, including J. Borges' sons and relatives, have their own studios in the town: **J. Miguel** (*BR-232, km 106, tel. 81/3728-3673*); **Amaro Francisco** and **Nena** (*Rua José Rufino, 135, Loteamento São José, tel. 81/3728-4038*) and **Givanildo** (*Rua José Pessoa Sobrinho, 232, São Pedro, tel. 81/ 9625-1406*). In the **Centro de Artesanato de Pernambuco** (*BR-232, km 107, tel. 81/3728- 2094*), there is a museum, store, auditorium, rooms for workshops and a design center. It also contains a collection with roughly 400 art works made in other regions of Pernambuco. It would be a shame not to visit **Lula Vassoureiro's Oficina de Papangu** (*Rua Otávia Bezerra Vila Nova, 64, Santo Amaro, tel. 81/9102-0665*). He creates the colorful masks for the local Carnival of Papangu, named after the dish *angu* or mush that in the olden days was served to Carnival revelers. In addition he also decorates the city's lampposts with giant masks from this century-old tradition.

SERRA DA CAPIVARA

At least 500 archeological sites are spread over the 130,000 hectares of **Parque Nacional da Serra da Capivara**, created in 1979 and recognized by Unesco as a World Heritage Site in 1991. The park is located in the **Serra da Capivara**, in São Raimundo Nonato, in the southeast of the state of Piauí. The Brazilian scientist Nìede Guidon, coordinator of archeological studies in the region for two decades, maintains that there is evidence that humans have lived in this region for at least 60,000 years (see next page). The idea is controversial because it contradicts widely accepted theories which held that this continent had been inhabited for only 20,000 years. Many trails through the Caatinga (semi-arid scrublands), with landscape dominated by canyons and rock formations, provide access to archeological sites, and some are physically demanding. The most interesting is **Pedra Furada**, named after a 15-meter (50-foot) diameter hole in a 60 meters (197

foot) high wall. The park offers excellent signage and impeccable maintenance. However, it lacks many hotel and restaurant options, as does the city of **Petrolina** on the São Francisco river at the border with the state of Bahia, which is the departure point for visiting Capivara, coming from Pernambuco. The city is 776 kilometers (482 mi.) from Recife, via highway BR-232. To get to the national park (*tel. 89/582-1612*) from there, you must take highway BA-235. It is a 310-kilometer (193-mi.) drive, on a paved road until you reach the city of São Raimundo Nonato where the **Museu do Homem Americano** is located. This museum of American man is run by Guidon. The city offers accommodations for those wishing to explore the park, 35 kilometers (22 mi.) away. One option is the **Hotel Serra da Capivara** (*tel. 89/582-1389*). You can also go to Petrolina by plane. There are flights departing from Recife, Rio, Brasília and other Brazilian cities.

Boqueirão da Pedra Furada: a valley surrounded by multi-colored rock walls

THE LONG TALE OF PREHISTORIC MAN

In 1963, when I was an archeologist at the Museu Paulista, the municipal government of São Raimundo Nonato showed me pictures of prehistoric rock drawings from the region. I immediately detected the differences between them and all that was known in the world in terms of rock drawings. That same year I arranged a trip to the region. I arrived in Casa Nova, in Bahia, but the rains had washed out a bridge and I wasn't able to continue on.

Other circumstances took me to live in France, and for many years those im ages were imprinted in my memory. I managed to come back in 1970, and local inhabitants showed me the first sites with paintings. At that time, everything was quite different. The local communities lived in complete isolation from the rest of the state. The only road leading to Teresina, the capital city, crossed a long stretch of sand along the Capivara gorge. Today, this stretch is a bustling tourist destination visited by over 400 people per day at times. But then we only had two choices: either get stuck in the sand or drive through at dangerously high speeds, skidding around and almost sliding off the side of the road. There was no electricity or running water in the city.

After 34 years in the region, we are able to retrace its cultural evolution, protect it and present it. The rock paintings represent the most abundant, conspicuous and astonishing manifestation left by prehistoric populations living in the area of the Parque Nacional da Serra da Capivara in remote times.

We took core samples and carried out excavations to date these paintings and situate them in their precise sociocultural context. This led the researchers to accelerate and expand the excavations to collect more data and document this discovery, which revolutionized theories of the peopling of the Americas.

Therefore, we know that men already lived in the area of the park 60,000 years ago. The human presence had been continuous until the arrival of white colonizers. The oldest sites in the area are rock-covered shelters (*tocas* in the regional language), formed by erosion that removed the low part of the rock walls, resulting in an outcropping overhead that serves as a roof.

Prehistoric men used these protected shelters as campsites, burial grounds and place where they could paint aspects of their oral tradition. These people lived

Anthropomorphic and human representations

Polychromatic panel

from hunting, gathering and fishing. The rock paintings portray in detail the sociocultural evolution over at least 15,000 years and is thus one of the most comprehensive and important archives on humanity currently available anywhere in the world.

These prehistoric societies lived in equilibrium with the environment, using it in different ways without ever depleting it. The economic model that we can infer from studies carried out in the area indicate that in the beginning, humans occupied an empty space, with no competitors. The first groups exploited certain limited areas, because there was plenty to hunt and they did not need to make great efforts. The raw materials used for their stone tools were always those located close at hand.

Over the last 8,000 years, pressured by climatic changes and a drop in production of ecosystems – probably caused by the disappearance of large game – humans underwent a process of adaptation, and developed a wide range of techniques for using all natural resources. They started to be more selective in terms of the raw materials used, at times bringing materials from far away in pursuit of greater quality, enabling improved efficiency in production of tools.

Starting 3,500 to 3,000 years ago, we find the first traces of an agricultural society. From 3,000 to 1,600 years ago, there is evidence of peoples who lived in round villages formed by ten to eleven elliptical houses, built around a central square. They occupied either the wide valleys in the peripheral low plains, or the top of the *chapada* (plateau) on sedimentary formations. Their burial ceremonies were very elaborate. They held secondary burials in urns or graves in the ground.

Archeological data provides a wealth and variety of information on these groups. All the original peoples of the Parque Nacional da Serra da Capivara were exterminated by white settlers. Today, all that is left from them is what archeology is able to discover. This legacy has helped us develop this extremely poor region, and offer visitors a structure where the rest points or destinations of the many trails are archeological sites. The Museu do Homem Americano presents a summary of more than thirty years of research amidst a very pleasant setting.

Nière Guidon,
Prehistorian and director of the Fundação Museu do Homem Americano

Human figures with adornments

A rock painting called Cena da Árvore (Tree Scene)

JOÃO PESSOA

Largo de São Pedro: Colonial houses in the historic center and the Igreja São Pedro Gonçalves

In 1930, João Pessoa, governor of the state of Paraíba, was assassinated in Recife. To honor him, his name was given to capital of the state. It was not the first time the city's name had changed: founded in 1585, its first name was Nossa Senhora das Neves, then Filipéia de Nossa Senhora das Neves, and also Frederica. The city, 120 kilometers (75 mi.) from Recife via highway BR-101, was founded on the banks of the Sanhauá river, a tributary of the Paraíba river, and spread out towards the sea. Today it has around 600,000 inhabitants and two big parks – **Arruda Câmara** and **Mata do Buraquinho**, with 515 hectares of Atlantic Rainforest.

IGREJA DE SÃO FRANCISCO AND CIDADE BAIXA

The walls covered with ceramic tiles that surround the courtyard portray scenes from the passion of Christ. Inside the church, take note of the pulpit's, wood carvings covered with gold leaf, and the choir's richly decorated pews. The **Capela da Ordem Terceira** is on the other side of the Moorish patio of the convent. Its large windows command a view of the Sanhauá river and the historical **Cidade Baixa** (Lower City). Visible is the former **Hotel Globo**, the first in the city, built in 1928 and surrounded by colorful houses that are being restored. *Praça São Francisco, Centro, tel. (83) 218-4505. Tue-Sun, 9am-noon and 2-5pm.*

PONTA DO SEIXAS

This stretch of land between the **Cabo Branco** and **Seixas** beaches is the easternmost part in the Americas. Here you are closer to Senegal, in Africa, than to São Paulo. You reach this point following the seafront avenue southward, to the hill with the Cabo Branco lighthouse. Enjoy the view while sipping a delicious coconut water – the most "oriental" coconut water in the continent.

Mercado de Artesanato Paraibano

There are some 100 stores with selling the arts and crafts of the state of Paraíba. You will find embroidery; laces like *bilro*, *renascença* and *labirinto*; woven articles such as hammocks, bed covers and carpets; and leather items. **Filipéia**, on the first floor, is one of the stores offering beautiful and high quality products.
Avenida Senador Rui Carneiro, 241, Tambaú, tel. (83) 247-3135. Mon-Sat, 9am-7pm. Sun, 9am-5pm.

Praia do Jacaré

Every single day, Jurandy do Sax, from the **Aldeia do Rio** bar, on the Jacaré beach (access via highway BR-230) repeats the same ritual: he takes his saxophone and plays Ravel's *Bolero* on the banks of the Paraíba river until the sun goes down. For those who believe that Ravel and twilight don't mix, there are other bars where you can have a cold drink watching the view.

South Coast

Following highway PB-008 to the south

Boats ply calm waters

Our Recommendation

|O| The pleasant restaurant **Mangai**, with its wood stove and rustic atmosphere, offers a buffet with more than 30 traditional dishes from the sertão paraibano (backlands of the state), and charges by the kilo. On Try regional specialties such as *rubacão* (rice, beans and meat cooked together) and *sovaco de cobra* (sun-dried meat, served with macaxeira, or manioc) (*Avenida General Édson Ramalho, 696, tel. 83/226-1615*).

Jacaré beach: bars, music and a beautiful landscape

coast, there is **Tambaba**, a beautiful nudist beach in the municipality of Conde. An expanse of white sand protected by cliffs and coconut trees, Tambaba has become an official refuge for naturists, where clothes and unaccompanied men are not allowed. Taking photographs and filming is also prohibited. Those who prefer a different environment can stop before the nudist area and enjoy the 200 meters (700 feet) of beach (before arriving at the nudist area) where bathing suits are welcome. You may also choose among the nearby beaches **Jacumã**, **Carapibus** and the almost untouched **Tabatinga**, **Coqueirinho** and **Bela**.

MAMANGUAPE AND PEIXE-BOI TO THE NORTH

The landscape of this coastal stretch makes up for its difficult access and the lack of services for tourists. To visit the beaches of **Campina**, **Oiteiro**, and **Barra do Mamanguape** follow highway BR-101 for 45 kilometers (28 mi.) from João Pessoa and turn right at the sign "Projeto Peixe-Boi/Barra do Mamanguape." Continue 30 kilometers (19 mi.) on a dirt road crossing a sugar cane plantation until you reach Campina, situated on hard sand by the open sea. Oiteiro, 5 kilometers (3 mi.) ahead, is protected by hills and offers good surfing and a panoramic view of the coast. Towards the direction of Campina is Barra do Mamanguape, where the river meets the sea. It's home to a peaceful fishing village and a station of the *peixe-boi-marinho* (manatee) conservation project.

FESTA DE SÃO JOÃO IN CAMPINA GRANDE

Campina Grande is in the interior of the state of Paraíba, in the **Serra de Borborema**, 130 kilometers (81 mi.) from João Pessoa. It can be reached by car on highway BR-230. Every June the city offers, according to some inhabitants, the most important "Festa de São João in the world", denoting the fierce dispute with Caruaru in the state of Pernambuco, a city that is also popular for its São João Festivities. In Campina Grande, land of *repentistas* (popular improvisors), *violeiros* (guitarists) and *vaquejadas* (rodeos), the traditional June Festival takes place in the **Parque do Povo**, a 42,500 m² (458,000 sq. ft) area in the city center. During the month, the event draws up to a million people. At least 200 stalls sell traditional dishes such as tapioca (not the dessert but rather a thin fried pancake of manioc flour), *pamonha* (a kind of steamed corn pud-

ding, like tamales), *batata-doce* (sweet potatoes), *bolo de fubá* (cornmeal cake), *macaxeira* (manioc), *cuscuz com carne guisada* (a molded corn meal porridge served with meat), *carne de bode* (goat meat) and locally made *cachaça*. Every day there are square dances and shows on different stages with traditional *forró* bands. The excitement has caught on, and local clubs now offer a variety of *forró* groups. Also worth a look are parallel events like the

collective wedding – based on faith in Santo Antônio, the matchmaker saint – and the *jegue* (donkey) race, where the donkeys run in groups of four after receiving a nickname, generally alluding to a Formula 1 driver. The **Trem Forroviário** is a train ride from Estação Velha de Campina Grande to the district of Galante. *Forró* trios with *sanfona* (accordion), triangle and *zabumba* (bass drum) play in the cars during the trip.

DESTINATION
NATAL

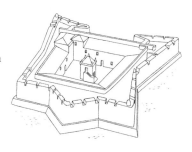

Rio Grande do Norte, in the extreme northeast of the country, is blessed by year-round sunshine. It's the right destination for those who seek peace and beautiful beaches. Genipabu boasts the most famous sand dunes in Brazil, and they can be explored by dune buggy. The most fashionable area is the coast of Pipa in the south, and the car trip from Natal is itself a delight. To the north, the natural pools of Maracajaú are great for diving. The area around Natal combines the good infrastructure of the capital with a constant breeze, bringing in some of the purest air in the country. In terms of food, the state is the proud birthplace of *carne-de-sol* (sun-dried meat), a traditional dish in most of the Northeast states. The capital gets crowded in early December when an off-season carnival, called Carnatal, takes place.

DESTINATION HIGHLIGHTS

NATAL
  Genipabu (25 km/16 mi.)
  Maracajaú (60 km/38 mi.)
  By Car to Pipa

PIPA (67 km/42 mi.)
  By Dune Buggy to Paraíba

All distances are from Natal

NATAL

Natal is the state's capital city, but most of the region's best attractions are outside city limits. These include Genipabu, the region's largest river, which is north of Potengi. The best accommodation options are nevertheless in Natal, especially along Via Costeira, a beautiful seafront avenue connecting the upper part of the city center to the trendy Ponta Negra.

PONTA NEGRA

A fashionable area with bars and restaurants, Ponta Negra has edged out the more centrally located Artistas beach to become *Natalenses'* favorite beach. Construction of a seafront promenade and installation of a sewage system revitalized the area, and the beach's warm waters and fine sand are now matched by good infrastructure. The neighboring beach **Morro do Careca** is closed to prevent further erosion of its sand dune.

CENTRO DE TURISMO

Handicraft markets are spread all over the city of Natal, but the Tourism Center seems to attract everyone. The former public prison dating from the 19th century was operational until the 1970's. It was listed as a historical heritage site in 1988. The restoration turned it into 36 stores and service posts. *Rua Aderbal de Figueiredo, 980, tel. (84) 211-6149. Daily, 8am-7pm.*

OUR RECOMMENDATION

 Considered the best hotel in Natal, the **Pestana Natal Beach Resort** combines the sophistication of its comfortable facilities with an extremely professional staff. The guests will have everything at hand while staying at this very pleasant stretch of coast: a great beach with private lifeguards, well-equipped rooms, accommodations for handicapped guests and children and recreational activities every day of the week.

Additional information begins on page 462.

Star-shaped Forte dos Reis Magos was captured by the Dutch in 1633

Boats navigate the coastline of Natal, a base for great tours

FORTE DOS REIS MAGOS

The Forte dos Reis Magos, with its five-pointed star shape and a commanding view of **do Forte** and **do Meio** beaches, is the oldest monument in the city. The fortification is located on the banks of the Potengi river; it was initially built with *taipa*, a wall of clay applied over a wood grid. Afterward, it was redecorated with stones brought from Portugal over a period of 30 years, from 1598 to 1628. Young guides of the state program Jovem Guia de Turismo tell the history of the fort. They give a detailed description of the battle of 1633, which lasted four days and culminated with an invasion of the Dutch, who would control the city for 21 years. The well-preserved fort has 14-meter-thick (46-foot) walls and cannons weighing 800 kilograms (1,764 lb) that can fire up to 800 meters (2,625 feet). The fortification was listed as a historical heritage site in 1949.

THE MEMORIAL CÂMARA CASCUDO

One of the most illustrious intellectuals of Rio Grande do Norte lends his name to three attractions of the capital. Luís da Câmara Cascudo (1898-1986) was a folklorist, historian, ethnographer, teacher and writer. He was the author of the 1944 *Antologia do Folclore Brasileiro* (*Brazilian Folklore Dictionary*), and the subject of the **Museu Câmara Cascudo** (*Avenida Hermes da Fonseca, 1,398, tel. 84/215-4192, Tue-Fri, 8-11:30am, entrance until 10:30, and 2-5pm; Sat and Sun, 1-5pm*). The collection explores subjects such as anthropology and archeology. His private library, with 10,000 titles, is in a 1875 building that also houses the **Memorial Câmara Cascudo** (*Praça André Albuquerque, 30, tel. 84/211-8408. Tue-Sun, 8am–5pm*). To visit the place where the scholar lived much of his life, and where he produced most of his work, go directly to **Casa de Câmara Cascudo** (*Avenida Câmara Cascudo, tel. 85/222-3293, Mon-Fri, 8am-5pm*).

Wind constantly reshapes the famous Genipabu sand dunes

GENIPABU

Although it has the most famous scenery of Natal, Genipabu is actually located 25 kilometers (16 mi.) away from the city in the municipality of Extremoz, with access by ferry boat from Ribeira. This fishing village is home to the most famous dunes in Brazil, with a cold water lagoon and several high-rise apartment buildings that clash with the natural scenery of the **Parque Ecológico Dunas de Genipabu**. It is also strange to see dromedaries walking across the sand. But if some tourists find the camel rides uncomfortable, the situation is even worse for the dromedaries, which suffer from the humidity of the region. The popular dune buggy tours are regulated by the state government to avoid accidents. Today, only licensed buggy drivers may enter the environmental conservation area. There are advantages to hiring a car and a driver in Natal – visitors won't have to worry about the route, which includes a ferry boat crossing from

Natal to Redinha (faster than by road, on highways RN-302 and RN-304). If the Genipabu beach is crowded, go visit the next beach, **Pitangui**, a wide stretch of fine sand facing a calm sea, or **Jacumã**, with its freshwater lagoon.

The popular dune-buggy ride in the park

MARACAJAÚ

Diving amidst the *parrachos* (reefs) of Maracajaú, accessible via highway BR-101, is like exploring an enormous 14 sq. km (5 sq. mi.) outdoor aquarium. This collection of coral reefs is located 7 kilometers (4 mi.) from **Maracajaú** beach, a fishing village 60 kilometers (37 mi.) north of Natal. The boats arrive at low tide, when the depth is only 3 meters (10 feet) and allows even inexperienced divers to see the bottom of the sea using only flippers, a mask and a snorkel. In the warm and crystalline waters, visitors can see shoals of fish swimming – and, with some luck, lobsters and shrimp.

ON THE MAINLAND

The tour to Maracajaú has become very popular, and contracting a full-day tour from Natal is a good way to enjoy it. (Taking the road without a guide requires many stops for directions, because there are few signs.) Another option is to see the beaches by dune buggy, which provides a fantastic tour. Drivers should check the tides beforehand. Besides the *parrachos*, Maracajaú has a pleasant beach lined with coconut trees, lagoons and good restaurants in front of the **Farol Tereza Pança**, a lighthouse built where the ship that bears its name sank. *Tour Operator: Porpinotur tel. (84) 3082-0341/9981-8553.*

OUR RECOMMENDATION

🍽 Tired of eating so much fish? On the way back to Natal, sample true Northeastern cuisine in the **Restaurante Mangai**. There are 50 mouth-watering specialties typical of the *sertão*, such as *buchada de bode* (goat tripe) and *carne-de-sol* (sun-dried meat) with *macaxeira* (manioc). Be sure to try *mangaba* or *cajá* juices; the restaurant does not serve alcoholic beverages. The waiters are called by bells tied to the tables (*Rua Amintas Barros, 3300, Lagoa Nova, tel. 84/206-3344*).

The boats stop miles from the coast, to allow visitors to swim over the ocean reefs

BY CAR TO PIPA

Plan to take your time if traveling by car along the highway RN-063, aka "Rota do Sol" (Sun Route), which connects Natal to the state's southern coast. The road winds along the coast and in just 30 minutes, at Búzios, visitors will find scenery very different from the urban landscape of Natal. On the way, in **Pirangi**, they can also see what is considered the biggest cashew tree in the world. Continue to **Pipa**, on the way to the border with the state of Paraíba, and stop to admire the scenery.

OUR RECOMMENDATION

🍽 There is no menu at the restaurant **Camamo Beijupirá**, at the beach Tibau do Sul. Every day, *chef* Tadeu Lubambo chooses the dishes. After sipping a drink, such as a cactus flower *caipiroska*, an appetizer and a salad, the main course might mix oysters au gratin with gorgonzola, pesto and Cointreau. The house, which receives at most five couples at a time, offers British porcelain and German cutlery with water and wine on the side (*Fazenda Pernambuquinho, access by highway RN-003, km 3, tel. 84/246-4195*).

❶ Búzios
Swimmers should enter the water only up to their waists in the stretch with strong waves. Holes in the bottom also require caution. This warm-water beach 35 kilometers (22 mi.) from Natal has dunes in its long sand stretch and an area with calm waters.

❷ Barra de Tabatinga
In Barra da Tabatinga, 5 kilometers (3 mi.) from Búzios, a coral reef runs a few feet from the sand, breaking the waves and forms calm rock pools which are perfect for swimming. On top of its cliffs, the Golfinho lookout is a mandatory stop – even if visitors don't spot any dolphins, the view of the Búzios beach is spectacular.

❸ Guaraíras (Malembar)
Deserted and untouched, the beach of Guaraíras is difficult to get to, but its white, fine sand faces the open sea. To get there, take the ferry boat that leaves from Tibau and crosses Guaraíras lagoon.

❹ Tibau do Sul
The beach that gives this municipality its name is famous for the point in the cliffs that provides a beautiful view of the sunset. To the south, coconut groves frame the gentle waves of the sea. To the north lies the place where Guaraíras lagoon meets the sea.

Tibau do Sul, 54 miles south of Natal: warm waters and a lookout point to watch the sunset

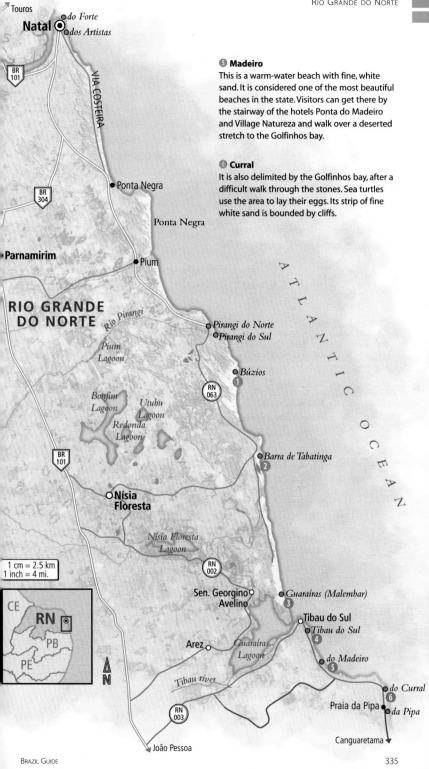

⑤ Madeiro

This is a warm-water beach with fine, white sand. It is considered one of the most beautiful beaches in the state. Visitors can get there by the stairway of the hotels Ponta do Madeiro and Village Natureza and walk over a deserted stretch to the Golfinhos bay.

⑥ Curral

It is also delimited by the Golfinhos bay, after a difficult walk through the stones. Sea turtles use the area to lay their eggs. Its strip of fine white sand is bounded by cliffs.

Touros

do Forte
Natal ◉ *dos Artistas*

BR 101

VIA COSTEIRA

BR 304

● Ponta Negra

Ponta Negra

Parnamirim

● Pium

**RIO GRANDE
DO NORTE**

Rio Pirangi

*Pium
Lagoon*

*Bonfim
Lagoon*

*Utubu
Lagoon*

*Redonda
Lagoon*

○ Pirangi do Norte
○ Pirangi do Sul

● *Búzios*
①

RN 063

BR 101

○ **Nísia
Floresta**

*Nísia Floresta
Lagoon*

● *Barra de Tabatinga*
②

1 cm = 2.5 km
1 inch = 4 mi.

RN 002

Sen. Georgino ○
Avelino

● *Guaraíras (Malembar)*
③

Tibau do Sul
○ *Tibau do Sul*
④

Arez ○

*Guaraíras
Lagoon*

● *do Madeiro*
⑤

Tibau river

○ *da Curral*
⑥

Praia da Pipa ● *da Pipa*

RN 003

Canguaretama ↓

↓ João Pessoa

CE

RN

PB

PE

N

ATLANTIC OCEAN

PIPA

The village of Pipa offers plenty of reasons why it is the greatest star of the state's coast. Nature decorated it with imposing reddish cliffs that contrast with its green waters, sporadically visited by dolphins and sea turtles. But the old fishing village has turned professional: visitors will eat well, and the lodgings are even better. Maintaining a spirit of nostalgia for the first hippies, Tibau do Sul attracts many visitors from Natal, 67 kilometers (42 mi.) away, as well as from abroad. Today, there are miles of crowded beaches for those who like excitement, as well as a good stretch of deserted beaches for those who want peace and quiet. The modernity brought by tourism did not eliminate the picturesque rustic buildings, but it did increase prices and make finding a place to park a test of patience.

EXCITEMENT AT YOUR DOORSTEP

Want excitement? Stay at the **Pipa** beach. It attracts all sorts of people, making it impossible to park after 11am. At low tide, the reefs form large warm-water pools just in front of the strip of soft white sand. It is quite developed, and it has the best infrastructure and nightlife.

PRAIAS DO AMOR AND MOLEQUE

Despite its rough sea, tranquility rules this small stretch of sand surrounded by cliffs. Its heart shape inspired the name **Praia do Amor** (love beach); **Moleque** beach lies to the south.

OUR RECOMMENDATION

🍽 The restaurant **La Provence**, commanded by the French chef Jean Louis Ferrari, serves traditional dishes from the south of France. Among them, creations like *cuisses de grenouilles*, frog's legs on the chef's special sauce. Cozy with torch lighting, it also offers a good wine selection (*Rua da Gameleira, tel. 84/246-2280*).

Heart-shaped Amor beach is one of the city's most tranquil

Central Pipa: the old fishing village has become a lively tourist destination

The beach is somewhat isolated, but it has kiosks serving large *pastéis* (pastry pockets). Surfers most frequently use the dangerous stairway embedded in the high wall. It starts in **Chapadão**, a large area of hardpacked earth that has become a lookout point for admiring the sunset, with a view up to **Formosa** Bay, almost in the state of Paraíba. The **Santuário Ecológico de Pipa** and the road to **Barra** do Cunhaú offer equally amazing panoramic views.

PRAIA DAS MINAS

Well preserved and undeveloped, **Minas** beach is also surrounded by cliffs that make waterfront difficult. Here, the steps down the cliff are more improvised and more dangerous. Those most inclined to run the risks to reach this stretch of the sand full of stones are the nudists who frequent the beach.

TO THE SLEEPY VILLAGES OF THE NORTH

While Pipa has surrendered to tourism, the north of the state is still largely unexplored. Above Maracajaú, beautiful deserted beaches and traditional villages with little infrastructure satisfy the curiosity of the most adventurous. The **Cabo de São Roque**, beside the dunes of **Barra de Maxaranguape**, is one of the closest points in the Brazilian coast to Africa. In the extreme northeast of Brazil, **Touros**, 85 kilometers(53 mi.) north of the capital has the highest lighthouse in Brazil – 62 meters (203 feet) high. Some 25 kilometers (16 mi.) further on, the bucolic village **São Miguel do Gostoso** preserves amidst its untouched beaches a replica of the first monument left by the Portuguese, in 1501. Closer to the state of Ceará, **Galinhos** beach is a backpacker's destination, accessible by boat. It is near **Macau**, 182 kilometers (113 mi.) northwest of Natal, in the salt producing region where **Ponta do Mel**, another almost deserted beach, is located.

With 6 kilometers (4 mi.) of sand, Formosa Bay's beach invites water sports

BY DUNE BUGGY TO PARAÍBA

Pipa is close to **Formosa** Bay, and it is the last town on the south coast of Rio Grande do Norte before the state of Paraíba. Visitors can visit its beautiful cliff-backed beaches by car departing from Pipa. Or even better, go along the beaches by dune buggy. Those who prefer the conventional road can opt for highway BR-101.

FORMOSA BAY

Fishermen and surfers are the most frequent visitors to this beach, 115 kilometers (72 mi.) south of Natal. Formosa Bay faces coral reefs and backs cliffs. The many boats create a colorful scene, and the area is good for water sports. The dune buggy route crosses the region of **Mata Estrela**, one of the last remaining areas of Atlantic Rainforest in the state, as well as a lagoon known as "**Coca-Cola**" because of its color.

PRAIA DO SAGI

The southernmost beach in the state covers 18 kilometers (11 mi.), with alternating stretches of rocks and soft, white sand. At the end of **Sagi** beach, the warm sea waters mix with the waters of Guaju river, which forms the boundary between the two states. The fishing village contributes to the Ibama project for the protection of the manatee, and villagers have even given a nickname – "Xuxu" – to one of the manatees that frequently visits the beach.

OUR RECOMMENDATION

Toca da Coruja Pousada, a inn in Pipa, has special areas for reading, resting and even romance. It is a member of *Roteiros de Charme* (a nonprofit association that rates hotels, inns and ecological resorts throughout Brazil) and offers sophisticated rooms especially for couples. Choose one of the double luxury chalets, with 120 m² (1291 sq. ft) of space, a large verandah with hammock, great beds and a porcelain bathtub in a private area. To get to the chalet, visitors need to walk over a wooden walkway built 1.5 meter (5 feet) above the ground to protect the vegetation.

Additional information begins on page 462.

DESTINATION
FORTALEZA

Ceará's exceptional climate attracts people from all over the world, making it one of Brazil's most popular vacation destinations. The perpetually sunny state has a coastline of about 573 kilometers (356 mi.) and offers 87 beaches dotted with the white sails of the *jangadas* (wooden boats) used for lobster fishing. Fortaleza, the capital city with a population around 2 million, offers a wide range of cultural attractions and has lively nightlife every night of the week. This is a striking contrast to the impoverished interior, where multitudes make the image of Father Cícero, in the town of Juazeiro do Norte, the focus of religious tourism in the Northeast. The state is also the birthplace of Brazilian writers Rachel de Queiroz and José de Alencar. Other highlights of the state include the cliffs of Beberibe and Canoa Quebrada east of Fortaleza, and, to the west, the sand dunes and lakes of Cumbuco and Jericoacoara.

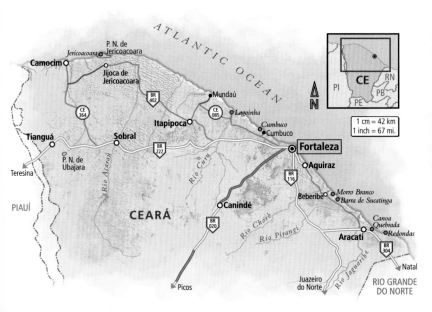

DESTINATION HIGHLIGHTS

FORTALEZA

CUMBUCO (30 km/18 mi.)

BEBERIBE (90 km/56 mi.)

CANOA QUEBRADA (167 km/104 mi.)

JERICOACOARA (300 km/186 mi.)
Jijoca de Jericoacoara
   (280 km/ 174 mi.)

All distances are from Fortaleza

Fortaleza

Fortaleza is famed for its 25 kilometers (16 mi.) of urban beaches, but it's got a good deal more to offer. The city's **Historical Center**, founded by the Portuguese in 1654, has more than 50 restored 19th century mansions. Every night, **Meireles** beach hosts an arts-and-crafts sale. At the neighboring **Iracema** beach, the Tabajaras street is famous for its active nightlife – and it's the best example of how Monday night can be just like Saturday. **Dragão do Mar** (*tel. 85/3488-8600*) is one of the busiest arts and cultural centers in the Northeast, and it is also located at Iracema beach. The *forró* at the **Bar do Pirata** (*tel. 85/3219-8030*), located in the cultural center, has become an obligatory tourist stop. In July, the city hosts the off-season carnival called *Fortal* and the streets are filled with revelers. The most popular lookout point to admire the sunset is at the **Ponte Metálica** (metal bridge) on the Iracema beach.

Praia do Futuro

With an enticing ocean and an average annual temperature of 27°C (81°F), it's hard to resist the beaches of Fortaleza. The best choice is **Futuro** beach, the most beautiful urban beach in Fortaleza accessible from **Avenida Santos Dumont**. On sunny days, it is the busiest beach and nicer than the popular downtown beaches of Iracema and Meireles, the departure points for the boat excursions along the urban shoreline. On Tuesdays and Thursdays, the action continues into the night, with live performances by bands playing everything from *forró* to Brazilian popular music. Futuro offers freshwater showers and food stands along the beach, which account for the action in front of the turquoise water. It is also a place where visitors can enjoy a nice meal. Try the sophisticated **Itapariká** and **Atlantizd**, as well as the traditional **Chico do Caranguejo**.

Fortaleza's urban shoreline: Ceará's capital offers culture and excitement

CENTRO DE TURISMO

This building was the former city jail; when it was constructed between 1850 and 1866 it was large enough to hold almost all of the city's population of 1,800 people. In 1991, the neoclassical building was transformed into the **Centro de Turismo** (tourist center), with 104 arts-and-crafts shops. In addition to the specialties of the Ceará state (such as bobbin and filet lace, wooden sculptures, hammocks and bottles filled with colored sand), there is also a tourist information center. The **Museu de Arte e Cultura Populares** displays the works of artists from Ceará depicting historical, cultural and religious subjects. There also is a food court and clean restrooms.

Rua Senador Pompeu, 350, Centro, tel. (85) 3488-7411. Mon-Sat, 7am-6pm; Sun, 7am-noon.

CENTRO DRAGÃO DO MAR DE ARTE E CULTURA

The main cultural center in Fortaleza was opened in 1998 in a spacious and well-structured area of 30,000 sq. mi. (7.5 acres). The center contains the **Museu de Arte Contemporânea do Ceará** and the city's planetarium as well as an amphitheater, movie theaters, auditoriums, library, bookstore, coffee shop and arts-and-crafts shop. The **Memorial da Cultura Cearense** has exhibits portraying local

---

CACHE OF CACHAÇA

The admirers of Brazilian *cachaça* (a sugar-cane spirit also known as *pinga*), will love the **Museu da Cachaça**, 30 kilometers (19 mi.) from Fortaleza, in the municipality of Maranguape. **Fazenda Ypioca** started to produce homemade *cachaça* when it was built in 1846, and it has a wide range of historical items such as enormous casks and the first sugarcane crusher. (One of the tanks has a 374,000-liter (98,800-gal.) capacity.) Documents, photographs and films can also be seen in this parkland setting at the foot of the **Maranguape** mountain range. The ranch no longer operates, but visitors may sample Ceará *pinga* at the end of the tour.

Rua Senador Virgílio Távora, tel. (85) 3341-0407; Tue-Sun, 8:30am-5pm.

scenes such as the daily routine of cowboys in the backlands of Cariri. The name **Dragão do Mar** (Sea Dragon) is in honor of Francisco José do Nascimento, a fisherman who led the abolition movement in Ceará. Dragão do Mar transformed the surrounding area. Now, with bars, restaurants and the square known as the **Quarteirão dos Artistas** (Artists' Block), it has a nightlife comparable to neighboring Rua Tabajaras.
Rua Dragão do Mar, 81, Iracema, tel. (85) 3488-8600. Tue-Sun, 2pm-9:30pm.

THEATRO JOSÉ DE ALENCAR

The 776-seat theater that opened in 1910 is one of Forteleza's most important historical buildings, and it was declared a historical heritage site. The architectural style combines a neoclassical façade with art nouveau stained-glass railings and auditorium. The metal structure of the museum was imported from Scotland. It has a movable stage and a lateral garden designed by landscape architect Burle Marx. The theater has a varied calendar that includes everything from hip-hop shows to exhibits. Tours with bilingual guides are available.
Praça José de Alencar, Centro, tel. (85) 3452-1581. Mon-Fri, 8am-5pm; Sat, 8am-noon.

OUR RECOMMENDATION

🍽 Characterized by its simple atmosphere and good service, the **Cantinho do Faustino** restaurant offers a perfect menu of regional dishes with wine and herb sauces. The cook and owner of the restaurant, Faustino, has not stopped creating new dishes since 1993, such as *paleta de cabrito* (kid goat pot roast) and *lagosta mocororó* (lobster cooked with green cashew apple wine). Other creations include exotic ice creams with flavors such as basil and brown-sugar candy (*Rua Delmiro Gouveia, 1520, tel. 85/3267-5348*).

🏨 Originally aimed at business travelers, the **Hotel Luzeiros** was so successful that it has started to focus on the tourist trade as well. It has a contemporary atmosphere, professional service and rooms with ocean views, and offers support for guests with disabilities. It is located next to Iracema beach on the Meireles beach, an ideal location for city walking tours.

Additional information begins on page 462.

BEACH PARK, A HAIR-RAISING ADVENTURE

Located in the city of Aquiraz, 29 kilometers (18 mi.) from Fortaleza, **Beach Park** is the largest water park in Latin America. There are 17 attractions, including water slides and wave pools. Only the most daring souls attempt the Insano (Insane) water slide, with a height of 41 meters – as high as a 14-story building. On the horseshoe-shaped Kalafrio (Chill), visitors slide down on an inflatable buoy in a ride that would give anyone goose bumps. Those who prefer relaxation to adventure can take advantage of the **Porto das Dunas** beach at the front of the park, with bar service on the beach, and can stay at the Beach Park Resort.

Rua Porto das Dunas, 2734, Aquiraz, tel. (85) 4012-3000. Daily, 11am-5pm. Closed Tue and Wed in the off-season.

Cumbuco beach, Fortaleza's neighbor, is an essential stop for seekers of tranquility

CUMBUCO

This is a small fishing village surrounded by dunes and lagoons, just 30 kilometers (18.5 mi.) from Fortaleza on highway CE-085. It has started to attract more and more tourists looking for a lush wilderness beach close to the urban center. A good one-day excursion, this beach has fine, white sand and coconut trees where visitors can hang hammocks and relax as they watch the world go by.

DUNES AND LAGOONS

Contracting a buggy driver at the Cooperativa de Bugueiros de Cumbuco is the best way to see the region. Along with the up-and-down ride over the sand dunes, the scenery includes the **Parnamirim** lagoon. The site is ideal for swimming and for using an *esquibunda*, a type of snow board that riders can sit on to slide down the dunes. Lined with summer homes, the **Banana** lagoon is a perfect location for water sports. With winds that are equally ideal for wind-surfing

and kite-surfing, the **Barra do Cauípe** also offers a remarkable view of the Atlantic Ocean and, behind the dunes, the **Lagamar do Cauípe**, which formed where the Cauípe river meets the ocean. Horseback riding and boat excursions can also be arranged in the village. Be prepared for persistent local tour guides who might try to convince drivers to take cars on the beach, because only buggies and four-wheel-drive vehicles can cross the soft sand without getting stuck.

WILDERNESS BEACHES

In addition to the lagoons in the middle of the dunes, Cumbuco has beautiful deserted beaches. **Icaraí, Tabuba, Pacheco** and **Cauípe** are fine examples, all lined with coconut trees. Icaraí and Tabuba have high waves and are separated by the **Barra Nova** river. Pacheco has great sand dunes. But the most beautiful of them all is **Cauípe**, at the mouth of the Cauípe river.

BEBERIBE

The shoreline to the east of Fortaleza is lined with cliffs and coconut trees in the direction of the village of **Canoa Quebrada** and the neighboring state of Rio Grande do Norte. The departure point to explore the region is the town of Beberibe, 90 kilometers (55 mi.) from Fortaleza on highway CE-040, starting from the scenic lookout point atop the high

Morro Branco cliffs: a natural maze

white cliffs of Morro Branco beach, which offers quality arts and crafts.

MORRO BRANCO'S ARTS AND CRAFTS

Try to avoid visiting Morro Branco on weekends, when tour buses bring crowds to **Labirinto das Falésias**. On weekdays, it is possible to enjoy the beautiful landscape and meet artisans who skillfully weave bobbin and filet lace. Some also transform colored sand from the cliff surfaces into bottle art depicting various scenes, such as the view from the top of the cliff with blue ocean speckled with rafts. It is impressive to watch the artists' continuous finger movements as the lace-makers skillfully manipulate wooden bobbins made from murity palm wood. Equally interesting to watch are cotton threads stretched over a wooden frame being transformed into a dress. After a friendly chat with the artisans, follow the guides licensed by the municipality into the Labirinto das Falésias, where the colorful sand is found.

BY BUGGY TO SUCATINGA

This is a classic tour. The buggy trip along the Ceará coastline is so enjoyable that it could last a few hours or many days, as in the case of the adventurers who travel the coast from Fortaleza to Natal. The half-day excursion from **Beberibe** to **Barra de Sucatinga** is unparalleled in beauty and may be made quickly along the 20 kilometers (12.5 mi.) of the paved highway CE-040. Hire a buggy driver – licensed, of course – and just sit back, relax and enjoy the wind in your face. The excursion starts at **Fontes** beach, which is flanked by multicolored sand walls. It makes its first stop at **Morro Branco** and continues to **Diogo** and **Uruaú** beaches, which have multicolored sand dunes. (The driver needs to put the pedal to the metal to avoid getting bogged down in the sand. And the terrain is very susceptible to accidents, so don't ask for a "thrill ride" like the radical maneuvers on the Genipabu sand dunes close to Natal.) Close to the Uruaú fishing village is the largest in the region: **Uruaú** lagoon, also called the **Cumbe** lagoon. The village is ideal for swimming, enjoying a drink at a food stands or practicing sports such as water skiing or jet-skiing. The ride to **Barra de Sucatinga**, at the end of the excursion, inspires contemplation as the buggy rolls along the edge of the ocean in the midst of coconut trees and boats. There is only one small fishing village to break the solitude.

EASTERN BEACHES

Other beautiful beaches lie on the way to Fortaleza in the opposite direction of **Barra de Tabatinga**. The highlight is the **Caponga** fishing village with calm waters, located close to **Barra Velha** at the edge of the mouth of the **Choro** river, and **Balbino**, lined with coconut trees. Visitors can buy quality regional handicrafts here, especially those made out of vines. On Saturdays, don't miss the traditional **Feira de São Bento** in Cascavel, fair held a 15 kilometers (9 mi.) away.

OUR RECOMMENDATION

The **Hotel Oásis Praia das Fontes**, facing the Fontes beach, is the best hotel in Beberibe. The price is "all inclusive" – meaning it covers everything from water to scotch whiskey. Guests have free access to the water theme park, and the comfortable, rustic chalets are spread over a large area. Choose a chalet carefully, because the ones in quiet areas away from the dance club are also very far from other areas of the resort.

Additional information begins on page 462.

Lace makers maintain the tradition of Ceará's handicrafts

CANOA QUEBRADA

A former hippie paradise, Canoa Quebrada is now a cosmopolitan beach town

In the 1970's, hippies discovered the fishing village Canoa Quebrada on top of the rust-colored cliffs, 167 kilometers (104 mi.) east of Fortaleza on highway CE-040. Facing beautiful sand dunes and a beach with white sand, this district of Aracati is no longer based on fishing, and it has witnessed an explosion of tourism that almost destroyed its tranquility. Some of the foreigners who moved there from all over the world and a certain nostalgic atmosphere remain in the now-globalized village. In addition to the mixture of different languages, Canoa Quebrada combines cyber cafés with *forró* clubs along the fashionable "Broadway," the main street lined with artisans displaying their goods. Luckily, the nature in and around Canoa Quebrada has maintained its charm. If the multitudes that sometimes invade the town become overwhelming, take a boat trip with the fishermen or contract a buggy driver to leave town.

THE SURROUNDING COASTLINE
Quieter than **Majorlândia**, the busiest beach in Canoa Quebrada, the eastern coast offers remarkable scenery that is usually explored by buggy excursions along the shoreline. Some of the eight local beaches are especially pleasant. A surprise at the deserted **Lagoa do Mato** beach are the small canyons shaped by the freshwater streams that run over the cliffs, such as **Garganta do Diabo** (devil's throat). The soft, white sand stretches to the calm **Ponta Grossa**, flanked by cliffs and a steeply sloping beach. There is also a fishing village of around 200 people. The village offers rustic restaurants and arts-and-crafts shops. The 30-kilometer (19 mi.) tour goes to **Redondas** beach, which has darker sand, fewer tourists and reddish cliffs along a green ocean. Every year on Aug. 15, it hosts a beautiful sea procession called Nossa Senhora dos Navegantes, or "guardian of navigators."

A DISPLAY OF BRAZILIAN FAITH IN JUAZEIRO DO NORTE

The interior of Ceará displays one of the strongest testaments of faith in the world's largest Catholic nation. In Juazeiro do Norte, 570 kilometers (354 mi.) south of Fortaleza, the myth surrounding the image of Father Cícero Romão Batista (popularly known as "*padim Ciço*") has made the city Brazil's second-largest pilgrimage center. First place still goes to the city of Aparecida, the home of Brazil's patron saint Nossa Senhora Aparecida and her *basílica* (principal church), 183 kilometers (114 mi.) from São Paulo. The *basílica* in Aparecida attracts 200,000 visitors in one day on Oct. 12, the Nossa Senhora Aparecida holiday.

And on Nov. 1, the Northeast comes to a halt to follow the pilgrimage to the land of Father Cícero, perhaps the most passionate religious event in Brazil. Approximately 500,000 of the faithful travel to Juazeiro at this time to worship the miraculous saint whose history is intermingled with the city's. Born in Crato in 1844, Cícero was ordained as a priest at age 26. Two years later, he heard Jesus asking him in a dream to take care of the poor people of Juazeiro, a village 10 kilometers (6 mi.) from his hometown. In 1872, riding a donkey, he entered the tiny village with only a few houses and a small chapel. Juazeiro do Norte was never again the same after his arrival, to the point that he is credited with founding the village.

The first miracle was reported soon after his arrival. During the communion of a devout woman, the consecrated wafer crumbled and turned to blood. Some parishioners claimed that their open wounds and illnesses had been cured, and that was sufficient for the fame of the priest to spread throughout the world and reach the Vatican.

Father Cícero was almost excommunicated and forbidden to celebrate mass. He ended up going into politics and was elected mayor. He died at age 90 in 1934, leaving a legacy of moral conduct that influenced a legion of rural parishioners.

Seventy years later, Juazeiro became the most densely populated city in the interior of Ceará, with approximately 250,000 residents living amidst the scrub vegetation in the valley of Cariri. Religious tourism boosted the local economy with the sale of spiritual items and visits to tourist attractions like the 27-meter statue of Father Cícero, the museum displaying his personal belongings and the memorial containing pictures and a retrospective of his life.

In addition to the pilgrimage day in November, Juazeiro also receives many caravans during the festival of Nossa Senhora das Dores (Our Lady of Sorrows) on Sept. 15, and on the anniversary of Cícero's death on July 20.

"Jeri" landscape: the town's development did not interfere with its charm

JERICOACOARA

The breezes of modernization that blow over the sand in Jericoacoara, 300 kilometers (186 mi.) west of Fortaleza, are still not strong enough to impact its natural beauty. The village is only accessible over a rough road by bus, buggy or four-wheel-drive pick-up from the neighboring Jijoca, around 20 kilometers (12.5 mi.) away. Although it has a cyber café, the fishing village has maintained its charm with *forró* dance clubs and packed-earth alleys. Not a single telephone pole spoils the scenery, because all the electric wiring is underground. It seems as the world passed the village by; however, the reality is that everybody has heard of Jeri, and many have fallen in love with it. The **Parque Nacional de Jericoacoara** opened in 2002, and a parking lot was constructed. Visitors can leave their cars there, because only buggies are allowed within the village limits. They can be hired on the main street for excursions to neighboring beaches and lagoons.

THE BEACHES OF JERI

Sand dunes, coconut trees, lagoons, reefs and rock formations grace Jericoacoara's landscape, but to see the nature that is protected by law in the area, visitors will have to like walking. At low tide, a 45-minute walk along the shoreline past **Pedra do Frade**, the **Gruta da Malhada** and the **Piscina da Princesa** leads to **Pedra Furada**. Everything is meticulously sculptured by nature. The view of the waves crashing against the

OUR RECOMMENDATION

Jeri's modernization is also reflected in the hotel developments. On the calmer side of the city, the **Pousada Vila Kalango** distributed its 11 bungalows at a strategic point of the beach: a coconut grove at the seashore beside the Pôr-do-Sol dune. The restaurant is exclusive to guests, and the rooms are decorated with products made from coconuts, straw and sticks. In the most lively area of the shore, the **Mosquito Blue** features an exit directly to the beach. It has a charming common area, with rooms facing a colorful flower garden surrounding a pool and hot tub.

Additional information begins on page 462.

rocks while the tide rises is second in beauty only to the remarkable July sunset, when the sun disappears on the horizon exactly in line with the span of the Pedra Furada. On the way back, if the tide is in, walk along the trail on top of the cliffs and admire the spectacular view. When guests reach the village, they should join the crowd at the 30-meter-high (98 foot) **Pôr-do-sol** dune to watch the sunset.

THE DUNES OF TATAJUBA

Tatajuba, west of Jericoacoara, was a fishing village that vanished under the sand dunes 30 years ago. A new Tatajuba emerged, however, and it can be visited on a buggy contracted from the Associação dos Bugueiros de Jericoacoara. The excursion passes through the **Mangue Seco** beach and takes the ferry across the mouth of the **Guriú** river. It runs through an estuary that separates Tatajuba from the area where the old fishing village used to be. and where the remains of the church and some houses still stand. Today, the river protects the village. During the

rainy season between January and July, water carries the sand deposited by the wind back to the ocean, which keeps the sand dunes from advancing further inland. The mouth of the other local river, Tatajuba, forms **Lago Grande**, a lagoon where people can go swimming and slide down the **Funil dune**. Visitors can relax in hammocks hung between the piles in the water while they wait for shrimp and lobster appetizers from one of four local food stands.

UBAJARA CAVE

A 1,120 meters (3,675 feet) cave in the heart of the **Ibiapaba mountain range**, located 320 kilometers (199 mi.) west of Fortaleza, is the highlight of the **Parque Nacional de Ubajara** (*tel. 88/3634-1388*). The 563 hectare (1,391 acre) park is Brazil's smallest national park, and its underground galleries have remarkable stalactites, stalagmites and other curious rock formations. There are two ways to descend the 535 meters (1755 feet) slope to reach the cave: the easiest is to take the aerial cable car, but sports enthusiasts may opt for the 2-hour hike. The scenery includes rock pools and waterfalls.

White sands spill into Ceará's waters

JIJOCA DE JERICOACOARA

An obligatory stop on the way to **Jeri** beach is the town of Jijoca de Jericoacoara, a paradise for water sports such as kite surfing and windsurfing. The **Lagoa Azul** and **Lagoa Paraíso**, where the trade winds blow all year long, are located 280 kilometers (174 mi.) west of Fortaleza via highways BR-222 and BR-402. The only way to reach these two lagoons is by buggy from Jeri village.

LAGOA AZUL

The classic excursion to Lagoa Azul will give visitors goose bumps as they zigzag through sand dunes along the route, like those at **Riacho Doce**. Upon reaching the lagoon, 30 minutes from Jijoca, travelers will understand why it is called "Lagoa Azul," or "Blue Lagoon." The pristine waters and white sand form a perfect complement with the sunlight to highlight the blue water. Tourists stay on an island formed by a sand bar that even has a restaurant. It is ideal for swimming, snorkeling and kayaking.

LAGOA PARAÍSO

Lagoa Paraíso is the second stop of the buggy excursion from Jeri. It has coarser sand and colder waters than Lagoa Azul, but they are still crystal clear. Also known as the **Lagoa de Jijoca**, its banks are covered with grass, coconut trees and cashew trees. The calm waters reflect the region's atmosphere. Boats with multicolored sails dominate the scenery and break the monotony of the white sand, blue ocean and blue sky. To preserve the peace, jet skis, motor boats and other motorized vessels are prohibited.

Jijoca: wind, sun and pristine lagoons

OUR RECOMMENDATION

🍽 To reach the lagoons, visitors can travel through either Jijoca de Jericoacoara or Preá beach. If they choose take the latter, they will pass in front of the restaurant **Azul do Mar**. The grilled *robalo* (snook fish) is a good option among the many delicious seafood specialties. Service could be better, but don't get bent out of shape by the lackadaisical attitude of the Northeast. Find a table by the beach, sit back and relax (*Praia do Preá, tel. 88/3660-3062*).

🍽 Small and informal, the **Chocolate** restaurant is close to the beach, and the tables offer a beautiful view of Jericoacoara's waters. But its best feature is a superb menu of pastas, risottos and seafood, not to mention the delicious desserts; the *petit gateau* is famous in the region. Reservations are advised (*Rua do Forró, 214, tel. 88/3669-2190*).

Additional information begins on page 462.

DESTINATION
SÃO LUÍS

Maranhão takes some visitors by surprise. The charming colonial town harbors a rich cultural mix that ranges from reggae music to the folkloric *bumba-meu-boi* performance, which retells the killing and resurrection of a prize cow in a tradition popular in the North and Northeast regions. Maranhão's beautiful seashore stretches for hundreds of miles and the winding coastline runs past striking dunes, lagoons and islands of both the ecological sanctuary Lençóis Maranhenses and, at the border with Piauí state, the Parnaíba delta. Heading towards the *sertão*, the landscape is dominated by *babaçu* palms. São Luís, a cultural heritage site, is a piece of living history. It's home to the most extensive Portuguese architectural legacy in Brazil. In the historic center, more than 3,500 large *sobrado* houses and other buildings sport façades of old-fashioned Portuguese tiles called *azulejos*.

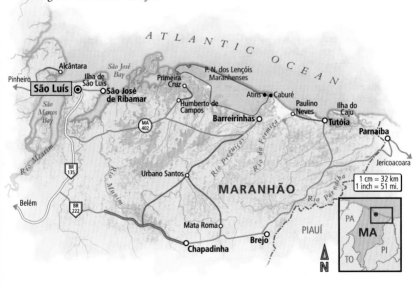

DESTINATION HIGHLIGHTS

SÃO LUÍS

ALCÂNTARA (22 km/14 mi.)

LENÇÓIS MARANHENSES (270 km/168 mi.)

PARNAÍBA DELTA
(500 km/311 mi.)
Ilha do Caju

All distances are from São Luís

SÃO LUÍS

São Luís is the only Brazilian state capital to have been founded by the French, in 1612, and was named after French King Louis XIII. But the Portuguese ultimately had the greater influence on this city. They took the city in 1615, and left their distinctive mark – literally – on the city's architecture: the *azulejo*-tiled *sobrados* in the historic center, along with the limestone cobblestones of the curbs and sidewalks. Starting in 1970, a revitalization program has been restoring the cobblestone streets. A leisurely stroll along the lanes and alleys of São Luís is a journey into the past. Vendors sell fruits, arts and crafts and fish in the charming **Ruas Portugal, do Giz, do Sol, da Estrela** and **do Egito**. Rivers crisscross São

Luís, as well as the eponymous island on which it's built. Some dark-water beaches have developed a little distance from the town. The construction of the new promenade on **Avenida Litorânea** made **Calhau** beach the best place to watch the sunset. But nothing is so impressive as the façades of the buildings in the city center and in the Praia Grande district, such as the **Solar da Baronesa de Anajatuba**, on Rua do Giz near Rua 14 de Julho, and the **Edificio São Luís**. Below is our suggestion for a three-hour walking tour, which strategically tackles hills and descents in an energy-conserving order. Try to take your tour in the afternoon, when the most tourist attractions are open.

① Palácio dos Leões (Louis' Palace)
The present seat of the state government, the palace was built by the French in 1612 and dubbed Saint Louis Fortress. The only original constructions remaining are the Saint Cosme and Saint Damião bastions, but all the architecture has been restored. The neo-classical building contains a rich collection of engravings and works of art.
Avenida D. Pedro II, tel. (98) 3232-1633. Mon, Wed and Fri, 2-5:30pm.

② Igreja Matriz da Sé
Nossa Senhora da Vitória
The most important church in São Luís, it was built in the 17th century, but transformed through countless

renovations by 1922, when it was restored in the neoclassical style. Projeto Reviver, the city's restoration project, has recently brought back the building's charm. A highlight is the main altar, from 1629, which was engraved in gold by Indians. A historical heritage site.
Praça D. Pedro II, Praia Grande, tel. (98) 3222-7380. Daily, 8-11:30am, 3-6:30pm. On Mondays open to 5:30pm.

③ Edifício São Luís
This imposing double-façaded three-story mansion is considered the largest colonial *azulejo*-tiled building in Brazil. *Rua de Nazaré, at the corner of Rua do Egito.*

❹ Teatro Arthur de Azevedo

Built in 1817, it was the second theater in Brazil. It was carefully restored from ruin in 1991. Crystal chandeliers, state-of-the-art stage technology and a U-shaped main auditorium now grace the hall with something akin to its former splendor.
Rua do Sol, 180, tel. (98) 3221-4587.

❺ Fonte do Ribeirão

Built in 1796 to supply the city with water, the fountain has a stone block patio. Its metal gates lead to fascinating underground passages that traverse the Historic Center.
Largo do Ribeirão

❻ Centro de Cultura Popular Domingos Vieira Filho

This three-story colonial mansion contains pieces representing various aspects of Maranhão traditions, both cultural (*tambor-de-crioula*, Carnival, *dança-do-coco*) and religious (*tambor-de-mina*, Festa do Divino). Bilingual guides lead tours.
Rua do Giz, 221, tel. (98) 3231-1557.
Tue-Sun, 9am-7pm.

❼ Convento das Mercês and Fundação da Memória Republicana

Built in 1654 and opened by Father Antônio Vieira, this building housed the convent of the Spanish religious order of the Mercedários. Today it is home to the Fundação da Memória Republicana, with documents and items belonging to former Brazilian president José Sarney.

Rua da Palma, 502, tel. (98) 3222-5182. Tue-Fri, 10am-6pm, Sat, 10am-2pm.

❽ Cafuá das Mercês

The former slave market in São Luís became the **Museu do Negro**. The two-story house contains a collection of African art and musical instruments.
Rua Jacinto Maia, 54. Mon-Fri, 9am-6pm.

❾ Casa de Nhozinho

This four-story mansion with *azulejo*-tiled eaves commemorates a local artist who made toys for poor children. It portrays daily life in Maranhão, with displays of Indian arts and crafts, pottery and fishing apparel. Offers guided tours.
Rua Portugal, 185. No phone, but information at (98) 3231-1557. Tue-Fri, 9am-7pm. Sat-Sun, 9am-6pm.

❿ Casa do Maranhão

This 19ᵗʰ century mansion is the best place to learn about the *bumba-meu-boi* performance, though its permanent display of the roots of this popular festivity.
Rua do Trapiche, Praia Grande. No phone, but information at (98) 3231-1557. Tue–Fri, 9am-7pm; Sat-Sun, 9am-6pm.

⓫ Rua Portugal

Only two blocks long, this street is lined with *azulejo*-tiled colonial mansions, cafés and bars. Ending your tour here in the evening will reveal a perspective of the city center as it was in former days, lit by the iron lamp posts.

ALCÂNTARA

Time seems to pass slowly on the steep streets of Alcântara. Founded in 1648, it was one of the richest towns of the Empire until the abolition of slavery at the end of the 19th century sent it into a period of economic decline. It was listed as a historical heritage site in 1948, due to its outstanding architectural heritage, with more than 300 mansions from the 17th and 18th centuries. But many of the tiled buildings (see detail) are in ruins. Even so, the mansions of **Praça Gomes de Castro** and **Rua Grande**, the **Museu Histórico de Alcântara** and the **Igreja de Nossa Senhora do Carmo**, dating from 1665, can be

visited on a one-day tour that leaves from São Luís. From the São Luís boat terminal, it's 22 kilometers (14 mi.) over here from Alcântara on the other side of the São Marcos Bay. Alcântara's rich heritage contrasts sharply with **Centro de Lançamento de Alcântara**, the Brazilian space agency's rocket-launching base four miles from the city, which is off limits to the public. The boat journey from São Luís to Alcântara departs from the port (Terminal Hidroviário), and the hour-and-a-quarter trip offers such comforts as air conditioning. Sunday is a good day for this trip, because many of São Luís's own attractions are closed then.

THE CELEBRATION OF BUMBA-MEU-BOI

The *festas juninas* refers to a trio of feasts, for the Saints John, Anthony and Peter, all held in June. They take on a special flavor in Maranhão due to the *bumba-meu-boi*, which may well be the richest expression of popular culture in the state. It combines aspects of Portuguese, African and Indian cultures, and uses theater, dance and music to tell the legend of Catirina. In each telling, the farm girl becomes pregnant and develops an uncontrollable craving for ox tongue. She persuades her husband Pai Francisco to kill the most beautiful bull on the farm, the farm owner's favorite. Apart from these characters, the troupes that stage *bumba-meu-boi* in the various cities of Maranhão introduce many other characters like the *caboclo* (Indian-Portuguese peasant), the cowboy,

the Indian and the white man to tell the story of the death and resurrection of the animal. Costumes and musical instruments mark the presentation of the various rhythms, like *matraca*, or frenetic sound; *zabumba*, one of the oldest styles, dominated by a kind of drum; and orchestra, with elaborated choreographies and a more harmonious sound of wind and string instruments. The extend-

ed festival mixes the sacred and the profane, superstition and religion, and its climax occurs on June 24th, Saint John's Day. Other major folk festivals in Maranhão are *tambor-de-crioula*, the *dança-do-coco*, *dança-do-caroço*, *dança-de-são-gonçalo* and the *Festa do Divino Espírito Santo*. The *Festa do Divino* held in Alcântara, in May, is one of the most colorful festivals of its kind in Brazil.

The lagoons, dunes and lush vegetation of Lençóis Maranhenses are accessible on foot or by boat

LENÇÓIS MARANHENSES

On the northeast coast, this half-time desert, interspersed with shape-changing lakes and dunes that rise as high as 40 meters (130 feet), has an ethereal beauty that takes many visitors by surprise. Some say the dunes look like a series of sheets spread out to dry in the sun. The water comes from the rain that the region receives in the first half of the year, making the period from July to December the best time to visit the region. The sun and the heat – up to 40°C (104°F) – is always present in the region of Lençóis Maranhenses, where the town of **Barreirinhas**, 270 kilometers (170 mi.) east of São Luís, offers the best base of operations for visitors. From the town, groups set out on foot or by boat along the **Preguiças** river, through part of the area designated a national park and covering 70 kilometers (43 mi.) of beaches and 50 kilometers (31 mi.) inland. For additional information, call the Ibama agency (*tel. 98/3231-3010*). Those coming from the Parnaíba delta, in the neighboring state of Piauí, can reach the park from the city of **Tutóia**, via a three-hour trip by four-wheel-drive vehicle, with a stop in **Paulino Neves**, also called **Rio Novo**.

BY JEEP TO THE LAGOONS

The waters of the lagoons of the **Parque Nacional dos Lençóis Maranhenses** are various shades of blue and green. After crossing the Preguiças river on a ferry boat departing from Barreirinhas, driving a four-wheel-drive jeep takes 45 minutes to reach the parking place in the park. From there, the tour along the desert is on foot, starting with a 15-minute walk to **Lagoa Azul**, a lagoon surrounded by dunes with very fine sand. Walk for another ten minutes to reach **Lagoa dos Peixes**, which has waters darkened by the algae but nevertheless ideal for a refreshing swim. Unlike Lagoa Azul, which evaporates by the end of each year, this lagoon never disappears, no matter the severity of the dry season. While the tour jeep parks at the banks of Lagoa dos Peixes for two hours, you can go for a walk over the dunes. But be careful: the dunes are surprisingly disorienting, and lots of people get lost in the area. After a one-hour drive in a jeep, you reach **Lagoa Bonita**, whose waters resembles Lagoa Azul except that they lack the surrounding

Lagoons and dunes as high as 40 meters (131 feet) resemble sheets spread out to dry in the sun

vegetation. Like the constantly shifting dunes, the lagoons are always changing their shape, as the wind blows back the sands carried to the beach by the Preguiças river.

A BOAT TRIP ALONG RIO PREGUIÇAS

Preguiças river is vital to the livelihoods of local residents, and is the best route of access to the many pleasant, nearby villages, outside the area of the national park. Any tour operator in Barreirinhas can arrange the boat trip, with daily departures at

OUR RECOMMENDATION

The **Porto Preguiças Resort** does not offer as many activities as some other resorts, but it is the best hotel in Barreirinhas. It has large chalets, equipped with comfortable beds, goose-down pillows, and cotton towels and bed linens. The waters of the large swimming pool get heated naturally each night by the sun-absorbing sand bottom. The staff serves a substantial breakfast from the capable kitchen.

Additional information begins on page 462.

8:30am, returning at 3pm. The first stopping point is **Vassouras**, after a 45-minute boat ride. A walk in the sands of **Pequenos Lençóis** beach is worth the detour, in a setting quite similar to that of the park. The tour continues on between the native vegetation on the riverbanks and some mangroves, passing **Espadarte**, **Morro do Boi**, and **Moitas** before reaching the village of **Mandacaru**. Take out your camera as soon as you see the first houses! The view of the village with the 35 meters (114 feet) high **Preguiças** lighthouse behind it is one of the most beautiful of the tour. Upon landing, go up the 160 steps of the lighthouse, built in 1940, and, from there, take in the unusual view of Lençóis Maranhenses. After leaving the village, it takes only five minutes for the boat to beach the sands of **Caburé**, another fishing village that is usually the last stop of the tour. Boats generally stop for 2.5 hours, which includes lunch, in this village. If you can't decide whether to go for a swim

on the Preguiças river on one side of the village, or to take a short walk until you reach the Atlantic Ocean, on the other side, do both! Or choose one of them and enjoy the rest of your time on shore relaxing in one of the hammocks of the many huts in Caburé.

A Walk in the Desert

If the short walks permitted during stops on boat or jeep tours isn't enough to get the blood in your legs flowing, take a hiking tour inside the Lençóis Maranhenses park. Just be prepared for scorching sun and desert-like sands. The tour leaves from Atins, a small village between Preguiças river and the ocean and which, instead of Caburé, is the final stop on some standard river boat trips. You can go from there to the villages **Baixa Grande** and **Queimada dos Britos**, inside the park, with a hard, one-day hike. This trip of Sahara desert conditions is only recommended for adventurers

that are in excellent physical condition, have a local guide, and are duly supplied with sun screen, a hat and lots of water.

A Taste of Maranhão

If you wish to sample specialties from the cuisine of Maranhão, start by sipping *tiquira*, a liquor made of manioc. Follow the aperitif with *arroz de cuxá*, a dish of rice accompanied by a sauce made with a base of leaves of *vinagreira* (red sorrel plant). That plant is also known as *caruru-azedo* (sour okra) or *azedinha*. Actually, this is just one of the ingredients of this African specialty that slaves incorporated into local cuisine. The gravy is prepared with toasted sesame seeds, dried shrimp pounded with manioc flour, onion, garlic, ginger and the okra cut in small pieces. While you relish the food, take the chance to sip Jesus-brand *guaraná*, a sweet pink soft drink with a touch of cinnamon that's been a regional concoction since 1920. For dessert there are exotic fruits such as *bacuri* (a roundish, yellow fruit with a white, slightly tart pulp), *murici* (the wild Amazon cherry, which is yellow and has sweet pulp of the same color) and *sapoti* (sapodilla).

Parnaíba Delta

Nature forged the largest delta in the Americas at the mouth of the Parnaíba river. Straddling the border between the states of Maranhão and Piauí, it consists of a lush, triangle-shaped labyrinth of multiple channels and 77 islands. It's accessible from the town of Parnaíba, itself a highlight of the short 66 kilometers (41 mi.) of Piauí coastline. The delta is an ecological sanctuary that includes a wide variety of eco-systems: coastal Caatinga (stunted, semiarid scrubland), sandbanks, mangrove swamps and *carnaubal* (a grove of wax palms).

Boat Rides

The traditional way to explore the delta's beaches, dunes and *igarapés,* or channels, is by hiring a boat. Tour operators' vessels leave from Porto das Barcas, in Parnaíba, but these tours are often noisy and take up to eight hours to cover could easily be done in three. We suggest hiring a private boat and sailing straight to the reserve on Ilha do Caju, which is in one of the Parnaíba delta's five bays. This journey takes one hour and a half. Along the way, the landscape is mostly *carnaubal.* The export of the wax of the *carnaúba* palm supported the state economy through the middle of the last century, and it attracted English traders who left their marks in the region.

The City of Parnaíba

Parnaíba, 335 kilometers (208 mi.) north of Teresina, the capital city of the state of Piauí, is the second-largest city in the state. It's about 500 kilometers (310 mi.) from each of the neighboring coastal capital cities: São Luís in the state of Maranhão and Fortaleza in the state of Ceará. Despite the recent recognition of the need to invest in tourism, this port still lacks much basic infrastructure in the way of hotels and restaurants. For an overnight stay, the best place is **Hotel Civico**, but that's not saying much.

The short coastline of Piauí features the delta's profusion of nature

Beautiful Ilha do Caju can be explored on horseback, by jeep or on foot

CAJU ISLAND

Above the mangrove swamps, the aerial ballet of the *guarás* – birds with a long and curved beak that resembles flamingoes – enthralls visitors… if they aren't already distracted spotting armadillos, foxes, cavies, herons, iguanas and other passing wildlife. Indeed, animals dominate this 100 sq. km (39 sq. mi.) area, which is accessible only after a 3.5-hour boat trip through the delta.

All the animals may frighten some visitors at first, but as hours go by, Ilha do Caju will seem like it has the most luxuriant ecosystem on earth. Apart from the animals, greenery, dunes and lagoons fill in the most important and preserved formation of the Parnaíba delta. The island's private owner, Ingrid Clark, inherited the lands that her British-derived family has owned since 1847. She relishes preservation of the flora and fauna. A decade ago, she established the **Refúgio Ecológico Ilha do Caju**, the only inn on the island. The inn is built in to be rustic, to better integrate its

structure with the environment. However, this means that it has no air conditioning, telephone or TV, and there's only cold water in the bathrooms! But don't panic. All steps were taken to ensure that guests will be able to relax in full harmony with nature. Therefore, all rooms have comfortable goose-down pillows and a king-size bed, for example. The inn's restaurant lets guests select what they eat, but they must place orders well in advance. Consider the regional *Piauiense* cuisine, featuring dishes like *maria-isabel*, a dish made of rice and salted, sun-dried meat, and *capote* made with Guinea fowl. Drinks include the delicious *cajuína*, a beverage made from the pulp of cashew apple. Only twenty people live on Ilha do Caju, and all of them work at the inn. Among other things they are responsible for guiding the guests on several tour options on horseback or by jeep, or for alligator watching at night. A tip: don't forget to bring along your insect repellent, a hat and a pair of boots.

NORTH

A visit to the North of Brazil is guaranteed to open the mind and spirit to remarkable surprises. This region is home to the Amazon Rainforest, which covers the states of Amazonas, Acre, Roraima, Rondônia, Pará, Amapá and Tocantins. We suggest three cities as principal destinations: Manaus, Belém and Palmas (see map below). From Manaus you can go to Parintins, home to one of Brazil's largest popular festivals. Close to Manaus, special wilderness hotels offer the best way to see first-hand the Amazon's fantastic biodiversity. The capital city of Belém has preserved both the architectural heritage and the indigenous culture from the past. From here, the tranquil fresh water beaches of Ilha de Marajó and Santarém are within striking distance. The city of Palmas is the departure point for journeys to Jalapão's amazing desert-like landscape.

Previous page: boy canoeing, Amazon. Cristiano Mascaro

DESTINATION
MANAUS

A mazonas is magnificent in every respect. Brazil's largest state, it covers more than 1.5 million km² (580,000 sq. mi.). Even with 3 million residents, that gives it a population density of less than 2 persons per square kilometer. It lays claim to the world's largest river both in volume and length, and contains the world's greatest biodiversity. A visit to Manaus provides a good understanding of the customs and essence of the Amazon, and even if you just visit the capital city and surrounding areas you will return home with pleasant memories. At least two days are needed to see the city and its historical monuments thoroughly. While settling in, schedule a boat trip to see the famous confluence of the Negro and Solimões rivers. A travel agency can arrange a boat trip, the classic means of transportation in a region with many rivers and few roads. Take the opportunity to try the typical *tambaqui* (red pacu) fish at a floating restaurant and visit the wilderness hotels that attract tourists throughout the year.

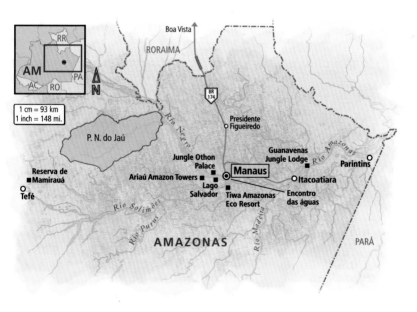

DESTINATION HIGHLIGHTS

MANAUS
Cultural Circuit
Wilderness Getaways

MANAUS

Although the highlights of any trip to the Amazon will be the forest and rivers, you should not completely skip the historical buildings in Manaus. The impressive buildings were constructed in the late 19th and early 20th century during the rubber boom, when the city became fabulously wealthy practically overnight. Before heading to a wilderness hotel for a few days to discover why this part of the country fascinates so many travelers,

schedule a layover in the capital city and make some discoveries that will be all your own. Since 2002, Manaus has benefited aesthetically from the Programa Monumenta, a federal government program aimed at saving the country's architectural heritage. Even though the excursion includes visits to buildings made from bricks and iron, nature is always present here, preparing your spirit for the trip to the jungle.

CULTURAL CIRCUIT

TEATRO AMAZONAS

The theatre, nestled in the heart of the Amazon wilderness, was superbly built in 1896. All the construction materials were imported from Europe, with the exception of the Brazilian woods used for the armchairs and parts of the floor. In the great hall, the flooring is made

up of 12,000 pieces of inlaid wood, and paintings by the Italian artist Domênico de Angelis adorn the walls and ceiling. The crystal light fixtures were imported from Murano, and the external finish of the cupola consists of 20,000 glass tiles in the colors of the Brazilian flag. The stage curtains display the merging

The neoclassical-style Teatro Amazonas: the historical landmark is undergoing restoration

The meeting of the waters of the Solimões and Negro rivers, where the Amazon begins

waters of the Negro and Solimões rivers. The annual opera festival takes place in April and May.
Praça São Sebastião, tel. (92) 622-1880. Daily, 9am-4pm.

MUSEU DE CIÊNCIAS NATURAIS DA AMAZÔNIA

The Amazonian Natural History Museum is on the outskirts of Manaus, and the signs pointing the way are not very helpful. Expect to ask for directions more than once. But for those interested in biology, which should be everyone coming to the Amazon, the trip is worth the trouble. The museum's collection consists of preserved stuffed examples of the many regional aquatic animals such as the *pirarucu* (giant arapaima) and the *piraíba* (kumakuma catfish).Both those fish grow to roughly 2.5 meters (8 feet) long and weigh more than 150 kilograms (330 lbs.). There are also giant beetles, spiders and butterflies from Amazon.
Estrada dos Japoneses, Colônia Cachoeira Grande, Aleixo, tel. (92) 644-2799. Mon-Sat and holidays, 9am-5pm.

MERCADO MUNICIPAL ADOLPHO LISBOA

This municipal market, a copy of the historic market of Les Halles in Paris, was built to face the Negro river. Ever since its completion in 1882, it has been the main market in Manaus for traditional Amazonian products. Take a leisurely stroll through the three warehouses selling meat, fish, fruits and vegetables and keep an eye out for unusual items like *jarina* – a seed also known as "Amazon ivory" that is used for costume jewelry and crafts. Curious attractions include the medicinal herb stands that promise to cure every type of ailment. Even if you buy nothing, you can discover a wealth of information talking to the herbalists about their plants.
Rua dos Barés, 46, Centro. Daily, 8am-6pm.

BOAT TRANSPORTATION

Water transport is essential to visit some of the best attractions close to Manaus. As well as traveling along the *igarapés*, as the narrow channels and inlets off the main river are called, you can schedule a one-day excursion to visit the wilderness hotels. A special highlight is the *encontro das águas*, or meeting of the waters, where you can see the merging of the dark waters of the Negro river with the muddy, brown current of the Solimões. If you prefer to avoid being crammed into a tourist boat with up to 90 other passengers, you can rent a boat at **Fontur** (*tel. 92/658-3052*) or at the **Associação dos Canoeiros Marina do David Fátima** (*tel. 92/658-6159*).
Lunch at the floating restaurant **Bicho Preguiça**, which is not on the route of the tourist boats, is bound to be a treat. Located on **Cacau** lake, its menu includes delicious *costelas de tambaqui* (red pacu fish), *picanha* (rump roast) and *caldeiradas* (fish stew).

Canoeing along the *igarapés*: during the rainy reason, only the tree crowns remain above water

WILDERNESS GETAWAYS

Staying in a wilderness hotel is a unique experience. The hotels offer guests good amenities and entertain them with nature walks, piranha fishing, nighttime alligators watching, canoe excursions along the *igarapés* and visits to the homes of people living on the river banks. Most of the wilderness hotels include shuttle transportation for tourists from Manaus by land, air or water.

IN THE HEART OF THE FOREST

Tefé, 663 kilometers (412 mi.) from Manaus, is worth flying to for a visit to the largest protected *várzea* (grassy floodplain) of the Amazon. A local environmental institute named **Instituto de Desenvolvimento Sustentável Mamirauá** is in charge of the upkeep of the **Mamirauá** reserve, and has an inn (*tel. 97/343-4672*) that offers an unforgettable three-night package for nature lovers. The trip includes excursions to see birds, monkeys and porpoises, canoe excursions and visits to local communities as well as seminars describing the Institute's ongoing research.

ARIAÚ AMAZON TOWERS

The largest wilderness hotel in the wilds of the Amazon is a tourist complex made up of 8 suspended towers connected by 8 kilometers (5 mi.) of walkways at treetop height. This is not an extravagance but rather a necessity to safeguard against frequent flooding. The impressive view from the top of two 41-meter (134-foot) towers allows you to take in a broad view of the Amazon region. The accommodations range from simple rooms with cold water showers to regular suites and luxury suites with the technological luxury of internet access. There are also the *Casas de Tarzan* (Tarzan Houses) – houses with up to four levels with two bedrooms and a whirlpool bath.

LAGO SALVADOR

The hotel located on and named after Salvador lake has the most exquisite scenery in the area. The accommodations include four chalets with three bedrooms each and a

verandah overlooking the water. The floating bar is a meeting place for the guests. For those seeking adventure, the hotel offers canopy tree climbing, rappelling and rafting.

JUNGLE OTHON PALACE
This is a good choice for lovers of the water and would-be mariners. The hotel is built on a steel barge anchored on an inlet off the Negro river, and it rocks in harmony with the waves. Although it only has 22 rooms, it offers amenities such as a convenience store, air conditioning and televisions in the rooms. The highlight is the restaurant, which offers a panoramic view of the nearby forest.

TIWA AMAZONAS ECO RESORT
Facing Manaus on the opposite bank of the Negro river, the hotel is run by a Dutch company for outdoor activities. Opened in 2003, it has comfortable wooden chalets with verandahs overlooking the river. The hotel offers activities such as rappelling and Tyrolean traverse, known as *tirolesa*.

GUANAVENAS JUNGLE LODGE
For those who want to get away from it all for a time, Guanavenas is the perfect spot. Located 350 kilometers (217 mi.) from Manaus, in Silves, it is well organized and offers a 30 meters (98 feet) observation tower. The local fruit trees attract numerous bird species.

Passionflower

Annato

THE AMAZON RAINFOREST:
BRAZIL'S GREATEST TREASURE

The Amazon is a world apart, the largest green reserve in the world. In the midst of this extraordinary biodiversity, it is one of the last places on Earth where tribal peoples still live much as they have since the Stone Age. Tribes live here that have virtually no history of contact with Western society and preserve pure habits developed during millennia of cultural isolation. The Amazon also is home to the largest reserve of fresh water in the world, and nowhere else in the world is there such a wealth of rivers. The Negro river alone has an average depth of 70 meters (230 feet), which means it could entirely submerge a 20-story building. The number of lakes and floodplains abound, and they are full of hundreds of species of plants, fish and other animals.

We are in the so-called "millennium of water," dedicated to that resource that is becoming dangerously scarce throughout the world. Consequently, the Amazon protects and represents a critical human resource. Those who have water have the oil of the future. Yet incredible as it seems, we are destroying this wealth. From any boat, along the shore of a river, you can easily see the momentum of deforestation caused by cattle ranching and other activities. Species vital to the area are being removed and destroyed and no one can guarantee that they will ever return to grow again.

In these times of deep divide between much of humanity and so much of nature, we must remember that we are part of both. We are killing something we are part of. That's why an increasing number of Brazilians consider it essential to develop controlled ecotourism, to become sufficiently acquainted with the Amazon to respect and protect this greatest of natural treasures.

To begin to understand this unique world, take a boat trip from Belém to Manaus. Take note of the sudden changes in the weather, three or four times throughout the day. Observe the density of light, the many variations of the sun, and the marvelous cloud formations. At times the sky turns lead-grey, creating a fantastic contrast with the green forest. Travel in a small boat so you can explore the inlets that appear along the river banks. You'll pass through various "lakes" that are actually flooded areas of the river. To discover the enchantment of the Amazon, travel leisurely without the rush of conventional tourism. Also at a leisurely pace, discover the lovely small towns of the region.

Make a note in your agenda, and underline it, that it is an absolute must to be in Parintins at the end of June. This is not another Carnival, as the press in the South of Brazil likes to call it, but rather a sensational 3-act opera, with remarkable costumes and decorations. I was so moved by the first representation I saw that I cried. It is a *bumba-meu-boi* with a distinct, traditional indigenous dance, without the usual African or Latin body movements of other popular rhythms. The entire pageant is portrayed and created by an incredible number of talented local artists.

A great civilization lives in the Amazon. I have had the opportunity to spend time with various Indian nations like the *ianomâmis*, *marubos* and *macuxis*. They have a profound knowledge of their forest. From plants, roots and sap of trees, they make natural medicines that correspond to, but have advantages over, antibiotics, anti-inflammatories, and other modern drugs. Large foreign laboratories are trying to patent these formulas, in an attempt to lay claim to ancient wisdom.

The Indians also have practical knowledge of soil fertility, and also know when to rotate their crops and how long the land should remain fallow in order to restore its vitality. These semi-nomadic peoples have an admirable "control" of the forest. There is a great deal of communication between the tribes and interaction among the villages.

This same mastery of the fruits of the land and resources of the region underpins the incredibly rich regional cuisine. The dishes include sophisticated combinations. A grilled *tambaqui* (red pacu) and *surubim* (catfish) are truly delicious. You'll also encounter – and enjoy – a large variety of fish with completely foreign identities. Another exceptional treat for the palate is to go to an ice cream parlor in Manaus or Belém. Take note of the various aromas and tastes. Good parlors offer at least 25 flavors of fruit sherbet, most of which even Brazilians from other regions have never heard of. Many of these fruits simply do not travel. Some have flavors so strong one has to develop a taste for them. But there are others known to make even unromantic visitors believe in love at first taste.

Despite the vast number of unique attractions found there, there are some things that cannot be found here, in spite of rumors. In Brazilian imaginations, the Amazon forest hides the dangerous *caipora*, or hobglobin, and the *mula-sem-cabeça*, a mythical priest's mistress who becomes a headless mule on Fridays and runs about frightening people. I hope that Brazilians overcome their fear of these myths, because it is essential to make Brazilians more aware of the importance of the Amazon. The region offers tourism opportunities for all pocketbooks and budgets. Ecotourism needs to be encouraged with responsibility. I hope that every Brazilian that visits the Amazon will become an activist, a defender of the preservation of Brazil's greatest heritage – the green of our flag.

Sebastião Salgado,
photographer

THE PARINTINS FESTIVAL

The date of June 28, 29 and 30 are just as sacred for the Amazon as Carnival is for Rio de Janeiro. During these days, the Parintins Folklore Festival takes place. The most important popular festival of northern Brazil, it's been celebrated in its current form since the 1960's. Every day of the festival, no fewer than 35,000 people from all over the Amazon as well as other states and countries congregate in the *bumbódromo* in **Parintins**, a town located on Tupinambarana island, 420 kilometers (260 mi.) from Manaus. They go there to watch the duel between the groups *Boi Caprichoso* and *Boi Garantido*.

The origin of the richly staged festival goes back to the arrival of migrants from the Northeast of Brazil at the end of the 19th century and the early the 20th century. In an arena a simple and monotonous melody called the *toada* envelops dancing players dressed in elaborate costumes. The main colors, blue for the *Caprichoso* and red for the *Garantido*, are reflected in the clothing of en-

thusiastic fan clubs. The fans do not boo as the rival group passes but watch the parade in absolute silence. In order to not give the impression that they favor one group over the other, the jury uses green pens to mark the scores of the parades. Even corporate sponsors adapt the colors of their logos to avoid offending either side.

Each presentation lasts three hours and symbolizes the same story. They use many elements of forest imagery and figures such as the porpoise. Each *Boi* consists of at least 4,000 participants and tells the folkloric story of a couple named Francisco and Catirina, the characters of the *bumba-meu-boi*. To fulfill his pregnant wife's desire, who wanted at any cost to eat cow tongue, Francisco kills his boss's prize animal. Sentenced to death, the man pleads for help from *pajés*, and these witch doctors resuscitate the cow. Not to spoil the ending, but Francisco is pardoned amidst great celebration. The legend is remembered today in the famous Festival of Parintins.

DESTINATION
BELÉM

Brazil's second largest state, Pará is the gateway to the Amazon. Within its roughly 1.2 million km² (463,000 sq. mi.), the capital Belém features the most remarkable colonial architecture. The city's ongoing renaissance has transformed the old docks of its port into a lively area of bars and restaurants, making it resemble Buenos Aires's hip Puerto Madero district. In addition, Pará maintains one of the most authentic and original culinary heritages in Brazil thanks to delectable freshwater fish and various fruits and seasonings. Belém's Mercado Ver-o-Peso has a great selection of this cornucopia. While traveling through the region take time to appreciate the ornate Marajoara and Tapajônica ceramics that can be found in Belém and on the large Ilha de Marajó, which is also famous for its buffalo ranches. Other state attractions are the freshwater beaches in the village of Alter do Chão, close to the city of Santarém, and the picturesque beaches 180 kilometers (112 mi.) from Belém to Algodoal, a rustic fishing village on the car-free island of Maiandeua.

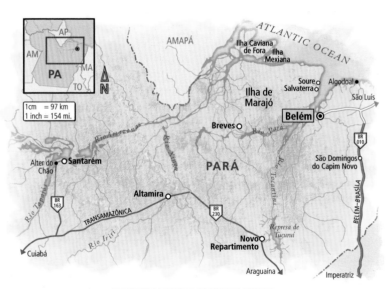

DESTINATION HIGHLIGHTS

BELÉM
    Núcleo Cultural Feliz Lusitânia
    Cultural Circuit
    Estação das Docas

ILHA DE MARAJÓ (three hours by boat)

SANTARÉM AND ALTER DO CHÃO
    (1526 km/948 miles)

All distances are from Belém

BELÉM

1 - Mercado Ver-o-Peso
2 - Museu de Arte Sacra
3 - Espaço Cultural Casa das Onze Janelas

4 - Museu Forte do Presépio
5 - Theatro da Paz
6 - Museu Paraense Emílio Goeldi

Belém was only effectively colonized after the Portuguese seized control of the area in the 16th century. Until then, it had been a site of colonial contention, mainly between the Dutch and British. Its colonial architecture has been well preserved, but the downtown area nevertheless lacks a certain amount of cleanliness. The capital's distinctive buildings include the **Theatro da Paz** and the cluster of buildings that form the **Núcleo Cultural Feliz Lusitânia**. A must-see is **Mercado Ver-o-Peso** (literally, See-the-Weight Market).

❶ MERCADO VER-O-PESO

A visit to this market, which opened in 1894, is crucial to acquaint the visitor with various facets of Pará culture. The former customs house was a compulsory stop to check the weight of merchandise, hence the name. The sprawling market has roughly 2,000 stands that sell delicacies to whet the appetite. However, the most interesting attractions are the "*mandingueiras,*" or witch doctors, who sell medicinal herbs, powdered plants and bottled solutions (mixtures of herbs and grain alcohol) for all ailments. They promise to cure everything from arthritis and diabetes to covetousness and envy. Lately, they've also taken to marketing "natural Viagra." The colors, aromas, flavors and hubbub are intoxicating, even if you skip the buzz-inducing homegrown remedies. Stop at the stands and awaken your taste buds: from the vast selection of fruits try *muruci* (golden spoon fruit), *bacuri*, *ingá* and *taperebá* (java plum).
Avenida Boulevard Castilhos França, Centro. Daily, 8am-6pm.

NÚCLEO CULTURAL FELIZ LUSITÂNIA

The capital's newly restored historical landmarks include colonial houses on **Rua Padre Champagnat**, the **Igreja de Santo Alexandre**, the **Museu de Arte Sacra,** the **Museu Forte do Presépio** and the **Espaço Cultural Casa das Onze Janelas**, located in the Praça Frei Caetano Brandão. You can visit them on foot.

② MUSEU DE ARTE SACRA
Built in 1883, this former Palácio Episcopal now houses one of the most important museums of religious art in Brazil. 340 pieces of religious objects, most of them 18th century wooden sculptures of saints, make up the collection. The museum, with images from Jesuit Baroque, is located beside the **Igreja de Santo Alexandre**.
Praça Frei Caetano Brandão, Cidade Velha, tel. (91) 219-1150. Tue-Fri, 1pm-6pm; Sat, Sun and holidays, 9am-1pm.

③ ESPAÇO CULTURAL CASA DAS ONZE JANELAS
The "house of eleven windows," designed by Italian Antonio Landi, was constructed in the 18th century and became famous for the façade windows. In 1768 it was converted into the Hospital Real and today it is a prestigious cultural space for the arts. The **Boteco das Onze**, located in the complex, offers a panoramic view of the Guajará Bay.
Praça Frei Caetano Brandão, Cidade Velha, tel. (91) 219-1105. Tue-Fri, 10am-6pm; Sat, Sun and holidays, 10am-8pm.

④ MUSEU FORTE DO PRESÉPIO
This 1616-built museum is inside the **Forte do Castelo**, which is at the exact center-point of downtown Belém. Fragments of cannons, swords and porcelain found during the restoration are now on display. Also located within the building is the **Museu do Encontro**, which relates the history of the Portuguese colonization of the Amazon. Relics from the Tapajó and Marajoara Indians discovered at various Amazon archeological sites are also on display.
Praça Frei Caetano Brandão, Cidade Velha, tel. (91) 219-1134. Tue-Fri, 10am-6pm; Sat, Sun and holidays, 10am-8pm.

Mercado Ver-o-Peso, a former customs house, overlooks the banks of Guajará Bay

CULTURAL CIRCUIT

⑤ THEATRO DA PAZ

Inspired by the Teatro Scala in Milan, Italy, and constructed in 1878 at the peak of the Amazon rubber boom, the theater was refurbished and reopened in 2002 in its original architectural splendor. In tours, guides reveal fascinating details about the theater. Pay special attention to the crystal light fixtures and mirrors and the parquet flooring made from Brazilian boxwood in the great hall. Also observe the painting on the ceiling of the auditorium by Italian Domênico de Angelis. It portrays Apollo entering Amazonia drawn by horses. Events held here include theatre performances, concerts, singing competitions and, between July and August, operas.

Rua da Paz, Centro, tel. (91) 224-7355 Tue-Fri, 9:30-11am; 12:30pm-2:30pm and 4pm-5pm; Sat, 9am–7pm.

Theatro da Paz, inspired by the Scala in Milan

UNIQUE FLAVORS

Pará's cuisine is distinct. Just the right combination of ingredients creates dishes like *pato no tucupi*, roast duck served with *tucupi*, a combination of manioc juice and *jambu* leaves which are similar to watercress. Another typical dish is *maniçoba*, also known as the "*feijoada* of Pará." Manioc leaves that are cooked for four days are used in place of beans. The dish is served with rice, manioc meal, and bonnet peppers, and various meats such as dried beef, smoked pork loin, pig ears and spareribs. You can try these delicacies at the **Lá em Casa** restaurant. If you prefer to try something out of the ordinary such as wild boar or ostrich the place to go is **O Ou tro**. Ice-cream lovers should stop by the **Cairu** ice-cream parlor, with *açaí* and *tapioca* flavors. Incidentally, in Pará they eat *açaí* with coarsely ground flours, and ordering it with *granola* and *guaraná*, which is common in some southeastern cities, is an offense.

---

⑥ MUSEU PARAENSE EMÍLIO GOELDI

Opened in 1866, this museum is internationally recognized for its research of Amazonian plants and animals as well as local customs. The **Parque Zoobotânico** covers an area of 5.2 hectares (13 acres) with roughly 800 species of trees such as kapoks and cedars, and some 600 animals including some that are threatened by extinction. Those interested in archeology shouldn't miss the collection of more than 81,000 pieces and fragments of ceramic and stone artifacts found at archeological sites in the region. The main attractions are the Tapajônica and Marajoara ceramic relics, some of which are believed to be 7,000 years old.

Avenida Magalhães Barata, 376, São Brás, tel. (91) 219-3369. Daily, 9am-5pm.

ESTAÇÃO DAS DOCAS

Belém's former port area, dating from 1902, was extremely run down before it was restored in 2000. The site got converted into one of the most fashionable tourist attractions in Belém, a small scale version of Puerto Madero in Buenos Aires. The three metal warehouses imported from England at the beginning of the 20th century were restored and now house 33 commercial establishments including a theater, stores, bars and restaurants.

A good option for a great meal is the **Lá em Casa** restaurant, an offshoot of the successful original that specializes in regional cuisine. Beer lovers, and anyone willing to try something new, should make a strategic stop at **Amazon Beer**, a brewery that makes its own beer flavored with the exotic fruit *bacuri*. At night, **Estação das Docas** becomes the place to be. Bands perform on a suspended stage that moves along the docks so that almost all of the bars and restaurants in the area have an unobstructed view of the show. The Estação also promotes temporary and permanent art and cultural exhibitions. The exhibit *Arqueologia, Memória e Restauro* (Archeology, Memory and Restoration) displays relics discovered during archeological excavations at São Pedro Nolasco Fort and *Memória do Porto de Belém* (Memories of the Belém Port) relates the port's history through photographs and objects. The Estação is also the departure point for day excursion on the region's waterways and is the ideal location to watch the sunset on Guajará Bay.

Avenida Boulevard Castilhos França, Centro, tel. (91) 212-5525. Mon-Wed, noon-midnight; Thu and Fri, noon-3am; Sat, 10am-3am; Sun, 9am-midnight.

CÍRIO DE NAZARÉ FAITH'S ULTIMATE EXPRESSION

On the second Sunday of October, an impressive demonstration of faith takes over the streets of Belém during one of Brazil's most popular religious celebrations. Two million people invade the city's streets to join the procession of tribute to Nossa Senhora de Nazaré (Our Lady of Nazareth), who is said to have performed miracles after a statue bearing her image was found on the banks of the Utinga *igarapé*, the present location of the **Basílica de Nazaré** (*Praça Justo Chermont, tel. 91/4009-8400*). Since 1793, pilgrims – who today come from all corners of the state and country – follow the procession of Círio de Nazaré, which carries the statue of the saint from the Igreja da Sé

to the basilica. During the procession the carriage that bears the saint is encircled by a rope barrier. The often-scorching sun does not deter the faithful, who try to hold the rope as they walk along the almost 5 kilometers (3 mi.) route. As there is not enough rope for everyone to hold, only an act of faith justifies the great sacrifice to at least try to place a finger on it. The religious fervor reaches its peak when the followers kneel by the thousands to celebrate the arrival of the Virgin of Nazareth at the basilica.

ILHA DE MARAJÓ

Two days are enough to visit Ilha de Marajó, the largest island in the world. It borders both fresh and salt water and covers 49,000 km² (19,000 sq. mi.) – larger than Switzerland or the state of Rio de Janeiro. From Belém it is a three-hour boat trip to **Salvaterra**, the island's main access point and also the location of the **Pousada dos Guarás**, the best hotel in the region. In the village it is worthwhile to visit the ruins of the Jesuit church that was constructed on the **Joanes** beach in the 17th century. In **Soure**, another village, the attractions include the famous buffalo ranches and the Marajoara ceramic studios that preserve the valuable inheritance of the island's ancestors.

CURTUME MARAJÓ
At Primeira Rua (First Street), 450, in the village of Soure, **Curtume Marajó** will give you an introduction to the treatment processes for buffalo leather. All stages of the leather treatment are completed here – salting, stripping (the removal of the hair and fat), tenderizing and tanning.

The smell, as you would expect, is far from pleasant. Then, it's transformed into items such as belts, sandals and horse saddles, which are sold in the tannery shop.

THE GREAT WAVE OF THE NORTH
Along with the meeting of the waters of the Negro and Solimões rivers in the upper Amazon, another of the country's greatest fresh water phenomena is the *pororoca*, or tidal bore. The word in Tupi means "a great roar," and the phenomenon reaches its peak in March and April when the water levels are highest. This phenomenon occurs when the water from the Atlantic Ocean meets with that of the various rivers, forming a wave that averages 3 meters (10 feet) in height. For this reason, the municipality of **São Domingos do Capim**, located 130 kilometers (81 mi.) upstream from Belém on the Rio Capim, has hosted the National Pororoca Surfing Competition since 1999. Along with Belém, the *pororoca* occurs in other regions of the North such as Canal do Perigoso (Dangerous Channel) between the islands of Mexiana and Caviana, in the archipelago of Marajó; Arari river in Maranhão; and Araguari river in Amapá. In the latter the *pororoca* travels a distance of up to 45 kilometers (28 mi.) in an hour and a half.

A ranch hand drives buffaloes in Marajó, where there are two of the beasts for every person

ANCESTRAL CERAMICS

Carlos Amaral is one of the few ceramics-makers who knows and faithfully reproduces the ancient art of the Marajoara Indians, and everyone in the village of Soure can give directions to his studio. The artisan proudly explains the details of the trade using samples from his small collection of original native works. These serve as the models for his creations. Amaral also describes the symbolism of the Marajoara art. The *cumaru uarabo*, for example, is a glass with a figure of a butterfly, which represents happiness; if the butterfly is accompanied by a frog, it is a symbol of health.

THE BUFFALO RANCH

Incredible as it may seem, there are more buffaloes than people – approximately 600,000 head of buffalo versus 250,000 residents – on the Ilha de Marajó. You see the lumbering animals in the streets pulling carts or serving as mounts for the police. At ranches, visitors have the chance to become better acquainted with this animal of Asian origin. The **Fazenda Bom Jesus** (*tel. 91/3741-1243*), located 12 kilometers (7.5 mi.) from Soure, offers an educational program. The owner, Eva Abufaiad, an agronomist and veterinarian, explains how to take care of the animals and urges visitors to ride them. The ride is not one of the most comfortable, but it is obligatory. To go to Marajó and not ride a buffalo is like going to Egypt and not riding a camel.

OUR RECOMMENDATION

The rustic accommodations are simple, but **Pousada dos Guarás** guarantees the guest a comfortable stay in Salvaterra. The rooms have air conditioning, minifridge and television, and from the inviting swimming pool there is access to Grande beach. The restaurant serves typical dishes like Marajoara filet (buffalo meat with melted buffalo cheese) and *frito do vaqueiro* (buffalo meat served with manioc meal).

Additional information begins on page 462.

SCARCE INDIGENOUS CERAMICS, ABUNDANT FACSIMILES

The largest center for ceramic handicrafts in the state of Pará, the town of **Icoaraci**, 18 kilometers (11 mi.) from Belém, has long ago stopped selling faithful reproductions of the pottery of the Tapajó and Marajoara Indians, respectively the ancient peoples of Santarém and Marajó island. The jars, vases and other items are produced in such large quantities that the local artisans do not have the time or the references to reproduce the pieces with the rigor that the technique demands. Although no one will admit this, what is really produced in the village is a distinctive local style, with a mix of designs of their own creation. For those wishing to purchase authentic reproductions, there are still a few good artists who respect the Marajoara style, with its stylized representations of animals, and the Tapajônico style, with its zoomorphic figures. Along with Carlos Amaral from Soure, another respected craftsman goes by the name of **Mestre Cardoso**. At 73, he still works in his ceramic studio at home (*Rua Oito de Maio, passagem São Vicente de Paula, 1, tel.*

91/247-0598) and has taught his son, José Levy, everything he knows, so that the Indigenous art may not disappear.

Fine sands and crystal waters of the beaches on Tapajós river dazzle visitors to Alter do Chão

SANTARÉM AND ALTER DO CHÃO

Alter do Chão, a village of unspoiled freshwater beaches, is accessible via Santarém, 35 kilometers (22 mi.) away. One of Santarém's few other attractions is the chance to purchase clothing and accessories made from the fibers of murity palm trees, banana trees, jute, Brazilian spiny club palm trees and hibiscus trees. This can be done at the studio of **Dica Frazão** (*Rua Floriano Peixoto, 281, tel. 93/522-1026*), who has made handkerchiefs for Pope John Paul II. The best way to get to the city, which mainly conducts soybean agriculture, is by boat or airplane.

RIVER BEACHES IN ALTER DO CHÃO
The crystal-clear water of Tapajós river has given beaches in the region the nickname of the "Amazon Caribbean." Boat travel is the best way to reach the more deserted beaches in Alter do Chão such as **Moça** and **Jacaré**. Other beautiful beaches, superior to many ocean beaches, are **Cururu**, **Ponta de Pedras** and **Ilha do Amor**, the most famous in Alter. The contrast between the white sand and the blue water is breathtaking.

BOAT EXCURSIONS
The lush nature here offers so many boat excursion options that it's difficult to settle on just one. A visit to the community of **Maguary** is most imperative. Two hundred people live in this immaculate village surrounded by fruit trees on the banks of Tapajós river. Eleven of the residents produce ecologically sensitive leather from rubber and demonstrate the entire process to visitors. Another excellent destination is **Lago Verde**, a rock pool full of fish whose water changes from green to blue throughout the day. To end the journey, entertain yourself fishing for piranhas in the **Furo do Jari**, which is a branch of the Amazon river.
Tour Operator: Santarém Tour, tel. (93) 522-4847.

OUR RECOMMENDATION

Located on the banks of Lago Verde in the municipality of Alter do Chão, the **Beloalter Hotel** is surrounded by well-kept grounds. There are 24 rooms with air conditioning, TV and solar-heated water. Two extra rooms are called "ecological suites" and have an exterior finish of thatching and an interior finish with a type of woven foliage. One even has a tree growing inside. The hotel offers boat excursions to remote beaches on the Tapajós river and organizes nature walks in the forest close to Lago Verde.

Additional information begins on page 462.

DESTINATION
JALAPÃO

The region of Jalapão covers approximately 34,000 sq. km (13,000 sq. mi.), a little smaller than the state of Rio de Janeiro. It has an abundance of waterfalls, rivers, dunes and lakes, and earns the state of Tocantins a spot on the ecotourism map. The best time to visit the region is during the dry season between May and September. Visiting the area requires a spirit of adventure, and will appeal to those willing to dispense with modern comforts in search of unusual places.

The state capital, Palmas, is the departure point for Ponta Alta. That city is the gateway to Jalapão, named after the locally abundant *jalapa* herb, which is used as a laxative. The 200 kilometers (124 mi.) trip on paved roads is uneventful, but from Ponte Alta on, the trip is pure adventure. There is no infrastructure and in the rainy season (October to April), conditions go downhill. There's a good chance visitors won't be able to traverse the eight municipalities that form Jalapão due to the amount of water that covers even the bridges.

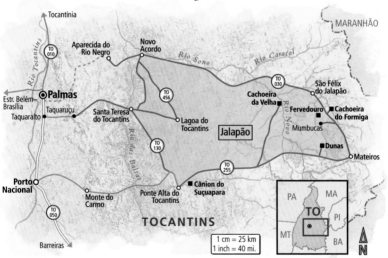

PALMAS

Established in 1990, Palmas is the newest capital city in the country. (Tocantins was only declared an independent state in 1988.) Before heading to Jalapão, travelers will have to stay overnight in Palmas. One option for accommodations is the **Pousada dos Girassóis**. The restaurant **Cabana do Lago** serves a delicious *galinha de cabidela* (chicken stewed in its blood, with tomatoes and onions). The best excursion in the area is to **Taquaruçu**, a region 32 kilometers (20 mi.) from the city center with more than 50 waterfalls. Visit **Cachoeira do Roncador**, a 50-meter-high (164-foot) waterfall.

For hotels and restaurants, see information beginning on page 462.

DESTINATION HIGHLIGHTS

PALMAS
Jalapão Classic (200 km/124 mi.)
Independent Adventure

Distance from Palmas

Natural erosion from the Espírito Santo mountain range (in the background) formed the Jalapão dunes

JALAPÃO CLASSIC

A travel agency provides the most practical way to become acquainted with Jalapão and its beautiful dunes and waterfalls. The more adventurous can choose travel packages with rafting on the **Novo** river between May and September.

SAND DUNES
Just cross a small stream to arrive at the sand dunes, which rise up to up to 40 meters (130 feet). The top of the rust-colored dunes offers a dazzling view of the Espírito Santo mountain range.

RAFTING ON THE RIO NOVO
A trip down the river takes three days. Going down the rapids, rafters can see macaws, capybaras and toucans. At night, camp on the riverbank beaches. The trip ends at the beautiful waterfall called **Cachoeira da Velha.**
Tour Operator: Venturas & Aventuras, tel. (11) 3872-0362.

CACHOEIRA DA VELHA
This horseshoe-shaped waterfall is the highest in Jalapão, 25 meters (82 feet) high and almost 100 meters (328 feet) wide. The water plunges into a deep pool that only good swimmers should risk entering. From there, a 1.2-kilometer (three-quarter mile) trail leads to the **Prainha**, a pleasant beach for bathing.

FERVEDOURO
An underground spring feeds this crystal-clear pool. Because the water is unable to flow downward, it gushes upwards under pressure, and the rising current keeps swimmers afloat.

CACHOEIRA DO FORMIGA
Although all the trees along the banks of the Formiga river have been cut down, this beautiful waterfall is worth a visit, as well as a dive in its clear greenish pool.

CÂNION DO SUÇUAPARA
A 15-meter-high (49-foot) crevice similar to a canyon is inside the Suçuapara grotto. Hikers can see the sky through the crevice, and an irresistible natural shower flows out of the wall.
Tour Operators: Freeway Adventures, tel. (11) 5088-0999; Propósito Turismo, tel. (21) 2549-6714; Venturas & Aventuras, tel. (11) 3872-0362.

INDEPENDENT ADVENTURE

Those with an independent streak can visit Jalapão on their own. But be warned that the region is inhospitable, with poor sand-covered roads. If visitors go by car, there are two essential requirements: a four-wheel-drive vehicle and a local guide. Without them, visitors risk getting lost or stuck in the sand, and depending on the time of year and the day of the week, there is no cell-phone signal and no sign of life in the region.

Along with a guide – which are available through the Associação dos Profissionais de Turismo (*tel. 63/9281-8373 and 218-2003*) – take lots of water and fuel and an extra tire. If you are no Indiana Jones but aren't interested in a standard tour, you can rent a vehicle with a driver and a guide (*Jalapão Tour, with the guider Cavalcante, tel. 63/9978-3695*). One good place to stay is **Fazenda Santa Rosa**, located 15 kilometers (9 mi.) from the center of Mateiros, with charming bungalows at the foot of the Espírito Santo mountain range, but don't go without making a reservation First. The **Panela de Ferro** restaurant in Mateiros serves a delicious home-cooked lunch.

Additional information begins on page 462.

GOLDEN GRASS

The village of **Mumbucas**, close to Mateiros, was a place without electricity, lost in time and hard to reach even by four-wheel-drive, until it became famous for its handicrafts made from *capim doura-do* (golden grass). Their products are now sold in stores in São Paulo and Rio de Janeiro.

The person responsible for putting the village on the map is a woman named Miúda, the matriarch of this old community of former slaves. She taught the residents how to weave the golden grass that is carefully harvested in September to preserve its characteristic color. Now this craft is spreading through the whole region, but the most beautiful baskets, purses, belts, bracelets and sandals in Jalapão are from Mumbucas. You can purchase them in the center of the village.

CENTRAL WEST

The Central West – made up of the Federal District and the states of Goiás, Mato Grosso and Mato Grosso do Sul – is the only region in Brazil that does not border the ocean. That distinction gives it unique natural and cultural attractions. Highlights include the spectacular architecture in Brasília and the lush flora and fauna of the Pantanal and the savannah (or "Cerrado"). No other region of the country provides such a profusion of animal life, from alligators and wood ibises to the fish in the crystal-clear waters of Bonito, Brazil's leading ecotourism location. The map below shows the cities we suggest as departure points for the itineraries outlined in the following pages. Cuiabá is the gateway to the Northern Pantanal and Campo Grande the gateway to the Southern Pantanal and Bonito. From Goiânia and Brasília, visitors can travel to historic towns where old traditions are still maintained and explore vast areas of exceptional natural beauty.

DESTINATION
BRASÍLIA

For enthusiasts of modernist architecture, a trip to Brasília is a must. Brazil's capital in the middle of the Central Plateau, was carefully planned and contains about 100 highly distinctive buildings. Unlike the world's other major capitals, where the machinery of government is largely housed in grim-looking, forbidding structures, Brasilia's public buildings are light, transparent and inviting. This feat is the result of three very talented people: the urban planner Lúcio Costa, the architect Oscar Niemeyer and the landscape artist Roberto Burle Marx. The city was the apple of former President Juscelino Kubitschek's eye, and it replaced Rio de Janiero as the country's capital in 1960. But Brasília is much more than just a political center, underlined by the fact that Unesco declared it a world heritage site in 1987. Brasília is the departure point for the Chapada dos Veadeiros and the towns of Goiás and Pirenópolis.

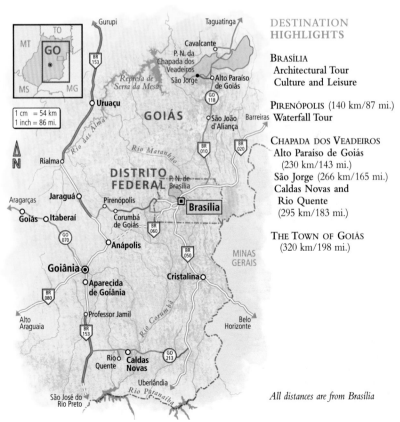

DESTINATION HIGHLIGHTS

BRASÍLIA
Architectural Tour
Culture and Leisure

PIRENÓPOLIS (140 km/87 mi.)
Waterfall Tour

CHAPADA DOS VEADEIROS
Alto Paraíso de Goiás
(230 km/143 mi.)
São Jorge (266 km/165 mi.)
Caldas Novas and
Rio Quente
(295 km/183 mi.)

THE TOWN OF GOIÁS
(320 km/198 mi.)

All distances are from Brasília

BRASÍLIA

If travelers are arriving by air, Brasília will astonish even before the plane touches down. In fact, the aerial view provides the best possible perspective of the city's layout – itself designed in the shape of a plane by Lúcio Costa, whose award-winning project won out over 26 others in a 1950 national contest.

The Eixo Monumental acts as a central axis, splitting this vast, planned city into north and south. The power center is located in the east, the plane's "cockpit," where the principal architectural buildings stand.

Flanked by the beautiful man-made lake, Paranoá, the city is divided into sections for hotels, residential buildings and manufacturing industries. A car is mandatory; hardly anyone walks in this city, where everything seems far away. Despite repeated criticisms of the design plan – for example, the lack of adequate signage – Brasília has an enviable traffic system and the wiring for street lamps is all underground. Most of the public buildings feature ornamental ponds to increase humidity, an absolute priority in an extremely dry location where summer temperatures exceed 30°C (86°F). The interiors are decorated with sculptures, murals and paintings by renowned 20th century national artists like Alfredo Volpi, Athos Bulcão, Bruno Giorgi, Carybé, Di Cavalcanti and Portinari. When the population of Brasília exceeded the 2 million mark, the federal capital became a true metropolis. Even so, it still has extensive green areas – even the route from the airport is lined with fruit-laden mango and jackfruit trees.

Universidade de Brasília

SUPERQUADRA NORTE

ASA NORTE

Lago do Paranoá

···· Helicopter Route

◁N

Palácio da Alvorada

Palácio da Justiça

Teatro Nacional

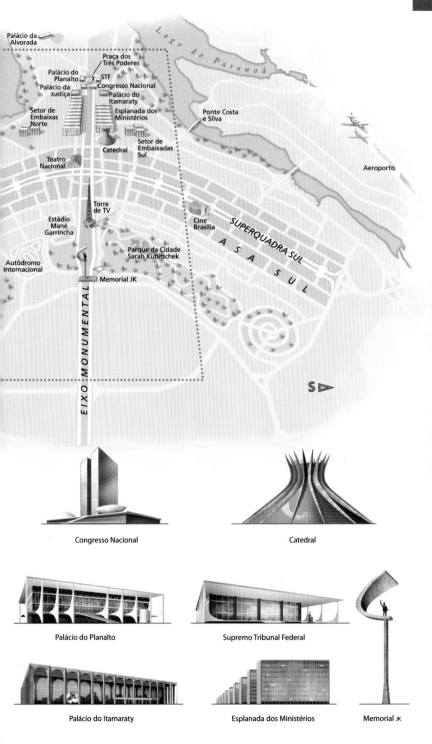

Palácio da
Alvorada

Praça dos
Três Poderes

Palácio do
Planalto

STF

Palácio da
Justiça

Congresso Nacional

Palácio do
Itamaraty

Setor de
Embaixas
Norte

Esplanada dos
Ministérios

Ponte Costa
e Silva

Catedral

Setor de
Embaixadas
Sul

Aeroporto

Teatro
Nacional

Torre
de TV

Cine
Brasília

SUPERQUADRA SUL

Estádio
Mané
Garrincha

A S A   S U L

Autódromo
Internacional

Parque da Cidade
Sarah Kubitschek

Memorial JK

EIXO MONUMENTAL

Lago do Paranoá

S ▷

Congresso Nacional

Catedral

Palácio do Planalto

Supremo Tribunal Federal

Palácio do Itamaraty

Esplanada dos Ministérios

Memorial JK

The *Meteoro*: the marble sculpture by Bruno Giorgi dominates the Palácio do Itamaraty water garden

ARCHITECTURAL TOUR

Start the city tour at the most interesting attraction: the **Praça dos Três Poderes**, the site of the **Palácio do Planalto**, the **Congresso Nacional** and the **Supremo Tribunal Federal**. The square also contains several sculptures, such as the famous 1959 bronze by Bruno Giorgi, *Os Guerreiros*, also known as *Candangos*. From there, visitors can also see the two parallel lines of the ministry buildings on the **Esplanada dos Ministérios**. Don't miss the square's underground area, where travelers can see the **Espaço Lúcio Costa**, which contains an enormous scale-model of the city's pilot plan as well as a number of texts and sketches by the urban planner.
Praça dos Três Poderes. Tue-Sun, 9am-6pm.

PALÁCIO DO PLANALTO
The presidential office building is open to the public on Sunday mornings. The highlight of the 30-minute tour is the visit to the

president's chambers, located behind a glass panel.
Praça dos Três Poderes, tel. (61) 411-2317. Sun, 9:30am-1pm.

SUPREMO TRIBUNAL FEDERAL (STF)
Brazil's highest courts, the **Supreme Court** and the **Court of Appeal**, are both located in Brasília. The **Supreme Court** is the headquarters of Judicial power, and it is open to the public for 30-minute guided tours of the court sessions and the museum. (If you plan to visit on weekends, it would be wise to book in advance.) Alfredo Ceschiatti's famous 1961 granite sculpture *A Justiça* stands in front of the building.
Praça dos Três Poderes, tel. (61) 217-4038. Visits only during the weekends, 10am-6pm.

PALÁCIO DO ITAMARATY
The Ministry of Foreign Affairs, better known as Itamaraty, the name given to its previous building in Rio de Janeiro, is one of Niemeyer's most

radiant buildings and a mandatory stop. The bridge over an enormous ornamental pool dotted with islands of tropical plants leads to one of the largest public art collections in Brazil. The massive 220-square-meter (2,368 sq. ft) main hall on the ground floor is free of columns and features a 2.3-meter-wide (7.5-foot) spiral staircase without a banister. Athos Bulcão created the embossed marble walls. Burle Marx designed the gardens, featuring plants from the Amazon region, and Bruno Giorgi carved the sculpture *Meteoro* from a single four-ton block of Carrara marble for the water garden in 1967. There are also numerous works by other great artists on display, including sculptures by Maria Martins, Victor Brecheret and Alfredo Ceschiatti, and paintings by Portinari, Manabu Mabe and Alfredo Volpi. Foreign artists such as Frans Post, Rugendas and Debret also depict scenes of Brazil's past. On the upper floor, visitors can see the desk Princess

Isabel used to sign the Lei Áurea (the law abolishing slavery) in 1888 and a triple-seat bench from Bahia with each of the places curiously baptized as *fofoqueira* (gossiper), *conversadeira* (chitchatter) and *namoradeira* (flirter). The guided tour lasts 40 minutes.

Esplanada dos Ministérios, Bloco H, tel. (61) 411-6148, Mon-Fri, 2pm-4:30pm; Sat, Sun and holidays, 10am-3:30pm.

PALÁCIO DA ALVORADA

Although the public is forbidden to enter the official presidential residence,

---

THE CANDANGOS

Brasília's building projects attracted thousands of construction workers, mainly from the Northeast of Brazil, who settled in the satellite cities around the outskirts and became known as *candangos*, a derogatory name African slaves gave the Portuguese. Today, however, the word has lost its derogatory connotation and is applied to city residents or natives.

Itamaraty: spiral staircase with symmetrical steps leading to the upper floors and internal gardens

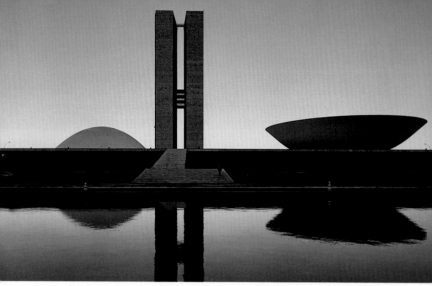

Congresso Nacional: The House of Representatives, Senate (in the background) and their office towers

also designed by Niemeyer, it is worth a visit just for the remarkable marble-and-glass façade supported by white columns.

Via Presidencial.

CONGRESSO NACIONAL

Brasília's greatest landmark houses the two federal legislative bodies: the **Senate**, with 81 senators, three from each of the 27 states, and the **House of Representatives**, with 513 deputies elected in line with the population of each state. The administrative machinery is in two 28-story buildings that form a vivid contrast to the vast flat landscape, flanked by two domes (one normal and the other inverted), where the elected members actually sit. When a session is in progress, a flag flies in front of the building. There are separate guided tours of the plenary buildings and the two Houses' museums. Both start from the **Salão Negro** (Black Room). Works by Athos Bulcão, Di Cavalcanti and Carybé, among others, are displayed in the rooms. The Senate tour is the best organized.

Câmara: tel. (61) 216-1771; Mon-Fri, 9:30am-11:30am and 2:30pm-4:30pm; Sat and Sun, 9am-4:30pm.
Senado: tel. (61) 311-2149; Mon-Fri, 9:30am-11:30am and 2:30pm-4:30pm; Sat and Sun, 9:30am-4:30pm.
Praça dos Três Poderes.

PALÁCIO DA JUSTIÇA

The **Ministry of Justice** building has the same architectural style as its neighbor across the street, the Palácio do Itamaraty, but it is distinguished by the falls over the water garden designed by Burle Marx. The Black Room hosts periodic exhibitions and the chair and desk of José Bonifácio de Andrada e Silva, the "Father of Independence," are on display in the library. The auditorium has an interesting peculiarity: this is where all films to be shown in movie theaters across the country are classified. The guided tour lasts for approximately 25 minutes and must be scheduled in advance.

Esplanada dos Ministérios, Bloco T, tel. (61) 429-3216. Mon-Fri, 8am-11am and 2pm-5pm.

THE JK MEMORIAL

A tribute to the founder of the city, Juscelino Kubitschek, the memorial is a pyramid-shaped building in white marble located in front of a 28-meter (92-foot) statue of the former president. Inaugurated in 1981, the building contains personal items belonging to Kubitschek and his wife, a private library with 3,000 books and a display close to the entrance showing the papers and documents that he had with him on the day he died in a 1976 car accident. Some of his clothes and his burial chamber are on the upper floor.

Eixo Monumental, Lado Oeste, Praça do Cruzeiro, tel. (61) 225-9451. Tue-Sun, 9am-6pm.

CATEDRAL METROPOLITANA

A city icon, the Metropolitan Cathedral's shape is different from any church travelers have ever seen. It also clashes somewhat with Niemeyer's more sober buildings, mainly due to the colorful stained-glass windows designed by Mariane Peretti. It was inaugurated in 1970 and includes paintings by Di Cavalcanti and Athos Bulcão. Alfredo Ceschiatti sculpted the three hanging angels from duralumin and the four bronze apostles in front of the building. Masses are held in the basement.

Esplanada dos Ministérios, tel. (61) 224-4073. Mon, 8am-5pm. Tue-Sun, 8am-6pm.

IGREJINHA NOSSA SENHORA DE FÁTIMA

This pretty little church dating from 1958, the first in the city, is proof that even in architecture, size is not everything. Kubitschek built it as a tribute to Nossa Senhora de Fátima, to repay a vow he and his wife made to the saint in return for curing their sick daughter, Márcia. The exterior of the building is shaped like a nun's coif. The church is finished in ceramic tiles designed by Athos Bulcão with stylized depictions of the Holy Ghost and the Star of the Nativity.

EQS 307/308, tel. (61) 242-0149. Mon, 9am-8pm; Tue-Sun, 6:30am-8pm.

The tiny Igrejinha Nossa Senhora de Fátima displays delicacy and originality of design

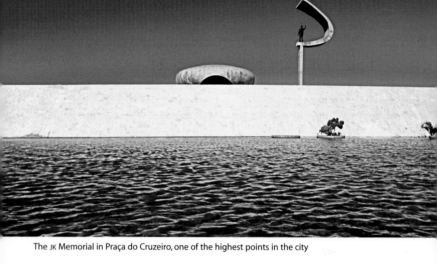
The JK Memorial in Praça do Cruzeiro, one of the highest points in the city

CULTURE AND LEISURE

Brasília has no notable museums, and the arts scene is focused on the cultural centers. For arts and crafts, check out the traditional **Feira da Torre** on Sundays under the **Torre de Televisão** (*Eixo Monumental Leste; tel. 61/321-7944*), and take advantage of the opportunity to visit the 75-meter-high (246-foot) observation deck with its panoramic view of the city (*Tue-Sun, 9am-6pm; Mon, 2pm-6pm*).

PARQUE DA CIDADE
The Parque Sarah Kubitschek, better known as the City Park, is the largest leisure area in Brasília. It spreads over 420 hectares (1,038 acres) of Burle Marx's lawns and landscaping. It is equipped with a go-cart track, restaurants, a horseback riding center, an amusement park, a bike lane and a walking and running track.
Eixo Monumental, tel. (61) 325-1092.

HELICOPTER TRIP
For an impressive view of the city, take the panoramic helicopter trip. The 12-minute flight takes travelers over the Paranoá lake, the Palácio da Alvorada, the Parque da Cidade, the JK Memorial, the Nelson Piquet race track and the Estádio Mané Garrincha.
Tour Operator: Esat Aerotaxi, tel. (61) 364-9933.

CENTRO CULTURAL BANCO DO BRASIL
Housed in a building designed by Oscar Niemeyer in 1993 and declared a historical heritage site, this cultural center was inaugurated in 2000 and hosts shows, plays, films and exhibitions. There is also a cafeteria and a bookstore that is part of Rio de Janeiro's **Livraria da Travessa** chain.
SCES, Trecho 2, Conj. 22, tel. (61) 310-7087. Tue-Sun, 10am-9pm.

CENTRO CULTURAL DA CAIXA
This cultural complex contains an art gallery and a theater with an eclectic agenda. Located beside the bank's headquarters in a cylindrical building, it is a distinctive landmark in the city's silhouette. Lourenço Heilmer designed te stained-glass windows in the atrium, one for each state.
SBS, Quadra 4, Lote 3/4, tel. (61) 414-9452. Tue-Sun, 9am-9pm.

PIRENÓPOLIS

This small town 140 kilometers (87 mi.) from Brasília and 125 kilometers (78 mi.) from Goiânia has a population of only 21,000. It was declared a historical heritage site in 1989. A traditional weekend destination for people from the capital, its bars and narrow lanes, thronged on Saturdays and Sundays, are so quiet during the week that most restaurants don't bother to open. The quaint streets in the original town center are paved with quartz cobblestones; the most charming is Rua Direita, where the town's first mansions were built in the 18th century. The pioneer explorers founded the town in 1727, when they discovered gold in the Almas river at the foot of mount Pireneus. The **Igreja Matriz Nossa Senhora do Rosário**, the state's first church, was built in 1732 and destroyed by fire in 2002. It is currently being restored, but the **Igreja do Bonfim**, dating from 1750, remains intact with its original gold-leafed altar and imposing figure of Senhor do Bonfim carved out of cedar. According to local legend, 250 slaves were required to bring it by foot from Bahia (*Rua do Bonfim, Alto do Bonfim*). During a tour of the town, stop by the **Cine Pireneus** and admire the art-deco façade designed in 1936 (*Rua Direita, Centro*).

GOIÂNIA

Also worth a visit is Goiânia, 210 kilometers (130 mi.) from Brasília. It is the capital of the state of Goiás, which has an economy based on cattle-raising. The hotel **Castro's Park** was built in the 1980's and is the most sophisticated in the city. For meals, try the **Aroeira**, which serves typical dishes such as *arroz com frango e pequi* (chicken with *pequi*, a local fruit, and rice), accompanied by manioc, kale, sausage and *feijão-tropeiro* (seasoned beans thickened with manioc meal).

The façade of Igreja Matriz Nossa Senhora do Rosário faces the sun all day

Rivers and waterfalls in the savannah's Pirenópolis region

Waterfall Tour

The natural beauty on the outskirts of Pirenópolis is dazzling. The rich savannah vegetation is preserved in places such as the **Reserva Ecológica de Vargem Grande**, the **Santuário de Vida Silvestre Vagafogo** and the **Parque Estadual da Serra dos Pireneus**, with a 1,385-meter-high (4,544-foot) mountain. Waterfalls are the principal attraction at all three, and 70 of them have been counted to date. Hikers should hire guides at the Associação dos Condutores de Visitantes de Pirenópolis (*tel. 62/331-2729 and 331-3440*) to make sure they don't get lost on the trails. The association also rents four-wheel-drive vehicles to tour the region.

Várzea do Lobo
The **Dragões** are a series of waterfalls located on land owned by Zen Buddhist monks in the Várzea do Lobo region. They vary in height from 3 to 60 meters (10 to 197 feet.); seven are suitable for swimming and one offers a picturesque view of the valley.

The entire trail can be completed in three hours, but the trip itself takes a whole day because of the 42 kilometers (26 mi.) of poorly preserved dirt roads leading to the falls. A maximum of 30 people are allowed in the area at any one time.

Vargem Grande and Pireneus
The **Reserva Ecológica de Vargem Grande** boasts Pirenópolis' most popular waterfalls. A bar, restrooms and a parking lot lie at the end of the well-marked trails. The trails are short: the **Santa Maria** waterfall, with its tiny beach, is just 500 meters (1/4 mi.) away, and the **Lázaro** only 1,800 meters (1 mi.). The same dirt road takes you to the **Parque Estadual da Serra dos Pireneus**, which has a chapel and offers an extensive view of the region at the end of a 600-meter (3/8 mi.) hike up a steep embankment. Five irresistible rock pools in the **Pocinhos do Sonrisal** are also close by.

CELEBRATION OF THE HOLY GHOST

Fifty days after Easter, Pirenópolis celebrates a glorious tradition. The Divino Espírito Santo festivity, one of the oldest and most popular religious events in the country, originated in the Middle Ages and was brought to Brazil by the Portuguese. It evolved over time in line with the particular characteristics of each town where it took root. In the case of Pirenópolis, the first such event was held in 1826 and is distinguished by its folkloric and dramatic focus. The celebrations combine the sacred and the profane in processions, fireworks, masked parades, medieval dances and dramatic presentations – the most important of which are the *Cavalhadas*.

Preparations begin around 20 days in advance as light-hearted celebrants tour the farms and ranches, begging for donations. Always with the Divino flag in hand, the groups hold daily masses and a novena. These last until Whitsunday, when the reigning emperor makes his celebratory procession and the emperor for the following year is selected, a great honor for the person chosen. If the new leader is wealthy he will bank the cost of the festivities himself; if not, he relies on the help of the people.

On the same day, the *Cavalhadas* begin at the town's football stadium. They consist of three days of simulated cavalry battles between the Christian warriors (led by Charlemagne, who was crowned Holy Roman Emperor by Pope Leo III in 800), and the Moors, determined to impose Islam on the Iberian Peninsula. On the first day, the Christians, dressed in blue, enter the stadium from the west while the Moors, dressed in red, enter from the east. Christians pretend to kill a Moorish spy who has infiltrated their side, and the battle begins. On the second day, the Christians stage the overthrow of the Moors, who are then baptized by a priest. On the final day, both sides enter together from the western side and take part in friendly competitions, consummating the Muslims' conversion.

CHAPADA DOS VEADEIROS

Murity palm trees punctuate the Cerrado on the upper elevations of the Planalto Central

Brazil has three main plateaus: Diamantina, Guimarães and Veadeiros. The Planalto Central's Veadeiros stands the tallest at 1,200 meters (3,937 feet), and it contains the headwaters of the region's various rivers. The immense **Parque Nacional da Chapada dos Veadeiros**, named after the traditional deer hunting practiced in the area, covers 235,000 hectares (580,695 acres) and acts as a reserve for the flora and fauna of the Cerrado. The town of **Alto Paraíso de Goiás**, 230 kilometers (143 mi.) from Brasília and with a population of 6,000, is the home base for hikes through the park's lush scenery and surroundings. Hiking is also a popular activity in the town of **Cavalcante**, 90 kilometers (56 mi.) away. Guides and four-wheel-drive vehicles are recommended for most of the attractions, because the dirt roads are not well marked. The best time to travel is during the dry season between May and September, when the rivers are clearer.

Both the Chapada dos Veadeiros and the ruins of Machu Picchu in Peru are located on latitude 14°. Because of this, and because the Chapada was famous for its quartz crystals, it became a mystical center at the end of the 20th century. But the world did not end in 2000 as predicted by the region's alternative communities, and the esoteric pilgrimages lost their impact – leaving nature as the main attraction.

OUR RECOMMENDATION

The **Casa Rosa Pousada das Cerejeiras** stands out among the few lodging options in Alto Paraíso. The former private home has been renovated and converted into four large rooms with bathrooms and eight comfortable chalets for up to five people each. Excellent service reinforces the inn's beauty.

Additional information begins on page 462.

ALTO PARAÍSO DE GOIÁS

Travelers along the GO-118 from Brasília will realize they have reached Alto Paraíso de Goiás when they spot buildings in the shape of pyramids or colored domes. This is the esoteric capital of the Planalto Central, where crystals, incense and new-age music are part of the inhabitants' daily routines. Locals now focus on nature preservation and ecotourism is their main source of income, but in the past they practiced prospecting, wheat farming and cattle ranching. Alto Paraíso has the best (albeit limited) tourist infrastructure in the region, and it serves as a base for visiting the Chapada dos Veadeiros.

The road leading to the village of **São Jorge**, which also leads to the entrance of the **Parque Nacional da Chapada dos Veadeiros** and the various waterfalls in the region, begins here. One of the town's favorite activities is to admire the sunset at the "airport," a landing strip originally built for UFOs but now abandoned. Although visitors are unlikely to see any extra-terrestrials, it is worth a visit to appreciate the beauty of the Chapada dusk.

VALE DO RIO MACACO

The waterfalls and canyons up to 100 meters (328 feet) tall along the Macaco river make a pleasant day trip. The journey involves a 40-kilometer (25-mi.) drive followed by a steep hike. During the dry season from May to October, travelers can practice rappelling and canyoning.

CACHOEIRA DE SÃO VICENTE

This beautiful combination of steep escarpments, five waterfalls stretching to 150 meters (492 feet) and a series of rock pools is located on the Couros river, 50 kilometers (31 mi.) from Alto Paraíso. The walk to the falls is comfortable.

Rocky escarpments and forest in the Alto Paraíso, a region full of canyons and waterfalls

São Jorge

The town of Alto Paraíso de Goiás looks like a metropolis compared to the sleepy village of São Jorge. Located 36 kilometers (22 mi.) from its closest neighbor on the GO-239, the village unites "alternative" travelers. Electricity was only installed 10 years ago, the tourist infrastructure is minimal and there is no bank. Travelers should be sure to bring cash to pay tour guides, almost all of whom are former prospectors who know the region like the backs of their hands. In addition to the national park, which can be visited in two days, travelers should find the astonishing **Lua** valley, a series of rock formations reminiscent of the moon's surface and bisected by the São Miguel river. The rock pools are ideal for swimming. Another spectacular excursion is the **Janela** and **Abismo** trail, which boasts a stunning view of the **Preto 1** and **2** river falls. Visit in the summer, during the rainy season, because the **Abismo** waterfall disappears in the winter. And be prepared – the steep 5.5 kilometers (3.5 mi.) hike leaves even the guides out of breath. None of the attractions have amenities for visitors such as restrooms or snack bars, so pack everything from water to insect repellent in a knapsack.

Parque Nacional da Chapada dos Veadeiros

The Parque Nacional da Chapada dos Veadeiros was established in 1961 (*tel. 62/459-3388, Tue-Sun, 8am-5pm*). Spring brings especially colorful vegetation, with orchids and bromeliads, and meadows covered with plants and murity palms. Typical savannah animals such as maned wolves, deer and rheas live here, but they are not easily spotted. With altitudes of between 1,400 and 1,700 meters (4,593-5,577 feet), the park offers two pleasant excursions. On the first day, take the 6 kilometers (4 mi.) trail to the 10-meter-high (33-foot) **Cariocas** waterfall and two

The Lua valley, 11 kilometers (7 mi.) from São Jorge: geological formations from 200 million years ago

Cariocas waterfall, where the Preto river tumbles from a height of 30 meters (98 feet)

Preto river canyons, uninspiringly named **Cânion 1** and **Cânion 2**. On the second, take the steeper trail (also 6 kilometers) leading to the two Preto river waterfalls: **Salto 1**, 80 meters (262 feet) high with a series of rock pools, and **Salto 2**, 120 meters (394 feet) high with a fantastic view of the valley. Visitors to the park must be accompanied by a guide at all times.

OUR RECOMMENDATION

🍽 Halfway between Sào Jorge and Alto Paraíso, the stark **Rancho do Waldomiro** restaurant is the only place in the surrounding area to try *matula*, also known as the *"feijoada of the Cerrado."* A traditional cattleman's dish hearty enough to survive extended cattle-drives of the old days, it contains beef jerky, sausage, pork offal, white beans and manioc meal (*Estrada Alto Paraíso–São Jorge, km 19*).

CALDAS NOVAS AND RIO QUENTE HOT SPRINGS

Goiás' most important tourist destination is the town of **Caldas Novas**, 159 kilometers (99 mi.) south of Goiânia and 295 kilometers (183 mi.) from Brasília. The town is famous throughout the country for entertaining and refreshing at least one million visitors per year in the various pools fed by hot underground springs with temperatures of up to 57°C (135°F). Just 31 kilometers (19 mi.) away is **Rio Quente**, which also has hot springs.

There is no lack of infrastructure, with a modern airport, water parks, hotels that function as clubs and enough entertainment to please the whole family, including children and grandparents attracted by the local waters' therapeutic properties. If visitors want peace and quiet, however, avoid the end of the year, when the town is invaded by hordes of students for graduation parties.

Rio Quente Resorts, a five-star hotel complex, employs almost all of the town's 2,000 inhabitants, but if visitors prefer a conventional hotel, a good option is the **Parque das Primaveras** in Caldas Novas. Guests can use the thermal facilities at **Hot Park** (*tel. 64/452-8000*). And if travelers can tear themselves away from the hot pools, they should check out the freezing waterfalls in the **Parque Estadual da Serra de Caldas Novas** (*tel. 64/453-5805*).

The charming city of Goiás Velho, flanked by the Serra Dourada mountains

CITY OF GOIÁS

Goiás Velho ("Old Goiás"), as everyone calls the town of Goiás, enchants visitors. The charm of its alleys and side streets with 18th century colonial buildings even won over the Unesco inspectors who declared it a world heritage site in 2001. Located 141 kilometers (87 mi.) west of Goiânia and 320 kilometers (199 mi.) from Brasília via the well-maintained GO-020, this town was founded in 1727 by the *bandeirante* Bartolomeu Bueno da Silva Filho, better known as Anhangüera. Once the home of the Goiás Indians, the town of 27,000 took root during the gold rush in an extremely disorganized fashion – so disorganized that the uneven, poorly planned stone-paved roads wreak havoc with traffic in the historical center to this day.

The best place for a bird's-eye view of this tangle of streets is the Alto de Santana lookout point in front of the **Igreja de Santa Bárbara**, a church at the top of 100 stairs on the street of the same name. The state capital until 1937, Goiás regains its former status every year between July 24 and 26, when the state government commemorates the town's anniversary on July 25. Two major annual events usually attract crowds of visitors: the **Procissão do Fogaréu** during Holy Week and the **International Environmental Film Festival** in June. On Mondays, most of the museums and restaurants are closed.

OUR RECOMMENDATION

🍴 The **Paróchia** is housed in a building belonging to the adjacent Matriz de Santana church. Inaugurated in 2002, the restaurant is famed for its marvelous sauces. Try the *filé ao conde D'Arcos*, filet mignon served with a mustard and caper sauce. On Saturdays, it serves *feijoada* (*Praça Dr. Tasso de Camargo, 18, Centro, tel. 62/371-3291/9982-3141*).

CASA DE CORA CORALINA

The small house of poet and Goiás native Cora Coralina is the city's main tourist attraction. Situated on the banks of the Vermelho river, the house was built in the 1770s and purchased in the 19th century by the poet's family. Cora, her mother and her grandfather were all raised there, and visitors can still see the spring used for drinking water in the backyard.

Coralina lived in the house until she was 22, when she moved to São Paulo, but returned when she was 66 and stayed there for the rest of her life. Although she left school at the age of 9, Cora was an avid reader; her first book was published when she was 75, and two more followed before her death in 1985 at the age of 95. Another six were published posthumously.

The bedroom, kitchen and living room where she wrote about life's simple pleasures have been kept exactly as she left them. In December 2001, the house flooded when the river rose during a storm, and it reopened in August 2002. The entire document collection was saved and is now being digitally copied.
Rua D. Cândido, 20, Centro, tel. (62) 371-1990. Tue-Sat, 9am-4:30pm; Sun, 9am-3:30pm.

IGREJA DE SÃO FRANCISCO DE PAULA

Goiás' third church, the Igreja de São Francisco de Paula, is also located on the bank of the Vermelho river. There is a beautiful staircase leading to the atrium; the ceilings of the chapel and the main church, built in 1761 and painted by André Antônio da Conceição in 1869, display scenes from the life of St. Francis.
Praça Zacheu Alves de Castro, Centro. Tue-Sun, 8am-noon.

THE FOGARÉU PROCESSION

It's not the KKK! Roughly 10,000 people fill the streets of Goiás Velho at Easter to watch a unique event: the Procissão do Fogaréu, religious event that has been celebrated for more than 200 years. At midnight on Wednesday during every Holy Week, all the lights in the city are turned off. Forty hooded men representing the Pharisees coming to arrest Jesus light their torches in front of the **Igreja da Boa Morte** (*Rua Luiz do Couto, Centro*) and proceed through the city to the sound of drums. A crowd holding candles joins the group along the way to the **Igreja do Rosário** (*Largo do Rosário, Centro*), where a table is prepared for the symbolic Last Supper. Af-terward, the medieval procession continues to the **Igreja de São Francisco de Paula**, representing the Garden of Gethsemane where the hooded men encounter Jesus, who is represented by an elegant banner that is a replica of the original painted by Veiga Vale, Goiás' Aleijadinho. The banner is lowered to the sound of bugles, the bishop delivers a sermon and Jesus is symbolically arrested and crucified.

Igreja de Nossa Senhora da Boa Morte, the starting point for the Fogaréu Procession

MUSEU DAS BANDEIRAS

This 1766 building housed the municipal government on its upper floor and the jail on its lower floor until 1937, when the capital was moved to Goiânia. In 1950, it was declared a historical heritage site. It is now a museum with 300 pieces from the 18th and 19th centuries relating the history of the occupation of the Central West and the formation of Goiás' society. The most interesting item is the *enxovia*, a dank dungeon where prisoners were kept and accessed directly from the courtroom via a trap door. If an accused man was found guilty, the trap door would open and he would be taken straight to the dungeon. A restoration of the museum was to be done in March 2005.
Praça Brasil Ramos Caiado, Centro, tel. (62) 371-1087. Tue-Fri, 8am-5pm; Sat, noon-5pm; Sun, 9am-1pm.

PALÁCIO CONDE D'ARCOS

Built in 1755, the palace was Goiás state's first seat of government and becomes so again every July 24-26 in celebration of the town's anniversary.

Ninety-eight governors from the colonial, imperial and republican eras have lived here.
Praça Dr. Tasso de Camargo, 1, Centro, tel. (62) 371-1200. Tue-Sat, 8am-5pm; Sun, 8am-noon.

SERRA DOURADA

This biological reserve, located in the magnificent mountain range that flanks the town of Goiás, can only be visited with a guide. Once visitors complete the challenging 47 kilometers (29 mi.) journey, some of it over dirt road, they will find themselves at 1,050 meters (3,445 feet), with many scenic trails leading to creeks, rock formations and lookout points on the edges of majestic escarpments.
Tel. (62) 9609-8903 and 9651-4979.

OUR RECOMMENDATION

"Charming" is the only word for the 200-year-old **Pousada Dona Sinhá**. This tiny inn with only five rooms is often entirely booked by large families. Originally a farmhouse, it is perfect for guests who appreciate a homey atmosphere. All the furniture is from the 18th century.

Additional information begins on page 462.

DESTINATION
NORTHERN PANTANAL AND
THE CHAPADA DOS GUIMARÃES

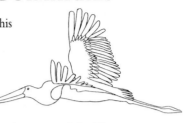

There is no place else like the Pantanal. This vast, ecologically unique area, covering some 230,000 km² (88,803 sq. mi.), hosts a huge diversity of fauna that is easier to observe than that of the Amazon. *Pântano* is Portuguese for swamp, but the Pantanal is actually a floodplain – the largest in the Americas. Its existence depends on natural flooding from October to April. None of this area in the extreme west of Brazil is more than 150 meters (500 feet) above sea level. The Northern Pantanal, in the state of Mato Grosso, encompasses Cuiabá, Cáceres and Barão de Melgaço, and has a national park that offers excellent fishing. Cuiabá, the capital city of Mato Grosso, is the main center and the departure point for the Transpantaneira Highway and Chapada dos Guimarães National Park.

DESTINATION HIGHLIGHTS

NORTHERN PANTANAL
(102 km/63 mi.)

CHAPADA DOS GUIMARÃES
(70 km/43 mi.)

CUIABÁ

Cuiabá, the capital of Mato Grosso and arrival point for visitors to the Northern Pantanal, is located on the banks of the Cuiabá river. It arose during the mineral prospecting that flourished here between 1717 and 1730. Tourist services are limited, but there is an excellent Arab restaurant, **Al Manzul**, and **Eldorado Cuiabá** is a good hotel option. Temperatures exceed 40°C (104°F) in the summer. Note: the city is one hour behind Brasília.
Additional information begins on page 462.

All distances are from Cuiabá

Wood ibises, emblems of the Pantanal, live on a giant floodplain where life follows the rhythm of the rains

NORTHERN PANTANAL

CALL OF THE TROPICAL WILD

Untouched nature is the Pantanal's greatest attraction. Everything else – the history of the arrival of the first pioneers and prospectors in the 18th century, the Indian arts and crafts and the influence of the neighboring Spanish-speaking countries on clothing and speech – is icing on the cake. The animals, in all their glory, live by the rhythms of the annual rise and fall of the rivers and the alternation of rainy and dry seasons. There are 1,700 plant species, 80 mammal species, 50 reptile species, 1,100 species of butterflies and 650 species of birds, many of which are migratory and remain here for only part of the year. Wood ibises, alligators and other animals abound. Photographers will find themselves in paradise, but hunting is strictly prohibited. The northern part of the Pantanal is just one-third of the entire area, so consider making time in your itinerary for the Southern Pantanal as well.

TRANSPANTANEIRA HIGHWAY BY CAR

Poconé, 102 kilometers (63 mi.) south of Cuiabá, is the starting point for the Transpantaneira highway, which runs across the Northern Pantanal parallel to the Cuiabá river to **Porto Jofre**, where the main attraction is fishing. There are more than 100 wooden bridges along the 150 kilometers (93 mi.) of unpaved road, which can be explored as day trips. Some stretches almost require a four-wheel-drive vehicle, but ranches along the way offer places to stop for lunch.

OUR RECOMMENDATION

Located alongside the Transpantaneira highway, the **Pousada Araras Eco Lodge** in Poconé has two observation towers for animal-watching. Since many foreign visitors stay here, they also have bilingual guides. There is good attention to detail, but the lodge doesn't have its own generator and the region is subject to frequent blackouts.

Additional information begins on page 462.

Daybreak and dusk are the best times to see the animals. You will not be the only one with binoculars in hand facing groups of alligators at 6am, but do not linger too long as the sun goes down, as animals on the road at night are a real danger. The Transpantaneira is also the access road for the **Parque Nacional do Pantanal** (*tel. 65/648-9141*), which contains several endangered animal species, including jaguars, giant anteaters and ocelots. It can only be visited by boat with a guide and previous authorization from Brazil's environmental institute, Ibama. There are various ranch-hotels and inns along the way. For the comfort of a traditional hotel, take off your boots at the **Sesc Porto Cercado**, 42 kilometers (26 mi.) from Poconé in the opposite direction from Porto Jofre.
Additional information begins on page 462.

FISHING RIVERS

The Northern Pantanal has considerably better fishing than its southern counterpart. Avid fishermen can stay at the ecotourism ranches in towns like Poconé and Porto Jofre or on the houseboat hotels in **Porto Cercado**. Another alternative is **Cáceres**, 215 kilometers (134 mi.) from Cuiabá, where the International Fishing Festival is held every September. Hotels can arrange licenses, bait and pilot-guides also known as *piloteiros*. The **Paraguay** river that crosses the region from north to south feeds the **Cuiabá**, as well as a network of other rivers, lakes and *corixos*, the natural canals that link the rivers to the marshes. Researchers have already counted at least 260 different fish species in these rivers such as the *pintado* (speckled catfish), *dourado* (golden dorado) and *piranha*. Note: fishing is permitted only between March and October, so as not to interfere with the spawning season.

A *dourado* leaping from the Paraguay river, which crosses the Pantanal from north to south

The Chapada dos Guimarães in the Roncador mountains has priceless natural and archeological treasures

CHAPADA DOS GUIMARÃES

Ranking second among Mato Grosso's great attractions after the Pantanal itself is the Chapada dos Guimarães, an impressive sheer red sandstone stack rising 800 meters (2625 feet) in the foreground of the immense flood-plain. Punctuating the flooded landscape with its distinctive savannah vegetation and escarpments, it extends for 280 kilometers (174 mi.) of the **Serra do Roncador** mountains. The town of Chapada dos Guimarães, 70 kilometers (43 mi.) north of Cuiabá, is home to the **Parque Nacional da Chapada dos Guimarães.** Despite its waterfalls, rock formations, scenic vantage points and archeological sites, tourist facilities are limited. The best time to visit is between April and October, during the dry season, when the water is clear.

THE NATIONAL PARK
Established in 1989, the national park covers 33,000 hectares (81,545 acres),

making it just about one-fifth the size of Bahia's Chapada Diamantina National Park, and is drastically lacking in adequate maintenance. Signposting on the trails is either poor or non-existent and a guide is essential (not least because of their acute awareness of the dangers of snakes). There is a visitors' center, but it doesn't always open at the designated time, and the place is full of noisy crowds on weekends (*tel. 65/301-1133, 8am-5pm*).

WATERFALL TOUR
There are dozens of waterfalls in the park, but one of the best routes, a scenic and refreshing half-day excursion to the **Sete de Setembro** river takes in seven of them – **Sete de Setembro, Sonrisal, Pulo, Degrau, Prainha, Andorinhas** and **Independência.** The 6 kilometers (4 mi.) trail is not marked, so a guide is helpful. Central de Guias hires them

out (*tel. 65/301-1687*). Another picturesque and easy-to-reach waterfall is the **Cachoeirinha**, located in a private area of the park. Perfect for families, it offers a small beach, restrooms with showers and a restaurant.

CIDADE DE PEDRA (CITY OF STONE)

The Chapada's rock formations are extremely peculiar, with odd shapes like alligators and mushrooms, making a trip to the so-called City of Stone an entertaining and enjoyable experience. The formations are located in the middle of a canyon with red sandstone embankments that are around 350 meters (1148 feet) high. The layout of the vegetation resembles the map of Brazil. The trip also includes a visit to the **Casa de Pedra** grotto and the **Pedra Furada**

OUR RECOMMENDATION

🍴 The **Morro dos Ventos** restaurant used to be a small family farm in the Chapada dos Guimarães. In 1997 the owners decided to transform part of the house into a restaurant and ended up creating the most pleasant place to eat in town. It shares a cliff with a scenic lookout point that offers a perfect view of the Chapada and the Amor waterfall. The menu specializes in the typical fish of the region. Begin with the *piranha* soup and try the *peixe do morro*, another typical dish that includes two versions of *pintado*, one fried and one stewed with tomatoes and onions, and *pacu* rib. In addition to serving excellent food, it offers a playground for children (*Estrada do Mirante, km 1, tel. 65/301-1030*).

🏨 The **Solar do Inglês** is a charming inn located at the top of the plateau. The 200-year-old main house at the front of the property contains four of the seven rooms, all of which are uniquely decorated. The proprietors' attention to detail is evident in everything from the starched table napkins and linen tablecloths used for afternoon tea to the convenience basket in each room. The decor was created by the owner Paula and her British husband Richard, an ex-hunter who has lived in the Pantanal for 30 years.

Additional information begins on page 462.

Red canyons rise above the Pantanal floodplain to a height of 800 meters (2,625 feet)

(Perforated Rock) which has been sculpted by the wind and rain over eons. It is thought that the Chapada dos Guimarães arose around 15 million years ago, when the emergence of the Andes forced the land downwards, generating the giant floodplain of the Paraguay river that today is the Pantanal. To reach the Cidade de Pedra, roughly 20 kilometers (12 mi.) from the center of Guimarães, you have to take an unmarked dirt road.

VÉU DA NOIVA (BRIDAL VEIL FALLS)

There are dozens of waterfalls in Brazil called "Bridal Veil," but this one tops them all. The Véu da Noiva da Chapada is the park's main attraction. It cascades 86 meters (282 feet) from the top of the canyon and cannot be approached up close. The walk to the lookout point does not require a guide. But it's worth taking another 40-minute walk to see the waterfall from below, and since that latter trail is extremely rugged, a guide is mandatory.

Bridal Veil Falls, the park's emblem

CLIMBING TO THE HIGH FOREST

The ecosystem around Alta Floresta, 780 kilometers (485 mi.) from Cuiabá, in the extreme north of Mato Grosso near the border with Pará, is different from any of the others in the Pantanal or the savannah. This is where the Amazon region starts. Resisting the depredations of the lumbermen so common in such areas, the virgin forest with centuries-old trees supports a wealth of animal species, including monkeys, tapir and deer, and more than 400 species of birds. There are at least two good accommo-dation options in the area for adventurers who wish to experience nature at its most untamed. The **Cristalino Jungle Lodge**, located on the banks of the Cristalino river and accessible by car and boat from Cuiabá, offers excursions to the beaches beside the crystal-clear rivers, as well as waterfalls with heights up to 40 meters (131 feet). During the trek along the trails your feet sink into layers of leaves, vines and branches up to 50 centimeters (20 in.) thick. If fishing is your passion, **Thaimaçu** inn offers you the chance to catch as many *tucunaré* (peacock bass), *piraíba* and *jaú* (two types of catfish) as you want. It is located on the banks of the São Benedito river that runs for 250 kilometers (155 mi.) within a state nature reserve. The Danish Prince Consort, Enrique de Monpezat, has stayed at this fishing paradise that is only accessible by car or plane. There are regular flights from Cuiabá to Alta Floresta. The dry season between May and October is definitely the best time to explore the beautiful riverside beaches. *Additional information begins on page 462.*

DESTINATION
SOUTHERN PANTANAL AND BONITO

The Southern Pantanal occupies two-thirds of the largest floodplain in the Americas. Campo Grande, the region's main city – and state capital of Mato Grosso do Sul, Aquidauana, Corumbá and Miranda – is the departure point for exploring the region, which includes the town of Bonito, one of the best ecotourism destinations in Brazil. As in its

northern counterpart, the Southern Pantanal's main attractions are wildlife and fishing. Most ranches here offer accommodation-activities packages for visitors and also open their properties during the day to non-guests who want to partake in activities. Visiting ranches offers visitors a chance to become acquainted with the highly distinctive customs of the *pantaneiros*, or local inhabitants. Corumbá, located on the Bolivian border, is the best place for fishing between March and October.

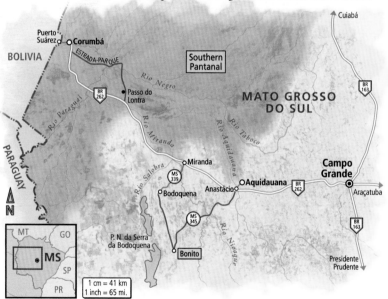

CAMPO GRANDE

Although Campo Grande itself does not offer any notable tourist attractions, it does have a great nightlife. The **Bristol Jandaia** is the city's most comfortable hotel and the **Fogo Caipira**, a first-class restaurant, serves delectable beef jerky with cream cheese in a hollowed out winter squash. If you have time, visit the **Museu Dom Bosco**, with its collection of around 40,000 items depicting Indian life and animals of the region (*Rua Barão do Rio Branco, 1843, tel. 67/312-6491*).
Additional information begins on page 462.

DESTINATION HIGHLIGHTS

SOUTHERN PANTANAL
  Independent Adventure

CORUMBÁ (403 km/250 mi.)

BONITO (280 km/174 mi.)
  Rivers and Rock Pools
  Extreme Sports

*All distances are from
Campo Grande*

Masters of the river: alligators bask in groups and can each reach 2.5 meters (8 feet) in length

SOUTHERN PANTANAL

ECOTOURISM AT THE RANCHES

Most tourism in the Pantanal involves observing wildlife, which you can frequently encounter right outside the front doors of inns, ranches and ranch-hotels. Thousands of animals live in the region's various ecosystems, including flooded areas, cattle pastures and riverbank forests. With easy access by land and well-made ranch-hotels, the city of **Miranda**, 200 kilometers (124 mi.) from Campo Grande via the BR-262, is the recommended base for exploring the Southern Pantanal. Bisected by the river of the same name, the surrounding region is usually filled with animals after the floods in the second half of the year. Visit if possible between May and September, when the water level recedes for the dry season.

IN SEARCH OF ANIMALS

The best time to appreciate the

Pantanal in all its natural glory is during the day. All accommodations offer excursions such as horseback riding, nature trails, boat trips, photo safaris, panoramic flights, bird watching (including the nesting grounds) and visits to observe the less elegant species such as snakes, alligators and capybaras. Bring adequate clothing, including a hat, waterproof boots, long-sleeved shirts and long pants to protect you against the insects. Binoculars are also extremely helpful for animal-watching during the day, while a flashlight is essential at night.

NIGHT LIFE IN NATURE

Nature's activity doesn't stop at the day's end, and neither should yours. After sunset, in itself a spectacular event, you can travel by car or by boat to do night viewing of alligators, deer, giant anteaters and raccoons. Of course, the animals don't make appear-

ances on a set schedule. They appear when – and if – they wish to, and you'd have to be extremely lucky, for example, to spot a jaguar. Both mammals and birds are abundant in the dry season, while in the rainy season mammals tend to remain hidden. Regardless of the time of year, however, the forests are always alive with the sounds of animals.

THE PANTANEIROS

While wildlife is the magnet for the Pantanal, take advantage of the opportunity to get to know some local people. The life of the *pantaneiros* revolves around cattle and they are becoming increasingly visible thanks to the trips around the ranch-hotels. Ranch hands here wear hats made of straw rather than the felt used in the country's colder regions. They use bullhorns to lead cattle to higher elevations during the floods and to bring them back to the plains in the dry season. Like their counterparts in Paraguay, they wear

colored bandannas and hunting knives strapped to their belts. They are also skilled with boats, since water transport is part of their daily routine. A typical *pantaneiro* lunch of fish is offered at virtually all the ranches both for guests and day visitors. Be sure to try *tereré*, a cold yerba maté tea.

OUR RECOMMENDATION

The **Fazenda Rio Negro** in Aquidauana, 135 kilometers (84 mi.) from Campo Grande, is deep in the heart of the Pantanal and can only be reached by air for most of the year, although cars can get there in the dry season. Easier to get to is the renowned **Refúgio Ecológico Caiman**, 36 kilometers (22 mi.) from the Miranda traffic circle. The most sophisticated hotel in the region, it is actually four separate inns. It offers a unique landscape thanks to its location in the transition zone between the Pantanal and savannah ecosystems, the latter being the most common in the rest of Central West Brazil. It also accepts day guests.

Additional information begins on page 462.

Master of the forest: the jaguar, threatened by extinction, is the largest cat in South America

INDEPENDENT ADVENTURE

If you are not on a tour organized by a travel agency, choose your accommodation carefully to get the most interesting experience possible. Ranch-hotels offer three and four-day packages that include a host of activities from horseback riding to fishing. An economical option for the more adventurous is to stay at a simpler hotel and use it as a base to visit ranches under the day-use system. The **Pousada Águas do Pantanal** (*tel. 67/242-1242*), owned by the Miranda government, offers a substantial breakfast and operates a tour agency that specializes in day trips. However, this type of independence is only possible if you are traveling by car in the Central region; if you are staying in places that are only accessible by plane and air-taxi from Campo Grande, you will be completely cut off.

JUST ONE DAY

In Miranda, the well-organized **Fazenda San Francisco** (*tel. 67/242-1088*) offers two-hour photo safaris and three-hour excursions along the rivers and bays in a *chalana*, or small flat-bottomed boat. If you are more interested in the countryside than wildlife observation, try the **Fazenda Santa Inês** (*tel. 67/324-2040*), which offers horseback riding, orchards, trails and a lake for fishing (although you have to return your catch to the water).

THE ESTRADA-PARQUE

For those with a four-wheel-drive vehicle, the most interesting way to see the Southern Pantanal is via the **Estrada-Parque do Pantanal**. Built by Marshal Cândido Rondon in the 19th century, it is a 120-kilometers (74-mi.) dirt road, with many treacherous wooden bridges, from where you can see many different kinds of animal, especially early in the morning. In any event, it is definitely an adventurous alternative if you arrive via the BR-262, which connects Campo Grande and Corumbá and passes through Miranda and Aquidauana. The exit for the Estrada-Parque is at the Buraco das Piranhas heading towards Passo do Lontra, where there is a police station. You have to cross the Paraguay river by ferry boat (6am-6pm) halfway through the trip. On no account drive at night as there are numerous potholes and animals crossing the road, and don't swim in the rivers without checking first whether or not they contain *piranha*. Schools of these fish can devour a person in minutes. A charming spot to spend the night or stay for a few days is the **Fazenda Bela Vista** (*tel. 67/9987-3660*), located alongside the Estrada in Corumbá.

CORUMBÁ

Corumbá, built on the banks of the Paraguay river near the Bolivian border, is one of Brazil's fishing meccas. Located 403 kilometers (250 mi.) from Campo Grande, and also accessible from the Estrada-Parque do Pantanal, it attracts visitors who like nothing better than spending their time on boats. In order to do so, you can stay at typical Pantanal ranches focused on ecotourism, on houseboats or even in special fishermen's hotels on the river banks, which will help to arrange boats, bait, equipment and *piloteiros*, or guide-pilots. The city itself, founded in 1776, played a strategic role in defending the Brazilian border during the Paraguay War (1865-1870), but it is now rather rundown. However, the lower section at least should be more attractive when the Programa Monumenta finishes restoring the historical sites. The fishing season runs from March to October, so as not to interfere with the spawning season (November to February), when the fish swim upstream to breed.

THE FISH OF THE PANTANAL

The most popular game fish are *dourado*, *pacu*, *pintado* and *piraputanga*. By law, sport fishing is limited to rod and reel and you obtain a license from a hotel in advance. The boat's structure must also comply with certain legal requirements. The houseboat hotels are comfortable alternatives for a one-week fishing trip, since they can anchor in the best spots and offer all the comforts of a conventional hotel, including TV, phone and hot showers. The luxurious **Millenium** (*tel. 67/231-3372/3470*) is one of the best.

Colorful macaws among the tree branches

OUR RECOMMENDATION

🍽 The only thing better than fishing for *pintado* and *dourado* is eating them. Pantanal cuisine also includes such exotic dishes as alligator meat and *piranha* soup. In the simple, family-run **Peixaria do Lulu**, the *pintado a urucum* is an unbeatable combination seasoned with *annatto* oil. The fish dishes are accompanied by rice and manioc and fish purée (*Rua Dom Aquino Correia, 700, tel. 67/232-2142*). The **Ceará**, a branch of the Campo Grande restaurant of the same name, serves the same specialties, but in a more refined atmosphere (*Rua Albuquerque, 516, tel. 67/231-1930*).

Blue Lake Grotto has yielded animal fossils as much as 6,000 years old

BONITO

Bonito is 280 kilometers (174 mi.) southwest of Campo Grande via the BR-262 to Aquidauana, and then the MS-345. With a population of 16,000, it could be just another sleepy Mato Grosso do Sul town, but as the Portuguese meaning of its name (beautiful) suggests, its wealth of natural beauty has made it one of Brazil's most sought-after eco-destinations. The local authorities do everything possible to minimize the impact of tourism on the beauty of the surroundings, so there are rules that visitors must obey. At times the precautions taken to protect the rivers, caves, plants and animals of the savannah can be a hindrance to their enjoyment, since you cannot simply dive impulsively into a river. The attractions are located on private lands, the number of guests is limited and you must be accompanied by an authorized guide from one of the local agencies. On holidays it is best to schedule excursions in advance.

Since it is all for a noble cause, just go with the flow and enjoy yourself.

RIVER "FLOATING" ON CRYSTAL
The crystal-clear rivers are like huge aquariums stocked with *dourado*, *piraputanga* and *pacu*. The high concentration of lime acts as a natural filter, making impurities settle to the river bed and leaving the water crystal-clear. As a result, Bonito is a paradise for "floating," a diversion that consists of floating in the rock pools with a mask and snorkel and watching the aquatic wildlife below. Relax as you drifts along and keep your feet from touching the bottom, as that will disturb the sand and cloud the water. To see fish undisturbed, look for less trafficked areas of the river.

GRUTA DO LAGO AZUL (BLUE LAKE GROTTO)
The Bonito region is dotted with hundreds of caves but the most famous is Lago Azul, 20 kilometers (12 mi.) from the town center, which is declared

an environmental heritage site. The gradual action of water running over the limestone has sculpted exquisite stalactites and stalagmites. Access to the interior is prohibited, but a 250-meter (820-foot) trail leads to the entrance, where 300 steps descend the slippery slope to an observation point with a view of the crystal-blue lake inside. If you are fortunate enough to be visiting between mid-December and mid-January, you will witness an astonishing sight – for about 20 minutes each day, between 8am and 9am, the sun shines directly on the turquoise water, the only time of the year when this happens. Several interesting finds have been made in the 70-meter-deep (230-foot) lake, including the skeletons of a saber-toothed tiger and a giant three-toed sloth, animals that are thought to have inhabited the site 6,000 years ago. A previously unknown species of albino shrimp has also been discovered here. The cave is the most popular tourist attraction in Bonito and offers good infrastructure, including rest rooms, a snack bar and a souvenir shop.

São Miguel Caves

Unlike Lago Azul, the caves in São Miguel, 18 kilometers (11 mi.) from Bonito, are open to the public and make for a perfect half-day trip. The main cavern, also made of limestone, is dry and full of stalactites and stalagmites. Mind your limbs and packs, however, as the formations are very fragile. Following the trail to the caves, an adventure in itself, requires crossing a 180-meter (590-foot) suspended bridge in the middle of dense forest.

Our Recommendation

Considered the best accommodation in Bonito, the **Zagaia Eco-Resort**, which opened in 1997, offers one-story chalets surrounded by greenery with various amenities such as a combined indoor heated pool and jacuzzi, and a glass-enclosed fitness room overlooking the stunning landscape. There are also facilities for infants and children such as a nursery and a games room with pinball machines.

Additional information begins on page 462.

The Sucuri river "aquarium": dissolved lime acts as a natural filter, leaving the water crystal-clear

RIVERS AND ROCK POOLS

Various rivers flow through the Bonito region whose waters are perfect for floating, the area's most fascinating activity. There are many options to choose from, including the **Olho D'Água, Prata, Formoso, Baía Bonita, Peixe, Anhumas** and **Miranda**, each with their own distinctive features. The water is so clear you can see entire schools of *piraputanga, pintado, curimba, dourado* and *piau* at a distance of 30 meters (100 feet). Equipment rentals, mask, snorkel and neoprene wetsuit are usually included in the excursion price. The **Aquidabã** and **Mimoso** rivers have beautiful waterfalls for swimming. At **Formoso** and its neighbor **Formosinho**, the most popular activities are boat trips and *bóia-cross* (floating down the river on inner tubes the size of truck tires). Warning: don't drink river water. Despite its transparency, it can contain a high level of magnesium, which is a powerful laxative.

RIO DA PRATA AND BURACO DAS ARARAS

The **Recanto Ecológico da Prata** is an ecological retreat 50 kilometers (31 mi.) from the center of Bonito. The excursion takes one day, and on part of the 2-kilometer (1.25-mi.) trail through the riverside forest you can see animals such as white-lipped peccaries and capuchin monkeys. The floating, which takes two to four hours, begins at the headwaters of Olho D'Água river and covers an 80-meter (262-foot) stretch of water inhabited by thousands of fish. When you reach the rapids, there is a 300-meter (984-foot) land detour before returning to a stretch of calm water that drains into the Prata river. Children must be over 8 to take part and each group is limited to a maximum of eight people. At the end of the day, pay a visit to the **Buraco das Araras**, a crater in the limestone surface that's more than 100 meters (328 feet) deep and contains a community of various birds.

AQUÁRIO DO RIO BAÍA BONITA

The **Reserva Ecológica Baía Bonita** is just 8 kilometers (5 mi.) from the center of Bonito. The ecological retreat contains a beautiful natural aquarium whose only peer is the one in the Prata river. The trail leading to the site is a 1.3-km (3/4 of a mi.) walk, but afterwards you can float for almost a kilometer (5/8 of a mi.) on the Bonita Baía river surrounded by aquatic plants and fish. Since the excursion can last an entire day and is fun for the whole family, take it easy and enjoy the other amenities. You can bounce on the trampoline installed in the middle of the river or try the "flying fox." A trail permits observation of the animals of the Cerrado.

RIO SUCURI

The ranch-hotel that provides floating on the Sucuri river also offers horseback riding and cycling. The excursion is similar to the Prata river one, but is more suitable for children since the floating course is only 1.4 kilometers (7/8 of a mi.). The hike is also shorter, only 500 meters (1/3 mi.).

RIO DO PEIXE WATERFALLS

The Peixe river offers a three-hour hike with floating at the end, and it has the added attraction of nearly a dozen waterfalls. You can also swim in the beautiful **Poço do Arco-Íris** (Rainbow Pond), eat a fantastic lunch, take a nap in the hammocks and try the flying fox. In the morning and late afternoon, the tree at the entrance to the ranch is visited by hordes of multi-colored macaws.

OUR RECOMMENDATION

🍽 The **Cantinho do Peixe** was located in one room of the owners' house when it opened in 2000, but it now occupies the entire building during the high season, when it can accommodate more than 250 guests. The main course is limited to *pintado*, but it gets served twenty different ways, including the typical *pintado a urucum*, accompanied by rice and a manioc-and-fish purée. The appetizer? What else but that other Pantanal tradition, *piranha* soup (*Rua Trinta e Um de Março, 1918, tel. 67/255-3381*).

Dourado swim past a school of *piraputangas* in the transparent waters of the Prata river

Rappelling in the Anhumas abyss, a 72-meter (236-foot) drop

EXTREME SPORTS

Bonito offers exceptional challenges for extreme adventurers. Local travel agencies organize deep diving in the **Gruta do Mimoso** cave, the **Anhumas** abyss and **Misteriosa** lake. At the lake, you can also practice canopy tree climbing, flying fox, *bóia-cross* and mountain biking. They also offer boat trips and all-terrain vehicle tours.

ABISMO ANHUMAS (ANHUMAS ABYSS)
Imagine lowering yourself by rope to the ground from the top of a 26-story building. Or imagine trying to climb the same. That's not a bad way to visualize the Anhumas abyss excursion, the most radical in Bonito. It includes rappelling into a 72-meter (236-foot) cave. At the bottom a beautiful 80-meter-deep (262-foot) pool awaits those who want to swim without equipment or licensed scuba divers who've brought their equipment down. The visibility of up to 40 meters (131 feet) ensures a stunning and relatively safe underwater journey between the enormous limestone stalactites and stalagmites. A boat tour is also available, as well as a walk through the cave galleries. The adventure demands a good level of physical fitness and a qualification test the day before. If you are visiting between mid-December and mid-January you can appreciate the spectacular view when, between 10am and 4pm, the sun shines directly on the water in the abyss.

THE TALLEST WATERFALL
The **Boca da Onça** waterfall is located on the outskirts of **Bodoquena**, 70 kilometers (43 mi.) from Bonito. At 156 meters (512 feet), it is the tallest waterfall in the state of Mato Grosso do Sul. After a 3-kilometer (1.8-mi.) hike past 12 smaller falls you can practice rappelling. On the way back there are two rock pools where you can observe fish.

A GENEROUS CUISINE

The natural wonders of the Pantanal can fool visitors into assuming that the region's beauty is all it has to offer. But if you look closer, you will discover much more. Its geographical peculiarities, combined with its diversity of flora and fauna, have created a unique and rich culture that shines through in personal relations, work habits – and, of course, the cuisine.

The cattle drives, which take livestock to higher pastures for the rainy season, is the origin of *tropeiro* food. It was influenced by the Creole cooking from the South of Brazil. Consider, for example, the yerba maté tea *tereré*, which is a chilled version of southerners' *chimarrão*, and *arroz-de-carreteiro*, which is also a staple in the southern Pampas. More important than the food itself, however, are the traditional cattleman customs that surround it. One example is the burning of garlic, a ritual performed by the lead hand, who travels ahead of the rest to prepare the food and choose a suitable place to set up camp for the night.

Just as typical as the burning of garlic is the tradition that surrounds the wild boar, an animal whose origin is bound up with the beginnings of cattle-breeding in the Pantanal. The boars here are descended from early settlers' domesticated pigs, some of which escaped and became feral. Whenever a ranch hand comes across one, he castrates it, cuts off the points of its ears and returns it to the wild. The next time the marked boar is encountered, it is ready to be slaughtered. It's a simple measure of population control that does not endanger the species but culls selectively for man's needs.

Talk of food in the Pantanal automatically turns to the abundance of fish, which has made the region one of the most popular sport-fishing destinations. But many people forget the cornucopia of fruit that supplies the local population throughout the year.

Pantanal cuisine is simple, almost crude, based on local ingredients and strongly rooted in working traditions. For those who consider some of these aspects – the ranch hand who prepares the food for the cattle drivers, the muleteer who presents a stranger with a capon, nature's offering of fish and fruit – there is only one conclusion: the only word that does justice to this cuisine – indeed, to this culture and place – is generosity.

Alex Atala,
chef and owner of D.O.M. restaurant in São Paulo

SOUTH

The southern stretches of Brazil, comprising the states of Paraná, Santa Catarina and Rio Grande do Sul, may defy familiar images of tropical lands. The climate is relatively cold for most of the year and the people are descended not from native and Latin blood but from German, Italian, Polish and Ukrainian immigrants. These groups settled here in the 19th and 20th centuries and still maintain their traditions in European-style towns. In the following pages, we have suggested several itineraries to discover the region. The departure points, highlighted on the map below, are the capital cities of the three states, from where you can travel to the magnificent waterfalls of Foz do Iguaçu, the fashionable beaches of Santa Catarina, and the mountains, vineyards and Jesuit ruins of Rio Grande do Sul.

Previous page: the *pampas*, Bagé, Rio Grande do Sul, 2002. Photograph by Edu Simões

DESTINATION
CURITIBA

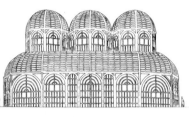

The capital of Paraná state is proud of its pioneering approach to public transport and public space, which has led to a considerable improvement in the inhabitants' quality of life in recent decades. A city full of green areas, it has 30 parks and woods, and plenty of bike lanes. It is also the site of several national cultural events, such as the annual theater festival in March. But remember to pack a sweater and a raincoat as summer temperatures are often cool and the winter can be downright harsh. Other attractions in Paraná include the breathtaking train trip from Curitiba over the mountains of the Serra do Mar to the coast. But the undisputed highlight is Foz de Iguaçu, whose falls are one of the continent's great natural wonders.

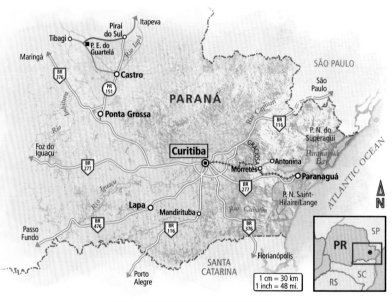

DESTINATION HIGHLIGHTS

CURITIBA
  Historic Center
  Cultural Circuit
  Parks
  Serra do Mar by Train

GUARTELÁ (215 km/133 mi.)

FOZ DO IGUAÇU (637 km/396 mi.)
  The Brazilian Side
  The Argentinean Side

All distances are from Curitiba

CURITIBA

HISTORIC CENTER

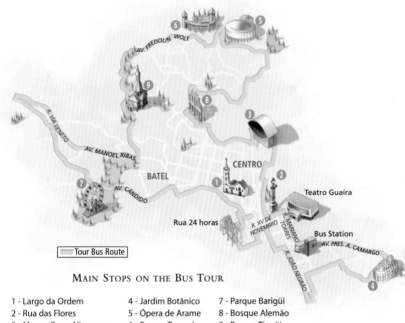

MAIN STOPS ON THE BUS TOUR

1 - Largo da Ordem	4 - Jardim Botânico	7 - Parque Barigüi
2 - Rua das Flores	5 - Ópera de Arame	8 - Bosque Alemão
3 - Museu Oscar Niemeyer	6 - Parque Tanguá	9 - Parque Tingüi

The **Linha Turismo**, a tour of 22 city attractions in a *jardineira* (a small bus), starts from **Praça Tiradentes**. It's one of the most comfortable options for exploring Curitiba. Tickets (*tel. 41/352-8000*) are good for four trips, and information is provided in Portuguese, Spanish and English. In the city center, you will find **Rua 24 Horas** (*tel. 41/324-7036*) Brazil's original 24-hour retail complex, though it's now somewhat rundown.

❶ LARGO DA ORDEM AND SURROUNDING AREA
The oldest group of buildings in the city includes the **Igreja da Ordem Terceira de São Francisco**, dating from 1737, and some fine examples of German-style

architecture. Also, the home of the local historian **Romário Martins**, another 18th century structure, is said to be the oldest house in Curitiba. On Sundays, the plaza hosts a popular arts and crafts fair with live music.

❷ RUA DAS FLORES
Rua Quinze de Novembro, in the heart of the city's commercial district, was Brazil's first pedestrian-only street. It's been closed to traffic since 1971. Since then, the Rua das Flores stretch has become a playground for the local kids on Saturday mornings. In December, a children's choir sings Christmas carols from the windows of the nearby **Palácio Avenida**.

CULTURAL CIRCUIT

Curitiba has an active and varied cultural calendar that you should check while planning your visit. Some destinations, however, deserve a place on every visitor's agenda.

❸ MUSEU OSCAR NIEMEYER

Built in 2002 to honor Brazil's most famous architect, the museum actually comprises two buildings, both designed by Niemeyer himself. The older of the two is a large, rectangular building built in the 1960's, which used to house government offices. To this, Niemeyer added the memorable "eye," with its striking interior.
There is a small exhibition on Niemeyer, but the collection and in particular the poor programming do not do justice to the building itself.
Rua Mal. Hermes, 999, tel. (41) 350-4400. Tue-Sun, 10am-6pm.

❹ JARDIM BOTÂNICO

One of Curitiba's landmarks, the Botanical Gardens are laid out in the French style. A greenhouse resembling something from London, a strip of native forest and a U-shaped gallery housing a collection of Frans Krajcberg's sculptures round out the attractions.
Rua Engenheiro Ostoja Roguski, tel. (41) 362-1800. Daily, 6am-8pm (9pm in the summertime).

❺ ÓPERA DE ARAME

Worth visiting only if you want to take pictures, not to watch performances. The acoustics leave much to be desired and the theater is more popular for graduation ceremonies than anything else, which says a lot. In fact, there is hardly any music or drama at all. If you like theater, then head for the traditional **Guaíra** (*tel. 41/304-7900*) in the city center.
Rua João Gava, tel. (41) 354-3266. Tue-Sun, 8am-10pm.

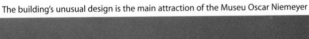

The building's unusual design is the main attraction of the Museu Oscar Niemeyer

Waterfall in Parque Tanguá: Curitiba has thirty parks and wooded areas

PARKS

Curitiba has more green areas – a total of some 18 million m² (4,448 acres) – than almost any other city in Brazil. Not surprisingly, it also has less air pollution than other Brazilian state capitals, ensuring a healthier life for its 1.5 million residents. Parks, squares and wooded areas dot the city, and some offer cultural attractions in tribute to the Polish, German, Ukrainian and Italian immigrants who colonized Paraná. Most are far from the center but can be reached on the tour bus (see *Linha Turismo*, on page 424). Note: you can only hire taxis at official taxi-stands or by phone; they do not pick up pedestrians on the street.

❻ PARQUE TANGUÁ
One of the city's most scenic parks is located on the site of a former stone quarry. There is a waterfall that plunges 40 meters (131 feet) from a plateau into a man-made lake. There is also a bike lane and a jogging track.
Rua Nilo Peçanha, tel. (41) 352-7607. Daily, 8am-5pm.

❼ PARQUE BARIGÜI
The city's largest park covers an area of 1.4 million m² (346 acres), and it always seems to be full of beautiful people working out. Although it's far from the city center, it is usually packed on weekends.
Rodovia do Café (BR-277), tel. (41) 339-8975. Daily, 8am-6pm.

❽ BOSQUE ALEMÃO
Offering one of the best views of the city, these woods are a tribute to Paraná's German immigrants and a paradise for kids. There is a trail with plaques that recount the story of Hansel and Gretel, as well as a children's library.
Rua Niccolo Paganini, tel. (41) 338-6835. Daily, 9am-5pm.

❾ PARQUE TINGÜI
This park is farthest away from the center. The main features are the **Memorial Ucraniano**, a replica of an Orthodox church, and an exhibition of paintings, embroidery and *pessankas* (painted eggs).
Avenida Fredolin Wolf, tel. (41) 338-1442. Tue-Sun, 8am-5pm.

SERRA DO MAR BY TRAIN

Built between 1880 and 1885, the 116 kilometers (72 mi.) Curitiba–Paranaguá Railway crosses over the mountains by way of 13 tunnels and 30 bridges. It offers the most spectacular train journey in Brazil, with the three-hour stretch to Morretes as the highlight. You can see the 86-meter-high (282-foot) **Véu de Noiva** waterfall, the **Ipiranga** canyon and the **Serra do Cadeado** mountains. The scenery on the descent is absolutely breathtaking; try to reserve a seat on the left side of the train, which will give you a better view of the Atlantic Rainforest dropping down to the ocean. First-class passengers are accompanied by bilingual tour guides. Along the way, you can get off at the **Parque Estadual do Marumbi**, a spectacular state park with great camping, hiking, and climbing on the 1,539-meter (5,049-foot) rocky face of Marumbi mountain. The best option for the return to Curitiba is by bus or, rather, van, via the scenic Estrada da Graciosa. That road dates from colonial times, and drivers have to take care on the cobbled stretches and when negotiating the switchbacks. An alternative is to take the *litorina* (an air-conditioned, self-propelled railway carriage), which follows the same route, and you can also return by road. The trip includes lunch and a tour to **Morretes** and the neighboring town of **Antonina**. That 18th century colonial town on **Paranaguá bay** would be a real delight if there were more accommodation options and the historical buildings were better preserved. Both trips are run by the Serra Verde Express (*tel. 41/323-4007*).

The Serra do Mar train route reveals natural beauty

OUR RECOMMENDATION

🍽 Don't leave Morretes without trying the *barreado*, a standard Paraná coastal dish of shredded beef, stewed for 12 hours, accompanied by manioc flour and banana. The name comes from *barrear*, meaning to seal the clay pot, a technique developed by the area's pioneer farmers. You can sample the dish at **Ponte Velha** (*Rua Almirante Frederico de Oliveira, 13, tel. 41/462-1674*), on the banks of the Nhundiaquara river, and **Armazém Romanus** (*Rua Visconde do Rio Branco, 141, tel. 41/462-1500*), which prepares a "light" version with less fat.

GUARTELÁ

Around 200 kilometers (124 mi.) north of Curitiba, you will find some of Brazil's best and most difficult whitewater rafting on the **Iapó** river. It plunges through **Guartelá** Canyon, which at 32 kilometers (20 mi.) is the sixth longest canyon in the world. The excursion can last up to two days, with an overnight stay by the river. You can also try the less difficult rapids on the **Tibagi** river, or practice trekking, rappelling or canyoning in the **Parque Estadual do Guartelá**, located between the towns of **Tibagi** and **Castro**. The trails are safe and well-signposted. Try the one leading to the **Ponte de Pedra** waterfall and the **Panelões do Sumidouro** rock pools.

Tour Operators: Ytayapé Ecotourismo e Aventuras, tel. (42) 275-1766 or 9982-0281; and Praia Secreta Expedições, tel. (41) 352-0520.

The Iapó river's whitewater carries experienced rafters through Guartelá canyon

LAPA: BRASIL'S FIRST SPA

The town of Lapa, located 67 kilometers (42 mi.) from Curitiba, has 14 blocks of well-preserved historical buildings that have been declared historical heritage sites, including the **Museu de Armas**, a weapons museum dating from 1871, and the **Igreja de Santo Antônio** (1874). Another attraction, the **Theatro São João** (1876), is one of only two theaters in Brazil with a circular auditorium and boxes around the stage in the Elizabethan style that Shakespeare popularized. On the outskirts of the town is the site of Brazil's first health spa. Since 1972, the **Lar Lapeano de Saúde**, also known as the *Lapinha*, has operated on a 550-hectare (1,359-acre) farm, which grows organic produce for the vegetarian menu served at the spa. Note: the rooms are not equipped with televisions or phones. The spa offers transport from São Paulo in a luxury coach, which departs from the Shopping Iguatemi mall every Sunday.

IGUAÇU FALLS

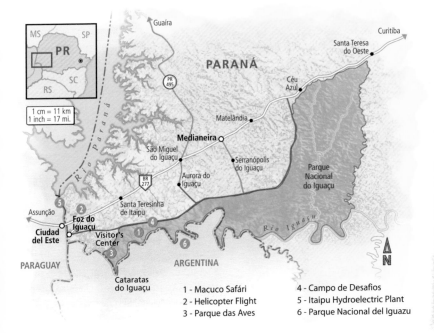

MS · SP
PR
SC
RS

1 cm = 11 km
1 inch = 17 mi.

Guaíra
Curitiba
Santa Teresa
do Oeste

PARANÁ

Céu
Azul

PR
495

Matelândia

Rio Paraná

Medianeira

São Miguel
do Iguaçu

Serranópolis
do Iguaçu

Parque
Nacional
do Iguaçu

Aurora do
Iguaçu

BR
277

Santa Teresinha
de Itaipu

Assunção

Foz do
Iguaçu

Ciudad
del Este

Visitor's
Center

Rio Iguaçu

PARAGUAY

ARGENTINA

N

Cataratas
do Iguaçu

1 - Macuco Safári
2 - Helicopter Flight
3 - Parque das Aves

4 - Campo de Desafios
5 - Itaipu Hydroelectric Plant
6 - Parque Nacional del Iguazu

Iguaçu Falls attracts half a million visitors a year to the city of Foz do Iguaçu, 637 kilometers (396 mi.) from Curitiba via the BR-277 and on the border of Brazil, Argentina and Paraguay. Although the 275 separate waterfalls, which have an average height of 60 meters (197 feet), are undoubtedly the area's main attraction, there are other things to see. The **Itaipu Hydroelectric Plant**, one of the greatest engineering feats in the world, is one. On the Brazilian side, the **Parque Nacional do Iguaçu** offers you the best view of the falls, plus the option to explore the region by boat or helicopter. On the Argentinean side, though, you can get much closer to the water.

THE CITY AND THE PARK

Foz do Iguaçu is a rarity among Brazilian cities. Everything works: the five tourist-information centers, the bilingual signs on the roads and the free phone information service in Portuguese, English and Spanish (*tel. 0800-451516*). There are many options for visitors, albeit pricey ones, except for the free tour of Itaipu and the trail that offers a panoramic view of the falls. All the attractions and most of the hotels are located on the Cataratas highway that connects Foz to the park. As for the city itself, the somewhat jumbled downtown area has no interesting stores or inviting restaurants, so just relax and enjoy the natural surroundings. Note: cars are not allowed on the reserve; everyone uses the double-decker buses.

Parque Nacional do Iguaçu: BR-469, km 18, tel. (45) 521-4400. Mon, 1pm-5pm; Tue-Sun, 8am-5pm; during the summer the park stays open until 6pm.

THE BRAZILIAN SIDE

❶ MACUCO SAFÁRI

The Macuco Safári is unquestionably the national park's most popular activity (*tel. 45/574-4244 and 529-6262*). An electric car with trilingual guides follows a 3-kilometer (1.8-mi.) route through the wilderness and stops at the top of a 600-meter (1968-foot) trail. If you don't want to walk down, you can always return in the car. The third part of the tour is a boat trip up the **Iguaçu** river in the direction of the falls. It ends where the spray of the **Mosqueteiros** waterfall begins. Take a raincoat if you don't want to get soaked.

❷ HELICOPTER FLIGHT

Those fond of aerial adventure shouldn't miss the 10-minute helicopter flight over the falls. There is an unforgettable instant in which the pilot hovers in front of the falls and slowly inches the nose downwards – a minute that seems to last for an eternity, accompanied by the noise of the rotor and the roar of the water. The flight costs US$60 per person. An extended trip (US$150 per person) also includes a bird's-eye view of **Itaipu** and the **Três Fronteiras** (Three Borders) landmark.
Tour Operator: Helisul, tel. (45) 529-7474/7327. Daily, 9am-6pm.

❸ PARQUE DAS AVES

This sanctuary, established in 1994, is home to 800 bird species, some of which are endangered. Ostriches wander around the parking lot. Walking through the aviaries, you will be surrounded by the chorus of birdsong and the vibrant colors of the macaws and flamingos. There are also marmosets and several species of reptile. The butterfly house, with more than fifty species, also merits a visit.
Rodovia das Cataratas, km 17.5, tel. (45) 529-8282. Daily, 8:30am-6pm (5:30pm in the winter).

A group heads up the Iguaçu river toward the falls

The most impressive view of the falls is from a helicopter

❹ CAMPO DE DESAFIOS

Founded in 2003, the Campo dos Desafios adventure park (*tel. 45/529-6040*) offers radical sports such as rappelling, rafting and rock climbing, with appropriate guides and safety equipment. Another option is canopy climbing, where you can wander among the tree-tops about 12 meters (39 feet) off the forest floor, before descending via a zip-line of steel cord.

❺ ITAIPU HYDROELECTRIC PLANT

Gather together enough steel and iron to build 380 Eiffel Towers and enough concrete for 210 Maracanã football stadiums. Add earth and rock equal to more than two times the volume of Rio's Sugarloaf mountain, and you will have one of the greatest engineering works in the world – the Itaipu Hydroelectric Plant. The dam supplies electricity for 25% of Brazil and 90% of Paraguay. The guided tour includes a film and a bus trip to the **vertedouro** (flood gate), where you can watch the gushing water fill the Itaipu reservoir to the point of overflowing, as well as a stop at the observation deck, which gives you a panoramic view of the plant.
Avenida Tancredo Neves, 6702, tel. (45) 520-6999. Mon-Sat, six tours daily.

THE ARGENTINEAN SIDE

6 PARQUE NACIONAL DEL IGUAZU
From the Brazilian side you get a
sense of the sheer magnitude of the
falls, but on the Argentinean side you
can feel their brute force up close.
Whether done on foot or by boat, the
close encounter will soak you to the
skin. There are three trails, the highest
one being both the shortest and
easiest. Extending for 650 meters
(1,969 feet), there are no steps to
climb and you get a view of the river
just a few meters before it tumbles
over the edge. The 1.2-kilometer
(3,937 foot) lower trail has many stairs
and you can almost touch the falls.
The fissure forming the spectacular
Garganta do Diabo (Devil's Throat)
waterfall allows you to get even closer,
and can be reached by a 1.1 kilometer
(3,609 feet) train ride. If you are in
good physical shape, you can hike for
five hours up a steep slope to **San
Martin** island, although the resulting
view is not as breathtaking, in both
senses of the word, as the trek itself.
Note: tourists need to present their
passport at the park entrance.
*Avenida Victoria Aguirre, 66, tel. (+54)
(3757) 42-3252/42-0180/42-0722.
Mon, 1pm-6pm; Tue-Sun, 8am-6pm
(7pm in spring and summer).
Boat Tour: Iguazu Jungle Explorer, tel.
(+54) (3757) 42-1696.*

OUR RECOMMENDATION

The **Tropical das Cataratas Eco
Resort**, a colonial-style Portuguese
building, overlooks the cataracts on the
Brazilian side of the Parque Nacional do
Iguaçu. A stay includes breakfast on the
verandah facing the falls where tables are
coveted. The only rooms with a similar
view are the two presidential suites and
the five luxury suites.

Additional information begins on page 462.

The Argentinean side offers the closest access to the falls

DESTINATION
FLORIANÓPOLIS

The majestic capital of the state of Santa Catarina straddles an island of 424 km² (164 sq. mi.), two-fifths of which is covered by Atlantic Rainforest, and on a small, 12 km² chunk of the mainland. It has 42 island beaches, catering to all tastes, and even more on the mainland. The proximity of forest and sea has made Florianópolis a popular tourist destination, and hordes of visitors descend for New Year's and Carnival, particularly since the widening of the main coastal highway, the BR-101, made driving through the state much easier. Although the beaches are the city's main attraction, it is a good idea to pack a jacket – the average temperature falls from 25°C (77°F) in the summer to 16°C (61°F) in the winter. For a capital, Florianópolis maintains a small-town atmosphere, and there are few attractions beyond the natural beauty. But who needs them?

DESTINATION HIGHLIGHTS

FLORIANÓPOLIS
  Beaches for All Kinds
  The Urban Coastline
  The Wild South
  The Lagoon and
    the Central Region
  Island Boat Trip

BOMBINHAS (60 km/37 mi.)

BALNEÁRIO CAMBORIÚ
  (80 km/50 mi.)

PENHA (120 km/75 mi.)

BLUMENAU (140 km/87 mi.)

SÃO FRANCISCO DO SUL
  (215 km/134 mi.)

GUARDA DO EMBAÚ (68 km/42 mi.)

GAROPABA (90 km/56 mi.)
  Rosa Beach

LAGUNA (121 km/75 mi.)

All distances are from Florianópolis

FLORIANÓPOLIS

The popularity contest among Florianópolis's 42 beaches hinges mainly on the quality of the scenery and water temperature. The warm waters of the northern coast attract families, and this region is more built-up than the rest. In the south, where the ocean is colder, virtually untouched beaches have retained their untamed charm and there is more greenery than elsewhere on the island. The fishing villages here survive without pressure from tourism. The east coast, facing the open sea, absorbs powerful breakers, which attract surfers to the beaches of Mole and Joaquina. At the latter, you might glimpse the island's most famous son, the tennis ace Gustavo Kuerten, with his board. In the central region, the Lagoa da Conceição is *the* place for nightlife, while the districts of Santo Antônio de Lisboa and Ribeirão da Ilha have the best-preserved examples of the architecture of the first immigrants, the Portuguese from the Azores Islands.

WALKING IS NOT AN OPTION

If you plan to tour the various beaches of Florianópolis, it's best to stay in the central region because you can get to all parts of the island from there. A car, nevertheless, is almost obligatory. The buses that run from the city center are unreliable, and taxis are virtually out of question due to the distances involved – the island is 50 kilometer (31 mi.) from top to bottom. As a result, you will see people fearlessly hitching rides all over the city, as if it were a country village. A more relaxing and safer alternative is just to set up your umbrella on your favorite beach and explore the immediate surroundings.

BEACHES FOR ALL KINDS

① Daniela
Three kilometer (1.8 mi.) long, with clear, warm and unruffled waters, Daniela is a family favorite. You can also take kayak or boat trips to the Forte de São José, on Forte beach.

② Jurerê Internacional
Calm waters and fine sand. There is a residential subdivision and good commercial services. Another pleasant family destination.

③ Ponta das Canas
Located far from the main roads, this fishing village attracts families looking for placid waters and a peaceful atmosphere.

④ Brava
The favorite hang-out of the young and well-heeled. *Brava* means "wild" in Portuguese and the waves here are higher than in the surrounding areas, much to the delight of surfers. Wild, too, is the daytime romance. (At night, head for Lagoa da Conceição.)

⑤ Santinho
This quiet beach also has high waves. Close to the Costão do Santinho resort you can see rock inscriptions dating from 5,000 years ago.

⑥ Moçambique
Thirteen kilometer (8 mi.) of untamed beach in the Parque Florestal do Rio Vermelho, a forest reserve. There are no food-stands, so bring lunch and water along with your umbrella and beach chair.

⑦ Barra da Lagoa
A fishing village with calmer waters than its neighbor Moçambique and a few modest inns and simple restaurants.

BR 101

BR 101

Porto Alegre

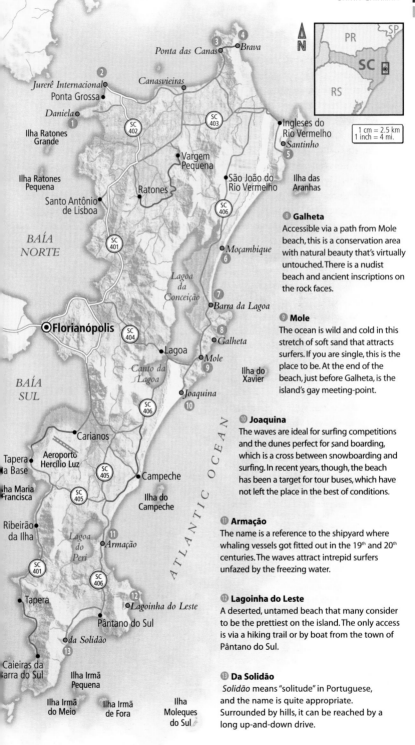

8 Galheta

Accessible via a path from Mole beach, this is a conservation area with natural beauty that's virtually untouched. There is a nudist beach and ancient inscriptions on the rock faces.

9 Mole

The ocean is wild and cold in this stretch of soft sand that attracts surfers. If you are single, this is the place to be. At the end of the beach, just before Galheta, is the island's gay meeting-point.

10 Joaquina

The waves are ideal for surfing competitions and the dunes perfect for sand boarding, which is a cross between snowboarding and surfing. In recent years, though, the beach has been a target for tour buses, which have not left the place in the best of conditions.

11 Armação

The name is a reference to the shipyard where whaling vessels got fitted out in the 19th and 20th centuries. The waves attract intrepid surfers unfazed by the freezing water.

12 Lagoinha do Leste

A deserted, untamed beach that many consider to be the prettiest on the island. The only access is via a hiking trail or by boat from the town of Pântano do Sul.

13 Da Solidão

Solidão means "solitude" in Portuguese, and the name is quite appropriate. Surrounded by hills, it can be reached by a long up-and-down drive.

THE URBAN COASTLINE

The north coast of Florianópolis, or Floripa as locals call it, has the calmest and warmest waters and was the first to attract tourists. The so-called "inner" beaches, which face the mainland, including **Canasvieiras**, **Jurerê** and **Ponta das Canas**, are particular crowd-pleasers. Not surprisingly, this coastline was also the first to be urbanized and has the greatest concentration of hotels and inns. On the "outer" side, facing the open sea, the pounding waves bring currents of cold water to **Ingleses** and **Brava** beaches. The latter is extremely popular with the younger set and is an alternative to the "in" spots in the central region such as **Joaquina** and **Mole**. Joaquina has suffered from its popularity, but the hills around Mole have protected it from being built up.

FAMILY AGENDA

If you are traveling with your family and appreciate the comforts of home, head for the condominiums to the north. The downside there is the crowds, which many consider excessive, attracted by the ample accommodations. This is particularly true of **Ingleses** and **Canasvieiras**. In fact, Canasvieiras receives so many visitors from Argentina and Uruguay that it has signs in both Portuguese and Spanish. The neighboring **Daniela**, **Ponta das Canas** and **Lagoinha de Ponta das Canas** beaches are also popular with families, as is **Jurerê**, which even has a shopping mall.

OUR RECOMMENDATION

The **Pousada da Vigia** is the only inn in Florianópolis that's listed by the *Roteiros de Charme*, an association that rates hotels, inns and resorts. It is protected by the serene Lagoinha da Ponta das Canas beach, a 250-meter (820-foot) strip of fine, white sand cradled in hills. As if its very exclusivity would not suffice, it also offers such amenities as a sauna, jacuzzis in the suites and on the deck, and a home-theater in every room.

Additional information begins on page 462.

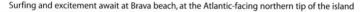

Surfing and excitement await at Brava beach, at the Atlantic-facing northern tip of the island

Lagoinha do Leste beach: limited access protects untamed nature

THE WILD SOUTH

According to local tradition, people born in Floripa are called "*manezinhos da ilha*", a nickname created by the German settlers on the mainland in reference to the huge number of Portuguese immigrants called Manuel on the island. In the south, its most traditional and untamed region, you still encounter real *manezinhos*, since the fishing villages and deserted bays attract fewer tourists. Note, however, that the ocean here is quite cold.

FISHING VILLAGES

Pântano do Sul and **Armação** beaches both have authentic fishing villages. The main attraction of Pântano do Sul is the seafood at the **Bar do Arante**. The eatery's walls are covered with messages left by customers, a tradition that began in the 1960's. In Armação, the fishermen have to cope with the high waves of a dangerous ocean.

UNTAMED BEACHES

The highlight of the local ecotourism route, **Lagoinha do Leste** beach is surrounded by hills and accessible by a 4-kilometer (2.5-mi.) path from Pântano do Sul. Many consider it the most beautiful beach in Floripa. To reach **Naufragados** at the extreme southern tip of the island, choose between a 3-kilometer (1.8-mi.) hike and a 20-minute boat ride from Caieira da Barra do Sul. Either way, the heavenly scenery is worth the effort. For trekking enthusiasts, there are other trails at **Solidão** beach.

"ZÉ PERRI" WAS HERE

The fishermen from Campeche beach insist that the famous French writer and pilot, Antoine de Saint-Exupéry, known here as "Zé Perri," regularly landed his plane on the beach when stopping over on his journeys between Paris and Buenos Aires in the early 20th century. In reference to this, the main access road to Campeche is named Avenida Pequeno Príncipe in homage to The Little Prince.

Florianópolis: ocean, sand dunes and lush vegetation

THE LAGOON AND THE CENTRAL REGION

LAGOA DA CONCEIÇÃO

Regardless of where one passes the day, almost everyone heads for the Lagoa da Conceição at night. Since it's in the middle of the island and on the route to the fashionable beaches of Joaquina and Mole, traffic around the lagoon is intense and jams are the norm during holiday periods. There are many restaurants and bars on the shoreline, but beware of the "all the shrimp you can eat" offers in the restaurants on Avenida das Rendeiras. The price may be great, but the quality is far from it.

CITY CENTER

Florianópolis has little to offer in terms of the usual urban services, architecture or culture. The main highlight of the city center, close to the Lagoa da Conceição and the airport, is the bridge known as Ponte Hercílio Luz. At 819 meters (2,687 feet), it is one of the longest suspension bridges in the world, and is particularly stunning at night when it is lit up. The bridge is closed to traffic. Another attractive destination is the **Mercado Público** (*Avenida Paulo Fontes*), or public market, which operates out of a 1898 building. Don't miss Boxe 32, a bar that is always packed with admirers of the deep-fried pastries (*pastéis*) stuffed with shrimp, that go down even better with hot-pepper sauce and the homemade *cachaça*. Equally interesting is the neighboring **Casa da Alfândega** (*Rua Conselheiro Mafra, 141, tel. 48/3028-8100 and 3028-8102. Mon-Fri, 9am-6pm; Sat, 8am-noon*). Built in 1876 as the customs house, it is now a gallery for Santa Catarina arts and crafts. Here, visitors can find lacework and figures from popular island festivals, such as the summer *boi-de-mamão* (a folkloric drama about the killing and resurrection of a prize cow). In addition, you can glimpse a little of the original Azorean architecture, especially the semi-detached houses made of crushed sea-shells and whale oil. The main bus station and the starting-points for all the buses to the beaches are also located downtown, as are most of the services. The hotels have a business profile, but may be a sensible option if you don't want to be restricted to a single beach.

ISLAND BOAT TRIP

ILHA DO CAMPECHE

If the big island does not satisfy your need for privacy, you can always escape to the surrounding islets. The virtually deserted Campeche, which has been declared a historical heritage site, has blue waters that are great for diving, as well as several trails leading to a cave with 150 ancient inscriptions. Although Campeche is located off the beach of the same name, the best ways to get there are actually from **Armação**, a 30-minute trip, or **Barra da Lagoa** (one hour).

ANHATOMIRIM AND RATONES

Unlike Campeche, whose heritage is truly an ancient one, the islands of **Anhatomirim** and **Ratones** guard more recent relics – forts built by the Portuguese in the 17th century to protect the colony, although they never actually had to fire a shot in anger. Many of the buildings have been restored by the Federal University of Santa Catarina and are open to visitors arriving by schooner from Canasvieiras and Trapiche da Beira-Mar Norte. The **Santa Cruz do**

Anhatomirim, dating from 1744, is the largest and oldest fort in Florianópolis. The schooner excursions also stop at the **Ratones Grande** island, where the **Santo Antônio de Ratones** fort is located. Take a look at the remains of the barracks and the powder magazine. There is also a trail through the Atlantic Rainforest that is worth exploring.
Tour Operator: Scuna Sul, tels. (48) 225-1806/225-4425/9971-1806 (City Center); (48) 266-1810/9982-1806 (Canasvieiras); (48) 232-4019 (Barra da Lagoa).

THE AZOREAN HERITAGE

Between 1748 and 1756, more than 6,000 immigrants from the Azores archipelago landed on Santa Cantarina island, escaping from a combination of overpopulation and a series of natural disasters. They supported themselves by whaling, fishing and growing manioc. Two and a half centuries later, their legacy remains in the distinctive local accent and in the villages of Santo Antônio de Lisboa and Ribeirão da Ilha. These, the immigrants' first settlements, contain Azorean style buildings dating from as early as 1755.

Bombinhas

Aficionados of the deep will be delighted with the visibility at the **Reserva Biológica Marinha do Arvoredo** marine reserve. When the ocean is calm, divers can see up to 25 meters (82 feet), making Bombinhas the best place for scuba diving in southern Brazil. Surrounded by beautiful beaches, the town was granted a 30,000 sq. m (7.4 acres) area for the **Parque Ambiental Família Schurmann**, which is owned by a family that circumnavigated the world in a sailboat. In the summer, Bombinhas is a popular spot for tourists and prices rise accordingly. Amenities such as grocery stores, drugstores, ATMs and phone booths can only be found at the main beaches.

Sea-bed treasures: a moray eel

Scuba diving in Bombinhas offers a riot of color

The Beaches

All of the town's 29 beaches have fine white sand, and at most of them – especially on the tranquil **Bombas**, **Bombinhas** and **Zimbros** – a mask and snorkel will open windows into new worlds. The large strip of Mariscal and the inlet of **Quatro Ilhas** face the open sea and are perfect for surfing. **Mariscal** also has a pleasant trail leading to **Macaco Hill**, while the tiny and isolated **Tainha** beach is worth the hairy drive over a dirt road.

Scuba Diving

The biodiversity in the Reserva Biológica Marinha do Arvoredo is so extensive that Ibama (Brazil's environmental agency) was forced to restrict the number of visitors while it prepares a plan to manage the area. Used to the restrictions, the local scuba-diving schools monopolize the excursions to see the underwater life at **Galé**, **Deserta** and **Arvoredo**, the three islands comprising the marine reserve. Unregistered divers can take the boat trip and go swimming with snorkel, mask and flippers only. But don't forget to take something for sea-sickness before leaving – the sometimes-rough trip over the open sea takes an hour.
Tour Operator: Patadacobra, tel. (47) 369-2119; Submarine, tel. (47) 369-2223/369-2473/369-2867; Trek e Dive, tel. (47) 369-2137/9973-0471.

Our Recommendation

Forget the noisy traditional resorts with crowds of teens. The charming **Ponta dos Ganchos Exclusive Resort** in Governador Celso Ramos, near Bombinhas, maintains a romantic and intimate atmosphere and prohibits guests under 18. All the bungalows are equipped with a fireplace, and other amenities include jacuzzi, sauna, and a chambermaid to help you pack and unpack.

Additional information begins on page 462.

BALNEÁRIO CAMBORIÚ

The mainland favorite of Santa Catarina's younger crowd, the beaches of Balneário Camboriú are usually packed in the summer. At night, the action moves to the night clubs and restaurants in Barra Sul. If you enjoy a crowded, festive atmosphere, the best places to stay are on Avenidas Atlântica or Brasil, which are parallel to one another. Save yourself the hassle of traffic and take the *bondindinho*, a sort of bus-streetcar that circulates along the two avenues 24 hours a day. If you prefer peace and quiet, however, head for **Amores** beach in the south, which is almost on the border with Itajaí, or the northern ones, such as **Pinho**, which is a nudist beach. You can reach both via the Interpraias road.

UNIPRAIAS AERIAL CABLE CAR

The pleasant cable car ride in the popular **Parque Unipraias** is 3.25 kilometer (2 mi.) long and gives you a spectacular view of the coastine. Departing from **Barra Sul** beach, the first stop is at the top of **Aguada** hill.

This station is called Mata Atlântica, an allusion to the typical Atlantic Rainforest vegetation that covers the trails leading to the lookout points. The park also has two tree canopy climbing circuits. The final stop is at **Laranjeiras** beach, which is much more enjoyable in the off season. The small beach offers calm, clear waters but it is just not equipped to handle the high-season crowds that flood in on the *bondindinho* or via the Interpraias road. A further warning to those with more discerning ears: the restaurants and bars here usually pump out earsplitting *axé* and *pagode* music from loudspeakers installed along the beach.

OUR RECOMMENDATION

The **Pousada Felíssimo**, with its Italian village atmosphere, is ideal for couples. All nine suites are equipped with jacuzzis and private verandahs. There is also an outdoor Japanese-style bath and a helicopter landing pad. It is located on Amores beach and is part of the *Roteiros de Charme* route.

Additional information begins on page 462.

The unforgettable view from the Unipraias cable car

Penha

Many think of the amusement park Beto Carrero World is as the feature attraction for Penha, but the town has a good deal more to offer. It is a major shellfish producer and has several attractive beaches, including the urban **Alegre** and the deserted **Vermelha** and **Lucas**. Locals take pride in their Azorean heritage, and let it shine through in their architecture and customs.

Beto Carrero World

The closest thing in Brazil to Disneyworld is still miles behind its American cousin. A massive undertaking, Beto Carrero World opened in 1991, and the 85 attractions cover 2 km² (494 acres) and attract 600,000 visitors per year. The park has seven theme areas, but the best two are Mundo Animal and Aventura Radical. The latter's exciting rides include the 100-meter (328-foot) Big Tower, which drops you in a 120 km/h (75 mph) free-fall, and the Tchibum, with its 80 km/h (50 mph) "rapids". Kids love the monkeys, tigers and camels and they will probably be the only ones to believe that the dinosaurs they meet while journeying on the little train from Magic Land to Beto Carrero's house are real. There are also many equestrian shows; not

Penha beach reflects strong Azorean influence

surprisingly given that horses are the passion of the park's creator, entrepreneur João Batista Sérgio Murad, better known as Beto Carrero. Pay attention to the show times, as they are held just once a day. A spectacular, nightly light show brightens the dusk.
Rua Inácio Francisco de Souza, 1597, Praia da Armação, tel. (47) 261-2000. Mar-Jun, Aug, Sep: Tue-Sun, 10am-6pm; Jan, Feb, Jul, Oct-Dec: daily, 9am-7pm.

Our Recommendation

🍽 **Pirão d'Água** restaurant in Penha, owned by chef Sarita Santos, serves traditional Azorean seafood dishes and rump in huge portions. This is not just a meal but a lesson in Portuguese culinary history. One interesting detail – there is no dessert. According to Sarita, the reason is that the early Portuguese settlers returned to work immediately after the main course. "Dessert for an Azorean is hard labor," says Sarita. But don't despair, she always has a cookie on hand to at least partially satisfy any sweet tooth (*Avenida São João, 954, Praia Armação do Itapocorói, tel. 47/345-6742*).

BLUMENAU

Santa Catarina's major German colony has gained national fame thanks to Oktoberfest (see below) and its industry. Blumenau is a picturesque city, with cobbled streets, exposed timber frame buildings and some streets where cars drive on the right. Its center is concentrated around Rua Quinze de Novembro, where shoppers can buy knitwear, linen, towels and crystal. Aside from Oktoberfest itself, there is also Strassfest mit Stammtisch, a popular street festival that takes place in March and September.

OKTOBERFEST

For 17 days every October, Blumenau becomes the beer capital of Brazil. Inspired by Munich's festival of the same name, the city breaks into dance, music and horseplay, all of it spiced with romance, especially among the younger crowd. Founded 20 years ago to raise funds after a flood, the festival is now a massive event for Blumenau's 261,000 inhabitants. During the day, the *Bierwagen* (literally, the "beer car") distributes free samples of draft beer along Rua Quinze de Novembro. It's well accompanied by a bratwurst sandwich. At night the party continues in the pavilion of the Proeb, an exhibition center, and the Vila Germânica, a lane filled with snack bars and souvenir shops. If you are averse to hordes of inebriated teenagers, however, forget it.

OUR RECOMMENDATION

🍽 At day's end, drop everything and enjoy the *café colonial* (a sort of marathon of an afternoon tea) at **Cafehaus Glória**. More than fifty items are served between 3 and 8pm, including delicious dishes and individual items such as deep-fried chicken pastries (*pastéis*), cheesecake, walnut bread, and apfelstrudel (*Rua Sete de Setembro, 954, tel. 47/322-6942*).

European-style timber-frame buildings enhance Blumenau's appeal

SÃO FRANCISCO DO SUL

Some inhabitants of this small town swear the spot was discovered by the Frenchman Binot Paulmier de Gonneville in 1504. They even celebrated the town's 500th anniversary in January, 2004, leaving cities like Salvador and Rio de Janeiro way behind in the oldest-town-in-Brazil stakes. Historians, on the other hand, are assured that it wasn't founded until 1658. In any event, there is no argument that the 150 colonial buildings deserve their status as historical heritage sites; they are currently being restored by the Monumenta Program. To see a few of them, take a walk down Rua Babitonga, and try to figure out just how old the town really is… Don't miss the **Igreja Matriz Nossa Senhora da Graça**, a church whose construction began in 1699 but which was only completed in the 19th century. In the surrounding area **Enseada**, **Ubatuba** and **Prainha** beaches offer the excitement that is missing in the center, while **Itaguaçu** preserves an air of tranquility. However, the town lacks quality hotels and restaurants, which becomes especially hard to ignore during Carnival.

MUSEU NACIONAL DO MAR

This warehouse complex houses a remarkable maritime collection, including an area dedicated to the navigator Amyr Klink, while Santa Catarina's fishing traditions are commemorated through a replica of a fisherman's house. The collection contains canoes, whaleboats, rafts and ships (as well as models) from Brazilian sites as far away as Maranhão.
Rua Manoel Lourenço de Andrada, 133, tel. (47) 444-1868. Daily, 10am-6pm.

OUR RECOMMENDATION

🍽 Catch a boat to the fishing village of Glória – just the 30-minute trip across breathtaking Babitonga Bay is worth the journey – and then head for **Jacizinho Batista**, where the food is divine.

Museu Nacional do Mar: collection of boats and models

GUARDA DO EMBAÚ

Powerful waves at Guarda do Embaú make for exciting surfing

At first glance, Guarda do Embaú, 68 kilometer (42 mi.) south of Florianópolis, is just another fishing village with beautiful deserted beaches and high waves. But since surfers love waves and girls love surfers, **Guarda** beach has one of the highest concentrations of young, suntanned, well-proportioned people per square foot in the state. However, there are few hotels and restaurants, so many visitors rent summer houses. To see more of the area's natural beauty, visit the **Parque Estadual da Serra do Tabuleiro**, the biggest conservation unit of Santa Catarina (*tel. 48/286-2624*).

SURFING PARADISE

Guarda beach has an abrupt drop near the shore that makes waves and attracts serious surfers. To reach the white-sand dunes you have to cross the Madre river by canoe or swimming.

However, surfing is prohibited between April and July. That period is the fishing season for mullet, the main source of income for the locals. There are five other nearby beaches that attract everyone from nudists to those who prefer calm waters.

OUR RECOMMENDATION

The highly exclusive **Ilha do Papagaio**, which houses the inn of the same name, is only for a select few. Although the island is part of the town of Palhoça, only guests staying in the 20 ocean-view chalets can land on it. Great attention is paid to detail – each room has a bottle of sparkling wine, chocolates and incense. The inn is owned by the Sehn family, who also lives on the island and welcomes all guests personally. The seafood served in the restaurant comes fresh from the family's own marine farm. The Sehns also offer water-skiing, sailing and diving.

Additional information begins on page 462.

Garopaba, a seafront village founded by immigrant Azorean whalers

GAROPABA

Discovered by surfers and hippies from the neighboring state of Rio Grande do Sul in the 1970's, Garopaba maintained its charm even as the village expanded and upgraded its services and infrastructure. Surfers represent most of the visitors. With the exception of Ferrugem, Garopaba's beaches are surrounded by hills, on which the hotels offering the best ocean views are perched. They are therefore quite some way from the shore.

THE BEACHES

Siriú and **Gamboa** are the most isolated and untamed beaches. The small **Garopaba**, in front of the village itself, is perfect for families, while **Silveira** is popular with surfers. If you like to party, however, **Ferrugem** is the place. The night begins at one o'clock in the morning, goes on until dawn and is thronged with young people. The beach is beautiful and the accommodation cheap, but beware: the water is freezing.

WHALE WATCHING

Every year from July to November, the southern part of Santa Catarina becomes an open-air aquarium for observing southern right whales. These cetaceans migrate from Antarctica to reproduce and suckle their young here. Hunted by Brazil until 1973, they have had shelter since 2000 in a marine protection area that's 140 kilometer (87 mi.) long. You can see them from the coast around Garopaba and Rosa beaches, but a boat trip provides a much more impressive encounter. Accompanying marine biologists explain the whales' habits as you approach.

Instituto Baleia-Franca: (48) 355-6111.

ROSA BEACH

Love at first site. Rosa, as it is known, is a 2-kilometer (1.25-mi.) strip of sand surrounded by green hills, lagoons and naturally the ocean. Some consider it one of the most beautiful beaches in the South of Brazil. It belongs to the municipality of Imbituba and offers more sophisticated accommodations and restaurants than its neighbor Garopaba, 18 kilometer (11 mi.) away. At the same time, it has preserved its rustic atmosphere. There isn't even a sidewalk in front of the steeply sloping beach. Most visitors are young surfers from Rio Grande do Sul, so almost every conversation is peppered with typical gaucho expressions like the interjections *bá* and *tchê*. It is also a popular destination for Argentineans and some have even settled here. Be extra careful when driving, especially when it's raining. As in Garopaba, the routes to the beaches are not adequately signposted, so it would be wise to park your car and walk, even though this involves a punishing up-and-down trek over hilly trails. You might also have to cross a seasonal lagoon by boat. The easiest trails are the one beside the Pousada Fazenda Verde do Rosa and those at the two extreme points of the beach. Although Rosa is not as popular as Ferrugem in Garopaba, it is also usually packed in the summer.

OUR RECOMMENDATION

If you are staying at Rosa, you will have to choose between an amazing view or easy access to the beach (rare in itself); there is no way to have both. If you opt for the view, try the **Pousada Quinta do Bucanero**, whose rooms are virtual observation decks. There is also a trail leading to the shore of the lagoon where you can take a boat to the beach. The inn is part of the *Roteiros de Charme* circuit.

Additional information begins on page 462.

Imbituba's Rosa beach combines beauty and simplicity

Laguna's center, with 600 historic buildings

LAGUNA

Laguna, 121 kilometer (75 mi.) south of Florianópolis, was founded in 1676 and is the second oldest town in the state. Even so, the thousands of tourists who visit every year seem to be more interested in its beaches and lagoons than in its rich historical heritage. Far from the commotion of the urban beaches, which are usually packed, especially during the street Carnival, **Prainha** is not only a magnet for surfers but is distinguished by the **Santa Marta** lighthouse, built in 1891.

HISTORICAL HERITAGE

The history of Laguna is recorded in its 600 houses and buildings that have been declared historical heritage sites. Worthy of special mention is the **Museu Anita Garibaldi**, housed in a building dating from 1747 where the so-called July Republic was proclaimed. The popular **Casa de Anita** has no collection. The best time to visit is in July when a cast of 300 presents an open-air drama re-enacting the town's capture by the revolutionary, Giuseppe Garibaldi.

ANITA GARIBALDI

Visitors to Laguna cannot help but hear the name of Anita Garibaldi. Laguna's most illustrious daughter was born in 1821 and married a cobbler at the age of 14. (Even the place where she dressed for the wedding has become a tourist attraction.) At the age of 18, she met the Italian rev-olutionary, Giuseppe Garibal-di, fell in love and joined his band of discontented farmers and ranchers from the south of Brazil. The so-called Re volução Farroupilha, a sepa-ratist movement against the imperial regime, lasted from 1835 to 1845. The rebels needed access to the ocean and captured Laguna, which provided them with a strategic port. Laguna became the headquarters of the short-lived July Republic in 1839, when what is now the state of Santa Catarina was incorpo-rated into the movement. However, it only remained in their hands for four months.

DESTINATION

PORTO ALEGRE

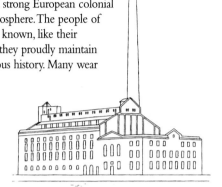

Rio Grande do Sul's cold climate and strong European colonial heritage give the state a unique atmosphere. The people of Brazil's major wine-producing region are known, like their Argentinean counterparts, as *gaúchos,* and they proudly maintain traditions that are steeped in their rebellious history. Many wear traditional pants and use drinking cups called *cuias de chimarrão,* which are fashioned from gourds, filled with yerba maté tea and emptied through a metal straw. In Porto Alegre, the capital, various cultural centers host major literary and artistic events. Some find Gramado the state's most charming city.

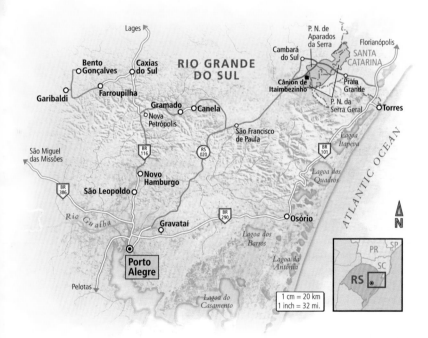

DESTINATION HIGHLIGHTS

PORTO ALEGRE
  Cultural Circuit
  Missões (500 km/311 mi.)

GRAMADO (120 km/75 mi.)
  The Southern Canyons
  (190 km/118 mi.)

CANELA (133 km/83 mi.)

BENTO GONÇALVES (128 km/80 mi.)

GARIBALDI (112 km/70 mi.)

All distances are from Porto Alegre

PORTO ALEGRE

CULTURAL CIRCUIT

Porto Alegre made recent international headlines by hosting events like the World Social Forum and the Mercosur Biennial art exhibition, but the city's cultural tradition is actually a long-established one underlined by the full program of events at museums and arts centers. Latin America's biggest outdoor book fair is held here in October and November, and the city also boasts the country's highest per capita book-reading and cinema-going rate. Nightlife is concentrated in the **Moinhos de Vento** and **Cidade Baixa** districts, along the **Rua da República** and in the **Centro Nova Olaria** complex's movie theaters and cafés.

❶ MEMORIAL DO RIO GRANDE DO SUL

The old Post Office & Telegraph building, dating from 1913, documents the state's history. It contains panels with photographs of local celebrities such as Lupicínio Rodrigues, Elis Regina and Érico Veríssimo.

Rua Sete de Setembro, 1020, tel. (51) 3224-7210. Tue-Sun, 10am-6pm.

❷ MARGS

The Museu de Arte do Rio Grande do Sul Ado Malagoli (MARGS), part of a recently restored complex of early 20th century buildings in the city center, contains the state's largest visual arts collection. It includes works by Lasar Segall, Di Cavalcanti and Cândido Portinari. There is also a bistro, a cafeteria and a store selling decorative items, books and clothing. *Praça da Alfândega, tel. (51) 3227-2311. Tue-Sun, 10am-7pm.*

❸ MERCADO PÚBLICO

This market sells everything from fish to *cuias de chimarrão*, but it also houses bars, restaurants and several stores selling Afro-Brazilian religious objects. The slaves who constructed the building in 1869 are believed to have dedicated the intersection of the four corridors to the god Bará, and the site

is used in the initiation rites for *pais-de-santo* (*candomblé* priests).
Largo Glênio Peres. Mon-Sat, 7:30am-7:30pm.

④ SANTANDER CULTURAL
This neoclassical building, which functioned as a bank between 1932 and 2001, is now a cultural center housing a large collection of national coins and medals and offering an extensive schedule of exhibitions, lectures, shows and films. There is also a restaurant, bookstore and a boutique, as well as a café, in the old safe-deposit vault.
Rua Sete de Setembro, 1028, tel. (51) 3287-5500. Mon, noon-8pm; Tue-Sat, 10am-8pm; Sun, 10am-6pm.

⑤ SCIENCE AND TECHNOLOGY MUSEUM
Visitors fond of science should make a point of seeing the Museu de Ciência e Tecnologia da PUC-RS. 750 interactive experiments cover all areas of knowledge – and guides help interpret exhibits. Although it is far away from most of the city's other cultural attractions, the museum is an unforgettable experience.

*Avenida Ipiranga, 6681, Pontifícia Universidade Católica do Rio Grande do Sul, T, tel. (51) 3320-3521.
Tue-Sun, 9am-5pm.*

⑥ CASA DE CULTURA MÁRIO QUINTANA
The renowned local poet Mário Quintana lived for many years in a room in the old Hotel Majestic, where former presidents also used to stay. Today, it serves as a lively cultural center with reading rooms, exhibition areas, libraries, cinemas and a center for theater and visual arts. The café on the top floor offers a wonderful view of the Guaíba river.
Rua dos Andradas, 736, tel. (51) 3221-7147. Tue-Fri, 9am-9pm; Sat, Sun and holidays, noon-9pm.

⑦ USINA DO GASÔMETRO
Constructed in 1928, this one-time thermal power plant was turned into a cultural center in 1989. Its location beside the Guaíba river makes it one of the best places to watch the sunset. It is also the departure point for boat trips on the river.
Avenida Presidente João Goulart, 551, tel. (51) 3212-5979. Tue-Sun, 9am-9pm.

View of Porto Alegre from Guaíba river: a city with extensive cultural offerings

MISSÕES

The ruins in the Missões region – situated 500 kilometers (311 mi.) west of Porto Alegre via the BR-386 highway to Carazinho and then the BR-285 – serve as a reminder of one of the most important eras in the colonization of the Americas. In the 17th and 18th centuries, the Kings of Spain and Portugal authorized Jesuit priests to settle here to convert the indigenous Guarani people to Catholicism. In the mid-18th century, when the movement was at its peak, the Indian population in the Jesuit-run towns, totaled hundreds of thousands. In 1768, however, the Jesuits were expelled from Brazil by the Marquis de Pombal and the missions fell into decline.

Almost 250 years later, the ruins of four of the seven Brazilian *reduções* are still standing. (There are also eight in Paraguay and another 15 in Argentina.) **São Nicolau, São Lourenço Mártir, São João Batista** and **São Miguel Arcanjo** are all worth visiting. The latter,

located in **São Miguel das Missões,** 485 kilometers (301 mi.) west of Porto Alegre, is the most important and the best preserved. Declared a World Heritage Site by UNESCO, it contains the ruins of the old 1745 church and the **Museu das Missões.** The Brazilian architect Lúcio Costa designed the museum, which contains Brazil's largest collection of missionary items. Every night, the ruins are illuminated for a 50-minute multimedia spectacular relating the history of the missions.

An alternative means of exploring the region is to take the **Caminho das Missões,** a walking tour inspired by the famous Santiago de Compostela pilgrimage in Spain. The seven-day journey along ancient indigenous roads, starting in Santo Ângelo, takes in five towns, and includes overnight stays in family homes or hostels and visits to the mission ruins.

More information at www.caminhodasmissoes.com.br.

Gramado: a popular destination featuring European architecture

GRAMADO

Located in the Serra Gaúcha mountains 120 kilometers (75 mi.) north of Porto Alegre via the BR-116, Gramado is a traditional tourist destination, particularly during the winter vacations when hotels are normally booked solid. This is particularly true during the first fortnight of August, when the town hosts Brazil's premiere film festival. Its attractions include the Bavarian architecture and Swiss-style chalets (it was originally colonized by Germans), the chocolate factories, colonial furniture shops and restaurants serving trout and fondue. The lookout point at the end of Avenida das Hortênsias offers a stunning view of the **Vale do Quilombo**. But make sure to bring some warm clothing, because temperatures can drop below freezing in the winter.

BUDDHIST TEMPLE
The Chagdud Khadro Ling, an unusual and very popular attraction, resembles a little piece of Tibet in the middle of the Serra Gaúcha mountains. Students give tours of the temple in Três Coroas, 20 kilometers (12 mi.) from Gramado; they explain the rich interior decoration, replete with ornate altars, delicate sculptures and wall-paintings portraying the life

NOVA PETRÓPOLIS CAFÉ

Nova Petrópolis, 34 kilometers (21 mi.) from Gramado on the RS-235, hosts the best *café colonial* in the country, a legacy of the German immigrants who settled in the region in the 19th century. The farmers lived so far from each other that any meeting was cause for celebration, and the best dishes were served. In the 1950's, Maria Hertel, the owner of a hotel in Nova Petrópolis started to serve customary dishes to her guests. And the tradition was carried on by restaurants like **Opa's Kaffehaus** (*Rua João Leão, 96, tel. 54/281-1273*), where visitors will find 45 varieties of cakes, bread, cold cuts and typical German jams. The **Colina Verde** also offers Italian specialties like *capeletti* soup and local standards like stuffed beef ribs (*BR-116, km 185.5, tel. 54/281-1388, Tue-Sun, 11:30am-3pm*).

Lago Negro: built in 1953 to reflect the landscape of Germany's Black Forest

of Buddha. It is customary to remove one's shoes when entering, not to take pictures or videos and to make a voluntary contribution for the maintenance of the buildings, because no admission is charged. Lodgings, stupas (large reliquaries) and statues surround the temple, all bathed in an atmosphere of silence.
RS-115, towards Gramado to Taquara, tel. (51) 546-8200. Wed-Sun, 9am-noon and 1pm-5pm, except Buddhist holidays (call to confirm).

FUN FOR THE KIDS

Gramado's parks and lakes are especially captivating for children. The **Lago Negro** has paddle boats and a path that takes visitors all the way round it. The **Parque Knorr**, with its wonderful view of the Quilombo valley, was originally an estate created in the 1940's as the home of businessman Oscar Knorr, but it has since been transformed into the **Aldeia do Papai Noel.** This Santa's Village has a gift factory, a nativity scene and an antique toy museum that

are open all year round *(tel. 54/286-7332, Mon-Fri, 1:30pm-9:30pm; Sat and Sun, 10:30am-9pm in the off season; 10:30am-10pm in the high season).*
Another theme park that is fun for both kids and grown-ups is **Minimundo.** It contains miniature replicas of the Igreja de São Francisco de Assis in Ouro Preto, the port area of Porto Alegre, the Neuschwanstein castle in Germany and Bariloche airport in Argentina, with the Andes mountains in the background *(Rua Horácio Cardoso, 291, tel. 54/286-4055, daily, 1pm-5pm).*

OUR RECOMMENDATION

🍽 **Chez Pierre**, hidden away in the basement of a pottery shop, was the first restaurant in Gramado to serve fondue. But travelers who want to go beyond dipping bread in melted cheese should try the *pierrade*, pieces of meat grilled on a hot stone. During the high season, there is a small dance floor where couples – which make up most of the clientele – can dance to jazz and French music *(Avenida Borges de Medeiros, 3022, tel. 54/286-2057).*

THE SOUTHERN CANYONS

Brazil's most impressive canyons, with an average depth of 800 meters (2,625 feet), are located 190 kilometers (118 mi.) north of Porto Alegre via the RS-020. They form the walls of the **Aparados da Serra** and **Serra Geral** national parks. The neighboring towns of **Cambará do Sul** in Rio Grande do Sul and **Praia Grande** in Santa Catarina lack decent services, but just walking among the Brazilian pine trees, rivers and waterfalls is an adventure in itself. Visibility is best in winter, when the fog disappears, but remember to take heavy clothing. **Gramado** and **Canela**, roughly 115 kilometers (71 mi.) away, are the most convenient departure points.

APARADOS DA SERRA

The highlight is the **Itaimbezinho** canyon, 5.8 kilometers (3.5 mi.) long and 720 meters (2,362 feet) deep. The **Parque Nacional de Aparados da Serra** has a visitor information center, a guide service and three well marked trails: Vértice, which takes 45 minutes; Cotovelo (a two-and-a-half hour trek); and Rio do Boi (which lasts for seven hours and requires prior authorization from Brazil's environmental agency, Ibama). *RS-429, 18 kilometers (11 mi.) from Cambará. Wed-Sun, 9am-5pm.*

SERRA GERAL

A continuation of Aparados da Serra, the **Parque Nacional da Serra Geral** is strictly for the adventurous, because there is no infrastructure or marked trails. But with a good guide, the trek is an amazing experience. The highlights are the Fortaleza canyon, which extends for 7.5 kilometers (4.5 mi.), the breathtaking views on the **Malacara** canyon trail and the **Pedra do Segredo** trail, which passes the **Tigre Preto** waterfall. *RS-429, 22 kilometers (13 mi.) from Cambará. Daily, 8am-6pm. Tour Operators: Atitude Ecologia e Turismo, tel. (54) 282-6305/9949-2495/9969-8220. Vida Livre Turismo, tel. (54) 282-1518.*

Monte Negro canyon in São José dos Ausentes provides a view of the ocean

WANDERING IN THE GAUCHO MOUNTAINS

Forget straight lines. Between the shore and the mountains, the shortest route between two points is a series of curves – at least along the stretch of coast where the Campos Gerais plateau hangs over the coastal plain. It looks like a basalt curtain slashed by canyons and threaded with roadways, where centuries ago, survey lines were traced by the hooves of mules. Following the muleteers' route, the visitors can swim in the ocean on a summer morning and relax in front of a fire at night; have fish for lunch and polenta for dinner; and contrast the fickle fashions of the beach with the austere figures of ranch hands clad in the traditional pants, hat and bandanna of Southern cowboys, as if they were rehearsing the roles of *gauchos* for TV.

The journey up the Serra do Mar extends for more than 100 kilometers and more than 1,000 meters in altitude. There are three main routes, but all of them share a style which is becoming increasingly rare in Brazil. It doesn't matter if visitors take the Rio do Rastro from Santa Catarina, whose smooth surface and nighttime illumination give it the appearance of an alpine highway, or the Corvo Branco, which offers more picturesque scenery and stretches of dirt road that are a real challenge for rental cars, or the Faxinal from Rio Grande do Sul, which resembles an off-road test track for four-wheel-drive vehicles during the rainy season.

Whichever path visitors choose, they will need a rapid course in driving etiquette to prepare for the standards of courtesy that await at the top. When a truck is having difficulty rounding a tight bend, all the other cars fall back as far as possible to help the maneuver. Overtaking is negotiated with almost diplomatic courtesy, and every shoulder that is a little wider than the norm is an unspoken invitation to park near a lookout point, where the sound of nearby waterfalls combined with the ocean view in the distance delights the senses.

It's sheer perfection – but this is just the beginning. Nineteenth-century naturalist Auguste de Saint-Hilaire described the scenery on the plateau bordering the canyons as paradise on earth. In fact, he was gazing at a forest of Brazilian pine, a native tree whose noble lineage extends back 250 million years. The Brazilian pine lives surrounded by meadows of wild flowers and misunderstandings. Born in the era of the dinosaurs, it resisted climatic changes and geological upheavals only to fall prey to the teeth of the lumber-saws that transformed the Southern states into voracious timber exporters in the 20th century. It was almost extinguished by the sawmills' greed. Under siege, the pines changed both their appearance and their company, no longer clumping together in extensive forests but retreating into isolation along the edges of fences and the back of pastures. The strategy has been so successful that it seems it had been that way forever. Although the tree appears all over the country, it flourishes in the region's cold climate. It has become a fixture on postcards promoting the snowy winters, reinforcing the idea that the region is really a piece of Europe in the heart of the Serra Gaúcha.

But visitors who believe this have no idea what the travel agencies are hiding. There's nothing wrong with Gramado's Christmas Lights, Nova Petrópolis' *Frühlingsfest*, Flores da Cunha's *Mangiare di Polenta*, Vale Real's *Krönenthalfest*, Bom Princípio's strawberries, Bento Gonçalves' wine cellars and vineyards, Urussanga's *Ritorno Alle Origini*, São Vendelino's twice-weekly German masses, and everything else the German, Italian, Polish and Ukrainian immigrants brought. With a good deal of sweat and not a little feasting, they built one of Brazil's finest tourist destinations. But it doesn't hurt to remember that it is also a perfect place for anyone suffering from homesickness for the real Brazil.

And this Brazil is hard to find in other parts of the country – a Brazil that is organized and welcoming, typifying the "predominantly agricultural country" that used to fill the schoolbooks of not-so-long ago. In this Brazil, entire municipalities are interlaced with national parks and flourishing green pastures that cattle have wandered since the 16th century, and its rustic place names bear witness to its rural origins.

In São José dos Ausentes, the major tourist attraction is a waterfall called Cachoeirão dos Rodrigues. Leave the map in the glove compartment, though, because getting lost is the best way to explore side-roads with no signs or names and discover the carefully cultivated valleys, tree-covered hills, water wheels, clear rivers, cattle grazing behind fences, chickens running loose and houses with their windows wide open. If drivers take a wrong turn, it doesn't matter – they'll wind up in a similar place. This in itself is a major achievement in an era when the slightest detour in most other states can lead to unexpected encounters with huge potholes or shantytowns.

This side of the mountain has more inns than hotels; most of them are part of farms, some historical but all productive. They are normally decorated with family furniture and the outbuildings are filled to the rafters with agricultural implements that any decorator would love to have hanging in his or her living room. Sleeping in the main house, which is customary, on pillows with the scent of sun-bleached clothing, guests awaken before dawn to the smell of bread baking in the kitchen. Morning greetings from the host are accompanied by an outstretched hand holding a gourd cup full of yerba maté tea. The food, taken at the family table, usually nestled close to the fire, is made from time-honored recipes with home-grown ingredients, seasoned by the smoke of the wood stove, and it has a flavor that awakens the palate and unlocks the memory. The food couldn't be more Brazilian – so Brazilian, in fact, it fits perfectly with the universal definition that Gianni Brera from Milan gave the traditional mountain cuisine of northern Italy: "Simple fare prepared with a civility that is almost refined." It seems straightforward enough, but just try finding something similar anywhere else in Brazil.

Marcos Sá Corrêa,
journalist and photographer

CANELA

Until 10 years ago, Canela lived in the shadow of Gramado, 8 kilometers (5 mi.) away – but a project to showcase the region's natural beauty changed all that. The town ditched its image of a winter vacation spot and opened an information center geared to ecotourists interested in exploring its trails, parks and canyons. Although it still falls short of Gramado in terms of hotels and restaurants, it does offer a range of attractions, including aerial cable cars, waterfalls and Brazilian pine trees throughout the nature reserves, which attract both children and adventurers.

SURROUNDING PARKS

Of Canela's six nature reserves, the main one is the **Parque Estadual do Caracol**, which attracts 350,000 visitors every year. Covering 100 hectares (247 acres), this forest reserve is equipped with trails, a train for children and the famous Caracol waterfall, which is 131 meters (430 feet) high and accessible by a stairway of 927 steps. (Check to make sure it is open before starting the trip to the observation deck.) A tower with a panoramic elevator offers another stunning view (*Estrada do Caracol, tel. 54/ 272-3035, daily, 8:30am-6pm*).
The neighboring **Parque Floresta Encantada** (*Estrada do Caracol, tel. 54/504-1405, daily, 9am-5pm*) has two waterfall lookout points as well as a 415-meter (1,362-foot) aerial cable car ride. The **Parque da Ferradura** (*Estrada do Caracol, information at the Hotel Laje de Pedra, tel. 54/278-9000, daily, 8:30am-6pm*), a private reserve, has several distinctive attractions. It includes the course of the Caí river, in the shape of a horseshoe, which is visible from the top of a 420-meter (1,378-foot) deep

Caracol waterfall: Canela's landmark

OUR RECOMMENDATION

The quality of the **Quinta dos Marques** inn more than makes up for its remote location. Surrounded by a hectare (2.5 acres) of greenery, all the suites are tastefully decorated – one even has an antique iron bathtub, and another boasts a jacuzzi and a fireplace. The leisure area has a Japanese-style bathhouse and massage service.

Additional information begins on page 462.

canyon, as well as the picturesque Caçador stream and waterfall.

GETTING WET

Visitors can participate in several outdoor sports in Canela, including trekking, horseback riding, rappelling, pendulum swinging and bicycling. The most popular, however, is rafting. Twice a day, an inflatable raft takes six people down the **Paranhana** river for two and a half hours or 4 kilometers (2.5 mi.) to **Três Coroas**. Because the river is calm, children who are seven and older can run the rapids, go over small waterfalls upstream and play on the water slide. It is a good idea to wear clothing and sandals that can handle a dunking. *JM Rafting & Expedições (tel. 54/282-1255/1542)* organize the river trips, while the other activities can be scheduled at the *Central de Aventuras* in the town center or at *Atitude Ecologia & Turismo (tel. 54/282-6305)*.

FOR THE KIDS

Kids love a sleigh-ride even if it isn't snowing. In **Alpen Park** (*Estrada do São João, 901, tel. 54/282-9752. Tue-Sun, 9am-6pm*), a small carriage descends for approximately 1 kilometer (3,280 feet) down a mountain with hairpin bends at speeds of up to 40 km/h (25 mph). Another great children's attraction is **Mundo a Vapor**, which sports steam-powered trains, tractors, a paper factory, sawmill, steel mill, pottery and a rice farm – all in miniature (*Rodovia Gramado–Canela, tel. 54/282-1125. Daily, 9:15am-5pm; closed on Wed in February*).

OUR RECOMMENDATION

The charming, centrally located **Pousada Cravo e Canela**, with its individually decorated rooms, was once a colonial-style mansion. It belonged to Ildo Meneghetti, a former governor of Rio Grande do Sul. Don't worry if you're not an early riser – the owner ignores convention and serves breakfast until noon.

Additional information begins on page 462.

Everyday life in the country: gauchos dressed in traditional fashion, drinking *chimarrão*

BENTO GONÇALVES

Bento Gonçalves, 128 kilometers (79.5 mi.) from Porto Alegre on the BR-116, RS-122 and RS-470, was settled by Italian immigrants who arrived in Rio Grande do Sul around 1875. Their descendants transformed it into the capital of Brazil's premiere grape and wine region. The town has a research center and a federal school dedicated to wine, as well as a producers' association that issues quality certificates for the local output. Visitors can also tour most of the vineyards in comfort.

VINEYARD TOUR

With only a little imagination, a drive along the RS-444 through the Vale dos Vinhedos evokes the magical landscape of Tuscany, especially in the harvest season between January and March when the trellises are bulging with grapes. Twenty-four of the vineyards in the region's hills are open to the public. Mandatory stops include **Miolo** (*tel. 0800-541-4165*), one of Brazil's largest vineyards, and **Casa Valduga** (*tel. 54/453-1154*), which offers wine-tasting lessons for guests staying at the vineyard's inn. Just on the edge of town is the **Cooperativa Aurora** (*tel. 54/455-2000*), a cooperative of 1,300 producers which turns out 45 million liters (11.9 million gallons) of wine a year.

CAMINHOS DE PEDRA

The majestic stone and timber houses, like those in the north of Italy, are located in **Colônia de São Pedro**, 13 kilometers (8 mi.) east of Bento Gonçalves. The 7 kilometers (4.25 mi.) Caminhos de Pedra tour leads past 23 of these late-19th-century houses, many of which operate as small commercial establishments selling sheep's milk cheese, shawls, handmade woolen clothing, homemade pasta, yerba maté tea and wine. *Giordani Turismo* organizes bus tours (*tel. 54/452-6042*). For private tours, guides can be hired at *Valleverde Turismo* (*tel. 54/459-1813*).

Italian immigrants turned the Serra Gaúcha into Brazil's largest wine-producing region

GARIBALDI

Garibaldi preserves Italian traditions in its architecture, cuisine and vineyards

The vineyards in Garibaldi, just 16 kilometers (10 mi.) from Bento Gonçalves, specialize in sparkling wines. The influence of the European immigrants who initiated this tradition is evident in the town's historical center. Other aspects of local culture can be appreciated during the 90-minute steam-train excursion between Garibaldi, Carlos Barbosa and Bento Gonçalves (*tel. 54/455-2788*). Several well-preserved buildings from the beginning of the 20th century display Italian, neoclassical and neo gothic styles. Most of them are on Rua Buarque de Macedo in the town center.

SPARKLING WINE TOUR

Garibaldi produces more than half of Brazil's sparkling wines. Visitors can taste them and learn how they are made by accompanying the specialized guides on the Garibaldi vineyard tour. **Georges Aubert** (*tel. 54/462-1155*) has a small museum, and the guides demonstrate *sabrage*, the art of opening a champagne bottle with a saber stroke. **Chandon** (*tel. 54/462-2499*), the most sought-out, only receives private parties and only sells its wine in cases of six bottles.

ESTRADA DO SABOR

Several farms and ranches around Garibaldi serve typical homemade meals to travelers along a route called the Estrada do Sabor (Gastronomic Tour). They also offer picnics, walks through the valleys and visits to caves and vineyards, as well as samples of wine, liqueurs, salami and bread. More information in the Centro de Informações Turísticas (*tel. 54/464-0796/462-2697*).

HOTELS, RESTAURANTS AND SERVICES

The information on the following pages is organized by geographical region: Southeastern, Northeastern, Northern, Central West and Southern. The pages have been color-coded to match the colors used in the corresponding regional chapter. Within each region, cities appear in alphabetical order.

Restaurants have been assigned price categories based on the cost of the most popular choice plus a 10% service fee.

Hotel rate categories correspond to the total charge for double-occupancy accommodations.

Addresses, telephone numbers, business hours and prices were provided by the establishments and checked by our team of reporters. Nevertheless, despite our efforts, there may be changes or discrepancies. Whenever possible, please confirm the information, particularly hours and services available, provided here before patronizing an establishment. Tourist information offices may not be open during the low season.

• HOTELS • RESTAURANTS • TOURIST INFORMATION
• LOCAL TOUR OPERATORS • CAR AND BOAT RENTAL • DIVING OPERATORS
• AIRPORTS • TOURIST POLICE STATIONS • TOURIST GUIDES
• CURRENCY EXCHANGE • AIR TAXI OPERATORS

ABBREVIATIONS OF THE BRAZILIAN STATES

AC – Acre	MT – Mato Grosso	RN – Rio Grande do Norte
AL – Alagoas	MS – Mato Grosso do Sul	
AP – Amapá	MG – Minas Gerais	RS – Rio Grande do Sul
AM – Amazonas	PA – Pará	RO – Rondônia
BA – Bahia	PB – Paraíba	RR – Roraima
CE – Ceará	PR – Paraná	SC – Santa Catarina
ES – Espírito Santo	PE – Pernambuco	SP – São Paulo
GO – Goiás	PI – Piauí	SE – Sergipe
MA – Maranhão	RJ – Rio de Janeiro	TO – Tocantins

SOUTHEAST

Anchieta – ES

AREA CODE 28 POPULATION 19,176
DISTANCES Vitória, 85 km (53 mi); Guarapari, 21 km (13 mi)
SITE www.anchieta.es.gov.br

HOTELS

Pontal de Ubu $
Simple accommodations situated on a strip of land with majestic views of the ocean and beaches. You'll feel like you're on a ship, thanks to the glass walls of the common area and the large bedroom windows. FACILITIES: 30 rooms, air-conditioning, phone, TV, bar, pool, playground, tennis court, restaurant, convention room, game room, sauna. CREDIT CARDS Not accepted.
R. General Oziel, 1, Praia de Ubu
TEL 3536-5065 FAX 3536-5115
www.hotelpontaldeubu.com.br

Pousada Aba Ubu $$
This simple inn on a street parallel to the beach, 50 meters from the sea, is run by a Swiss owner who speaks English, French, German, Italian and Japanese. Fondue is served in wintertime. From March to November, it opens only on weekends and holidays. FACILITIES: 29 rooms, air-conditioning, TV, ceiling fan, bar, pool, tennis court, restaurant, game room, sauna. CREDIT CARDS Diners, MasterCard, Visa.
R. Manuel Miranda Garcia, Praia de Ubu
TEL 3536-5067 FAX 3536-5068
www.abaubu.com.br

RESTAURANT

Peixada do Garcia $$
This simple and traditional restaurant faces the beach. In addition to *moquecas* (stewed seafood with coconut milk, onions and coriander), there are several lobster options. In the ice cream parlor next door, try the delicious homemade ice cream and sweets such as the crystallized jack fruit candy. The restaurant has a branch on Costa Sul beach, in Iriri. CUISINE Fish and Seafood. CREDIT CARDS All. HOURS Daily, 10am-10pm.
Av. Beira-Mar, Praia de Ubu
TEL 3536-5050

SERVICES

TOURIST INFORMATION

Centro de Informações Turísticas
Av. Carlos Lindemberg, Centro
TEL 3536-1800/3261-5575. HOURS 7am-6:20pm

Angra dos Reis – RJ

AREA CODE 24 POPULATION 119,247
DISTANCE Rio de Janeiro, 150 km (93 mi)
SITE www.angra.rj.gov.br

HOTELS

Blue Tree Park Angra dos Reis $$$$
This hotel has the most complete leisure equipment and facilities on the Rio–Santos highway, including kayaks, water skiing and multipurpose sports court. Parents may relax at the spa while children have fun with the mini race track or the computer game network. FACILITIES: 319 rooms, air-conditioning, phone, TV, cable TV, bar, boating, football field, recreation team, pool, jogging track, playground, football court, tennis court, restaurant, convention room, fitness room, game room, massage room, sauna, spa. CREDIT CARDS All.
Estrada Vereador Benedito Adelino, 8413
TEL 3379-2800 FAX 3379-2801 RESERVATIONS 08007037272
www.bluetree.com.br

Hotel do Frade and Golf Resort $$$$
This large leisure complex offers water sports opportunities, such as water skiing and motorboat, and outdoor entertainment, including horseback riding and horse-drawn carts. Rooms on the ground floor open onto the beach, while the more private digs upstairs have small balconies. The golf course has 18 holes and instructors for novice players. FACILITIES: 178 rooms, air-conditioning, phone, TV, cable TV, bar, boating, football field, golf course, horses, recreation team, heated pool, jogging track, playground, football court, tennis court, restaurant, convention room, fitness room, game room, massage room, sauna, spa. CREDIT CARDS All.
Praia do Frade, BR 101, km 513
TEL 3369-9500 FAX 3369-2254
www.hoteldofrade.com.br

Pestana Angra Beach Bangalôs $$$$
One of the most sophisticated resorts in Angra dos Reis Bay, this hotel is unique among large hotels. Its greenery-enveloped bungalows have ocean views and offer privacy in a romantic setting. The large, comfortable rooms are equipped with DVD players. The hotel also has a restaurant with a panoramic view, recreation service and a heliport. FACILITIES: 27 rooms, air-conditioning, phone, TV, ceiling fan, bar, pool, playground, restaurant, convention room, fitness room, game room, massage room, sauna. CREDIT CARDS All.
Estrada Benedito Adelino, 3700
TEL 3364-2005 FAX 3367-2654 RESERVATIONS 08007044796
www.pestanahotels.com.br

RESTAURANT

Le Bistrot Chez Dominique $$
This relaxed atmosphere with outdoor tables by the river serves up delicious *crevettes du chef* (shrimps, mushrooms, herbs, white wine and rice with palm tree hearts). CUISINE French. CREDIT CARDS All. HOURS Tue-Sun, 1pm-11pm.
Condomínio Porto Frade, BR-101, km 512 towards Paraty
TEL 3369-5458

RESTAURANTS $ up to R$50 $$ from R$51 up to R$100 $$$ from R$101 up to R$150 $$$$ above R$150

SERVICES

TOURIST INFORMATION

Centro de Informações Turísticas
Av. Ayrton Senna, 580, Praia do Anil
HOURS Mon-Sat, 8am-8pm; Sun, 8am-5pm

Arraial do Cabo – RJ

AREA CODE 22 POPULATION 23,877
DISTANCE Rio de Janeiro, 158 km (98 mi)
SITE www.arraialdocabo-rj.com.br

HOTELS

Capitão n'Areia Pousada $$
A boat "docked" inside the hotel functions as a bar. Another bar, outside the hotel, offers a fine spot to watch the sunset, with a view of Anjos beach. Not all rooms have air-conditioning. FACILITIES: 32 rooms, phone, TV, ceiling fan, bar, boating, pool, restaurant, fitness room, sauna. CREDIT CARDS All.
R. Santa Cruz, 7, Praia dos Anjos
TEL 2622-2720
www.capitaopousada.com.br

Pousada Caminho do Sol $$
The interior garden makes this inn especially charming. All the rooms have air-conditioning. Many suites have a panoramic view of the city. FACILITIES: 25 rooms, phone, TV, cable TV, bar, pool, restaurant, sauna. CREDIT CARDS All.
R. do Sol, 50, Praia Grande
TEL 2622-2029
www.caminhodosol.com.br

RESTAURANTS

Saint Tropez $$
Each day, local fishermen supply fresh fish to this restaurant, and the menu varies according to what's availability. House specialties are black grouper, comb grouper, dourado (dorado) and anchovy. Ask for a table on the verandah. CUISINE Fish and seafood. CREDIT CARDS Diners, MasterCard, Visa. HOURS Daily, 10am-11pm; May-June, daily, 5pm-11pm.
Pça. Daniel Barreto (pça. Cova da Onça), 2, Praia dos Anjos
TEL 2622-1222

Viagem dos Sabores $
Cuisine with a Mediterranean touch. The Provençal shrimp (with tomatoes and seasonings) is highly popular. CUISINE Varied. CREDIT CARDS Diners, MasterCard, Visa. HOURS Daily, 1pm-10:30pm; closed on Sundays in the off-season.
R. Santa Cruz, 12, Praia dos Anjos
TEL 2622-2892

Bananal – SP

AREA CODE 12 POPULATION 9,713
DISTANCE São Paulo, 300 km (186 mi)
SITE www.bananal.com.br

HOTEL

Fazenda Boa Vista $
Built in 1780, this farm has been a backdrop for soap operas and miniseries. The rooms are simple. FACILITIES: 22 rooms, air-conditioning, phone, TV, bar, football field, horses, lake for fishing, pool, heated pool, tennis court, restaurant, game room, sauna. CREDIT CARDS Not accepted.
Rodovia dos Tropeiros, km 327
TEL 3116-1539
www.bananal.com.br/hotelfazendaboavista

RESTAURANT

Dona Licéia $
Most of the ingredients used are produced in the farm. The duck with orange and the caipira (free-range) chicken are delicious. The dessert buffet, with over thirty choices, adds a sweet finish to any meal. Reservations required. Closed in August. CUISINE Brazilian. CREDIT CARDS Diners, MasterCard. HOURS Tue-Sun, noon-5:30pm.
Fazenda Caxambu, Rodovia dos Tropeiros, SP-068, km 20
TEL 3115-1412

Belo Horizonte – MG

AREA CODE 31 POPULATION 2,238,526
DISTANCE São Paulo, 586 km (364 mi); Rio de Janeiro, 444 km (276 mi)
SITE www.pbh.gov.br/belotur

HOTELS

Mercure Belo Horizonte Lourdes $$
Great location, near the hubbub of Savassi district. The hotel has an international restaurant, coffee shop, cigar store and rooms for smokers, and disabled or allergy-sensitive guests. FACILITIES: 360 rooms, air-conditioning, phone, cable TV, bar, heated pool, restaurant, convention room, fitness room, sauna. CREDIT CARDS All.
Av. do Contorno, 7315, Lourdes
TEL 3298-4100 RESERVATIONS 08007037000

Ouro Minas Palace $$
This hotel has a "menu" with a choice of pillows, rooms for allergy-sensitive guests and other options such as rooms specially for women, which have hairdryers, skirt hangers and magnifying mirrors. FACILITIES: 344 rooms, air-conditioning, phone, cable TV, bar, heated pool, restaurant, convention room, fitness room, massage room, sauna. CREDIT CARDS All.
Av. Cristiano Machado, 4001, Ipiranga
TEL 3429-4001 RESERVATIONS 0800314000

RESTAURANTS

Bar Maria de Lourdes $
Serves homemade light, creamy and dark draft beers. It's packed on Saturdays, when feijoada (stew of beans and pork) is the special. On the other days, try the mineirinho (crackling, sausage, sun-dried meat) and mandioquinha (a kind of root similar to potato). CUISINE Appetizers. CREDIT CARDS All. HOURS Mon-Fri, 6pm-1am; Sat and Sun, noon-1am.
R. Barbara Heliodora, 141, Lourdes
TEL 3292-6905

PRICES	HOTELS (couple)	$ up to R$150	$$ from R$151 up to R$300	$$$ from R$301 up to R$500	$$$$ above R$500

Bar Tip Top $
Founded in 1929 and located here since the late 1970's. The bar's specialties are potato salad with large sausage and pork knuckle with sauerkraut. CUISINE Appetizers. CREDIT CARDS All. HOURS Mon-Fri, 11am-midnight; Sat and Sun, from 11am until late.
R. Rio de Janeiro, 1770, Lourdes
TEL 3275-1880

Boca do Forno $
This is the place for finger foods, sweets and a Minas specialty, cheese bread. Check out the hot sandwiches, the salads, crepes and juices. You may also buy frozen finger foods. Boca do Forno has thirteen branches throughout the city. CUISINE Regional. CREDIT CARDS Diners, MasterCard, Visa. HOURS Daily, 8am-11pm.
Av. André Cavalcanti, 571, Gutierres
TEL 3334-6377

Quintal $
The owners of this rustic, family-style restaurant serve a choice of meats. The most popular options are boar leg and *leitão à pururuca* (roast stuffed suckling pig with a crisp skin). Reservations required. CUISINE Meat. CREDIT CARDS Visa. HOURS Thu and Fri, from 6pm until late.
R. Sebastião Antônio Carlos, 350, Bandeirantes
TEL 3443-5559

Taste Vin $
Smoked *surubim* soufflé and fresh tuna are famous here, but the highlight is the extensive wine list, with labels from the world's best wine regions. The shop next-door has a wide range of labels. CUISINE French. CREDIT CARDS Diners, MasterCard, Visa. HOURS Mon-Thu, 7:30pm-midnight; Fri and Sat, until 1am.
R. Curitiba, 2105, Lourdes
TEL 3292-5423

Xapuri $$
Regional dishes of Minas are prepared in a wood-burning stove. The grilled, homemade sausage is famous all over the city. From Wed to Sun, there are Brazilian country music performances. Suggestions: *frango preguento do Bento* (Bento's chicken) and *carne-seca na moranga* (sun-dried meat in winter squash), which serves four. CUISINE Regional of Minas. CREDIT CARDS Diners, MasterCard, Visa. HOURS Tue-Thu, noon-11pm; Fri and Sat, noon-2am; Sun, noon-6pm.
R. Mandacaru, 260, Trevo
TEL 3496-6455

SERVICES

AIRPORTS

Aeroporto da Pampulha / Pampulha Airport
Pça. Bagatelle, 204, Pampulha
TEL 3490-2001

Aeroporto Internacional Tancredo Neves Tancredo Neves International Airport
Rodovia MG-010, Estrada Velha de Confins
TEL 3689-2700

TOURIST POLICE STATION

Delegacia de Atendimento ao Turista
R. Pernambuco, 282, Funcionários
TEL 3277-9777. HOURS Mon-Fri, 9am-6pm

TOURIST INFORMATION

Centro de Informações Turísticas
Pça. Bagatelle, 204, Pampulha
TEL 3277-7400. HOURS Daily, 8am-10pm

Centro de Informações Turísticas
Av. Afonso Pena, 1055, Centro
TEL 3277-7666. HOURS Mon-Fri, 8am-7pm; Sat and Sun, 8am-3pm

EXCHANGE SHOP

American Express
R. Paraíba, 626, Loja 4, Funcionários
TEL 3261-2601. HOURS Mon-Fri, 9am-3pm

Brotas – SP

AREA CODE 14 POPULATION 18,886
DISTANCE São Paulo, 245 km (152 mi)
SITE www.brotas.tur.br

HOTELS

Estalagem Quinta das Cachoeiras $$
This English-style inn serves a delicious breakfast, which can be delivered to the room or enjoyed on a charming balcony with colorful stained glass windows. FACILITIES 14 rooms, air-conditioning, phone, TV, bar, pool, game room, sauna. CREDIT CARDS Not accepted.
R. João Rebecca, 225
TEL 3653-2497 FAX 3653-4493
www.quintadascachoeiras.com.br

Pousada Sítio Recanto Alvorada $$
This farm hotel is perfect for families with children. Staff monitor various recreation activities. Some rooms have a fireplace, others overlook the lake. FACILITIES 22 rooms, air-conditioning, fireplace, phone, TV, ceiling fan, bar, boating, football field, horses, recreation team, pool, rock pool, playground, tennis court, restaurant, convention room, fitness room, game room, sauna. CREDIT CARDS Not accepted.
Rodovia Brotas–Torrinha (SP-197), km 12.5
TEL 3656-6332 FAX 3656-5082
www.recantoalvorada.com.br

RESTAURANT

Malagueta $
Located on the town's main avenue, this restaurant serves grilled dishes and homemade pasta. It is dimly lit and decorated with motifs of chili peppers. CUISINE Varied. CREDIT CARDS Visa. HOURS Thu and Fri, 7pm-midnight; Sat and Sun, noon-midnight.
Av. Mário Pinotti, 243
TEL 3653-5491

RESTAURANTS $ up to R$50 $$ from R$51 up to R$100 $$$ from R$101 up to R$150 $$$$ above R$150

SERVICES

LOCAL TOUR OPERATORS

Brotas Aventura
Av. Mário Pinotti, 113
TEL 3653-1015/4463. HOURS 8am-7pm

Mata Dentro
Av. Mário Pinotti, 230
TEL 3653-1915. HOURS 9am-6pm

TOURIST INFORMATION

Diretoria de Turismo e Cultura/Culture and Tourism Department
R. Lourival Jaubert da Silva Braga, 101
TEL 3653-5282/2288

Búzios – RJ

AREA CODE 22 POPULATION 18,204
DISTANCE Rio de Janeiro, 165 km (102 mi)

HOTELS

Colonna Park Hotel $$$
This hotel's design exploits the view of João Fernandes and João Fernandinho beaches. Some suites have whirlpool tubs. FACILITIES 63 rooms, air-conditioning, phone, TV, cable TV, bar, pool, restaurant, convention room, game room, massage room, sauna. CREDIT CARDS All.
Praia de João Fernandes, Quadra J
TEL 2623-2245 FAX 2623-7102
www.colonna.com.br

El Cazar Space Club $$$$
The hotel sits at the top of Humaitá Hill, with views of Armação beach and Bardot shore. FACILITIES 19 rooms, air-conditioning, phone, TV, cable TV, bar, pool, tennis court, restaurant, convention room, game room, sauna. CREDIT CARDS All.
R. A, Lote 6, Morro do Humaitá
TEL 2623-1620
www.buzioselcazar.com.br

Fazendinha Blancpain $$$
This farm has chalets with double beds and two single beds and an on-site French restaurant. The green garden, the orchard and the animals are very popular with children. FACILITIES 6 rooms, air-conditioning, phone, TV, ceiling fan, football field, golf course, horses, pool, restaurant. CREDIT CARDS Not accepted.
Estrada Búzios–Cabo Frio, km 5, at the entrance of Praia de Caravelas
TEL 2623-6490
www.buziosonline.com.br/blancpain

Galápagos Inn $$$$
This inn is a favorite of celebrities, and many of their pictures are inserted into the decorative murals. Almost all windows afford a view of beautiful João Fernandinho beach. FACILITIES 37 rooms, air-conditioning, phone, TV, cable TV, bar, pool, playground, restaurant, convention room, fitness room, game room, massage room, sauna. CREDIT CARDS All.
Praia de João Fernandinho, Lote 3, Quadra B
TEL 2623-6161 FAX 2623-2297
www.galapagos.com.br

Hotel Vila Boa Vida I $$$
This colonial-style hotel is located on one of the ends of the Ferradura beach, close to the beautiful mansions of the Búzios resort. It has beautiful gardens with flowers. FACILITIES 35 rooms, air-conditioning, phone, TV, bar, pool, restaurant, fitness room, massage room, sauna. CREDIT CARDS All.
R. Q, Lote 12, Praia da Ferradura
TEL 2623-6767
www.vilaboavida.com.br

Hotel Vila Boa Vida II $$$
Only a 20-minute walk from Vila Boa Vida I, this hotel nests on a hill to the south of Ferradura bay. It has large gardens and fruit trees. FACILITIES 45 rooms, air-conditioning, phone, TV, bar, pool, restaurant, convention room, game room, sauna. CREDIT CARDS All.
R. I, Lote 1, Praia da Ferradura
TEL 2623-4222
www.vilaboavida.com.br

Pousada Pedra da Laguna $$$
Located on Lagoinha peninsula, this is one of the most charming inns in town. Rooms for disabled guests available. FACILITIES 23 rooms, air-conditioning, phone, TV, cable TV, ceiling fan, bar, pool, tennis court, restaurant, convention room, fitness room, game room, massage room, sauna. CREDIT CARDS All.
R. 6, Lote 6, Quadra F, Praia da Ferradura
TEL 2623-1965
www.pedradalaguna.com.br

RESTAURANTS

Bar dos Pescadores $$
The tables are set on a patio, under the trees, beside the fish market. The location lacks aesthetic ambiance, but the food is great. Service is slow, so while you wait try the shrimp and crab pastéis (fried turnovers). CUISINE Fish and seafood. CREDIT CARDS Not accepted. HOURS Daily, 10am-8pm.
Av. José Bento Ribeiro Dantas, next to the Manguinhos fish market

Capricciosa $
This pizza parlor faces the sea and was the first of the pizza chain that became popular in Rio de Janeiro. 38 great toppings. CUISINE Pizza. CREDIT CARDS All. HOURS 6pm-1am.
Av. José Bento Ribeiro Dantas, 500, Orla Bardot
TEL 2623-1595

Chez Michou $
This traditional crepe shop in Búzios has opened branches in Rio, Cabo Frio and Brasília. The pancakes and fillings are delicious. CREDIT CARDS Not accepted. HOURS Mon-Tue, 5:30pm until late; Wed-Sun, noon until late.
R. das Pedras, 90, Centro
TEL 2623-2169

PRICES	HOTELS (couple)	$ up to R$150	$$ from R$151 up to R$300	$$$ from R$301 up to R$500	$$$$ above R$500

Cigalon $$
This bistro has become one of the best restaurants in town. The menu rotates periodically, and the wines are carefully selected. Ask for a table on the verandah. CUISINE French. CREDIT CARDS All. HOURS 6pm-midnight; Sat and Sun, 1pm-midnight.
R. das Pedras, 199, Centro
TEL 2623-6284/0932

Satyricon $$
This is the original Satyricon, the forerunner of the famous Rio restaurant. It offers top-quality fresh fish and lobsters kept in a special tank. Tables are set on the large verandah overlooking Bardot sea front, a very busy spot in the evening. CUISINE Fish and seafood. CREDIT CARDS All. HOURS Daily, 5pm-2am.
Av. José Bento Ribeiro Dantas, 500, Orla Bardot
TEL 2623-1595

Sawasdee $$
The owner studied culinary arts in Thailand and prepares dishes from the wok in this neat restaurant. The menu includes seafood, pork meat and pasta. CUISINE Thai. CREDIT CARDS All. HOURS Daily, 6pm-2am.
Av. José Bento Ribeiro Dantas, 422, Orla Bardot
TEL 2623-4644

SERVICES

LOCAL TOUR OPERATORS

Escuna Queen Lovy
Orla Bardot, 89
TEL 2623-1179/2286

BOAT RENTAL

Escuna Queen Lovy
Orla Bardot, 89
TEL 2623-1179/2286

BUGGY RENTAL

Oficina de Turismo
TEL 2623-8045

TOURIST INFORMATION

Secretaria de Turismo
Pórtico de entrada (Town's Gateway)
TEL 0800249999. HOURS 8am-10pm

Cabo Frio – RJ

AREA CODE 22 POPULATION 126,828
DISTANCE Rio de Janeiro, 148 km (92 mi)
SITE www.cabofrioturismo.rj.gov.br

HOTELS

Acapulco $$
Close to the town's white sand dunes, but far from Forte beach. FACILITIES 64 rooms, air-conditioning, phone, TV, bar, recreation team, pool, playground, restaurant, convention room, game room, sauna. CREDIT CARDS All.
R. João Antonio Rocha, 373, Praia das Dunas
TEL 2647-1212 FAX 2643-5445
www.hotelacapulco.com.br

La Plage $$
The rear of this well-placed hotel overlooks Peró beach. The service is good. FACILITIES 43 rooms, air-conditioning, phone, TV, ceiling fan, bar, pool, playground, restaurant, convention room, game room, massage room, sauna, spa. CREDIT CARDS Not accepted.
R. dos Badejos, 40, Praia do Peró
TEL 2647-1746
www.redebela.com.br

Pousada do Leandro $$$
The rustic décor makes this inn the most charming in town. It is tranquil in spite of its proximity to busy Forte beach. FACILITIES 22 rooms, air-conditioning, phone, TV, bar, pool, restaurant, sauna. CREDIT CARDS All.
Av. Nilo Peçanha, 333, Centro
TEL 2645-4658
www.pousadaleandro.com.br

Pousada Portoveleiro $$
This secluded and pleasant inn is close to Peró and Conchas beaches, near the Canal and Japonês island. There is a computer with internet connection available to guests at the lobby. FACILITIES 25 rooms, air-conditioning, phone, TV, cable TV, bar, pool, restaurant, convention room, sauna. CREDIT CARDS All.
Av. dos Espadartes, 129, Ogiva
TEL 2647-3081 RESERVATIONS 2647-3124
www.portoveleiro.com.br

RESTAURANTS

Hippocampus $
The tables on the sidewalk face the recently opened Canal Boulevard, by the Canal. The menu changes frequently, but it always features specialties from the sea. CUISINE Fish and seafood. CREDIT CARDS All. HOURS Daily, 11am-midnight.
R. Marechal Floriano, 283, São Bento
TEL 2645-5757/6369

Zeppelin $
From the tables on the verandah, diners can watch the action on the street parallel to Canal Boulevard. Although seafood is not the house specialty, there are good options in the menu such as the black grouper. CUISINE Varied. CREDIT CARDS Diners, MasterCard, Visa. HOURS Daily, noon-midnight.
R. Major Billgard, 525, Centro
TEL 2645-6164

SERVICES

BUGGY RENTAL

Casa do Buggy
Av. Vereador Antônio Ferreira dos Santos, 836, Braga
TEL 2645-3939/9215-9974

RESTAURANTS $ up to R$50 $$ from R$51 up to R$100 $$$ from R$101 up to R$150 $$$$ above R$150

TOURIST INFORMATION

Secretaria de Turismo
Av. Américo Vespúcio
TEL 2647-1689/6227. HOURS Mon-Fri, 9am-5pm; Sat, Sun and holidays, 9am-4:30pm.

Campos do Jordão – SP

AREA CODE 12 POPULATION 44,252
DISTANCE São Paulo, 167 km (104 mi)

HOTELS

Canadá Lodge $$$$
The building and the décor resemble a Canadian ski station. The rooms are comfortable, with king-size beds and bathroom with heated floor. Guests may use the pool of neighboring Ludwig restaurant. FACILITIES 20 rooms, phone, TV, cable TV, game room. CREDIT CARDS Diners, MasterCard, Visa
R. Plínio de Godói, 403
TEL 3663-1677 FAX 3663-6641
www.canadalodge.com.br

Frontenac $$$$
This French-style luxury hotel offers goose-feather pillows and quilts. English-speaking staff provides efficient service. Unfortunately, the hotel is located in a busy spot and the rooms are not sound-proof. FACILITIES 47 rooms, air-conditioning, phone, TV, cable TV, bar, pool, tennis court, restaurant, convention room, fitness room, game room, massage room, sauna. CREDIT CARDS All.
Av. Dr. Paulo Ribas, 295
TEL 3669-1000
www.frontenac.com.br

Grande Hotel – Hotel-Escola Senac $$$$
Built in 1944, this hotel became Senac's hotel school in 1998, after extensive renovation. It is exquisitely decorated, with French clocks, Belgian tapestries and art nouveau furniture. It also has a heliport, a restaurant for children and a recreation team, in addition to a theater open to non-guests. Suites with whirlpool tubs. FACILITIES 95 rooms, phone, TV, cable TV, bar, recreation team, heated pool, playground, tennis court, restaurant, convention room, fitness room, game room, massage room, sauna. CREDIT CARDS All.
Av. Frei Orestes Girardi, 3549
TEL 3668-6000 FAX 260-6100 RESERVATIONS (11) 3673-1311
www.sp.senac.br/ghj

La Villete Pousada $$$
The owner of this unique and cozy English-style inn is inviting and welcomes guests as if they were her friends. Each apartment has unique décor. Breakfast (or brunch) is served until 1pm. FACILITIES 8 rooms, air-conditioning, phone, TV, cable TV, bar, restaurant, game room. CREDIT CARDS Diners, MasterCard, Visa.
R. Cantídio Pereira de Castro, 100
TEL 3663-2767 FAX 3663-1278
www.lavillettepousada.com.br

Pousada Vila Natal $$$
This very comfortable house is decorated with Persian rugs and collectibles inherited by the owner. Breakfast is actually a full brunch. It is far from the hubbub of the town center and on the way to Pedra do Baú. FACILITIES 11 rooms, air-conditioning, TV, cable TV. CREDIT CARDS All.
R. Serafim Capela, 390
TEL 3664-4524
www.guiacampos.com/pousadavilanatal/

Pousada Villa Capivary $$
Located in the main district, this comfortable inn has ample rooms with balconies. The beds have a "heating lining" that may be controlled so that each side of the bed has a different temperature. Breakfast is delicious. FACILITIES 15 rooms, phone, TV, bar, game room. CREDIT CARDS All.
Av. Vitor Godinho, 131
TEL 3663-1736 FAX 263-1746
www.villacapivary.com.br

Toriba $$$$
One of the most traditional hotels in Campos do Jordão, Toriba celebrated its 60th anniversary in 2003. Almost all the rooms have ample and neat balconies. The bathrooms have hairdryers and goat-milk soap. The reading room has internet access and the on-site restaurant serves fondue. FACILITIES 32 rooms, phone, TV, cable TV, bar, recreation team, pool, jogging track, playground, restaurant, convention room, fitness room, game room, massage room, sauna. CREDIT CARDS All.
Av. Ernesto Diederichsen, 2962
TEL 3668-5000 FAX 262-4211 RESERVATIONS 0800178179
www.toriba.com.br

RESTAURANTS

Harry Pisek $
Since 1997, Harry Pisek, a Brazilian of Austrian ancestry, has home-made an array of frankfurters. There are over fifteen varieties, some with white pepper and herbs, *ementhal* cheese, pork or beef (*schlubig*). CUISINE German. CREDIT CARDS Diners, MasterCard. HOURS Mon-Fri, 9am-6pm; Sat, 9am-11pm; Sun, 9am-6pm.
Av. Pedro Paulo, 857, on the way to the Horto (park)
TEL 3663-4030

Ludwig Restaurant $$
This is one of the best restaurants in town, with a cozy atmosphere and attentive staff. Game meat is the specialty. The wine list is a highlights. CUISINE French and Swiss. CREDIT CARDS All. HOURS Mon-Fri, from 6pm until the last customer; Sat and Sun, from noon until the last customer.
R. Aristides de Souza Melo, 50
TEL 3663-5111/9771-5162

SERVICES

LOCAL TOUR OPERATORS

Altus Turismo Ecológico
TEL 3663-4122

Verticália – Aventura no Rancho
Av. Pedro Paulo, 7997, on the way to the Horto (park)
TEL 3663-7400

PRICES	HOTELS (couple)	$ up to R$150	$$ from R$151 up to R$300	$$$ from R$301 up to R$500	$$$$ above R$500

TOURIST INFORMATION

Portal da Cidade (Town's Gateway)
TEL 3664-3525

Catas Altas – MG

AREA CODE 31 POPULATION 4,241
DISTANCE Belo Horizonte, 142 km (88 mi)
SITE www.catasaltas.hpg.ig.com.br

RESTAURANT

Histórias Taberna $
This simple eatery is the best option for those visiting the Caraça Natural Park. Suggestions: grilled pork loin or tilapia with manioc puree. CUISINE Varied. CREDIT CARDS Not accepted. HOURS Fri, 8am-2am; Sat, 11am-4pm and 8pm-2am.
R. Monsenhor Barros, 230, Centro
TEL 3832-7615.

Cunha – SP

AREA CODE 12 POPULATION 23,090
DISTANCE São Paulo, 222 km (138 mi)

HOTEL

Pousada Recanto das Girafas $
The chalets are comfortable and have verandahs with hammocks and king-size beds. Breakfast is served by the pool at a large, communal table. The owner gives tips on the region and entertains guests by playing the piano. In dinner, food is prepared in a wood-burning stove. FACILITIES 8 rooms, TV, bar, pool, restaurant, sauna. CREDIT CARDS MasterCard, Visa.
R. Professor Agenor de Araújo, 251
TEL 3111-1330 FAX 3111-1965
www.recantodasgirafas.com.br

SERVICES

TOURIST INFORMATION

Cunhatur
Pça. Coronel João Olímpio, 17, Centro
TEL 3111-2634

Portal da Cidade (Town's Gateway)
Av. Francisco da Cunha Menezes
HOURS Tue-Sun, 9am-5pm, closed on Mondays.

Diamantina – MG

AREA CODE 38 POPULATION 44,259
DISTANCE Belo Horizonte, 285 km (177 mi)
SITE www.diamantina.com.br

HOTELS

Pousada Jardim da Serra $$$
Recently built in the upper area of town, this inn is near some good trails. It has a beautiful view of the city center and the neighboring mountains. FACILITIES 21 rooms, phone, TV, bar, rock pool, lake for fishing, restaurant, sauna. CREDIT CARDS Not accepted.
Estrada do Cruzeiro Luminoso
TEL 9106-8561
www.jardimdaserra.com.br

Tijuco $
Oscar Niemeyer designed this charming, Modernist building in the 1950's, and it still has the original furniture. The rooms are large and airy. The lobby is beautiful and features a very high ceiling. FACILITIES 27 rooms, phone, TV. CREDIT CARDS All.
R. Macau do Meio, 211
TEL 3531-1022 FAX 3531-3763

RESTAURANTS

Caipirão $
This restaurant serves the regional dishes of Minas cooked in a wood-burning stove. Dinner is à la carte; you may pay by the kilo at lunch. Near Rua da Quitanda, the busiest street in town. CUISINE Regional of Minas. CREDIT CARDS MasterCard, Visa. HOURS Mon-Sat, 11am-1am; Sun, 11am-4pm.
R. Campos Carvalho, 15
TEL 3531-1526

O Garimpeiro $
This restaurant, located inside the Pousada do Garimpo inn, specializes in regional cuisine: steak with spinach-like ora-pro-nobis, feijão tropeiro (cooked beans with olive oil, garlic, onion, parsley and chive, thickened with manioc flour), fern sprouts with pork loin, and xinxim da Chica (chicken, okra, onions and seasonings). CUISINE Regional of Minas. CREDIT CARDS All. HOURS 6pm-11pm; Sat and Sun, noon-11pm.
Av. da Saudade, 265
TEL 3531-1044

Restaurante do Raimundo Sem Braço $
The regional food of Minas and charcoal barbecue are the house specialties. CUISINE Barbecue, Minas cuisine, varied. CREDIT CARDS Not accepted. HOURS Mon-Thu, 10:30am-4pm; Fri and Sat, 6pm-midnight; Sun, 10:30am-5pm.
R. José Anacleto Alves, 18, BR-367,
exit to Belo Horizonte
TEL 3531-2284

Domingos Martins – ES

AREA CODE 27 POPULATION 30,559
DISTANCE Vitória, 50 km (mi.)
SITE www.domingosmartins.com.br

HOTELS

Aroso Paço $$
This huge building with its incredible Roman columns contrasts with the beautiful mountain range landscape around it. The atmosphere is opulent and kitsch inside the building as well: Roman columns ring the pool too. The rooms are more classical and simple. Suites have whirlpool tub and fireplace. The hotel has a heliport. FACILITIES 48 rooms, air-conditioning, phone,

RESTAURANTS	$ up to R$50	$$ from R$51 up to R$100	$$$ from R$101 up to R$150	$$$$ above R$150

TV, ceiling fan, bar, football field, recreation team, heated pool, playground, tennis court, restaurant, game room, sauna. **CREDIT CARDS** Diners, MasterCard, Visa.
Rodovia BR-262, km 89, Aracê (54 km from the center of Domingos Martins)
TEL 3248-1147 **FAX** 3248-1180
www.pedraazul.com.br/aroso

Pousada dos Pinhos $$
This inn offers a good amenities for families with children. The small farm where the inn is situated has a lake and trails, and the hotel has a recreation team year round and baby-sitter services. Some rooms and chalets have a fireplace and whirlpool tubs. **FACILITIES** 38 rooms, phone, TV, ceiling fan, bar, football field, horses, recreation team, pool, heated pool, playground, football field, tennis court, restaurant, convention room, fitness room, game room, massage room, sauna. **CREDIT CARDS** MasterCard, Visa.
Rodovia BR-262, km 90, Aracê (50 km from the center of Domingos Martins)
TEL 3248-1283 **FAX** 3248-1115
www.pedraazul.com.br/pousadadospinhos

Pousada Eco da Floresta $$
This inn has a good leisure services for adults and children. It's situated in a ten-thousand-hectare area covered with Atlantic Rainforest, with a view of Pedra Azul. The suites and chalets have a fireplace and whirlpool tub. The chalets are far from the common areas and have no cable TV, which is a boon to those who seek some isolation. **FACILITIES** 88 rooms, air-conditioning, phone, TV, bar, football field, horses, recreation team, pool, heated pool, tennis court, restaurant, convention room, fitness room, game room, sauna. **CREDIT CARDS** Diners, MasterCard, Visa.
Rodovia BR-262, km 96, Aracê (62 km from the center of Domingos Martins)
TEL 3248-1196 **FAX** 3248-1198
www.ecodafloresta.com.br

Pousada Oriundi $
The facilities are simple, but this inn sits in a forest full of trails and waterfalls that invite excursions. The owner is a famous chef of the Oriundi restaurant in Vitória. Open Fri-Sun, and holidays. **FACILITIES** 12 rooms, air-conditioning, phone, TV, football field, horses, pool, playground, restaurant, game room, sauna. **CREDIT CARDS** Not accepted.
Estrada to Paraju, km 12, access off km 56 of BR-262 (31 km from the center of Domingos Martins)
TEL 3249-1018 **RESERVATIONS** 3227-6989
www.oriundi.com.br

Pousada Peterle $$
Pedra Azul, just 3 km away, is visible from this inn. Much of the charm of this inn can be credited to its rustic style. The chalets built in eucalyptus logs have a living room with fireplace, one bedroom each, and a verandah. There are also rooms built in stone. **FACILITIES** 14 rooms, fireplace, phone, TV. **CREDIT CARDS** MasterCard, Visa.
BR-262, km 88, Aracê (51 km from the center of Domingos Martins)
TEL 3248-1243 **FAX** 3248-1171
www.pousadapeterle.com.br

RESTAURANT

Italiano $
The pork-leg sausage is a popular appetizer. The restaurant also serves mouthwatering, homemade pasta with organic sauces. The garden has a small playground. **CUISINE** Italian. **CREDIT CARDS** MasterCard, Visa. **HOURS** Mon-Thu, 11am-3pm; Fri and Sat, 11am-midnight; Sun, 11am-5pm.
Av. Duque de Caxias, 16, Centro
TEL 3268-1420

SERVICES

LOCAL TOUR OPERATOR

Emoções Radicais
R. do Lazer (r. João Batista Wernersbach), 194, Centro
TEL 3268-2165. **HOURS** 8am-7pm

TOURIST INFORMATION

Casa de Cultura
R. do Lazer (r. João Batista Wernersbach), Centro
TEL 3268-1471. **HOURS** 7am-1pm

Guarapari – ES
AREA CODE 27 **POPULATION** 88,400
DISTANCE Vitória, 58 km (36 mi)
SITE www.guaraparitotal.com.br

HOTELS

Hotel Fazenda Flamboyant $$
Located near the Aquamania theme park, this hotel offers great amenities for leisure on a genuine farm. The hotel has four pools, a fitness room, orchard, animals and nautical equipment such as kayaks and jet ski. It also offers canopy tree walking. **FACILITIES** 90 rooms, air-conditioning, phone, TV, bar, football field, horses, recreation team, pool, heated pool, playground, tennis court, restaurant, convention room, game room, sauna. **CREDIT CARDS** MasterCard, Visa.
Fazenda Querência, Amarelos
TEL and **FAX** 3229-0066
www.hotelflamboyant.com.br

Porto do Sol $$
Its prime location at the end of a beach affords a view of the Praias do Morro and Muquiçaba, and also gives access to these beaches. It has a neat and ample common area. The rooms are spacious and have a verandah, but need renovation. **FACILITIES** 88 rooms, air-conditioning, phone, TV, bar, recreation team, pool, football field, tennis court, restaurant, convention room, fitness room, game room, massage room, sauna. **CREDIT CARDS** All.
Av. Beira-Mar, 1, Praia do Morro
TEL 3361-1100 **FAX** 3261-2929
www.geocities.com/portodosol

Pousada Enseada Azul $
Glass, handicrafts and artworks decorate this inn, just 300 m (1,000 feet) away from Macunã Madeira beach. The rooms are small but have a large verandah and

| PRICES | HOTELS (couple) | $ up to R$150 | $$ from R$151 up to R$300 | $$$ from R$301 up to R$500 | $$$$ above R$500 |

470
BRAZIL GUIDE

ocean view. The service is efficient. **FACILITIES** 33 rooms, air-conditioning, phone, TV, bar, pool, convention room, massage room, sauna. **CREDIT CARDS** MasterCard, Visa.
R. Alegre, 367, Nova Guarapari
TEL and **FAX** 3272-1092
www.enseadaazul.com.br

RESTAURANTS

Cantinho do Curuca $$
The décor is rustic with a sand floor in part of the restaurant. Fried shrimp (complimentary) arrive before the house specialties, *moquecas* (seafood stew with coriander and coconut milk) with rice, *pirão* (manioc meal and fish broth) and *moqueca de banana-da-terra* (plantain). **CUISINE** Regional of Espírito Santo. **CREDIT CARDS** Visa. **HOURS** Daily, 11am-10pm.
Av. Santana, 96, Praia de Meaípe
TEL 3272-1262

Gaeta $$
Very simple restaurant located on the avenue alongside the beach, beside Cantinho do Curuca. The locally devised *moqueca de banana-da-terra*, which accompanies the traditional seafood *moquecas*, is complimentary. They serve their own version of coconut pie. There are other options such as lobster au gratin and grilled shrimp. **CUISINE** Regional of Espírito Santo. **CREDIT CARDS** Diners, MasterCard, Visa. **HOURS** Daily, 11am-10pm.
Av. Santana, 45, Praia de Meaípe
TEL 3272-1202

Guaramare $$
There's no menu. You may choose from the fresh fish, shrimp, lobsters and other seafood placed on a large tray carried by the owner and chef. Your choice is then to have them charcoal-grilled or prepared in paella. Shaped like a boat, the restaurant is exquisitely decorated with gardens, a fountain and a verandah that stretches to a lagoon. Reservations required. **CUISINE** Fish and seafood. **CREDIT CARDS** Not accepted. **HOURS** Thu-Sat, 8pm-1am; Sun, noon-6pm.
Av. Meaípe, 716, Nova Guarapari
TEL 3272-1300

SERVICES

LOCAL TOUR OPERATOR

Praiatour Receptivo
Av. José Ferreira Ferro, 99, Loja 1, Praia do Morro
TEL 3361-5858/3327-6834

TOURIST INFORMATION

Secretaria de Turismo de Guarapari
R. Camilo Gianordoli, 193
TEL 3361-2322. **HOURS** noon-6pm

DIVING OPERATORS

Acquasub
R. Anísio Fernandes Coelho, 30, Loja 01, Jardim da Penha (in Vitória)
TEL 3325-0036

Atlantes
R. José Barcellos de Matos, 341, Centro
TEL 3361-0405

Guarujá – SP

AREA CODE 13 **POPULATION** 264,812
DISTANCE São Paulo, 87 km (54 mi)
SITE www.guiaguaruja.com.br

HOTEL

Casa Grande $$$
Facing busy Enseada beach, this large and comfortable colonial-style manor is the most luxurious hotel of Guarujá. It has many restaurants and a complete leisure area for children and adults. Attractions include a spa. **FACILITIES** 265 rooms, air-conditioning, phone, TV, cable TV, bar, recreation team, pool, heated pool, jogging track, playground, tennis court, restaurant, convention room, fitness room, game room, massage room, sauna, spa. **CREDIT CARDS** All.
Av. Miguel Estéfano, 1001
TEL 3389-4000
www.casagrandehotel.com

RESTAURANTS

Rufino's $$
This restaurant serves delicious seafood in a relaxed atmosphere by the beach. Be patient for service. **CUISINE** Fish and seafood. **CREDIT CARDS** Visa. **HOURS** Sun-Thu, noon-11pm; Fri and Sat, until 1am.
Av. Miguel Estéfano, 4795, Praia da Enseada
TEL 3351-5771

Thai $$
Thai cuisine is the highlight here, at the only such restaurant on this stretch of coast. The décor and the uniform of the employees are Thai-themed. It belongs to the Casa Grande Hotel. **CUISINE** Thai. **CREDIT CARDS** All. **HOURS** Tue-Sun, 7pm-midnight.
Av. Miguel Stéfano, 1001
TEL 3389-4000

SERVICES

TOURIST INFORMATION

Centro de Informações Turísticas
Av. Marechal Deodoro da Fonseca, 723, Centro
TEL 3387-7199. **HOURS** Mon-Fri, 8am-6pm; Sat and Sun, 10am-6pm

Ilha Grande – RJ

AREA CODE 24
DISTANCE Rio de Janeiro, 150 km (93 mi) to Angra dos Reis, plus 90 minutes by boat

HOTELS

Eco and Dive Resort Ilha Grande $$
Surrounded by greenery, the rooms have a spectacular view of Bananal bay. The owner gives diving class-

es. **FACILITIES** 18 rooms, air-conditioning, TV, ceiling fan, bar, kayaks, pool, restaurant, fitness room, game room, sauna. **CREDIT CARDS** MasterCard, Visa.

Costeira do Bananal
TEL 3367-2274
www.ecodiveresort.com

Pousada Sankay $$

This inn is situated on the waterfront at the foot of a hill – a great location for diving. The daily rate includes a boat excursion. Closed the first two weeks of July. **FACILITIES** 12 rooms, air-conditioning, ceiling fan, bar, playground, restaurant, fitness room, game room, sauna. **CREDIT CARDS** Visa.

Enseada do Bananal
TEL 3365-1090 **RESERVATIONS** 3365-4065
www.pousadasankay.com.br

Sagu Mini Resort $$

This resort is totally integrated with nature, with a beautiful view of Abraão bay, but also conveniently close to the town center. The rooms have no TV and are ideal for those seeking isolation. **FACILITIES** 9 rooms, air-conditioning, phone, ceiling fan, bar, restaurant, spa. **CREDIT CARDS** All.

Praia Brava, Enseada do Abraão
TEL 3361-5660 **FAX** 3361-5896
www.saguresort.com

RESTAURANTS

Lua e Mar $

This restaurant serves the best shrimp *moqueca* on the island. The atmosphere is basic, and tables are placed under a large tree. The owner serves guests, while his wife cooks. **CUISINE** Fish and seafood. **CREDIT CARDS** Diners, MasterCard, Visa. **HOURS** 11am-10pm; closes on Wed.

R. da Praia, Praia do Abraão
TEL 3361-5113

Reis e Magos $$

This charming restaurant and studio is carefully decorated in rustic style. The food and service are good. The restaurant is on the waterfront and features live MPB (Brazilian Popular Music). It has a private dock and boats to transport customers. Meals may be served in boats anchored nearby. **CUISINE** Fish and seafood. **CREDIT CARDS** Not accepted. **HOURS** Daily, from 11am.

Entrada do Saco do Céu
TEL 9258-2490/3367-2812

Ilhabela – SP

AREA CODE 12 **POPULATION** 20,836
DISTANCE São Paulo, 224 km (140 mi)

HOTELS

Mercedes $$

The building resembling a medieval castle is not part of the hotel. But the rooms are neat, and overlook the ocean or the river that crosses the estate. The pool built by the beach is its major attraction. **FACILITIES** 41 rooms, air-conditioning, phone, TV, bar, pool, rock pool,

restaurant, game room. **CREDIT CARDS** All.

Av. Leonardo Reali, 2222
TEL 3896-1071 **FAX** 3896-1074
www.hotelmercedes.com.br

Porto Pacuiba $$

The German owners of this inn provide customized service. In addition to restaurant meals, there are also homemade cakes and breads. **FACILITIES** 18 rooms, air-conditioning, phone, TV, cable TV, ceiling fan, bar, pool, restaurant, game room, massage room, sauna. **CREDIT CARDS** All.

Av. Leonardo Reale, 2392
TEL 3896-2466
www.portopacuiba.com.br

Pousada Canto da Praia $$$

This inn operates in the owner's beautiful home. Each room is uniquely decorated and the common areas (game room, pool, breakfast room) are part of the main house. Children are not allowed. **FACILITIES** 4 rooms, air-conditioning, ceiling fan, boating, pool, game room. **CREDIT CARDS** American Express, Diners, MasterCard.

Av. Força Expedicionária Brasileira, 793
TEL 3896-1194 **FAX** 3896-6415
www.cantodapraiailhabela.com.br

Pousada do Capitão $$

The inn's décor imitates the interior of a ship. The comfortable rooms look like cabins, with Egyptian cotton sheets and goose-feather pillows. **FACILITIES** 21 rooms, air-conditioning, phone, TV, bar, pool, game room, sauna. **CREDIT CARDS** All.

R. Almirante Tamandaré, 272, Praia de Itaguassu
TEL 3896-1037/2253
www.pousadadocapitao.com.br

RESTAURANTS

Deck $$

Try *casquinha de siri* (crab ragout with dende oil and coconut milk) and shrimp with tangerine sauce. Serves appetizers and drinks on the beach kiosk. **CUISINE** Varied. **CREDIT CARDS** All. **HOURS** noon-2am.

Av. Almirante Tamandaré, 805, Praia de Itaguassu
TEL 3896-1489

Free Port Café $

This sophisticated café, next to a fancy shop, serves espresso, champagne and wine, in addition to excellent pies and sweets. Live piano music on weekends. **CUISINE** Pies and coffee. **CREDIT CARDS** All. **HOURS** Mon-Fri, 11am-11:30pm; Sat and Sun, noon-12:30.

R. Dr. Carvalho, 112, Centro
TEL 3896-2237

Viana $

This restaurant is simple and very busy but its delicious dishes are worth the hassle. The beach kiosk in front of the restaurant serves appetizers and drinks. **CUISINE** Fish and seafood. **CREDIT CARDS** Not accepted. **HOURS** 1pm-11:30pm; closed Mon-Thu in the low season.

Av. Leonardo Reale, 1560, Praia do Viana
TEL 3896-1089

PRICES | **HOTELS** (couple) | **$** up to R$150 | **$$** from R$151 up to R$300 | **$$$** from R$301 up to R$500 | **$$$$** above R$500

SERVICES

TOURIST INFORMATION

Secretaria de Turismo
R. Bartolomeu de Gusmão, 140, Pequeá
TEL 3896-6737/2440. HOURS Daily, 9am-6pm

Itatiaia – RJ

AREA CODE 24 POPULATION 24,739
DISTANCE Rio de Janeiro, 175 km (109 mi); São Paulo, 250 km (155 mi)

HOTELS

Donati $$
This hotel has an attractive living room and a cave bar that serves drinks and fondue. FACILITIES 23 rooms, fireplace, TV, bar, recreation team, pool, heated pool, restaurant, sauna. CREDIT CARDS All.
Estrada do Parque Nacional, km 9.5
TEL 3352-1110 RESERVATIONS (11) 3817-4453
www.hoteldonati.com.br

Pousada Esmeralda $$
Nestled in the National Park, this inn has four types of chalets. The "de luxe" chalets have a fireplace and the "double de luxe" ones overlook the lake. You may fish for carps, go horseback riding, ride bikes, take the park trails and play volleyball. FACILITIES 14 rooms, fireplace, TV, horses, heated pool, playground, restaurant, game room, sauna. CREDIT CARDS All.
Estrada do Parque Nacional, km 4
TEL 3352-1643 FAX 3352-1769
www.pousadaesmeralda.com.br

Itaúnas – ES

AREA CODE 27
DISTANCE Vitória, 270 km (167 mi)
SITE www.guiaitaunas.com.br

HOTELS

Casarão Parque de Itaúnas $
This hotel enjoys a quiet location, amidst trees and lawns. The rooms are spacious but basic with optional air-conditioning or ceiling fan. Boiler-heated showers. FACILITIES 12 rooms, air-conditioning, TV, ceiling fan, pool, and playground. CREDIT CARDS MasterCard.
Estrada de Itaúnas, km 20
TEL and FAX 3762-5000
www.itaunas.com.br

Pousada Casa da Praia $
A fresh breeze coming from the river blows onto the common outdoor area. Rooms with a verandah or a mezzanine. No pool. FACILITIES 11 rooms, air-conditioning, TV, bar. CREDIT CARDS Not accepted.
R. Profa Deolinda Lage, Centro
TEL and FAX 3762-5028
www.casadapraiaitaunas.com.br

Pousada do Coelho $
Its leisure area is located by the river. It offers rooms and chalets, most with a mezzanine. FACILITIES 10 rooms, air-conditioning, ceiling fan, bar, pool. CREDIT CARDS MasterCard, Visa.
R. Projetada
TEL 3762-5216 FAX 3314-2537
www.pousadadocoelho.com

Pousada Garça Real $
The owners have shown flair in decorating the rooms. Open December to February, in July and on holidays. Close to the town center. FACILITIES 9 rooms, air-conditioning, TV, ceiling fan, bar, pool. CREDIT CARDS Diners, MasterCard.
R. Antenor Cabral da Silva
TEL 3762-5219 FAX 3765-2413
www.pousadagarcareal.com.br

RESTAURANT

Céu-Mar $
Very simple house with a wood-burning stove used to prepare great *bonito* with herbs and white wine, served with basil rice. CUISINE Fish and seafood. CREDIT CARDS Visa.
HOURS 11am-midnight (open December to March).
Av. Bento Daher, Centro
TEL 3762-5081 (information)

SERVICES

LOCAL TOUR OPERATOR

Casinha de Aventuras
Av. Bento Daher
TEL 3762-5081

Jacaraípe – ES

AREA CODE 27
DISTANCE Vitória, 30 km (19 mi)

RESTAURANT

Estação Primeira de Manguinhos $$
The restaurant has a large yard by the sea with tables placed under kiosks covered with native *piassava* straw. The *peixe à jardineira* is a must: muttonfish, red grouper, mero or red snapper roasted in olive oil with vegetables. As the cooking time is long, enjoy the beach while you wait. There's a train car beside the restaurant that hosts exhibits and cultural events. CUISINE Fish and seafood. CREDIT CARDS Diners, MasterCard, Visa. HOURS Tue-Sat, 8am-10pm; Sun, 8am-6pm.
Av. Atapuã, at the corner of R. Piraquira, Praia de Manguinhos
TEL 3243-2687

Linhares – ES

AREA CODE 27 POPULATION 112,617
DISTANCE Vitória, 138 km (86 mi)

HOTEL

Hotel da Reserva Natural da Vale do Rio Doce $$
Situated in an Atlantic Rainforest Natural Reserve, this

---

hotel offers plenty of comforts while giving guests the enjoyment of being inside the forest. There are cozy chalets and simpler rooms. Trekkers and bikers will love the trails in the forest. The hotel also offers a tropical orchard, a lake, a rock pool and whirlpool. **FACILITIES** 50 rooms, air-conditioning, phone, TV, cable TV, bar, football field, recreation team, pool, rock pool, playground, restaurant, convention room, game room, sauna. **CREDIT CARDS** MasterCard, Visa.
Rodovia BR-101 Norte, km 120, 30 km to the north of Linhares
TEL 3371-9797 **FAX** 3273-1277
www.cvrd.com.br/linhares

Mangaratiba – RJ

AREA CODE 21 **POPULATION** 24,901
DISTANCE Rio de Janeiro, 100 km (62 mi)

HOTELS

Club Med Rio das Pedras $$$
This luxurious resort, with complete facilities, is better for those wanting leisure-time activities than those seeking quiet and silence. The hotel was named after the beautiful river that crosses the estate. Biologists supervise trekking in the Atlantic Rainforest. **FACILITIES** 325 rooms, air-conditioning, phone, TV, cable TV, bar, football field, recreation team, pool, jogging track, tennis court, restaurant, convention room, fitness room, game room, massage room, sauna. **CREDIT CARDS** All.
Rodovia Rio–Santos, BR-101, km 445.5
TEL 2688-9191 **FAX** 2688-3333
www.clubmed.com

Portobello Resort Safari $$$$
All rooms overlook the sea and have a verandah with hammock. The 36 "beach rooms" have an exit onto the sands. Leisure activities include a photography safari where guests see zebras, deer, monkeys and many other animals. **FACILITIES** 150 rooms, air-conditioning, phone, TV, cable TV, bar, horses, recreation team, pool, rock pool, playground, football field, tennis court, restaurant, convention room, fitness room, game room, massage room, sauna, spa. **CREDIT CARDS** All.
Rodovia Rio–Santos, BR-101, km 438
TEL 2789-8000 **FAX** 2689-3011
www.hotelportobello.com.br

Niterói – RJ

AREA CODE 21 **POPULATION** 459,451
DISTANCE Rio de Janeiro, 17 km (10.5 mi)

RESTAURANT

Caneco Gelado do Mário $$
Mário, the Portuguese proprietor, has run this simple restaurant for 35 years. It seats 400 people on the ground-floor tables and counter. Located 400 meters from the Rio–Niterói bridge, the restaurant has an entrance at rua Marquês de Caxias, 49. The traditional menu includes *moqueca* (serves three) and a savory dry salty cod fritter. No reservations on Friday, the busiest day. **CUISINE** Fish and seafood; Portuguese. **CREDIT CARDS** Not accepted. **HOURS** Mon-Fri, 9am-11pm; Sat, 9am-7pm.
R. Visconde do Uruguai, 288, Loja 5, Centro
TEL 2620-6787

Ouro Preto – MG

AREA CODE 31 **POPULATION** 66,277
DISTANCE Belo Horizonte, 99 km (61.5 mi)

HOTELS

Grande Hotel de Ouro Preto $$
This no-frills hotel is a beautiful modernist construction, one of Oscar Niemeyer's early designs from the 1940's. The roof tiles ensure that the building blends in with the surrounding colonial architecture. Each suite of two adjoining rooms has a verandah with a great view of the town. The restaurant also offers a picturesque view. **FACILITIES** 36 rooms, phone, TV, bar, pool, restaurant, and convention room. **CREDIT CARDS** All.
R. das Flores, 164
TEL 3551-1488 **FAX** 3551-5028
www.hotelouropreto.com.br

Pousada do Mondego $$
This inn operates in a manor built in 1747. It's in a prime location, next to the São Francisco church, one of the most important buildings in town. The busy soapstone handicraft fair takes place in the church square. **FACILITIES** 22 rooms, phone, TV, bar, restaurant, and convention room. **CREDIT CARDS** All.
Lgo. de Coimbra, 38
TEL 3551-2040 **FAX** 3551-3094
www.mondego.com.br

Solar do Carmo $$
This inn, in a private 18th century house, has limited capacity. The owner accepts only recommended guests. **FACILITIES** 4 rooms, cable TV, massage room. **CREDIT CARDS** Not accepted.
R. Brigadeiro Mosqueira, 66
TEL and **FAX** 3552-2804 **RESERVATIONS** (21) 2282-1364

Solar Nossa Senhora do Rosário $$
Built in 1830, this house became an inn in 1994. It is located beside the Rosário church. Its French restaurant is one of the most famous in town. **FACILITIES** 46 rooms, air-conditioning, phone, cable TV, bar, pool, restaurant, convention room, fitness room, sauna. **CREDIT CARDS** All.
R. Getúlio Vargas, 270
TEL 3551-5200 **FAX** 3551-4288 **RESERVATIONS** 3227-1444
www.hotelsolardorosario.com.br

RESTAURANTS

Casa dos Contos $
This restaurant operates in former slave quarters at the rear of an 18th century house. It's decorated with antique utensils and serves a regional buffet at lunch and à la carte dinner. They serve *cachaça* that was aged on the premises. Try the fried turnovers with corn porridge and mincemeat filling. **CUISINE** Regional

PRICES	HOTELS (couple)	$ up to R$150	$$ from R$151 up to R$300	$$$ from R$301 up to R$500	$$$$ above R$500

foods of Minas. **CREDIT CARDS** All . **HOURS** Wed-Sat, 11am-10pm; Sun, Mon and Tue, 11am-5pm.
R. Camilo de Brito, 21
TEL 3551-5359

Chafariz do Paço $

This restaurant has been open for 40 years and in the last 25 the kitchen has been run by Dona Teresa. Regional dishes compose the buffet, and old photos of the owners' family adorn the walls. Open only for lunch. **CUISINE** Regional of Minas. **CREDIT CARDS** All. **HOURS** Tue-Sun, 11am-4pm
R. São José, 167
TEL 3551-2828

Le Coq d'Or $

Located in the Solar Nossa Senhora do Rosário hotel, it combines regional and French cuisine: *surubim* with chestnuts, stuffed duck. Chef Eduardo Avelar studied at Cordon Bleu, in Paris. **CUISINE** French. **CREDIT CARDS** All. **HOURS** Sun-Fri, 7pm-11pm; Sat, noon-3pm and 7pm-11pm.
R. Getúlio Vargas, 270
TEL 3551-5200

Perypatus $

It operates in the Grande Hotel de Ouro Preto. The best tables are on the verandah with a wonderful view of the historic part of the town. **CUISINE** Regional, varied. **CREDIT CARDS** All. **HOURS** Daily, noon-3pm and 7pm-10pm; in the high season, noon-10pm.
R. Senador Rocha Lagoa, 164
TEL 3551-1488

SERVICES

TOURIST INFORMATION

Centro de Informações Turísticas

Pça. Tiradentes, 41, Centro
TEL 3559-3269. **HOURS** Mon-Fri, 8am-6pm; Sat and Sun, 8am-5pm

Paraty – RJ

AREA CODE 24 **POPULATION** 29,544
DISTANCE Rio de Janeiro, 248 km (154 mi); São Paulo, 350 km (217.5 mi)

HOTELS

Pousada Arte Urquijo $$

This inn and art gallery operates in a 17th century manor. The rooms are individually decorated and have goose-feather pillows and bathrobes. Guests leave their shoes at the entrance and wear straw slippers. Many of the objects and pictures that decorate the inn are for sale. Children are not allowed. **FACILITIES** 6 rooms, air-conditioning, TV, bar, pool. **CREDIT CARDS** Diners, MasterCard, Visa.
R. Dona Geralda, 79, Centro Histórico
TEL 3371-1362
www.urquijo.com.br

Pousada da Marquesa $

Quiet and sophisticated, this 18th century manor has

antique furniture and a pool. Choose one of the rooms in the manor, as the six standard rooms located in a building across the street are less charming. **FACILITIES** 28 rooms, air-conditioning, phone, TV, bar, pool. **CREDIT CARDS** All.
R. Dona Geralda, 99, Centro Histórico
TEL 3371-1263 **FAX** 3371-1299
www.pousadamarquesa.com.br

Pousada do Ouro $$

Located in a colonial manor in the historic center, this inn is very comfortable. The rooms are set around a beautiful internal garden. **FACILITIES** 25 rooms, air-conditioning, phone, TV, bar, pool, convention room, fitness room, game room, sauna. **CREDIT CARDS** All.
R. Dr. Pereira, 145 (R. da Praia)
TEL 3371-1378 **FAX** 3371-1311
www.pousadaouro.com.br

Pousada do Sandi $$$

This charming 18th century manor is located in the busy historic center. It offers comfort and friendly service. **FACILITIES** 26 rooms, air-conditioning, phone, TV, pool, restaurant, game room, sauna. **CREDIT CARDS** All.
Lgo. do Rosário, 1
TEL 3371-2100 **RESERVATIONS** 0800232100
www.pousadadosandi.com.br

Pousada Pardieiro $$$

This manor is located in the historic center but far from the busy spots. The rooms have a view of the large garden. There is a contained area that contains macaws, and dozens of saki monkeys that live free in the trees and are used to being fed by the guests. Children under 15 are not allowed. **FACILITIES** 27 rooms, bar, pool, restaurant, sauna. **CREDIT CARDS** All.
R. do Comércio, 74, Centro Histórico
TEL 3371-1370 **FAX** 3371-1139
www.pousadapardieiro.com.br

Santa Clara $$$

Located 10 km from the city, this inn is surrounded by mountains and the Atlantic Rainforest and has a beautiful ocean view. In the rooms, decorated with light colors, you will find Brazilian fruit soaps such as Barbados cherry (*acerola*) and large-flowered cocoa (*cupuaçu*). **FACILITIES** 34 rooms, air-conditioning, phone, TV, cable TV, bar, pool, restaurant, game room, massage room, sauna. **CREDIT CARDS** Diners, MasterCard, Visa.
Rodovia Rio–Santos, km 567
TEL 3371-8900
www.santaclarahotel.com.br

RESTAURANTS

Banana da Terra $

This traditional restaurant has a relaxed atmosphere and savory dishes such as a shellfish risotto called *lambe-lambe*. They also prepare creative drinks. **CUISINE** Fish and seafood. **CREDIT CARDS** All. **HOURS** noon-midnight; closed Tue.
R. Dr. Samuel Costa, Centro Histórico
TEL 3371-1725

Hiltinho $$

Serves the best *casadinho* shrimp in the region: giant

RESTAURANTS	$ up to R$50	$$ from R$51 up to R$100	$$$ from R$101 up to R$150	$$$$ above R$150

prawns stuffed with shrimp *farofa* (manioc meal). It has a branch on the Algodão island (Fri-Sun and holidays, 11am-5pm). CUISINE Fish and seafood. CREDIT CARDS All. HOURS Daily, 11am-11pm.
R. Marechal Deodoro, 233, Centro Histórico
TEL 3371-1432/2155

Kontiki $$
This sophisticated restaurant has a boat to take customers from the Paraty dock to the island (10 min). While customers wait for their orders to arrive, they can enjoy the private beach in front of the restaurant. CUISINE Fish and seafood. CREDIT CARDS Diners, Master-Card, Visa. HOURS Daily, 9am-5:30pm; closed on Wed from February to December.
Ilha Duas Irmãs
TEL 3371-1666/6056

Le Gite d'Indaiatiba $$
Hidden in the mountains beside a beautiful waterfall, this restaurant is an hour far from the center. The crab *moqueca* (cooked in dende oil, coconut milk, onions and coriander) with palm tree hearts is worth the visit. Heliport available. CUISINE French; fish and seafood. CREDIT CARDS Not accepted. HOURS Daily, 1pm-9pm; closed in May.
Estrada para Graúna, km 4, access off km 562 in the Rio–Santos highway
TEL 3371-7174/9999-9923

Merlin o Mago $$
This restaurant has a cosy atmosphere, perfect for couples. Its French cuisine has Asian and Brazilian influence. The lobster and shrimp dishes are the highlights of the menu. CUISINE French. CREDIT CARDS Diners, MasterCard, Visa. HOURS 7pm-1am; closed on Wed.
R. do Comércio, 376, Centro Histórico
TEL 3371-2157

Refúgio $$
Very popular with couples, this restaurant has candle-lit tables. The *camarão à espanhola* (shrimps cooked in a clay pot with garlic and olive oil) is one of the menu's highlights. Reservations advised. CUISINE Fish and seafood. CREDIT CARDS Diners, MasterCard, Visa. HOURS noon-midnight.
Pça. do Porto, 1, Loja 4
TEL 3371-2447

Thai Brasil $$
The red curry with shrimp, served in a pineapple, is a favorite with diners at this Thai restaurant. The tables and chairs are decorated with amusing animal (cow, giraffe and zebra) motifs painted by the artist-owner. CUISINE Thai. CREDIT CARDS MasterCard, Visa. HOURS From 6pm until the last customer.
R. Dona Geralda, 345, Centro Histórico
TEL 3371-0127

SERVICES

TOURIST INFORMATION

Centro de Informações Turísticas
Av. Roberto Silveira, 1, Centro
TEL 3371-1897. HOURS Daily, 9am-9pm.

Penedo – RJ

AREA CODE 24
DISTANCES Rio de Janeiro, 165 km (102 mi); São Paulo, 267 km (165 mi)

HOTELS

Pequena Suécia $$
Located on a quiet street, this is the best option to stay close to the town center and still enjoy greenery. The owner, of Swedish descent, produces different types of bread, biscuits and cakes following Swedish recipes. Excellent restaurant. FACILITIES 17 rooms, air-conditioning, fireplace, phone, TV, cable TV, bar, pool, restaurant, fitness room, game room, massage room, sauna. CREDIT CARDS All.
R. Toivo Suni, 33
TEL 3351-1275/1343
www.pequenasuecia.com.br

Pousada Serra da Índia $
Perched on a mountain top 2 km from the center, this inn has a stunning view. Two chalets with whirlpool tubs and sound systems are ideal for couples. The others are scattered on the mountain and require some effort to climb steep stairs. FACILITIES 12 rooms, air-conditioning, fireplace, phone, TV, pool, restaurant, fitness room, game room, sauna. CREDIT CARDS All.
Estrada Vale do Ermitão
TEL 3351-1185 RESERVATIONS 3351-1804
www.serradaindia.com.br

RESTAURANTS

Koskenkorva $
If you've never had Finnish food before, why not try it here in Brazil? The owner, a visual artist, has decorated the exuberant garden with his own sculptures. CUISINE Finnish. CREDIT CARDS Not accepted. HOURS Daily, noon-midnight.
Estrada das Três Cachoeiras, 3955
TEL 3351-2532

Pequena Suécia $
This small, cozy restaurant operates next to the hotel described above and features music and dance performances in addition to soirees. Try the herring with potatoes, yogurt and shallots. CUISINE Swedish. CREDIT CARDS All. HOURS Daily, noon-11pm.
R. Toivo Suni, 33
TEL 3351-1275

Rei das Trutas $
In a relaxed atmosphere, it serves the best trout in the region. For entree order the trout *casquinha* (trout ragout with coconut milk and seasoning) with *caipirinha*. CUISINE Fish. CREDIT CARDS All. HOURS Daily, 11am-11pm.
Av. das Mangueiras, 69
TEL 3351-1387

Vikings $
Serves homemade-style trout in a dill-cream sauce with capers, spinach and potatoes. CUISINE Scandinavian. CREDIT CARDS Not accepted. HOURS Mon-Fri, 6pm-

PRICES	HOTELS (couple)	$ up to R$150	$$ from R$151 up to R$300	$$$ from R$301 up to R$500	$$$$ above R$500

11pm; Sat and Sun, noon-midnight.
Av. Brasil, 800
TEL 9219-1516

Zur Sonne $

This German restaurant is 15 km (9.3 mi) from Penedo, of which 4 km (2.5 mi) are on dirt road. The seasonings come all the way from Germany. The owner personally welcomes customers at the door and prepares the dishes. Children under 12 are not allowed at dinner. CUISINE German. CREDIT CARDS Not accepted. HOURS Mon-Fri, upon reservation; Sat, Sun and holidays from noon; reservations required for dinner.
Estrada da Serrinha, km 4, Serrinha de Resende
TEL 3381-7108/9258-8362

Peruíbe – SP

AREA CODE 13 POPULATION 51,451
DISTANCE São Paulo, 128 km (80 mi)
SITE www.peruibe.sp.gov.br

HOTEL

Waldhaus Hotel $

The rooms are simple, as if not to distract from the stunning view. The hotel has its own ecotourism agency, Eco Adventure. Remo, the Germanic owner, can take you to neighboring Juréia and the trail that starts in the hotel and leads to a belvedere. FACILITIES 9 rooms, TV, pool, restaurant, game room, massage room. CREDIT CARDS MasterCard.
R. Gaivota, 1201
TEL 3457-9170
www.jureiaecoadventure.com.br

RESTAURANT

A Ponte $

Decorated with fishing gear, fish and pictures of fishing boats, this is one of the most genuine restaurants of Peruíbe. It is very simple and customers are welcomed by the owner, José Carlos, a former fisherman. The stuffed mullet or swordfish with seafood risotto is recommended. CUISINE Fish and seafood. CREDIT CARDS MasterCard. HOURS Daily, noon-9pm.
R. José Veneza Monteiro, 76
TEL 3455-5444

SERVICES

LOCAL TOUR OPERATOR

Eco Adventure (canoeing, jeep rides and trekking)
Av. Central, 880, Guaraú
TEL 3457-9170/9390

Ecotur
Offers jeep and jardineira (tractor-pulled wagon) rides to beaches and waterfalls.
TEL 3455-8083

Petrópolis – RJ

AREA CODE 24 POPULATION 286,537

DISTANCE Rio de Janeiro, 65 km (40 mi)
SITE www.petropolis.rj.gov.br

HOTELS

Bomtempo Raquete and Resort $$$$

Tennis is the main attraction of this resort: there are four clay courts, one of which is roofed, in addition to squash, peddle, football and volley courts. There's a cigar shop and an ofurô tub. Couples with children are very welcome. There is a large recreation area for children with games, animals and a recreation team. FACILITIES 30 rooms, air-conditioning, fireplace, phone, cable TV, bar, football field, horses, recreation team, heated pool, playground, tennis court, restaurant, convention room, fitness room, game room, massage room. CREDIT CARDS MasterCard, Visa.
Estrada da Cachoeira, 400, Santa Mônica–Itaipava
TEL 2222-9922
www.bomtemporesort.com.br

Fazenda das Videiras $$$

Cozy chalets have skylights in the bathroom over the whirlpool tub. Children under 14 are not allowed. FACILITIES 7 rooms, fireplace, phone, TV, bar, natural pool, restaurant, game room, and sauna. CREDIT CARDS None.
Estrada Paulo Meira, 6000, access via the Araras–Vale das Videiras road
TEL 2225-8090
www.videiras.com.br

Hotel Pousada dos Pirineus $$$

The owners, Marisa and her son Bruno, provide excellent service. The chalets are semi-detached, but two of them are being renovated to provide greater privacy. The pool is heated and roofed. The generous breakfast, freshly prepared, is served until 1pm. In the basement, there are tables for meat and chocolate fondue. FACILITIES 5 rooms, fireplace, TV, ceiling fan, bar, heated pool, restaurant, game room, and sauna. CREDIT CARDS Diners, MasterCard.
R. dos Lírios, 790, access via the Bernardo Coutinho road, km 4.7
TEL 2225-1729
www.pousadapirineus.com.br

Locanda della Mimosa $$$

Six rooms are in two different buildings: three rooms overlook a pool, two overlook a garden and one overlooks a vegetable patch. When guests return from dinner they find chocolates on their pillows. The owner of this inn is a famous chef who also owns a restaurant of the same name. FACILITIES 6 rooms, air-conditioning, minibar, phone, TV, heating, ceiling fan, bar, heated pool, restaurant, game room, sauna. CREDIT CARDS Not accepted.
Al. das Mimosas, 30, Vale Florido, access off km 72 of BR-040, Araras
TEL 2233-5405
www.locanda.com.br

Parador Santarém $$$

This complete leisure complex offers great options to children. Serves homemade cheese and butter and organic vegetables. Fondue is served in the base-

ment, where there's also wine tasting. Heliport available. FACILITIES 14 rooms, air-conditioning, phone, TV, cable TV, bar, mini-golf course, horses, pool, jogging track, playground, football court, tennis court, restaurant, convention room, fitness room, game room, massage room, sauna. CREDIT CARDS All.
Estrada Correia da Veiga, 96, Santa Mônica–Itaipava
TEL 2222-9933
www.paradorsantarem.com.br

Pousada da Alcobaça $$$
Once the summer house of the owner's grandfather, this inn has since been renovated. The ventilation system distributes air heated by the main hall's fireplace to the rooms. Beautiful gardens surround the building. FACILITIES 10 rooms, air-conditioning, phone, TV, bar, pool, tennis court, restaurant and sauna. CREDIT CARDS American Express, MasterCard, Visa.
R. Dr. Agostinho Goulão, 298, Correas
TEL 2221-1240 FAX 2229-3162
www.pousadadaalcobaca.com.br

Pousada das Araras $$$
This 15-hectare estate is at the foot of the Maria Comprida rock. There are internal trails across the Atlantic Rainforest, and two pools, one with natural and the other with treated water. The chalets are fitted with whirlpool tubs. FACILITIES 24 rooms, fireplace, phone, TV, bar, rock pool, heated pool, restaurant, convention room, game room, massage room, sauna. CREDIT CARDS MasterCard.
Estrada Bernardo Coutinho, 4570, Araras–Vale das Videiras road
TEL 2225-0555
www.pousadadasararas.com.br

Pousada das Flores $$$
This Inn of Flowers is worthy of its name. The garden has some 300 species of plants and flowers, especially hydrangeas, sunflowers and orchids. The rooms are for couples only. The inn is distant from the town, which is great if you're looking to relax in isolation. There are bathtubs in three chalets and in three suites. FACILITIES 19 rooms, air-conditioning, phone, TV, ceiling fan, bar, recreation team, pool, tennis court, restaurant, convention room, game room, sauna. CREDIT CARDS Diners, MasterCard, Visa.
Estrada União–Indústria, 34750, Posse
TEL 2259-1546
www.pousadadasflores.com.br

Pousada Tambo los Incas $$$
Tambo means "hut" or "inn" in the native language Quechuan. Objects such as a collection of pre-Colombian ceramics and Latin American handicrafts decorate the house. There are two suites fitted with whirlpool tubs and one fitted with an ofurô tub. The inn has an on-site delicatessen and a wine cellar with 400 labels. Children under 12 are not permitted. FACILITIES 9 rooms, fireplace, phone, TV, bar, heated pool, restaurant, convention room, fitness room, game room, sauna. CREDIT CARDS All.
Estrada Ministro Salgado Filho, 2761, Vale do Cuiabá
TEL 2222-5666 FAX 2222-5668
www.tambolosincas.com.br

Tankamana $$$$
Details make the difference here: all chalets have heated towel racks, king-size beds, fireplaces, cable TV and video players. Archery and horseback riding instructors are available at no extra cost. The inn's restaurant specializes in trout. FACILITIES 16 rooms, fireplace, phone, TV, ceiling fan, bar, horses, pool, rock pool, restaurant, game room, sauna. CREDIT CARDS All.
Estrada Júlio Capúa, Vale do Cuiabá–Itaipava
TEL 2222-9182 FAX 2222-9181 RESERVATIONS 2222-9183
www.tankamana.com.br

RESTAURANTS

Alvorada $
"Peking" spring chicken and delicious, crispy, sun-dried meat with battered onions, pumpkin and roasted banana are prepared in a wood-burning stove. A creek crosses the garden, making the atmosphere bucolic and pleasant. CUISINE Varied. CREDIT CARDS All. HOURS Fri-Sun, 1pm-midnight; closed Mon-Thu.
Estrada Bernardo Coutinho, 1655
TEL 2225-1118

Chico Veríssimo $$
Serves trout, *escargots*, boar ribs, pâtés and salads carefully prepared by chef Christina Heilborn. The backdrop to this quality cuisine is the atmosphere created by the sound of a nearby waterfall and the gurgling of a river. CUISINE Contemporary. CREDIT CARDS All. HOURS Wed-Sat, 1pm until the last customer; Sun, 1pm-7pm.
R. Agostinho Goulão, 632, Correas
TEL 2221-3049

Clube do Filé $$
Located in an old farm and surrounded by a beautiful garden with a fountain, this restaurant offers a variety of fish, beef, and chicken fillets prepared in different manners and with classical sauces. There is an adjoining Expand wine import shop. CREDIT CARDS Not accepted. HOURS Thu, noon-4pm; Fri and Sat, 1pm-6pm and 8pm-midnight; Sun, 1pm-6pm.
Estrada União–Indústria, 9153
TEL 2222-8891

Fazenda das Videiras $$$
The inn has two dining rooms, one with a fireplace and the other with a gorgeous view of the mountains. The dishes are prepared in a wood-burning stove. Reservations advised. On Friday evenings try the cheese, meat or chocolate fondue with one of the more than 200 wine labels available. CUISINE French. CREDIT CARDS Not accepted. HOURS Fri, 9pm-11pm; Sat, 1pm-4pm and 9pm-11pm; Sun, 1pm-4pm.
Estrada Paulo Meira, 6000, Vale das Videiras
TEL 2225-8090

Granum Salis $$
This restaurant is surrounded by a beautiful garden and has an adjoining art gallery. The antique china and the glass sculptures add a sophisticated touch to the atmosphere and are a perfect backdrop to the exquisite recipes. Don't miss the cream cheese foam with walnut dust and the spinach gnocchi with butter and crispy sage. CUISINE Contemporary. CREDIT CARDS

PRICES	HOTELS (couple)	$ up to R$150	$$ from R$151 up to R$300	$$$ from R$301 up to R$500	$$$$ above R$500

Not accepted. **HOURS** Fri and Sat, from 10am until the last customer; Sun, 10am-5pm.
Estrada Bernardo Coutinho, 3575, Araras
TEL 2225-0516/2247-7574

Locanda della Mimosa $$$

Award-winning chef Danio Braga is one of the most renowned chefs of Rio de Janeiro. His name draws many gourmets to Locanda, and he has one of the best wine cellars of Brazil. The seasonings produced in a private garden add a special touch to their contemporary Italian dishes. **CUISINE** Italian. **CREDIT CARDS** Not accepted. **HOURS** Thu, 8pm-11:30pm; Fri and Sat, 12:30-3:30pm and 8pm-11:30pm; Sun 12:30-3:30pm and 7pm-11pm.
Al. das Mimosas, 30, Vale Florido
TEL 2233-5405

Parador Valencia $$

Spanish cuisine, featuring spectacular paellas and squids filled with black rice. Chef Paquito lives in the house where the restaurant operates. His paintings, sculptures and personal furniture decorate the place. **CUISINE** Spanish. **CREDIT CARDS** All. **HOURS** Fri and Sat, noon-11pm; Sun, noon-6pm.
R. Servidão Celita de O. Amaral, 189, Estrada União–Indústria, 11389
TEL 2222-1250

Parrô do Valentim $$

Since the late 1970's, this has been the place for genuine Portuguese cuisine. The restaurant is run by Guilhermina and Valentim. *Toucinhos do céu* (convent sweets), cod fish and charcoal grilled sardines are the highlights, accompanied by Portuguese wine. Take some of the delicious sweets home from the adjoining shop. **CUISINE** Portuguese. **CREDIT CARDS** MasterCard, Visa. **HOURS** Tue-Thu, and Sun, 11:30am-10pm; Fri and Sat, 11:30am-midnight.
Estrada União–Indústria, 10289, Itaipava
TEL 2222-1281

Pousada da Alcobaça $

The cozy restaurant at this inn has only six tables, but even non-guests may walk in and enjoy the colonial-style breakfast. The traditional Saturday *feijoada* (beans stewed with sun-dried meat, smoked pork and sausages) and trout with delicate sauces are menu highlights. Reservations advised. **CUISINE** Varied. **CREDIT CARDS** Not accepted. **HOURS** Daily, 8am-noon and 1:30pm-10pm.
R. Dr. Agostinho Goulão, 298, Correas
TEL 2221-1240

SERVICES

LOCAL TOUR OPERATOR

Campos de Aventuras Paraíso Açu

Estrada do Bonfim, 3511, Correas
TEL 2221-3999

Haras Analu (horse breeding farm)

Estrada Ministro Salgado Filho, 5230, Vale do Cuiabá, Itaipava
TEL 2222-9666/2527-1044

Haras Fazenda do Moinho (horse breeding farm)

Estrada do Moinho, Vale do Cuiabá
TEL 2222-9599

Rios Brasileiros Rafting

R. Silva Jardimi, 514/104, Centro
TEL 2243-4372/9811-6523

TOURIST INFORMATION

Casa do Barão de Mauá

Pça. da Confluência, 3, Centro
HOURS Mon-Sat, 9am-6:30pm; Sun, 9am-5pm.

Centro Histórico

Pça. dos Expedicionários, next to the Museu Imperial (Imperial Museum)
HOURS 9am-6pm.

Disque Turismo

TEL 0800241516/2246-9377
HOURS Mon and Tue, 9am-6:30pm; Wed-Sat, 9am-8pm; Sun, 9am-4pm.

Pórtico da Quitandinha

Av. Ayrton Senna
HOURS 8am-7pm.

Rio de Janeiro – RJ

AREA CODE 21 **POPULATION** 5,857,904
SITE www.rio.rj.gov.br

HOTELS

Caesar Park $$$$

Considered the most luxurious hotel in Ipanema, the Caesar's prime location facing Posto 9 puts it at the center of the bustle of this famous beach. It is also close to the best shops and restaurants. While most rooms have wonderful views of the beach, the view from the top floor and from the gym is breathtaking. **FACILITIES** 226 rooms, air-conditioning, phone, TV, cable TV, bar, pool, restaurant, convention room, fitness room, massage room, sauna. **CREDIT CARDS** All.
Av. Vieira Souto, 460, Ipanema
TEL 2525-2525 **FAX** 2521-6000 **RESERVATIONS** 2525-2500
www.caesar-park.com

Copacabana Palace $$$$

Orson Welles got involved in some steamy scandals at this hotel, famous for attracting interesting people from places like Hollywood. The octogenarian building has been declared a historical heritage site. Have a *caipirinha* by the pool and see why it is considered a gem. The rooms are spacious and the original furniture is well maintained. Cipriani, the on-site restaurant run by chef Francesco Carli, is one of the best dining spots in town. The Copacabana Palace is guaranteed glamour. **FACILITIES** 216 rooms, air-conditioning, phone, TV, cable TV, bar, pool, tennis court, restaurant, convention room, fitness room, massage room. **CREDIT CARDS** All.
Av. Atlântica, 1702, Copacabana

RESTAURANTS $ up to R$50 $$ from R$51 up to R$100 $$$ from R$101 up to R$150 $$$$ above R$150

TEL 2548-7070 FAX 2235-7330
www.copacabanapalace.com.br

JW Marriott $$$$
Located by Copacabana beach, this hotel opened in 2001. Some rooms overlook the patio, so ask for one with a view. Chairs, parasols, and towels are available to beach-bound guests. FACILITIES 245 rooms, air-conditioning, phone, TV, cable TV, bar, pool, restaurant, convention room, fitness room, massage room, sauna. CREDIT CARDS All.
Av. Atlântica, 2600, Copacabana
TEL 2545-6500 FAX 2545-6555
www.marriottbrasil.com

Lancaster $$$
The charming building – and the current hotel – dates back to the 1940's and has spacious rooms with large verandahs, but needs renovation. The "de luxe" rooms are in better condition and overlook the beach. FACILITIES 69 rooms, air-conditioning, phone, TV, restaurant. CREDIT CARDS All.
Av. Atlântica, 1470, Copacabana
TEL 2543-8300

Le Meridien $$$$
One of the tallest buildings of Rio, this hotel has an award-winning restaurant on the 37th floor, with a breathtaking view. On New Year's Eve, a firework cascade falls from the top floor down the façade, and is one of the highlights of New Year's celebrations. The hotel was renovated in 2000 and has a good facilities for conventions, business travelers and leisure travelers. FACILITIES 496 rooms, air-conditioning, phone, TV, cable TV, bar, pool, restaurant, fitness room, sauna. CREDIT CARDS All.
Av. Atlântica, 1020, Leme
TEL 3873-8850/0800257171 FAX 3873-8777
www.meridien-br.com

Marina All Suites $$$$
Located by Leblon beach, this hotel has good facilities and 38 suites with ocean view. Eight of these are "design suites" that were designed by well-regarded interior designers and architects. FACILITIES 38 rooms, air-conditioning, phone, TV, cable TV, pool on the penthouse floor, restaurant, fitness center, fitness room, massage room, video room, sauna. CREDIT CARDS All.
Av. Delfim Moreira, 696, Leblon
TEL 2172-1100 RESERVATIONS 2172-1101
www.marinaallsuites.com.br

Ouro Verde Hotel $$$
Built for the 1950 World Cup games, this hotel still has a 1950's vintage charm, and 1950's furniture. It's less suitable for the ones who expect modern facilities. Ask for a room with a verandah and a view of Copacabana beach. FACILITIES 61 rooms, air-conditioning, phone, TV, bar, restaurant, convention room. CREDIT CARDS All.
Av. Atlântica, 1456, Copacabana
TEL 2543-4123 FAX 2543-4776

Sheraton Barra $$$$
This hotel, opened in 2003, is the best in Barra da Tijuca. The wide building has fifteen floors and many corridors. The rooms are well equipped, some with microwave ovens and stereo system. Offers a good services for business travelers. FACILITIES 292 rooms, air-conditioning, phone, TV, cable TV, bar, recreation team, pool, playground, restaurant, convention room, fitness room, massage room, sauna, spa. CREDIT CARDS All.
Av. Lúcio Costa (Sernambetiba), 3150, Barra da Tijuca
TEL 3139-8000
www.sheraton.com/barra

Sheraton Rio Hotel and Towers $$$$
This huge hotel has a nice private beach, but it's rather distant from other tourist attractions. The whole leisure infrastructure is excellent, from the pool to the gym. In the bar by the pool there's a sushi bar. The view of the Cagarras islands and the Leblon and Ipanema coastlines is gorgeous. FACILITIES 559 rooms, air-conditioning, phone, TV, bar, recreation team, heated pool, tennis court, restaurant, convention room, fitness room, game room, massage room, sauna. CREDIT CARDS All.
Av. Niemeyer, 121, São Conrado
TEL 2274-1122 RESERVATIONS 2239-1173
www.sheraton-rio.com

Sofitel Rio de Janeiro $$$
Located between Copacabana and Ipanema, this hotel operates in a building that used to belong to the traditional Rio Palace. The afternoon tea, served in the halls overlooking Copacabana beach, is a tradition that dates back to the 1940's, and it still offers the same great beach view. FACILITIES 388 rooms, air-conditioning, phone, TV, bar, recreation team, heated pool, tennis court, restaurant, convention room, fitness room, game room, massage room, sauna. CREDIT CARDS All.
Av. Atlântica, 4240, Copacabana
TEL 2525-1232 FAX 2525-1230

RESTAURANTS

Adega do Pimenta $
This restaurant, with rustic décor, has been operating for 20 years in the bohemian district of Santa Teresa. It specializes in popular German delicacies such as pork knuckle (eisbein) with sauerkraut. Dishes serve two. Reservations advised. It has branches in Leblon, Barra and in the city of Itaipava. CUISINE German. CREDIT CARDS MasterCard, Visa. HOURS Mon and Wed-Fri, 11:30am-10pm; Sat, 11:30am-8pm; Sun, 11:30am-6pm.
R. Almirante Alexandrino, 296, Santa Teresa
TEL 2224-7554

Adega do Valentim $$
This is a traditional Portuguese restaurant, with abundant servings for two. Widow Neide de Souza has run the business since the death of her husband, Commander Valentim. CUISINE Portuguese. CREDIT CARDS All. HOURS Daily, noon-1am.
R. da Passagem, 178, Botafogo
TEL 2541-1166

Adegão Português $$$
This traditional restaurant in the northern region of Rio is serious about cod fish. The menu has a myriad of cod fish dishes. Servings are very generous. CUISINE Portuguese. CREDIT CARDS All. HOURS Mon-Sat, 11:30am-

PRICES	HOTELS (couple)	$ up to R$150	$$ from R$151 up to R$300	$$$ from R$301 up to R$500	$$$$ above R$500

11:30pm; Sun, 11:30am-8pm.
Campo de São Cristóvão, 212, São Cristóvão
TEL 2580-7288/8689

Alda Maria Doces Portugueses $

Alda Maria sells, in her own house, sweets made from the recipes of her Portuguese grandmother. Popular choices are *pastel de nata* (custard tart), *toucinho do céu* and *bem-casado* (convent sweets). The entrance of the house, decorated with blue-and-white ceramic tiles, resembles Portuguese buildings. CUISINE Portuguese pastries. CREDIT CARDS Not accepted. HOURS Mon-Fri, with appointment; Sat and Sun, 2pm-7pm.
R. Almirante Alexandrino, 1116, Santa Teresa
TEL 2232-1320

Alessandro and Frederico Café $

Choose a table on the large verandah to enjoy the bold sandwiches which mix apricot and Parma ham, cheddar cheese and sausage. CUISINE Sandwiches. CREDIT CARDS All. HOURS Daily, 9am-1am.
R. Garcia d'Ávila, 134, Ipanema
TEL 2521-0828

Alfaia $$

This small Copacabana restaurant's most famous dish is *bacalhau à patuscada*. That combination of cod fish, boiled potatoes, broccoli, eggs, garlic and lots of olive oil serves one or two. Another good choice is octopus *à moda*, which follows the house style – and contains no ice cream! For dessert, try the delicious *pastel de nata* (custard tart). CUISINE Portuguese. CREDIT CARDS All. HOURS Daily, 11am-midnight.
R. Inhangá, 30, Loja B, Copacabana
TEL 2236-1222

Amarelinho $

This bar has attracted Rio's bohemian set for more than 80 years. That history rather than the quality of its food accounts for its fame.
CUISINE Brazilian. CREDIT CARDS All. HOURS Daily, 11am-midnight.
Pça. Floriano, 55, Cinelândia
TEL 2240-8434

A Marisqueira $$

This traditional seafood restaurant has welcomed the former president of Portugal, Mário Soares, who tried the cod fish dish by the same name. The dish however was not named in his honor, but after the two owners, Mario and Soares. The second most popular choice is *Zé do Pipo* cod fish. CUISINE Portuguese. CREDIT CARDS All. HOURS Daily, 11am-midnight.
R. Barata Ribeiro, 232, Copacabana
TEL 2547-3920

Antiquarius $$

Located close to Leblon beach, this restaurant is one of the best in town. The waiting room is in the mezzanine, where an antique shop operates. Serves delicious Portuguese dishes with several cod fish options. CUISINE Portuguese. CREDIT CARDS Diners, MasterCard. HOURS Daily, noon-2am.
R. Aristides Espíndola, 19, Leblon
TEL 2294-1049/1496

Aprazível $$

With a unique view of the city, outdoor tables and Brazilian dishes prepared by chef Ana Castilho, this restaurant is a Rio institution. CUISINE Brazilian, Contemporary. CREDIT CARDS All. HOURS June through August: Thu-Sun, noon-6pm; rest of the year: Thu, 8pm-midnight; Fri and Sat, noon-midnight; Sun and holidays, 1pm-7pm.
R. Aprazível, 62, Santa Teresa
TEL 2508-9174/3852-4935

Azul Marinho $$

This restaurant has a great view of Ipanema and Arpoador beaches, and features seafood dishes from all over Brazil. Suggestions: mixed shrimp and fish *moqueca*. CUISINE Fish and seafood. CREDIT CARDS All. HOURS From noon until the last customer.
Av. Francisco Bhering, Arpoador
TEL 2513-5014

B! $

This trendy restaurant operates in the mezzanine of a bookstore, Livraria da Travessa, in Ipanema, and has a short menu. It is frequented by artists and intellectuals. CUISINE Contemporary. CREDIT CARDS All. HOURS Tue-Sat, 9am-11pm; Sun and Mon, noon-11pm.
R. Visconde de Pirajá, 572, Ipanema
TEL 2249-4977

Balada Sumos $

This traditional fruit juice shop has been serving up tasty beverages at its counter for 30 years. There are combinations for all tastes, such as orange juice with eggplant and passion fruit with vanilla ice cream. CUISINE Sandwiches. CREDIT CARDS Not accepted. HOURS Sun-Thu, 7am-2am; Fri and Sat, 7am-3am.
Av. Ataulfo de Paiva, 620, Loja B, Leblon
TEL 2239-2699

Belmonte $

The bar has been operating in the district of Flamengo since 1952. It serves finger foods, including its specialty, the turnover with sun-dried meat filling. There are over 30 labels of *cachaça* on offer from the state of Minas Gerais. The bar has branches in Ipanema and Leblon. CUISINE Bar. CREDIT CARDS Not accepted. HOURS Daily, 7am-3am.
Praia do Flamengo, 300
TEL 2552-3349

Bip Bip $

Although very small, this bar draws a huge number of people thanks to the *rodas de samba* (samba jam session). First-class artists such as Walter Alfaiate and Nelson Sargento have been known to show on Sundays. On Mondays it features *chorinho* and on Wednesdays, *bossa nova*. Once in a while a famous "friend" shows up and performs. CUISINE Finger food. CREDIT CARDS Not accepted. HOURS Daily, 7pm-1am.
R. Almirante Gonçalves, 50-D, Copacabana
TEL 2267-9696

Bira $$$

This restaurant has been situated here above Marambaia Spit for 14 years. It offers different types of two-

| RESTAURANTS | $ up to R$50 | $$ from R$51 up to R$100 | $$$ from R$101 up to R$150 | $$$$ above R$150 |

person *moquecas* in addition to fresh fish and seafood. The most popular choice is snook fillet with lemon and shrimp rice. **CUISINE** Fish and seafood **CREDIT CARDS** Not accepted. **HOURS** Thu and Fri, noon-6pm; Sat and Sun, noon-8pm.
Estrada da Vendinha, 68, Barra de Guaratiba
TEL 2410-8304

Bar Brasil $

This *boteco* (bar) is one of the most famous in Rio and dates back nearly a century. It operates in an old, high-ceilinged manor that's very airy, in the district of Lapa. Notice the draft beer keg, in bronze. German dishes are the highlights of the menu: pork knuckle, veal and smoked ribs. **CUISINE** German. **CREDIT CARDS** Diners, MasterCard, Visa. **HOURS** Mon-Fri, 11:30am-11pm; Sat, 11:30am-4pm.
Av. Mem de Sá, 90, Centro
TEL 2509-5943

Bar Devassa $

The main attractions at this bar are the four varieties of homebrewed *chope* (draft beer): blonde, red-headed, black and mulatto. True to its name, the last is a blend of the other three. To eat, try the croquette. **CUISINE** Bar. **CREDIT CARDS** American Express, MasterCard. **HOURS** Mon-Thu, 6pm-1am; Fri, 6pm-3am; Sat, Sun and holidays, 2pm-2am.
R. General San Martin, 1241, Leblon
TEL 2540-6087

Bar do Arnaudo $

This restaurant grew out of an older bar established 33 years ago. Today, it's a point of reference for Brazilian Northeastern cuisine in Rio. Chef Arnaudo is the only one the kitchen has seen, and the staff and facilities have been unchanged for decades. **CUISINE** Regional from the Northeast. **CREDIT CARDS** Not accepted. **HOURS** Tue-Fri, noon-11pm; Sat and Sun, noon-8pm.
R. Almirante Alexandrino, 316-B, Santa Teresa
TEL 2252-7246

Bar do Zé $

One of this theme bar's owners, José "Zé" Antônio Esteves, decided to pay tribute to his namesakes, and has placed illustrations and pictures of anonymous or famous "Zés," such as José Sarney (a former president of Brazil) and São José (Saint Joseph). The menu has plenty of dishes named after one José or another. The most popular is *picadinho* (chopped meat) *do Zé Antônio*. The atmosphere is very relaxed especially on Wednesdays, Thursdays and Fridays from 6:30pm on, when the samba performances start. **CUISINE** Brazilian. **CREDIT CARDS** All. **HOURS** Mon-Fri, from noon until late.
R. do Carmo, 38, Centro
TEL 2517-3586

Bar Lagoa $

The beautiful art deco styling of this bar, with its high ceiling, dates back to the 1930's. It has a roofed balcony with a view of the Rodrigo de Freitas lagoon. The menu features German dishes such as pork knuckle and sausages. **CUISINE** German. **CREDIT CARDS** All. **HOURS** Mon, 6pm-2am; Tue-Sun, noon-2am.

Av. Epitácio Pessoa, 1674, Lagoa
TEL 2523-1135

Bar Luiz $

This bar, one of the best in town, serves famous *chope* (draft beer). It opened in 1887, but moved to the current address in 1927. The decor and the architecture take customers back to the Rio of old. It serves dishes such as pork and veal sausages. **CUISINE** German. **CREDIT CARDS** All. **HOURS** Mon-Sat, 11am-11:30pm; Sun 11am-5pm.
R. da Carioca, 39, Centro
TEL 2262-6900

Bar e Restaurant Urca $

This small bar, decorated with sea motifs, is the most traditional in Urca. It serves fresh fish bought from local fishermen. **CUISINE** Fish and seafood. **CREDIT CARDS** Diners, MasterCard, Visa. **HOURS** Sun-Tue, 11am-5pm; Wed-Sat, 11am-11pm.
R. Cândido Gaffrée, 205, Urca
TEL 2295-8744

Bofetada $

This bar draws a gay clientele. On the menu, in addition to the creamy *chope* (draft beer), there's a wide variety of *caipirinhas* (fruit with *cachaça*, ice and sugar): lime, Mexican lime, pineapple, grape, tangerine, passion fruit, kiwi, mango and strawberry. For an appetizer, sun-dried meat ragout is popular for good reason. **CUISINE** Bar. **CREDIT CARDS** All. **HOURS** Daily, from 8am.
R. Farme de Amoedo, 87, Loja A, Ipanema
TEL 2227-1675

Bracarense $

This busy bar in Leblon has plastic tables on the sidewalk. The place has earned a reputation in the last 30 years for its cold and well-poured *chope* (draft beer), which goes well with dried cod fish or shrimp fritters. **CREDIT CARDS** Not accepted. **HOURS** Mon-Sat, 7am-midnight; Sun, 9:30am-10pm.
R. José Linhares, 85-B, Leblon
TEL 2294-3549

Cais da Ribeira $$

The restaurant operates in the Pestana Rio hotel, on Av. Atlântica. A new menu features Portuguese dishes by chef Leonel Pereira, who works for the Pestana chain, and includes more sophisticated options. The servings are smaller than those offered by many similar restaurants. **CUISINE** Portuguese. **CREDIT CARDS** All. **HOURS** Daily, 6am-10:30am, noon-3pm and 7:30pm-11:30pm.
Av. Atlântica, 2964, Copacabana
TEL 2548-6332

Cais do Oriente $

This great restaurant was built with the demolition materials of two abandoned houses and is decorated with wood carvings and rattan furniture. Fish and seafood are the highlights of the menu. On the second floor there's a piano bar with jazz, MPB (Brazilian Popular Music) and *bossa nova* performances on Friday and Saturday evenings. **CUISINE** Mediterranean; Asian. **CREDIT CARDS** All. **HOURS** Sun and Mon, noon-4pm; Tue-Sat, noon-midnight.

PRICES	HOTELS (couple)	$ up to R$150	$$ from R$151 up to R$300	$$$ from R$301 up to R$500	$$$$ above R$500

R. Visconde de Itaboraí, 8, Centro
TEL 2233-2531/2203-0178

Capricciosa $

Although Italian cuisine is traditionally stronger in São Paulo, inhabitants of Rio love to say that the best Brazilian pizza is made here in their hometown. Test their claim for yourself with any of 32 options. Capricciosa has three branches, but the Ipanema one is oldest and most famous. CUISINE Pizza. CREDIT CARDS All. HOURS Daily, 6pm-2am.
R. Vinicius de Moraes, 134, Ipanema
TEL 2523-3394

Carême Bistrô $

This bistro run by chef Flávia Quaresma now offers pasta prepared by young Italian chef Nelo Garaventa. The simple, charming place calls itself a "bistro with a carioca (native of Rio) accent." The menu changes every three months. CUISINE French. CREDIT CARDS All. HOURS Tue-Sat, 8pm-midnight.
R. Visconde de Caravelas, 113-D, Botafogo
TEL 2537-2274/2226-0085

Carioca da Gema $

In the hubbub of the nightlife of Lapa, this bar features samba performances every evening from 9pm, and customers are always dancing by last call. Great singers such as Monarco, Teresa Cristina and Noca da Portela perform here. CUISINE Brazilian. CREDIT CARDS Not accepted. HOURS Mon-Fri, from 6pm on; Sat, from 9pm on.
Av. Mem de Sá, 79, Lapa
TEL 2221-0043

Carlota $

This is the Rio branch of the original restaurante Carlota of São Paulo, run by chef Carla Pernambuco. It's one of the most charming streets of Leblon, close to other top-notch restaurants and many bookstores. CUISINE Contemporary. CREDIT CARDS All. HOURS Mon-Thu, 7pm-12:30am; Fri, 7pm-1am; Sat, 1pm-5:30pm and 7pm-1am; Sun, 1pm-6pm.
R. Dias Ferreira, 64, Leblon
TEL 2540-6821

Casa Cavé $

Specialized in Portuguese sweets, it is famous for making the best pastel de nata (custard tart) of Brazil. Since 1860 customers have flocked to this small house to buy toucinhos do céu and dom-rodrigos (convent sweets), millefoglie (crisp puff pastry with layers of cream) and others. CUISINE Portuguese. CREDIT CARDS Not accepted. HOURS Mon-Fri, 9am-7pm; Sat, 9am-1pm.
R. Sete de Setembro, 137, Centro
TEL 2221-0533/2222-2358

Casa da Feijoada $

Located near Ipanema beach, this restaurant has been serving one of the best feijoadas in town for over 15 years. Choose the types of meat you want in the feijoada. There is a wide variety of lovingly prepared cachaças, the perfect drink to accompany feijoada. CUISINE Brazilian. CREDIT CARDS All. HOURS Daily, noon-midnight.
R. Prudente de Moraes, 10-B, Ipanema
TEL 2247-2776/2523-4994

Celeiro $$

Soups, a variety of breads, and 30 salad options are part of the menu. There's also a wide variety of meat dishes, pasta and quiches. Everything is surprisingly good, which explains the long waiting lines. CREDIT CARDS All. HOURS Mon-Sat, 10am-6pm.
R. Dias Ferreira, 199, Leblon
TEL 2274-7843

Cervantes $

Open throughout the night, this restaurant serves great sandwiches and chope (draft beer) to attract bohemians and night owls. It has been in business for 50 years and has an amazing "assembly line": even the most complicated sandwiches are swiftly prepared with quality much superior to that of a fast food chain. CUISINE Sandwiches, Varied. CREDIT CARDS Visa. HOURS Tue-Thu and Sun, noon-4am; Fri and Sat, noon-6am.
Av. Prado Júnior, 335, Copacabana
TEL 2275-6147

Cipriani $$$

Renowned chef Francesco Carli runs this Copacabana Palace restaurant. The ambience is refined and the menu changes frequently but is always excellent. One of its highlights is the view of the famous pergola of the hotel's pool. CUISINE Italian. CREDIT CARDS All. HOURS Mon-Thu and Sun, 12:30pm-3pm and 7pm-midnight; Fri and Sat, 12:30pm-3pm and 7pm-1am.
Av. Atlântica, 1702, Copacabana
TEL 2548-7070

Comuna do Semente $

This small bar, at the foot of the Lapa arches, is a hangout of musicians such as Yamandú Costa and Nicolas Kraffik, and has jam sessions of choro and instrumental Brazilian music on Thursdays, and roda de samba (samba jam session) on Sundays. It offers only one brand of beer: Itaipava, produced in the interior of the state of Rio de Janeiro. CUISINE Sandwiches and cold cuts. CREDIT CARDS Not accepted. HOURS Thu, from 9pm on; Sun, 5pm-11pm.
R. Joaquim Silva, 138, Lapa
TEL 2509-3591

Confeitaria Colombo $

This tea house has become the most important icon of the belle époque in Rio since it opened in 1894. It still has its original Belgian mirrors, French stained glass windows, Carrara marble and Portuguese flooring. It's on Rua Gonçalves Dias, which was one of the busiest of Rio at the turn of the 20th century. Its afternoon tea is a tradition in Rio. CUISINE Sandwiches, varied. CREDIT CARDS All. HOURS Mon-Fri, 8am-8pm; Sat, 8am-5pm.
R. Gonçalves Dias, 32, Centro
TEL 2232-2300

D'Amici $$

The four owners, all from state of Ceará, take turns to ensure the efficient service that has earned the restaurant a good reputation. One of them, Valmir Pereira, is steward of the 500-label wine cellar. The durum wheat (grano duro) pasta is homemade. CUISINE

Italian. **CREDIT CARDS** All. **HOURS** Daily, noon-1am.
R. Antônio Vieira, 18-B, Leme
TEL 2541-4477/2543-1303

Da Brambini $$
This little and charming *trattoria* is almost hidden in one of the ends of the Leme beach. The menu was inspired by the cuisine of Crema, a town in the Italian region of Lombardia, where the family owns another restaurant. The owner, Gilberto Brambini, partly owns Gibo and La Forneria. **CUISINE** Italian. **CREDIT CARDS** All. **HOURS** Daily, noon-1am.
Av. Atlântica, 514-B, Leme
TEL 2275-4346/2542-8357

Degrau $
This very casual restaurant is ideal for hungry beach-goers coming straight from the sands. If you have no shirt, the restaurant will slap one on your back. How's that for service? It serves the most delicious turnovers of Rio, with meat, cheese or shrimp fillings. **CUISINE** Varied. **CREDIT CARDS** All. **HOURS** 11am-1am.
Av. Ataulfo de Paiva, 517-B, Leblon
TEL 2259-3648/2259-2842

Enotria $$
The original restaurant opened in Copacabana, but the one in the Barra Shopping mall is the only one still open. The clientele consists mostly of businessmen. It offers good quality Italian food. **CUISINE** Italian. **CREDIT CARDS** All. **HOURS** Daily, noon-4pm and 7pm-11pm.
Av. das Américas, 4666, Loja 129-B (Barra Shopping Expansão), Barra da Tijuca
TEL 2431-9119

Esplanada Grill $$
This Rio branch of the original São Paulo restaurant opened 17 years ago. Unlike other barbecue restaurants which offer *rodízio* (shwarma-style rotisserie meat), this one offers an *à la carte* choice of meat. The menu features meats such as ostrich and veal imported from the Netherlands, accompanied by side dishes of the customer's choice. **CUISINE** *Churrasco* (barbecue). **CREDIT CARDS** All. **HOURS** Mon-Thu, noon-4pm and from 7pm until late; Fri-Sun, from noon until late.
R. Barão da Torre, 600, Ipanema
TEL 2512-2970

Filé de Ouro $$
This bar serves top quality food and has waiting lines usually found only in trendier places. The tenderloin and striploin servings are generous and come with several side dishes. The Oswaldo Aranha tenderloin, with garlic, rice, beans, egg *farofa* (manioc meal, eggs and seasonings) and potatoes is a good choice. **CUISINE** Meat. **CREDIT CARDS** Not accepted. **HOURS** Mon-Sat, noon-10pm.
R. Jardim Botânico, 731, Jardim Botânico
TEL 2259-2396

Garcia e Rodrigues $
Chef Christophe Lidy has adapted his French dishes to the Brazilian climate, but with more types of oil and vegetables. At the front of the restaurant, a pastry shop that's one of the best of Rio gets especially busy for breakfast. **CUISINE** Varied. **CREDIT CARDS** All. **HOURS** Mon-Thu, 8am-12:30am; Fri and Sat, 8am-1am; Sun, 8am-midnight.
Av. Ataulfo de Paiva, 1251, Leblon
TEL 3206-4120

Gero $$
The traditional Fasano family, of São Paulo, has won a huge clientele in Rio with this Ipanema branch of Gero. Its beautiful, pleasant ambience is more sophisticated than most Italian restaurants in town. Try the veal osso buco with saffron risotto. **CUISINE** Italian. **CREDIT CARDS** All. **HOURS** Mon-Fri, noon-4pm and 7pm-1am; Sat and Sun, noon-midnight.
R. Aníbal de Mendonça, 157, Ipanema
TEL 2239-8158

Gibo $$
This restaurant belongs to Gilberto Brambini, who also owns Da Brambini, in Copacabana, and Forneria, in Ipanema. Gibo is the most sophisticated of the three. The menu highlights Mediterranean dishes inspired by the cuisine of the owner's northern Italian hometown of Crema. **CUISINE** Italian. **CREDIT CARDS** All. **HOURS** Daily, noon-1am.
R. Jangadeiros, 28 A e B, Ipanema
TEL 2521-9610

Guimas $
This traditional restaurant has been in the Baixo Gávea district for over 20 years. The dry, salted cod fish fritters are a must, unless you're tempted by the duck with honey and pear rice. **CUISINE** French. **CREDIT CARDS** All. **HOURS** Daily, noon-1am.
R. José Roberto Macedo Soares, 5, Gávea
TEL 2259-7996

Gula Gula
The standard menu offers salads and grilled meats, but every day there are specials such as quiches and pasta. All are prepared to be light and wholesome meals, a hallmark of the chain. There are branches in Leblon, Centro, Gávea, São Conrado and Barra da Tijuca. **CUISINE** Varied. **CREDIT CARDS** All. **HOURS** Sun-Thu, noon-midnight; Fri and Sat, noon-1am.
R. Aníbal de Mendonça, 132
TEL 2259-3084

Hipódromo $
A meeting point since 1937 for a varied clientele in the region of Baixo Gávea. Saturday's *feijoada* is a classic. **CUISINE** Meat, Pizza. **CREDIT CARDS** All. **HOURS** Daily, from 8am on 2am.
Pça. Santos Dumont, 108, Gávea
TEL 2274-9720

Jobi $
This Leblon bar has been in business for almost half a century, and is a refuge for Rio's bohemians, musicians, artists and journalists. It's well-poured *chope* (draft beer) is a must. **CUISINE** Bar. **CREDIT CARDS** American Express. **HOURS** Daily, 9am-4am.
R. Ataulfo de Paiva, 1166, Leblon
TEL 2274-0547/5055

PRICES	HOTELS (couple)	$ up to R$150	$$ from R$151 up to R$300	$$$ from R$301 up to R$500	$$$$ above R$500

Lamas $

This 130-year-old restaurant serves traditional dishes of Rio such as Oswaldo Aranha fillet and fish fillet with shrimp sauce. CUISINE Brazilian. CREDIT CARDS All. HOURS Mon-Fri, 9:30am-3:45am; Sat, 9:30am-4am.
R. Marquês de Abrantes, 18, Flamengo
TEL 2556-0799

Le Pré Catelan $$$

This French restaurant seats 65 and is run by chef Roland Villard. One highlight of its menu is that it changes every two weeks and features three different options for entree, main course and dessert. CUISINE French. CREDIT CARDS All. HOURS Mon-Sat, 7pm-midnight.
Av. Atlântica, 4240, Copacabana
TEL 2525-1160

Mangue Seco $

In a relaxed atmosphere, on an alley in Lapa, the self-styled "first *cachaçaria* (cachaça house) of Rio de Janeiro" offers seafood, especially crabs and *bobó de camarão* (dried shrimp with manioc, coconut milk, cashew nuts, peanuts and dende oil). Wash it all down with cold beer while listening to samba and *seresta* (serenade) on Tuesday, Friday and Saturday evenings. CUISINE Finger foods, fish and seafood. CREDIT CARDS All. HOURS Mon, 11am-3pm; Tue-Sat, from 11am.
R. do Lavradio, 23, Lapa
TEL 3852-1947

Margutta $

Enjoy *pesce al cartoccio* (fish in a pouch), prepared by chef Paolo Neroni, in a cozy atmosphere. The restaurant specializes in fish and seafood. CUISINE Italian. CREDIT CARDS All. HOURS Mon-Fri, 6pm-1am; Sat and holidays, noon-1am; Sun, noon- midnight.
Av. Henrique Dumont, 62, Ipanema
TEL 2259-3718

Mil Frutas Café $

The Ipanema shop is different from the other branches of this chain. Here, not only ice cream but also coffee, sandwiches, wraps, soups and salads are served. Weekends feature a generously portioned breakfast. Visit the Jardim Botânico branch, too. CUISINE Ice cream, wraps, soups and salads. CREDIT CARDS Diners, MasterCard. HOURS Mon-Thu, 10:30am-12:30am; Fri and Sat, 9:30am-1:30am; Sun, 9:30am-12:30am.
R. Garcia D'Ávila, 134, Loja A, Ipanema
TEL 2521-1384/2247-2148

Na Pressão $

This Southern-style *choperia* serves *chope* (draft beer) in cold mugs. Accompanies include turnovers and finger foods such as croquettes. CUISINE Brazilian. CREDIT CARDS All. HOURS Mon-Fri, from 4pm until the last customer; Sat and Sun, from 11am.
R. Conde Bernadotte, 26 E e F, Leblon
TEL 2259-5044

Oásis $$

This *churrascaria* (barbecue restaurant) opened in the Centro district in 1985 serves *rodízio* (rotisserie meat). One of the highlights is *picanha* (cap of rump) prepared the *gaucho* way. There are two other branches:

one in São Conrado (Estrada do Joá, 136) and one on the Dutra highway (Via Dutra, km 171.5). CUISINE Meat, *churrasco* (barbecue). CREDIT CARDS All. HOURS Mon-Fri, 11am-4pm.
R. Gonçalves Dias, 56, Sobreloja, Centro
TEL 2252-5521

Olympe $$

After some renovation, the dimly-lit restaurant now is all white, with an almost minimalist atmosphere. The menu includes the most famous dishes created by chef Claude Troisgros. The restaurant was renamed to honor the chef's mother. The extensive wine list is kept up to date. CUISINE French. CREDIT CARDS American Express, MasterCard, Visa. HOURS Mon-Thu, 7:30pm-12:30am; Fri, 12:30pm-4pm and 7:30pm-12:30am; Sat, 7:30pm-12:30am.
R. Custódio Serrão, 62, Jardim Botânico
TEL 2539-4542

Osteria Dell'Angolo $$

A favorite of the singer and composer Chico Buarque, this restaurant specializes in the cuisine of Northern Italy. Excellent risottos and *polenta with funghi porcini* are recommended. CUISINE Italian. CREDIT CARDS American Express, Diners, MasterCard. HOURS Mon-Fri, noon-4pm and 6pm-1am; Sat and Sun, from noon until late.
R. Paul Redfern, 40, Ipanema
TEL 2259-3148

Penafiel $

This restaurant has maintained early 20th century decor. In the long corridor, always packed with customers, it serves good Portuguese dishes: slices of *bacalhau* (salted cod fish) and Porto-style tripe. CUISINE Portuguese. CREDIT CARDS Diners, MasterCard, Visa. HOURS Mon-Fri, 11am-3:30pm.
R. Senhor dos Passos, 121, Centro
TEL 2224-6870

Pérgula $$

A glass hall in Copacabana Palace, by the wide sidewalk, overlooking the hotel's pool, adds a dose of glamour to breakfast, afternoon tea, champagne at sunset, or Sunday brunch. CREDIT CARDS All. HOURS Daily, 7am-10:30am and noon-midnight.
Av. Atlântica, 1702
TEL 2545-8744

Plataforma $$

This *churrascaria* (barbecue restaurant) was very fashionable in the 1980's in the southern area of the city. Famous clientele included Tom Jobim and Chico Buarque. Unfortunately it was renovated and lost much of its charm and some of its customers. The old decor has recently been restored. The meat and cheese bread are still excellent. CUISINE Meat, *churrasco* (barbecue). CREDIT CARDS All. HOURS noon-1am.
R. Adalberto Ferreira, 32, Leblon
TEL 2274-4022

Polis Sucos $

Juice shops are scattered all over Rio de Janeiro, but this is one of the oldest. A diverse clientele is equally likely to include churchgoers or beachgoers. Sand-

RESTAURANTS	$ up to R$50	$$ from R$51 up to R$100	$$$ from R$101 up to R$150	$$$$ above R$150

wiches and juices are served at the counter. The most popular choices are the tenderloin steak with *Palmira* cheese sandwich and the *fruta-do-conde* (sugar apple) juice. **CUISINE** Sandwiches. **CREDIT CARDS** Not accepted. **HOURS** Daily, 8am-midnight.
R. Maria Quitéria, 70-A, Ipanema
TEL 2247-2518

Porcão $$
The most traditional barbecue *rodízio* (rotisseries meat) offers fantastic meat and an extensive, quality salad buffet. It has become a brand name, with branches abroad as well. **CUISINE** Meat, *churrasco* (barbecue). **CREDIT CARDS** All. **HOURS** Daily, noon-midnight.
R. Barão da Torre, 218, Ipanema
TEL 2522-0999

Quadrifoglio $$
Run by chef Silvana Bianchi, this is one of the best Italian restaurants in town. The menu takes inspiration from the cuisine of Lombardy, in northern Italy. Try novelties such as spicy watermelon *gazpacho* and Guinea fowl with pink pepper. **CUISINE** Italian. **CREDIT CARDS** Diners, MasterCard, Visa. **HOURS** Mon-Fri, noon-3:30pm and 7:30pm-midnight; Sat, 7:30pm-1am; Sun, noon-5pm.
R. J. J. Seabra, 19, Jardim Botânico
TEL 2294-1433

Quinta $$
This restaurant is on a small farm. From seating on the verandah, you can see the funny *micos-estrelas* (common marmoset monkeys). The house, which looks like an old farm manor, was constructed with reused building materials. **CUISINE** Brazilian, contemporary, fish and seafood. **CREDIT CARDS** Diners, MasterCard, Visa. **HOURS** Sat, Sun and holidays, 1pm-7pm.
R. Luciano Gallet, 150, Vargem Grande
TEL 2428-1396/2568

Rio Minho $$
This traditional restaurant opened in 1884 and frequently served the Baron of Rio Branco. Another distinguished customer was Antônio Houaiss, a famous linguist. A delicious fish dish, with garlic and saffron, was named in his honor. **CREDIT CARDS** All. **HOURS** Mon-Fri, 11am-4pm.
R. do Ouvidor, 10
TEL 2509-2338

Rio Scenarium $
This three-story manor is one of the best places in Rio for live music and dance. During the day, an antique shop operates here. There is even a carriage and an antique pharmacy, complete with furniture and objects. Late in the afternoon, there are performances of *chorinho*, MPB (Brazilian Popular Music) and *samba* on Tuesdays, and of *forró* and *maracatu* (dance music from the Northeast) on Saturdays. And lots of *gafieira* (a ballroom variation of samba). **CUISINE** Bar. **CREDIT CARDS** All. **HOURS** Tue-Sat, from 7pm on.
R. do Lavradio, 20, Lapa
TEL 3852-5516/2233-3239

Satyricon $$$
This prestigious restaurant is a temple of seafood.

Shrimp, oysters, crayfish, snapper and lobsters are served, sometimes to celebrities such as Madonna or famous Spanish chef Ferran Adrià. **CUISINE** Mediterranean. **CREDIT CARDS** All. **HOURS** Mon-Thu and Sun, noon-midnight; Fri and Sat, noon-1am.
R. Barão da Torre, 192, Ipanema
TEL 2521-0627

Shirley $$
With only twelve tables, this simple place is very traditional and is already 50 years old. Spanish dishes are the highlights of the menu and the abundant paella is the house specialty. **CUISINE** Spanish. **CREDIT CARDS** Not accepted. **HOURS** Daily, noon-1am.
R. Gustavo Sampaio, 610, Leme
TEL 2542-1797

Sobrenatural $$
This Santa Teresa restaurant serves its own catch of fish. The tambouril *moqueca* with shrimp sauce, rice, *pirão* (manioc meal with fish broth) or yellow *farofa* (manioc flour) will leave a couple satisfied. **CUISINE** Brazilian. **CREDIT CARDS** Diners, MasterCard, Visa. **HOURS** Daily, from noon.
R. Almirante Alexandrino, 432, Santa Teresa
TEL 2224-1003

Sushi Leblon $$
It is one of the first Japanese restaurants in town. The menu features special crunch salmon and squid stuffed with *shiitake* and *shimeji* mushrooms. The sushi bar is neat and the *sake* list is good. **CUISINE** Japanese. **CREDIT CARDS** All. **HOURS** Mon-Fri, noon-4pm and 7pm-1:30am; Sat, noon-1:30am; Sun, 1:30pm-midnight.
R. Dias Ferreira, 256, Leblon
TEL 2512-7830

Tia Palmira $
This restaurant has been drawing Rio inhabitants to distant Barra de Guaratiba for 40 years, thanks to its home-style seafood. The trip is worth it: the fried shrimp, risottos and *moquecas* are delicious. **CUISINE** Fish and seafood. **CREDIT CARDS** All. **HOURS** Tue-Fri, 11:30am-5pm; Sat, Sun and holidays, 11:30am-6pm.
Caminho do Souza, 18, Barra de Guaratiba
TEL 2410-8169

Traiteurs de France $
This 16-year-old restaurant is run by chef Patrick Blancard and *pâtissier* (pastry-chef) Philippe Bryem, who used to work together at Le Meridien. Suggestion: goat cheese quiche with Provence olive oil. **CUISINE** French, varied. **CREDIT CARDS** MasterCard, Visa. **HOURS** Sun-Thu, noon-4:30pm; Fri and Sat, noon-4:30pm and 7pm-11pm.
Av. Nossa Senhora de Copacabana, 386, Copacabana
TEL 2548-6440

00 $
This restaurant operates in the city Planetarium. On weekends, the clientele dances to the sound of DJs and live music. The restaurant has diverse programs including theatrical performances and short film screenings. **CUISINE** Contemporary. **CREDIT CARDS** Ameri-

PRICES	**HOTELS** (couple)	$ up to R$150	$$ from R$151 up to R$300	$$$ from R$301 up to R$500	$$$$ above R$500

can Express, Diners, MasterCard. **HOURS** Daily, from 8:30pm (dinner) and from 10pm (DJs).
Av. Padre Leonel Franca, 240, Gávea
TEL 2540-8041

Zuka $$

An overnight success, this restaurant belongs to the owner of Sushi Leblon. It's one of the best places in Rio for those looking for innovation and bold combinations in the style of Spanish chef Ferran Adrià. Two good choices are octopus with sherry vinaigrette and foie gras with shiitake mushrooms. **CUISINE** Contemporary. **CREDIT CARDS** American Express, MasterCard, Visa. **HOURS** Mon, 7pm-1am; Tue-Fri, noon-4pm and 7pm-1am; Sat, 1pm-1am; Sun, 1pm-10pm.
R. Dias Ferreira, 233, Leblon
TEL 3205-7154

SERVICES

AIRPORT

Aeroporto Internacional do Rio de Janeiro – Galeão/Antônio Carlos Jobim
Av. Vinte de Janeiro, Ilha do Governador
TEL 3398-5050/4106

Aeroporto Santos Dumont
Pça. Senador Salgado Filho, Centro
TEL 3814-7070

TOURIST POLICE STATION

Delegacia Especial de Atendimento ao Turista
Av. Humberto Campos, 315, Leblon
TEL 3399-7170. **HOURS** 24 hours

TOURIST INFORMATION

Centro de Atendimento ao Turista
Av. Princesa Isabel, 183, Copacabana
TEL 2541-7522/2542-8004 **HOURS** Mon-Fri, 9am-6pm.

EXCHANGE SHOP

Casa Aliança
R. Miguel Couto, 35, Loja B, Centro
TEL 2509-6546. **HOURS** Mon- Fri, 9am-5:30pm

Santa Bárbara – MG

AREA CODE 31 **POPULATION** 24,180
DISTANCE Belo Horizonte, 105 km (65 mi)

HOTEL

Quadrado $
Opened in 1917, this hotel was fully restored in 2002. It caters for visitors to the Caraça Park who enjoy comfortable accommodations. The flooring is original, and some spots show a bit of the old walls. **FACILITIES** 15 rooms, air-conditioning, phone, TV, bar. **CREDIT CARDS** Not accepted.
Pça. da Matriz, 136
TEL 3832-3106

Santos – SP

AREA CODE 13 **POPULATION** 417,983
DISTANCE São Paulo, 85 km (53 mi)

HOTELS

Mendes Plaza $$
Located on a busy commercial street, beside a shopping mall, this hotel is two blocks from the beach. The pool on the penthouse floor overlooks the ocean. It offers complete business services. **FACILITIES** 104 rooms, air-conditioning, phone, TV, cable TV, bar, pool, restaurant, convention room, fitness room, game room, sauna. **CREDIT CARDS** All.
Av. Marechal Floriano Peixoto, 42
TEL 3289-4243
www.grupomendes.com.br

Parque Balneário $$
The original building, from 1914, was torn down in the 1970's to allow the construction of this personality-deficient edifice. Nevertheless, its interior makes it the most luxurious hotel in town. It's only half a block from the beach and offers courteous service. The presidential suite and the "balneária" suite have a private garden and pool. The pool on the top of the building has a beautiful view of the coastline. It's next to a shopping mall. **FACILITIES** 120 rooms, air-conditioning, phone, TV, cable TV, bar, recreation team, pool, restaurant, convention room, game room. **CREDIT CARDS** All.
Av. Ana Costa, 555
TEL 3289-5700
www.grupomendes.com.br

RESTAURANTS

Paco Paquito $$
A Spanish family has long tended this eatery. Although simple and not very close to the beach, it draws many people thanks to its fresh seafood and paella. **CUISINE** Fish and seafood. **CREDIT CARDS** Not accepted. **HOURS** Tue-Sat, from 11am until late; Sun, 11am-5pm.
R. Constituição, 607, Encruzilhada
TEL 3233-2594

Tamariz $$
Facing the José Menino beach, this traditional restaurant is more sophisticated than others of its rank. It specializes in fish and seafood. The caldeirada (bouillabaisse) serves three. **CUISINE** Brazilian. **CREDIT CARDS** Diners, MasterCard, Visa. **HOURS** Daily, noon-midnight.
Av. Presidente Wilson, 88, Pompéia
TEL 3237-6234

Último Gole $$
Located on a little alley by the Gonzaga beach, this traditional Portuguese restaurant serves delicious bacalhoada (dried codfish stew) and the best salted codfish fritters in town. **CUISINE** Portuguese. **CREDIT CARDS** All. **HOURS** Daily, 11am-1am.
R. Carlos Afonseca, 214, Gonzaga
TEL 3284-0508

RESTAURANTS $ up to R$50 $$ from R$51 up to R$100 $$$ from R$101 up to R$150 $$$$ above R$150

Vista ao Mar $
One of the most traditional restaurants in town, it has earned a reputation for its Valencia-style paella, which serves four. The facilities are simple but close to the sea. CUISINE Fish and seafood. CREDIT CARDS All. HOURS Daily, 11am-midnight.
Av. Bartolomeu de Gusmão, 68, Embaré
TEL 3236-9469/3273-4411

SERVICES

TOURIST INFORMATION

Centro de Informações Turísticas
Pça. Paulo Viriato Corrêa da Costa (former Ilha da Conveniência)
TEL 0800173887. HOURS Daily, 8am-8pm

São José do Barreiro – SP

AREA CODE 12 POPULATION 4,139
DISTANCE São Paulo, 270 km (149 mi)

HOTELS

Porto da Bocaina $$
Located by the Funil dam, this hotel has a stunning view, spacious and comfortable rooms, and good amenities for water sports. The spa offers programs for those wanting to get in shape or relax. FACILITIES 35 rooms, air-conditioning, phone, TV, cable TV, ceiling fan, bar, recreation team, pool, tennis court, restaurant, convention room, fitness room, game room, sauna, spa. CREDIT CARDS All.
Rodovia dos Tropeiros, km 260
TEL 3117-1102/1192 FAX 3117-1303
www.hoteisdabocaina.com.br

Pousada Vale dos Veados $$$
Reach this inn via Porto da Bocaina hotel along 42 km (26 mi) of dirt road that's fit only for 4-wheel vehicles. The farm manor was built in 1926, with pine logs and stones. There's a bathroom for every two rooms in the main house. The suites have a private bathroom and a fireplace. FACILITIES 9 rooms, bar, horses, restaurant, game room, sauna. CREDIT CARDS Diners, MasterCard, Visa.
Estrada da Bocaina, km 42, Parque Nacional da Serra da Bocaina
TEL 3117-1102/1221 FAX 3117-1303
www.hoteisdabocaina.com.br

São Paulo – SP

AREA CODE 11 POPULATION 10,434,252
DISTANCES Curitiba, 408 km (253.5 mi); Rio de Janeiro, 429 km (266.5 mi)

HOTELS

Bourbon $
Located in the downtown area, one block from Praça da República, this hotel has charming decor. All rooms have a work station. FACILITIES 129 rooms, air-conditioning, phone, TV, cable TV, bar, restaurant, convention room, fitness room, sauna. CREDIT CARDS All.

Av. Dr. Vieira de Carvalho, 99, Centro
TEL 3337-2000 FAX 3337-1414
www.bourbon.com.br

Emiliano $$$$
This luxury boutique hotel, designed by Arthur de Mattos Casas, offers guests massage and butler services. The rooms are huge. The fitness room and sauna have panoramic city views. Pieces of furniture designed by famous brothers Fernando and Humberto Campana decorate the lobby. FACILITIES 57 rooms, air-conditioning, phone, TV, cable TV, bar, restaurant, convention room, fitness room, sauna, spa. CREDIT CARDS All.
R. Oscar Freire, 384, Jardins
TEL 3069-4369
www.emiliano.com.br

Fasano $$$$
Opened in 2003, it is one of the most luxurious hotels of São Paulo. It belongs to the Fasano family, which also owns award-winning restaurants such as Gero, Parigi and Fasano. The last now occupies the ground floor of this building. The ground floor also houses Baretto, a bar for jazz lovers. Designed by architects Isay Weinfeld and Márcio Kogan, the hotel has many imported pieces of furniture dating back to the 1940's. Fasano is located in the district of Jardins, close to many restaurants, fashionable shops and the trendy Oscar Freire street. FACILITIES 64 rooms, air-conditioning, phone, TV, cable TV, bar, heated pool, restaurant, convention room, fitness room, massage room, sauna, spa. CREDIT CARDS All.
R. Vitório Fasano, 88, Jardins
TEL 3896-4077
www.fasano.com.br/hotel

George V Jardins $$$
This conveniently located hotel has rooms with marble whirlpool bathtubs and a fully equipped mini-kitchen with stove, fridge, dish washer and microwave oven. Some suites are vast. FACILITIES 64 rooms, air-conditioning, phone, TV, cable TV, bar, heated pool, restaurant, convention room, fitness room, massage room, sauna, spa. CREDIT CARDS All.
R. José Maria Lisboa, 1000, Jardins
TEL 3088-9822 FAX 3082-7431
www.george-v.com.br

Gran Meliá Mofarrej $$$
This hotel near park Trianon has a stately lobby. The rooms are spacious, comfortable and exquisitely decorated. Non-smoking rooms are available. FACILITIES 244 rooms, air-conditioning, phone, TV, cable TV, bar, pool, heated pool, restaurant, fitness room, massage room, sauna, spa. CREDIT CARDS All.
Al. Santos, 1437, Jardins
TEL 3146-5900 FAX 3146-5901
RESERVATIONS 08007033399
www.granmeliamofarrej.somelia.com

Gran Meliá WTC São Paulo $$$$
Although far from Jardins and from Paulista Avenue, this is the ideal hotel for executives doing business in the Luís Carlos Berrini area. The executive rooms and suites have bathtub, broadband internet access, butler and

PRICES	HOTELS (couple)	$ up to R$150	$$ from R$151 up to R$300	$$$ from R$301 up to R$500	$$$$ above R$500

open bar services. The rooms are spacious. It is next to Shopping D&D, one of the most sophisticated malls in town, specialized in furniture, furnishings, and design. **FACILITIES** 300 rooms, air-conditioning, phone, TV, cable TV, bar, pool, tennis court, restaurant, convention room, fitness room, massage room, sauna. **CREDIT CARDS** All.

Av. das Nações Unidas, 12559, Brooklin
TEL 3055-8000 **FAX** 3055-8002
www.granmeliawtcsaopaulo.solmelia.com

Grand Hyatt São Paulo $$$

One of the newest and most attractive hotels in town, this Grand Hyatt is on Luís Carlos Berrini Avenue, an important business area. It has an Italian, a Japanese and a French restaurant, two bars and a lounge with live music. The impressive "wine library" has more than 2,500 bottles and over 280 labels. air-conditioning, phone, TV, cable TV, bar, heated pool, restaurant, fitness room, massage room, sauna, spa. **CREDIT CARDS** All.

Av. das Nações Unidas, 13301, Brooklin
TEL 6838-1234 **FAX** 6838-1235
www.saopaulo.grand.hyatt.com

Hilton $$$$

Yet another luxury hotel in the Luís Carlos Berrini business district, this hotel faces the charmless Pinheiros River and is miles away from the major tourist attractions. The "relaxing" rooms have whirlpool tubs, aromatherapy, special music, and massage devices. The standard rooms include no breakfast, which is charged at a fixed price per person. **FACILITIES** 485 rooms, air-conditioning, phone, TV, cable TV, bar, heated pool, restaurant, convention room, fitness room, massage room, sauna, spa. **CREDIT CARDS** All.

Av. das Nações Unidas, 12901, Brooklin
TEL 6845-0000 **FAX** 6845-0001
www.saopaulomorumbi.hilton.com

L'Hotel $$$$

On a street off Paulista Avenue, this hotel is decorated in classic style and has few rooms but gives each guest spacious and pleasant quarters. It offers services according to guests' nationality, for example Japanese guests might get *ikebana* flower arrangements, Oriental china for tea, and Japanese newspapers in the rooms. It has an Italian restaurant and a pub. **FACILITIES** 80 rooms, air-conditioning, phone, TV, cable TV, bar, heated pool, restaurant, convention room, fitness room, massage room, sauna. **CREDIT CARDS** All.

Al. Campinas, 266, Jardins
TEL 2183-0500 **FAX** 2183-0505
www.lhotel.com.br

Mercure Downtown $$

Built in the site of an old tram station, the hotel kept the beautiful original arches of the station. Comfortable and charming, it is located in the heart of São Paulo, one block from Praça da República. **FACILITIES** 260 rooms, air-conditioning, phone, TV, cable TV, bar, heated pool, restaurant, convention room, fitness room. **CREDIT CARDS** All.

R. Araújo, 141, Centro
TEL 3120-8400 **FAX** 3120-8401
www.accorhotels.com.br

Pergamon $$

Although located in a rundown area of São Paulo, this hotel is near many tourist attractions in the old city center (Centro Velho). It's also close to some of the best theaters. It's a design-conscious hotel, with halls decorated in different forms and colors. The rooms are spacious and charming. A small library is available to guests. **FACILITIES** 123 rooms, air-conditioning, phone, TV, cable TV, bar, restaurant, convention room, fitness room. **CREDIT CARDS** All.

R. Frei Caneca, 80, Centro
TEL 3123-2021
www.pergamon.com.br

Sofitel $$$

This hotel is close to Parque do Ibirapuera and it has large executive clientele. It offers services tailored to Arab and Asian guests, such as their favorite foods. Businesswomen are welcomed with fruit baskets and other perks. The hotel has three bars and two restaurants in addition to a charming *boulangerie*. Pets are welcome. **FACILITIES** 219 rooms, air-conditioning, phone, TV, cable TV, bar, pool, tennis court, restaurant, convention room, fitness room, massage room, sauna. **CREDIT CARDS** All.

R. Sena Madureira, 1355, Vila Mariana
TEL 5087-0800 **FAX** 5575-4544
www.accorhotels.com.br

Unique $$$$

The unusual building, designed by Ruy Ohtake, has the shape of a slice of gigantic watermelon. Its round windows afford a view of Ibirapuera Park. The rooms are decorated in light colors. The penthouse floor houses Skye, a restaurant run by Emmanuel Bassoleil and a trendy bar, by a red pool, with a magnificent view of the city. It is a favorite among fashion models, designers and the publicity people of the São Paulo Fashion Week, a fashion show held in the nearby Bienal building. **FACILITIES** 95 rooms, air-conditioning, phone, TV, cable TV, bar, pool, heated pool, restaurant, convention room, fitness room, massage room, sauna. **CREDIT CARDS** All.

Av. Brigadeiro Luís Antônio, 4700, Jardins
TEL 3055-4710 **FAX** 3889-8100 **RESERVATIONS** 08007708771
www.hotelunique.com.br

RESTAURANTS

A Figueira Rubaiyat $$$

The restaurant's 50-foot fig tree is an attraction on its own, and makes the outdoor seating especially pleasant. The extensive menu features meat, pasta and fish. *Feijoada* is Saturday's special. **CUISINE** Varied. **CREDIT CARDS** Visa. **HOURS** Mon-Fri, noon-3:30pm; Mon-Thu, 7pm-midnight; Fri, 7pm-12:30 am; Sat and Sun, noon-1am.

Rua Haddock Lobo, 1738, Jardins
TEL 3063-3888

Acrópoles $

The most genuine Greek restaurant of São Paulo, established in 1963, it has resisted the decline of the neighborhood thanks to the loyalty of its customers. The place is simple and rather chaotic: customers

---

RESTAURANTS	$ up to R$50	$$ from R$51 up to R$100	$$$ from R$101 up to R$150	$$$$ above R$150

look at the pots and pans in the kitchen and choose what they want to eat. The waiter then takes their order to the table. It serves great stews and roasts. It is close to Pinacoteca, one of the best museums in town. **CUISINE** Greek. **CREDIT CARDS** Visa. **HOURS** Daily, 6:30am-11:30pm.
R. da Graça, 364, Bom Retiro
TEL 223-4386

Antiquarius $$

This São Paulo branch of the Rio restaurant opened in the early 1990's and soon became one of the best restaurants in town. The atmosphere is sophisticated and the Portuguese dishes are excellent. The menu features several excellent choices of *bacalhau* (codfish). **CUISINE** Portuguese. **CREDIT CARDS** Diners, MasterCard, Visa. **HOURS** Tue-Thu, noon-3pm and 7pm-1am; Fri, until 2am; Sat, noon-2am; Sun, noon-6pm; Mon, 7pm-1am.
Al. Lorena, 1884, Jardins
TEL 3082-3015/3064-8686

Arábia $

Located in Jardins, near the trendy shops of Oscar Freire street, this is one of the best Arab restaurants in town. It has a high ceiling and its diverse clientele includes executives, families and couples. **CUISINE** Arab. **CREDIT CARDS** American Express, Diners, MasterCard. **HOURS** Mon-Thu, noon-3pm and 7pm-midnight; Fri, noon-3:30pm and 7pm-1am; Sat, noon-1am; Sun, noon-midnight.
R. Haddock Lobo, 1397, Jardins
TEL 3061-2203

Astor $

Located in the bohemian district of Vila Madalena, it is one of the most charming bars of São Paulo, with 1950's-vintage decor. The excellent *chope* (draft beer) and savory dishes served are ideal to accompany a nice chat. Be prepared to wait, especially on weekends. **CUISINE** Bar. **CREDIT CARDS** Diners, MasterCard. **HOURS** Mon-Thu, 6pm-2am; Fri and Sat, noon-4am; Sun, noon-7pm.
R. Delfina, 163, Vila Madalena
TEL 3815-1364

Baby-Beef Rubaiyat $$

Exceptional meat is the specialty of this restaurant run by Spaniard Belarmino Iglesias, but the *feijoada*, served on Saturdays, is also great. It is packed with executives on weekdays and with a more diverse clientele on weekends. You may opt for the buffet or choose from the menu. **CUISINE** Churrasco (barbecue). **CREDIT CARDS** Visa. **HOURS** Mon-Fri, 11:30am-3pm and 7pm-12:30am; Sat and Sun, noon-5pm.
Al. Santos, 86, Jardins
TEL 3141-1188

Bar Brahma $

This 1940's-era bar reopened after a brief hibernation in the early 2000's and is now one of the highlights of the São Paulo night scene. It sits at the most famous corner of São Paulo, between Ipiranga and São João avenues, and is one of the most charming bars in town. It features great samba and *chorinho* performances. **CUISINE** Bar. **CREDIT CARDS** All. **HOURS** Daily, from 11am until the last customer.
Av. São João, 677, Centro
TEL 3333-0855

Bar do Sacha $

This is one of the busiest bars in Vila Madalena, and is a favorite hangout for Romeos and flirts. It has a relaxed atmosphere, with tables on the sidewalk and long waiting lines. Beer is always perfect and the slow-roasted short ribs are delicious. **CUISINE** Bar, Brazilian. **CREDIT CARDS** Diners, MasterCard, Visa. **HOURS** Mon-Sat, noon-1am; Sun, noon-midnight.
R. Original, 89, Vila Madalena
TEL 3815-7665

Bar Léo $$

This traditional *botequim* (bar) in the city center is always packed during happy hour. It serves one of the best *chopes* (draft beer) in town, and the dried codfish fritters make an excellent accompaniment. **CUISINE** Finger food. **CREDIT CARDS** MasterCard, Visa. **HOURS** Mon-Fri, 11am-8:30pm; Sat, 11am-4pm.
R. Aurora, 100, Santa Ifigênia
TEL 221-0247

Barbacoa $$

This great *churrascaria* in Itaim also has an excellent buffet with different types of cold cuts, cheese and salads. Like its similar counterparts, it can be very noisy in busy days. **CUISINE** Churrasco (barbecue). **CREDIT CARDS** All. **HOURS** Mon-Fri, noon-3:30pm and 7pm-12:30am; Sat, noon-5pm and 7pm-1am; Sun, from noon.
R. Dr. Renato Paes de Barros, 65, Itaim Bibi
TEL 3168-5522

Bárbaro $$

This Argentinean restaurant seats 60. Among the good choices of meat is *tapa de cuadril* (cap of rump). Each serving is a whopping 600 grams (1.3 lb), but you can order a half serving. Side dishes include French fries, fried onions or *quimérica* potato, a dumpling made of mashed potatoes and covered with cream cheese and Parmesan cheese. **CUISINE** Meat. **CREDIT CARDS** All. **HOURS** Mon-Sat, noon-midnight; Sun, 1pm-6pm.
R. Dr. Sodré, 241, Vila Olímpia
TEL 3845-7743

Bistrô Charlô – Jockey Club $$

Located in the Jockey Club, this restaurant belongs to renowned chef Charlô Whately, and has a beautiful view of the race track and of the skyscrapers alongside Pinheiros River. The atmosphere is refined and very pleasant. Open only for lunch, except on Mondays when dinner is served during the races. **CUISINE** French. **CREDIT CARDS** All. **HOURS** Mon, noon-3pm and 7pm-11pm; Tue-Fri, noon-3pm; Sat and Sun, noon-5pm.
Av. Lineu de Paula Machado, 1263, Cidade Jardim
TEL 3811-7799

Bolinha $$

The most traditional *feijoada* of São Paulo started haphazardly. Bolinha opened in 1946 as a pizza parlor,

PRICES | **HOTELS** (couple) | $ up to R$150 | $$ from R$151 up to R$300 | $$$ from R$301 up to R$500 | $$$$ above R$500

490   BRAZIL GUIDE

and later became an international restaurant. It served *feijoada* for the first time to celebrate the victory of the owner's team in a local championship. That was in 1952, and since then Bolinha has been serving the prized dish in traditional clay pots. **CUISINE** Brazilian. **CREDIT CARDS** All. **HOURS** Daily, 11am-midnight.
Av. Cidade Jardim, 53, Jardins
TEL 3061-2010

Bráz $

Some consider this the best *pizzaria* in São Paulo. That's no small achievement in a city that boasts hundreds of prideful pizza parlors. The decor smacks of old times, and the place is always busy, with groups clustered around large tables. It has branches in Moema (R. Graúna, 125) and Higienópolis (R. Sergipe, 406). **CUISINE** Pizza. **CREDIT CARDS** Diners, MasterCard. **HOURS** Daily, from 6:30pm until the last customer.
R. Vupabussu, 271, Pinheiros
TEL 3037-7975

Bread and Co. $

This bakery is a meeting point for young people and adults, especially those who frequent Ibirapuera Park. There's a wide variety of sweets, bread and savories. The chocolate puff pastry stands out. The menu includes risottos and salads. **CUISINE** Brazilian, sandwiches. **CREDIT CARDS** Diners, MasterCard, Visa. **HOURS** Daily, 7am-8pm.
R. Lourenço de Almeida, 470, Vila Nova Conceição
TEL 3842-5156

Buttina $

This Italian restaurant serves good food and great gnocchi. At the back of the house there are tables under *jabuticaba* trees and there are tables in a roofed garden. Oscar Niemeyer has enjoyed their pasta and donated a drawing that now hangs on one of the walls. **CUISINE** Italian. **CREDIT CARDS** All. **HOURS** Mon-Thu, noon-2:30pm and 8pm-11:30pm; Fri, until 12:30am; Sat, 1pm-4pm and 8pm-12:30am; Sun, 1pm-5pm.
R. João Moura, 976, Pinheiros
TEL 3083-5991

Café Antique $$

The atmosphere is refined and formal, and the restaurant takes its name from the next-door antique shop. The innovative cuisine of Erick Jacquin and the excellent wine list stand out. **CUISINE** French. **CREDIT CARDS** All. **HOURS** Mon-Thu, noon-3pm and 7pm-midnight; Fri, until 1am; Sat, noon-4:30pm and 7pm-1am.
R. Haddock Lobo, 1416, Jardins
TEL 3062-0882

Camelo $

Camelo serves some of the best thin, crispy-crust pizza in town. The trendy spot has long lines on weekends. The restaurant is simple, and tables packed close together. There is a branch in Itaim Bibi (av. Presidente Juscelino Kubitschek, 151). **CUISINE** Pizza. **CREDIT CARDS** All. **HOURS** Mon-Sat, 6pm-1am; Sun, 6pm-midnight.
R. Pamplona, 1873, Jardins
TEL 3887-8764/6004

Capim Santo $

One of the best things to do on sunny Sundays is to have lunch at this restaurant in Vila Madalena, which has outdoor tables, under mango trees, and a buffet of Brazilian dishes. On Wednesdays and Saturdays, the menu is *feijoada*. On the other days, service is *à la carte*. **CUISINE** Contemporary. **CREDIT CARDS** American Express, Diners, MasterCard. **HOURS** Mon-Thu, noon-3pm and 7pm-12:30am; Fri, noon-4:30pm and 7:30pm-1am; Sat, 12:30pm-4:30pm and 8pm-1am; Sun, 12:30pm-5pm.
R. Arapiraca, 152, Vila Madalena
TEL 3813-9103

Capuano $

The photos on the walls tell the story of this traditional *trattoria* in Bexiga. The menu features good Italian dishes such as *fusilli al sugo*. **CUISINE** Italian. **CREDIT CARDS** MasterCard, Visa. **HOURS** Tue-Fri, 11:30am-3pm and 7pm-midnight; Sun, noon-4:30pm.
R. Conselheiro Carrão, 416, Bexiga
TEL 3288-1460

Carlota $

This small and charming restaurant in Higienópolis, run by Carla Pernambuco, offers refined options such as salmon with Moroccan couscous and duck *magret* with mustard. There's a often-crowded lounge upstairs. **CUISINE** Contemporary. **CREDIT CARDS** All. **HOURS** Tue-Thu, noon-3pm and 7:30pm-midnight; Fri, until 12:30am; Sat, 12:30pm-4:30pm and until 12:30am; Sun, 12:30pm-4:30pm; Mon, from 7:30pm.
R. Sergipe, 753, Higienópolis
TEL 3661-8670

Casa Búlgara $

This is a standby option for Bulgarian finger food. *Burekas* (round-shaped puff pastry) made according to the recipe of the Levi family are the house specialty. There are two branches: one in Higienópolis (r. Baronesa de Itu, 375) and one in Morumbi (Hipermercado Extra, av. das Nações Unidas, 16741). **CREDIT CARDS** Not accepted. **HOURS** Mon-Fri, 9am-6:30pm; Sat, 9:30am-2pm.
R. Silva Pinto, 356, Bom Retiro
TEL 222-9849

Casa Garabed $

Located in Santana, in the north of town and far from most gourmands' itineraries, this is a simple bar-like house. Once known only to local Armenians, it became famous thanks to its typical dishes prepared in a wood-burning stove. *Esfiha* (small open-faced meat pie) and raw kibbeh are great options. **CUISINE** Armenian. **CREDIT CARDS** All. **HOURS** Tue-Sun, noon-9pm.
R. José Margarido, 216, Santana
TEL 6976-2750

Castelões $

Many consider it the best pizza parlor in town. The original restaurant in Brás, the oldest *pizzaria* of São Paulo, is located on a street that gets almost deserted at night, and is difficult to find. But it is worth the sacrifice. Photos and newspaper articles hanging on the walls retell the establishment's history. There's a branch in Itaim Bibi (av. Presidente Juscelino Kubitschek, 373), which is easier to get to, but lacks the

---

charm of the original. CUISINE Italian. CREDIT CARDS Not accepted. HOURS Daily, 11am-4pm and 6pm-midnight.
R. Jairo Góes, 126, Brás
TEL 3229-0542

Colher de Pau $$

A branch of a restaurant in Fortaleza, in Northeastern Brazil, it serves typical food from the Northeast such as *peixada* (fish stew), sun-dried meat and *cearense* shrimp. CUISINE Regional from the Northeast. CREDIT CARDS All. HOURS Mon-Sat, noon-3:30pm; Sun, noon-6pm; Tue-Thu, 7pm-11pm; Fri and Sat, 7pm-midnight.
R. Dr. Mário Ferraz, 563, Itaim Bibi
TEL 3168-8068/2617

Consulado Mineiro $

Regional dishes from Minas are the specialty here. On weekdays it's frequented mostly by young people from neighboring Vila Madalena. On Saturdays it's packed with the crowd that flocks to the handicraft and antique fair held in Benedito Calixto square. It's a great experience, but be prepared to wait for hours. CUISINE Brazilian, regional from Minas. CREDIT CARDS All. HOURS Tue-Sun, noon-midnight.
Pça. Benedito Calixto, 74, Pinheiros
TEL 3064-3882

DeliParis $

With its delicious quiches and mouthwatering sweets, this charming and casual bakery located in Vila Madalena is an excellent choice for brunch or for an afternoon snack. CUISINE French. CREDIT CARDS Not accepted. HOURS Daily, 7am-10pm.
R. Harmonia, 484, Vila Madalena
TEL 3816-5911

D.O.M. $$$

Chef Alex Atala, who is greatly influenced by Spanish chef Ferran Adrià, runs one of the most acclaimed restaurants in São Paulo. Using Brazilian ingredients, Atala creates exquisite delicacies that combine different flavors, temperatures and textures. CUISINE: Contemporary. CREDIT CARDS All. HOURS Mon-Fri, noon-3pm and 7pm-midnight; Fri and Sat, 7pm-1am.
R. Barão de Capanema, 549, Jardins
TEL 3088-0761

Don Curro $$$

This traditional Spanish restaurant offers the best and most famous paella of São Paulo. It has its own vivarium with up to 800 lobsters. You can see them in an aquarium before they're prepared. The restaurant was named after the bullfighter (now deceased) who established the restaurant over 40 years ago. His sons now run it. CUISINE Spanish. CREDIT CARDS American Express, Diners, MasterCard. HOURS Tue-Thu, noon-3pm and 7pm-midnight; Fri, noon-3pm and 7pm-1am; Sat, noon-1am; Sun, noon-5pm.
R. Alves Guimarães, 230, Pinheiros
TEL 3062-4712

Espírito Capixaba $$

Several types of *moqueca capixaba* (from Espírito Santo) are served here. Unlike *moqueca* from Bahia, which is made with coconut milk and dende oil, the *mo-*

queca capixaba is lighter and incorporates olive oil and urucum (a palm) oil. CUISINE Brazilian, regional from Espírito Santo. CREDIT CARDS All. HOURS Tue-Fri, noon-3pm and 6:30pm-11:30pm; Sat, noon-midnight; Sun, noon-6pm.
R. Francisco Leitão, 57, Pinheiros
TEL 3062-6566

Fasano $$$

For many people this is the most sophisticated restaurant of Brazil. It is located in the hotel of the same name, with a very high ceiling and impeccable decoration. Chef Salvatore Loi prepares dishes inspired by contemporary Italian cuisine. The wine steward, Manoel Beato, is often considered the best in Brazil, and he commands a comprehensive wine list. CUISINE Contemporary, Italian. CREDIT CARDS All. HOURS Mon-Sat, 7:30pm-1am.
R. Vittorio Fasano, 88, Jardins
TEL 3896-4000

Feijoada da Lana $

Unlike most *feijoada* places, which serve the dish only on Saturdays, this casual restaurant in Vila Madalena serves the Brazilian specialty every day. There are tables in the outdoor patio. CUISINE Brazilian, *feijoada*. CREDIT CARDS American Express, Diners, MasterCard. HOURS Mon-Fri, noon-3:30pm; Sat and Sun, 12:30pm-6pm.
R. Aspicuelta, 421, Vila Madalena
TEL 3814-9191

Filial $

This informal bar, located in the bohemian Vila Madalena district, is always packed. There are plenty of caricatures of Brazilian artists on the walls. The clientele is mostly made up of artists, intellectuals and journalists. It serves an excellent *chope* (draft beer). CUISINE Bar, Brazilian, Italian. CREDIT CARDS All. HOURS Daily, 5pm-4am.
R. Fidalga, 254, Vila Madalena
TEL 3813-9226

Fogo de Chão $$

This *churrascaria*'s *rodízio* (rotisserie barbecue) is said to offer some of the best meats in town. The waiters dress in gaucho clothing typical of the Pampas, and are very efficient. There are two other branches in São Paulo: one on av. Santo Amaro, 6824, and one on av. Moreira Guimarães, 964, both in the Southern region. The chain headquarters opened 25 years ago in Porto Alegre. There are also branches in the United States. CUISINE Brazilian, *churrasco* (barbecue). CREDIT CARDS All. HOURS Mon-Fri, noon-4pm and 6pm-midnight; Sat, noon-midnight; Sun, noon-10:30pm.
Av. Bandeirantes, 538, Vila Olímpia
TEL 5505-0791

Fornaio d'Italia $

This is a very informal, simple and entertaining restaurant. The owner, Italian Vito Simone, welcomes customers himself and suggests dishes, since there's no menu. He also prepares good pasta and meat dishes while he draws on the paper tablecloths. Reservations required. CUISINE Italian. CREDIT CARDS Not accepted. HOURS Mon-Fri, noon-2pm and 7:30pm-9:30pm.

PRICES	HOTELS (couple)	$ up to R$150	$$ from R$151 up to R$300	$$$ from R$301 up to R$500	$$$$ above R$500

R. Manoel Guedes, 160, Itaim Bibi
TEL 3079-2473

Forneria San Paolo $

This sandwich shop is part of the top-rate Fasano group. There are several choices of savory *panini*, prepared with pizza dough in a wood-burning stove with lots of imported ingredients. Its charming ambience, high ceiling and the glassed-in kitchen draw a large clientele, including celebrities. CUISINE Italian, sandwiches. CREDIT CARDS All. HOURS Mon-Thu, noon-4pm and 6pm-2am; Fri, noon-4pm and 6pm-4am; Sat, noon-4am; Sun, noon-2am.
R. Amauri, 319, Itaim Bibi
TEL 3078-0099

Frevinho $

Opened in the mid-1950's, Frevinho still has the same old casual look. Its *beirute* sandwich is very traditional: toasted pita bread, filled with roast beef, cheese, tomato and oregano. It stays open until late and attracts hungry night owls. There's a branch on r. Augusta, 1563. CUISINE Brazilian, sandwiches. CREDIT CARDS All. HOURS Sun-Thu, 10:30am-1am; Fri, 10:30am-2am; Sat, 10:30am-3am.
R. Oscar Freire, 603, Jardins
TEL 3082-3434

Galeria dos Pães $

The four-story building accommodates a bakery and pastry shop, a buffet (brunch, breakfast, lunch and afternoon tea), sandwich shop and a convenience store that sells wine and imported food as well. It's a meeting point for bohemians in the small hours. CUISINE Breakfast, fast food. CREDIT CARDS All. HOURS 24 hours.
R. Estados Unidos, 1645, Jardins
TEL 3064-5900

Gero $$

One of the best and most sophisticated Italian restaurants in town, it is owned by the Fasano family, but is less formal than Fasano (see above). The veal ravioli is classic. The simple and elegant architecture, with its brick walls, was designed by Aurelio Martinez Flores. CUISINE Italian. CREDIT CARDS All. HOURS Mon-Thu, noon-3pm and 7pm-1am; Fri and Sat, noon-4:30pm and 7pm-1:30am; Sun, noon-4:30pm and 7pm-midnight.
R. Haddock Lobo, 1629, Jardins
TEL 3064-0005

Gero Café Iguatemi $$

Located at the Shopping Iguatemi mall, this branch of Gero is more casual than the original restaurant (see above). In addition to the dishes offered at Gero, this branch offers finger foods, sandwiches, cakes and tea. CUISINE Italian. CREDIT CARDS All. HOURS Mon-Sat, 11:30am-11pm; Sun, 11:30am-10pm.
Av. Brigadeiro Faria Lima, 2232, Jardins
TEL 3813-8484

Govinda $$

The typical Indian decor, with imported sculptures and ornaments, and the Indian ambient music transport patrons to another continent. It attracts many couples and those who love spicy Indian food. There is a cigar smoking area. CUISINE Indian. CREDIT CARDS All. HOURS Mon-Sat, noon-3pm and from 6pm until late; Sun, noon-5pm.
R. Princesa Isabel, 379, Brooklin
TEL 5092-4816

Jardim di Napoli $

This genuine Italian *trattoria* opened more than 30 years ago. The tables are covered with checked tablecloths and it is always packed, with long lines. The highlight is the marvellous *polpetone*: meatloaf filled with mozzarella cheese, with tomato sauce and Parmesan cheese. CUISINE Italian. CREDIT CARDS American Express, Visa. HOURS Mon-Fri, noon-3pm and 6:30pm-midnight; Sat and Sun, noon-4pm and 6:30pm-midnight.
R. Dr. Martinico Prado, 463, Higienópolis
TEL 3666-3022

Jun Sakamoto $$$

For many gourmets, this Japanese restaurant serves the best *sushi* in São Paulo. Trust the famous chef Jun Sakamoto to pick your food for you, and order the tasting menu. Every dish, whether a traditional Japanese recipe or a bold innovation, is a delicious surprise. The restaurant is small, busy and very sophisticated. Reservation is essential. CUISINE Japanese. CREDIT CARDS MasterCard. HOURS Mon-Thu, 6:30pm-12:30am; Fri and Sat, 7pm-1am.
R. Lisboa, 55, Pinheiros
TEL 3088-6019

Kinoshita $$

In the traditional district of Liberdade, Kinoshita stands out for its Japanese menu and the surprises created by chef Tsuyoshi Murakama on the tasting menu (which must be ordered in advance). CUISINE Japanese. CREDIT CARDS Visa. HOURS Mon-Sat, 11:30am-2pm and 6:30pm-10pm.
R. da Glória, 168, Liberdade
TEL 3105-4903

Konstanz $

A most acclaimed German restaurant, it serves several traditional dishes with different options of sausages and pork knuckle. The menu also features different types of fondue. The German town of Konstanz, after which the restaurant was named, is near the German-Swiss border. CUISINE German, Swiss, varied. CREDIT CARDS American Express, Diners, MasterCard, Visa. HOURS Tue-Thu, noon-3pm and 6pm-midnight; Fri and Sat, noon-1am; Sun, noon-6pm.
Av. Aratãs, 713, Moema
TEL 5543-4813

Koyama $$

Try *omakase*, a complete meal with fish, *sushi*, *tempuras* and dessert. The menu features Japanese dishes, although some have been adapted to Brazilian tastes. The ambience reflects this attitude too: there are Japanese-style tables and *tatame* rooms where you'll have to take your shoes off. CUISINE Japanese. CREDIT CARDS All. HOURS Mon-Thu, noon-2:30pm and 7pm-11pm; Fri and Sat, noon-2pm and 7pm-11:30pm.
R. Treze de Maio, 1050, Bela Vista
TEL 3283-1833

RESTAURANTS	$ up to R$50	$$ from R$51 up to R$100	$$$ from R$101 up to R$150	$$$$ above R$150

La Casserole $

This traditional bistro opened in 1954 and is less formal than most French restaurants in town. The oysters, the roast mutton leg, and the *mandioquinha* (baroa potato) cream with confit of partridge have become classics. The location is very pleasant, in front of the Flower Market of Largo do Arouche. CUISINE French. CREDIT CARDS All. HOURS Tue-Thu, noon-3pm and 7pm-midnight; Fri, noon-3pm and 7pm-1am; Sat, 7pm-1am; Sun, noon-4pm and 7pm-11pm.
Lgo. do Arouche, 346, Centro
TEL 3331-6283/221-2899

La Tambouille $$

In the early 1970's, chef-owner Giancarlo Bolla converted a house into a restaurant, but left it decorated like a real house. As a result, the place has a homey charm. CUISINE French, Italian. CREDIT CARDS All. HOURS Mon-Fri, noon-3pm; Sat and Sun, noon-5pm; Mon-Thu, 7pm-1am; Fri and Sat, 7pm-2am; Sun, 7pm-12:30am.
Av. Nove de Julho, 5925, Itaim Bibi
TEL 3079 6277

La Vecchia Cucina $$

Its brick walls, reminiscent of Tuscany, create a rustic environment. Chef Sérgio Arno changes the menu frequently, but pasta is the highlight here, with different choices every week. CUISINE Italian. CREDIT CARDS All. HOURS Mon-Fri, noon-3pm; Sun, noon-5pm; Mon-Thu, 7pm-12:30am; Fri and Sat, 7pm-1am.
R. Pedroso Alvarenga, 1088, Itaim Bibi
TEL 3167-2822, ext. 1005/3079-7115

Laurent $$

This very sophisticated restaurant offers French classics suffused with Brazilian ingredients and flavors. They are all created by the highly acclaimed chef Laurent Suaudeau, who studied with Paul Bocuse. Try the cream of sea urchin with fresh coriander emulsion, shrimp Napoleon with fresh palm tree hearts, and green corn gnocchi with cream of Parmesan and Port wine. CUISINE Contemporary, French. CREDIT CARDS All. HOURS Tue-Fri, noon-3pm; Sun, noon-5pm; Mon-Thu, 7pm-midnight; Fri and Sat, 7pm-1am.
Al. Lorena, 1899, Jardins
TEL 3062-1452

Le Vin Bistrô $

This charming bistro belongs to the same owner of Café Antique. It serves delicious dishes in a romantic atmosphere, such as the duck *confit* with sautéed potatoes. The ambience is elegant though more casual and relaxed than Antique's. CUISINE French. CREDIT CARDS American Express, MasterCard, Visa. HOURS Mon-Thu, noon-midnight; Fri and Sat, noon-1am; Sun, noon-11pm.
Al. Tietê, 184, Jardins
TEL 3081-3924

Martín Fierro $

Argentinean meat cuts, such as *bife de chorizo* (sirloin steak) are the highlights here, but don't miss the *empanadas* (meat-filled baked turnovers). It is located in a busy spot in Vila Madalena and you'll probably have to wait to be served. There are also outdoor tables. CUISINE Meat. CREDIT CARDS All. HOURS Mon-Fri, 11:30am-11pm; Sat and Sun, 11:30am-5:30pm.
R. Aspicuelta, 683, Vila Madalena
TEL 3814-6747

Massimo $$$

Extremely refined and expensive, this was the second restaurant opened by the Ferrari family. In the 1950's they opened Cabana, a *churrascaria* that operated until 1993. Massimo opened in 1976 and has become one of the town's most important Italian restaurants. The menu features some of the famous options offered by Cabana, such as spaghetti *al cartoccio* (in a pouch) with tomato and basil. The wine list has over 100 Italian labels. CUISINE Italian. CREDIT CARDS Not accepted. HOURS Mon-Thu, noon-3pm and 7:30pm-midnight; Fri, noon-3pm and 7:30pm-1am; Sat and Sun, noon-4:30pm; Sat, 7:30pm-1am; Sun, 7:30pm-11pm.
Al. Santos, 1826, Cerqueira César
TEL 3284-0311

Mercearia do Conde $

This fast-food casual restaurant serves great quiches, crepes, sandwiches and salads. The unusual decoration has handicraft-style pieces with kitschy flourishes. It is usually busy and draws a hype clientele, especially on weekends. CUISINE Varied. CREDIT CARDS Not accepted. HOURS Mon, 12:30pm-4pm and 7pm-midnight; Tue-Sun, 12:30pm-midnight.
R. Joaquim Antunes, 217, Jardins
TEL 3081-7204

Mestiço $

This busy and casual restaurant is packed on weekends. The menu, with a mix of Thai food and regional cuisine from Bahia offers good options such as *samui* (chicken with cashew nuts) and *hua hin* (chicken with shiitake mushrooms and ginger). CUISINE Contemporary, Thai. CREDIT CARDS All. HOURS Daily, from 11:45am until late.
R. Fernando de Albuquerque, 277, Consolação
TEL 3256-3165/3259-1539

Oficina de Pizzas $

In a relaxed atmosphere, with brick walls and rustic tables and chairs, this pizza parlor serves one of the best pizzas of the bohemian Vila Madalena district. CUISINE Pizza. CREDIT CARDS All. HOURS Sun-Thu, 7pm-midnight; Fri and Sat, 7pm-1am.
R. Purpurina, 517, Vila Madalena
TEL 3816-3749

Osteria Don Boseggia $

Chef Luciano Boseggia offers tasty pizza topping choices such as Du Boseggia, with Brie cheese, asparagus and tomato. CUISINE Italian. CREDIT CARDS All. HOURS Mon-Fri, 7pm-12:30am; Sat and Sun, noon-midnight.
R. Diogo Jacome, 591, Vila Nova Conceição
TEL 3842-5590

Padaria Barcelona $

In business for almost 30 years, this bakery in Higienópolis has a loyal clientele drawn from all over town. Those in the know come to taste its sweet breads. CUISINE Sandwiches. CREDIT CARDS Diners, MasterCard, Visa. HOURS Daily, 6am-10pm.

PRICES	HOTELS (couple)	$ up to R$150	$$ from R$151 up to R$300	$$$ from R$301 up to R$500	$$$$ above R$500

R. Armando Penteado, 33, Higienópolis
TEL 3826-4911

Pandoro $$

This restaurant, bar and pastry shop is one of the most traditional in town. The delicious *caju-amigo* ("Friendly cashew", with vodka, cashew apple, sugar and ice) was created here almost 50 years ago. It offers a complete breakfast and lunch buffet. CUISINE Varied. CREDIT CARDS All. HOURS Daily, 8:30am-1am.
Av. Cidade Jardim, 60, Jardim Europa
TEL 3083-0399

Parigi $$$

Owned by the Fasano family, Parigi is romantic and refined in the evenings, while businessmen pack its premises at lunch. Chefs Salvatore Loi and Eric Berland run the kitchen and offer Italian and French dishes. CUISINE French, Italian. CREDIT CARDS All. HOURS Mon-Thu, noon-3pm and 7pm-1am; Fri, noon-4pm; Sat, 7pm-1:30am; Sun, noon-5pm.
R. Amauri, 275, Itaim Bibi
TEL 3167-1575

Ponto Chic $

Opened in 1922, this snack bar is known for having created the *bauru*, a sandwich made on bread with roast beef, cheese and tomato. There are other branches, but none is as good as the charming original shop. CUISINE Brazilian, sandwiches. CREDIT CARDS All. HOURS Mon-Sat, 10am-midnight.
Lgo. do Paissandu, 27, Centro
TEL 222-6528

Rincón de Buenos Aires $

The meat choices such as *ojo de bife* (rib-eye steak) and *parrillada* (mixed grilled meat) are the highlights of this restaurant in *porteño* atmosphere. On Fridays, there are tango shows and live *bolero*. CUISINE Meat. CREDIT CARDS All. HOURS Mon-Fri, noon-3:30pm and 7pm-midnight; Sat, noon-midnight; Sun, noon-6pm.
R. Santa Justina, 99, Vila Olímpia
TEL 3849-0096

Ritz $

This bar has been a meeting point for celebrities for decades. It serves fast food options, including an exceptional hamburger. It is a gay and lesbian spot in the evening. There's a branch in Itaim. CUISINE Contemporary. CREDIT CARDS All. HOURS Mon-Fri, noon-3pm and 8pm-1:30am; Sat and Sun, 1pm-1:30am.
Al. Franca, 1088, Jardins
TEL 3088-6808

São Cristóvão $

Football fans especially appreciate this charming bar. The walls are decorated with photos, flags, t-shirts and team memorabilia. The Saturday special *feijoada* stands out, and the *chope* (draft beer) is good. CUISINE Varied. CREDIT CARDS All. HOURS Daily, noon-2am.
R. Aspicuelta, 533, Vila Madalena
TEL 3097-9904

Skye $$

Located on the top floor of the Unique Hotel, it offers a wonderful, cosmopolitan view that takes in even Ibirapuera Park and the district of Jardins. The bar, in what used to be the restaurant's waiting area, is now a must. Try the "PF risotto", included in the menu created by chef Emmanuel Bassoleil. CUISINE Varied. CREDIT CARDS All. HOURS Mon-Thu, 7am-11am, noon-3pm and 7pm-midnight; Fri, 7pm-1am; Sat, noon-4pm and 7pm-1am; Sun, noon-4pm.
Av. Brigadeiro Luís Antônio, 4700, Jardins
TEL 3055-4702

Speranza $

Visit the district of Bexiga and try Speranza's *tortano* (bread with sausage). Their pizzas are also tasty, especially the *margherita* (cheese and basil) and *calabresa* (Calabrian-style sausage) ones. CUISINE Pizza. CREDIT CARDS Visa. HOURS Mon-Fri, 6pm-1:30am; Sat, until 2am; Sun, until 1am.
R. Treze de Maio, 1004, Bexiga
TEL 3288-8502

Spot $

Surrounded by glass walls, this highly fashionable restaurant is the ideal place to see and be seen. The service is fast, the food great, and the drink options many. CUISINE Contemporary. CREDIT CARDS All. HOURS Mon-Fri, noon-3pm; Sat and Sun, 1pm-5pm; Daily, 8pm-1am.
Al. Ministro Rocha Azevedo, 72, Cerqueira César
TEL 3284-6131

St. Etienne $

This is a busy and casual meeting point in Vila Madalena, especially for Sunday brunch, when it offers great sandwiches and sweets. CUISINE Sandwiches. CREDIT CARDS Diners, MasterCard, Visa. HOURS Mon-Fri, 6am-11pm; Sat and Sun, 7am-10pm.
R. Harmonia, 699, Vila Madalena
TEL 3819-2578

Suplicy $

This café offers a selection of coffee beans, from several farms, ground to the customer's taste. There are also sweets, pastries and savories. CUISINE Bar. CREDIT CARDS Diners, MasterCard, Visa. HOURS Mon-Thu, 8:30am-midnight; Fri, 8:30am-1am; Sat, 9:30am-1am; Sun, 9:30am-midnight.
Al. Lorena, 1430, Jardins
TEL 3061-0195

Sushi Lika $

Lika, a *sushiman* from Bahia, in Northeastern Brazil, prepares delicious *negui-toro*, a dumpling with salmon and tuna. Another suggestion is salmon *teppan*. CUISINE Japanese. CREDIT CARDS Diners, MasterCard, Visa. HOURS Mon-Sat, 11:30am-2:30pm and 6:30pm-12:30am.
R. dos Estudantes, 152, Liberdade
TEL 3207-7435

Sushi Yassu $$$

Opened in 1972, it is one of the most established Japanese restaurants in town. It serves exotic dishes such as *uni sushi*, *sushi* with sea urchin filling. There's a branch on r. Manoel da Nóbrega, 199, Paraíso. CUISINE Japanese. CREDIT CARDS All. HOURS Mon-Fri, 11:30am-

---

RESTAURANTS $ up to R$50 $$ from R$51 up to R$100 $$$ from R$101 up to R$150 $$$$ above R$150

2:30pm and 6pm-11:30pm; Sat, noon-3:30pm and 6pm-midnight; Sun, noon-10pm.
R. Tomás Gonzaga, 98, Liberdade
TEL 3209-6622

348 Parrilla Porteña $$
With a friendly atmosphere, this Argentinean meat restaurant serves traditional cuts such as *bife de chorizo* (sirloin steak) and rib-eye steak. CUISINE Meat. CREDIT CARDS All. HOURS Tue-Fri, noon-3pm and 7pm-midnight; Sat, noon-midnight; Sun, noon-6pm.
R. Comendador Miguel Calfat, 348, Vila Olímpia
TEL 3849-5839

Totó Ristorante $
Chef Luiza Bistolfi runs the kitchen under the influence of Northern Italy. One of the highlights of the menu is *tortellini* with rabbit filling. CUISINE Italian. CREDIT CARDS All. HOURS Tue-Thu, noon-3pm and 7pm-11pm; Fri, noon-3pm and 7pm-midnight; Sat, 1pm-4pm and 8pm-midnight; Sun and holidays, 1pm-5pm.
R. Dr. Sodré, 77, Vila Olímpia
TEL 3841-9067

Varanda Grill $
It serves Brazilian cuts such as *picanha* (cap of rump), Argentinean cuts such as *bife de lomo* (tenderloin), and North American cuts such as porterhouse steak. The wine list is good. Order *biro-biro* rice (with egg, bacon and seasoning) as a side dish. CUISINE Meat. CREDIT CARDS All. HOURS Mon-Fri, noon-3pm and 7pm-midnight; Sat, noon-midnight; Sun, noon-5pm.
R. General Mena Barreto, 793, Jardim Paulista
TEL 3887-8870

Vecchio Torino $$
Very cheerful and charming, this restaurant serves great dishes such as the *tortelloni alla piemontese*, with duck filling. The wine cellar contains almost 6,000 bottles, so do your duty and help them make some space down there. CUISINE Italian. CREDIT CARDS All. HOURS Tue-Sat, noon-4pm and 7pm-midnight; Sun, noon-4pm.
R. Tavares Cabral, 119, Pinheiros
TEL 3816-0592/0560

Vinheria Percussi $
A trellised vine at the entrance sets the tone of this restaurant, which used to be a wine house. The pasta, such as the one filled with Brie cheese and *prosecco* sauce, is delicious. CUISINE Italian. CREDIT CARDS All. HOURS Tue-Thu, noon-3pm and 7pm-11:30pm; Fri, noon-3pm and 7pm-1am; Sat, noon-4:30pm and 7pm-1am; Sun, noon-4:30pm.
R. Cônego Eugênio Leite, 523, Pinheiros
TEL 3088-4920

Z Deli $
This delicatessen offers a wide variety of Jewish food. There are two branches, on r. Haddock Lobo, 1386, and other on al. Gabriel Monteiro da Silva, 1350. CUISINE Jewish. CREDIT CARDS American Express, Diners, MasterCard. HOURS Mon-Fri, noon-6pm; Sat, noon-4:30pm.
Al. Lorena, 1689, Jardins
TEL 3088-5644

SERVICES

AIRPORT

Aeroporto Internacional de São Paulo/Guarulhos
Rodovia Hélio Smidt, Cumbica
TEL 6445-2945

Aeroporto Internacional de Congonhas
Av. Washington Luiz, Campo Belo
TEL 5090-9000

TOURIST POLICE STATION

Delegacia de Atendimento ao Turista
Av. São Luís, 91, Centro
TEL 3214-0209. HOURS Daily, 9am-7pm

TOURIST INFORMATION

Centro de Informações Turísticas
Pça. da República, Centro
TEL 3231-2922. HOURS Daily, 9am-6pm

Centro de Informações Turísticas
Av. Paulista, across from Parque Trianon
TEL 3251-0970. HOURS Daily, 9am-6pm

EXCHANGE SHOP

Cotação S/A
Av. Paulista, 807, 19º andar, cj. 1901
TEL 3178-8900. HOURS Mon-Fri, 9am-4pm

São Sebastião – SP

AREA CODE 12 POPULATION 57,886
DISTANCE São Paulo, 214 km (133 mi)

HOTELS

Juquehy Praia $$$
This hotel is virtually on the beach, and the beautiful pool seems to be a continuation of the sea. The rooms, though simple, are spacious and comfortable, making it ideal for families. FACILITIES 54 rooms, air-conditioning, phone, TV, ceiling fan, bar, pool, tennis court, restaurant, convention room, fitness room, sauna. CREDIT CARDS All.
Av. Mãe Bernarda, 3221, Praia de Juqueí
TEL 3891-1000
www.juquehy.com.br

Maresias Beach $$$
This comfortable hotel is located in the most fashionable beach of São Sebastião. Rooms overlook the sea and the mountains, and each has a balcony. A recreation team offers activities for children. It's very pleasant for couples, too. FACILITIES 92 rooms, air-conditioning, phone, TV, ceiling fan, bar, football field, recreation team, pool, playground, tennis court, restaurant, convention room, fitness room, game

PRICES	HOTELS (couple)	$ up to R$150	$$ from R$151 up to R$300	$$$ from R$301 up to R$500	$$$$ above R$500

room, sauna. **CREDIT CARDS** Diners, MasterCard, Visa.
Av. Francisco Loup, 1109, Praia de Maresias
TEL 3891-7500 **FAX** 3891-7509
www.maresiashotel.com.br

Sambaqui $$

This hotel is decorated in rustic style and has a family-like atmosphere. Each room has been individually decorated and six of them overlook the sea. Closed in May. **FACILITIES** 16 rooms, air-conditioning, TV, cable TV, ceiling fan, bar, pool, restaurant, convention room, sauna. **CREDIT CARDS** Diners, MasterCard.
R. Xavantes, 57, Praia da Juréia
TEL 3867-1291
www.hotelsambaquicom.br

Villa Bebek $$

This hotel was built in Thai style and the rooms are arranged around the pool, which is narrow, long and sinuous, like a river. The service is very friendly. **FACILITIES** 21 rooms, air-conditioning, phone, TV, cable TV, ceiling fan, bar, pool, restaurant, massage room. **CREDIT CARDS** MasterCard, Visa.
R. do Zezito, 251, Camburizinho
TEL 3865-2123
www.villabebek.com.br

RESTAURANTS

Acqua $$

Very charming and refined, this restaurant sits on top of a hill, and has a stunning view of the Camburi beach. Try the *gamberoni* (grilled shrimp). **CUISINE** Fish and seafood. **CREDIT CARDS** Diners, MasterCard, Visa. **HOURS** Fri and Sat, 2pm-1am; Sun, 1pm-10pm; Daily in the summer, 2pm-1am.
Estrada do Camburi, 2000
TEL 3865-1866

Manacá $$

Hidden in an alley in Camburizinho and surrounded by greenery, this is the best restaurant on the São Paulo coast. The menu changes frequently but there are fixed options such as seafood risotto, sole with orange sauce, and fish stuffed with *farofa* (manioc flour with seasoning). Reservations advised. **CUISINE** Fish and seafood. **CREDIT CARDS** All. **HOURS** Thu, 6pm-11pm; Fri and Sat, 1pm-11pm; Sun, 1pm-9pm.
R. Manacá, 102
TEL 3865-1566

SERVICES

TOURIST INFORMATION

Centro de Informações Turísticas
R. Altino Arantes, 174, Centro
TEL 3892-1808. **HOURS** Mon-Fri, 8am-6pm

Teresópolis – RJ

AREA CODE 21 **POPULATION** 138,081
DISTANCES Rio de Janeiro, 87 km (54 mi); **São Paulo**, 484 km (300.7 mi); **Belo Horizonte**, 405 km (252.6 mi)

HOTELS

Bromélia, Sabiá and Cia. $$

The decorations show how well traveled the owners are. Breakfast is served in a round stone room illuminated by the immense skylight on the roof. Children under 14 are not allowed. **FACILITIES** 5 rooms, phone, TV, bar, rock pool, sauna. **CREDIT CARDS** All.
Estrada do Araken, 1231, Granja Guarany
TEL 2642-2239
www.bromeliasabia.com.br

Hotel Fazenda Rosa dos Ventos $$$

Situated between Teresópolis and Nova Friburgo, this hotel combines comfort and country life. There are plenty of leisure options and a wine cellar where there's wine tasting and fondue is served. The rooms are spacious, with large beds. **FACILITIES** 42 rooms, phone, TV, ceiling fan, bar, boating, horses, pool, heated pool, restaurant, convention room, fitness room, game room, massage room, sauna. **CREDIT CARDS** All.
Estrada Teresópolis–Nova Friburgo,
km 22.5 Campanha
TEL 2644-9900 **FAX** 2642-8174 **RESERVATIONS** 2532-1197
www.hotelrosadosventos.com.br

Pousada Urikana $$$

This inn nests on a plateau of dos Órgãos mountains, 3281 ft above sea level, in an area with private woods where guests can hike trails. Some chalets have a whirlpool tub and a 29" TV. **FACILITIES** 17 rooms, air-conditioning, fireplace, phone, TV, ceiling fan, minigolf course, pool, restaurant, fitness room, game room, sauna. **CREDIT CARDS** All.
Estrada Ibiporanga, 2151, Parque do Imbuí
TEL 2641-8991
www.pousadaurikana.com.br

Toca-Terê Pousada $$$

There are 11 chalets on this several-acre lot, 5 of which have *ofurô* bathtubs overlooking the vegetation. The paths between the two restaurants and the chalets cross suspended bridges and rocks. **FACILITIES** 11 rooms, fireplace, phone, TV, cable TV, bar, recreation team, rock pool, heated pool, restaurant, convention room, fitness room, game room, massage room, sauna. **CREDIT CARDS** All.
Pça. dos Namorados, Parque do Ingá
TEL 2642-5020 **FAX** 2642-5021
www.tocatere.com.br

RESTAURANTS

Cremerie Genève $

This restaurant, on a goat farm, has ready access to some of the best goat cheese in the country. There are twelve types. The menu features classical French recipes, such as duck *magret* with cassis sauce and rabbit with mustard or wine sauce. Kids love the goats, especially the kids. Book visits ahead. **CUISINE** French. **CREDIT CARDS** Diners, MasterCard. **HOURS** Fri and Sat, noon-10pm; Sun, noon-8pm.
Estrada Teresópolis–Nova Friburgo, km 16
TEL 3643-6391

RESTAURANTS	**$** up to R$50	**$$** from R$51 up to R$100	**$$$** from R$101 up to R$150	**$$$$** above R$150

Dona Irene $$

Set two hours aside to enjoy this genuine Russian banquet. The meal begins with *piroskis* (meat turnovers) and herrings accompanied by homemade vodka. Then comea a Kiev soup of beets and chicken, and the "real" stroganoff, among other delicacies. Reservation advised. CUISINE Russian. CREDIT CARDS Not accepted. HOURS Wed-Sat, noon-midnight; Sun, noon-6pm.
R. Tenente Luiz Meirelles, 1800, Bom Retiro
TEL 2742-2901

Manjericão $

Located in the district of Alto, this is reputed to be the best pizza parlor in the region. The crust is thin and light. The Parmesan cheese, cream and walnut topping is a great choice. CUISINE Pizza. CREDIT CARDS American Express, MasterCard. HOURS Thu and Fri, 6pm-11pm; Sat and Sun, noon-11pm.
R. Flávio Bortoluzzi de Souza, 314, Alto
TEL 2642-4242

SERVICES

LOCAL TOUR OPERATORS

Centro de Excursionistas de Teresópolis (CET)
TEL 2643-1177/2742-9791

TOURIST INFORMATION

Secretaria de Turismo
Av. Rotariana, Town's Gateway
TEL 2642-1737/2094. HOURS Mon-Fri, 9am-6pm; Sat, 9am-5pm; Sun, 9am-1pm

Tiradentes – MG

AREA CODE 32 POPULATION 5,759
DISTANCE Belo Horizonte, 215 km (133.6 mi)

HOTELS

Pousada dos Inconfidentes $$$
This colonial-style inn opened recently. All the rooms are spacious, comfortable, and centrally heated. Some have a fireplace, others have a balcony. The pool, in the shape of an "L", is 25 meters long. Children under 16 are not allowed. FACILITIES 13 rooms, fireplace, phone, TV, bar, pool, restaurant, fitness room, sauna. CREDIT CARDS All.
R. João Rodrigues Sobrinho, 91, Condomínio Parque dos Bandeirantes
TEL 3355-2215 FAX 3355-2135 RESERVATIONS 3355-2341
www.pousadadosinconfidentes.com.br

Pousada Villa Paolucci $$$
This 200-year-old estate used to be the family's farm. It was restored with discarded wood. The rooms are spacious and airy, and genuine articles of old furniture mix with replicas. Notice especially the garden pergola and the large kitchen, which makes the inn the most important venue of the town's Gastronomy Week in August. Children under 16 are not welcome in the high season. FACILITIES 10 rooms, fireplace, phone, TV, pool, tennis court, restaurant, sauna. CREDIT

CARDS MasterCard, Visa.
R. do Chafariz
TEL 3355-1350
www.villapaolucci.cjb.net

Solar da Ponte $$$
This inn offers colonial-style lodgings, matching the style of the historical town of Tiradentes. The owners, Anna Maria and John Parsons, welcome guests with the congenial hospitality typical of the state of Minas, and offer abundant breakfast and afternoon tea. Anna is a specialist in baroque art. FACILITIES 18 rooms, heater, minibar, phone, TV, bar, pool, internet access, TV and video room, sauna. CREDIT CARDS All.
Pça. das Mercês
TEL 3355-1255 FAX 3355-1201
www.solardaponte.com.br/page.htm

Xica da Silva Pousada $$$
The owner lives in the inn, and provides customized service. She collects antiques and displays them all around. Some rooms are very spacious. It is far from the center. One of the few inns that accept children and has an adequate amenities for them. FACILITIES 16 rooms, fireplace, phone, TV, bar, heated pool, playground, restaurant, game room, massage room, sauna. CREDIT CARDS American Express, Diners, MasterCard.
Av. Governador Israel Pinheiro, 400
TEL 3355-1874
www.xicadasilva.com.br

RESTAURANTS

Padre Toledo $
This restaurant has been open for more than 30 years and is near one of the oldest and most important streets of the town, next to an inn. The decoration of the 19th century house is austere, with furniture in *jacaranda* hard wood. It serves great food and a famous *pinga* or *cachaça* (white rum) called Pedro Toledo. CUISINE Regional from Minas. CREDIT CARDS All. HOURS Daily, 11am-10pm.
R. Direita, 250, Centro
TEL 3355-1222/3355-2132

Tragaluz $
This is one of the newest restaurants in town, although it operates in a 300-year-old house. It serves light-style regional dishes with an innovative touch. The lighting and decoration provide a friendly atmosphere. CUISINE Contemporary, regional from Minas. CREDIT CARDS All. HOURS 7pm-10pm; closed on Tuesdays.
R. Direita, 52, Centro
TEL 3355-1424

Uai $
This is a simple and familial restaurant, with a fireplace and a wood-burning stove. The home-style cooking is delicious. Try the chicken with *ora-pro-nobis* (spinach-like leaves) or okra and *feijão-tropeiro* (cooked beans with olive oil, garlic, onion, parsley and chive, thickened with manioc flour) or *tutu à mineira* (bean purée with pork sausage, manioc flour and seasoning). All dishes serve two. CUISINE Regional from Minas. CREDIT CARDS Not accepted. HOURS Daily, noon-11pm.

PRICES	HOTELS (couple)	$ up to R$150	$$ from R$151 up to R$300	$$$ from R$301 up to R$500	$$$$ above R$500

Travessa do Chafariz, 73
TEL 3355-2370

Viradas do Largo $

This traditional restaurant presents its wood-burning stove very close to the dining room. There are novelties added to traditional dishes. Try the *tutu* (bean purée with pork sausage, manioc flour and seasoning) with spare ribs or smoked pork knuckle (serves three). CUISINE Regional from Minas. CREDIT CARDS Diners, MasterCard, Visa. HOURS Wed-Mon, noon-10pm.
R. do Moinho, 11, Centro
TEL 3355-1111

Ubatuba – SP

AREA CODE 12 POPULATION 66,861
DISTANCE São Paulo, 235 km (146 mi)

HOTELS

Itamambuca Eco Resort $$$

Located inside a small ecological reserve, this resort offers its guests plenty of sports activities and environmental education programs. The rooms are comfortable and have a balcony overlooking the reserve. FACILITIES 52 rooms, phone, TV, bar, recreation team, pool, playground, tennis court, restaurant, convention room, fitness room, game room, massage room. CREDIT CARDS Not accepted.
Rodovia Rio–Santos, km 36
TEL 3834-3000
www.itamambuca.com.br

Pousada Maranduba $$

This inn has spacious rooms with verandahs overlooking the ocean, and a nice living room as well. The owner himself provides the service. There are kayaks and a boat. FACILITIES 12 rooms, air-conditioning, phone, TV, bar, boat, playground, restaurant, game room. CREDIT CARDS All.
Av. Marginal, 899
TEL 3849-8378 RESERVATIONS 3849-8408
www.pousadamaranduba.com.br

Recanto das Toninhas $$$

Decorated in rustic style, this inn has spacious rooms with verandahs. The kid's club organizes activities for children almost all day. The *feijoada* served on Saturdays is included in the rate. FACILITIES 54 rooms, air-conditioning, phone, TV, cable TV, bar, recreation team, pool, heated pool, tennis court, restaurant, convention room, fitness room, game room, massage room, sauna. CREDIT CARDS All.
Rodovia SP-055, km 56.5
TEL 3842-1410 FAX 0800177557 RESERVATIONS (11) 288-2022
www.toninhas.com.br

Solar das Águas Cantantes $$

Hidden between the beaches of Lázaro and Sununga, this friendly hotel was built in colonial style and has an efficient staff. It serves delicious *moquecas* by the pool and the beautiful garden. It is simple and romantic. FACILITIES 20 rooms, air-conditioning, phone, TV, ceiling fan, bar, pool, restaurant, game room. CREDIT CARDS MasterCard, Visa.

Estrada do Saco da Ribeira, 253
TEL 3842-0178 RESERVATIONS 3842-0288
www.solardasaguascantantes.com.br

RESTAURANTS

Juju Balangandã $

This charming restaurant overlooks the sea on one side and the Ubatumirim river on the other. It specializes in healthy foods, such as grilled dishes, seafood, fish and salads, and has no fried options. Tables are virtually placed on the sand, and food is served in fish-shaped wooden vessels. Under the trees are hammocks for an after-meal nap. CUISINE Fish and seafood. CREDIT CARDS Not accepted. HOURS Sat and Sun, 9am-5pm; in the high season, daily, 9am-6pm.
Praia do Ubatumirim (last bar before the river)
TEL 9145-0879

Peixe com Banana $$

This restaurant prepares the best *azul-marinho* (navy blue) of the region, with slices of fish (such as red grouper) and green Cavendish banana, cooked in an iron pot. The banana turns slightly blue, thus the name of the dish. CUISINE Fish and seafood. CREDIT CARDS Diners, MasterCard, Visa. HOURS Daily, noon-11pm.
R. Guarani, 255, Itaguá
TEL 3832-1712

Solar das Águas Cantantes $$

This well-regarded restaurant is located inside a hotel by the same name (see separate listing above). The tasty grouper and shrimp *moqueca*, served by the pool, is the house specialty. Pay attention to the small signs that indicate the way on the bumpy, unpaved roads between the Lázaro and Sununga beaches. CUISINE Fish and seafood. CREDIT CARDS Diners, MasterCard, Visa. HOURS Mon-Fri, noon-2pm and 6pm-10pm; Sat and Sun, noon-10pm.
Estrada do Saco da Ribeira 253, Praia do Lázaro
TEL 3842-0178/0288

Terra Papagalli $$

Located on the sea front, this restaurant changes its menu every week, but you can always put your money on the day's special. CUISINE Fish and seafood. CREDIT CARDS American Express, Diners, MasterCard. HOURS Mon and Wed-Fri, 6pm-midnight; Sat and Sun, noon-midnight. From December 15 through January 31, open daily, noon-midnight.
R. Xavantes, 537, Itaguá
TEL 3832-1488

SERVICES

TOURIST INFORMATION

Centro de Informações Turísticas

Av. Iperoig, 331, Centro
TEL 08007717400. HOURS Daily, 8am-6pm

Vassouras – RJ

AREA CODE 24 POPULATION 31,451
DISTANCE Rio de Janeiro, 111 km (69 mi)

RESTAURANTS $ up to R$50 $$ from R$51 up to R$100 $$$ from R$101 up to R$150 $$$$ above R$150

HOTELS

Hotel Fazenda Galo Vermelho $$$

This hotel has a good services for nature-oriented recreation, and more than 1,000 acres to play in, nearly half of which are clad in Atlantic Rainforest. There are itineraries for hiking trails and horseback riding, and a vacation resort for kids. In the low season it is available for day use. FACILITIES 14 rooms, air-conditioning, phone, TV, cable TV, ceiling fan, football field, horses, pool, volleyball court, restaurant, fitness room. CREDIT CARDS Not accepted.
Estrada RJ-121, 6814
TEL 2471-1244 FAX 2471-7200
www.hotelfazendagalovermelho.com.br

Mara Palace $

The unit in the center of Vassouras has simple amenities, but the country resort, 7 km (4.3 mi) from there has a lake for fishing, sauna, trails, tennis courts, football field and pool. FACILITIES 65 rooms, air-conditioning, phone, cable TV, boat, football field, horses, recreation team, pool, playground, football court, tennis court, restaurant, convention room, fitness room, game room, massage room, spa. CREDIT CARDS All.
R. Chanceler Raul Fernandes, 121, Centro
TEL 2471-1993 FAX 2471-2524 RESERVATIONS 08007041994
www.marapalace.com.br

Vila Velha – ES

AREA CODE 27 POPULATION 345,965
DISTANCE Vitória, 3 km (1.9 mi)
SITE www.vilavelha.es.gov.br

HOTEL

Quality Suítes Vila Velha $$

This hotel, part of the Atlântica Hotel chain, is on the avenue alongside the beach. It offers business facilities as well as amenities for leisure, such as chairs and parasols. It also has an exclusive entry for beach goers. The rooms have a living room and a bedroom. Senior rooms have a minikitchen. FACILITIES 136 rooms, air-conditioning, phone, TV, cable TV, ceiling fan, bar, pool, restaurant, convention room, fitness room, game room, sauna. CREDIT CARDS All.
Av. Antônio Gil Veloso, 856, Praia da Costa
TEL 3399-5454 RESERVATIONS 0800555855 FAX 3349-3947
www.atlanticahotels.com.br

RESTAURANTS

Atlântica $$

A traditional option on the seaside, this restaurant opened in the 1960's. Paintings by local artists, all for sale, decorate the simple facilities. In addition to the mixed (fish and seafood) *moqueca*, it also serves *moquecas* of grouper, shrimp, lobster and *sururu* (mussel). CUISINE Fish and seafood. CREDIT CARDS All. HOURS Mon and Wed-Sat, 11:30am-midnight; Sun and Tue, 11am-5pm.
Av. Antônio Gil Veloso, 80, Praia da Costa
TEL 3329-2341

Café do Museu $

This café operates from inside an old train car, in the patio of the Pedro Nolasco station, next to the Museu Ferroviário (Railway Museum). The short menu features Italian dishes. CUISINE Varied. CREDIT CARDS Visa. HOURS Tue, Wed and Sun, 10am-6pm; Thu-Sat, 10am-1am.
R. Vila Isabel, Estação Pedro Nolasco, Argolas (Museu da Vale do Rio Doce)
TEL 3326-8190/9279-8459

SERVICES

TOURIST INFORMATION

Casa do Turista

Av. Presidente Lima, 516, Centro
TEL 3289-0202/3139-9015. HOURS Mon-Fri, 8am-6pm

Posto de Informação Turística – Convento da Penha

R. Vasco Coutinho, Prainha
TEL 3329-0420/3329-9290. HOURS Daily, 9am-5pm

Visconde de Mauá – RJ

AREA CODE 24
DISTANCE Rio de Janeiro, 200 km (124 mi)

HOTELS

Bühler $$$

This is one of the few hotels of the region that welcomes children. It lies in the state of Minas, in Maringá, just over the border from Rio de Janeiro. The two-room chalets are comfortable. Baby-sitter service is available. FACILITIES 21 rooms, fireplace, TV, cable TV, bar, minigolf course, pool, rock pool, heated pool, jogging track, playground, multipurpose court, football field, tennis court, volleyball courts, restaurant, convention room, fitness room, game room, massage room, sauna. CREDIT CARDS All.
Pça. Maringá
TEL 3387-1204 FAX 3387-1378
www.hotelbuhler.com.br

Fronteira $$$$

Far from the center, this hotel has a stunning view of the mountains. Heliport available. The chalets are enormous and have been individually decorated. The owner provides customized service. Children under 14 are not allowed. FACILITIES 10 rooms, fireplace, TV, DVD player, CD player, bar, rock pool, restaurant, sauna. CREDIT CARDS Not accepted.
Estrada Mauá–Campo Alegre, km 4
TEL 3387-1219 RESERVATIONS 3387-1366
www.hotelfronteira.com.br

Hotelaria Mauá Brasil $$$

This new and rather exclusive inn is a good option for those seeking peace and quiet. The large chalets are scattered on top of a hill with a view of the mountain range. The rooms are nicely decorated and have a fireplace and a whirlpool tub with a panoramic view. FACILITIES 9 rooms, fireplace, TV, bar, heated pool, restaurant, sauna. CREDIT CARDS Diners, MasterCard.
Estrada Visconde de Mauá–Campo Alegre, km 4
TEL 3387-2077
www.mauabrasil.com.br

PRICES	HOTELS (couple)	$ up to R$150	$$ from R$151 up to R$300	$$$ from R$301 up to R$500	$$$$ above R$500

500

BRAZIL GUIDE

Jardins do Passaredo $$

This inn is on the side of the mountains that's inside the state of Minas. The owner is a talented landscaper, and a large and luxuriant garden has hundreds of species of bromeliad, orchids, pines and palms. The rooms have goose-feather pillows and quilts and there is a shallow pond in front of each chalet. The two flats have kitchen, cable TV and CD player with a collection of jazz CDs. Children under 12 are not allowed. **FACILITIES** 6 rooms, TV, rock pool, sauna. **CREDIT CARDS** Not accepted.
Estrada Maringá, km 6
TEL 3387-1190
www.jardinsdopassaredo.com.br

Terra da Luz Pousada $$$

Located in the heart of the village of Maringá, in the state of Minas, this pleasant inn has a great restaurant. The service is friendly and on weekends there are jazz performances. Children discouraged. **FACILITIES** 6 rooms, fireplace, phone, TV, bar, restaurant, massage room, sauna. **CREDIT CARDS** American Express, Diners, MasterCard.
Estrada Maringá, km 6.5
TEL 3387-1306 **RESERVATIONS** 3387-1545
www.pousadaterradaluz.com.br

Verde que te Quero Ver-te $$$

Frequented mostly by couples, this inn has spacious chalets, surrounded by plenty of green and a well-tendered garden. Breakfast is served anytime. The rooms have CD player, coffeemaker, fireplace and whirlpool tub. Children under 16 are not allowed. **FACILITIES** 7 rooms, fireplace, phone, TV, bar, pool, restaurant, game room, massage room, sauna. **CREDIT CARDS** All.
Estrada Mauá–Maringá, km 7.5
TEL 3387-1322
www.verdequetequeroverte.com.br

RESTAURANTS

Gosto com Gosto $

In a rustic atmosphere, this restaurant serves several regional dishes from the state of Minas, including traditional foods and its own creations, such as pork loin with orange sauce. There's a dessert buffet and a stunning 400 types of *cachaça*. Don't try them all in one evening. **CUISINE** Regional from Minas. **CREDIT CARDS** All.
HOURS Sun-Thu, noon-6pm; Fri and Sat, noon-10pm.
R. Wenceslau Braz, 148
TEL 3387-1382

Rosmarino Officinalis $$

Surrounded by green mountains, with an area of 1.23 acre, this restaurant offers candle-lit dinners. The food is some of the most acclaimed of the region. Chef Julio Buschinelli prepares excellent pastas in a wood-burning stove and seasons them with herbs from his own garden. **CUISINE** Varied. **CREDIT CARDS** All. **HOURS** Mon-Thu, 7pm-10pm; Fri and Sat, 1pm-5pm and 7pm-midnight; Sun, 1pm-6pm. Open every evening in January and July.
Estrada Mauá–Maringá, km 4, Maringá
TEL 3387-1550

Terra da Luz $$

Located in the inn of the same name, it has a roman-tic atmosphere, and offers jazz performances on Saturdays. The best choices are *risotto al funghi* with trout, lamb with couscous and cheese fondue. **CUISINE** Contemporary. **CREDIT CARDS** American Express, Diners, MasterCard. **HOURS** Fri-Sun, 8pm-1am.
Estrada Maringá, km 6.5
TEL 3387-1306

Vitória – ES

AREA CODE 27 **POPULATION** 292,304
DISTANCES Rio de Janeiro, 525 km (326 mi); Belo Horizonte, 526 km (326.8 mi); São Paulo, 958 km (595 mi)
SITE www.vitoria.es.gov.br

HOTELS

Ilha do Boi $$

This school-hotel of Senac College is situated on the top of a hill on Boi island, overlooking the third bridge and the bay. There's a separate leisure area with a marina, tennis court and playground. The rooms are spacious, and have a simple decorations and a verandah. The service falls short of expectations. **FACILITIES** 95 rooms, air-conditioning, phone, cable TV, bar, boat, pool, playground, tennis court, restaurant, convention room, sauna. **CREDIT CARDS** All.
R. Bráulio Macedo, 417, Ilha do Boi
TEL 3345-0111 **RESERVATIONS** 08002839991
www.hotelilhadoboi.com.br

Novotel Vitória $$

Located on the avenue alongside the beach, the building has ample common areas and modern decor. There's a business center, a 24-hour cyber café, a recreation room and a videogame room. It's great for both executives and tourist looking for leisure and beaches. It offers towels, chairs and parasols to beach goers. **FACILITIES** 162 rooms, air-conditioning, phone, TV, cable TV, bar, pool, restaurant, convention room, fitness room, sauna. **CREDIT CARDS** All.
Av. Saturnino de Brito, 1327, Praia do Canto
TEL 3334-5300 **FAX** 3334-5333 **RESERVATIONS** 08007037000
www.accorhotels.com.br

RESTAURANTS

Lareira Portuguesa $$

This restaurant is elegant, quiet and has a well-trained staff that can suggest wines from the cellar. Dona Elizete and her son, Fernando, the chef, have been running it since 1979. They prepare tasty charcoal-grilled codfish, *lagareira*-style codfish (*au gratin*, with peppers and capers) and a *mariscada* (a type of bouillabaisse) that includes codfish. **CUISINE** Portuguese. **CREDIT CARDS** American Express, Visa. **HOURS** Mon-Sat, 11:30am-3pm and 7pm-midnight; Sun, 11:30am-3pm.
R. Saturnino de Brito, 260, Praia do Canto
TEL 3345-0329

Oriundi $$

This small, congenial restaurant has efficient service. Chef-owner Juarez is usually visible in the glassed-in kitchen, where he prepares fillet *crosta* (crusted fillet) with powdered mushrooms and risotto with shiitake,

---

RESTAURANTS $ up to R$50 $$ from R$51 up to R$100 $$$ from R$101 up to R$150 $$$$ above R$150

in addition to *penne gambere* with shrimp and mush-room sauce. There's a wine cellar. **CUISINE** Italian. **CREDIT CARDS** Not accepted. **HOURS** Tue-Sat, 11:30am-2:30pm and 7pm-midnight; Sun and Mon, noon-3:30pm.
R. Elias Tomasi Sobrinho, 130, Santa Lúcia
TEL 3227-6989

Pirão $$
This pleasant restaurant, one of the most sophisticat-ed in town, serves a famous *moqueca* that's carefully prepared with fresh ingredients. The salted grouper and the *capixaba* pie are some of the house special-ties. The *pastelzinho de Belém*, a Portuguese convent sweet, is a favorite dessert. **CUISINE** Regional. **CREDIT CARDS** MasterCard. **HOURS** Mon-Sat, 11am-4pm and 6pm-10:30pm; Sun, 11am-5pm.
R. Joaquim Lírio, 753, Praia do Canto
TEL 3227-1165

SERVICES

AIRPORT

Aeroporto de Vitória Eurico Sales
Av. Fernando Ferrari
TEL 3235-6300

LOCAL TOUR OPERATORS

Avitures Receptivo
Av. Saturnino de Brito, 258, Edifício Kiara, Room 206, Praia do Canto
TEL 3227-8269

Fomatur
R. Manoel Vivacqua, 464, Jabour
TEL 3200-3155/9944-0685

Vitória Receptive
R. Tarciano Abaurre, 225, Centro Empresarial da Praia, Room 303, Enseada do Suá
TEL 3325-3637

BOAT RENTAL

Dolphin Pesca Oceânica
R. Paula Miled, 63/201, Barro Vermelho
TEL 3345-9455/9981-3699

Iate Clube do Espírito Santo
Pça. do Iate, 200, Praia do Canto
TEL 3225-0422

TOURIST POLICE STATION

Delegacia de Turismo
TEL 3137-9117

TOURIST INFORMATION

Posto de Informação Turística
Av. Américo Buaiz, 200, Enseada do Suá, Shopping Vitória

DIVING OPERATORS

Acquasub
R. Anísio Fernandes Coelho, 30, Loja 01, Jardim da Penha
TEL 3325-0036

Flamar
R. Almirante Tamandaré, 255, Praia do Suá
TEL 3227-9644

NORTHEAST

Andaraí – BA

AREA CODE 75 **POPULATION** 13,884
DISTANCE Salvador, 414 km (257 mi); Lençóis, 101 km (62.5 mi)
SITE www.pmandarai.com.br

HOTELS

Pousada Pedras do Igatu $
A century-old manor that belonged to a powerful *Coronel* (local political chief) accommodates the inn's common areas. The rooms are new, and have been decorated with local handicraft. They overlook the pa-tio, which has plenty of mango trees. **FACILITIES** 15 rooms, ceiling fan, bar, rock pool, restaurant. **CREDIT CARDS** Diners, MasterCard.
R. São Sebastião, Centro, distrito de Xique-Xique do Igatu, 12 km from Andaraí
TEL and **FAX** 335-2281
www.igatu.com.br/pousada

Pousada Sincorá $
Helder and Ana Lúcia made their home into an inn. Helder, who knows the Chapada region very well, is a tour guide and plans and organizes excursions and hikes. Ana Lúcia prepares delicious breakfasts. **FACILITIES** 5 rooms, air-conditioning, TV. **CREDIT CARDS** Diners, Master-Card, Visa.
Av. Paraguaçu, 120, Centro
TEL 335-2210 **FAX** 335-2486
www.sincora.com.br

SERVICES

TOURIST GUIDES

Associação dos Condutores de Visitantes de Andaraí (ACVA)
TEL 335-2255/2242. **HOURS** 9am-5pm.

Associação dos Condutores de Visitantes de Igatu (ACVI)
TEL 335-2445/2478 (public phones)

PRICES	HOTELS (couple)	$ up to R$150	$$ from R$151 up to R$300	$$$ from R$301 up to R$500	$$$$ above R$500

TOURIST INFORMATION

Prefeitura Municipal de Andaraí
R. Santa Bárbara (Pça. do Sol), Centro
TEL 335-2118 HOURS Mon-Sat, 8am-noon and 5pm-8pm

Aquiraz – CE

AREA CODE 85 POPULATION 60,469
DISTANCE Fortaleza, 24.7 km (15.3 mi)

HOTEL

Beach Park Suites Resort $$
Suites for two or four people have verandahs overlooking the ocean. Enjoy the comfort and privacy of the resort's beach, which is part of the Beach Park. Breakfast and dinner included in the rate. FACILITIES 198 rooms, internet, air-conditioning, individual safe, minibar, phone, TV, cable TV, bar, recreation team, convenience store, pool, playground, tennis court, restaurant, convention room, fitness room, game room, massage room, video room, sauna, hiking trails. CREDIT CARDS American Express, MasterCard, Visa.
R. Porto das Dunas, 2734, Porto das Dunas
TEL 4012-3000 FAX 4012-3040
www.beachpark.com.br

Aracaju – SE

AREA CODE 79 POPULATION 461,534
DISTANCE Salvador, 330 km (205 mi); Maceió, 290 km (180 mi)
SITE www.emsetur.com.br

HOTEL

Celi Praia Hotel $$
The airy and pleasant atmosphere attracts all types of visitors, including executives and artists. Located in front of the Atalaia beach, it offers business services and has a cyber café. FACILITIES 93 rooms, air-conditioning, phone, TV, cable TV, bar, pool, football court, restaurant, convention room, fitness room, game room, massage room, sauna. CREDIT CARDS All.
Av. Oceânica, 500
TEL 2107-8000
www.ffb.com.br

Arembepe – BA

AREA CODE 71
DISTANCE Salvador, 40 km (25 mi)

RESTAURANTS

Mar Aberto $
The great atmosphere and the carefully prepared food have brought good repute to this restaurant in the center of the village. Run by a Belgian and a Brazilian, it specializes in *escabeche* (pickled) fish and shrimp *bobó* (fresh shrimp, manioc meal, coconut milk, cashew nuts, peanuts, dende oil), and it sits right on the beach. CUISINE Fish and seafood, regional. CREDIT CARDS All. HOURS Mon-Thu, 11am-10pm; Fri and Sat,

11am-midnight; Sun, 11am-7pm.
Lgo. de São Francisco
TEL 624-1257

Arraial d'Ajuda – BA

AREA CODE 73
DISTANCES Salvador, 715 km (444 mi), Porto Seguro, 4 km (2.5 mi) plus 10 minutes by boat
SITE www.portosegurotur.com.br

HOTELS

Arraial d'Ajuda Eco Resort $$$
The hotel sits on a large plot on a strip of land, with the river on one side and the sea on the other, facing the town of Porto Seguro. It has its own ferryboat to take guests to the town and vans to take them to and from the beaches. Water-based leisure options include motorboats, jet ski, diving and free access to the Water Park. The hotel offers a nursery, kid's club, and an "aesthetic" and relaxation center. Decorated with local handicraft. Half the rooms have bathtubs. FACILITIES 169 rooms, air-conditioning, phone, TV, cable TV, ceiling fan, bar, boating, recreation team, pool, playground, restaurant, convention room, fitness room, game room, massage room, sauna, spa. CREDIT CARDS All.
Ponta do Apaga-Fogo, Praia do Apaga-Fogo
TEL 575-1010 FAX 575-1016
www.arraialecoresort.com.br

Estação Santa Fé $$
This hotel, just 50 meters (55 yd) from the beach, has Mexican-inspired architecture and decor. Village craftsmen made the furniture, the mosaic floor and the ornamental objects. The rooms are very pleasant, with large verandahs overlooking the garden or the pool. FACILITIES 29 rooms, air-conditioning, phone, TV, cable TV, bar, pool, restaurant, game room, sauna. CREDIT CARDS Visa.
Estrada do Arraial, 2020
TEL and FAX 575-2237
www.santafehotel.com.br

Hotel Pousada Manacá $$
This hotel is located near the historical center and stands out for the magnificent view of Arraial and Porto Seguro beaches from the pool and the restaurant. Rooms face a small verandah in the front and a garden in the back. FACILITIES 21 rooms, air-conditioning, phone, TV, cable TV, bar, pool, restaurant. CREDIT CARDS American Express, Visa.
Estrada Arraial–Trancoso, 500, Centro
TEL and FAX 575-1442
www.pousadamanaca.com.br

Pousada Beijo do Vento $$
Located on a quiet spot, close to the historical center, this inn has a great view of the coast. It is decorated with artworks and items handmade by the owner, a native of São Paulo. Her husband, a Frenchman, runs the kitchen, and prepares crepes and croissants for breakfast. Children under 8 are not allowed. Closed from May 15-June 30. FACILITIES 10 rooms, air-conditioning, phone, TV, cable TV, bar, pool. CREDIT CARDS

RESTAURANTS	$ up to R$50	$$ from R$51 up to R$100	$$$ from R$101 up to R$150	$$$$ above R$150

American Express, MasterCard, Visa.
Located off Estrada do Mucugê, 730
TEL and FAX 575-1349
www.beijodovento.com.br

Pousada Canto d'Alvorada $$

The Swiss owner speaks five languages and gracious-
ly welcomes all visitors. The inn sits on a 3-acre garden
by the sea. A single building surrounded by a verandah contains the rooms, and there are also chalets
with rustic decoration. The inn has internet access
and a tent on the beach. FACILITIES 20 rooms, air-conditioning, phone, cable TV, ceiling fan, bar, pool,
playground, restaurant, game room, massage room,
sauna. CREDIT CARDS All.
Estrada do Arraial, 1993, Praia de Araçaípe
TEL 575-1218
www.cantodaalvorada.com.br

Pousada Pitinga $$$

The lodgings are actually colorful hut-like constructions, thatched with piassava and decorated with local handicraft, in a garden covered in bromeliads. All
huts have an ample verandah and an ocean view.
Children under 12 are not allowed. FACILITIES 19 rooms,
air-conditioning, amphitheater, library, bar, pool,
restaurant, convention room, game room, massage
room, sauna, spa. CREDIT CARDS All.
Estrada da Pitinga, 1633, Praia da Pitinga
TEL 575-1067 FAX 575-1035
www.pousadapitinga.com.br

Privillage Hotel Pousada $$

This inn is situated on the fashionable Pitinga beach.
The brightly colored decor adds cheer to the com-
mon areas. The rooms are well equipped but small.
Closed in May. FACILITIES 24 rooms, air-conditioning,
phone, TV, bar, pool, restaurant, massage room. CREDIT
CARDS American Express, MasterCard, Visa.
Estrada da Pitinga, 1800, Praia da Pitinga
TEL 575-1646
www.privillage.com.br

Saint Tropez Praia $$$

Located on the seaside, this is a sizeable hotel compared to others in the Arraial area. There are different
types of accommodations in several colorful blocks:
suites with whirlpool tub, chalets for up to six people
and rooms. A toy library and baby sitter service ensure
parents' peace of mind. FACILITIES 60 rooms, air-conditioning, phone, TV, cable TV, bar, pool, tennis court,
restaurant, massage room, sauna. CREDIT CARDS All.
Estrada da Pitinga, 100, Praia do Parracho
TEL 288-7700 FAX 288-7785
www.saint-tropez.com.br

RESTAURANTS

Rosa dos Ventos $$

Close to the historical center, this restaurant has a
green garden and an orchard, and uses seasonal ingredients to prepare classical and regional dishes,
such as fish with pineapple. On Sundays the menu
features typical dishes of the countryside, like chick-
en, duck, and suckling pig. CUISINE Fish and seafood.

CREDIT CARDS Not accepted. HOURS Mon, Tue and Thu-
Sat, 5pm-midnight; Sun, 2pm-10pm.
Al. dos Flamboyants, 24
TEL 575-1271

SERVICES

LOCAL TOUR OPERATOR

Brasil 2000 Turismo

Estrada do Mucugê, Centro
TEL 575-1815. HOURS 9am-10pm

EXCHANGE SHOP

Brasil 2000 Turismo

Estrada do Mucugê, Centro
TEL 575-1815. HOURS 9am-10pm

Barra de Santo Antônio – AL

AREA CODE 82 POPULATION 11,351
DISTANCE Maceió, 56 km (35 mi)

HOTEL

Captain Nikolas $$

This is the best option in town, but it's somewhat rundown. The reception closes at night. It sits on a lush
patch of turf by the sea. The chalets are spacious and
each has a minibar-equipped living room, a bedroom
and a bathroom. FACILITIES 39 rooms, air-conditioning,
phone, TV, ceiling fan, bar, pool, tennis court, restaurant,
convention room, fitness room, sauna. CREDIT CARDS Visa.
Rodovia AL-101 (Norte), km 40
TEL 291-2145

Barra de São Miguel – AL

AREA CODE 82 POPULATION 6,379
DISTANCE Maceió, 34 km (21 mi)

RESTAURANT

La Tablita $

This simple restaurant specializes in traditional Span-
ish cuisine including *tortillas*, variations on octopus
and *paella* (the latter must be ordered ahead). CUISINE
Spanish, varied. CREDIT CARDS Not accepted. HOURS Fri-
Sun, 11am-11pm; from March-November.
R. Salvador Aprato, 30

Barra Grande – BA

AREA CODE 73
DISTANCE Salvador, 460 km (286 mi)
SITE www.barragrande.net

HOTELS

Kiaroa Beach Resort $$$$

This exclusive and comfortable resort occupies an
area of 59.3 acres in an environmental protection area
off Três Coqueiros beach. The huts have been built
with bamboo and wood blending perfectly into the

PRICES	HOTELS (couple)	$ up to R$150	$$ from R$151 up to R$300	$$$ from R$301 up to R$500	$$$$ above R$500

environment. There's a large pool with an Olympic lane. The hotel also has diving equipment available and a lighted tennis court. Schooner excursions available. Regular flights from Salvador land on the hotel's own runway. Children under 14 are not permitted. FACILITIES 32 rooms, air-conditioning, phone, TV, cable TV, bar, boat, pool, tennis court, restaurant, fitness room, game room, massage room, sauna. CREDIT CARDS All. Praia dos Três Coqueiros
RESERVATIONS (71) 272-1320/272-0454
www.kiaroa.com.br

Pousada dos Tamarindos $$

This inn is located barely 10 m (300 ft) from the sea, in a plot with plenty of fruit trees and a lake stocked with ornamental fish. The service, provided by a family of Japanese descent, is very friendly. The decoration and the architecture have an Asian touch. FACILITIES 16 rooms, air-conditioning, phone, TV, bar, restaurant. CREDIT CARDS Not accepted.
R. José Melo Pirajá, 21, Centro
TEL 258-6017 RESERVATIONS 258-6064
www.pousadadostamarindos.com.br

Pousada Fruta-Pão $

Many fruit trees and a century-old breadfruit tree surround the rustic chalets and rooms made of wattle, daub, bricks and wood. The owner speaks French. Basic, no-frills accommodations and service. FACILITIES 6 rooms, air-conditioning. CREDIT CARDS Not accepted.
R. Maraú, Centro
TEL 258-6083
www.barragrande.net

Pousada Lagoa do Cassange $$

With an excellent location, between the lagoon and the sea, this inn provides transportation to nearby airports and excursions in the region. Individual chalets, made of wood and glass, with large verandahs, provide up-close contact with nature. FACILITIES 13 chalets, air-conditioning, phone, ceiling fan, bar, restaurant. CREDIT CARDS MasterCard, Visa.
Praia do Cassange, 19 km (12 mi) from Barra Grande
TEL 258-2166 FAX 255-2348
www.maris.com.br

Pousada Taipú de Fora $$$

Situated on a seaside 180-acre farm of coconut and dende palm trees, this inn offers tranquility near the magnificent beach of Taipu de Fora. Ask for one of the rooms with an ocean view. The hotel has a runway and provides transfer to and from Ilhéus and Salvador airports. FACILITIES 12 rooms, phone, TV, ceiling fan, pool. CREDIT CARDS MasterCard, Visa.
Praia de Taipus de Fora
TEL and FAX 258-6278
www.taipudefora.com.br

RESTAURANTS

Bar do Francês $

This bar offers friendly service in a relaxed atmosphere, with rustic tables and benches scattered on the beach. The name (Frenchman's Bar) refers to the owner, a Frenchman who also speaks English. It serves finger food, fresh fish and seafood. HOURS 8am-10pm; March-June and August-November, 8am-5pm. CREDIT CARDS Not accepted.
Praia de Taipus de Fora, 8 km (5 mi) from Barra Grande
TEL 255-2225

Café Latino $

The owner, Juan Pablo, is a photographer and owns the adjoining gallery of photos. The menu's highlights are the homemade pasta and the grilled dishes, in addition to 18 different types of iced and hot coffee. CUISINE Varied. CREDIT CARDS Not accepted. HOURS 6pm-midnight; in February, closed on Tuesdays.
R. Dr. Chiquinho, 9, Centro
TEL 258-6188

Do Jorge $

The restaurant serves lobsters and *guaiamuns* (land crabs) that customers can select live from tanks. While you wait, try the "confusion drink", made with allspice leaves. The restaurant has no phone. CUISINE Fish and seafood. CREDIT CARDS Not accepted. HOURS Daily, 11am-6pm.
Ilha do Sapinho, access by boat from the Barra Grande or Camamu dock

Matataúba $

The cheerful Italian couple who owns the restaurant serves specialties of their homeland, especially pizza baked in the oven adjoining the house and seasoned with herbs grown in the garden. The tables are set under a mango tree, by the Carapitangui river. CUISINE Italian, pizza. HOURS noon-10pm from Christmas to Carnival; during low season, open upon reservation. CREDIT CARDS Not accepted.
Rio Carapitangui, Ilha do Campinho, Maraú
TEL 258-6265

Tubarão $

Their large, rustic wooden tables and benches are placed on the sand, under piassava-thatched kiosks near the dock. The eatery specializes in seafood dishes, such as grilled lobster or octopus and lobster risotto, that are generous enough to serve three. Delicious fruit juices are served in the yard. CUISINE Fish and seafood. CREDIT CARDS Not accepted. HOURS 7am-10pm.
Praia de Barra Grande
TEL 258-6006

SERVICES

LOCAL TOUR OPERATOR

Camamu Adventure

Av. Beira-Mar, Píer nº 1, Casa Tangerina, Porto de Camamu
TEL 255-2138

Naturemar

Av. Beira-Mar, 8, Centro, Camamu
TEL 255-2343

Sollarium Taipus Ecoturismo

TEL 258-6151/6191

RESTAURANTS	$ up to R$50	$$ from R$51 up to R$100	$$$ from R$101 up to R$150	$$$$ above R$150

BOAT RENTAL

Camamu Adventure
Av. Beira-Mar, Píer nº 1, Casa Tangerina,
Port of Camamu
TEL 255-2138

Naturemar
Av. Beira-Mar, 8, Centro, Camamu
TEL 255-2343

Barreirinhas – MA

AREA CODE 98 POPULATION 39,669
DISTANCE São Luís, 265 km (164.5 mi)

HOTELS

Hotel Pousada do Buriti $$
Near the center of Barreirinhas, this hotel offers efficient service and spacious but simple accommodations. The pool may be used during the evening. The
decoration and the menu lack local color. FACILITIES 29
rooms, air-conditioning, phone, TV, pool, playground,
restaurant. CREDIT CARDS MasterCard, Visa.
R. Inácio Lins
TEL 3349-1338/1800 FAX 3349-1053
www.pousadadoburiti.com.br

Porto Preguiças Resort $$
Quiet and far from the center, this hotel has a great,
sandy-bottomed pool. Although simple, the rooms offer perks such as spring mattresses, goose-feather pillows and towels in Egyptian cotton. Breakfast is good.
FACILITIES 27 rooms, air-conditioning, TV, ceiling fan, bar,
pool, restaurant, game room. CREDIT CARDS MasterCard.
Estrada do Carnaubal, Carnaubal
TEL 3349-1220 FAX 3349-0620
www.portopreguicas.com.br

SERVICES

AIRPORT

Aeroporto Municipal de Barreirinhas
R. Cincinato Ribeiro

LOCAL TOUR OPERATOR

Guará Ecoturismo
R. Inácio Lins, 200, Centro
TEL 3349-1313

Beberibe – CE

AREA CODE 85 POPULATION 42,343
DISTANCE Fortaleza, 90 km (56 mi)
SITE www.municipios-ce.com.br/beberibe

HOTELS

Hotel Oásis Praia das Fontes $$$$
This is an all-inclusive hoTEL The chalets are distant
enough from the nightclub to guarantee a peaceful
sleep. The club opens daily in the high season. Guests
have access to the water park of the neighboring hotel, Parque das Fontes. FACILITIES 253 rooms, air-conditioning, phone, TV, cable TV, bar, football field, mini-golf
course, recreation team, pool, football court, tennis
court, restaurant, convention room, game room,
sauna. CREDIT CARDS All.
Av. Coronel Antônio Teixeira Filho, 3
TEL 3327-3000 FAX 3327-3039
www.hoteloasispraiadasfontes.com.br

Parque das Fontes $$
This hotel faces Fontes beach, and is ideal for families
with children. The water park has pools with 3 tobog-
gans and slides, and is great entertainment for smaller children. FACILITIES 211 rooms, air-conditioning,
phone, TV, bar, pool, jogging track, restaurant, convention room, fitness room, sauna. CREDIT CARDS All.
Av. Coronel Antônio Teixeira Filho, 3
TEL 3327-3100 FAX 3327-3144
www.hotelparquedasfontes.com.br

Cabo de Santo Agostinho – PE

AREA CODE 81 POPULATION 152,977
DISTANCE Recife, 37 km (23 mi)
SITE www.cabo.pe.gov.br

HOTEL

Blue Tree Park Cabo
de Santo Agostinho $$$$
This resort has exceptional amenities, modern facilities, and plenty of leisure activities. It stands out for the
kid's club and ocean-based activities that include jet
ski, sail boats and motorboats. Dinner is included in
the rate. FACILITIES 304 rooms, air-conditioning, phone,
TV, cable TV, bar, boat, football field, horses, recreation
team, pool, playground, football court, tennis court,
restaurant, convention room, fitness room, game
room, massage room, sauna. CREDIT CARDS All.
Av. Beira-Mar, 750, Suape
TEL 3521-6000 FAX 3521-6010 RESERVATIONS 0800789200
www.bluetree.com.br

RESTAURANT

Bar do Artur $$
The known-about-town owner runs a bar synonymous with Calhetas beach. It serves as a meeting
point for artists. The extensive menu includes dishes
such as fish stew and shrimp "a la Greek," and finger
foods. Servings are abundant. CUISINE Fish and seafood,
varied. CREDIT CARDS All. HOURS Daily, 8am-6pm.
R. dos Carneiros, 17, Praia de Calhetas
TEL 3522-6382

Cachoeira – BA

AREA CODE 75 POPULATION 30,416
DISTANCE Salvador, 116 km (72 mi)

HOTEL

Pousada do Convento $
The original architecture of the 1767 Carmelite con-

| PRICES | HOTELS (couple) | $ up to R$150 | $$ from R$151 up to R$300 | $$$ from R$301 up to R$500 | $$$$ above R$500 |

506   BRAZIL GUIDE

vent has been preserved, including the thick wattle and daub walls with the traditional *conversadeiras* (stone benches) by the windows. The antique furniture and the original wooden floor in the rooms make up for the simple accommodations. The rooms on the ground floor are not very airy. **FACILITIES** 26 rooms, air-conditioning, TV, bar, pool, playground, restaurant. **CREDIT CARDS** Diners, MasterCard, Visa.
Pça. da Aclamação
TEL 3425-1716

RESTAURANT

A Confraria $
This restaurant has tables both in the dining room and on the verandah of the internal patio of Pousada do Convento. It serves regional dishes such as *maniçoba* (bitter cassava leaves stewed with smoked pork meat and sausage, bacon, sun-dried meat), *xinxim de galinha* (served on Saturdays: chicken, dried smoked shrimps, dende oil, cashew nuts, ginger, seasonings) and fresh fish. For dessert, try the homemade regional fruit sweets. **CUISINE** Regional. **CREDIT CARDS** All. **HOURS** noon-4pm and 7pm-9:30pm.
Praça da Aclamação
TEL 3425-1716

SERVICES

TOURIST INFORMATION

Centro de Atendimento ao Turista
Pça. da Aclamação, Centro
TEL 3425-2686 (information). **HOURS** Mon-Sat, 8am-6pm.

Canavieiras – BA

AREA CODE 73 **POPULATION** 35,322
DISTANCE Salvador, 560 km (348 mi)

HOTEL

Ilha de Atalaia Resort Hotel $$
Located among coconut and fruit trees, this resort is surrounded by the sea and the Patipe river. The rooms are simple, but half of them have an ocean view. The resort organizes fishing excursions and outings in the region. In the high season there's a recreation team. **FACILITIES** 31 rooms, air-conditioning, phone, TV, cable TV, bar, horses, recreation team, pool, playground, restaurant, game room, massage room. **CREDIT CARDS** American Express, MasterCard, Visa.
Praia da Costa Norte, km 6.7 km (4.3 mi) from the Center
TEL 3284-2101 **FAX** 3284-2102 **RESERVATIONS** (11) 5549-0900

RESTAURANT

Le Poivre $
The restaurant serves steaks and seafood in a remodeled building near the port. Late in the afternoon, outdoor tables pop up. There's live music on weekends. **CUISINE** Varied. **CREDIT CARDS** Visa. **HOURS** Daily, 11am-midnight.
Av. Dr. Felinto Mello, 26, Centro Histórico
TEL 3284-3855

SERVICES

BOAT RENTAL

Royal Charlotte Sport Fishing
Av. Filinto Melo, 16, Centro
www.royalcharlotte.com.br

Canoa Quebrada – CE

AREA CODE 88
DISTANCE Fortaleza 167 km (104 mi)

HOTELS

Village Long Beach $$
This inn is 150 meters (500 ft) from the beach and only slightly farther from the main street. It has four pools in the leisure area. The chalets have an ocean view and king-size beds. **FACILITIES** air-conditioning, TV, cable TV, ceiling fan, bar, pool. **CREDIT CARDS** Diners, MasterCard, Visa.
R. Quatro Ventos
TEL 3421-7405
www.villagelongbeach.com

Caraíva – BA

AREA CODE 73
DISTANCES Salvador, 765 km (475 mi); Porto Seguro, 65 km (40 mi)

HOTELS

L'Unico $$$
This hotel is inside a residential condominium, on the top of a cliff. There are trails down to the beach and an ample common area, with a brick floor that runs into the restaurant. The rooms and bungalows are spacious. Italian chef-owner Orlando Giordan provides customized service in English, Portuguese and Italian. Reservation advised. **FACILITIES** 22 rooms, air-conditioning, phone, TV, ceiling fan, bar, horses, pool, restaurant, fitness room, sauna. **CREDIT CARDS** Not accepted.
Viela da Vista, 80, Condomínio Outeiro das Brisas, access off the Caraíva–Trancoso (BA-001) road, 22 km from Trancoso
TEL 3668-1481
www.lunicohotel.com.br

Pousada da Barra $
This inn sits in a coconut grove between the river and the sea. The rooms are small and simple, with verandahs overlooking the beach or the river. The showers are heated with solar energy. **FACILITIES** 11 rooms, ceiling fan, bar. **CREDIT CARDS** Not accepted.
R. dos Navegantes
TEL 9985-4302 **RESERVATIONS** (21) 3437-4273
www.caraiva.com

Pousada Lagoa $
Colorful and charming chalets lie scattered across a 1.7-acre area, near the sea. The inn has a boat for river outings. The simple lodgings are decorated with handicrafts, but only four have hot water. **FACILITIES** 4

---

rooms (1 with a hot shower), 3 bungalows. CREDIT CARDS Not accepted.
Beco da Lagoa
TEL 9985-6862
www.caraiva.com.br

Pousada do Baiano $$$$
Located on the waterfront, this inn has a common area that stretches onto the sand and offers hammocks and sofas near the restaurant. The suites are charming, spacious, and all have an *ofurô* tub and king-size bed. FACILITIES 19 rooms, phone, TV, ceiling fan, bar, restaurant. CREDIT CARDS Diners, MasterCard.
Praia do Espelho, 22 km from the center
TEL and FAX 3668-5020
www.pousadadobaiano.com

Pousada Flor do Mar $$
This charming, candle-lit inn on a large plot by the sea, is rustic, with torches on the patio, cold showers, wood walkways. The wattle and daub chalets are very well finished inside. FACILITIES 6 rooms, bar. CREDIT CARDS Not accepted.
R. da Praia
TEL 9985-1608

Pousada Porto Espelho $$$
The common areas extend down to the beach and are decorated with flair. The spacious suites have bathtubs and an exit to the beach. The rooms are located in the garden. The inn may be reached by car, boat, helicopter or small plane. FACILITIES 11 rooms, air-conditioning, ceiling fan, bar, restaurant. CREDIT CARDS Not accepted.
Praia do Espelho, 22 km (13.6 mi) from Trancoso
TEL 668-5031

Pousada Vila do Mar $$
This inn has a power generator, solar heating, and internet access. The rooms have mosquito nets. FACILITIES 11 rooms, air-conditioning, TV, ceiling fan, bar, pool. CREDIT CARDS Not accepted.
R. 12 de Outubro, Praia de Caraíva
TEL 3668-5111/9993-1393
www.pousadaviladomar.com.br

Pousada Vindobona $$
This small, simple inn, with pleasant and airy rooms, is inside a residential condominium. A trail across the cliff leads to the beach. The owner, Karl Würzl, speaks German and provides customized service. FACILITIES 6 rooms, ceiling fan. CREDIT CARDS Not accepted.
Condomínio Outeiro das Brisas, access through the Caraíva–Trancoso (BA-001) road, 22 km (13.6 mi) from Trancoso
TEL 3668-1482

RESTAURANTS

Boteco do Pará $$
This neat restaurant on the riverside has outdoor and indoor tables. The owner has a fishing boat, which guarantees fresh catch. The desserts are locally famous. CUISINE Fish and seafood. CREDIT CARDS Not accepted. HOURS Daily, 11am-midnight; in the low

season, daily, 11am-8pm.
Av. dos Navegantes
TEL 9991-9804

Da Silvinha $
This is a good option for those wanting to spend the day in Espelho-Curuípe. There are only three tables on the beach and no menu. Silvinha, the owner, suggests and prepares delicious Thai dishes, such as smoked fish with spicy passion fruit sauce, and chicken and vegetable skewers with peanut sauce. Reserve at least one day in advance. CUISINE Thai. HOURS Only upon reservation.
Praia do Espelho, 22 km (13.6 mi) from Trancoso
TEL 9985-4157

Do Baiano $$
This waterfront restaurant has deck chairs on the lawn over the sand. *Baiano*, which means native of state of Bahia, serves the tables and creates dishes such as grilled fish with soy sauce, and lobster. Enjoy the beach after you order, as it usually takes some time to prepare the dishes. CUISINE Fish and seafood. CREDIT CARDS Diners, MasterCard. HOURS Daily, 7am-11pm.
Praia do Espelho, 22 km from the center
TEL 3668-5020

L'Unico $
This restaurant, next to the hotel, has a large brick oven near the dining hall. There's no need for a menu, as the six daily options cover Italian, Mediterranean, and some regional dishes with slight adaptations such as lobster risotto with mango or fillet of golden *dourado* with Indian sauce. CUISINE Mediterranean. CREDIT CARDS Not accepted. HOURS 8am-9:30pm.
Viela da Vista, 80, Condomínio Outeiro das Brisas, access through Estrada Caraíva–Trancoso (BA-001), 22 km
TEL 3668-1481

SERVICES

LOCAL TOUR OPERATORS

Cia. do Mar
Pça dos Patachós, Porto Seguro
TEL 3288-2107

Comando Verde
TEL 9142-5808

Caravelas – BA

AREA CODE 73 POPULATION 20,103
DISTANCES Salvador 886 km (550 mi), Porto Seguro, 210 km (130.5 mi)

HOTELS

Farol Abrolhos Hotel late Clube $
The amenities are basic, with small chalets scattered in the garden along the Caravelas river. There are boats and motorboats, with guides and diving equipment available. FACILITIES 15 rooms, air-conditioning, TV, bar, boat, pool, restaurant, game room. CREDIT CARDS Diners, MasterCard, Visa.

| PRICES | HOTELS (couple) | $ up to R$150 | $$ from R$151 up to R$300 | $$$ from R$301 up to R$500 | $$$$ above R$500 |

508 BRAZIL GUIDE

Estrada Caravelas–Barra, km 1, Quitongo
TEL 297-1173/297-1515

Marina Porto Abrolhos $$
This hotel is in a coconut grove, by the sea, far from the center. Rooms have verandahs and hammocks. There are suites with two adjoining bedrooms. FACILITIES 32 rooms, air-conditioning, phone, TV, bar, mini-golf course, pool, playground, tennis court, restaurant, convention room, game room, massage room, sauna. CREDIT CARDS All.
R. da Baleia, 333, Praia do Grauçá, Barra de Caravelas, 10 km
TEL 3674-1060 FAX 3674-1082 RESERVATIONS (11) 3208-4526
www.marinaportoabrolhos.com.br

RESTAURANT

Encontro dos Amigos $
One of the few options in town, this no-frills restaurant serves fresh fish and seafood. CREDIT CARDS Not accepted. HOURS Mon-Sat, 11:30am-10pm.
R. das Palmeiras, 370
TEL 3297-1600

SERVICES

LOCAL TOUR OPERATORS

Abrolhos Embarcações
Av. Ministro Adalício Nogueira, 1294
TEL 3297-1172

Abrolhos Turismo
Pça. Dr. Imbassay, 8, Centro
TEL 3297-1149/1332

Iate Clube Abrolhos
Estrada Caravelas–Barra, km 1, Iate Clube intersection
TEL 3297-1173/297-1515

Paradise Abrolhos
R. das Palmeiras, 313, Centro
TEL 3297-1352

TOURIST INFORMATION

Secretaria de Turismo
Pça. Santo Antônio, 28, Centro
TEL 3297-1404 HOURS Mon-Fri, 7am-1pm

DIVING OPERATORS

Abrolhos Embarcações
Av. Ministro Adalício Nogueira, 1294
TEL 3297-1172

Abrolhos Turismo
Pça. Dr. Imbassay, 8, Centro
TEL 297-1149/1332

Iate Clube Abrolhos
Estrada Caravelas–Barra, km 1, Iate Clube intersection
TEL 3297-1002

Paradise Abrolhos
R. das Palmeiras, 313, Centro
TEL 3297-1352

Carpina – PE

AREA CODE 81 POPULATION 63,811
DISTANCE Recife, 56 km (35 mi)

RESTAURANT

Panela Cheia $
This is the locals' favorite churrascaria. It stands out for the costela no bafo (slow-roasted short ribs), which cooks in low heat for hours. CUISINE Churrasco (barbecue). CREDIT CARDS Diners, MasterCard. HOURS Mon-Sat, 11am-10pm; Sun, 11am-5pm.
Rodovia PE-90, 1516, km 0, Carpina intersection
TEL 3621-1278

Caruaru – PE

AREA CODE 81 POPULATION 253,634
DISTANCE Recife, 134 km (83 mi)

HOTELS

Caruaru Park Hotel $$
The colorful chalets are basic, but well tended. "Superluxe" rooms have a verandah overlooking the town. FACILITIES 68 rooms, air-conditioning, phone, TV, cable TV, pool, playground, restaurant, convention room, game room. CREDIT CARDS All.
Rodovia BR-232, km 128, on the way to Recife
TEL and FAX 3722-9191
www.caruaruparkhotelonline.com.br

Village Caruaru $
Although it is near the highway, this well-located hotel is quiet. It is only five minutes from the center, where the famous handicraft fair is held, and not far from Alto do Moura, the craftsmen district. The inn offers a hearty breakfast, with typical food from the sertão (hinterlands). FACILITIES 61 rooms, air-conditioning, phone, TV, cable TV, pool, playground, restaurant, convention room, fitness room, game room, sauna. CREDIT CARDS All.
Rodovia BR-232, km 135, in the Recife-Arcoverde direction
TEL 3722-5544 FAX 3722-7033
www.hoteisvillage.com.br

RESTAURANT

Lengo Tengo $
Here you'll be able to taste goat meat prepared in genuine sertanejo (hinterland) style, either roasted or in sausages. The outdoor tables under a mango tree create a congenial ambience. CUISINE Regional. CREDIT CARDS Not accepted. HOURS Daily, 11am-midnight.
R. Mestre Vitalino, 450, Alto do Moura
TEL 3722-4377

Conde – BA

AREA CODE 75 POPULATION 20,426
DISTANCE Salvador, 190 km (118 mi)
SITE www.bahia.com.br

HOTEL

Resort Itariri $$
Despite its name, this is more of a farm hotel than a

resort. The hotel is on a beautiful beach, and the facilities are quite old. The service is simple. It is ideal for those seeking tranquility. Closed in April. FACILITIES 30 rooms, air-conditioning, TV, bar, boat, football field, horses, pool, playground, restaurant, convention room, game room. CREDIT CARDS MasterCard, Visa.
Rodovia BA-099, km 131, Linha Verde, and another 8 km of dirt road to Itariri
TEL 3449-1142 FAX 3449-1212
www.itaririresort.com

Costa do Sauípe – BA

AREA CODE 71
DISTANCE Salvador, 105 km (65 mi)
SITE www.costadosauipe.com.br

HOTELS

Marriott Resort and Spa $$$$
This hotel has two advantages as compared to others in the complex: a lobby with air-conditioning and an on-site spa. The most traditional of the five hotels, it is decorated following the chain's global standards. FACILITIES 256 rooms, air-conditioning, phone, TV, cable TV, bar, boat, football field, golf course, mini-golf course, horses, recreation team, riding club, pool, jogging track, football court, tennis court, restaurant, convention room, fitness room, game room, massage room, sauna, spa. CREDIT CARDS All.
Rodovia BA-099, km 76, Mata de São João
TEL 3465-3000 FAX 3465-3001 RESERVATIONS 08007031512
www.marriottbrasil.com

Renaissance Resort $$$$
This hotel belongs to the Marriott chain but has a more relaxed atmosphere. The guests may avail themselves of on-site facilities or instead use those of the nearby Marriot. A "total vacation" package includes full board and locally produced beverages during meals. FACILITIES 237 rooms, air-conditioning, phone, TV, bar, boat, football field, golf course, mini-golf course, horses, recreation team, riding club, pool, jogging track, playground, football court, tennis court, convention room, fitness room, game room, massage room, sauna, spa. CREDIT CARDS All.
Rodovia BA-099, km 76, Mata de São João
TEL 2104-7300 FAX 2104-7301 RESERVATIONS 08007031512
www.renaissancehotels.com/ssabr

Sofitel Costa do Sauípe $$$$
This is the largest, most beautiful and best decorated hotel of the complex. It has a huge pool and plenty of convention rooms. FACILITIES 404 rooms, air-conditioning, phone, TV, bar, boat, football field, golf course, horses, recreation team, riding club, pool, playground, football court, tennis court, restaurant, convention room, fitness room, game room, massage room, sauna. CREDIT CARDS All.
Rodovia BA-099, km 76, Mata de São João
TEL 2104-7600 FAX 2104-7601 RESERVATIONS (11) 3747-7477
www.accorhotels.com.br

Sofitel Suítes Costa do Sauípe $$$$
This is the smallest and coziest hotel of the complex. It is decorated with cocoa motifs. FACILITIES 198 rooms, air-conditioning, phone, TV, cable TV, bar, boat, football field, golf course, horses, recreation team, riding club, pool, playground, football court, tennis court, convention room, fitness room, game room, massage room, sauna. CREDIT CARDS All.
Rodovia BA-099, km 76, Mata de São João
TEL 2104-8000 FAX 2104-7601 RESERVATIONS (11) 3747-7477
www.accorhotels.com.br

Super Clubs Breezes Costa do Sauípe $$$$
This is the most happenin' hotel in the complex. Plenty of daytime activities keep things interesting, and in the evening there's a busy nightclub. Meals, drinks (including those of the minibar) and activities are included in the rate. FACILITIES 324 rooms, air-conditioning, phone, TV, cable TV, bar, football field, golf course, horses, recreation team, riding club, pool, playground, football court, tennis court, restaurant, convention room, fitness room, game room, massage room, sauna. CREDIT CARDS All.
Rodovia BA-099, km 76, Mata de São João
TEL 3463-1000 FAX 3463-1010 RESERVATIONS 08007043210
www.superclubs.com.br

Cumuruxatiba – BA

AREA CODE 73
DISTANCES Salvador, 828 km (514.5 mi); Porto Seguro, 236 km (145.5 mi)

HOTELS

Pousada É $
The ocean breeze blows gently through the hotel's common areas, and fruit trees surround rooms and suites of various sizes. Swiss owner Hans Fritsch speaks many languages and maintains a library with classics and a collection of whiskey. FACILITIES 12 rooms, TV, ceiling fan, bar, mini-pantry, pool, fitness room, game room. CREDIT CARDS Diners, MasterCard.
Al. Roberto Pompeu, 8, Praia do Rio do Peixe Grande, 3.5 km (2 mi) from the center
TEL 3573-1007 FAX 3573-1160
www.portonet.com.br/pousadae

Pousada Mandala $$
New Age music plays in the common areas, which are decorated with handicrafts and artworks. The rooms are spacious, with a verandah and an ocean view. A wood bridge over the Do Peixe river connects the garden and the pool to the beach. The Swiss owner speaks English, French and German. FACILITIES 9 rooms, TV, ceiling fan, pool. CREDIT CARDS Not accepted.
Al. Roberto Pompeu, Praia do Rio do Peixe Grande, 2 km (1.2 mi) from the center
TEL and FAX 3573-1143
www.pousadamandala.com.br

Pousada Rio do Peixe $
The whole inn overlooks the ocean. The rooms have verandahs and hammocks. FACILITIES 12 rooms, air-conditioning, phone, TV, bar, pool, restaurant, game room. CREDIT CARDS Diners, MasterCard, Visa.
Al. Roberto Pompeu, 26, Praia do Rio do Peixe Grande, 3.5 km (2 mi) from the center
TEL and FAX 3573-1213
www.pousadariodopeixe.com.br

| PRICES | HOTELS (couple) | $ up to R$150 | $$ from R$151 up to R$300 | $$$ from R$301 up to R$500 | $$$$ above R$500 |

Vista Mar Praia $$

This hotel has the best facilities in the town center. There are spacious common and leisure areas. The standard rooms are small and have no air-conditioning, so consider getting "de luxe" digs, which have verandahs and king-size beds. During the high season, the hotel promotes MPB (Brazilian Popular Music) performances. FACILITIES 40 rooms, air-conditioning, phone, TV, bar, pool, playground, restaurant, game room. CREDIT CARDS MasterCard, Visa.
Av. Beira-Mar, Centro
TEL 3573-1065 FAX 3573-1045 RESERVATIONS (11) 5543-9444
www.cumuruxatiba.com.br

RESTAURANTS

Asa Branca $

Grab a bench at one of this rustic restaurant's long tables if you want a change from seafood. Situated near the dam close to the town's entrance, it has become famous thanks to the *carne-de-sol de picanha* (sundried cap of rump), with *pirão de leite* (manioc meal and milk porridge with coriander) and rice. CUISINE Regional. CREDIT CARDS Not accepted. HOURS 10am-8pm; March-June and August-November, closed on Sundays.
Av. Treze de Maio, Centro
TEL 3573-1205

Catamarã $

This restaurant sits atop a cliff, 45 meter above the town's entrance, and has a stunning view. Stairs and a ramp lead down to the beach. If you can spare 90 minutes for preparation, order *polvo à napolitana* (Naples-style whole octopus), with white wine sauce. An unusual device is used to serve those who prefer to stay on the beach: a rope and pulley takes down a basket with the menu, paper, pen and a whistle. Customers write down their selections, send them up and the chosen dishes are sent down in the basket when ready. CUISINE Fish and seafood. CREDIT CARDS Not accepted. HOURS 11am-8:30pm.
Access by the Prado-Cumuruxatiba road, bairro Areia Preta, 2 km from the center
TEL 3573-1124

Hermes $

Brothers Hermes and Geraldo have upgraded an old beach tent and created a glassed-in room, and a deck with outdoor tables. The menu has delicious options, of which we suggest red parrotfish with lemon and herbs, cooked in banana leaves. The servings are generous. CUISINE Fish and seafood. CREDIT CARDS MasterCard, Visa. HOURS Daily, 10am-11pm; March-June and August-November, daily, 9am-9pm.
Av. Beira-Mar, Praia de Cumuruxatiba, Centro
TEL 573-1155

Mama África $$

This casual restaurant by the sea has a menu featuring grouper with curry and tenderloin with *morillo* (mushrooms imported from Switzerland) and several codfish options. Try some of the *caipifrutas*, made with *cachaça* from the state of Minas Gerais and fruit from the restaurant's own orchard. CUISINE Contemporary. CREDIT CARDS Not accepted. HOURS Daily, 2pm-10pm;

March-November, open upon reservation.
Al. Roberto Pompeu, 4, Praia do Rio do Peixe Grande, 3 km (1.8 mi)from the center
TEL 3573-1274

SERVICES

LOCAL TOUR OPERATOR

Aquamar

Av. Beira-Mar, 7, Praia de Cumuruxatiba, Centro
TEL 3573-1360. HOURS 8am-8pm

BOAT RENTAL

Sr. Antônio Carlos
TEL 3573-1127

Fernando de Noronha – PE

AREA CODE 81 POPULATION 2,051
DISTANCES Natal, 360 km (223.7 mi), Recife, 545 km (338.6 mi)
SITE www.noronha.pe.gov.br

HOTELS

Pousada Maravilha $$$$

This inn with sophisticated architecture offers a stunning view of Sueste Bay. There are three Bali-style rooms and five bungalows with *ofurô* tubs. FACILITIES 8 rooms, air-conditioning, phone, TV, cable TV, bar, pool, restaurant. CREDIT CARDS All.
Rodovia BR-363, Sueste
TEL 3619-1290 FAX and RESERVATIONS 3619-0028
www.pousadamaravilha.com.br

Pousada Zé Maria $$$$

Bungalows with king-size beds, whirlpool tubs, 29" satellite TV and CD players let guests relax. The view of imposing Pico Rock is magnificent. FACILITIES 19 rooms, air-conditioning, phone, TV, cable TV, bar, pool, restaurant. CREDIT CARDS Diners, MasterCard, Visa.
R. Nice Cordeiro, 1, Floresta Velha
TEL 3619-1258
www.pousadazemaria.com.br

RESTAURANTS

Ecologiku's $$

This is the best option to eat outside the Maravilha and Zé Maria inns. It serves classical recipes such as lobster with butter and *moquecas*. CUISINE Fish and seafood. CREDIT CARDS MasterCard. HOURS Daily, 7pm-10:30pm.
Estrada Velha do Sueste (access through the airport)
TEL 3619-1807

Maravilha $$

The on-site restaurant of this exclusive inn has a short menu of international dishes. The wine list is good and the view of Sueste Bay is beautiful. CUISINE Varied. CREDIT CARDS All. HOURS Daily, noon-3pm and 8pm-11pm.
Rodovia BR-363, Sueste
TEL 3619-1290

Museu do Tubarão $

This bistro is located in the Shark Museum and offers

RESTAURANTS	$ up to R$50	$$ from R$51 up to R$100	$$$ from R$101 up to R$150	$$$$ above R$150

many shark dishes. Some of the highlights are the shark salad, *tubaburguer* (a shark hamburger) and *tubalhau* (shark meat and potato fritters). Be aware that many shark species are heavily overfished. There are also healthy, environmental friendly sandwiches and seafood. CUISINE Fish and seafood. CREDIT CARDS All. HOURS Mon-Sat, 8:30am-6:30pm; Sun, 9am-4pm.
Av. Joaquim Ferreira Gomes, 40, Vila do Porto
TEL 3619-1365

Triboju $$
This famous buffet offers about 20 dishes. After lunch, there's a talk show with music and interviews with customers. Reservation advised. CUISINE Fish and seafood, varied. CREDIT CARDS Diners, MasterCard. HOURS Tue and Thu, 8pm-11:30pm.
R. Amaro Preto, 113, Floresta Velha
(setor de chácaras)
TEL 3619-1389

Zé Maria $$
Thin fillets of yellowtail, walnut purée and flambé shrimp are some of the options. Celso Freire, chef of the Boulevard Restaurant, in Curitiba, created the menu. There's a sushi bar and, on Wednesdays and Saturdays, a fixed-price buffet. CUISINE Varied. CREDIT CARDS Diners, MasterCard, Visa. HOURS Daily, 7:30am-10:30am and noon-11:30pm.
R. Nice Cordeiro, 1, Floresta Velha
TEL 3619-1258

SERVICES

TOURIST INFORMATION

Centro de Informações Turísticas
Palácio São Miguel – Vila dos Remédios
TEL 3619-1378. HOURS Mon-Fri, 8am-5pm

Fortaleza – CE

AREA CODE 85 POPULATION 2,141,402
DISTANCE Natal, 552 km (343 mi)
SITE www.fortaleza.ce.gov.br

HOTELS

Caesar Park Fortaleza $$$
On one of the busiest beaches in town, this hotel has become famous thanks to the *feijoada* served in the on-site Mucuripe restaurant, one of the hotel's three eateries. The hotel is a favorite among executives and conventions planners, but recent renovations have been carried out to add more charm to the hotel and draw more tourists. The pool is small and rooms have no verandah. FACILITIES 230 rooms, air-conditioning, phone, TV, bar, pool, restaurant, convention room, fitness room, massage room, sauna. CREDIT CARDS All.
Av. Beira-Mar, 3980, Praia de Mucuripe
TEL 3466-5000 FAX 3466-5111 RESERVATIONS 3466-5222
www.caesarpark-for.com.br

Luzeiros $$$
One of the newest and best-equipped hotels in town, Luzeiros offers a hearty breakfast. The best view is afforded from the rooms between the 15th and 21th

floors. FACILITIES 202 rooms, air-conditioning, phone, TV, ceiling fan, bar, pool, restaurant, convention room, fitness room, massage room, sauna. CREDIT CARDS All.
Av. Beira-Mar, 2600, Meireles
TEL 4006-8585 FAX 4006-8587 RESERVATIONS 4006-8586
www.hotelluzeiros.com.br

Marina Park $$
Families make up most of this hotel's clientele. It has a marina and a large leisure area. It has spacious rooms, but the decoration and facilities have been a bit neglected. It's rather far from the tourist attractions but offers transportation to Beira-Mar Avenue. FACILITIES 315 rooms, air-conditioning, phone, TV, bar, recreation team, pool, jogging track, playground, tennis court, restaurant, convention room, fitness room, massage room, sauna. CREDIT CARDS All.
Av. Presidente Castelo Branco, 400, Iracema
TEL 3455-9595 FAX 253-1803
www.marinapark.com.br

Othon Palace $$
This hotel has a good Italian restaurant, La Terrace Alfredo, and a great location. Another place popular with business travelers, it has efficient service and good facilities, but it lacks the charm and leisure opportunities that attract other tourists. FACILITIES 133 rooms, air-conditioning, phone, TV, bar, pool, restaurant, convention room, fitness room, massage room, sauna. CREDIT CARDS All.
Av. Beira-Mar, 3470, Meireles
TEL 3466-5500 FAX 3466-5501
www.othon.com.br

RESTAURANTS

Al Mare $$
This restaurant overlooking Mucuripe beach specializes in fresh seafood, and dishes it up in prodigious servings. The decor resembles that of a ship's interior. Mussels in wine sauce, black grouper fillet and *grelhado al maré* (grilled shrimp, shrimp and other catch) are menu highlights. CUISINE Fish and seafood. CREDIT CARDS All. HOURS noon-midnight.
Av. Beira-Mar, 3821
TEL 3263-3888

Cantinho do Faustino $
This restaurant stands out for its creative regional cuisine, with herb-based sauces, a great *moqueca*, and goat-kid shoulder. For dessert, see if you can avoid the temptation of basil and *rapadura* (lump of brown sugar) ice cream, created by the restaurant, with banana flambé. CUISINE Regional. CREDIT CARDS All. HOURS Tue-Fri, noon-3pm and 7pm-midnight; Sat, noon-midnight; Sun, noon-4pm.
R. Delmiro Gouveia, 1520, Varjota
TEL 3267-5348

Cemoara $$
The decoration changes often and the loyal clientele usually orders wine to accompany the fresh catch. CUISINE Fish and seafood. CREDIT CARDS All. HOURS Mon-Thu, noon-3pm and 7pm-midnight; Fri and Sat, noon-3pm and 7pm-1am; Sun, noon-5pm.

| PRICES | HOTELS (couple) | $ up to R$150 | $$ from R$151 up to R$300 | $$$ from R$301 up to R$500 | $$$$ above R$500 |

512

BRAZIL GUIDE

2

Av. da Abolição, 3340, Meireles
TEL 3263-5001

Colher de Pau $
Located on a street that's lively at night, the restaurant serves good regional food, such as the popular sun-dried meat, as well as tasty seafood options. The waiters do their best to handle the large crowds, but the place is understaffed. There are no natural juices, only those made with frozen pulp. CUISINE Fish and seafood, regional. CREDIT CARDS All. HOURS 6pm-1am.
R. dos Tabajaras, 412, Iracema
TEL 3219-3605

Nostradamus $$
This restaurant, with only eight tables, maintains a sophisticated ambience that contrasts with the other, mostly informal restaurants in town. Chef Laurent Suaudeau created the menu. Some of the highlights are grilled lobster, tournedos *rossini* and snapper. There's a good wine list, and whites arrive at the table chilled. Reservation advised. Don't go in t-shirt and shorts. CUISINE Varied. CREDIT CARDS All. HOURS Mon-Thu, 7pm-midnight; Fri and Sat, 7pm-2am.
R. Joaquim Nabuco, 166, Meireles
TEL 3242-8500

SERVICES

AIRPORT

Aeroporto Internacional Pinto Martins
Av. Senador Carlos Jereissati, 3000, Serrinha
TEL 3477-1030

LOCAL TOUR OPERATORS

Aeroway Viagens e Turismo Ltda.
Av. Santos Dumont, 5420
TEL 4011-1515

**Ernanitur Viagens
e Receptivo Turístico Ltda.**
Av. Barão Studart, 1165, Conjuntos 101 a 107, Aldeota
TEL 3244-9363

Hippopotamus Agência de Viagens e Turismo Ltda.
Av. Abolição, 2950, Loja 5, Meireles
TEL 3242-9191

TOURIST POLICE STATIONS

Divisão de Apoio ao Turista (DAT)
Av. Almirante Barroso, 805, Praia de Iracema
TEL 3219-1538. HOURS 24 hours

TOURIST INFORMATION

Aeroporto Internacional Pinto Martins
Av. Senador Carlos Jereissati, 3000, Serrinha
TEL 3477-1667. HOURS 6am-3am

Antigo Farol do Mucuripe
R. Vicente Castro
TEL 3263-1115. HOURS 8am-5pm

Centro Administrativo Virgílio Távora
Av. Ministro José Américo, Cambeba
TEL 3488-3858/3900. HOURS Mon-Fri, 8am-noon and 2pm-6pm

Centro de Turismo
R. Senador Pompeu, 350, Centro
TEL 3488-7411. HOURS Mon-Sat, 8am-6pm

Novo Mercado Central
Av. Alberto Nepomuceno, Centro
HOURS Mon-Fri, 8am-6pm

Pça. do Ferreira
Between Major Fecundo and Floriano Peixoto Streets, Centro
HOURS Mon-Fri, 8am-6pm

Posto de Informações Turísticas
Av. Beira-Mar, Meireles
TEL 3242-4447. HOURS 1pm-5pm

Praia de Iracema
Calçadão da Praia de Iracema
HOURS 8am-6pm

Genipabu – RN

AREA CODE 84
DISTANCE Natal, 25 km (15.5 mi)

HOTEL

Genipabu Hotel $$
This hotel provides surprising tranquility given its busy location. It sits on a high, isolated spot. All the rooms have a view of Genipabu and Barra do Rio beaches. There's a good spa for those wanting a healthy session to keep in shape. FACILITIES 24 rooms, air-conditioning, phone, TV, ceiling fan, bar, pool, playground, restaurant, convention room, spa. CREDIT CARDS All.
Praia de Genipabu, road to Natal, km 3
TEL 3225-2063 FAX 3225-2071 RESERVATIONS 3206-8840
www.genipabu.com.br

RESTAURANT

Bar 21 $
Made entirely of wood, with a deck overlooking the sea, this bar sits by the sea on the Genipabu dunes, one of the region's finest sights. It serves large dishes such as *peixada* (fish stew). CUISINE Fish and seafood. CREDIT CARDS All. HOURS Daily, 9am-6pm.
Av. Beira-Mar, Praia de Genipabu
TEL 3224-2484

Ilha de Boipeba – BA

AREA CODE 75 POPULATION 4,920
DISTANCES Salvador, 30 min by motorboat, and an additional 321 km (199.5 mi)
SITE www.ilhaboipeba.org.br

HOTELS

Pousada dos Ventos $
This small farm by the sea is covered in native vegeta-

tion and bisected by a river. The bungalows are rustic, ample in size and thatched with piassava. The inn organizes boat excursions, horse rides and hikes in the region. It can also arrange to transfer guests from Velha Boipeba, Morro de São Paulo or Torrinha. **FACILITIES** 5 rooms, ceiling fan, bar, horses. **CREDIT CARDS** Not accepted.
Praia de Moreré, access by boat, trail or tractor, 6 km (3.7 mi) from the Velha Boipeba village
TEL 9994-8789/9987-0659

Pousada Maliale $$
This inn sits occupies an island on Inferno river, with woods, trails and river beaches, near the village of Boipeba. There's a motorboat available to take guests to the village. Rooms are very airy, with screened windows and doors. **FACILITIES** 16 rooms, air-conditioning, TV, ceiling fan, pool, game room. **CREDIT CARDS** Not accepted.
Ilha São Miguel
TEL 3653-6134 **RESERVATIONS** (11) 4794-7474
www.pousadamaliale.com.br

Pousada Vila Sereia $
From your bed, you'll be able to see the beach and the river. The wood bungalows, with a mezzanine, are airy and have mosquito nets. **FACILITIES** 4 rooms, TV, ceiling fan. **CREDIT CARDS** Not accepted.
Praia da Barra
TEL 3653-6045

RESTAURANT

Mar e Coco $
Hammocks hang from the coconut trees and the view of Moreré Beach is superb. Everything is freshly prepared, so it's better to order ahead. The shrimp *moqueca* with green banana is delicious. To kick back, try the fruit *caipirinha* (*cachaça*, sugar, ice and fruit) or the coconut *batida* (coconut milk, sugar, ice and *cachaça*). **CUISINE** Fish and seafood. **CREDIT CARDS** Not accepted. **HIGH SEASON:** Mon-Fri, 10am-4pm and 6pm-10pm; Sat and Sun, 10am-4pm. **LOW SEASON:** 10am-4pm.
Praia de Moreré
TEL 3653-6013

SERVICES

BOAT RENTAL

Miguel Lanchas
TEL 3653-6018/3641-3233

Ilha do Caju – MA

AREA CODE 86 POPULATION 60

HOTEL

Refúgio Ecológico Ilha do Caju $$
This is the only lodging option on this very rustic island. There's no TV, phone or air-conditioning, and the shower is cold. To compensate for their simplicity, the chalets have large beds and goose-feather pillows. The inn offers jeep and horse excursions on the trails. The restaurant has a diverse menu. Armadillos, cavies, large lizards, foxes and herons will cross your path on the trails. **FACILITIES** 16 rooms, boat, horses, restaurant. **CREDIT CARDS** Not accepted.
Araioses (Ilha do Caju), 3:30 hours by boat, departing from Parnaíba
TEL 321-1179 / 9983-3331
www.ilhadocaju.com.br

Ilhéus – BA

AREA CODE 73 POPULATION 222,127
DISTANCE Salvador, 464 km (288.3 mi)
SITE www.ilheus.ba.gov.br/turismo.php

HOTELS

Cana Brava Resort $$$
This hotel sits in a large swath of Atlantic Rainforest by the sea, and it's crossed by the Jairi river. There are enclosures for small animals, a private beach and a dam. There are also surfboards, body boards, kayaks and bikes for rent. The suites have whirlpool tubs. **FACILITIES** 179 rooms, air-conditioning, phone, TV, cable TV, bar, recreation team, pool, football court, tennis court, convention room, fitness room, game room, massage room, sauna. **CREDIT CARDS** All.
Rodovia Ilhéus–Canavieiras (BA-001), km 24, Praia de Canabrava, Olivença
TEL 3269-8000 **RESERVATIONS** (11) 3255-6500
www.canabravaresort.com.br

Ecoresort Tororomba $$$
Attractions at this resort include mud baths in the Jairi river, with its mineral-rich waters, hiking trails in the Atlantic Rainforest, and a large leisure area that's also open to non-guests. The "de luxe" rooms overlook the sea. **FACILITIES** 86 rooms, air-conditioning, phone, TV, cable TV, bar, recreation team, pool, playground, football court, restaurant, convention room, fitness room, game room, massage room, sauna. **CREDIT CARDS** All.
Rodovia Ilhéus–Canavieiras (BA-001), km 21, Praia de Canabrava, Olivença
TEL 3269-1200 FAX 269-1090 **RESERVATIONS** (11) 3262-3718
www.tororomba.com.br

La Dolce Vita $$
The rooms, concentrated in three blocks, have exits to the beach. The "de luxe" rooms and suites face the sea. The twelve suites are spacious and have verandahs and whirlpool tubs. **FACILITIES** 44 rooms, air-conditioning, phone, TV, cable TV, bar, pool, restaurant, fitness room, sauna. **CREDIT CARDS** American Express, Visa.
R. A, 114, access by the Rodovia Ilhéus–Canavieiras (BA-001), km 2.5
TEL 3234-1212 FAX 3234-1213
www.ladolcevita.com.br

Transamérica Ilha de Comandatuba $$$$
This resort offers a wide range of services and ample leisure amenities, especially for water sports. There's a golf course, a L'Occitane spa, shops, five restaurants, six bars, and a nightclub. **FACILITIES** 363 rooms, air-conditioning, phone, TV, cable TV, bar, boat, football field, golf course, recreation team, pool, jogging track, playground, football court, tennis court, restaurant, convention room, fitness room, game room, massage

PRICES	HOTELS (couple)	$ up to R$150	$$ from R$151 up to R$300	$$$ from R$301 up to R$500	$$$$ above R$500

room, sauna, spa. **CREDIT CARDS** All.
Ilha de Comandatuba, municipality of Una
TEL 686-1122 **FAX** 686-1457 **RESERVATIONS** 0800126060
www.transamerica.com.br

RESTAURANTS

Boca du Mar $$
Facing Pontal Bay, this restaurant has outdoor tables by the river, verandah and a sushi bar, with live music daily. It specializes in fish and pasta with seafood. **CUISINE** Varied. **CREDIT CARDS** All. **HOURS** Tue-Fri, from 6pm until the last customer; Sat and Sun, from 11:30am until the last customer.
Av. Lomanto Júnior, 15, Pontal
TEL 231-3200/2822

Cabana Gabriela $
This simple eatery serves finger food and fish from a large kiosk on the beach. Tables are on the sand and also indoors. **CUISINE** Fish and seafood. **CREDIT CARDS** All. **HOURS** 8am-8pm.
Rodovia Ilhéus–Olivença, km 4
TEL 632-1836

Sheik $
The glassed-in hall has a wonderful view of Ilhéus and Pontal coastline. There are five independent kitchens: Arab, Italian, Portuguese, Japanese and regional from Bahia, but everything is served in the same hall. Live MPB (Brazilian Popular Music) rings out daily. **CUISINE** Varied. **CREDIT CARDS** All. **HOURS** Daily, from 6pm until late.
Alta de São Sebastião, Oiteiro
TEL 634-1799/231-0197

SERVICES

AIRPORT

Aeroporto de Ilhéus
R. Brigadeiro Eduardo Gomes, Pontal
TEL 231-7629

LOCAL TOUR OPERATOR

NV Turismo
R. General Câmara, 27, Centro
TEL 634-4101

TOURIST INFORMATION

Prefeitura Municipal de Ilhéus
Av. Soares Lopes, 1741, Centro
TEL 234-5050

Itacaré – BA

AREA CODE 73 **POPULATION** 18,120
DISTANCES Salvador, 440 km (273 mi); Ilhéus, 66 km (41 mi)
SITE www.itacare.com.br

HOTELS

Aldeia da Mata Ecolodge $$$
Relax here, and soak up some nature. The bungalows are scattered across 44.5 acres of Atlantic Rainforest, with 300 meters (100 ft) of beach. Made of wood, bamboo and piassava, the bungalows are very charming and cozy. Some sit on pillars almost 3 meters (10 ft) tall. There is a suspended spa in the forest. **FACILITIES** 10 rooms, TV, ceiling fan, pool, massage room, spa. **CREDIT CARDS** Not accepted.
Praia do Pé da Serra, district of Uruçuca, access by the rodovia Itacaré–Ilhéus (BA-001), km 31.5
TEL 231-7112
www.aldeiadamata.com.br

Aldeia do Mar Chalés $$
The chalets are in one end of the beach, near an attractive, vegetation-covered and divided by a river. They offer plenty of tranquility and darkness at night, which allows night owls to contemplate the stars. The common areas and spacious chalets are decorated with handicrafts and paintings with Indian motifs. **FACILITIES** 13 rooms, air-conditioning, phone, TV, cable TV, bar, restaurant. **CREDIT CARDS** All.
Praia da Concha, Centro
TEL 251-2230 **FAX** 357-3822 **RESERVATIONS** (71) 356-4344
www.aldeiadomar.tur.br

Burundanga Pousada $$
The decor combines colonial elements with handicrafts, antiques and mosaic floors. Located 100 meters (330 ft) from the beach, the inn has spacious rooms with verandahs and hammocks, hair dryers and coffeemakers. Children under 14 are not allowed. Closed in May. **FACILITIES** 6 rooms, air-conditioning, phone, TV, cable TV, ceiling fan, pool. **CREDIT CARDS** MasterCard.
Praia da Concha, Centro
TEL 251-2543
www.burundanga.com.br

Itacaré Eco Resort $$$$
This resort is inside a condominium by a private beach. The surrounding 543-acre environmental reserve used to be a cocoa farm. There are several trails, a waterfall and a belvedere. The rooms have verandahs with hammocks and views of the river and forest. Private vehicles are not allowed in the area, so guests must use the hotel's vans. **FACILITIES** 25 rooms, air-conditioning, phone, TV, cable TV, bar, recreation team, pool, rock pool, restaurant, convention room, fitness room, game room, sauna. **CREDIT CARDS** All.
Praia de São José, access by the Rodovia Itacaré–Ilhéus (BA-001), km 64.5
TEL 251-3133
www.ier.com.br

Pousada Ilha Verde $
The French owner is crazy about Afro-Brazilian culture, and established this simple inn, with an architecture and decoration that combine native Brazilian and African elements. There are common areas outdoors with an *ofurô* tub, a massage tent, a kiosk for reading, a large hut with sofas and large cushions, and a suspended deck for *capoeira* (an African-derived martial art) and African dance classes. **FACILITIES** 8 rooms, air-conditioning, ceiling fan, pool, massage room. **CREDIT CARDS** Visa.
R. Ataíde Setubal, 234, Centro

RESTAURANTS	**$** up to R$50	**$$** from R$51 up to R$100	**$$$** from R$101 up to R$150	**$$$$** above R$150

TEL 251-2056
www.ilhaverde.com.br

Pousada Sage Point $$$

The chalets of this inn are very charming and comfortable. Built from *canduru* wood, which is now listed as a threatened species, they are scattered on plateaus along the rocky coast. Most items served for breakfast are prepared in the inn. **FACILITIES** 17 rooms, ceiling fan, restaurant, sauna, spa for relaxation. **CREDIT CARDS** Diners, MasterCard, Visa.
Praia de Tiririca, 65
TEL 251-2030
www.pousadasagepoint.com.br

Txai Resort $$$$

This resort is on an old cocoa farm surrounded by Atlantic Rainforest. There's a large common area, decorated rustically, which includes a reading room with 24-hour internet access and a piano room. There are rooms facing the beach and bungalows with CD players, some of which also have a whirlpool tub. There's a semi-Olympic pool by the beach, surf classes and a relaxation center with therapeutic massage. **FACILITIES** 26 rooms, air-conditioning, phone, TV, cable TV, pool, tennis court, restaurant, game room, massage room, sauna. **CREDIT CARDS** All.
Praia de Itacarezinho, access by the Rodovia Itacaré–Ilhéus (BA-001), km 48
TEL 634-6936 **FAX** 634-6956
www.txai.com.br

Villa de Ocaporan Hotel Village $$

The beautiful woods that crosses the beaches of Concha and Resende can be seen from a belvedere. There are accommodations with one or two bedrooms and suites. There's a hut with hammocks and sofas in the garden. **FACILITIES** 31 rooms, air-conditioning, phone, TV, cable TV, ceiling fan, bar, pool, playground, restaurant, game room. **CREDIT CARDS** Diners, MasterCard, Visa.
R. Jacarandá, Condomínio Conchas do Mar II,
Praia da Concha
TEL 251-2470 **FAX** 251-3116
www.villadeocaporan.com.br

RESTAURANTS

Boca do Forno $

This pizza parlor is located in the Beco das Flores gallery, a charming place, decorated with typical regional handicrafts and old-fashioned furniture. It serves thin crust pizza, with traditional and innovative toppings. For dessert, order the pies and sweets from Armazém de Minas Café. **CUISINE** Pizza. **CREDIT CARDS** All.
HOURS Daily, 6pm-1am.
R. Lodônio de Almeida, 108, Centro (Beco das Flores)
TEL 251-3121

Casa Sapucaia $

Chef Marina Ribeiro, from São Paulo, and Frenchman Mathieu Hourcade decided to move to Itacaré to this colonial-style house. The menu features modern French recipes and inventive options based on the cuisines of other countries. **CUISINE** Varied. **CREDIT CARDS** MasterCard, Visa. **HOURS** Mon-Sat, 7pm-11pm.

R. Lodônio de Almeida, 84, Centro (Beco das Flores)
TEL 251-3091

Dedo de Moça $

This restaurant is well decorated, with colorful lamps, sofas and an outdoor terrace. Its nice atmosphere enhances the taste of the shrimp *bobó* (fresh shrimp, dried shrimp, manioc meal, dende oil, coconut milk, cashews and peanuts, seasoning), as well as the fish with walnuts and the beef tenderloin medallion with red wine sauce. Good list of wine and *cachaça*. **CUISINE** Contemporary. **CREDIT CARDS** All. **HOURS** High season, noon-midnight; low season, 7pm-midnight.
R. Plínio Soares, 26, Centro
TEL 251-3372

Estrela do Mar $

This restaurant lies between the sea and the river, and combines rustic and sophisticated items in an ambience reminiscent of a fishing village. The menu emphasizes fish and regional food, but also features international dishes. **CUISINE** Fish and seafood. **CREDIT CARDS** Diners, MasterCard, Visa. **HOURS** 8am-10pm.
Praia da Concha, Centro
TEL 251-2230

Itacarezinho $

This is the only restaurant on Itacarezinho beach, 20 km (12.3 mi) from the center. There are tables under piassava-thatched huts, on a deck amidst coconut trees. It serves finger foods and starters such as *acarajé* (beans purée deep-fried in dende oil, and served with ground dried shrimp), sun-dried meat with onions and banana, and fish and seafood options. **CUISINE** Fish and seafood, snacks. **CREDIT CARDS** Diners, MasterCard. **HOURS** 10am-6pm.
Praia de Itacarezinho, rodovia Itacaré–Ilhéus (BA-001), km 50 (20 km [12.3 mi] from the center)
TEL 239-6154

Restaurante do Miguel $

Home-style fish and seafood dishes get served up in a simple, pleasant setting. After lunch, rest in a hammock and take in the beautiful landscape. **CUISINE** Fish and seafood. **CREDIT CARDS** Not accepted. **HOURS** Daily, 11am-6pm.
Ilha de Manguinhos, accessible by canoe on the Contas river

SERVICES

LOCAL TOUR OPERATORS

Ativa Rafting

Estrada da Pancada, Taboquinhas
TEL 696-2219

Caminho da Terra

R. do Pituba, 165
TEL 251-3053/3060. **HOURS** 4pm-10pm

Itacaré Ecoturismo

R. Lodônio Almeida, 117, Centro
TEL 251-2224/2443. **HOURS** 8am-noon and 2pm-9pm

PRICES	HOTELS (couple)	$ up to R$150	$$ from R$151 up to R$300	$$$ from R$301 up to R$500	$$$$ above R$500

Jacumã – PB

AREA CODE 83
DISTANCE João Pessoa, 25 km (27 mi)

RESTAURANT

Canyon de Coqueirinho $
This restaurant serves several versions of *moqueca* at outdoor tables that afford magnificent views of Coqueirinho Beach. As a starter, try the needlefish fillet. **CUISINE** Fish and seafood. **CREDIT CARDS** Not accepted. **HOURS** Daily, 9am-5pm.
Praia do Coqueirinho
TEL 9301-1990/9309-9094

Japaratinga – AL

AREA CODE 82 **POPULATION** 6,868
DISTANCES Maceió, 110 km (120.3 mi)

HOTEL

Pousada do Alto $$
This inn sits atop a hill with a stunning ocean view. There's a large deck with plenty of deck chairs. Paintings by artists such as João Câmara, antiques and modern design pieces give the place an eclectic look. Children under 12 are not allowed. **FACILITIES** 10 rooms, air-conditioning, ceiling fan, restaurant. **CREDIT CARDS** Not accepted.
Sítio Biquinha, Centro
TEL 297-1268
www.pousadadoalto.com.br

Jericoacoara – CE

AREA CODE 88
DISTANCE Fortaleza, 300 km (328 mi)
SITE www.jericoacoara.tur.br

HOTELS

Mosquitoblue Jeri $$
Open only since 2004, this hotel faces the beach. Its common area is charming, and the rooms overlook flowery gardens. The central part of the garden houses the lighted pool and a jacuzzi. The restaurant serves only breakfast. **FACILITIES** 44 rooms, air-conditioning, phone, TV, cable TV, bar, recreation team, pool, restaurant, fitness room, game room, sauna. **CREDIT CARDS** All.
R. Ismael, Jericoacoara
TEL 3669-2203 **FAX** 3669-2204
www.mosquitoblue.com.br

Pousada e Windsurfcenter Sítio Verde $$
This quiet inn sits by Paraíso lagoon, and the chalets are simple and neat. There's no phone or TV in the rooms, but breakfast is made to order. A great place for windsurfing. **FACILITIES** 5 rooms, air-conditioning, ceiling fan, bar, restaurant, fitness room, game room. **CREDIT CARDS** Visa.
Córrego do Urubu, Lagoa Paraíso
TEL 3669-1151
www.jericoacoara.tur.br/sitioverde

Pousada Vila Kalango $$
This rustic and charming inn is decorated with local elements, made with coconut, straw and twigs. One of its highlights is the lounge with hammocks and ottomans and a reading area, all facing the beach, near a sand dune and a coconut grove. The stilt cabins, built 3 meters (10 ft) above the ground, are a good option for couples. **FACILITIES** 18 rooms, ceiling fan, bar, restaurant, game room. **CREDIT CARDS** MasterCard, Visa.
R. das Dunas, 30
TEL 3669-2290 / 3669-2289 **FAX** 3669-2291
www.vilakalango.com.br

RESTAURANTS

Azul do Mar $
The large servings draw regulars from Preá beach, 12 km (7.5 mi) outside of Jericoacoara. One of the menu's highlights is the grilled snook. The restaurant is very simple, with tables set inside a kiosk facing the beach. There's no written menu, and no fruit juice. **CUISINE** Fish and seafood. **CREDIT CARDS** Not accepted. **HOURS** Daily, noon-6pm.
Praia do Preá, Cruz
TEL 3660-3062

Chocolate $
This small, cozy restaurant of wood accommodates only 30 diners at a time. There is a good choice of risottos, pasta, salads and desserts such as the *petit gâteau* (dark chocolate cake with a soft chocolate filling served with vanilla ice cream). **CUISINE** Varied. **CREDIT CARDS** All. **HOURS** Daily, 6pm-11pm.
R. do Forró, 213/214
TEL 3669-2190

SERVICES

LOCAL TOUR OPERATORS

Clube dos Ventos
R. das Dunas
TEL 3669-2288

Jeri Off Road Viagens e Turismo
R. Principal, 208, Centro
TEL 3669-2022/9961-4167

Koala Passeios
R. do Forró
TEL 3421-7044/3421-7063/9962-0934

João Pessoa – PB

AREA CODE 83 **POPULATION** 597,934
DISTANCES Natal, 180 km (112 mi); Recife, 120 km (74.5 mi)
SITE www.joaopessoa.pb.gov.br

HOTELS

Hardman Praia $$
This executive-quality hotel has good facilities and is well located in the district of Manaíra, facing the beach. The restaurant, on the first floor, has a beautiful night view. **FACILITIES** 120 rooms, air-conditioning,

---

RESTAURANTS $ up to R$50 $$ from R$51 up to R$100 $$$ from R$101 up to R$150 $$$$ above R$150

phone, TV, cable TV, bar, pool, restaurant, convention room, fitness room, game room, sauna. **CREDIT CARDS** All.
Av. João Maurício, 1341
TEL 246-8811
www.hotelhardman.com.br

Tropical Tambaú Vacation $$
This hotel's distinctive round shape dates from the 1970's. It occupies a large parklike area between the beaches of Tambaú and Manaíra. Though comfortable, the hotel is a bit dated. **FACILITIES** 172 rooms, air-conditioning, phone, TV, cable TV, bar, recreation team, pool, restaurant, convention room, fitness room, game room, massage room, sauna. **CREDIT CARDS** All.
Av. Almirante Tamandaré, 229, Tambaú
TEL 218-1919 **FAX** 247-1070 **RESERVATIONS** 08007012670
www.tropicalhotel.com.br

RESTAURANTS

Badionaldo $
This restaurant has been serving its famous Brazilian *peixada* (fish stew), prepared with tomatoes, potatoes, peppers and onions for over 40 years. The atmosphere is relaxed and the place is very simple. **CUISINE** Fish and seafood. **CREDIT CARDS** Visa. **HOURS** Mon, 11am-4pm; Tue-Sat, 11am-9pm; Sun, noon-5pm.
R. Vitorino Cardoso, 196, Praia do Poço (Cabedelo)
TEL 250-1299

Mangai $
The perfect place to sample regional cuisine, this restaurant offers more than 30 dishes typical of the *sertão* (the Brazilian hinterland). Examples include *rubacão* (beans, pork meat, sun-dried meat, rice, butter, cheese and seasoning), *mungunzá* (hominy and coconut milk pudding) and *sovaco de cobra* (shredded sun-dried beef, corn and onions). All the dishes are prepared with fresh, organic ingredients, and served in a nice "per kilo" buffet. No alcoholic beverages available. **CUISINE** Regional from the Northeast of Brazil. **CREDIT CARDS** Visa. **HOURS** Tue-Sun, 6am-10pm.
Av. General Édson Ramalho, 696, Manaíra
TEL 226-1615

Porto Madeiro $
Frequented by locals, this restaurant serves pasta and sushi in the evening, from Tuesdays to Saturdays. **CUISINE** Varied. **CREDIT CARDS** All. **HOURS** Mon and Tue, 6pm-midnight; Wed-Fri, noon-4pm and 6pm-midnight; Sat, 6pm-midnight; Sun, noon-4pm.
R. Antônio Carlos Araújo, 60, Cabo Branco
TEL 247-1594

SERVICES

AIRPORT

Aeroporto Presidente Castro Pinto
TEL 232-1200

TOURIST POLICE STATION

Delegacia de Apoio ao Turista (Deatur)
Av. Almirante Tamandaré, 100
TEL 214-8022/8023

TOURIST INFORMATION

Disque Turismo
TEL 08002819229

Empresa Paraíbana de Turismo
Av. Almirante Tamandaré, 100, Tambaú
TEL 214-8297. **HOURS** 8am-4pm

Lençóis – BA

AREA CODE 75 **POPULATION** 8,910
DISTANCE Salvador, 415 km (256 mi)

HOTELS

Canto das Águas $$
This hotel, in the town center by the Lençóis river, is filled with the relaxing gurgling of the rapids. The architecture and decoration are charming and welcoming, and blend into the rosy rocks and curves of the river. **FACILITIES** 44 rooms, air-conditioning, phone, TV, bar, pool, restaurant, convention room, game room, massage room, sauna. **CREDIT CARDS** All.
Av. Senhor dos Passos, 1, Centro
TEL 334-1154 **FAX** 334-1279
www.lencois.com.br

Estalagem do Alcino $
Artist-owner Alcino Menezes restored a derelict manor dating from 1890. To do so, he consulted old photographs and added antique furniture, handicraft and his own artwork. The result is exquisite. The inn is simple, but breakfast is excellent. **FACILITIES** 7 rooms, ceiling fan. **CREDIT CARDS** Not accepted.
R. Tomba Surrão, 139 (r. General Viveiros), Tomba
TEL 334-1171

Portal de Lençóis $$$
This spacious and comfortable hotel has a rather formal service. There are rooms, mezzanines and bungalows with two rooms and two bathrooms that are great for families or groups. It's far from the town center, but a scheduled shuttle service runs for guests. **FACILITIES** 84 rooms, air-conditioning, phone, TV, ceiling fan, bar, pool, jogging track, playground, restaurant, convention room, fitness room, game room, massage room, sauna. **CREDIT CARDS** All.
R. Chácara Grota, Altina Alves
TEL and **FAX** 334-1233
www.portalhoteis.tur.br

RESTAURANTS

Cozinha Aberta $
In this small historical house, the kitchen opens onto two small rooms that seat fourteen. The young owner, Débora Doitschinoff, serves mouthwatering and aromatic dishes typical of the various countries where she studied culinary arts. **CUISINE** Contemporary. **CREDIT CARDS** Not accepted. **HOURS** Daily, 1pm-11pm.
R. da Baderna, 111, Centro
TEL 334-1066

La Pérgola $
The owner, Paulo Alcântara de Meirelles, studied culi-

| **PRICES** | **HOTELS** (couple) | $ up to R$150 | $$ from R$151 up to R$300 | $$$ from R$301 up to R$500 | $$$$ above R$500 |

518   BRAZIL GUIDE

nary arts in France, where he worked in several restaurants. Before you go, check whether he is on duty in the kitchen. Try the traditional steak *au poivre* or innovations such as *tucunaré* (peacock bass) with herbs. Great salads. CUISINE French. CREDIT CARDS Diners, MasterCard. HOURS 7pm-11pm.
Pça. do Rosário, 70, Centro
TEL 334-1241/1387

Neco's Bar $

The congenial Neco and his family draw customers to this small restaurant. It serves sun-dried meat, mutton, free range chicken and *tucunaré* (peacock bass) with varied side dishes. Many of the ingredients are produced in the family's farm. CUISINE Regional. CREDIT CARDS Not accepted. HOURS noon-10pm (reservation required).
Pça. Maestro Clarindo Pacheco, 15
TEL 334-1179

SERVICES

AIRPORT

Aeroporto Coronel Horácio de Matos
BR-242, km 209, 25 km (15.5 mi) from the center
TEL 625-8100

LOCAL TOUR OPERATORS

Andrenalina
R. das Pedras, 121, Centro
TEL 334-1689

Cirtur
R. da Baderna, 41, Centro
TEL 334-1133

Edivaldo (horseback riding)
TEL 334-1729

Explorer Brasil
Pça. Maestro Clarindo Pacheco, 5, Centro
TEL 334-1183

Lentur
Av. Sete de Setembro, 10, Centro
TEL 334-1271

Marimbus Ecoturismo
TEL 334-1718/1292

Nativos da Chapada
R. Miguel Calmon, 29, Centro
TEL 334-1314/9966-0131

Pé de Trilha
Pça. Horácio de Matos, Centro
TEL 334-1124/1635

Velozia Cicloturismo
R. do Lagedo, 68, Centro
TEL 334-1700

Zentur
Pça. das Nagôs, Centro
TEL 334-1397

TOURIST GUIDES

Associação dos Condutores de Visitantes de Lençóis (ACVL)
Av. Senhor dos Passos, 61
TEL 334-1425

Kristine Nicoleau
TEL 334-1308

Roy Funch
TEL 334-1305

TOURIST INFORMATION

Prefeitura Municipal de Lençóis
TEL 334-1121

Maceió – AL

AREA CODE 82 POPULATION 797,759
DISTANCES Aracaju, 290 km (180 mi); Recife 253 km (157 mi)

HOTELS

Jatiúca Resort $$$$
This resort is located in one of the town's best areas, rather than being isolated like some similar hotels. The atmosphere is relaxed. The main door opens onto the promenade, and the garden stretches to the beach. Dinner is included. FACILITIES 179 rooms, air-conditioning, phone, TV, cable TV, ceiling fan, bar, recreation team, pool, tennis court, restaurant, convention room, fitness room, game room, massage room. CREDIT CARDS All.
R. Dr. Mário Nunes Vieira, 220, Mangabeiras,
Praia de Jatiúca
TEL 355-2020 FAX 355-2121
www.hoteljatiuca.com.br

Meliá Maceió $$$
This luxury hotel on the waterfront lacks character, but has an excellent view of the coastline. The lobby's sushi bar invites guests to settle in for an afternoon drink. FACILITIES 184 rooms, air-conditioning, phone, TV, cable TV, bar, recreation team, pool, playground, tennis court, restaurant, convention room, fitness room, game room, massage room, sauna. CREDIT CARDS All.
Av. Álvaro Otacílio, 4065, Jatiúca
TEL 325-5656 FAX 325-3784 RESERVATIONS 08007033399
www.meliamcz.com.br

Ritz Lagoa da Anta $$$
Frequented by executives, it also attracts tourists. The first floor is exclusively convention space. On the fifth floor, the Bali Floor, the rooms are decorated in Balinese fashion and the corridor is dimly lit. The Design Floor (the sixth) has modern furniture which gives a contemporary touch to the businessmen's floor. FACILITIES 200 rooms, air-conditioning, phone, TV, cable TV, bar, recreation team, pool, playground, tennis court, restau-

RESTAURANTS $ up to R$50 $$ from R$51 up to R$100 $$$ from R$101 up to R$150 $$$$ above R$150

rant, convention room, fitness room, game room, massage room, sauna, spa. CREDIT CARDS All.
Av. Brigadeiro Eduardo Gomes, 546,
Praia da Lagoa da Anta
TEL 2121-4000 FAX 2121-4123
www.ritzmaceio.com.br

Venta Club Pratagy $$$$

Mostly Italian tourists frequent this rustic hotel, and all information is written both in Portuguese and Italian. It sits amid greenery and has leisure facilities on the beach. Almost everything is included in the daily rate, except lobster, shrimp and imported beverages. It is far from the most fashionable beaches. FACILITIES 164 rooms, air-conditioning, phone, TV, cable TV, ceiling fan, bar, football field, recreation team, pool, tennis court, restaurant, convention room, fitness room, game room, sauna. CREDIT CARDS All.
Rodovia AL-101 Norte, km 10, Pratagy
TEL 2121-6200 FAX 2121-6201
www.pratagy.com

RESTAURANTS

Canto da Boca $$

Simplicity, from the cutlery to the menu layout, belies the fame-garnering quality of the food. The octopus and shrimp *moqueca* and the shrimp *bobó* are highlights. CUISINE Fish and seafood. CREDIT CARDS Diners, MasterCard, Visa. HOURS Mon, Wed and Thu, noon-midnight; Fri and Sat, noon-1am; Sun, noon-6pm.
Av. Dr. Júlio Marques Luz, 654, Jatiúca
TEL 325-7346

Divina Gula $

You'll feel like you're in Minas Gerais. The most fashionable restaurant of Maceió serves dishes such as chicken with okra, and *tutu à mineira* (bean purée with pork sausage, manioc flour and seasoning). It also offers a good variety of *cachaça*. CUISINE Regional from the state of Minas. CREDIT CARDS All. HOURS Tue-Sat, noon-2am; Sun, noon-midnight.
R. Engenheiro Paulo Brandão Nogueira, 85, Jatiúca
TEL 235-1262

Recanto do Picuí $

This is the best place to taste genuine regional dishes. It's all here: sun-dried meat, manioc and cowpea, all in generous servings. CUISINE Regional. CREDIT CARDS MasterCard, Visa. HOURS Mon-Thu and Sun, 11:30am-midnight; Fri and Sat, 11:30am1:30am; From March-November, closed on Tuesdays.
Av. Álvaro Calheiros, 110, Mangabeiras
TEL 325-7537

Wanchako $

You may find it odd to see a Peruvian restaurant in Maceió, but you'll think it perfectly natural to return after your first visit. Peruvian cuisine produces sophisticated fish dishes, and the menu is prepared with mastery. Try the *ceviche* (fish or seafood marinated in lemon). CUISINE Peruvian. CREDIT CARDS Diners, MasterCard, Visa. HOURS Tue-Fri, noon-3pm and 7pm-11:30pm; Sat, 7pm-1am; Sun, noon-5pm.
R. São Francisco de Assis, 93, Jatiúca
TEL 327-8701

SERVICES

AIRPORT

Aeroporto Zumbi dos Palmares
Rodovia BR-104, km 91
TEL 214-4000

TOURIST POLICE STATION

Delegacia de Turistas
Av. Fernandes Lima, Farol
TEL 338-3507. HOURS Mon-Fri, 8am-6pm

TOURIST INFORMATION

Secretaria Estadual de Turismo (Setur)
Av. Dr. Antônio Gouveia, 1143, Pajuçara
TEL 315-1603. HOURS Mon-Fri, 8am-6pm

Secretaria Municipal de Turismo (Seturma)
R. Sá e Albuquerque, 310, Jaraguá
TEL 336-4409. HOURS Mon-Fri, 8am-7pm; Sat and Sun, 8am-8pm

Mangue Seco – BA

AREA CODE 75
DISTANCE Salvador, 246 km (152 km)

HOTELS

Pousada Asa Branca $

One of the newest inns in the village, this simple spot is near the docks where the motorboats from Sergipe arrive from across the river. It has few offerings for leisure activities. FACILITIES 20 rooms, air-conditioning, TV, ceiling fan, bar, pool, restaurant. CREDIT CARDS MasterCard, Visa.
R. da Frente, 4, Praia do Rio Real
TEL 445-9053 / 9985-2580
www.infonet.com.br/asabranca

Pousada O Forte $

This simple inn is run by Argentinean Eduardo and Uruguayan Gabriela. The two of them make you feel at home. Ask for one of the rooms higher up the estate, so you can overlook the Real river. Three rooms have air-conditioning. FACILITIES 13 rooms, air-conditioning, TV, bar, restaurant. CREDIT CARDS MasterCard.
Praia da Costa
TEL 445-9039
www.pousadaoforte.com

Village Mangue Seco $

This inn sits on a large strip of land in front of mangroves, very close to the beach. The restaurant is good, and Eliane, the chef, prepares delicious cashew sweets. Some rooms have cold shower only. FACILITIES 20 rooms, air-conditioning, TV, bar, pool, playground, restaurant. CREDIT CARDS Diners, MasterCard.
Caminho da Praia
TEL (79) 224-2965 / 9982-5553
www.villagemangueseco.com.br

PRICES	HOTELS (couple)	$ up to R$150	$$ from R$151 up to R$300	$$$ from R$301 up to R$500	$$$$ above R$500

Maragogi – AL

AREA CODE 82 **POPULATION** 21,832
DISTANCE Maceió, 141 km (87.6 mi)

HOTEL

Club Hotel Salinas do Maragogi $$$
This rustic resort sits by the beach on a plot cut across by the Maragogi river. A family-oriented resort, it offers plenty of activities for children. Dinner is included in the rate. **FACILITIES** 205 rooms, air-conditioning, phone, TV, cable TV, bar, boat, football field, horses, recreation team, pool, playground, football court, tennis court, restaurant, convention room, fitness room, game room, massage room, sauna. **CREDIT CARDS** All.
Rodovia AL-101 Norte, km 124, Praia de Maragogi
TEL 296-3000 **FAX** 296-1158
www.salinas.com.br

RESTAURANTS

Ponto de Embarque $$
This beachside restaurant specializes in baked whole fish filled with shrimp and banana. The dish serves three, but needs to be ordered an hour ahead. The owner organizes boat excursions to the rock pools. **CUISINE** Fish and seafood. **CREDIT CARDS** Visa. **HOURS** 11am-5pm.
R. Beira-Mar, 327
TEL 296-1400

Restaurante do Mano $$
Established some three decades ago, this waterfront restaurant has become a benchmark for seafood in town. The service is friendly and the food is well made and plentiful. **CUISINE** Fish and seafood. **CREDIT CARDS** Not accepted. **HOURS** 9am-9pm.
R. Semião Ribeiro de Albuquerque, 82,
Praia de São Bento
TEL 296-7106

Morro de São Paulo – BA

AREA CODE 75
DISTANCE Salvador, 248 km (154 mi) by car, plus 90 minutes by boat or 30 minutes by fast motorboat
SITE www.morrodesaopaulo.com.br

HOTELS

Catavento Praia Hotel $$
This hotel is located on a quiet spot, far from the hubbub of the village. Guests are welcomed at the dock or at the runway, and there's a regular shuttle service to the village. The rooms are spacious, with king-size beds, and the leisure area has a collection of toys and a large pool. Heliport available. **FACILITIES** 20 rooms, air-conditioning, phone, TV, cable TV, pool, tennis court, fitness room, game room, massage room, sauna. **CREDIT CARDS** All.
Quarta Praia, 2.5 km (1.5 mi) from the village
TEL 483-1052 **FAX** 483-1444
www.cataventopraiahotel.com.br

Hotel Fazenda Vila Guaiamu $$
This hotel sits on a crab preservation area. The *guaia-mun* crabs can be seen in the garden. The rooms are spacious and rustic, with windows, verandahs and hammocks. Closed in May and June. **FACILITIES** 21 rooms, air-conditioning, TV, ceiling fan, restaurant. **CREDIT CARDS** American Express, MasterCard, Visa.
Terceira Praia, 1 km (0.6 mi) from the village
TEL 483-1035 **FAX** 483-1073
www.vilaguaiamu.com.br

Patachocas Eco-Resort $$
On an old farm by the sea, this resort offers transfers from Salvador (the hotel has its own runway and airport) or Valença, and to the village. The bungalows, with a verandah and hammock, are located alongside coconut alleys. **FACILITIES** 52 rooms, air-conditioning, phone, TV, bar, pool, restaurant, game room. **CREDIT CARDS** Diners, MasterCard, Visa.
Quarta Praia, 4.5 km (2.8 mi) from the village
TEL 483-2129 **RESERVATIONS** 483-2130
www.patachocas.com.br

Portaló $$$
Standing near the docks and the historical Portaló, the 18th century arch at the town's entrance, the hotel stretches along the sides of a hill. It overlooks the ocean and the islands. There are hair dryers, bathrobes and whirlpool tubs in the master chalets. The massage kiosk on the deck offers an ocean view. **FACILITIES** 19 rooms, air-conditioning, phone, TV, cable TV, bar, pool, fitness room, game room, massage room, sauna. **CREDIT CARDS** Diners, MasterCard, Visa.
Lad. da Igreja, Pça. do Portaló, Centro
TEL 483-1374 **FAX** 483-1354
www.hotelportalo.com

Porto do Zimbo Small Resort $$$
This hotel faces rock pools and possesses gardens full of coconut trees and piassava-thatched walkways. Some rooms have whirlpool tub, enhancing the general tropical atmosphere. Each room is equipped with hair dryer, cordless phone with answering machine and CD player. **FACILITIES** 16 rooms, air-conditioning, phone, TV, bar, horses, pool, restaurant, convention room, game room. **CREDIT CARDS** All.
Quarta Praia, 3 km (1.8 mi) from the village
TEL 483-1278 **FAX** 483-1299
www.hotelportodozimbo.com.br

Pousada Charme $$
The inn's common area faces the village's busiest spot, and rooms scattered on the side of a hill have a beautiful ocean view. One of the rooms has an outdoor whirlpool tub and is ideal for couples. **FACILITIES** 8 rooms, air-conditioning, phone, TV, cable TV, bar, pool, restaurant, massage room. **CREDIT CARDS** All.
R. da Prainha, 25, in the center of the village
TEL and **FAX** 483-1306
www.charmepousada.com.br

Pousada Fazenda Caeira $$
This 617-acre coconut farm has a runway, pastures and some Atlantic Rainforest. The inn sits by the sea and has gardens, extensive lawns, and colonial-style decor. Closed in May and June. **FACILITIES** 24 rooms, air-conditioning, TV, bar, horses, pool, restaurant, game room.

RESTAURANTS $ up to R$50 $$ from R$51 up to R$100 $$$ from R$101 up to R$150 $$$$ above R$150

CREDIT CARDS Diners, MasterCard, Visa.
Terceira Praia, 1.5 km (1 mi) from the village
TEL and FAX 483-1042
www.fazendacaeira.com.br

Praia do Encanto $$

The distance from the village – 6 km (3.7 mi) – may
be a disadvantage, but this is offset by the access to
the rock pools and by the tranquility of the setting,
which is surrounded by 247 acres of forest. The service is good, and lodgings are simple, in rooms and
chalets. Leisure includes kayaks, bikes and horses.
Closed in June. FACILITIES 22 rooms, air-conditioning,
bar, horses, pool, playground, restaurant, game room,
massage room. CREDIT CARDS Diners, MasterCard, Visa.
Praia do Encanto (Quinta Praia), 6 km (3.7 mi)
from the village
TEL 483-1288 FAX 483-1020
www.praiadoencanto.com.br

Provence Villegaignon Resort $$

The common areas are located by the beach. The spacious rooms are distributed in several blocks along long
alleys. FACILITIES 89 rooms, air-conditioning, phone, bar,
recreation team, pool, playground, tennis court, restaurant, game room, sauna. CREDIT CARDS MasterCard, Visa.
Terceira Praia, 2 km (1.2 mi) from the village
TEL 483-1010 FAX 483-1012 RESERVATIONS 08007049089
www.redeprovence.com.br

Villa das Pedras Pousadas $$

This inn has a garden and a pool by the beach. There's
a fashionable plaza adjoining the inn, with boutiques
and a cachaçaria that serves sugarcane rum. The
rooms are simple, with access through walkways on
the sand floor. FACILITIES 24 rooms, air-conditioning, TV,
bar, pool, restaurant. CREDIT CARDS All.
Segunda Praia
TEL 483-1075 FAX 483-1122
www.villadaspedras.com.br

RESTAURANTS

El Sitio $$

This cheerful restaurant has a small verandah overlooking the busy street along the beach. The dining room is
candle-lit. The menu is eclectic: there's grilled Argentinean picanha (cap of rump) and lobster au gratin with
aromatic herbs and white wine. CUISINE Varied. CREDIT
CARDS Diners, MasterCard, Visa. HOURS Daily, 5pm-1am.
R. Caminho da Praia, center of the village
TEL 483-1527

O Casarão $$

Outdoor tables overlook the village's main square. It
serves international and regional fish recipes, including moqueca and bobó. Meat and fowl dishes on the
menu serve two. CUISINE Varied. CREDIT CARDS All. HOURS
Daily, 6pm-11pm.
Pça. Aureliano Lima, 190, center of the village
TEL 483-1022

Piscina $$

The restaurant and the beach tent are rustic, and have
large tables and benches in two floors, with a view of

the rock pools. Moquecas, bobó and grilled or baked
seafood are the highlights. CUISINE Fish and seafood.
CREDIT CARDS Diners, MasterCard, Visa. HOURS 9am-10pm.
Quarta Praia
TEL 483-1461

SERVICES

LOCAL TOUR OPERATORS

Centro de Informações Turísticas (CIT)

Pça. Aureliano Lima, Centro
TEL 483-1083. HOURS 8:30am-10pm

Madalena Tur

Segunda Praia
TEL 483-1317/9148-3234. HOURS 8am-9pm

Marlins Ecotur

Caminho da Praia
TEL 483-1242/1385. HOURS 8am-midnight

Tirolesa do Morro

Morro do Farol
TEL 8805-9796. HOURS 10am-6pm

TOURIST INFORMATION

Centro de Informações Turísticas

Pça. Aureliano Lima
TEL 483-1083/1589

DIVING OPERATORS

Companhia do Mergulho

Primeira Praia (Prainha)
TEL 483-1200

AIR TAXI

Addey Táxi-Aéreo

Caminho da Praia
TEL 483-1242/1385

Aero Star Táxi-Aéreo

TEL 483-1083/(71) 377-4406

Mucugê – BA

AREA CODE 75 POPULATION 13,682
DISTANCES Salvador, 460 km (285 mi), Lençóis, 150 km
(93 mi)
SITE www.infochapada.com

HOTELS

Alpina Resort Mucugê $

This resort overlooks the town of Mucugê from a
perch 1,200 meters (4000 ft) above the sea level. It offers a rural, alpine atmosphere, and horseback and
cart riding amid lots of greenery. The rooms have
king-size beds and DVD players. FACILITIES 32 rooms, TV,
ceiling fan, bar, football field, horses, pool, restaurant,
convention room, game room. CREDIT CARDS All.
Rodovia Andaraí–Mucugê (BA-142), km 40, 6 km (3.7

| PRICES | HOTELS (couple) | $ up to R$150 | $$ from R$151 up to R$300 | $$$ from R$301 up to R$500 | $$$$ above R$500 |

mi) from the center
TEL 338-2150 RESERVATIONS (71) 451-4900
www.alpinamucuge.com.br

Pousada Mucugê $

This 19th century manor has been remodeled and now has a modern building attached to it. Local stone has been used for the flooring. The inn organizes excursions for the guests and has its own guides. FACILITIES 30 rooms, phone, TV, ceiling fan, bar, pool, restaurant, game room. CREDIT CARDS Diners, MasterCard, Visa.
R. Dr. Rodrigues Lima, 30, Centro
TEL 338-2210 FAX 338-2170
www.pousadamucuge.com.br

RESTAURANT

Dona Nena $

Cross the living room, pantry and kitchen to get to the tables and benches set in the yard of this simple house. The structure has made the historical heritage list. Try the sun-dried meat, free range chicken and fish, accompanied by *godó* de banana-verde (sun-dried meat and green banana stew), *cortado* of green papaya (chopped green papaya with minced meat), or *cortado* of palma (a type of cactus with minced meat or cod fish). CUISINE Regional. HOURS Daily, 11:30am-8pm.
R. Direita do Comércio, 140, Centro
TEL 338-2153

SERVICES

LOCAL TOUR OPERATORS

KM

Pça. Coronel Douca Medrado, 126, Centro
TEL 338-2277/2152

Venturas and Aventuras

R. Dr. Rodrigues Lima, 49
TEL 338-2284

TOURIST GUIDES

Associação dos Condutores de Visitantes de Mucugê (ACVM)

TEL 338-2414

TOURIST INFORMATION

Centro de Atendimento ao Turista (CAT)

R. Coronel Douca Medrado, 71, Centro
TEL 338-2255. HOURS 8am-noon and 2pm-10pm

Natal – RN

AREA CODE 84 POPULATION 712,317
DISTANCES Fortaleza, 552 km (343 mi), João Pessoa, 180 km (112 mi)

HOTELS

Escola de Turismo e Hotelaria Barreira Roxa $$

Senac's school hotel stands out for its regional cuisine restaurant and for the 18 rooms decorated with handicraft from the nine states of Northeastern Brazil. The pool is small. The hotel is well located, but its not possible to bath or swim along the stretch of beach in front. FACILITIES 53 rooms, air-conditioning, phone, TV, cable TV, jogging track, restaurant, convention room. CREDIT CARDS All.
Via Costeira, 4020, Parque das Dunas
TEL 209-4000
www.barreiraroxa.com.br

Esmeralda $$$$

This brand-new hotel is well located. The large verandah, actually an extension of the reception area, overlooks Ponta Negra beach. There's no room service, leisure services are limited and the fitness room has only three devices. FACILITIES 120 rooms, air-conditioning, phone, TV, cable TV, bar, pool, restaurant, convention room, fitness room, massage room. CREDIT CARDS All.
R. Francisco Gurgel, 1160, Ponta Negra
RESERVATIONS 4005-0000 FAX 219-5994
www.hotelesmeralda.com.br

Manary Praia $$$

The ambience and the rooms are very charming thanks to the plentiful use of wood and straw in construction. A varied and hearty breakfast includes homemade cakes and bread. The "de luxe" rooms overlook the sea and have a verandah with a hammock. The "de luxe superior" have whirlpool tubs. Twenty-four-hour room service is available. There's a tour operator that promotes excursions to the *sertão* (hinterland), including the Cariri valley. FACILITIES 24 rooms, air-conditioning, phone, TV, cable TV, bar, pool, restaurant, convention room, game room. CREDIT CARDS All.
R. Francisco Gurgel, 9067, Ponta Negra
TEL and FAX 219-2900
www.manary.com.br

Ocean Palace Hotel and Resort $$$$

This resort is well placed on an excellent bathing beach that has a lifeguard on duty. There are twenty bungalows with verandahs that overlook the sea, far from the noise of the pool, where there are two bars. FACILITIES 233 rooms, air-conditioning, phone, TV, cable TV, bar, recreation team, pool, playground, football court, restaurant, convention room, fitness room, game room, massage room, sauna. CREDIT CARDS All.
Via Costeira, km 11, Praia de Barreira D'Água
TEL 219-4144 FAX 219-3081 RESERVATIONS 0800844144
www.oceanpalace.com.br

Pestana Natal Beach Resort $$$$

This is the most luxurious hotel in town. It has panoramic elevators, spacious rooms and an excellent pool, with an exit to the beach. There are plenty of activities for children. Foreign tourists make up many of the guests. FACILITIES 189 rooms, air-conditioning, phone, TV, cable TV, bar, recreation team, pool, playground, football court, tennis court, restaurant, convention room, fitness room, game room, massage room, sauna. CREDIT CARDS All.
Via Costeira, 5525, Parque das Dunas
TEL 220-8900 FAX 220-8920 RESERVATIONS 0800266332
www.pestana.com

RESTAURANTS	$ up to R$50	$$ from R$51 up to R$100	$$$ from R$101 up to R$150	$$$$ above R$150

RESTAURANTS

Camarões $
Abundant servings at affordable prices make this place a favorite among shrimp lovers. At peak times, you might wait an hour to be served. CUISINE Fish and seafood. CREDIT CARDS All. HOURS Mon-Sat, 11:30am-3:30pm and 6:30pm-midnight; Fri and Sat, until 1am; Sun, 11:30am-4pm and 6:30pm-11pm.
Av. Engenheiro Roberto Freire, 2610, Ponta Negra
TEL 219-2424

Mangai $
This casual restaurant is the city's temple of regional cuisine. It is a branch of Mangai of João Pessoa. It is frequented by locals who appreciate the 50 Northeastern dishes typical of the *sertão* (hinterland) such as *buchada de bode* (stuffed goat's stomach) and sundried meat with manioc. CUISINE Regional. CREDIT CARDS Visa. HOURS Tue-Fri, 7am-10pm; Sat and Sun, 6am-10pm.
Av. Amintas Barros, 3300, Lagoa Nova
TEL 206-3344

Paçoca de Pilão $
Although 25 km (15.5 mi) from Natal, the restaurant may be well worth the visit. The ambience is simple and pleasant, especially if you eat under the large cashew tree. The house specialty shares its name with the restaurant itself: sun-dried meat with banana, rice, string beans, manioc and *coalho* (rennet) cheese. CUISINE Regional. CREDIT CARDS Diners, Master-Card. HOURS From 11 am until late; in the low season, Mon-Thu, 11am-6pm; Fri and Sat, 11am-11pm; Sun, 11am-8pm.
R. Deputado Márcio Marinho, 5708, Praia de Pirangi do Norte, Parnamirim
TEL 238-2088

Peixada da Comadre $
This traditional restaurant stands out for the fish served, and draws many local families. Dishes serve two. CUISINE Fish and seafood. CREDIT CARDS Diners, MasterCard, Visa. HOURS Tue-Sat, 11:30am-3:30pm and from 6:30 until the last customer leaves; Sun, 11:30am-5pm.
Av. Praia de Ponta Negra, 9048, Ponta Negra
TEL 219-3016

SERVICES

AIRPORT

Aeroporto Internacional Augusto Severo
Rodovia BR-101, km 8, Parnamirim
TEL 644-1000

LOCAL TOUR OPERATORS

Cascadura Turismo e Viagens Ecológicas Ltda.
Av. Engenheiro Roberto Freire, 576, Ponta Negra
TEL 219-6334/9409-2393

Luck Receptivo Nataltur
Av. Praia de Ponta Negra, 8884, Ponta Negra
TEL 219-2966/2967

Manary Ecotours
R. Francisco Gurgel, 9067, Ponta Negra
TEL 219-2900

Scandinavian Plus
Av. Engenheiro Roberto Freire, 9028, Ponta Negra
TEL 236-5114

Supertur Viagens e Turismo Ltda.
Av. Prudente de Morais, 4283, Lagoa Nova
TEL 234-2790/1000

TOURIST POLICE STATION

Delegacia do Turista
Av. Engenheiro Roberto Freire, 8790, Praia Shopping (Ponta Negra)
TEL 232-7404

TOURIST INFORMATION

Tourist Information Kiosk at Aeroporto Internacional Augusto Severo
Av. Torquato Tapajós, km 8, Parnamirim
It has no phone. HOURS 8am-midnight

Secretaria Estadual de Turismo
R. Mossoró, 359, Tirol
TEL 232-2486/2518

Secretaria Municipal de Turismo
R. Enéas Reis, 760, Petrópolis
TEL 232-9061. HOURS Mon-Fri, 8am-6pm

Olinda – PE

AREA CODE 81 POPULATION 367,902
DISTANCE Recife, 7 km (4.4 mi)
SITE www.olinda.pe.gov.br

HOTELS

Pousada do Amparo $$
This historical manor is on one of the main streets of Olinda. Works by local artists decorate the cozy common area. At the rear, there's a yard with a garden and an extraordinary view of the center of Recife. FACILITIES 11 rooms, air-conditioning, phone, TV, cable TV, ceiling fan, bar, pool, sauna. CREDIT CARDS Diners, Master-Card, Visa.
R. do Amparo, 199, Centro Histórico
TEL 3439-1749 FAX 3429-6889
www.pousadadoamparo.com.br

Sete Colinas $$
Set in a wooded area of 3.7 acres, this is a quiet spot in the historical center. It's a good place to enjoy Carnival. The rooms with verandahs are decorated with woodcuts. FACILITIES 39 rooms, air-conditioning, phone, TV, cable TV, bar, pool, restaurant, convention room, sauna. CREDIT CARDS All.
Lad. do São Francisco, 307
TEL 3439-6055
www.hotel7colinas.com.br

PRICES	HOTELS (couple)	$ up to R$150	$$ from R$151 up to R$300	$$$ from R$301 up to R$500	$$$$ above R$500

RESTAURANTS

Goya $
This combination studio-restaurant is run by artists and chefs Petrúcio Nazareno and Antônio Cabral. The menu features many sweet-and-sour dishes, such as Goya lobster, which is served with diced pineapple. CUISINE Contemporary, fish and seafood. CREDIT CARDS All. HOURS Mon and Wed-Sat, noon-5pm and 6pm-midnight; Sun, until 10pm.
R. do Amparo, 157, Centro Histórico
TEL 3439-4875

Kwetú $
This is one of the most acclaimed restaurants in town. Belgian chef Brigitte Anckaerte combines French cuisine with Indian and Moroccan influences. She can always spare a minute to chat with customers. CUISINE French, fish and seafood. CREDIT CARDS Diners, MasterCard, Visa. HOURS Mon-Fri, 6pm-midnight; Fri-Sun, noon-3pm and 6pm-midnight.
Av. Manoel Borba, 338, Pça. do Jacaré
TEL 3439-8867

Oficina do Sabor $$
A meal here is a must in Olinda. Creative chef César Santos reinvents the regional cuisine of Pernambuco and creates sophisticated dishes by combining local ingredients such as *jerimum* (pumpkin) and *macaxeira* (manioc) with seafood. CUISINE Regional from the Northeast, fish and seafood. CREDIT CARDS All. HOURS Tue-Thu, noon-4pm and 6pm-midnight; Fri, noon-4pm and 6pm-1am; Sat, noon-1am; Sun, noon-5pm.
R. do Amparo, 335, Centro Histórico
TEL 3429-3331

Palmeiras – BA

AREA CODE 75 POPULATION 7,518
DISTANCE Salvador, 453 km (281.5 mi), Lençóis, 86 km (53.5 mi)
SITE www.infochapada.com

HOTELS

Pousada Candombá $
When Frenchman Claude Samuel moved to the Chapada (plateau), he kept the habits of his homeland. He owns an orchard where he organically grows almost all the ingredients used in the inn, including coffee, and he offers good wine from his cellar. He also knows the area very well and provides information to guests with the support of guides, maps and models. FACILITIES 7 rooms, bar, restaurant, sauna. CREDIT CARDS Visa.
R. das Mangas, Vale do Capão, district of Caeté-Açu, 65 km (40.4 mi) from Lençóis
TEL and FAX 344-1102

Pousada do Capão $
This self-sustained farm is surrounded by the beauties of Vale do Capão. The rooms and chalets are simple. There's an internet room and a room with a fireplace. FACILITIES 14 rooms, phone, ceiling fan, bar, rock pool, restaurant, game room, massage room, sauna. CREDIT CARDS Diners, MasterCard.
R. do Chamego, Vale do Capão, district of Caeté-Açu
TEL and FAX 344-1034
www.pousadadocapao.com.br

SERVICES

LOCAL TOUR OPERATORS

Pé no Mato
Ladeira da Vila, 2, district of Caeté-Açu
TEL 344-1105. HOURS 8am-10pm

Tatu na Trilha
R. da Vila, district of Caeté-Açu
TEL 344-1124. HOURS Mon-Sat, 8am-noon and 2pm-6pm

TOURIST GUIDES

Associação dos Condutores de Visitantes do Vale do Capão (ACVVC)
TEL 229-4019

TOURIST INFORMATION

Secretaria de Turismo
Pça. Dr. José Gonçalves, 11, Centro
TEL 332-2211. HOURS Mon-Fri, 8am-noon and 2pm-8pm

Parnaíba – PI

AREA CODE 86 POPULATION 132,282
DISTANCE Teresina, 350 km (217.5 mi)

HOTELS

Cívico $
Although it may be the best hotel in town, Cívico's 30-years-old facilities need renovation. Only the "de luxe" rooms have TV and minibar. The ones in front overlook a busy street and are rather noisy. FACILITIES 29 rooms, air-conditioning, phone, bar, pool, restaurant, convention room. CREDIT CARDS Diners, MasterCard, Visa.
Av. Governador Chagas Rodrigues, 474, Centro
TEL 322-2470 FAX 322-2028
www.hotelcivico.com.br

Penedo – AL

AREA CODE 82 POPULATION 56,993
DISTANCE Maceió, 173 km (107.5 mi)
SITE www.rotasdealagoas.com.br/site/penedo.html

HOTEL

Pousada Colonial $
This simple inn offers a beautiful view of São Francisco river from its 1734 manor. The rooms on the side of the manor are cozier, although they have no air-conditioning. FACILITIES 12 rooms, air-conditioning, phone, TV, ceiling fan, restaurant.
Pça. 12 de Abril, 21, Centro
TEL 551-2355

RESTAURANT

Forte da Rocheira $
The specialty here is alligator meat with coconut

RESTAURANTS	$ up to R$50	$$ from R$51 up to R$100	$$$ from R$101 up to R$150	$$$$ above R$150

sauce. The owners have a permit from Ibama (the Brazilian Environmental Protection Agency) to grow and ranch alligators on a farm. The view of São Francisco river is excellent. CUISINE Varied. CREDIT CARDS Visa. HOURS Daily, 11am-4pm and 6pm-10pm.
R. da Rocheira, 2
TEL 551-3273/4151

Piaçabuçu – AL

AREA CODE 82 POPULATION 16,775

HOTEL

Pousada Chez Julie $

This is a good option for those wanting to visit São Francisco river and its surroundings. It's 18 km (11 mi) from Piaçabuçu, and cars need to ride on the sand to reach it. Roeland Eniel, a Belgian-born Brazilian, who also owns an agency that organizes excursions in the river, runs this simple inn. FACILITIES 10 rooms, air-conditioning, TV, bar, pool, restaurant. CREDIT CARDS Visa.
Av. Beira-Mar, 53, Praia de Pontal do Peba
TEL 557-1217

Ponta do Corumbau – BA

AREA CODE 73
DISTANCES Salvador, 844 km (524.5 mi); Porto Seguro, 220 km (136.7 mi)

HOTELS

Jocotoka Eco Resort $$

This coconut farm by the sea has 700 meters (2300 feet) of beach, a river at the back and an area with trails for hiking and biking. The lodgings are spacious bungalows decorated with tropical motifs. The resort stands out for its watersports and marine leisure options including schooner, motorboats and boats, which can also be used to transport guests from Porto Seguro airport. FACILITIES 15 rooms, ceiling fan, bar, boat, pool, playground, restaurant, game room, massage room. CREDIT CARDS Not accepted.
Praia de Corumbau, access by the Rodovia Itamaraju–Corumbau, 70 km, or by boat from Cumuruxatiba or Porto Seguro
TEL 294-1244 FAX 288-2540 RESERVATIONS 288-2291
www.jocotoka.com.br

Pousada São Francisco $$$$

This charming inn is located on a coconut farm that, in addition to 1,000 meters (3,300 ft) of exclusive beach, has a river at the back with mangroves and islands for hikes and excursions. There are long chairs under the coconut trees. The rooms and chalets are spacious and decorated with handicrafts and antiques. There's a heliport. Children under 11 are not welcome in the high season. FACILITIES 8 rooms, air-conditioning, bar, boating, horses, restaurant, massage room. CREDIT CARDS Not accepted.
Praia de Corumbau, 2 km (1.2 mi) from the Corumbau village, access by the Rodovia Itamaraju–Corumbau, 70 km, or by boat from Cumuruxatiba or Porto Seguro

TEL 9994-9842 RESERVATIONS (11) 3085-9616/9993
www.corumbau.com.br

Vila Naiá $$$$

In addition to the almost-exclusive beach, this old coconut farm has a 49-acre preserved area of salt marsh and mangrove trees. Local craftsmen built everything of wood – and no nails, following the region's time-honored construction methods. FACILITIES 8 rooms, ceiling fan, bar, restaurant, fitness room, massage room. CREDIT CARDS MasterCard, Visa.
Praia de Corumbau, 4 km (2.5 mi) from the Corumbau village, access by the Rodovia Itamaraju–Corumbau, 70 km, or by boat from Cumuruxatiba or Porto Seguro
TEL 573-1006 RESERVATIONS (11) 3062-6214

Porto de Galinhas – PE

AREA CODE 81
DISTANCE Recife, 65 km (40.4 mi)

HOTELS

Nannai Beach Resort $$$$

This charming resort sits by the beautiful, quiet Muro Alto beach. Couples on honeymoon love the place. The wooden Polynesian-style bungalows have simple decor. The vast pool stretches to the guests' door. FACILITIES 73 rooms, air-conditioning, phone, ceiling fan, bar, boat, recreation team, pool, playground, football court, tennis court, restaurant, fitness room, game room, massage room, sauna. CREDIT CARDS All.
Rodovia PE-09, km 3, Muro Alto
TEL 3552-0100 FAX 3552-1474
www.nannai.com.br

Pousada Porto Verde $

The decoration combines colors and regional motifs in a large plot of land with plenty of vegetation. The inn is in the heart of the village, but the sound of forró (typical dance music) from the main street does not bother the guests. FACILITIES 14 rooms, air-conditioning, TV, ceiling fan, bar, pool. CREDIT CARDS Diners, MasterCard, Visa.
Pça. 1, Praia de Porto de Galinhas
TEL 3552-1410
www.pousadaportoverde.com.br

Pousada Tabajuba $$

The service is very good and the staff is cheerful. Located by the beach, the inn is frequented by couples on honeymoon. Children under 12 are not allowed. FACILITIES 24 rooms, air-conditioning, phone, bar, pool, fitness room. CREDIT CARDS Diners, MasterCard, Visa.
Rodovia PE-09, km 6.5
TEL 3552-1049 FAX 3552-1006
www.tabajuba.com

Summerville Beach Resort $$$$

There are many leisure activities, including in the pool that stretches over a large part of the property. There is a recreation team that caters to children and adolescents, a children's restaurant and a nursery. There's a "pillow menu" with over 10 choices of herb stuffing

| PRICES | HOTELS (couple) | $ up to R$150 | $$ from R$151 up to R$300 | $$$ from R$301 up to R$500 | $$$$ above R$500 |

526   BRAZIL GUIDE

for the cushions. FACILITIES 250 rooms, air-conditioning, phone, ceiling fan, bar, boat, football field, mini-golf course, recreation team, pool, heated pool, playground, football court, tennis court, restaurant, convention room, fitness room, game room, massage room, sauna. CREDIT CARDS All.
Rodovia PE-09, Praia de Muro Alto
TEL 3302-5555 RESERVATIONS 03007894844 FAX 3302-4445
www.summervilleresort.com.br

RESTAURANTS

Beijupirá $
Almost all the dishes are prepared from *beijupirá* (black king fish), hence the restaurant's name. The most fashionable in Porto de Galinhas, it's a great choice for tourists looking for good food and a pleasant atmosphere. CUISINE Fish and seafood, regional. CREDIT CARDS All. HOURS Daily, noon-1am (Reservation advised for dinner).
R. Beijupirá
TEL 3552-2354

Peixe na Telha $$
This restaurant provides good food, informal service and tables by the beach. It stands out for the fish and seafood prepared, which are served on clay tiles. CUISINE Fish and seafood, varied. CREDIT CARDS All. HOURS 11am-10pm.
Av. Beira-Mar, Praia de Porto de Galinhas
TEL 3552-1323

Porto Seguro – BA

AREA CODE 73 POPULATION 95,721
DISTANCE Salvador, 715 km (444 mi)
SITE www.portosegurotur.com.br

HOTELS

Brisa da Praia $$
In this modern building facing the beach, the large glassed-in areas let in natural light and afford a magnificent view of the ocean. The corridors are roofed with transparent material. The common areas are decorated with local handicrafts. The rooms are spacious and the suites have two whirlpool tubs: one in the bathroom and one in the verandah. FACILITIES 121 rooms, air-conditioning, phone, TV, bar, recreation team, pool, playground, restaurant, convention room, fitness room, game room, massage room, sauna. CREDIT CARDS All.
Av. Beira-Mar, 1860, Praia de Mundaí
TEL 288-8600 FAX 288-8636
www.brisadapraia.com.br

La Torre $$
Located 30 meters (100 feet) from the beach, this congenial inn has a small internal garden, a small flowing lake and discreet decoration in the rooms. Access for disabled people is available in all areas. The inn owns its own tent on the beach, with a massage kiosk available. The Italian owner speaks many languages. FACILITIES 80 rooms, air-conditioning, phone, TV, bar, pool, playground, restaurant, fitness room, game room,

massage room, sauna, spa. CREDIT CARDS All.
Av. Beira-Mar, 9999, Praia de Mutá
TEL 672-1243 FAX 672-1616
www.latorreaparthotel.com.br

Porto Seguro Praia $$
This hotel has a beautiful 12.3-acre wooded area and gardens on the avenue that runs along the beach. The simply decorated rooms are spacious and have large verandahs with hammocks. Five suites have extraordinary ocean views and whirlpool tubs. FACILITIES 150 rooms, air-conditioning, phone, TV, cable TV, bar, recreation team, pool, playground, fitness room, game room, massage room, sauna. CREDIT CARDS All.
Av. Beira-Mar, Praia de Curuípe
TEL 288-9393 FAX 288-2069
www.portoseguropraiahotel.com.br

Vela Branca Resort $$
Situated on the upper city, near the historical site, with a magnificent view of the coastline and the town, this resort has great services and leisure services. It covers a sizable estate of gardens and lawns. Accommodations are available in rooms, duplex rooms, or suites with 2 or 3 rooms. The hotel has a beach tent in Taperapuã. FACILITIES 125 rooms, air-conditioning, phone, TV, bar, football field, recreation team, pool, playground, tennis court, restaurant, convention room, fitness room, game room, massage room, sauna. CREDIT CARDS All.
R. Dr. Antonio Ricaldi, 177, Cidade Alta
TEL 288-2318 FAX 288-2316
www.velabranca.com.br

Villaggio Arcobaleno $$$
On the avenue alongside the beach, this hotel has a high standard of service and facilities. The common area in the front blocks the noise and music from the Axé Moi beach kiosk nearby. The rooms are distributed in seven blocks, which are painted in rainbow colors. The rooms and suites are large and have balconies and bathtubs (the suites have whirlpool tubs.). There is a beach tent and the restaurant's menu changes every night. FACILITIES 161 rooms, air-conditioning, phone, TV, cable TV, bar, recreation team, pool, playground, tennis court, restaurant, convention room, fitness room, game room, massage room, sauna. CREDIT CARDS All.
Av. Beira-Mar, Praia de Taperapuã
TEL 679-2000 RESERVATIONS 08002845222 FAX 679-1269
www.hotelarcobaleno.com.br

RESTAURANTS

Bistrô da Helô $
This restaurant operates in a historical house in Passarela do Álcool (Alcohol Promenade). From the small dining room, you'll see Helô in the glassed-in kitchen. It serves creative fish and seafood and recipes with a French touch. CUISINE Fish and seafood and varied. CREDIT CARDS Diners, MasterCard. HOURS 6:30-midnight; March-June and August-November, closed on Sundays
Travessa Assis Chateaubriand, 29 (back) (Beco)
TEL 288-3940

RESTAURANTS	$ up to R$50	$$ from R$51 up to R$100	$$$ from R$101 up to R$150	$$$$ above R$150

Cabana Recanto do Sossego $$
This informal, waterfront restaurant is run by chef Ettore Dertoni, who has lived in Porto Seguro for 14 years and prepares fish the Italian way. CUISINE Fish and seafood. CREDIT CARDS Not accepted. HOURS Daily, 8am-5pm.
Av. Beira-Mar, 10130, Praia do Mutá
TEL 672-1266

Tia Nenzinha $
One of the oldest restaurants in town, Tia operates in a historical building near Passarela do Álcool (Alcohol Promenade). It is simple and serves good fish, meat and chicken options. CUISINE Fish and seafood. CREDIT CARDS Visa. HOURS noon-midnight.
Av. Portugal, 170, Passarela do Álcool
TEL 288-1846

SERVICES

AIRPORT

Aeroporto Internacional
Estrada do Aeroporto, Cidade Alta
TEL 288-1880/2010

LOCAL TOUR OPERATOR

Adeltour Turismo e Câmbio
Av. Vinte e Dois de Abril, 100 (Shopping Avenida), Centro
TEL 288-1888/3484

EXCHANGE SHOP

Adeltour Turismo e Câmbio
Av. Vinte e Dois de Abril, 100 (Shoppping Avenida), Centro
TEL 288-1888/288-3484

TOURIST INFORMATION

Secretaria de Turismo
Pça. dos Pataxós, 66, Centro
TEL 288-4124 / 288-1009

DIVING OPERATOR

Portomar
R. Dois de Julho, 178, Centro
TEL 288-2606

Praia da Pipa – RN

AREA CODE 84
DISTANCE Natal, 80 km (49.7 mi)
SITE www.praiadapipa.com.br

HOTELS

Sombra e Água Fresca $$$
The restaurant of this quiet, family-oriented hotel is on the highest part of Pipa, and overlooks Amor and Moleque beaches. Beach chairs, deck chairs and parasols are loaned to guests. The executive suite has a private pool. FACILITIES 19 rooms, air-conditioning, phone, TV, cable TV, ceiling fan, bar, pool, restaurant. CREDIT CARDS Diners, MasterCard, Visa.
R. Praia do Amor, 1000
TEL 246-2258 FAX 246-2144
www.sombraeaguafresca.com.br

Toca da Coruja Pousada $$$
This inn has well-tended gardens, numerous fruit trees and areas for resting and reading. There are four "double de luxe" chalets, each with 120 sq meters (143 sq yd), a king-size bed, a bathtub and a verandah with hammocks. A wooden walkway, built 1.5 meters (4.9 ft) off the ground, leads to the rooms while preserving the native vegetation below. The hotel serves copious breakfast. FACILITIES 15 rooms, air-conditioning, phone, TV, cable TV, ceiling fan, bar, pool, restaurant, fitness room, massage room, sauna. CREDIT CARDS All.
Av. Baía dos Golfinhos
TEL 246-2225 FAX 246-2226
www.tocadacoruja.com.br

RESTAURANT

La Provence $$
This is a quiet restaurant for couples wanting to enjoy a torch-lit dinner. The dishes look beautiful and the flavors have a touch of Provence, where chef-owner Jean Louis Ferrari comes from. The wine list is varied. CUISINE French, varied. CREDIT CARDS Not accepted. HOURS noon-4pm and 7pm-11pm; in the low season and in May and July, closed on Tuesdays.
R. da Gameleira
TEL 246-2280

Praia do Forte – BA

AREA CODE 71
DISTANCE Salvador, 91 km (56.5 mi)
SITE www.praiadoforte.org.br

HOTEL

Praia do Forte Eco Resort $$$$
On one of the most pleasant beaches in Bahia, this is among Brazil's best resorts. The great pools make guests feel lazy and reluctant to go to the beach. Preservation of nature is emphasized here. Biologists organize hikes and give talks on environmental conservation. FACILITIES 250 rooms, air-conditioning, phone, bar, boats, football field, horses, nautical center with boats and windsurfing, recreation team, pool, playground, football court, tennis court, restaurant, convention room, fitness room, game room, massage room. CREDIT CARDS All.
Av. do Farol
TEL 676-4000 FAX 676-1112 RESERVATIONS 0800118289
www.ecoresort.com.br

RESTAURANT

Caramuru e Catarina $
In a manor with a large verandah, this restaurant serves home cooking, such as spaghetti with tomato sauce and seafood such as *moqueca*. There's an array of choices of homemade desserts. Try the chocolate

PRICES	HOTELS (couple)	$ up to R$150	$$ from R$151 up to R$300	$$$ from R$301 up to R$500	$$$$ above R$500

and apricot pie. The service is rather slow. **CUISINE** Brazilian. **CREDIT CARDS** Diners, MasterCard, Visa. **HOURS** Mon-Sat, noon-4pm; Sun, noon-5pm; in the high season, open from noon-1am.
Al. da Felicidade
TEL 676-1343

Recife – PE

AREA CODE 81 POPULATION 1,422,905
www.recife.pe.gov.br

HOTELS

Atlante Plaza $$
This well-located business hotel features modern architecture and three panoramic elevators, which afford a beautiful view of the Boa Viagem coast. **FACILITIES** 233 rooms, air-conditioning, phone, TV, cable TV, bar, pool, heated pool, restaurant, convention room, fitness room, game room, sauna. **CREDIT CARDS** All.
Av. Boa Viagem, 5426, Boa Viagem
TEL 3302-3333 FAX 3302-4445 RESERVATIONS 3302-4446
www.atlanteplaza.com.br

Dorisol $$
A former Sheraton hotel, it now belongs to the Portuguese chain Dorisol. In the transition, the building's structure was preserved, while the decor was updated with reed and wicker furniture. It is located in front of Piedade beach, far from the center and 15 minutes from the airport. **FACILITIES** 198 rooms, air-conditioning, phone, TV, cable TV, bar, pool, restaurant, convention room, fitness room, game room, massage room, sauna. **CREDIT CARDS** All.
Av. Bernardo Vieira de Melo, 1624, Piedade (Jaboatão dos Guararapes)
TEL and FAX 2122-2700
www.dorisol.com.br

Mar Hotel Recife $$
This large hotel is near trendy Boa Viagem beach, but not on the sea front itself. There's a good leisure area, a large pool, and a good services for both casual tourists and business executives. Burle Marx designed the water park landscape. **FACILITIES** 207 rooms, air-conditioning, phone, TV, cable TV, bar, pool, restaurant, convention room, fitness room, game room, massage room, sauna. **CREDIT CARDS** All.
R. Barão de Souza Leão, 451, Boa Viagem
TEL 3302-4444 FAX 3302-4445 RESERVATIONS 3302-4446
www.marhotel.com.br

Pousada Casuarinas $
This is not a luxury inn. The key words here are cheerfulness and personalized service. Located 200 meters (660 feet) from Boa Viagem beach, it operates in the owner's house, which was built in the 1960's and converted into an inn in 1994. **FACILITIES** 12 rooms, air-conditioning, TV, ceiling fan, pool. **CREDIT CARDS** Not accepted.
R. Antônio Pedro Figueiredo, 151, Boa Viagem
TEL 3325-4708 FAX 3465-2061
www.pousadacasuarinas.com.br

Recife Palace $$
This large, classical-style hotel is on Boa Viagem beach, just 10 minutes from Shopping Center Recife. The rooms are decorated with woodcuts by J. Borges and family. It caters to tourists and executives alike. **FACILITIES** 295 rooms, air-conditioning, phone, cable TV, bar, pool, restaurant, convention room, fitness room, massage room, sauna. **CREDIT CARDS** All.
Av. Boa Viagem, 4070, Boa Viagem
TEL 3464-2500 FAX 3464-2525 RESERVATIONS 0800813161
www.lucsimhoteis.com.br

RESTAURANTS

Anjo Solto $
The modern decoration, good-looking staff, independent local bands, and electronic music contribute to create a stylish ambience that draws trendy people. As for the food, the crepes are very good. **CUISINE** Crepes. **CREDIT CARDS** Not accepted. **HOURS** Sun-Thu, from 6pm until late; Fri and Sat, from 7pm until late.
Av. Herculano Bandeira, 513 (Galeria Joana d'Arc), Pina
TEL 3325-0862

Casa de Banhos $
The short menu features *peixada* (fish stew) and *caldinho de sururu* (mini-mussel soup). It operates in a simple building, similar to a stilt house, by Capibaribe river, in Brasília Teimosa. It can be reached by boat (10 min), from Marco Zero. This used to be a medicinal bath resort area. **CUISINE** Fish and seafood. **CREDIT CARDS** Diners, MasterCard. **HOURS** Wed and Thu, noon-5pm; Fri and Sat, until midnight; Sun, noon-7pm; From April-August, closed in the evening.
Molhes do Porto, Brasília Teimosa
TEL 3075-8776

Casa dos Frios $$
This cozy, sophisticated bistro opened just recently. It seats only 40 people. Its *bolo-de-rolo* (roll cake) is very popular. The menu features mostly fish and seafood, and it has a great wine list. **CUISINE** Varied. **CREDIT CARDS** Diners, MasterCard, Visa. **HOURS** Mon-Sat, 9am-10pm; Sun, 9am-6pm.
Av. Engenheiro Domingos Ferreira, 1920, Boa Viagem
TEL 3327-0612/6794

Entre Amigos – O Bode $
Goat dishes, which are sadly looked down on by Brazilian haute cuisine, are the highlights here. There are 15 options of goat meat, including the basic goat stew, the traditional *buchada* (stuffed goat stomach) and a fantastic goat leg that weighs up to one kilo and serves five. **CUISINE** Regional from the Northeast. **CREDIT CARDS** All. **HOURS** Daily, from 11 am until late.
R. da Hora, 695, Espinheiro
TEL 3222-6705

Famiglia Giuliano $
The façade, which imitates a medieval castle, is not very encouraging, but this restaurant stands out for the *feijoada* served on Wednesdays and Saturdays. The tasty *feijoada* and more than twenty side dishes such as *paio* (a pork sausage), spare ribs and pork loin have earned this place some fame. It also serves pasta. **CUISINE** Varied. **CREDIT CARDS** All. **HOURS** Daily, noon-1am.
Av. Engenheiro Domingos Ferreira, 3980,

RESTAURANTS	$ up to R$50	$$ from R$51 up to R$100	$$$ from R$101 up to R$150	$$$$ above R$150

Boa Viagem
TEL 3465-9922

La Cuisine Bistrô $

This bistro serves light dishes such as sandwiches and salads, and French classics such as *steak au poivre*. It seats 70 people in a climate-controlled dining room and a terrace with a view of Boa Viagem beach. CUISINE Varied. CREDIT CARDS Diners, MasterCard. HOURS Mon-Thu and Sun, noon-11pm; Fri and Sat, noon-1am.
Av. Boa Viagem, 560, Boa Viagem
TEL 3327-4073

Leite $

This restaurant is a mainstay in the center of Recife. Decorated with dark wood, mirrors and green curtains, it has been open since 1882, making it one of the oldest restaurants of the country. The seafood menu draws lawyers, executives, and politicians. The service is very efficient. Try the *cartola* (banana, rennet cheese and molasses) for dessert. CUISINE Varied. CREDIT CARDS All. HOURS Mon-Fri and Sun, 11am-4:30pm.
Pça. Joaquim Nabuco, 147, Santo Antônio
TEL 3224-7977

Parraxaxá $

This restaurant brings a glimpse of the *sertão* (hinterlands) to Boa Viagem beach. The buffet has typical dishes such as mutton leg, *paçoca* (lean sun-dried meat, onions, manioc meal, coriander) and *baião-de-dois* (cowpea, bacon, crackling, rice, coriander, sun-dried meat, rennet and seasonings). Food is served in a simple ambience featuring brick walls, rustic furniture, calabashes and baskets. The waiters dress like *cangaceiros*, in the typical leather clothes of the *sertão*. CUISINE Regional from the Northeast. CREDIT CARDS Visa. HOURS Daily, 11:30am-4pm and 5:30-11pm.
R. Baltazar Pereira, 32, Boa Viagem
TEL 3463-7874

Portoferreiro $

This is one of the best restaurants in town. The decoration is elegant and simple, and the menu has dishes with Portuguese, Italian and French influences. It stands out for the wine list which features bottles of Barca Velha, a rare and acclaimed wine. CUISINE Varied. CREDIT CARDS Diners, MasterCard, Visa. HOURS noon-4pm and 7pm-midnight; Fri and Sat, until 2am; Sun, noon-3:30pm.
Av. Rui Barbosa, 458, Graças
TEL 3423-0854/2795

Recanto Lusitano $$

Forget the decor, which is a bit outdated, and focus on the house specialty: codfish, particularly Narcisa codfish sauteed in olive oil with onions and garlic, and served with boiled potatoes. CUISINE Portuguese. CREDIT CARDS All. HOURS Tue-Thu, 11:45am-3pm and 7pm-11pm; Fri and Sat, until 1am; Sun, noon-4pm.
R. Antônio Vicente, 284, Boa Viagem
TEL 3341-9790

Restaurant da Mira $

This is a truly theme restaurant. The menu-man, Edmílson, son of owner Alzemira Pereira, will introduce you to the kitchen, or, rather, the "surgery room," to *galinha ao molho pardo* (chicken cooked in a sauce

with its blood), or rather "indexed chicken" and to the "UTI" (intensive care unit), a room with a bed and all that is needed for relaxing or for an after-lunch nap. Despite the jokes, they're serious about regional cuisine and the food is great. CUISINE Regional from the Northeast. CREDIT CARDS Not accepted. HOURS Daily, noon-7pm.
Av. Doutor Eurico Chaves, 916, Casa Amarela
TEL 3268-6241

Wiella Bistrô $

This new restaurant has yet to be discovered by gourmets. The efficient staff, the modern but tasteful decor and the creative dishes will soon make it known as one of the best. The acoupa weakfish with shrimps and walnuts and the salmon with saffron risotto are excelent. CUISINE Contemporary, varied. CREDIT CARDS All. HOURS Tue-Sat, noon-midnight; Sun, noon-5pm.
Av. Engenheiro Domingos Ferreira, 1274, Boa Viagem
TEL 3463-3108

SERVICES

AIRPORT

Aeroporto Internacional dos Guararapes
Pça. Ministro Salgado Filho, Imbiribeira
TEL 3464-4188

TOURIST POLICE STATION

Delegacia do Turista
Aeroporto dos Guararapes
TEL 3303-7217/3464-4088

TOURIST INFORMATION

Disque Recife Turístico
TEL 3425-8409

Empresa de Turismo de Pernambuco (Empetur)
Complexo Viário Vice-governador Barreto Guimarães (Olinda)
TEL 3427-8183. HOURS 8am-5pm

Posto de Informações Turísticas
Pça. Ministro Salgado Filho (Aeroporto dos Guararapes)
TEL 3462-4960/3341-6090

Posto de Informações Turísticas
Pça. do Arsenal da Marinha, Recife Antigo (r. da Guia)
TEL 3224-2361. HOURS 9am-11pm

Salvador – BA

AREA CODE 71 POPULATION 2,443,107
DISTANCE Maceió, 617 km (383.4 mi)
SITE www.emtursa.ba.gov.br

HOTELS

Catharina Paraguaçu $$

This hotel is a favorite thanks to the historical manor that houses it, the tasteful decoration, and efficient service. It is decorated with tiles painted by local artists

PRICES	HOTELS (couple)	$ up to R$150	$$ from R$151 up to R$300	$$$ from R$301 up to R$500	$$$$ above R$500

and handicrafts from Maragogipinho. Breakfast includes couscous of *tapioca* (manioc starch) and a wonderful *bolinho de estudante* (manioc starch sweet fritter with cinnamon). FACILITIES 32 rooms, air-conditioning, phone, restaurant. CREDIT CARDS All.
R. João Gomes, 128, Rio Vermelho
TEL 334-0089
www.hotelcatharinaparaguacu.com.br

Club Med Itaparica $$$

This is the oldest resort in Brazil and it keeps up with the high standards of the Mediterranean chain. It is the most rustic of the three Brazilian villages. There are lots of activities for children and adults during the day and evening. It operates on an all-inclusive and "day use" basis, which allows non-guests to visit and enjoy the resort. FACILITIES 330 rooms, air-conditioning, phone, boating, football field, golf course, horses, recreation team, riding club, pool, jogging track, football court, tennis court, restaurant, convention room, fitness room, game room, massage room, sauna. CREDIT CARDS All.
Rodovia Bom Despacho, km 13, Nazaré,
Ilha de Itaparica
TEL 681-8800 RESERVATIONS 08007073782
www.clubmed.com.br

Pestana Bahia $$$

This classical and well-decorated hotel used to belong to the Meridien chain but was acquired by the Portuguese group Pestana, which remodeled it in 2001. It sits on a cliff with a stunning ocean view. FACILITIES 433 rooms, air-conditioning, phone, TV, cable TV, bar, pool, restaurant, convention room, fitness room, game room, massage room, sauna. CREDIT CARDS All.
R. Fonte do Boi, 216, Rio Vermelho
TEL 2103-8000/8001 RESERVATIONS 0800266332
www.pestanahotels.com.br

Pousada das Flores $$

Run by a French couple, this inn operates in an 18th century manor just a 5-minute walk from Pelourinho. Some rooms have a verandah with a view of Todos os Santos Bay. The spacious rooms are furnished with antique furniture. FACILITIES 9 rooms, phone, ceiling fan, restaurant. CREDIT CARDS Visa.
R. Direita de Santo Antônio, 442, Centro Histórico
TEL 243-1836
www.pflores.com.br

Pousada do Boqueirão $$

Decorated with flair, this is one of the most charming inns in town. It is efficiently run by Italian Fernanda Cabrini, a tour guide with 12 years' experience who knows all about Salvador. No wonder tourists feel at home. Closed in June. FACILITIES 11 rooms, air-conditioning, phone. CREDIT CARDS American Express, MasterCard, Visa.
R. Direita do Santo Antônio, 48, Centro Histórico
TEL 241-2262 TEL 241-8064
www.pousadaboqueirao.com.br

Redfish $$

This inn just opened in 2004. You'll hear a mix of accents: the owners are Charles Ruler, an Englishman, and his wife, Helena, a Bahian. Guests come from all over the world. It operates in a manor, on a quiet street near Pelourinho. FACILITIES 8 rooms, air-conditioning.
CREDIT CARDS Visa.
R. Ladeira do Boqueirão, 1, Centro Histórico
TEL 241-0639 RESERVATIONS 243-8473
www.hotelredfish.com

Sofitel Salvador $$$

This elegant and luxurious hotel offers flawless and environmentally-friendly service: it has implemented selective waste collection, sewage treatment and sensors to save energy. The pool is quite large. Although far from the center, it is ideal for those wanting to enjoy the best beaches. FACILITIES 206 rooms, air-conditioning, phone, TV, bar, football field, golf course, pool, playground, football court, tennis court, restaurant, convention room, fitness room, game room, massage room, sauna. CREDIT CARDS All.
R. da Passárgada, Itapuã
TEL 374-8500/6946 RESERVATIONS 08007037000
www.accorhotels.com.br

Solar Santo Antonio $$

This is a real melting pot: the owner Dimitri was born in Morocco, lived in Portugal for many years and decided to settle down in Salvador. There are only 2 rooms in this three-story 18th century manor. Being a guest here will give you the chance of delving into the culture of Bahia, since the host is one of the town's cultural mainstays. FACILITIES 2 rooms, ceiling fan. CREDIT CARDS Not accepted.
R. Direita de Santo Antônio, 177, Centro Histórico
TEL 242-6455
www.solarsantoantonio.com.br

Vila Galé Bahia $$

Opened in 2002, this inn has an excellent location: just a 10-minute walk from Pelourinho, it is also near Barra and Rio Vermelho, two of the busiest districts in town. But the best thing about this hotel is the ocean view. FACILITIES 224 rooms, air-conditioning, phone, TV, bar, pool, restaurant, convention room, fitness room, game room, massage room, sauna. CREDIT CARDS All.
R. Morro do Escravo Miguel, 320, Ondina
TEL 263-8888 FAX 263-8800 RESERVATIONS 08002848818
www.vilagale.pt

RESTAURANTS

Galpão $$

Acclaimed chef Laurent Suaudeau created menu, and the modern, clean decor draws an eclectic clientele that ranges from tourists to politicians. Try the lobster with manioc purée, plantain and *acarajé* chips (chips of bean purée deep-fried in *dendê* oil, with dried shrimps and seasonings). Don't miss the delicious desserts, such as crust cashew with *cachaça* emulsion. CUISINE Contemporary. CREDIT CARDS All. HOURS Mon-Sat, noon-3pm and 7pm-midnight.
Av. do Contorno, 660, Cidade Baixa
TEL 266-5544

Jardim das Delícias $

Regional dishes such as shrimp *bobó* and green coconut sweet are great. Service is slow and indifferent. CUISINE Regional. CREDIT CARDS All. HOURS From noon.
R. João de Deus, 12, Pelourinho
TEL 321-1449

RESTAURANTS	$ up to R$50	$$ from R$51 up to R$100	$$$ from R$101 up to R$150	$$$$ above R$150

Maria Mata Mouro $$

This restaurant is a gourmet favorite that provides good service. The shrimp dishes are particularly well prepared. Located in Pelourinho, it has a more formal dining room in the front, and a less formal one in the back, under a jasmine tree. CUISINE Varied. CREDIT CARDS All. HOURS Daily, from noon.
R. Inácio Accioly, 8, Pelourinho
TEL 321-3929

Mistura Fina $

The manor, with an pleasant verandah, is near Itapuã. Highlights include the combination of Italian dishes with seafood and a buffet with cold cuts and salads. CUISINE Fish and seafood. CREDIT CARDS All. HOURS Mon-Thu, 11:30am-midnight; Fri and Sat, 11:30am-1am; Sun, 11:30am-11pm.
R. Professor Souza Brito, 41, Farol de Itapuã
TEL 375-2623

Paraíso Tropical $$

This restaurant serves a lighter version of regional dishes using the *dendê* fruit rather than *dendê* oil, and coconut pulp instead of coconut milk. The place is simple, but busy because of the excellent food. Other highlights are the service, which is very informal, and the location: it operates on a verandah, on the owner's small farm. CUISINE Regional. CREDIT CARDS All. HOURS Mon-Sat, noon-11pm; Sun, noon-10pm.
R. Edgar Loureiro, 98-B, Cabula
TEL 384-7464

Trapiche Adelaide $$

Located in the old docks, facing Todos os Santos Bay, this restaurant is close to many design shops. The cliché "it is the place to see and be seen" applies here. Acclaimed chef Luciano Boseggia's menu features meat, pasta and seafood. Shorts and t-shirts are not permitted. CUISINE Varied. CREDIT CARDS All. HOURS Mon-Sat, noon-4pm and 7pm-1am; Sun, noon-4pm.
Pça. dos Tupinambás, 2,
Bahia Design Center, Comércio
TEL 326-2211

Yemanjá $$

Salvador's most traditional seafood restaurant devotes little attention to ambience and much to food. It serves 12 types of *moqueca*, of which the one with shrimp is the favorite. There's a branch in Rio de Janeiro on Rua Visconde de Pirajá, 128, Ipanema. CUISINE Regional from Bahia, fish and seafood. CREDIT CARDS All. HOURS Sun-Thu, 11:30am-4pm and 6pm-midnight; Fri and Sat, 11:30am-4pm and 6pm-1am.
Av. Otávio Mangabeira, 4655, Jardim Armação
TEL 461-9008/9010

SERVICES

AIRPORT

Aeroporto Deputado Luís Eduardo Magalhães

Pça Gago Coutinho, São Cristóvão, 28 km (17.3 mi) from the center of Salvador
TEL 204-1010

TOURIST POLICE STATION

Delegacia de Proteção ao Turista (Deltur)

R. Cruzeiro de São Francisco, 14, Pelourinho, Centro Histórico
TEL 322-7155/1188 HOURS 24 hours

TOURIST INFORMATION

Bahiatursa

R. das Laranjeiras, 12, Pelourinho
TEL 321-2463 HOURS 8:30am-9pm

Emtursa

Av. Vasco da Gama, 206, Centro Histórico
TEL 380-4200 HOURS Mon-Fri, 8am-noon and 2pm-6pm

Santo André – BA

AREA CODE 73
DISTANCES Salvador, 660 km (410 mi); Porto Seguro, 30 km (18.5 mi) and an additional 10 min by boat

HOTELS

Costa Brasilis Resort $$$

Situated by the beach, this resort has beautiful gardens and woods. The rooms are spacious and have a colonial touch, except the Premium room, decorated in Bali style with a whirlpool tub. There are plenty of leisure options, especially maritime activities such as marlin fishing by motorboat. The spa created by actress Tânia Alves operates in the hotel FACILITIES 51 rooms, air-conditioning, phone, TV, cable TV, ceiling fan, bar, boat, recreation team, pool, playground, football court, tennis court, restaurant, convention room, fitness room, game room, massage room, sauna, spa. CREDIT CARDS All.
Av. Beira-Mar, 2000, access via the Rodovia BA-001, km 46
TEL 671-4056/4057
www.resortcostabrasilis.com.br

Pousada Gaili $$

This inn is situated in an area of 20 acres of garden by the mouth of João de Tiba river. The accommodations in rooms or chalets are simple but pleasant. The owner is a Swiss baker and chef and prepares bread, cakes and pies for breakfast. FACILITIES 10 rooms, air-conditioning, TV, ceiling fan, bar, pool, jogging track, restaurant, massage room. CREDIT CARDS MasterCard, Visa.
Av. Beira-Rio, 1820
TEL 671-4060/4108
www.gaili.com

Toca do Marlin $$$$

The construction is opulent, with a high ceiling and structure made with trumpet tree hard wood. Artworks and antiques decorate the hotel. There's a bakery and areas for horseback riding. The suites are good-sized, with Swiss-made adjustable beds and gold-plated fittings in the bathrooms. Chef Laurent Suaudeau created the menu for this all-inclusive facility. The beach is not terribly nice, but the pool is enormous. FACILITIES 10 rooms, air-conditioning,

| PRICES | HOTELS (couple) | $ up to R$150 | $$ from R$151 up to R$300 | $$$ from R$301 up to R$500 | $$$$ above R$500 |

532   BRAZIL GUIDE

phone, TV, cable TV, bar, horses, pool, restaurant. **CREDIT CARDS** Visa, American Express.
Rodovia BA-001 Via Belmonte, km 40.5, Praia das Tartarugas
TEL 9985-0380
www.tocadomarlin.com.br

RESTAURANTS

Gaili $
This restaurant adjoins the inn by the beach of João de Tiba river. The Swiss chef serves dishes such as bratwurst (veal sausage) and regional dishes such as *moquecas* . **CUISINE** Varied. **CREDIT CARDS** MasterCard, Visa. **HOURS** Daily, noon-5pm and 7pm-10pm.
Av. Beira-Rio, 1820, Praia de Santo André
TEL 671-4060

Maria Nilza $$
This piassava-thatched hut has benches and straw mats in the almost deserted Guaiú beach. Nilza herself cooks fish and regional dishes such as *vatapá* (purée of dried smoked shrimp, ground peanuts and cashew nuts, bread crumbs, coconut milk and dende oil). **CUISINE** Regional. **CREDIT CARDS** Not accepted. **HOURS** 11am-5pm.
R. da Praia, 380, Praia de Guaiú
TEL 671-2047

São Cristóvão – SE

AREA CODE 79 **POPULATION** 64,647
DISTANCES Aracaju, 23 km (14.3 mi); Salvador, 330 km (250 mi)

RESTAURANT

Solar Parati $
This restaurant operates on the second floor of a re-modeled 18th century manor. The service is cheerful. The sun-dried meat with manioc purée and buttered manioc flour is a real treat for gourmets. **CUISINE** Varied. **CREDIT CARDS** Diners, MasterCard, Visa. **HOURS** Tue-Sun, 10am-5pm.
Praça da Matriz, 40
TEL 261-1712

São Luís – MA

AREA CODE 98 **POPULATION** 870,028
DISTANCES Belém, 803 km (499 mi); Teresina, 445 km (276.5 mi)

HOTELS

Pousada do Francês $
It stands out for its great location, in the historical center. Choose the Mirante rooms that are more spacious and have a superb view. **FACILITIES** 29 rooms, air-conditioning, phone, TV, bar, restaurant. **CREDIT CARDS** All.
R. Sete de Setembro, 121, Centro Histórico
TEL 3231-4844 **TEL** 3232-0879

São Luís Park Hotel $$$
Considered to be the best hotel in town, it offers spacious and comfortable rooms with bathtubs. Macaws and peacocks walk freely in the pool area. **FACILITIES** 112 rooms, air-conditioning, phone, TV, cable TV, bar, football field, pool, playground, tennis court, restaurant, convention room, fitness room, game room, sauna. **CREDIT CARDS** All.
Av. Aviscênia, Calhau
TEL 2106-0505
www.saoluisparkhotel.com.br

RESTAURANTS

A Varanda $
In the airy and lush yard of the cook's house, you'll be able to enjoy freshly made shrimp and fish dishes, though they take quite some time to prepare. The homemade sweets, such as the cashew sweets, are a must. **CUISINE** Fish and seafood. **CREDIT CARDS** Not accepted. **HOURS** Mon-Sat, from noon until late.
R. Genésio Rego, 185, Monte Castelo
TEL 3232-8428/ 3232-7291

Cabana do Sol $
This very successful regional restaurant serves banquet-worthy dishes for three people such as sun-dried meat from the North with *baião-de-dois* (cowpea, bacon, crackling, rice, coriander, sun-dried meat, *coalho* [rennet] cheese and seasonings), rice, string beans, *paçoca* (sun-dried meat with banana, rice, string beans, manioc and *coalho*), baroa potato purée, boiled manioc, battered and deep-fried banana and clarified butter. The facilities are simple, and the service is efficient. For dessert, try cream of *cupuaçu* (a tropical fruit). **CUISINE** Regional. **CREDIT CARDS** All. **HOURS** Mon-Thu, 11am-midnight; Fri-Sun, 11am-2pm.
R. João Damasceno, 24-A, Farol de São Marcos
TEL 3235-2586

SERVICES

AIRPORT

Aeroporto Marechal Cunha Machado
Av. dos Libaneses, Tirirical
TEL 3217-6133/3217-6105

LOCAL TOUR OPERATORS

Caravelas Turismo Ltda.
Av. Dom Pedro II, 231, Centro
TEL 3232-6606/9991-6606

Marencanto Viagens e Turismo
R. dos Holandeses, 400 B, Ponta do Farol
TEL 3227-9444/9991-3161

Máxima Aventura Turismo
R. da Estrela, 401, Armazém da Estrela
TEL 3221-0238

Taguatur Turismo Ltda.
R. do Sol, 141, loja 15/16, Centro
TEL 3213-6400

TOURIST POLICE STATION

Delegacia de Turismo
R. da Estrela, 427, Centro
TEL 3232-4324. **HOURS** Mon-Fri, 8am-6pm

RESTAURANTS $ up to R$50 $$ from R$51 up to R$100 $$$ from R$101 up to R$150 $$$$ above R$150

TOURIST INFORMATION

Aeroporto Marechal Cunha Machado
Av. dos Libaneses, Tiririca
TEL 3244-4500 HOURS 24 hours

Lagoa de Jansen
Av. Ana Jansen, Ponta D'Areia
TEL 3227-8484 HOURS 8am-8pm

Shopping do Cidadão
Av. Jaime Tavares, 26 B, Praia Grande
TEL 3231-2000 HOURS Mon-Fri, 7:30am-6pm

São Miguel dos Milagres – AL

AREA CODE 82 POPULATION 5,860
DISTANCE Maceió, 100 km (62 mi)
SITE www.saomigueldosmilagres.com.br

HOTELS

Pousada Côte Sud $
This very charming, no-frills inn is run by a French-woman and her Belgian husband. The decoration is very pleasant and the chalets provide privacy to guests. The inn offers horseback riding, bikes and boats that take guests to the rock pools. FACILITIES 9 rooms, air-conditioning, bar, horses, restaurant. CREDIT CARDS Not accepted.
Praia de Porto da Rua
TEL 295-1283
www.geocities.com/pousadacotesud

Pousada do Caju $
This charming inn operates in an airy house and is run by Antônio, a Brazilian, and Jerome, a Frenchman. It is only 150 meters (500 ft) from the beach. The decoration is clean, and the rooms are white, clean and neat. FACILITIES 7 rooms, air-conditioning, bar, restaurant. CREDIT CARDS Not accepted.
Praia do Toque
TEL 295-1103
www.pousadadocaju-al.com.br

Pousada do Toque $$
The couple Nilo and Gilda provides attentive service. The bungalows have large beds, flat panel TV sets and CD and DVD players. The main bungalow, called Toque, is comfortable and spacious, with an ofurô tub and a private pool. Breakfast is served anytime. The furniture was designed by Fernando Jaeger. There's a library with a small collection of cigars. FACILITIES 11 rooms, air-conditioning, TV, bar, pool, restaurant. CREDIT CARDS Not accepted.
R. Felisberto de Ataíde, Praia do Toque
TEL 295-1127
www.pousadadotoque.com.br

RESTAURANTS

Cantinho de Nanã $
Located by the Porto da Rua beach, this restaurant offers peixada (fish stew) and a carefully prepared rice with octopus. The superb coconut baked sweet is a must for dessert. CUISINE Fish and seafood, regional.

CREDIT CARDS Not accepted. HOURS 9am-7pm.
R. Ana Marinho Braga, Praia de Porto da Rua
TEL 295-1573

São Raimundo Nonato – PI

AREA CODE 89 POPULATION 26,890
DISTANCE Recife, 1125.4 km (699 mi)

HOTEL

Hotel Serra da Capivara $
This is a good lodging option for visitors to Serra da Capivara National Park. The rooms are comfortable and the hotel has guides for hiking. FACILITIES 19 rooms, air-conditioning, minibar, TV, restaurant, pool. CREDIT CARDS Diners, MasterCard, Visa.
Rodovia PI-140, km 0, Santa Luzia
TEL 582-1389 TEL 582-1760

Tibau do Sul – RN

AREA CODE 84 POPULATION 7,749
DISTANCE Natal, 75 km (46 mi)

HOTELS

Marinas Tibau Sul $$
All chalets have an ocean view. There's a good variety of leisure options such as cavalgadas (horseback riding), fishing in the lagoon, trails across the Atlantic Rainforest and night boat rides (not included in the rate). The crepe shop, built on stilts above the sea, is a great place to watch the sunset. FACILITIES 32 rooms, air-conditioning, phone, TV, cable TV, ceiling fan, bar, boat, football field, horses, pool, playground, restaurant. CREDIT CARDS MasterCard, Visa.
R. Governador Aluísio Alves (street alongside the beach)
TEL 246-4111/4228
www.hotelmarinas.com.br

Ponta do Madeiro $$$
This charming, quiet hotel contrasts with the hubbub of Pipa. From the top of the cliff, you can see Golfinhos (Dolphin) Bay. Flights of stairs with 195 steps lead down to Madeiro beach. Complimentary fruit and champagne are served by the pool. The large green area softens the intense heat. FACILITIES 32 rooms, air-conditioning, phone, TV, cable TV, bar, pool, restaurant. CREDIT CARDS All.
Rodovia Rota do Sol, km 3, Pipa
TEL 246-4220 RESERVATIONS 502-2377
www.pontadomadeiro.com.br

RESTAURANT

Camamo Beijupirá $$$
In the refined and cozy ambience of this farm, chef Tadeu Lubambo welcomes his clientele. Meals may last for hours, so do not hurry. Dinner is a special occasion. The menu changes daily but there's always a green salad, oysters and shrimp. Reservation is essential as only 5 couples are served every evening. Only water and wine are served. CUISINE Fish and seafood. CREDIT CARDS Not accepted. HOURS From 9:15pm until late.
Fazenda Pernambuquinho, access via the Rodovia RN-003, km 3
TEL 246-4195/8816-4195

PRICES	HOTELS (couple)	$ up to R$150	$$ from R$151 up to R$300	$$$ from R$301 up to R$500	$$$$ above R$500

Trancoso – BA

AREA CODE 73

DISTANCES Salvador, 735 km (456.7 mi); Porto Seguro (via boat and Arraial D'Ajuda), 25 km (15.5 mi), or 47 km (29.2 mi) via BA-001.

SITE www.trancosobahia.com.br

HOTELS

Club Med Trancoso $$$$

Perched above a mountainous coastline, this Club Med affords a beautiful view of the rivers and beaches from the common areas. A long flight of stairs lead to the beach, or you may take a van down there. The multicolored blocks, with spacious rooms and rustic decoration are reminiscent of the architecture of Quadrado (Square) de Trancoso. Meals and drinks are included in the rate. There's a wide variety of leisure options, including archery, a golf court with 18 holes and motorboats. FACILITIES 250 rooms, air-conditioning, phone, TV, cable TV, bar, boat, football field, golf course, horses, recreation team, nightclub with a DJ, pool, playground, football court, tennis court, restaurant, convention room, fitness room, game room, massage room, sauna, spa. CREDIT CARDS All.

Estrada do Arraial, km 18, Praia de Taípe
TEL 575-8400/8484 RESERVATIONS 08007073782
www.clubmed.com.br

Pousada Capim Santo $$

Woods and gardens cover the area around the inn, which has an outdoor *ofurô* tub and massage kiosks. In Beco da Flor there's a beauty parlor. Beauty treatments are available too. The ambience is rustic but comfortable. There are small and charming rooms and large suites, with mezzanine and whirlpool tub. FACILITIES 15 rooms, air-conditioning, phone, TV, bar, pool, restaurant, massage room. CREDIT CARDS American Express, Visa.

Pça. São João, Quadrado
TEL 668-1122
www.capimsanto.com.br

Pousada do Quadrado $$

This congenial inn has large garden common areas with sofas, tables and deck chairs. Sig Bergamin designed the decoration, at once rustic and sophisticated. The 3 duplex rooms have a mezzanine and a private verandah. FACILITIES 11 rooms, air-conditioning, TV, bar, restaurant. CREDIT CARDS Visa.

Pça. São João, 1, Quadrado
TEL 668-1808/1811
www.pousadadoquadrado.com.br

Pousada Estrela d'Água $$$$

This inn used to be Gal Costa's home. A wood walkway over the river separates the inn from the beach. The pools and the charming common areas have an ocean view. The ambience is rustic: the reception is in a wattle-and-daub hut, with sand floor, but antique pieces decorate the place. The suites and rooms are scattered in several acres of tropical gardens. The chalets have an *ofurô* tub and the master suite has a private pool. FACILITIES 26 rooms, air-conditioning, phone, TV, bar, pool, tennis court, restaurant, fitness room, massage room. CREDIT CARDS All.

Estrada Arraial D'Ajuda

TEL 668-1030 RESERVATIONS (21) 2287-1592
www.estreladagua.com.br

Pousada Etnia $$

This is a boutique inn, in an area full of trees, decorated with artworks, antiques and exclusive furniture designed by the owners and designers André Zanonato and Corrado Tini, who provide personalized service to guests. Each chalet has Egyptian-cotton sheets, goose-feather pillows, canopied bed, winter garden and verandah. Adults only. FACILITIES 5 rooms, air-conditioning, phone, TV, cable TV, bar, pool, restaurant, massage room. CREDIT CARDS Visa.

Av. Principal, Centro
TEL 668-1137
www.etniabrasil.com.br

RESTAURANTS

Capim Santo $$

The owners are natives of São Paulo and have lived in Trancoso for more than 20 years. They serve fish and seafood and other regional ingredients prepared creatively. Some dishes are made with lemon balm (*capim-santo* in Portuguese). The best choice is shrimp with curry and lemon balm. The owners' daughter owns the São Paulo branch in Vila Madalena. CUISINE Fish and seafood. CREDIT CARDS American Express. HOURS Mon-Sat, 5pm-11pm.

Pça. São João, Quadrado
TEL 668-1122

Jacaré $$

Located in the charming Pousada do Quadrado inn, this restaurant has a relaxed atmosphere with tables in the verandah and garden, and offers romantic candle-lit dinner. The menu is changed every season but fish and seafood, and regional ingredients always stand out. CUISINE Varied. CREDIT CARDS Visa. HOURS Daily, 5pm-midnight (open only in high season).

Pça. São João, Quadrado
TEL 668-1808

SERVICES

LOCAL TOUR OPERATORS

Bahia Alegria
TEL 575-1690/8802-5033

Latitude 16 Expedições
TEL 668-2260/8803-0016

Natural Cicloturismo e Aventura
TEL 668-1955/8804-5557

Solomar e Nique Cavalgadas
TEL 668-1637

Trancoso Receptivo
Pça. São João Quadrado
TEL 668-1333

BOAT RENTAL

Jarbá Lanchas
TEL 668-1479

RESTAURANTS $ up to R$50 $$ from R$51 up to R$100 $$$ from R$101 up to R$150 $$$$ above R$150

NORTH

Belém – PA

AREA CODE 91 **POPULATION** 1,280,614
DISTANCE São Luís, 803 km (499 mi)
SITE www.prefeituradebelem.com.br

HOTELS

Equatorial Palace $$
A renovation will upgrade the 30-year old facilities and bring them up to the standards of business clientele. Ask for one of the renovated rooms. **FACILITIES** 126 rooms, air-conditioning, phone, TV, cable TV, bar, pool, restaurant, convention room. **CREDIT CARDS** All.
Av. Brás de Aguiar, 612, Nazaré
TEL 3181-6000/6001 **RESERVATIONS** 0800995222
www.equatorialhotel.com.br

Hilton Belém $$$
Located in the city center, beside Theatro da Paz, this hotel caters to executives and offers them two exclusive floors with a bilingual secretary, fax and computer. Efficient service. Promotional rates on weekends attract tourists. **FACILITIES** 361 rooms, air-conditioning, phone, TV, cable TV, bar, pool, jogging track, restaurant, convention room, fitness room, massage room, sauna. **CREDIT CARDS** All.
Av. Presidente Vargas, 882, Centro
TEL 4006-7000/2942 **RESERVATIONS** 0800780888
www.belem.hilton.com

RESTAURANT

Amazon Beer $
Located in Estação das Docas, one of Belém's tourist spots, it is always crowded in the happy hour. This brewery produces five types of beer and serves great food such as Amazon shrimp and fish fillet with risotto. **CUISINE** Brazilian. **CREDIT CARDS** All. **HOURS** Mon-Wed, 5pm-1am; Thu and Fri, 5pm-3am; Sat, 11am-3pm; Sundays and holidays, 11am-1am.
Av. Boulevard Castilhos França, Armazém 1, Estação das Docas
TEL 212-5400

Lá em Casa $
Tourists make up most of the clientele. The eatery serves regional food such as duck stew with *tucupi* (manioc milk), *maniçoba* (sun-dried meat, sour manioc leaves, smoked pork meat and bacon), *farofa de pirarucu* (manioc meal with *pirarucu*, a freshwater fish) and grilled *filhote* (catfish). Choose the regional menu from Pará to taste small servings of regional dishes. There's an adjoining hall, more comfortable than this one, where another restaurant by the same owner, O Outro, operates. **CUISINE** Regional. **CREDIT CARDS** All. **HOURS** Mon-Sat, noon-3pm; Mon-Wed, 7pm-11:30pm; Thu-Sat, 7pm-1am; Sun, noon-4pm.
Av. Governador José Malcher, 247, Nazaré
TEL 223-1212

O Outro
Chef-owner Paulo Martins lets his creativity run free in this modern restaurant, which adjoins Lá em Casa (see above). The menu changes every two months, except for the always-available house specialty, a delicious roasted lamb. **CREDIT CARDS** All. **HOURS** Fri and Sat, 7pm-1am; Sun, noon-4pm.
Av. Governador José Malcher, 247, Nazaré
TEL 223-1212

SERVICES

AIRPORT

Aeroporto Internacional de Belém
Av. Júlio César, 12 km
TEL 210-6039

LOCAL TOUR OPERATORS

Rumo Norte Expedições
Av. Serzedelo Correa, 895, Vila Augusta, 59, 2nd floor
TEL 222-6442

Valeverde Turismo
R. Alcindo Cacela, 104, Pedreira
TEL 241-7333

TOURIST POLICE STATION

Delegacia de Turismo
Companhia Integrada de Policiamento de Turismo (Ciptur)
TEL 230-0549/241-1751

TOURIST INFORMATION

Belemtur – Companhia de Turismo de Belém
Av. Governador José Malcher, Passagem Bolonha, 38, Nazaré
TEL 283-4851/4850 **HOURS** Mon-Fri, 8am-6pm

Mosqueiro
Pça. Matriz do Mosqueiro, Praia Bar
TEL 3771-3624 **HOURS** Mon-Fri, 8am-1pm

Paratur – Companhia Paraense de Turismo
Pça. Maestro Waldemar Henrique, Reduto
TEL 212-0669/9135 **HOURS** Mon-Fri, 8am-6pm

Posto de Informações Turísticas (Belemtur) at Aeroporto Internacional de Belém
Av. Júlio César, 12 km
TEL 210-6272 **HOURS** 8am-10pm

Posto de Informações Turísticas (Paratur) at Aeroporto Internacional de Belém
Av. Júlio César, 12 km
TEL 210-6330 **HOURS** 8am-9pm

PRICES	HOTELS (couple)	$ up to R$150	$$ from R$151 up to R$300	$$$ from R$301 up to R$500	$$$$ above R$500

Ilha de Marajó – PA

AREA CODE 91

HOTEL

Pousada dos Guarás $

This inn has a large natural area with a direct exit to Grande beach. Typical dishes such as *marajoara* steak and *frito do vaqueiro* (fried buffalo meat with manioc meal) stand out. It is rustic but has some of the best facilities in the island. FACILITIES 50 rooms, air-conditioning, phone, TV, football field, horses, pool, restaurant, convention room, game room, massage room. CREDIT CARDS All.
Av. Beira-Mar, Praia Grande
(access off km 24 of Rodovia PA-154)
TEL 3765-1133 RESERVATIONS 4005-5658
www.pousadadosguaras.com.br

Jalapão – TO

AREA CODE 63
DISTANCE Palmas, 200 km (125 mi)

HOTEL

Fazenda Santa Rosa $$$$

This inn sits in one of the most stunning locations of Jalapão, near the dunes and at the foot of the Espírito Santo mountains. The bungalows are stylishly rustic. Reservations advised. FACILITIES 6 rooms, restaurant.
CREDIT CARDS MasterCard.
Estrada do Jalapão, 15 km (9.3 mi)
from the city of Mateiros
TEL 534-1033

RESTAURANT

Panela de Ferro $

Located in Mateiros, this is a good option for homemade food. It serves only rice, beans, salad and meat.
CUISINE Brazilian. CREDIT CARDS Not accepted. HOURS 11am-2:30pm and 6pm-8:30pm.
Av. Tocantins, Quadra 7, Lote 15, Centro
TEL 534-1038

Manaus – AM

AREA CODE 92 POPULATION 1,405,835
DISTANCE Brasília, 3.490 km (2.168 mi)

HOTELS

Ariaú Amazon Towers $$$

This hotel is 2 hour and 30 minutes by boat from Manaus. It's the largest hotel in the jungle and is built on suspended towers that are interconnected by 8 km (5 mi) of walkways at the height of the trees' canopy. There are two observation towers, each 41 meters (134 ft) high, to enjoy a view of the jungle. The rooms have only cold water and the suites have electric showers and a stunning view. There are also Tarzan-style rooms, with whirlpool tubs. FACILITIES 50 rooms, air-conditioning, phone, TV, football field, horses, pool, restaurant, convention room, game room,

massage room. CREDIT CARDS All.
Lago Ariaú
TEL 2121-5000 and 233-5615 RESERVATIONS 08007025005
www.ariau.tur.br

Guanavenas Pousada Jungle Lodge $$$

This is one of the farthest hotels from Manaus. You'll have to travel 350 km (218 mi) into the jungle. The trip by bus and motorboat takes 5 hours. It was also a pioneer enterprise. The hotel is very organized and clean, with a very good leisure services, in addition to a common area with plenty of greenery. There are lots of *igarapés* (narrow channels) that can be seen from a 30-meter (100 ft) tower. Since there are many fruit trees around, there are also many species of birds in the area.
FACILITIES 50 rooms, air-conditioning, phone, TV, football field, horses, pool, restaurant, convention room, game room, massage room. CREDIT CARDS All.
Lago do Canaçari, island of the municipality of Silves
TEL 238-1211 RESERVATIONS 656-1500
www.guanavenas.com.br

Hotel de Selva Lago Salvador

Four huts have verandahs overlooking a crystal-clear lake. The view is spectacular. The hotel offers rafting, canopy walking, and rappelling. Choose hut nº 1 if you prefer to stay close to the restaurant, as you have to walk on trails or take a canoe to get from room to dining table. FACILITIES 50 rooms, air-conditioning, phone, TV, football field, horses, pool, restaurant, convention room, game room, massage room. CREDIT CARDS All.
Lago Salvador, municipality of Iranduba, right bank of Negro river
TEL 658-3052/3512
www.salvadorlake.com.br

Jungle Othon Palace $$$

This floating hotel was built on a steel raft which allows it to rise and fall with the river's water level. It is one of the smallest hotels of its class. The restaurant has a belvedere. FACILITIES 50 rooms, air-conditioning, phone, TV, football field, horses, pool, restaurant, convention room, game room, massage room. CREDIT CARDS Diners, MasterCard, Visa.
Igarapé do Tatu, left bank of Negro river
TEL 633-6200/5530
www.junglepalace.com.br

Tiwa Amazonas Ecoresort $$$

This, the newest jungle hotel in the Amazon, is positioned across Negro river from Manaus, which gives visitors the impression of not being in the forest. The wood chalets are comfortable but have cold showers. Activities such as rappelling and flying fox require a 20-minute walk on walkways. FACILITIES 50 rooms, air-conditioning, phone, TV, football field, horses, pool, restaurant, convention room, game room, massage room.
CREDIT CARDS Not accepted.
Município de Iranduba, right bank of Negro River
TEL 3088-4676
www.tiwaamazone.nl/portugees/frameport.htm

Tropical Manaus Eco Resort Experience $$$$

Located 15 km (9.3 mi) from the center, this is one of the most complete and luxurious hotels in the region.

There are many attractions for guests, especially children, including a wave pool and a mini-zoo. There are good restaurants and well-equipped lodgings. FACILITIES 589 rooms, air-conditioning, phone, TV, cable TV, bar, football field, recreation team, pool, jogging track, playground, tennis court, restaurant, convention room, game room, massage room, sauna. CREDIT CARDS All.
Av. Coronel Teixeira, 1320, Ponta Negra
TEL 659-5000/5026 RESERVATIONS 08007012670
www.tropicalhotel.com.br

RESTAURANTS

Açaí e Cia $
This restaurant gets busy on Friday and Saturday evenings, when there's live music. It is very traditional, with a relaxed atmosphere, and frequented by locals. The house specialties are *tacacá*, a typical Amazon soup with manioc, dry shrimp, green leaves and *tucupi* (manioc milk), *caldeirada de tambaqui (bouillabaisse* of a large freshwater fish) and *açaí* fruit with manioc meal. CUISINE Fish and seafood, regional. CREDIT CARDS All. HOURS Sun and Mon, 4am-midnight; Tue and Wed, 11am-midnight; Thu-Sat, 11am-1pm.
R. Acre, 92, Vieiralves
TEL 635-3637

Bicho Preguiça Restaurant Flutuante $
With a very quiet atmosphere and kiosks on a wood deck, this restaurant is more stylish than others of its class. Enjoy the beautiful view of the waters while eating *tambaqui (a large freshwater fish)* ribs or charcoal grilled *picanha* (cap of rump). CUISINE Varied. CREDIT CARDS Not accepted. HOURS Daily, from 11am.
Lago do Cacau
TEL 9148-0215/9604-3594

Canto da Peixada $
On one of the tables you'll see a stuffed, 30-kg (66-lb) *tambaqui* (a freshwater fish). This should inspire you to order the charcoal-grilled *tambaqui* ribs, the delicious specialty of this informal place. CUISINE Fish. CREDIT CARDS American Express. HOURS Mon-Sat, 11:30am-3:30pm and 6:30pm-11:30pm.
R. Emílio Moreira, 1677, Praça 14 de Janeiro
TEL 234-3021/066

SERVICES

AIRPORT

Aeroporto Internacional Eduardo Gomes
Av. Santos Dumont, 1350, Tarumã
TEL 652-1212

LOCAL TOUR OPERATORS

Agência Selvatur
Pça. Adalberto Vale, 17, Centro
TEL 622-2577/2580

Amazon Explorers Ltda.
Av. Djalma Batista, 2100, sala 225/226, Chapada
TEL 633-3319/8802-3733

Equipol Turismo
R. Rio Branco, 24, Quadra 37, Sala A, Vieiralves
TEL 633-4400/6017

Fontur – Fonte Turismo Ltda.
Av. Coronel Teixeira, 1320, Ponta Negra
TEL 658-3052/3438

Paradise Turismo Ltda.
Av. Eduardo Ribeiro, 520, Sala 108, Centro
TEL 633-1156

TOURIST POLICE STATION

Polícia de Turismo (Politur)
TEL 622-4986

TOURIST INFORMATION

Centro de Atendimento ao Turista at Aeroporto Internacional Eduardo Gomes
Av. Santos Dumont, 1350, Tarumã
TEL 652-1120. HOURS 8am-11pm

Centro de Atendimento ao Turista no Amazonas Shopping Centro
Av. Djalma Batista
TEL 236-5154

Centro de Atendimento ao Turista Eduardo Ribeiro
Av. Eduardo Ribeiro, 666, Centro
TEL 622-0767

Manaustur – Fundação Municipal de Turismo
Av. Sete de Setembro, 157, Centro
TEL 622-4986

Palmas – TO

AREA CODE 63 POPULATION 137,355
DISTANCES Belém, 1243 km (772.5 mi); Brasília, 847 km (526.3 mi)
SITE www.amatur.to.gov.br

HOTEL

Pousada dos Girassóis $
Located in the town center, this nice inn is ideal for a night's rest before heading to Jalapão. It is one of the oldest inns in town. FACILITIES 61 rooms, air-conditioning, phone, TV, bar, pool, convention room, game room. CREDIT CARDS All.
103 Sul, conjunto 3, Lote 44
TEL 219-4500 and 215-2321
www.pousadadosgirassois.com.br

RESTAURANT

Cabana do Lago $
This is the best eatery in town. It serves typical food. CUISINE Regional from the Northeast. CREDIT CARDS All. HOURS Daily, from 11am until late.
103 Sul, R. SO 09, Lote 5
TEL 215-4989

PRICES	HOTELS (couple)	$ up to R$150	$$ from R$151 up to R$300	$$$ from R$301 up to R$500	$$$$ above R$500

SERVICES

AIRPORT

Aeroporto de Palmas
Av. Joaquim Teotônio Segurado/Aureny III
(Expansão Sul area)
TEL 219-3700

Santarém – PA

AREA CODE 93 POPULATION 262,672
DISTANCE Belém, 1526 km (948 mi)

HOTEL

Beloalter $$
The accommodations are surrounded by forest. The suites of Casa da Praia stand out. One of them, the Lago Verde suite, accommodates up to 5 people. It is organized, clean and has an exit to the continuation of the Alter do Chão beach. FACILITIES 26 rooms, air-conditioning, phone, TV, cable TV, boat, pool, restaurant, convention room. CREDIT CARDS American Express, Diners, MasterCard, Visa.
R. Pedro Teixeira, Alter do Chão
TEL 527-1247/1230
www.beloalter.com.br

SERVICES

LOCAL TOUR OPERATORS

Santarém Tur – Empreendimentos Turísticos de Santarém Ltda.
Av. Adriano Pimentel, 44, Centro
TEL 522-4847

CENTRAL WEST

Alta Floresta – MT

AREA CODE 66 POPULATION 46,982
DISTANCE Cuiabá, 820 km (509.5 mi)

HOTELS

Cristalino Jungle Lodge $$
Located next to Parque Estadual do Cristalino, a state park, in the jungle, it has a 50-meter (164-ft) tall observation tower. The hotel is reached via dirt road (39 km/24 mi) plus 30 minutes by boat. FACILITIES 18 rooms, ceiling fan, bar, boat, restaurant. CREDIT CARDS All.
Av. Perimetral Oeste, 2001
TEL 512-7100/2221
www.cristalinolodge.com.br

Pousada Thaimaçu $$$$
A good option for those interested in sport fishing. Guests are allowed to catch species like *tucunaré* and *jaú*, although the fish have to be freed afterwards. The sport-fishing package includes 8 days from Saturday-Saturday. FACILITIES 20 rooms, air-conditioning, boat, restaurant. CREDIT CARDS Not accepted.
R. C2, 228
TEL 521-3587 RESERVATIONS 521-2331
www.thaimacu.com.br

Alto Paraíso de Goiás – GO

AREA CODE 62 POPULATION 6,182
DISTANCES Brasília, 230 km (143 mi); Goiânia, 440 km (273.4 mi)
www.agetur.go.gov.br/municipios/paraiso.htm

HOTELS

Casa Rosa Pousada das Cerejeiras $
This converted inn is located in a beautiful spot and offers efficient service. There are four spacious rooms and 8 chalets for up to 5 guests. FACILITIES 12 rooms, TV, pool. CREDIT CARDS Not accepted.
R. Gumercindo Barbosa, 233, Centro
TEL 446-1319
www.pousadacasarosa.com.br

Pousada Portal da Chapada $$
The spacious and comfortable wood chalets are near a waterfall and a suspended ecological trail. There's a camping ground. The inn offers a "day use" system for those wanting to use the facilities by day but not stay. FACILITIES 11 rooms, bar, playground, football court, restaurant, game room, massage room, sauna. CREDIT CARDS Not accepted.
Rodovia GO-327, km 9
TEL 9669-2604 RESERVATIONS 446-1820
www.portaldachapada.com.br

SERVICES

LOCAL TOUR OPERATORS

Alpatur Ecoturismo
R. das Nascentes, 129
TEL 446-1820

Alternativas Ecoturismo
Av. Ary Valadão Filho, 1331
TEL 446-1000

Transchapada Turismo
R. dos Cristais, 7, sala 01
TEL 446-1345

Travessia Ecoturismo
Av. Ary Valadão Filho, 979
TEL 446-1595

RESTAURANTS $ up to R$50	$$ from R$51 up to R$100	$$$ from R$101 up to R$150	$$$$ above R$150

Aquidauana – MS

AREA CODE 67 POPULATION 43,440
DISTANCE Campo Grande, 130 km (80.7 mi)

HOTELS

Fazenda Rio Negro $$$
The access to the farm may be by car in the dry season, from the end of July-the beginning of October by the most dicey. For those who prefer not to take risks, it's better to take the plane year round. The hotel has bilingual tourist guides. FACILITIES 13 rooms, bar, restaurant. CREDIT CARDS All.
On the banks of Negro river
TEL 326-0002 FAX 326-8737
www.fazendarionegro.com.br

Pousada Aguapé $$
The place is charming but only for those who like adventure. The dirt road with 53 km (33 mi) road can get really rough during the summer rainy season. There's a camping ground. FACILITIES 14 rooms, air-conditioning, ceiling fan, football field, pool, restaurant. CREDIT CARDS American Express, Visa.
Access via the Rodovia BR-262
TEL/FAX 686-1036
www.aguape.com.br

Bonito – MS

AREA CODE 67 POPULATION 16,956
DISTANCE Campo Grande, 280 km (174 mi)
SITE www.bonito-ms.com.br

HOTELS

Wetega $$$
Wetega means "stone" in the language of the Kadineu tribe. The hotel is built on wood logs and has excellent rooms with verandahs. It is near the town's commercial center. There are no leisure services for children. FACILITIES 67 rooms, air-conditioning, phone, TV, cable TV, bar, pool, restaurant, convention room, game room. CREDIT CARDS Diners, MasterCard, Visa.
R. Coronel Pilad Rebuá, 679
TEL 255-1699
www.wetegahotel.com.br

Zagaia Eco Resort $$$
This greenery-surrounded resort has chalets on the ground. Request a "de luxe" one, as these have better bathrooms. There's a heated pool with whirlpool tub and a fitness room overlooking the woods. FACILITIES 100 rooms, air-conditioning, phone, TV, cable TV, bar, football field, horses, recreation team, pool, heated pool, playground, tennis court, restaurant, convention room, fitness room, sauna. CREDIT CARDS All.
Rodovia Bonito–Três Morros, km 0
TEL 255-1280/1710 RESERVATIONS 0800994400
www.zagaia.com.br

RESTAURANT

Cantinho do Peixe $
This restaurant serves only fillets of *pintado* (a kind of catfish) but you can take your pick from 20 choic-

es of sauce. Try *surubi* with *urucum* (a palm fruit), with cream and *mozzarella* cheese, with rice and *pirão* (manioc meal porridge with fish broth). *Caldo de piranha* (piranha fish broth) is served as a starter. CUISINE Brazilian. CREDIT CARDS MasterCard, Visa. HOURS Mon-Sat, 11am-3pm and 6pm-10pm; Sun, 11am-3pm.
R. Trinta e Um de Março, 1918
TEL 255-3381

SERVICES

LOCAL TOUR OPERATORS

Tamanduá
R. Coronel Pilad Rebuá, 1890, Centro
TEL 255-5000

Ygarapé Tour
R. Coronel Pilad Rebuá, 1956, Centro
TEL 255-1733

TOURIST INFORMATION

Secretaria de Turismo
R. Coronel Pilad Rebuá, 1780, Centro
TEL 255-1850 HOURS Mon-Sat, 7am-5pm

Brasília – DF

AREA CODE 61 POPULATION 2,051,146
DISTANCE Goiânia, 136 km (84.5 mi)
SITE www.setur.df.gov.br

HOTELS

Blue Tree Park Brasília $$$
Designed by Ruy Ohtake, this hotel faces Paranoá Lake, next to the Alvorada Palace. Request on of the rooms that overlooks the lake. FACILITIES 387 rooms, air-conditioning, phone, TV, cable TV, bar, boat, pool, jogging track, football court, floating restaurant, convention room, fitness room, massage room, sauna, spa. CREDIT CARDS All.
Setor Hoteleiro Turístico Norte, Trecho 1, Conjunto 1B, Bloco C
TEL 424-7000/7001 RESERVATIONS 0800150500
www.bluetree.com.br

Naoum Plaza Hotel $$$$
From the doorman to the manager, the whole staff is kind and efficient. The clientele is mostly business travelers. There's a business center with bilingual secretaries and a non-smoking floor. FACILITIES 190 rooms, air-conditioning, phone, TV, cable TV, bar, pool, jogging track, restaurant, convention room, fitness room, massage room, sauna. CREDIT CARDS All.
Setor Hoteleiro Sul, Quadra 5, Bloco H/I
TEL 322-4545/4949 RESERVATIONS 0800614844
www.naoumplaza.com.br

RESTAURANTS

Bargaço $$
The best dish here is the shrimp *moqueca* with rice, *pirão* (manioc meal porridge) and dende-flavored man-

PRICES	HOTELS (couple)	$ up to R$150	$$ from R$151 up to R$300	$$$ from R$301 up to R$500	$$$$ above R$500

ioc flour. **CUISINE** Regional from Bahia, fish and seafood.
CREDIT CARDS MasterCard, Visa. **HOURS** Mon-Thu, noon-
midnight; Fri and Sat, noon-1am; Sun, noon-11pm.
Setor de Comércio Sul, 405, Bloco D, Loja 36
TEL 443-8729/364-6090

Dudu Camargo $$$
Frequented by politicians and business people, this is
one of the most sophisticated restaurants in town. It
combines different textures in dishes such as sun-
dried meat with crisp collard greens and soft collard
greens. The duck risotto also stands out. **CUISINE** Contemporary. **CREDIT CARDS** All. **HOURS** Mon-Thu, noon-3pm
and 7pm-11:30pm; Fri, noon-4pm and 7pm-2am; Sat,
7pm-2am; Sun, noon-5pm.
Setor Comércio Local Sul, Quadra 303, Bloco A, Loja 3
TEL 323-8082

Lagash $
Arab dishes are prepared following family recipes. The
apricot salad, which combines leaves, honey,
chanclich cheese and apricot and the soft Moroccan
mutton stands out. For dessert we suggest *lagash*, a
puff pastry with walnut, chestnut and honey. **CUISINE**
Arab. **CREDIT CARDS** All. **HOURS** Mon-Sat, noon-4pm and
7pm-midnight; Sun, noon-4pm.
Setor Comercial Norte 308, Bloco B, Loja 11/17
TEL 273-0098

O Convento $$
This beautiful house was assembled from recovered
building materials. There's no name sign at the door,
but you'll be ushered in by waiters dressed like Franciscan priests. We suggest *rogai por nós, pecadores*
("pray for us, sinners"), a tasty pumpkin cream soup
with sun-dried meat, or *cordeiro dos deuses* ("lamb of
the gods"), with passion fruit and apple sauce. **CUISINE**
Regional from Minas. **CREDIT CARDS** Diners, MasterCard,
Visa. **HOURS** Tue-Sat, noon-4pm and 8pm-midnight;
Sun, 1pm-4pm.
Setor de Habitações Individuais Sul, Quadra 9, Conjunto 9, Casa 4
TEL 248-1211/3149

Patu Anú $
Far from the city center and hard to reach, this spot is
worth the detour. The ambience is cozy and integrated with nature, offering a view of Paranoá Lake. It
serves tasty game and fish dishes such as Yapuana
sole, with honey, orange and pink pepper. Reservations are essential. **CUISINE** Contemporary. **CREDIT CARDS**
All. **HOURS** Tue-Sat, 8:30pm-1am; Sun, 1:30-6pm.
Setor de Mansões do Lago Norte, Trecho 12, Conjunto 1, Casa 7
TEL 369-2788/9202-8930

SERVICES

AIRPORT

Aeroporto Internacional de Brasília Presi-
dente Juscelino Kubitschek
This is one of the most modern airports of Brazil and
has a complete services for tourists.
TEL 364-9000

TOURIST INFORMATION

Setur
Setor Comercial Norte – Centro Empresarial Varig,
4º andar
TEL 429-7635 **HOURS** Mon-Fri, 9am-6pm

Caldas Novas – GO
AREA CODE 64 **POPULATION** 49,660
DISTANCES Brasília, 290 km (180 mi); Goiânia, 170 km
(105.6 mi)
www.caldas.tur.br

HOTEL

Parque das Primaveras $$
This is an oasis of silence in a region full of noisy hotels. The chalets are located in a large grassy area. All
the rooms have a whirlpool tub and verandah. **FACILI-
TIES** 23 rooms, air-conditioning, phone, TV, cable TV,
bar, playground, football court, restaurant, game
room, sauna. **CREDIT CARDS** Diners, MasterCard, Visa.
R. do Balneário, 1
TEL 453-1355/1294
www.hpprimaveras.com.br

Campo Grande – MS
AREA CODE 67 **POPULATION** 663,621

HOTEL

Hotel Jandaia $$
This hotel is at the intersection of two busy streets,
but nevertheless a good place to spend the night.
There are floors for non-smoking and guests with al-
lergies. **FACILITIES** 140 rooms, air-conditioning, phone,
TV, bar, pool, restaurant, convention room, fitness
room, game room. **CREDIT CARDS** All.
R. Barão do Rio Branco, 1271, Centro
TEL 3167-7000
www.jandaia.com.br

RESTAURANT

Fogo Caipira $
This inviting restaurant has a beautiful garden at the
back. Dishes take about 30 minutes to prepare, so
plan on a wait. Try the sun-dried beef cooked in winter squash with *requeijão* (cream cheese). **CUISINE** Regional. **CREDIT CARDS** All. **HOURS** Mon-Thu, 5pm-10pm; Fri
and Sat, 11am-midnight; Sun, 11am-4pm.
R. José Antonio Pereira, 145
TEL 324-1641/382-0731

SERVICES

AIRPORT

Aeroporto Internacional de Campo
Grande
It is small and clean, and there is a tourist information
kiosk, but it gives out little information.
Access via Av. Duque de Caxias
TEL 368-6000

RESTAURANTS $ up to R$50 $$ from R$51 up to R$100 $$$ from R$101 up to R$150 $$$$ above R$150

LOCAL TOUR OPERATOR

Impacto Tour
This agency specializes in ecotourism.
R. Padre João Crippa, 686
TEL 325-1333

EXCHANGE SHOP

Intercâmbio
TEL 324-1515

TOURIST INFORMATION

Morada dos Baís
This is a beautiful historical building. Tourist information is provided by Sebrae-MS. There are several brochures of tourist attractions of Mato Grosso do Sul (including Pantanal and Bonito) and material in English. HOURS Tue-Sat, 8am-7pm; Sun, 9am-noon.
Av. Noroeste, 5140 (on the corner of Av. Afonso Pena)
TEL 324-5830

AIR TAXI

Amapil Táxi-Aéreo
R. Belizário Lima, 677
TEL 321-0733

Chapada dos Guimarães – MT

AREA CODE 65 POPULATION 15,755
DISTANCE Cuiabá, 70 km (43.5 mi)

HOTELS

Pousada Penhasco $$
Many of the rooms overlook the Chapada (plateau). There are services for families and two roofed thermal pools with whirlpool tub. Also available for "day use". There's video karaoke in the dining room. FACILITIES 44 rooms, air-conditioning, phone, TV, cable TV, ceiling fan, bar, football field, pool, heated pool, jogging track, playground, restaurant, convention room, game room, sauna. CREDIT CARDS Diners, MasterCard, Visa.
Av. Penhasco
TEL 301-1555 RESERVATIONS 624-1000
www.penhasco.com.br

Solar do Inglês $$
The main house, where 4 of the 7 rooms are located, is 200 years old. Each room has unique décor that was selected by the owner and her English husband, a former hunter who lived in Pantanal for 30 years before establishing the inn. Every detail is taken care of, from the linen napkins and tablecloths used for afternoon tea to the convenience basket of the rooms. FACILITIES 7 rooms, phone, TV, ceiling fan, bar, pool, sauna. CREDIT CARDS Not accepted.
R. Cipriano Curvo, 142
TEL 301-1389
www.chapadadosguimaraes.com.br/solardoingles

RESTAURANT

Morro dos Ventos $
This restaurant is located in a private condominium that charges an entrance fee. The view of the Chapada (plateau) and the Amor waterfall is beautiful. The quintessential dish is peixe do morro: surubi moqueca, pacu (a freshwater fish) ribs and fried surubi fish fillets. CUISINE Regional. CREDIT CARDS Not accepted. HOURS 8am-6pm.
Estrada do Mirante, km 1
TEL 301-1030/2059/1059

SERVICES

LOCAL TOUR OPERATOR

Ecoturismo Cultural
Pça. Dom Wunibaldo, 464
TEL 301-1393/1639

TOURIST GUIDES

Central de Guias
Pça. Dom Wunibaldo , 464, sala 103
TEL 301-1687/9246-2449

Corumbá – MS

AREA CODE 67 POPULATION 95,701
DISTANCE Campo Grande, 403 km (250.5 mi)
SITE www.corumba.ms.gov.br

HOTEL

Fazenda Bela Vista $$
The Portuguese owners (he's an architect and she's a biologist) live there and take care of everything themselves. The meat, eggs, milk and most of the fruit served in the hotel come from the farm. FACILITIES 10 rooms, air-conditioning, phone, TV, ceiling fan, bar, boat, football field, horses, pool, football court, game room, sauna. CREDIT CARDS Not accepted.
Estrada Parque, km 26
TEL and RESERVATIONS 9987-3660
www.pousadabelavista.com

Yacht Millennium $$$
This boat-hotel navigates Paraguay river and its tributaries either towards São Lourenço river or Negra Bay. Choose the excursions in the high season, from August-October. During piracema (upstream spawning migration), from November-January, only ecological excursions are available as fishing is forbidden at this time of year. The five-day package includes full board, drinks, bait and gasoline. The boat rents sport fishing equipment. It's better to make a group reservation for 20 or 30 people. FACILITIES 10 rooms, Internet access, air-conditioning, minibar, phone, TV, bar, motorized canoes, fishing equipment, restaurant, game room. CREDIT CARDS Not accepted.
R. Manoel Cavassa, 225, Porto Geral
TEL 231-3372/3470
www.opantaneirotur.com.br

RESTAURANTS

Ceará $
This is a traditional fish restaurant with efficient service. The house specialty is surubi with urucum (palm fruit): fried fish with tomato sauce, cream and mozzarella.

PRICES	HOTELS (couple)	$ up to R$150	$$ from R$151 up to R$300	$$$ from R$301 up to R$500	$$$$ above R$500

CUISINE Regional. CREDIT CARDS Visa. HOURS Tue-Sun, 11am-2:30pm and 7pm-11pm.
R. Albuquerque, 516
TEL 231-1930

Peixaria do Lulu $

This simple, family-style restaurant is known for its tasty seasonings. The *surubi* with *urucum* (palm fruit) with tomato sauce, mozzarella and cream, served with rice and *pirão* (manioc porridge with fish broth) stands out. CUISINE Regional. CREDIT CARDS Not accepted. HOURS 10am-4pm and 6pm-midnight; in the low season (Nov-Jan), closed on Sundays.
R. Dom Aquino Correia, 700
TEL 232-2142

SERVICES

AIRPORT

Aeroporto Internacional de Corumbá
R. Santos Dumont
TEL 231-3322

Cuiabá – MT

AREA CODE 65 POPULATION 483,346
SITE www.cuiaba.mt.gov.br

HOTEL

Eldorado Cuiabá $$

This is the best lodging option in Cuiabá for those en route to Pantanal or Chapada dos Guimarães. Choose a room on an upper floor, far from the traffic noise below. FACILITIES 139 rooms, air-conditioning, phone, TV, cable TV, bar, pool, restaurant, convention room. CREDIT CARDS All.
Av. Isaac Póvoas, 1000
TEL 319-3000/1480
www.hoteiseldorado.com.br

RESTAURANT

Al Manzul $$

10 km (6.2 mi) from the city and difficult to reach, this Arab eatery is worth every minute of you're the detour. The couple who owns and manages it prepares delicacies. The specialties include raw *kibbeh* with mint and eggplant sauce, mutton and okra with pomegranate sauce, in addition to traditional options such as hummus dip, *baba ghanouj*, yogurt and grape leaf stuffed rolls. Reservation essential. CUISINE Arab. CREDIT CARDS Not accepted. HOURS Thu and Fri, 6pm-10:30pm; Sat, noon-3pm and 6pm-10:30pm; Sun, noon-3pm.
Av. Arquimedes Pereira Lima, Estrada do Moinho. It's the farm near Brahma Beer Factory.
TEL 663-2021/2237/2393

SERVICES

AIRPORT

Aeroporto Internacional Marechal Rondon
Av. João Ponce Arruda (Várzea Grande)
TEL 614-2500

LOCAL TOUR OPERATORS

Anaconda
Av. Isaac Póvoas, 606
TEL 624-6242

Pantanal Explorer
Av. Governador Ponce de Arruda, 670
(Várzea Grande)

Goiânia – GO

AREA CODE 62 POPULATION 1,093,007
DISTANCE Brasília, 209 km (130 mi)

HOTEL

Castro's Park Hotel $$

Located in the city center, this old hotel is still the best option in town. FACILITIES 173 rooms, air-conditioning, phone, TV, cable TV, recreation team, heated pool, playground, restaurant, convention room, fitness room, game room, massage room, sauna. CREDIT CARDS All.
Av. República do Líbano, 1520, Setor Oeste
TEL 0800623344/225-7070
www.castrospark.com.br

RESTAURANT

Aroeira Restaurante e Bar $

This restaurant has a rustic ambience and live music. Customers help themselves to the food, served in clay and iron pots placed on a large stove. You can also order à la carte. The menu features *aroeira* steak (grilled steak with rice, *feijão tropeiro* [cooked beans with olive oil, garlic, onion, parsley and chive, thickened with manioc flour] and fried banana), a typical dish of the state of Goiás. CUISINE Regional from Goiás and Minas Gerais. CREDIT CARDS Visa. HOURS Tue-Fri, 11:30am-3pm and 6pm-midnight; Sat and Sun, 11:30am-midnight.
R. 146, 570, Setor Marista
TEL 241-5975

SERVICES

TOURIST INFORMATION

Agetur
TEL 201-8100

Goiás – GO

AREA CODE 62 POPULATION 27,120
DISTANCES Brasília, 320 km (199 mi); Goiânia, 136 km (84.5 mi)

HOTELS

Hotel Fazenda Manduzanzan $$

This quiet, well-located hotel is named after two of the region's rivers, the Mandu and the Zanzan. The food is good and the owners, a couple that lives in the farm, provide friendly service. FACILITIES 10 rooms, air-conditioning, TV, football field, horses, pool, rock pool, restaurant, game room, sauna. CREDIT CARDS Not accepted.
Rodovia Municipal do Assentamento do Mosquito, km 7

TEL 9982-3373
www.manduzanzan.com.br

Pousada do Ipê $
The old part of the house dates back to 1798, but guests usually prefer the new building, which faces the pool. Although the rooms are small, the inn is very charming. FACILITIES 21 rooms, TV, bar, pool. CREDIT CARDS Not accepted.
R. do Fórum, 22, Centro
TEL 371-2065/3802

Pousada Dona Sinhá $
There are only 5 rooms, decorated with 18th century furniture. The house is 200 years old and used to be the manor house of a farm, but has been successfully converted into an inn. FACILITIES 5 rooms, pool. CREDIT CARDS Not accepted.
R. Padre Arnaldo, 13
TEL 371-1667

RESTAURANTS

Goiás Pontocom $
This is the place for home-style, tasty food. For lunch, it serves only meat and salad, the so-called "executive lunch." Dinner is à la carte. CUISINE Varied. CREDIT CARDS Not accepted. HOURS Tue and Wed, 11am-3:30pm; Thu-Sat, 11am-3:30pm and 7pm-midnight; Sun, 11am-3:30pm.
Pça. do Coreto, 19
TEL 371-1691

Paróchia $
It is located next to the Matriz Santana church. A good option is the *conde d'arcos* steak, with mustard and caper sauce. On Saturdays it serves *feijoada* . CUISINE Contemporary. CREDIT CARDS Diners, MasterCard. HOURS Tue and Fri, 7:30pm-midnight; Sat and Sun, noon-3pm and 7:30pm-1am.
Pça do Coreto, 18
TEL 371-3291

Miranda – MS

AREA CODE 67 POPULATION 23,007
DISTANCE Campo Grande, 194 km (120.5 mi)
SITE www.miranda.ms.gov.br

HOTELS

Fazenda San Francisco $$
Apart from being a conventional hotel, it is also one of the best "day-use" resorts in the region. The place is well tended and the staff are pleasant. Two-thirds of the guests are Brazilian and just a third foreign. "Day-use" excursions last 3 hours (photographic safari) and 2:30 hours (a *chalana* boat ride). FACILITIES 9 rooms, air-conditioning, minibar, pool, restaurant. CREDIT CARDS Diners, MasterCard, Visa.
Rodovia BR-262, km 583
TEL 242-1088/1088
www.fazendasanfrancisco.tur.br

Fazenda Santa Inês $$
This is a small, well-tended farm that caters to outdoor-oriented visitors. It offers horseback riding, fishing on a "catch and free" basis, climbing wall and rappel. Available for "day use". FACILITIES 6 rooms, air-conditioning, TV,

bar, horses, pool, restaurant. CREDIT CARDS All.
Zona Rural (19 km/11.8 mi of unpaved road from the municipal stadium)
TEL 9988-4082 RESERVATIONS 384-9862
www.fazendasantaines.com.br

Pousada Águas do Pantanal Inn $
This is a good option for those who do not want to buy the 3 or 4-day packages offered by other farms of the region. There's a local tour operator that specializes in one-day excursions. The hotel offers a good breakfast. The standard rooms are very small. The "de luxe" rooms have TV, minibar and air-conditioning. FACILITIES 17 rooms, air-conditioning, pool. CREDIT CARDS Visa.
Av. Afonso Pena, 367
TEL 242-1242/1497 RESERVATIONS 242-1314
www.aguasdopantanal.com.br/pousada.htm

Refúgio Ecológico Caiman $$$$
The region's most sophisticated option, this complex occupies an area of 138,378 acres. It consists of 4 separate inns that are 36 km (22.4 mi) from the Miranda intersection. Each one has its own leisure facilities: pool, bar and cuisine. The lodgings offer kayaks, horses and fishing equipment. Each group is guided by two guides: a biologist and one that knows the region well. It is possible to go on one-day excursions. FACILITIES 17 rooms, air-conditioning, pool, ceiling fan, bar, football field, horses, restaurant. CREDIT CARDS All.
Estância Caimã, Zona Rural
TEL 242-1450 RESERVATIONS (11) 3079-6622
www.caiman.com.br

Pirenópolis – GO

AREA CODE 62 POPULATION 21,245
DISTANCES Goiânia, 115 km (71.5 mi); Brasília, 140 km (87 mi)

HOTELS

Estalagem Alter Real $$
This charming lodge operates near a Lusitano horse breeding farm. There are horseback riding trails. The chalets have verandahs and 4 of them offer whirlpool tubs. FACILITIES 11 rooms, TV, ceiling fan, bar, horses, pool, heated pool, playground, restaurant, fitness room, sauna. CREDIT CARDS MasterCard.
Estrada Bonsucesso, km 3
TEL 331-1656/1931
www.alterreal.com.br

Pousada dos Pireneus Resort $$
This resort nests in a wooded area, in the city's elevated area, and the restaurant has a beautiful view. There are good leisure services for families. FACILITIES 105 rooms, air-conditioning, phone, TV, cable TV, bar, football field, pool, playground, tennis court, restaurant, convention room, fitness room, game room, sauna. CREDIT CARDS Diners, MasterCard, Visa.
Chácara Mata do Sobrado, 80, Bairro do Carmo
TEL 331-1345/1345
www.pousadadospireneus.com.br

RESTAURANT

Le Bistrô $
This candle-lit bistro offers dishes such as the Provençal

PRICES	HOTELS (couple)	$ up to R$150	$$ from R$151 up to R$300	$$$ from R$301 up to R$500	$$$$ above R$500

steak, with herb sauce, served with rice with mint. Open for dinner only. **CUISINE** Contemporary. **CREDIT CARDS** Not accepted. **HOURS** Mon-Wed, 7pm-11pm; Fri, 7pm-midnight; Sat, 1pm-2am; Sun, 1pm-midnight.
R. do Rosário, 23 (R. do Lazer), casa 3, Centro Histórico
TEL 331-2150

Poconé – MT

AREA CODE 65 **POPULATION** 30,773
DISTANCE Cuiabá, 102 km (64 mi)

HOTELS

Pousada Araras Eco Lodge $$$
With bilingual guides and towers that allow guests to spot animals, this hotel draws mainly foreigners. Reservation are essential. **FACILITIES** 15 rooms, air-conditioning, ceiling fan, boat, horses, pool, restaurant. **CREDIT CARDS** MasterCard, Visa.
Estrada Transpantaneira, km 33
TEL 9603-0529 **RESERVATIONS** 682-2800
www.araraslodge.com.br

Sesc Porto Cercado $
This hotel is located inside a natural reserve of 261,930 acres. Request a room in block "E", as these are the newest. There are ample leisure opportunities for children: a baby-care room, a toy library and a cinema for children. There's a butterfly enclosure and a garden. **FACILITIES** 108 rooms, air-conditioning, phone, TV, cable TV, bar, boating, football field, horses, recreation team, pool, playground, restaurant, convention room, fitness room, game room. **CREDIT CARDS** Diners, MasterCard, Visa.
Estrada Poconé–Porto Cercado (MT-370), km 43
TEL 688-2021/688-2005
www.sescpantanal.com.br

Rio Quente – GO

AREA CODE 64 **POPULATION** 2,097
DISTANCES Goiânia, 165 km (102.5 mi); Brasília, 295 km (183.5 mi)

HOTEL

Rio Quente Resorts $$$
This thermal water resort has 3 hotels and 3 managed apartments. There are 2 water parks, the Hot Park and the Parque das Fontes. Stay at Hotel Turismo, which offers the best accommodation, and request Parque das Fontes, the most charming park. The Hot Park welcomes non-guests for day use. **FACILITIES** 122 rooms (in Hotel Turismo), air-conditioning, phone, TV, cable TV, bar, restaurant. **CREDIT CARDS** All.
At the end of the Estrada GO-507
TEL 452-8000/8575 **RESERVATIONS** 452-8080
www.aguasquentes.com

São Jorge – GO

AREA CODE 61
DISTANCE Brasília, 266 km (165 mi)

HOTEL

Casa das Flores $$
This hotel offers candle-lit rooms, breakfast served on the verandah and outdoor whirlpool tub. Some rooms have air-conditioning, minibar and in-room safes. **FACILITIES** 122 rooms, air-conditioning, phone, TV, cable TV, bar, restaurant. **CREDIT CARDS** Not accepted.
R. 10, Quadra 2, Lote 14
TEL 234-7493
www.pousadacasadasflores.com.br

RESTAURANT

Rancho do Waldomiro $
The place is rustic, but if you want to taste *matula* (the *feijoada* of *cerrado*, the Brazilian savannah) you'll have to come here. This typical dish of the *peões* (cowboys) of the Chapada dos Veadeiros includes four types of meat, beans and manioc meal. **CUISINE** Regional. **CREDIT CARDS** Not accepted.
Estrada Alto Paraíso–São Jorge, km 19

SOUTH

Balneário Camboriú – SC

AREA CODE 47 **POPULATION** 73,455
DISTANCE Florianópolis, 80 km (50 mi)
SITE www.secturbc.com.br

HOTELS

Pousada Felíssimo $$$
The suites have a whirlpool tub and a private verandah with an outdoor *ofurô* tub, in addition to amenities such as Egyptian-cotton sheets and a choice of pillows. It is far from the beach and busy spots, but offers bikes. Ideal for those seeking peace and quiet. **FACILITIES** 9 rooms, air-conditioning, phone, TV, cable TV, bar, pool, restaurant, massage room, sauna. **CREDIT CARDS** All.
R. Alles Bleu, 201, Praia dos Amores, access by Av. Osvaldo Reis
TEL 360-6291 **FAX** 360-8281
www.pousadafelissimo.com.br

Recanto das Águas $$$
This complete resort includes a private beach and is only 5 minutes from the center. It is also a spa. Guests can take golf carts around the property. The "super de luxe" suites have a whirlpool and *ofurô* tubs, and DVD player. **FACILITIES** 70 rooms, air-conditioning, phone, TV, cable TV, bar, football field, recreation team, pool, heated pool, playground, tennis court, restaurant, convention room, fitness room, game room, massage room,

RESTAURANTS	$ up to R$50	$$ from R$51 up to R$100	$$$ from R$101 up to R$150	$$$$ above R$150

sauna, spa. **CREDIT CARDS** All.
Estrada da Rainha, 800, Praia dos Amores
TEL 261-0300 **FAX** 261-0361 **RESERVATIONS** 261-0391
www.hotelrecantodasaguas.com.br

RESTAURANT

Vieira's $$
Located in the hubbub of Barra Sul, at the near end of
Atlântica Avenue, this is a typical coastal town seafood
restaurant, with an extensive menu, large servings and
simple facilities. In the high season, things get a bit
hectic and some services options are not available. **CUI-
SINE** Fish and seafood. **CREDIT CARDS** All. **HOURS** Tue-Sun, 11
am-5pm and 6pm-2 am; high season, open Mon
Av. Atlântica, 570, Barra Sul
TEL 361-0842

SERVICES

LOCAL TOUR OPERATORS

CCHTour
TEL 361-8441

CG Tour
TEL 360-7950

EXCHANGE SHOPS

Silva Center
Av. Brasil, 1259, Sala 2A
TEL 367-0878

Traveler's Câmbio e Turismo
Av. Brasil, 1148
TEL 367-0405

TOURIST INFORMATION

Posto de Informações Turísticas – bus station
Av. Santa Catarina
HOURS 6am-midnight

Bento Gonçalves – RS

AREA CODE 54 **POPULATION** 91,486
DISTANCE Porto Alegre, 128 km (79.6 mi)
SITE www.bentoonline.com.br

HOTELS

Dall'Onder Vittoria $$
The suites have a living room and TV in both the bedroom and the living room. The "superior de luxe"
rooms have a mini-kitchen equipped with a microwave oven and a small stove. **FACILITIES** 109 rooms,
air-conditioning, phone, TV, cable TV, bar, pool, restaurant, convention room, fitness room. **CREDIT CARDS** All.
R. Treze de Maio, 800, São Bento
TEL 455-3000 **FAX** 452-7633
www.dallondervittoria.com.br

Pousada Valduga $$
The inn operates inside a winery that shares its name.
Simple rooms overlook the vineyards. Breakfast is

served in the cellar. Tour with wine tasting included.
FACILITIES 14 rooms, phone, TV, ceiling fan, pool, restau-
rant. **CREDIT CARDS** Diners, MasterCard, Visa.
Linha Leopoldina, access by the Rodovia RS-470 highway
TEL and **RESERVATIONS** 453-1154
www.casavalduga.com.br

Villa Michelon $$
The most comfortable hotel of Vale dos Vinhedos
(Vineyard Valley), Michelon has a large convention
center and excellent leisure amenities, including a
pool, playground and sports courts. Reservation advised. **FACILITIES** 50 rooms, air-conditioning, phone, TV,
cable TV, bar, recreation team, heated pool, jogging
track, playground, football court, tennis court, restaurant, convention room, fitness room, game room,
sauna. **CREDIT CARDS** Diners, MasterCard, Visa.
**Rodovia RS-444, km 18.9, Vale dos Vinhedos,
access by the Rodovia RS-470**
TEL 08007033800 **RESERVATIONS** 459-1800
www.villamichelon.com.br

RESTAURANTS

Don Ziero $
Are you tired of eating spring chicken? One of the few
alternatives is Don Ziero, an Italian restaurant like virtually all the others of the region – except that it offers à la carte choices in addition to salads, pasta and
meat. **CUISINE** Italian. **CREDIT CARDS** Diners, MasterCard,
Visa. **HOURS** Tue-Sun, noon-3pm; Wed, Fri and Sat,
noon-3pm and 7pm-11pm.
**Rodovia RS-470, km 219, Vinícola Cordelier, at the
entrance of Vale dos Vinhedos**
TEL 453-7593

Giuseppe $
From the outside it looks like a typical roadside
restaurant, to be avoided by discriminating customers. But the food and service here are surprisingly good. The *galeterias*, which specialize in spring
chicken, are a tradition in the Gaucho mountains. And
here you will find the best spring chicken of the region. **CUISINE** Italian. **CREDIT CARDS** All. **HOURS** 11am-3pm.
**Rodovia RS-470, km 221.5, between Garibaldi and
Bento Gonçalves**
TEL 463-8505

SERVICES

LOCAL TOUR OPERATORS

Giordani Turismo
TEL 452-6042/6455

Rio das Antas Turismo
TEL 451-2844

Valle Verde Turismo
TEL 459-1813

EXCHANGE SHOP

Banco do Brasil
R. Marechal Floriano, 85, Centro
TEL 451-3666

PRICES	HOTELS (couple)	$ up to R$150	$$ from R$151 up to R$300	$$$ from R$301 up to R$500	$$$$ above R$500

Blumenau – SC

AREA CODE 47 **POPULATION** 261,808
DISTANCE Florianópolis, 140 km (87 mi)
SITE www.blumenau.com.br

HOTELS

Himmelblau Palace $$
This hotel is almost 30 years old, but the rooms were renovated in 2002. It is near Shopping Neumarket (a mall) and the town center. **FACILITIES** 125 rooms, air-conditioning, phone, TV, cable TV, bar, pool, restaurant, convention room, sauna. **CREDIT CARDS** All.
R. Sete de Setembro, 1415, Centro
TEL 326-5800
www.himmelblau.com.br

Plaza Blumenau $$
Albeit a bit aged (it is 30 years old) this is one of the most comfortable hotels in town. The rooms ending in 3 and 4 have been renovated. The "de luxe" rooms have a whirlpool tub. **FACILITIES** 131 rooms, air-conditioning, phone, TV, bar, pool, restaurant, convention room, fitness room. **CREDIT CARDS** All.
R. Sete de Setembro, 818, Centro
TEL 231-7000 **FAX** 231-7001 **RESERVATIONS** 0800471213
www.plazahoteis.com.br

Viena Park $$
This hotel is far from the center, and sits on a large, green estate. The 4 duplex suites have a whirlpool tub in the bathroom and in the balcony. There's a complete leisure infrastructure. **FACILITIES** 90 rooms, air-conditioning, phone, TV, bar, recreation team, pool, playground, football court, tennis court, restaurant, convention room, fitness room, game room, massage room, sauna. **CREDIT CARDS** All.
R. Hermann Huscher, 670, Vila Formosa
TEL 326-8888
www.vienahotel.com.br

RESTAURANTS

Cafehaus Glória $
Café colonial (full afternoon tea) is served in a buffet and includes more than 50 items. The favorite options are strudels, *cucas* (banana pies), chicken pie, cheese pie and whole-wheat bread with walnuts. **CUISINE** Café colonial. **CREDIT CARDS** All. **HOURS** 3pm-8pm.
R. Sete de Setembro, 954, Centro
TEL 322-6942

Cervejaria Biergarten $
Enjoying the local Eisenbahn *chope* (draft beer), by the Itajaí-Açu river, is a must after walking on Quinze de Novembro Street. The *choperia* is just like a famous *biergarten* of Munich, down to the food. **CUISINE** German. **CREDIT CARDS** MasterCard, Visa. **HOURS** 10am-midnight.
R. Quinze de Novembro, 160, Centro
TEL 326-8380

Frohsinn $$
This is one of the most elegant restaurants of Blumenau, with a beautiful view of the town. It serves generous helpings of standard fare such as stuffed *marreco* (garganey), *einsbein* (pork knuckle), but there are also choices of pasta and meat. **CUISINE** German. **CREDIT CARDS** Diners, MasterCard, Visa. **HOURS** 11:30am-12:30pm.
R. Gertrud Sierich
TEL 322-2137

SERVICES

LOCAL TOUR OPERATORS

CGTur Turismo Receptivo
R. Getúlio Vargas, 196, sala 4, Centro
TEL 222-1804

Gardentur Turismo
Al. Rio Branco, 21
TEL 322-7733/326-0145

TOURIST INFORMATION

Blumenau Convention Visitors Bureau
R. Quinze de Novembro, 420
TEL 322-6933 **HOURS** 8am-8pm

Castelinho do Turismo
R. Quinze de Novembro, 1050
TEL 326-6931 **HOURS** Mon-Fri, 8am-7pm; Sat and Sun, 9am-3pm

Terminal Rodoviário – Seterb
R. Dois de Setembro, 1222, Itoupava Norte
TEL 323-2155

Bombinhas – SC

AREA CODE 47 **POPULATION** 8,716
DISTANCE Florianópolis, 60 km (37.3 mi)
SITE www.bombinhas.sc.gov.br

HOTELS

Atlântico $$
This leisure hotel is located on Mariscal Beach, the largest and quietest beach of Bombinhas. Request a suite in the old wing: the ones in the new wing are more modern but are located across the avenue and have no ocean view. **FACILITIES** 110 rooms, air-conditioning, phone, TV, ceiling fan, bar, recreation team, pool, restaurant, convention room, game room, massage room, sauna. **CREDIT CARDS** All.
Av. Aroeira da Praia, 500, Mariscal
TEL 393-9100
www.hotelatlantico.com.br

Morada do Mar $$
This hotel on Bombas Beach caters to families and offers a good leisure options for children, beach service and recreation. **FACILITIES** 40 rooms, air-conditioning, phone, TV, ceiling fan, bar, recreation team, playground, restaurant, convention room, game room. **CREDIT CARDS** Diners, MasterCard, Visa.
Av. Leopold Zarling, 1221, Bombas
TEL 393-6090
www.moradadomar.com.br

RESTAURANTS $ up to R$50 $$ from R$51 up to R$100 $$$ from R$101 up to R$150 $$$$ above R$150

Pousada Mauna Lani $$$
This inn faces Bombas beach, one of the busiest in town. There's a deck with bar that extends to the beach. FACILITIES 18 rooms, air-conditioning, phone, TV, bar, pool. CREDIT CARDS All.
Av. Leopoldo Zarling, 2183, Bombas
TEL and FAX 369-2674
www.pousadamaunalani.com.br

Pousada Quintal do Mar $$
This inn is a converted beach house. There are only 4 suites, decorated with local fruit and flower motifs. In the yard there's a verandah with hammocks. In the living room, a home theater with a small collection of films and CDs. Children are not allowed. FACILITIES 4 rooms, air-conditioning, TV, cable TV, restaurant. CREDIT CARD MasterCard.
Av. Aroeira da Praia, 1641, Mariscal
TEL 393-4389/9980-2100
www.quintaldomar.com.br

Pousada Tortuga do Mariscal $$$
This Mediterranean-style inn, painted in vivid colors, sports a fountain with carps and turtles that gives it its name. The rooms contain a fully equipped kitchen. FACILITIES 24 rooms, air-conditioning, phone, TV, ceiling fan, bar, pool, restaurant. CREDIT CARDS MasterCard, Visa.
Av. dos Coqueiros, 3423, Mariscal
TEL 393-4560
www.pousadatortuga.com.br

Pousada Vila do Coral $$
Even though location is the great advantage of this inn, which faces Bombinhas beach, most of the rooms face the other way. It is simply decorated but comfortable. There's no restaurant. FACILITIES 28 rooms, air-conditioning, phone, TV, cable TV, bar, pool, game room. CREDIT CARDS All.
Av. Vereador Manoel José dos Santos, 215, Bombinhas
TEL 393-9333
www.viladocoral.com.br

Pousada Vila do Farol $$$
This inn resembles an Azorean village, with colorful two-story houses. All the rooms have a complete kitchen and an ocean view. There's a recreation room, and a commercial complex with shops and restaurants near the inn. FACILITIES 56 rooms, air-conditioning, phone, TV, cable TV, bar, recreation team, pool, playground, restaurant, convention room, game room. CREDIT CARDS All.
Av. Vereador Manoel José dos Santos, 800, Bombinhas
TEL 393-9000 FAX 393-9005
www.viladofarol.com.br

Pousada Villa Paradiso $$$$
This Balinese-style inn is located on the side of a hill at the end of Bombinhas beach. There are high-ceiling bungalows with a verandah, deck with 10 whirlpool tubs, pools, *ofurô* tubs and tents for relaxation. There's no restaurant and breakfast is served in the bungalows. FACILITIES 17 rooms, air-conditioning, fireplace, phone, TV, cable TV, ceiling fan, bar, pool. CREDIT CARDS Diners, MasterCard, Visa.
Av. Garoupas, 5, at the end of the Bombinhas beach
TEL 369-0005/0069
www.villaparadiso.com.br

RESTAURANTS

Berro d'Água $$
It is worth coming here to this fishing village at Zimbros beach, if only to taste Asian shrimp with soy sauce, bacon and mushrooms, or salmon with honey-mustard. The place is one of the best in the region thanks to the nice decor, good food and service. CUISINE Fish and seafood. CREDIT CARDS Diners, MasterCard, Visa. HOURS Mon-Sat, 10am-5pm and 8pm-midnight; Sun, 9am-midnight.
R. Rio Juquiá, Praia de Zimbros
TEL 393-3666

Casa da Lagosta $$
This is a simple option in the center, with abundant seafood dishes. Despite the name (Lobster House), lobster is not really the house specialty. Opt instead for the *moquecas* and shrimp dishes. CUISINE Fish and seafood. CREDIT CARDS Diners, MasterCard, Visa. HOURS 11am-11pm.
Av. Vereador Manoel José dos Santos, 987, Centro
TEL 369-2235

SERVICES

LOCAL TOUR OPERATORS

Altura Climb (adventure sports)
TEL 369-0070

Hy Brazil (diving)
Av. Vereador Manoel José dos Santos, 205
TEL 369-2545/9102-7177

EXCHANGE SHOP

Casa de Câmbio
Av. Vereador Manoel José dos Santos, 822

TOURIST INFORMATION

Citur
Rodovia SC-412 (BR-101 exit to Porto Belo)
TEL 369-6050. HOURS 8am-10pm (high season), 9am-6pm (low season)

Posto de Informações Turísticas – Prefeitura
Av. Vereador Manoel José dos Santos, 662
TEL 393-7080. HOURS 8am-11pm (high season), 8:30am-6pm (low season)

Projeto Viva Trilha
TEL 369-3653/393-7080

Cambará do Sul – RS

AREA CODE 54 POPULATION 6,840
DISTANCE Porto Alegre, 180 km (112 mi)
SITE www.cambaradosul.com.br

HOTEL

Parador Casa da Montanha $$
The hotel looks like a charming camping ground. In-

| PRICES | HOTELS (couple) | $ up to R$150 | $$ from R$151 up to R$300 | $$$ from R$301 up to R$500 | $$$$ above R$500 |

548   BRAZIL GUIDE

stead of rooms or chalets, there are electrically heated tents with double bed, sink and toilet. The showers are in a separate bath house. The daily rate includes full board. FACILITIES 8 rooms, ceiling fan, horses, restaurant. CREDIT CARDS Diners, MasterCard, Visa.
Estrada do Faxinal, between Cambará and Itaimbezinho Canyon
TEL 504-5302/9973-9320 FAX and RESERVATIONS 286-2544
www.paradorcasadamontanha.com.br

SERVICES

LOCAL TOUR OPERATORS

Atitude Ecologia e Turismo
TEL 282-6305

Canyon Turismo
TEL 251-1027

TOURIST INFORMATION

Posto de Informações Turísticas
R. Adail Valim, 39, Pça. São José
TEL 251-1320 HOURS 8am-8pm (high season); 8am-noon and 1:30pm-5:30pm (low season)

Canela – RS

AREA CODE 54 POPULATION 33,625
DISTANCE Porto Alegre, 133 km (82.7 mi)
SITE www.canelaturismo.com.br

HOTELS

Pousada Cravo e Canela $$$
This inn occupies an old colonial manor. Each room is uniquely decorated, and breakfast is served until noon. FACILITIES 12 rooms, fireplace, phone, TV, cable TV, ceiling fan, heated pool, convention room, game room, sauna. CREDIT CARDS All.
R. Tenente Manoel Correia, 144, Centro
TEL 282-1120
www.pousadacravoecanela.com.br

Pousada Quinta dos Marques $$
This inn occupies a remodeled 1930 manor far from the town center. The rooms have been decorated with flair. The suites sport canopied beds and skylights. Paulo Marques, the owner, provides customized service. FACILITIES 12 rooms, phone, TV, bar, heated pool, restaurant, game room, massage room. CREDIT CARDS Diners, MasterCard, Visa.
R. Gravataí, 200, Santa Teresinha, access by the Rua Borges de Medeiros
TEL 282-9812
www.quintadosmarques.com.br

Pousada Solar Don Ramon $$
This inn is far from the center, on the way to Caracol Park. The rooms are uniquely decorated and 5 suites have fireplace. FACILITIES 11 rooms, phone, TV, ceiling fan, pool, game room. CREDIT CARDS Not accepted.
R. José Pedro Piva, 745, Estrada do Caracol
TEL 282-3306/3812
www.donramoncom.br

SERVICES

LOCAL TOUR OPERATORS

Atitude Ecologia e Turismo
TEL 282-6305

Brocker Turismo
TEL 282-2668

Macuco Aventura
TEL 3031-0273

TOURIST INFORMATION

Central de Aventuras
R. Dona Carlinda, 455, Centro
TEL 282-7822. HOURS 8am-8pm

Centro de Informações Turísticas
Lgo. da Fama, 227, Centro
TEL 282-2200. HOURS 9am-9pm (high season); 8am-7pm (low season)

Curitiba – PR

AREA CODE 41 POPULATION 1,587,315
DISTANCES Florianópolis, 304 km (189 mi); São Paulo, 408 km (253.7 mi)
SITE www.viaje.curitiba.pr.gov.br

HOTELS

Four Points Sheraton $$
Executives make up most of the clientele. There's a floor exclusively for women, where rooms are equipped with scales, toiletry kit and pantyhose. FACILITIES 176 rooms, air-conditioning, phone, TV, cable TV, bar, heated pool, restaurant, convention room, fitness room, massage room, sauna. CREDIT CARDS All.
Av. Sete de Setembro, 4211
TEL 340-4000 FAX 340-4001
www.fpsc.com.br

Full Jazz $$
This is one of the few boutique hotels of Curitiba. The rooms are equipped with 29" TV sets, DVD players and computers with internet access. A fitness room is the only leisure option. FACILITIES 84 rooms, air-conditioning, phone, TV, cable TV, bar, restaurant, convention room, fitness room. CREDIT CARDS All.
R. Silveira Peixoto, 1297, Batel
TEL 312-7000 RESERVATIONS 08007043311
www.hotelfulljazz.com.br

Grand Hotel Rayon $$$
One of the most luxurious hotels in town, it offers a beauty parlor and masseuses, a gym and a pool that is open day and night. The rooms have bathtubs. It is near the 24-hour street. FACILITIES 133 rooms, air-conditioning, phone, TV, cable TV, bar, heated pool, restaurant, convention room, fitness room, massage room, sauna. CREDIT CARDS All.
R. Visconde de Nacar, 1424
TEL 3027-6006 RESERVATIONS 3021-1222
www.rayon.com.br

RESTAURANTS $ up to R$50 $$ from R$51 up to R$100 $$$ from R$101 up to R$150 $$$$ above R$150

Rockfeller $

This hotel is one of the newest in town, though it occupies a 1940's-era building behind the Centro de Convenções Estação (convention center). The wide hallways are illuminated with natural light. This is a theme hotel: everything here relates to New York in the 1920's. There are 2 Jacuzzis in the sports area. **FACILITIES** 78 rooms, air-conditioning, phone, TV, cable TV, bar, restaurant, convention room, fitness room, massage room, sauna. **CREDIT CARDS** All.
R. Rockfeller, 11, Rebouças
TEL 3023-2330 **RESERVATIONS** 08007042330
www.hotelslaviero.com.br

San Juan Palace $

The hotel's charm prevails over its location. It occupies a beautiful renovated building that housed the first hotel of Curitiba. Request one of the rooms in the front, which are more spacious and have wood floors. The hotel is near a stop of Linha Turismo (Tourist Line), but be careful when walking there at night. **FACILITIES** 24 rooms, air-conditioning, phone, TV, restaurant. **CREDIT CARDS** American Express, MasterCard, Visa.
R. Barão do Rio Branco, 354
TEL 3028-7000 **FAX** 3028-7026 **RESERVATIONS** 0800415505
www.sanjuanhoteis.com.br

RESTAURANTS

Bar Curityba $

This bar serves traditional finger foods, such as "jaguar meat" (steak tartar sandwich). The furnishings tell a bit of the city's history: the windows came from Colégio Sion and the wood table tops are made with sleepers of the old Curitiba–Paranaguá railway line. **CREDIT CARDS** Diners, MasterCard, Visa. **HOURS** Mon-Sat, 6pm-1am.
Av. Presidente Taunay, 444, Batel
TEL 3018-0444

Beto Batata $

Swiss-style (*rosti*) potato is a traditional dish of Curitiba. It is type of fried pie made of pre-cooked, grated potatoes with various fillings. This restaurant in the Alto da Quinze district offers the best *rosti* potato in town. There's live music, too, especially MPB (Brazilian Popular Music) and *chorinho* at lunch and dinner. **CREDIT CARDS** Diners, MasterCard, Visa. **HOURS** Daily, 11am-2pm.
R. Professor Brandão, 678, Alto da Quinze
TEL 262-0840

Boulevard $$

This restaurant, run by Celso Freire, has received many awards from specialized publications and is considered the best in town. The menu features contemporary dishes influenced by French and Italian cuisine. The wine list has been awarded recognition by *Wine Spectator*. **CUISINE** French, Italian. **CREDIT CARDS** All. **HOURS** Mon-Fri, noon-2:30pm and 7:30pm-11:30pm; Sat, 7:30pm-11:30pm.
R. Voluntários, 539, Centro
TEL 224-8244

Cantinho do Eisbein $

This simple restaurant, located far from the center, has a short menu that includes eisbein (pork knuckle), stuffed *marreco* (garganey) and *kassler* (smoked pork steak). It is "the" place for German food, prepared following the recipes of the friendly owner's mother. **CUISINE** German. **CREDIT CARDS** All. **HOURS** Tue-Sat, 11am-3pm and 6pm-11:30pm; Sun, 11am-3pm.
Av. dos Estados, 863, Água Verde
TEL 329-5155/3023-5155

Durski $

At this traditional restaurant, order the Slav banquet, similar to a tasting menu that includes specialties from Poland, Ukraine and Russia such as *platzki* (potato pancakes), *holopti* (cabbage rolls stuffed with meat), *borscht* (beet soup) and *pierogi* (a type of ravioli with potato filling). **CUISINE** Slavic. **CREDIT CARDS** All. **HOURS** Tue-Sat, 11:30am-2:30pm and 7:30pm-11:30pm; Sun, 11:30am-4pm.
Av. Jaime Reis, 254, São Francisco
TEL 225-7893

Estrela da Terra $

This is a great idea for Sundays: have lunch at Estrela da Terra before or after going to the handicraft fair in Largo da Ordem. The restaurant's lack of sophistication is offset by Curitiba's best *barreado*, a dish of slow-cooked lean meat, bacon, tomato, onions, seasonings. There's a "per kilo" buffet on weekdays and a buffet with regional dishes on Saturdays and Sundays. **CUISINE** Regional. **CREDIT CARDS** Diners, MasterCard. **HOURS** Daily, 11:30am-3:30pm.
Av. Jaime Reis, 176, lgo. da Ordem
TEL 222-5007

Spaghetteria Passaparola $

Italian food is carefully prepared and served here. The restaurant operates in a residential area and specializes in dishes with mushrooms imported from Italy. **CUISINE** Italian. **CREDIT CARDS** Not accepted. **HOURS** Tue-Sun, 7:30pm-11pm.
Av. Vicente Machado, 3031, Batel
TEL 242-2482

SERVICES

AIRPORT

Aeroporto Internacional Afonso Pena

Av. Rocha Pombo
TEL 381-1515

LOCAL TOUR OPERATORS

BWT

Av. Presidente Afonso Camargo, 330, Jardim Botânico
TEL 322-0277

Esatur

R. Marechal Deodoro, 235, 1º andar
TEL 322-7667

Onetur

R. Marechal Floriano Peixoto, 228, 11º andar
TEL 224-8509

EXCHANGE SHOP

AVS Câmbio e Turismo

Av. Marechal Deodoro, 630, conjunto 504
TEL 223-2828/323-1747

| **PRICES** | **HOTELS** (couple) | $ up to R$150 | $$ from R$151 up to R$300 | $$$ from R$301 up to R$500 | $$$$ above R$500 |

550　　　　　　　　　　　　　　　　　　　　　　　　　　　　　BRAZIL GUIDE

Jade Turismo e Câmbio
R. Quinze de Novembro, 467, 1º andar
TEL 322-1123

TOURIST INFORMATION

Diretoria Municipal de Turismo
R. da Glória, 362, Centro
TEL 352-8000. HOURS Mon-Fri, 8am-noon and 2pm-6pm

Disque Turismo (Paraná Turismo)
R. Deputado Mário de Barros, 1290, Centro
TEL 313-3500. HOURS Mon-Fri, 8:30am-noon and
1:30pm-6pm

Florianópolis – SC

AREA CODE 48 POPULATION 342,315
DISTANCES Curitiba, 304 km (189 mi); Porto Alegre, 474
km (294.7 mi)
SITE www.florianopolisturismo.sc.gov.br

HOTELS

Blue Tree Towers Florianópolis $$
Located beside the Beiramar shopping mall, this hotel offers rooms with bathtubs and services such as round-the-clock laundry. It's a good option for executives but is far from the most fashionable beaches. FACILITIES 95 rooms, air-conditioning, phone, TV, cable TV, bar, pool, restaurant, convention room, fitness room, massage room, sauna. CREDIT CARDS All.
R. Bocaiúva, 2304, Centro
TEL 251-5555 FAX 251-5500 RESERVATIONS 251-5554
www.bluetree.com.br

Costão do Santinho $$$$
One of the largest resorts of Brazil, this place has a marina, kayaks, motorboats, spa, trails in the woods and an outdoor archaeology museum. The rooms in the village include a complete kitchen, but the ones in Hotel Internacional are newer. Dinner is included. FACILITIES 695 rooms, air-conditioning, phone, TV, cable TV, bar, football field, horses, recreation team, pool, heated pool, playground, football court, tennis court, restaurant, convention room, fitness room, game room, massage room, sauna, spa. CREDIT CARDS All.
Estrada Vereador Onildo Lemos, 2505,
Praia do Santinho
TEL 261-1000 RESERVATIONS 08007019000
www.costao.com

Hotel Fazenda Engenho Velho $$
This farm hotel is in the city and has horses, woods, a lake, sports courts, game room and an ecotourism operator that offers rappelling and mountain climbing in the region. FACILITIES 45 rooms, air-conditioning, fireplace, phone, TV, ceiling fan, bar, football field, horses, recreation team, pool, playground, tennis court, restaurant, convention room, game room, massage room. CREDIT CARDS All.
Rodovia João Gualberto Soares, 8290
TEL 269-7000
www.engenhovelho.com.br

Jurerê Beach Village $$$
This family-pleasing inn is in the Jurerê Internacional

condominium, at Jurerê Beach. The suites include a complete kitchen. FACILITIES 242 rooms, air-conditioning, phone, TV, cable TV, bar, recreation team, heated pool, playground, restaurant, convention room, fitness room, game room, massage room, sauna. CREDIT CARDS All.
Al. César Nascimento, 646
TEL 261-5100 FAX 261-5200 RESERVATIONS 0800480110
www.jurere.com.br

Majestic Palace Hotel $$$
This downtown hotel is far from the beaches but close to the nightlife action. It is luxurious and formal, and attracts the businessmen. FACILITIES 245 rooms, 12 presidential suites, air-conditioning, cable TV, safe, broadband internet, fridge, internacional cuisine restaurant, scenic view restaurant, piano bar, conventional center, coffee shop, 24-hour room service, gift shop, concièrge, exercise room, pool, spa, helipad. CREDIT CARDS All.
Av. Beira Mar Norte, 2746, Centro
TEL 231-8000 FAX 231-8008 RESERVATIONS 231-8000
www.majesticpalace.com.br

Pousada da Vigia $$$
This hillside inn has a beautiful view of the beach. Suites have a whirlpool tub in the bathroom and on the deck, home theater with DVD player, barbecue and microwave oven. Closed in June. FACILITIES 10 rooms, air-conditioning, phone, TV, ceiling fan, bar, heated pool, restaurant, fitness room, massage room, sauna. CREDIT CARDS Diners, MasterCard, Visa.
R. Cônego Walmor Castro, 291, Praia de Lagoinha de Ponta das Canas
TEL 284-1789 FAX 284-1108
www.pousadavigia.com.br

Pousada Pénareia $$
Opened recently, this inn faces the sea. The owners, a young couple from São Paulo, serve breakfast. The rooms are well decorated and the bathrooms are spacious. FACILITIES 13 rooms, phone, TV, ceiling fan. CREDIT CARDS Not accepted.
R. Hermes Guedes da Fonseca, 207,
Praia da Armação
TEL 338-1616 FAX 338-7156
www.pousadapenareia.com.br

Pousada Villas del Sol y Mar $$
This Mexican-style inn is just 50 meters from the sand, but it has no ocean view. The suites have a mini-kitchen with a microwave oven. English and Spanish are spoken. FACILITIES 24 rooms, air-conditioning, phone, TV, ceiling fan, fitness room, sauna. CREDIT CARDS All.
R. Jorge Cherem, 84, Jurerê
TEL 282-0863
www.villasdelmar.com.br

Praia Mole Park Hotel $$$
The facilities are not very well maintained, but the location is great: 22.7 acres that stretch from the Mole beach to the Conceição lagoon. There's a sushi bar on the beach and an orchid glasshouse with over 5000 species. No room service. FACILITIES 84 rooms, air-conditioning, phone, TV, ceiling fan, bar, boating, football field, mini-golf course, recreation team, pool, heated

pool, playground, tennis court, restaurant, convention room, fitness room, game room, massage room, sauna, spa. CREDIT CARDS All.
Rodovia Jornalista Manoel de Menezes, 2001, Praia Mole
TEL 232-5231 FAX 232-5482 RESERVATIONS 0800480008
www.praiamole.com.br

Villa Del'Este $$

Hidden in a quiet corner of the Conceição lagoon, it offers complete rooms, with kitchen and utility area. Breakfast is served in the rooms until 11am. FACILITIES 6 rooms, air-conditioning, phone, TV, ceiling fan, pool, massage room. CREDIT CARDS Diners, MasterCard.
Beco dos Coroas, 370, Barra da Lagoa
TEL 232-3253
www.villadeleste.com.br

RESTAURANTS

Bar do Arante $

This is one of the tourist attractions in town, and offers fish and shrimp *à moda*. The walls are covered with notes left by customers who maintain a tradition dating back to the 1960's. Back then, the bar was a meeting point for young campers, who used to leave notes to communicate with their friends. CUISINE Fish and seafood. CREDIT CARDS Diners, MasterCard. HOURS Daily, from 11:30am on.
R. Abelardo Otacílio Gomes, 254,
Praia do Pântano do Sul
TEL 389-2622/237-7022

Bistrô D'Acampora $$

Chef Zeca D'Acampora owns a sophisticated restaurant, which is also part art gallery. Reservation required. The menu changes weekly and fish and shrimp dishes stand out. CUISINE French, Italian. CREDIT CARDS Visa. HOURS 8pm-11:30pm; in summer, closed Sundays and Mondays; off season, closed Sundays, Mondays and Tuesdays.
Rodovia SC-401, km 10, 10300
TEL 235-1073

Bistrô Isadora Duncan $$

The service could be a bit speedier and more friendly, but this bistro is charming and has a beautiful view of the Conceição lagoon. It is ideal for couples. The outdoor tables are the best. CUISINE Contemporary. CREDIT CARDS MasterCard, Visa. HOURS Daily, Mon-Sat, 7pm-1am.
Rodovia Jornalista Manoel de Menezes, 2658, Praia Mole
TEL 232-7210

Box 32 $

Located inside the Mercado Público (public market), this bar is a happy-hour favorite and is always packed. Order the popular turnovers with abundant shrimp filling and iced *chope* (draft beer). The bar serves its own *cachaça*. CUISINE Fish and seafood. CREDIT CARDS All. HOURS Mon-Fri, 10am-10pm; Sat, 10am-3pm.
Inside the Mercado Público Municipal, boxe 32
TEL 224-5588

Chef Fedoca – Marina Ponta de Areia $$

In a marina by the Conceição lagoon, this 20-year-old restaurant serves the most famous and generously portioned *moqueca* in Florianópolis. CUISINE Fish and seafood. CREDIT CARDS Diners, MasterCard, Visa. HOURS Tue-Sat, 11:30am-3pm and 7:30pm-midnight; Sun, noon-6pm; in summer, 11:30am-midnight.
R. Senador Ivo de Aquino Neto, 133, Barra da Lagoa
TEL 232-0759

Gugu $

The owner, a former fisherman, has created Azores-influenced recipes. The seafood bouillabaisse and blanched mullet are very tasty. The ambience is simple. Customers are served by the owner's family. CUISINE Fish and seafood. CREDIT CARDS Diners, MasterCard, Visa. HOURS Mon, 6:30pm-11:30pm; Tue-Thu, 11:30am-3pm and 6pm-11:30pm; Sat and Sun, 11:30am-5pm and 6:30pm-11:30pm.
R. Antonio Dias Carneiro, 747, Sambaqui
TEL 335-0288

Rancho Açoriano $$

This is a good place to enjoy oysters. Its recipe of oysters *au gratin* has won twice the Fenaostra, a local gourmet festival. CUISINE Fish and seafood. CREDIT CARDS Diners, MasterCard, Visa. HOURS 11am-11pm.
Rodovia Baldisero Filomeno, 5634, Ribeirão da Ilha
TEL 337-0848

Restinga Recanto $$

This restaurant is decorated with motifs of the *boi-mamão* festival, the local version of the *bumba-meu-boi* folkloric festival, in which ox-costumed dancers celebrate the death and resurrection of an ox. The menu features grilled anchovy or mullet and mixed *moqueca*. Try the *pirão* (manioc meal porridge with fish broth). CUISINE Fish and seafood. CREDIT CARDS Not accepted. HOURS Tue, 5pm-midnight; Wed-Sun, 11am-midnight.
R. Geral do Sambaqui, 2759
TEL 235-2093

Santo Antonio Spaghetteria e Café $

This spaghetti shop is a good option for those who are tired of having fish and seafood. There's an adjoining handicraft shop, and the restaurant is in a typical Azorean neighborhood. CUISINE Italian, fish and seafood. CREDIT CARDS Diners, MasterCard, Visa. HOURS noon-midnight; in the low season, closed Mondays.
R. Cônego Serpa, 30, Santo Antônio de Lisboa
TEL 235-2356

Toca de Jurerê $$

The restaurant's owner is a diver and catches the fish served in the mouthwatering mixed *moqueca*. CUISINE Fish and seafood. CREDIT CARDS Not accepted. HOURS noon-3pm and 7pm-midnight.
R. Acácio Mello, 78, Jurerê
TEL 282-0795

Um Lugar $$

This is a spot for people-watching. The atmosphere is modern and casual. The dishes, such as curry shrimp and tuna with sesame seeds, are beautiful. There's an adjoining handicraft shop. CUISINE Contemporary. CREDIT CARDS All. HOURS Tue-Sat, 8pm-midnight; in winter, closed Sundays and Mondays.

PRICES	HOTELS (couple)	$ up to R$150	$$ from R$151 up to R$300	$$$ from R$301 up to R$500	$$$$ above R$500

R. Manoel Severino de Oliveira, 371
TEL 232-2451

SERVICES

AIRPORT

Aeroporto Hercílio Luz
Av. Deputado Diomício Freitas, 3393, Carianos
TEL 331-4000

LOCAL TOUR OPERATOR

Triptur
TEL 369-5847

EXCHANGE SHOPS

Centaurus Câmbio
Av. Osmar Cunha, 183, loja 26, Centro
TEL 224-3318
HOURS 11am-4pm

Banco do Brasil
Praça Quinze de Novembro, 321
TEL 221-1600
HOURS 10am-4pm

TOURIST POLICE STATION

Delegacia do Turista
Av. Paulo Fontes, 1101, Centro
TEL 222-4065
HOURS 24 hours

TOURIST INFORMATION

Postos de Informações Turísticas
Av. Engenheiro Max de Souza, 270 (at the near end of the Colombo Salles bridge)
TEL 271-7028/221-1516 HOURS 8am-8pm

Foz do Iguaçu – PR

AREA CODE 45 POPULATION 258,543
DISTANCES Curitiba, 637 km (396 mi); São Paulo, 1019 km (633.7 mi)
SITE www.fozdoiguacu.pr.gov.br/turismo

HOTELS

Bourbon Cataratas Resort Convention Center $$$$
This 30-year old hotel is in very good condition. The rooms in the new wing are better, especially those overlooking the pool. There's great leisure activity options for kids, including a water park and a game room. FACILITIES 311 rooms, air-conditioning, phone, TV, bar, football field, recreation team, pool, heated pool, jogging track, playground, restaurant, convention room, fitness room, game room, massage room, sauna. CREDIT CARDS All.
Rodovia das Cataratas, km 2.5
TEL 529-0123 FAX 529-0000 RESERVATIONS 0800451010
www.bourbon.com.br

Mabu Thermas and Resort $$$$
This is the only resort in town with thermally heated waters. There are 5 pools, with a temperature ranging from 32º to 36º C (89.6º to 96.8ºF). It operates on an all-inclusive basis, which also includes locally produced beverages. Rooms overlook the pools, the garden or the woods, with the first being the noisiest. FACILITIES 208 rooms, air-conditioning, phone, TV, cable TV, bar, football field, horses, recreation team, pool, heated pool, jogging track, playground, tennis court, restaurant, convention room, game room, massage room, sauna. CREDIT CARDS All.
Rodovia das Cataratas, km 3.5, 3175
TEL 521-2000 FAX 529-6361 RESERVATIONS 0800417040
www.hotelsmabu.com.br

Tropical das Cataratas Eco Resort $$$$
This is the only hotel inside Iguaçu National Park. It faces waterfalls that can be seen from some of the rooms and from the verandah. FACILITIES 202 rooms, air-conditioning, phone, TV, cable TV, bar, football field, recreation team, pool, playground, football court, tennis court, restaurant, convention room, game room. CREDIT CARDS All.
Parque Nacional do Iguaçu, Rodovia das Cataratas, km 28
TEL 521-7000 FAX 521-1688 RESERVATIONS 08007012670
www.tropicalhotel.com.br

SERVICES

AIRPORT

Aeroporto Internacional de Foz do Iguaçu
Entrance via Rodovia das Cataratas, km 16.5
TEL 521-4200

TOURIST POLICE STATION

Delegacia do Turista
Av. Brasil, 1374
TEL 523-3036 HOURS Mon-Fri, 8:30am- 6pm

TOURIST INFORMATION

Posto de Informações Turísticas
Pça. Getúlio Vargas, 69, Centro
Portuguese, English and Spanish spoken
TEL 0800451516 HOURS 7am-11pm

Garibaldi – RS

AREA CODE 54 POPULATION 28,337
DISTANCE Porto Alegre, 112 km (69.5 mi)

HOTEL

Casacurta $$
This very charming, highly traditional hotel has been in business for over 5 decades. The decor dates back to the 1950's and is in good condition even in the oldest rooms. FACILITIES 31 rooms, air-conditioning, phone, TV, cable TV, ceiling fan, pool, playground, restaurant, convention room, fitness room, game room. CREDIT CARDS All.
R. Luís Rogério Casacurta, 510, Centro

RESTAURANTS $ up to R$50 $$ from R$51 up to R$100 $$$ from R$101 up to R$150 $$$$ above R$150

TEL 462-2166 FAX 462-2354
www.hotelcasacurta.com.br

RESTAURANT

Hosteria Casacurta $
This is the best restaurant of its kind in town. It adjoins the hotel and offers its own pasta. The menu features *penne al champagne*, *ravioli* with veal filling with shitake sauce and steak with mushroom sauce. CUISINE Italian. CREDIT CARDS All. HOURS Mon-Sat, 7:30pm-11:30pm.
R. Luís Rogério Casacurta, 510, Centro
TEL 462-2166

SERVICES

TOURIST INFORMATION

Centro de Informações Turísticas
TEL 464-0796

Museu de Garibaldi
R. Dr. Carlos Barbosa, 77
TEL 462-3483. HOURS Mon-Fri, 8:30am-11:30am and 1:30pm-5pm; Sat and Sun , 9am-11:30am

Secretaria de Turismo
Av. Júlio de Castilho, 254
TEL 462-2627/3876. HOURS 8am-11:30am and 1:30pm-5pm.

Garopaba – SC

AREA CODE 48 POPULATION 13,164
DISTANCE Florianópolis, 90 km (56 mi)
SITE www.garopaba.sc.gov.br

HOTELS

Morro da Silveira Eco Village $$
One of the newest hotels in Garopaba, this establishment sits atop Da Silveira hill. All rooms have a view of the beach. Though rustic the hotel is comfortable. The approach to the rooms may be too steep for the disabled. FACILITIES 22 rooms, air-conditioning, phone, TV, cable TV, ceiling fan, bar, pool, heated pool, restaurant, convention room, fitness room, game room, massage room, sauna. CREDIT CARDS Diners, MasterCard, Visa.
Rodovia GRP-454, 80, Morro da Silveira
TEL 354-1740
www.morrodasilveira.com.br

Pousada Basfak Praia $$
This Garopaba Beach inn caters to families. The large and bright rooms have kitchen with fridge, microwave oven and electric stove. It is just one block away from the main avenue and 3 blocks away from the beach. FACILITIES 31 rooms, air-conditioning, phone, TV, cable TV, bar, pool, restaurant, game room. CREDIT CARDS Diners, MasterCard, Visa.
R. Santa Rita, 41, Praia de Garopaba
TEL 254-4507
www.pousadabasfak.com.br

SERVICES

LOCAL TOUR OPERATORS

Ailton Coelho
TEL 254-3259

Irapuá Turismo
TEL 354-3259

CURRENCY EXCHANGE

Banco do Brasil
R. Prefeito João Orestes de Araújo, 740, Centro
TEL 254-3210 HOURS Mon-Fri, 10am-3pm

BESC
R. Aderbal Ramos da Silva, 100, Centro
TEL 254-3171. HOURS Mon-Fri, 10am-3pm

TOURIST INFORMATION

Secretaria de Turismo Municipal
Pça. Governador Ivo Silveira, 296 (Prefeitura/City Hall)
TEL 254-3106. HOURS 9am-noon and 2pm-6pm

Governador Celso Ramos – SC

AREA CODE 48 POPULATION 11,598
DISTANCE Florianópolis, 40 km (24.8 mi)
SITE www.govcelsoramos.com.br

HOTEL

Ponta dos Ganchos Resort $$$$
This exclusive resort is part of the "charm route", 60 km (37 mi) from Florianópolis, and sleeps at most 34 guests. Many guests are honeymooning couples. People under 18 are not allowed. FACILITIES 13 rooms, air-conditioning, fireplace, phone, TV, cable TV, ceiling fan, bar, boating, heated pool, tennis court, restaurant, fitness room, game room, massage room. CREDIT CARDS All.
R. Elpídio Alves do Nascimento, 104, Praia de Ganchos de Fora
TEL 2262-5000 RESERVATIONS 08006433346
www.pontadosganchos.com.br

SERVICES

TOURIST INFORMATION

Secretaria de Turismo
Pça Seis de Novembro, 1, Centro
TEL 262-2090 HOURS 8am-7pm

Gramado – RS

AREA CODE 54 POPULATION 28,593
DISTANCE Porto Alegre, 120 km (74.6 mi)
SITE www.gramadosite.com.br

HOTELS

Estalagem La Hacienda $$$$
Located in an old 168-acre farm, far from the town

center, this lodge has comfortably rustic stone chalets for up to 4 guests each. It offers horseback riding and hiking within the estate. FACILITIES 6 rooms, fireplace, phone, TV, cable TV, horses, pool, tennis court, restaurant, convention room, fitness room, game room. CREDIT CARDS All.
Estrada Serra Grande, 4200, off km 110 of the BR-115 highway, toward Taquara
TEL 286-8186 RESERVATIONS (51) 3029-8196
www.lahacienda.com.br

Estalagem St. Hubertus $$$
This lodge faces Negro lake and sits in a quiet area though not very far from the busy spots. There's a TV and reading room, with complimentary tea and cakes every afternoon. FACILITIES 26 rooms, air-conditioning, phone, TV, cable TV, ceiling fan, heated pool, convention room, game room, sauna. CREDIT CARDS All.
R. da Carrière, 974
TEL 286-1273
www.sthubertus.com

Ritta Höppner $$$
This Bavarian-style inn is one of the most traditional in town, and it has a winter garden. There are chalets with private thermal pools. Guests have free access to neighboring Minimundo (Mini-world), a children's park with miniature replicas of landmark buildings from various countries. FACILITIES 14 rooms, air-conditioning, phone, TV, cable TV, pool, playground. CREDIT CARDS Diners, MasterCard.
R. Pedro Candiago, 305
TEL 286-1334 FAX 286-3129 RESERVATIONS 286-4055
www.minimundo.com.br

Varanda das Bromélias Boutique Hotel $$$$
This boutique hotel offers high-ceiling lofts, and spacious suites and cabins. Breakfast is served to the room until noon, at no extra cost. FACILITIES 17 rooms, air-conditioning, phone, TV, cable TV, bar, heated pool, fitness room, game room, massage room, sauna. CREDIT CARDS All.
R. Alarisch Schulz, 158
TEL 286-6653
www.varandadasbromelias.com.br

RESTAURANTS

Casa da Velha Bruxa $
This cafeteria of the Prawer chocolate factory serves snacks, sandwiches, pizza, different types of coffee and of course chocolate. It is a meeting point during the Gramado Festival of Cinema. CREDIT CARDS All. HOURS Daily, 11am-11pm.
Av. Borges de Medeiros, 2746
TEL 286-1551

Chez Pierre $
In the basement of a ceramics shop, this eatery has the atmosphere of a French cave. The menu features raclettes and fondues. In the high season, the clientele, made up mostly by couples, dances to the sound of jazz. CUISINE Swiss. CREDIT CARDS Diners, MasterCard, Visa. HOURS Daily, Mon-Sat, 7pm-1am.

Av. Borges de Medeiros, 3022
TEL 286-2057

Gasthof Edelweiss $$
The wine cellar has a wide variety of labels. If you find yourself admiring any of the objects on display, just ask about the price: the place is also an antique shop. The trout with almonds is a great choice. Free transfer is offered to and from all the hotels. The restaurant is located by Negro Lake. CUISINE German. CREDIT CARDS All. HOURS Daily, noon-3pm and 7:30pm-11pm.
R. da Carrière, 1119
TEL 286-1861

La Caceria $$
Game meats are the highlights here. Only the deer is wild; the other animals are bred in captivity. The menu features pigeon, pheasant, quail, boar, partridge, capybara. It is inside the Casa da Montanha hotel. CREDIT CARDS All. HOURS Tue-Sun, 7pm-midnight.
Av. Borges de Medeiros, 3166
TEL 286-2544

Le Petit Clos $$
This restaurant specializes in fondues and other delicacies of Swiss cuisine. Chairs lined with sheep wool enhance the intimate atmosphere, making it a favorite among sweethearts. CUISINE Swiss. CREDIT CARDS Diners, MasterCard, Visa. HOURS Daily, 7pm-midnight.
R. Demétrio Pereira dos Santos, 599
TEL 286-1936

SERVICES

LOCAL TOUR OPERATORS

Bella Tur
Av. das Hortênsias, 2040, Sala 6
TEL 286-2087/2115

Turistur
Av. Borges de Medeiros, 3165, Sala 2A
TEL 286-3939

EXCHANGE SHOP

Swisstur Turismo e Câmbio
TEL 3036-0070

TOURIST INFORMATION

Pórtico via Nova Petrópolis (Nova Petrópolis Gateway)
Rodovia RS-235
TEL 286-2803 HOURS Tue-Sun, 9am-noon and 1pm-4pm

Pórtico via Taquara
Rodovia RS-115
TEL 286-8171 HOURS Tue-Sun, 9am-noon and 1pm-4pm

Posto de Informações Turísticas – Centro
Av. Borges de Medeiros, 1674, pça. Major Nicoletti
TEL 286-1475 HOURS Mon-Fri, 9am-7pm; Sat and Sun, 9am-9pm

RESTAURANTS $ up to R$50 $$ from R$51 up to R$100 $$$ from R$101 up to R$150 $$$$ above R$150

Laguna – SC

AREA CODE 48 POPULATION 47,568
DISTANCE Florianópolis, 121 km (75.2 mi)
SITE www.lagunagolfinho.com.br

RESTAURANT

Arrastão $

Just 150 meters (500 ft) from the beach, this restaurant specializes in seafood. CUISINE Fish and seafood. CREDIT CARDS All. HOURS 11am-3pm and from 6pm; in winter, 10am-2pm and 6pm-10pm.
Av. Senador Gallotti, 629, Praia de Mar Grosso
TEL 647-0418

SERVICES

TOURIST INFORMATION

Portal Turístico
Av. Calistrato Müller Salles
TEL 644-2441 HOURS 8am-6pm

Lapa – PR

AREA CODE 41 POPULATION 41,838
DISTANCES Curitiba, 60 km (37.3 mi)
SITE www.lapa.pr.gov.br

HOTEL

Lapinha – Lar Lapeano de Saúde $$$
This is Brazil's original spa. It is located in a 1,360-acre farm that produces its own organic food. The rooms are Spartan, with no TV or phone, and guests should be at their rooms by 9pm. But alternative therapies, massage and physical activities relax and help guests get fit. FACILITIES 35 rooms, horses, recreation team, heated pool, tennis court, restaurant, fitness room, game room, massage room, sauna, spa. CREDIT CARDS All.
Estrada da Fazenda Margarida, Lapa –
Campo do Tenente, km 16
TEL 622-1044 RESERVATIONS 08006431090
www.lapinha.com.br

RESTAURANT

Lipski $
This is a simple restaurant that offers 13 different dishes for a fixed price (called the rodízio system). Two regional dishes stand out: quirera lapeana (corn, fried spare ribs), and virado de feijão (cooked beans, bacon, manioc meal, clover, and seasonings). CUISINE Regional. CREDIT CARDS All. HOURS Mon-Sat, 11am-3pm and 7pm-10pm; Sun, 11am-4pm.
Av. Manoel Pedro, 1855
TEL 622-1202

SERVICES

LOCAL TOUR OPERATOR

Sprintur
TEL 622-5989

TOURIST INFORMATION

Specialized Guides at Centro Histórico de Lapa
Márcio: 622-1422

Posto de Informações Turísticas
Pça. General Carneiro, 106
TEL 622-7401 HOURS 9am-5pm.

Morretes – PR

AREA CODE 41 POPULATION 16,077
DISTANCE Curitiba, 62 km (38.5 mi)

RESTAURANT

Armazém Romanus $
In addition to seafood, this restaurant serves a light version of barreado (slow-cooked lean meat, bacon, tomato, onions, and seasonings). CUISINE Regional. CREDIT CARDS All. HOURS Mon, 11am-4pm; Tue-Sat, 11am-4pm and 7pm-10pm; Sun, 11am-6pm.
R. Visconde do Rio Branco, 141
TEL 462-1500

Ponte Velha $
Located on the bank of Nhundiaquara river, Ponte Velha serves traditional barreado and other dishes. CUISINE Regional. CREDIT CARDS American Express, Visa. HOURS Thu-Tue, 11am-4pm.
R. Almirante Frederico de Oliveira, 13
TEL 462-1674

Nova Petrópolis – RS

AREA CODE 54 POPULATION 16,891
DISTANCE Porto Alegre, 101 km (62.8 mi)
SITE www.novapetropolis.com.br

RESTAURANTS

Colina Verde $
Café colonial (a hearty version of the afternoon tea) is more like a brunch, with German specialties such as eisbein (pork knuckle), Italian specialties such as capeletti in brodo, and specialties from the state of Rio Grande do Sul such as matambre (stuffed flank steak) and manioc fritters. CUISINE Café colonial. CREDIT CARDS Diners, MasterCard. HOURS Tue-Sun, 11:30am-3pm.
Rodovia BR-116, km 185.5
TEL 281-1388

Opa's Kaffehaus $
This is the most famous restaurant in the region. It offers 45 choices of cake, bread, cold cuts and jelly. Eat as much as you have space for; everything is delicious. CUISINE Café colonial. CREDIT CARDS Not accepted. HOURS Tue-Fri, 2pm-8pm; Sat, from 1pm; Sun, from noon.
R. João Leão, 96
TEL 281-1273

PRICES	HOTELS (couple)	$ up to R$150	$$ from R$151 up to R$300	$$$ from R$301 up to R$500	$$$$ above R$500

SERVICES

TOURIST INFORMATION

Pórtico
Av. Quinze de Novembro, 100, intersection with BR-116
TEL 281-1398 HOURS 8am-6pm

Palhoça – SC

AREA CODE 48 POPULATION 102,742
DISTANCE Florianópolis, 68 km (42.3 mi)
SITE www.palhoca.sc.gov.br

HOTEL

Pousada Ilha do Papagaio $$$
Visitors can reach this inn by boat only. The owner, Renato Sehn, welcomes guests on the beach. There are trails, a pool and a beach in an Atlantic Rain Forest preservation area. Closed in August. FACILITIES 20 rooms, air-conditioning, fireplace, phone, TV, bar, boating, pool, restaurant, convention room, fitness room, massage room, sauna. CREDIT CARDS Diners, MasterCard, Visa.
Ilha do Papagaio, Praia da Ponta do Papagaio (Praia do Sonho)
TEL 286-1242 FAX 286-1243
www.papagaio.com.br

RESTAURANT

Seacoquille $$
The owner's house becomes a restaurant between December and March. Shrimp with coconut and green mango headlines the menu. CUISINE Fish and seafood. CREDIT CARDS Diners, MasterCard. HOURS Mon, 6pm-midnight; Tue-Sun, noon- midnight.
R. da Antena, Guarda do Embaú
TEL 283-2559

SERVICES

TOURIST INFORMATION

Portal do Lazer
Rodovia BR-101, km 224, adjoining the Cambirela gas station. HOURS 9am-6pm

Penha – SC

AREA CODE 47 POPULATION 17,678
DISTANCE Florianópolis, 120 km (74.6 mi)
www.cidadedepenha.com.br

HOTEL

Pousada Pedra da Ilha $$
This inn faces the beach and caters to families with small children. There are suites with a whirlpool tub and rooms for disabled guests. FACILITIES 31 rooms, air-conditioning, phone, TV, ceiling fan, bar, pool, rock pool, heated pool, playground, convention room, game room, massage room, sauna. CREDIT CARDS Diners, MasterCard, Visa.
R. Abraão João Francisco, 46, Praia Alegre

TEL and FAX 345-0542
www.pedradailha.com.br

RESTAURANT

Pirão d'Água $$
Chef-owner Sarita Santos has added many dishes typical of Azorean cuisine to the menu. The restaurant serves generous *alcatra* (rump), fish and seafood servings. CUISINE Portuguese. CREDIT CARDS Not accepted. HOURS 12:30pm-3:30pm and 7pm-11:30pm; in winter, Fri-Sun, 6pm-10:30pm
Av. São João, 954, Praia Armação do Itapocorói
TEL 345-6742

Porto Alegre – RS

AREA CODE 51 POPULATION 1,360,590
DISTANCE Florianópolis, 474 km (295 mi)
SITE www.portoalegre.rs.gov.br/turismo

HOTELS

Blue Tree Millenium Porto Alegre $$
This is a well-located serviced apartment next to Shopping Praia de Belas (a mall). Each room has a living room and a kitchen with a microwave oven. The fitness room is on the penthouse level: exercise watching the sunset on Guaíba River. FACILITIES 146 rooms, air-conditioning, phone, TV, cable TV, bar, pool, restaurant, convention room, fitness room, sauna. CREDIT CARDS All.
Av. Borges de Medeiros, 3120
TEL 3026-2200 FAX 3026-6704 RESERVATIONS 0800150500
www.bluetree.com.br

Blue Tree Towers Porto Alegre $$
This hotel attracts business clientele. The "de luxe" rooms have living rooms and balconies. From the 5th floor up, the rooms afford a view of Guaíba River. FACILITIES 131 rooms, air-conditioning, phone, TV, cable TV, bar, restaurant, convention room, fitness room, massage room, sauna. CREDIT CARDS All.
Av. Coronel Lucas de Oliveira, 995, Bela Vista
TEL 3333-0333 FAX 3330-5233 RESERVATIONS 0800150500
www.bluetree.com.br

Plaza São Rafael $$
This is one of the most traditional hotels in Porto Alegre. Shops sell antiques and jewelry in the lobby. The pool is in another building, across the street. FACILITIES 284 rooms, air-conditioning, phone, TV, cable TV, bar, pool, restaurant, convention room, fitness room, massage room, sauna. CREDIT CARDS All.
Av. Alberto Bins, 514, Centro
TEL 3220-7000 FAX 3220-7001 RESERVATIONS 3220-7259
www.plazahoteis.com.br

Sheraton Porto Alegre $$$$
In one of the fanciest districts, next to a shopping mall, this is the best hotel in town. Each room has a bathtub, 29" TV set, 2 telephone lines and high-speed Internet connection. FACILITIES 173 rooms, air-conditioning, phone, TV, cable TV, bar, heated pool, restaurant, convention room, fitness room, massage room, sauna. CREDIT CARDS All.
R. Olavo Barreto Viana, 18, Moinhos de Vento

TEL 3323-6000 FAX 3323-6010 RESERVATIONS 0800893566
www.sheraton-poa.com.br

Tryp Porto Alegre $$

This hotel is surrounded by the green of Parque Moinhos de Vento. The best view of the park is from upper-floor rooms with numbers ending in 4 and 5. FACILITIES 80 rooms, air-conditioning, phone, TV, cable TV, restaurant, convention room, fitness room, massage room, sauna. CREDIT CARDS All.
R. Comendador Caminha, 42
TEL 3323-9300 FAX 3323-9301
www.solmelia.com

RESTAURANTS

Al Dente $$

This restaurant serves freshly prepared pasta in a refined atmosphere. It specializes in the cuisine of Northern Italy. CUISINE Italian. HOURS Mon-Sat, 7pm-midnight. CREDIT CARDS All.
R. Mata Bacelar, 210, Auxiliadora
TEL 3343-1841

Barranco $

One of the best churrascarias in town, this simple place stays busy. Service is à la carte. CUISINE Churrasco (barbecue). CREDIT CARDS All. HOURS 11am-2am.
Av. Protásio Alves, 1578, Petrópolis
TEL 3331-6172

Koh Pee Pee $$

The Thai-style inn's main kitchen is in the middle of the hall, to re-create the atmosphere of a food-kiosk-cluttered Bangkok street layout. Fried rice with vegetables and shrimp, conger eel with curry sauce and seafood pasta are the specialties. CUISINE Thai. CREDIT CARDS Diners, MasterCard, Visa. HOURS Mon-Sat, 7:30pm-midnight.
R. Schiller, 83, Moinhos de Vento
TEL 3333-5150

Mercado del Puerto $

Uruguayan churrasco (barbecue) is served here. The meat is charcoal grilled without skewers. The abundant servings have an average 350 grams (12 oz) of meat and chimichurri sauce. CUISINE Uruguayan. CREDIT CARDS All. HOURS Mon-Fri, 7pm-2am; Sat, Sun and holidays, from noon.
Av. Cairu, 1487, São João
TEL 3337-1066

Orquestra de Panelas $

This restaurant operates in the first floor of a charming building in the midst of the town's hubbub. The menu features contemporary dishes such as wild boar with mango chutney and sole with shrimp. Reservation advised. CUISINE Contemporary. CREDIT CARDS Diners, MasterCard, Visa. HOURS Mon-Sat, noon-3pm and 7pm-11pm.
R. Padre Chagas, 196, 1º andar, Moinhos de Vento
TEL 3346-9439

Polska $

There's a fixed charge per person. The most popular choices are pierogi (pasta stuffed with ricotta cheese and potato) and placek (potato pancake with goulash filling). CUISINE Polish. CREDIT CARDS Not accepted. HOURS Tue-Sat, 7pm-midnight; Sun, noon-3pm.
R. João Guimarães, 377, Santa Cecília
TEL 3333-2589

SERVICES

AIRPORT

Aeroporto Internacional Salgado Filho

Av. Severo Duilius, 90010
TEL 3358-2000

LOCAL TOUR OPERATOR

Fellini Turismo

R. General Bento Martins, 24, Sala 401
TEL 3228-6388/3227-5400

TOURIST INFORMATION

Posto de Informações Turísticas – Mercado do Bom Fim

Av. Osvaldo Aranha, Loja 12, Parque Farroupilha
TEL 3333-1873. HOURS 9am-8pm

Posto de Informações Turísticas – Mercado Público

Lgo. Glênio Peres
HOURS 8am- 8pm

Serviço de Atendimento ao Turista

TEL 0800517686. HOURS 9am-8pm

Praia do Rosa – distrito de Imbituba – SC

AREA CODE 48
DISTANCE Florianópolis, 78 km (48.5 mi)
SITE www.praiadorosa.tur.br

HOTELS

Fazenda Verde do Rosa $$$$

This is one of the few places with an exit to the beach. There are 3 restaurants by the sea, with different menus. The hotel offers trails, paddle court, horseback riding and surf school. The cabins have a complete kitchen but no TV set. FACILITIES 36 rooms, fireplace, phone, ceiling fan, horses, recreation team, pool, playground, restaurant, massage room. CREDIT CARDS All.
Estrada Geral do Rosa
TEL 355-7272
www.fazendaverde.com

Morada dos Bougainvilles $$

This small and charming inn stands out for its restaurant. Guests are welcomed with chocolate, incense and champagne. The "de luxe" and the standard bungalows overlook the beach, 400 meters (1300 ft) away. FACILITIES 7 rooms, air-conditioning, phone, TV, ceiling fan, recreation team, pool, playground, restaurant. CREDIT CARDS Diners, MasterCard, Visa.
Caminho do Alto do Morro

| PRICES | HOTELS (couple) | $ up to R$150 | $$ from R$151 up to R$300 | $$$ from R$301 up to R$500 | $$$$ above R$500 |

558   BRAZIL GUIDE

TEL 355-6100
www.pousadabougainville.com.br

Pousada Caminho do Rei $$

This hilltop inn has a great view of Rosa beach. The "de luxe" suite has a fireplace and the others have a whirlpool tub. In the low season the restaurant is closed and the owners serve the meals in their own house. FACILITIES 8 rooms, phone, TV, ceiling fan, pool, restaurant, game room. CREDIT CARDS Visa.
Caminho do Alto do Morro
TEL 355-6062 RESERVATIONS 355-6071
www.caminhodorei.com.br

Quinta do Bucanero $$$

The rooms have a beautiful ocean view. The drawback is that the beach is down a trail and you'll have to cross a lagoon to get there. The inn has a small boat to take guests there. Children under 14 are not allowed. Closed in July. FACILITIES 10 rooms, air-conditioning, phone, TV, ceiling fan, bar, pool, restaurant, game room. CREDIT CARDS Diners, MasterCard, Visa.
Estrada Geral do Rosa
TEL 355-6056
www.bucanero.com.br

Regina Guest House $

This inn adjoins Bistrô Pedra da Vigia, and has only 2 rooms with a deck and a hut for 4 guests, with a verandah. The inn has a view of the beach and of the Ibiraquera lagoon, in Imbituba. The restaurant has a beautiful ocean view. FACILITIES 3 rooms, TV, ceiling fan. CREDIT CARDS All.
Caminho do Alto do Morro
TEL 355-6066/6247
www.praiadorosa-brasil.com.br

RESTAURANTS

Bistrô Pedra da Vigia $

This bistro has a French atmosphere but the kitchen is open, in the American way. On Thursdays it serves Japanese food. The fish and seafood are in the authentic style of the state of Santa Catarina. CUISINE French. CREDIT CARDS Diners, MasterCard, Visa. HOURS 7:30pm-12:30am; in the low season, Thu-Sat, 6:30pm-11:30pm.
Caminho do Alto do Morro
TEL 355-6247

Margherita $

This pizza parlor is so popular as a meeting point in the Rosa neighborhood that a branch has been opened on the southern portion of the beach. Three sizes of pizza are served. CUISINE Pizza. CREDIT CARDS Visa. HOURS Daily, from 7pm on.
Estrada Geral do Rosa
TEL 355-6010

Tigre Asiático $

This is one of the best Thai restaurants in southern Brazil. The most popular choices are chicken with rice served in a pineapple, and shrimp and fish with coconut milk. There's a sushi bar. CUISINE Thai. CREDIT CARDS Diners, MasterCard, Visa. HOURS Daily, 7pm-midnight.
Estrada Geral do Rosa
TEL 354-0170/355-7045

São Francisco do Sul – SC

AREA CODE 47 POPULATION 31,519
DISTANCE Florianópolis, 215 km (133.7 mi)

HOTEL

Bristol Villa Real $$

This villa has good leisure facilities, such as a marina. Ask for a room on one of the upper floors, which have been remodeled recently. FACILITIES 71 rooms, air-conditioning, phone, TV, cable TV, bar, recreation team, pool, heated pool, playground, restaurant, convention room, fitness room, game room. CREDIT CARDS All.
R. Francisco Machado de Souza, 1135
TEL 444-2010
www.bristolhoteis.com.br

RESTAURANT

Jacizinho Batista

To enjoy its great all-you-can-eat seafood *rodízio*, you'll have to take a boat or a ferryboat to the fishing village of Glória. It takes half an hour to cross the bay, with its stunning natural beauty, which will stimulate your appetite. Shrimp, crab, fish and shellfish are served until you've had enough. CUISINE Fish and seafood. CREDIT CARDS Not accepted. HOURS Daily, 11:30am-10pm.
Estrada Geral do Estaleiro, Vila da Glória
TEL 492-1056/449-5124

SERVICES

LOCAL TOUR OPERATOR

Estação Turismo

R. Barão do Rio Branco, 363, Centro
TEL 444-6981. HOURS Mon-Fri, 9am-noon and 2pm-6pm

BOAT RENTAL

Marujo Amigo

R. Macapá, 1332
TEL 449-0875/9974-3986

TOURIST INFORMATION

Secretaria de Turismo

R. Marechal Floriano Peixoto, 220, Centro
TEL 444-5257/5380. HOURS 7am-6pm

RESTAURANTS $ up to R$50 $$ from R$51 up to R$100 $$$ from R$101 up to R$150 $$$$ above R$150

USEFUL INFORMATION

Airports

Most of Brazil's airports have tourist information desks that provide useful information such as accommodations listings and telephone numbers for the city's tourist police. Most airports offer internet access at cybercafes or designated computer terminals. The addresses and telephone numbers of the airports mentioned in this guidebook are listed in the Hotel, Restaurant and Services Section.

Airline Companies

BRA – Avenida São Luís, 94, São Paulo, São Paulo, tel. (11) 3017-5454; www.voebra.com.br

GOL – Rua dos Tamoios, 246, São Paulo, São Paulo, tel. (11) 5033-4200; other locations: 0300-789-2121 (ticket sales) / 0800-701-2131 (information); www.voegol.com.br

RICO – Eduardo Gomes International Airport – Manaus, Amazonas, tel. (92) 652-1652; other locations: 0300-789-8333; www.voerico.com.br

TAM – Rua Jurandir, 856, lote 4, São Paulo, São Paulo, tel. (11) 3123-1000; other locations: 0300-123-1000; www.tam.com.br

VARIG – Rua da Consolação, 372, São Paulo, São Paulo, tel. (11) 5091-7000; other locations: 0300-789-7000; www.varig.com.br

VASP – Praça Comandante Lineu Gomes, Congonhas Airport, São Paulo, São Paulo, tel. (11) 5532-3000; Rio de Janeiro: (21) 2462-3363; other locations: 0300-789-1010; www.vasp.com.br

HIGHWAYS

Road quality and driving safety vary greatly throughout Brazil. Mainly in the Southeastern region, private companies maintain many highways, as well as their rest areas, and also services such as medical and rescue assistance and towing. Federal and state toll highways are usually in a better state of repair and offer more complete services. Before heading out on a road trip, contact the federal and state highway patrols about road maintenance conditions along the highways that you plan to travel, available services and toll fees. The Brazilian Road Association's web site also displays much of this information. (Associação Brasileira das Concessionárias de Rodovias; www.abcr.org.br).

State Highway Patrol

Alagoas – (82) 324-0599
Bahia – (71) 301-9440
Ceará – (85) 3383-2444
Espírito Santo – (27) 3222-8000
Goiás – (62) 201-4771 or 0800-620040
Mato Grosso – (65) 631-1251
Mato Grosso do Sul – (67) 388-7700
Minas Gerais – (31) 3332-4988
Paraná – (41) 342-7111
Pernambuco – (81) 227–2965
Rio de Janeiro – (21) 2625-1530
Rio Grande do Sul – (51) 3339-6799
Santa Catarina – (48) 240-0433
São Paulo – (11) 3327-2727
Sergipe – (79) 259-3099

Federal Highway Patrol

Alagoas – (82) 324-1135 /1395
Amazonas – (92) 648-6406

Bahia – (71) 254-2200
Ceará – (85) 3295-3591
Distrito Federal – (61) 394-3000
Espírito Santo – (27) 3235-6900
Maranhão – (98) 3225-2563
Mato Grosso – (65) 667-1000
Mato Grosso do Sul – (67) 325-3600
Minas Gerais – (31) 3333-2999
Pará – (91) 255-2100
Paraíba – (83) 231-3366
Paraná – (41) 267-4446
Pernambuco – (81) 3303-6623
Piauí – (86) 233-1011 or 191
Rio de Janeiro – (21) 2471-6111
Rio Grande do Norte – (84) 203-1550
Rio Grande do Sul – (51) 3374-0003
Santa Catarina – (48) 251-3200
São Paulo – (11) 6954-1814
Sergipe – (79) 261-1495
Tocantins – (63) 312-3491 (in Gurupi)

CAR RENTALS

Most car rental agencies accept only major credit cards and rent only to drivers 21 or older who have been licensed for at least two years. Some destinations have a surcharge during the high season of tourism and on long weekends. Shop around for a bargain and ask about additional charges for items such as insurance, which can be as high as 25% of the rental cost. Before driving away from the rental agency, look over your vehicle for damage, check the state of the tires and the spare tire, and make sure directional signals and brakes work. Stop at the closest gas station and verify the maximum air pressure for cold tires. Rent a model appropriate for the road conditions you may face.

Car Rental Agencies

AVIS – Rua Clélia, 1500, São Paulo, São Paulo, tel.(11) 4225-8456; other locations: 0800-198-456; www.avis.com.br

ALAMO – Rua Sete de Abril, 127, conj. 41, 4th floor, São Paulo, São Paulo, tel. (11) 3257-8855; www.suncrowne.com.br

HERTZ – Rua da Consolação, 429, São Paulo, São Paulo, tel. (11) 3258-9384; other locations: 0800-701-7300; www.hertz.com.br

LOCALIZA – Rua da Consolação, 419, São Paulo, São Paulo, tel. (11) 3231-3055; other locations: 0800-99-2000; www.localiza.com.br

MOBILITY – Rua Barão do Triunfo, 464, conj. 51, 5th floor, São Paulo, São Paulo, tel. 0800-160-525; www.mobility.com.br

NATIONAL – Avenida Nove de Julho, 3229, #501, 5th floor, São Paulo, São Paulo, tel. 0800-555-150; international calls: 1-800-227-7368 www.nationalcar.com

Taxis

Find taxis at official taxi stands or call the central office. When requesting the service, check if the company charges for the trip to pick up the passenger. If there has been a recent price adjustment and the meter has not been recalibrated, a new price table pasted on the window will show the corrected value in relation to the meter reading. Prices are higher at night, in the early morning hours, and on Sundays and holidays. There is a surcharge to use the trunk or boot. In some locations, taxis charge a fixed rate for a trip from the airport to the city's downtown area.

SAFETY

IN THE CITIES: Avoid displaying valuable items such as jewelry and watches. Cameras, video cameras and notebook computers require particular safeguards. Keep your money close to your body, preferably distributed among several pockets, and avoid showing it unnecessarily in public. In cities, avoid secluded and poorly lit places. Keep a firm hold on purses and re-consider carrying knapsacks on your back; it is safer to carry them in front of your body. Whenever possible, lock suitcases and backpacks with padlocks.
ATMs: If it is necessary to make a withdrawal at an ATM, look for one that is in a heavily trafficked building such as a mall. In some locations the withdrawal limit is reduced between 10pm and 6am. Never accept a stranger's help with a transaction .
IN CARS: Do not hitchhike or pick up hitchhikers, even if you are not alone. Even in areas with plenty of activity, avoiding lingering in a parked car, especially at night. In large cities, keep the windows closed even during the day, no matter how stifling it may be.
AT THE BEACH: Do not take expensive articles or your wallet to the beach. It's better to take just enough money for the day. Do not leave money or objects on the sand while you walk along the beach or go swimming. Instead, keep everything close to you and in sight. At outdoor food stands, bars and restaurants, do not leave your purse hanging on the back of the chair.
AT FOOTBALL STADIUMS: Brazilian stadiums are slowly being modified to conform to the new security standards, but there is still a long way to go. Major teams' games easily attract 50,000 to 70,000 fans. Fans of oppositing fans sit apart, separated by barricades and police. The expense of each ticket corresponds to have safe area of the stands it is in. Select a seat in the numbered section rather than the bleachers where the majority of the public sits. If you can choose a seat in a covered area, even better. Do not take valuable objects to the stadium. To avoid potentially unruly crowds, arrive approximately 40 minutes before game time and leave after the majority of people have left. Do not wear a shirt of any team that might attract the attention of an adversary. Do not use public transportation to go to the stadium on game days, as there are often confrontations between rival fans. Go by car or taxi instead, keeping the windows closed, and expect traffic jams. If driving, park in an established lot and avoid provisional parking spots. People who offer to watch your car are generally unreliable.

Tourist Police Divisions

Various states offer specialized police divisions with officers trained to handle crimes involving tourists and foreigners. In locations that do not offer this service, complaints may be registered at the regular police stations.
BAHIA (Salvador): Rua Cruzeiro de São Francisco, 14, Pelourinho, tel. (71) 322-7155.
CEARÁ (Fortaleza): Avenida Almirante Barroso, 805, Praia de Iracema, tel. (85) 3219-1538.
ESPÍRITO SANTO (Vitória): Rua Dr. João Carlos de Souza, 740, Santa Luísa, tel. (27) 3137-9117.

MARANHÃO (São Luís): Rua da Estrela, 427, Centro, tel. (98) 3232-4324.
PARÁ (Belém): Travessa Avertano Rocha, 417, Batista Campos, tel. (91) 212-3626.
PARAÍBA (João Pessoa): Avenida Tamamdaré, 100, Loja 1, Tambaú, tel. (83) 214-8022.
PERNAMBUCO (Recife): Guararapes Airport, tel. (81) 3303-7217.
RIO DE JANEIRO (Rio de Janeiro): Rua Humberto de Campos, 315, Leblon, tel. (21) 3399-7170.
RIO GRANDE DO NORTE (Natal): Avenida Engenheiro Roberto Freire, 8790, Praia Shopping, tel. (84) 232-7404.
SÃO PAULO (São Paulo): Avenida São Luís, 91, Centro, tel. (11) 3214-0209.
SERGIPE (Aracaju): Avenida Santos Dumont, Praia de Atalaia, tel. (79) 255-2155.

Police Reports by Internet

In some states, a police report may be registered by internet for the loss or theft of documents.
RIO DE JANEIRO – www.delegaciavirtual.rj.gov.br
RIO GRANDE DO SUL – www.pc.rs.gov.br
SANTA CATARINA – www.ssp.sc.gov.br
SÃO PAULO – www.policiacivil.sp.gov.br

HEALTH

Yellow fever is a hazard in the North and Central-West regions, the states of Maranhão and Minas Gerais and the areas southwest of Piauí, west of Bahia, west of Paraná, west of Santa Catarina, northwest of Rio Grande do Sul and northwest of São Paulo. This infectious disease is transmitted by mosquito bites. Those planning to travel in these regions should get vaccinated ten days before traveling. Vaccines are available at the ports, airports and border posts. There is no vaccine for malaria, also transmitted by a mosquito bite, which is primarily a problem in the Amazon region. The best protection is to use repellents on all exposed skin, sleep in places protected by window screens and mosquito nets, wear long pants and long sleeved shirts, preferably with light colors, and use insecticides in all rooms.
Diarrhea is very common among travelers. To prevent it, avoid eating raw vegetables and foods from street stands or other locations with questionable hygiene standards. Avoid nonpasteurized milk. Safer bets include dry foods like breads and crackers, peeled fruits, bottled or boiled water. Piping-hot cooked meals are fine, as long as hands, plates and utensils are clean. Do not drink water from fountains or taps even if it appears clear; also avoid ice. Sunscreens are essential, throughout the country, due to the strong tropical sun.

Medical Assistance for the Traveler

São Paulo has medical centers specializing in vaccinations for tourists at the Congonhas and Guarulhos airports, among other places. There are also two referral services:
CLÍNICA DE MEDICINA DO VIAJANTE (Instituto de Infectologia Emílio Ribas): Avenida Dr. Arnaldo, 165, Cerqueira César, tel. (11) 3896-1200. Open Tuesdays from 4:30pm – 5:30pm.
AMBULATÓRIO DOS VIAJANTES (Centro de Imunização – Hospital das Clínicas): Avenida Dr. Enéas de Carvalho Aguiar, 155 4th floor, Cerqueira César (Prédio dos Ambulatórios), tel. (11) 3069-6392. Daily 8am – 3:30pm; emergencies 24hrs.
In Rio de Janeiro go to Centro de Informação em Saúde para Viajantes (Traveler's Medical Assistance

Information Center):**CIVES**, Cidade Universitária da UFRJ (Ilha do Fundão), Hospital Universitário, 5th floor, South Wing, #2.

PUBLIC RESTROOMS

Public Restrooms in Brazil are limited to airports, bus stations, malls and locations with masses of people. In emergencies, find a hotel, bar, bakery or restaurant that look adequate. It is often not necessary to purchase anything to use the facilities.

CURRENCY EXCHANGE

Exchange rates are published daily in all major Brazilian newspapers and are announced on the evening TV news. Banks generally offer better rates that currency exchange agencies, but the process is usually more bureaucratic and there are additional fees. The exchange agencies located in the major cities accept traveler's checks issued by major international institutions.

INTERNET

Even most small towns have access to the Worldwide Web via and computers in cyber cafés, hotels, libraries, malls and post offices. The telephone companies are also introducing computer terminals with internet access that depend on telephone calling cards.

TIME ZONES

Brazil has four time zones but the majority of the country is within the Brasília time zone (3 hours behind GMT). Mato Grosso, Mato Grosso do Sul, Rondônia, Roraima, most of the Amazon and half of Pará are 1 hour behind Brasília. Acre and the southwestern portion of the Amazon is two hours behind Brasília. Fernando de Noronha located east of Brasília is 1 hour ahead. The southeast, south and central-west regions adjust their clocks for Daylight Saving Time between October and February, which puts them 1 hour ahead of their normal time relative to the rest of the country. If you are traveling close to the time change dates, verify the exact dates and check your flight times with the airline companies.

CLIMATE

Brazil's tropical location makes for a hot climate that, whether it's humid or not, has minimal differences between minimum and maximum temperatures. Throughout most of Brazil, between December and February, the somewhat hotter summer season is usually rainy. A colder and dryer winter prevails from June through August. The climatic differences of spring from September to December and autumn from March to June are less distinct. In the summer, the high relative humidity makes the atmosphere oppressive. In Rio de Janeiro the temperature at the beach may vary between 30°C (86°F) and 40°C (104°F). Porto Alegre, in Rio Grande do Sul, is cooler but is even more humid and heavy-aired. The northeastern coast is even hotter, although the humidity is lower and the constant ocean breeze alleviates discomfort. In the southern states there is a more distinct difference between the four seasons, and the winter is much colder. In some parts of the Gaucho Mountains, it even snows. Bitterly cold winds can sweep over the pampas and hills, pushing the cold air masses to Minas Gerais, São Paulo and Espírito Santo.

It rains all year, long although with different intensities, especially in the Amazon Region. Belém in Pará is one of the wettest cities in the world, and an downpour every afternoon is almost guaranteed. The region is more humid than hot, in contrast to the northeastern interior, with its long dry periods and torrential rains in the summer.

HOLIDAYS

Brazil's National Holidays include:
January 1st – New Year's Day
February / March – Carnival (floating date)
March / April – Easter (floating date)
April 21st – Tiradentes (in memory of the man who was hung for leading an independence movement in Brazil against the Portuguese crown)
May 1st – Labor Day
May / June – Corpus Christi (floating date)
September 7th – Independence Day
October 12th – Our Lady Aparecida
November 2nd – All Soul's Day
November 15th – Declaration of the Republic
December 25th – Christmas
There are also various regional holidays, such as São João, which is celebrated on June 24th in the rural areas in the Northeast.

CLIMATE & DRESS.

Visitors from the Northern Hemisphere need to keep in mind that the seasons in Brazil are the reverse of what they're used to. The southern region of the country experiences the most noticeable seasonal changes, ranging from steadily rainy in winter (June to August) to hot and humid in summer (December to February). This guide's map insert details average temperatures by month for different regions of the country. The wam average temperatures discourage formal clothing. Rio is particularly informal. Sao Paulo, on the other hand, favors more conservative fashion, in line with its business-minded orientation. For natural areas, where mosquitoes carry diseases, bring clothing that's long, loose-fitting, and preferably light in color.
HOURS Brazil uses military time, so 9am appears as 9h00, and 5pm appears as 17h00. Typical business hours are from 9am to 5pm.

EMERGENCY NUMBERS

The telephone numbers for emergency and support services are standardized throughout the country. They are toll-free numbers and calls may be made from any public telephone.
Military Police –190
Federal Highway Patrol – 191
Ambulance – 192
Fire Department – 193
Federal Police – 194
Civil Police – 147
State Highway Patrol – 198
Civil Defense – 199
Public Health and Drug and Food Administration – 150
Procon (Consumer Protection) – 151
Ibama (Brazilian Institute of Environmental and Renewable Natural Resources) – 152
Municipal Police – 153
Department of Transportation – 154
Emergencies in the Mercosul Region – 128

CONSULATES

ARGENTINA
Belo Horizonte – MG
Tel: (31) 3281-5288
Fax: (31) 3281-5288
Curitiba – PR
Tel: (41) 222-0799
Fax: (41) 223-0799
Florianópolis – SC
Tel: (48) 224-2841
Fax: (48) 224-5666
Foz do Iguaçu – PR
Tel: (45) 574-2969
Fax: (45) 574-2877
Porto Alegre – RS
Tel: (51) 3321-1360
Fax: (51) 3321-1360
Recife – PE
Tel: (81) 3327-1451
Fax: (81) 3327-1450
Rio de Janeiro – RJ
Tel: (21) 2553-1646
Fax: (21) 2552-4191
Salvador – BA
Tel: (71) 3241-4863
Fax: (71) 3241-4862
São Paulo – SP
Tel: (11) 3897-9522
Fax: (11) 3082-8019

AUSTRALIA
São Paulo – SP
Tel: (11) 3085-6247
Fax: (11) 3082-4140
www.cdasp.org.br

AUSTRIA
Rio de Janeiro – RJ
Tel: (21) 2102-0020
Fax: (21) 2521-6180

BELGIUM
Rio de Janeiro
Tel: (21) 2543-8558
Fax: (21) 2543-8398
www.diplobel.org
São Paulo – SP
Tel: (11) 3171-1599
Fax: (11) 3288-6869
www.diplomatie.br/saopaulo

BOLIVIA
Cuiabá - MT
Tel: (65) 381-5961
Fax: (65) 321-6833
Rio de Janeiro - RJ
Tel: (21) 2552-5490
Fax: (21) 2551-2395
São Paulo -SP
Tel: (11) 3081-1688
Fax: (11) 3068-0243

BULGARIA
Rio de Janeiro - RJ
Tel: (21) 2532-3912
Fax: (21) 2532-4604
www.bulgariario.org.br

CANADA
Belo Horizonte – MG
Tel: (31) 3261-1017
Fax: (31) 3261-1017

Rio de Janeiro – RJ
Tel: (21) 2543-3004
Fax: (21) 2275-2195
www.canada.org.br
São Paulo – SP
Tel: (11) 5509-4321
Fax: (11) 5509-4260

CHILE
Belém - PA
Tel: (91) 4005-5207
Fax: (91) 4005-5469
Belo Horizonte – MG
Tel: (31) 422-4415
Fax: (31) 422-4415
Campo Grande – MS
Tel: (67) 389-9052
Fax: (67) 324-8703
Curitiba – PR
Tel: (41) 225-1369
Fax: (41) 223-6980
Florianópolis – SP
Tel: (48) 224-2394
Fax: (48) 222-3360
Manaus – AM
Tel: (92) 236-9941
Fax: (92) 236-6888
Porto Alegre – RS
Tel: (51) 3346-3970
Fax: (51) 3346-3970
www.congechile.com.br
Recife - PE
Tel: (81) 3224-3740
Fax: (81) 3224-2834
Rio de Janeiro – RJ
Tel: (21) 2552-5349
Fax: (21) 2553-6371
Salvador – BA
Tel: (71) 3345-4141
Fax: (71) 3248-3618
São Paulo – SP
Tel: (11) 3284-2044
Fax: (11) 3284-2097

CHINA
São Paulo – SP
Tel: (11) 3082-9877
Fax: (11) 3064-2531
www.embchina.org.br

COLOMBIA
São Paulo – SP
Tel: (11) 3078-0322
Fax: (11) 3078-0298

COSTA RICA
Rio de Janeiro – RJ
Tel: (21) 2522-8899
Fax: (21) 2522-8833

CROATIA
São Paulo – SP
Tel: (11) 3815-4375
Fax: (11) 3815-4375

CUBA
São Paulo - SP
Tel: (11) 3873-2800
Fax: (11) 3864-5052

CZECH REPUBLIC
São Paulo – SP
Tel: (11) 3814-3728

Fax: (11) 3031-1822
www.mzv.cz/saopaulo

DENMARK
São Paulo – SP
Tel: (11) 3061-3625/3068-9867
Fax: (11) 3068-9867

DOMINICAN REPUBLIC
São Paulo – SP
Tel: (11) 3288-2459
Fax: (11) 3288-2459

ECUADOR
São Paulo – SP
Tel: (11) 3031-7004
Fax: (11) 3031-7004
www.consulecuadorsp.com.br

FINLAND
São Paulo - SP
Tel: (11) 5087-9542
Fax: (11) 5087-9520
www.finlandia.org.br

FRANCE
Belo Horizonte – MG
Tel: (31) 4501-3649
Fax: (31) 4501-3601
Campo Grande - MS
Tel: (67) 321-0339
Fax: (67) 321-0339
Curitiba – PR
Tel: (41) 320-5805
Fax: (41) 320-5805
Florianópolis – SC
Tel: (48) 221-9900
Fax: (48) 221-9901
Foz do Iguaçu – PR
Tel: (45) 529-6850
Fax: (45) 529-6850
Maceió – AL
Tel: (82) 221-9001
Fax: (82) 221-9001
Natal- RN
Tel: (84) 217-4558
Porto Alegre – RS
Tel: (51) 3222-6467
Fax: (51) 3222-6467
www.consulfrance-sp.org
Porto Seguro – BA
Tel: (73) 668-1661
Fax: (73) 668-1661
Recife – PE
Tel: (81) 3465-3290
Fax: (81) 3466-3599
Salvador – BA
Tel: (71) 3241-0168
Fax: (71) 3245- 5648
São Luís - MA
Tel: (98) 3231- 4458
Fax: (98) 3232-7746
São Paulo – SP
Tel: (11) 3371-5400
Fax : (11) 3371-5410
www.consulfrance-saopaulo.org
Rio de Janeiro – RJ
Tel: (21) 3974-6699
Fax: (21) 3974-6861
Vitória – ES
Tel: (27) 3331-3400
Fax: (27) 3322-6133

GERMANY
Belo Horizonte – MG
Tel: (31) 3213-1568
Fax: (31) 3213-1567
Curitiba - PR
Tel: (41) 222-6920
Fax: (41) 222-0322
Fortaleza – CE
Tel: (85) 3246-2833/2091
Fax: (85) 3246-7099
Manaus - AM
Tel: (92) 622-8800
Fax: (92) 622-8800
Porto Alegre – RS
Tel: (51) 3224-9255
Fax: (51) 3226-4909
www.alemanha.org.br/portoalegre/
Recife – PE
Tel: (81) 3463-5350
Fax: (81) 3465-4084
www.alemanha.org.br/recife/
Rio de Janeiro – RJ
Tel: (21) 2554-0004
Fax: (21) 2553-0184
www.alemanha.org.br/riodejaneiro/
Salvador – BA
Tel: (71) 3334-7106
Fax: (71) 3334-7106
São Paulo - SP
Tel: (11) 3097-6644
Fax: (11) 3815-7538
www.alemanha.org.br/saopaulo/
Vitória
Tel: (27) 3224-5387
Fax: (27) 3345-8202

GREECE
São Paulo - SP
Tel: (11) 3251-0675/283-1231
Fax: (11) 3289-0178

GUATEMALA
São Paulo - SP
Tel: (11) 3285-0586
Fax: (11) 3266- 6603

GUYANA
Brasília - DF
Tel: (61) 248-0874
Fax: (61) 248-0886

HONDURAS
São Paulo – SP
Tel: (11) 3088-2993
Fax: (11) 3088-2993

HUNGARY
São Paulo – SP
Tel: (11) 5506-5011
Fax: (11) 5506-4321
www.hungria.org.br

ICELAND
Rio de Janeiro – RJ
Tel: (21) 2285-1795
Fax: (21) 2205-0581

INDIA
São Paulo – SP
Tel: (11) 3171-0340/0341
Fax: (11) 3171-0342
www.indiaconsulate.org.br

IRAN
Brasília – DF
Tel: (61) 242-5733
Fax: (61) 244-9640

IRELAND
São Paulo – SP
Tel: (11) 3287-6362

ISRAEL
Brasília – DF
Tel: (61) 2105-0500
Fax: (61) 2105-0555

ITALY
Belo Horizonte – MG
Tel: (31) 3281-4211/4224
Fax: (31) 3281-4408
www.conbelo.org.br
Curitiba – PR
Tel: (41) 304-1750
Fax: (41) 304-6451
www.concuri.org.br
Porto Alegre – RS
Tel: (51) 3230-8200
Fax: (51) 3230-8222
www.italconsulpoa.org.br
Recife – PE
Tel: (81) 3466-4200
Fax: (81) 3466-4320
www.italconsulrecife.org.br
Rio de Janeiro – RJ
Tel: (21) 2282-1315
Fax: (21) 2262-6348/2220-3460
www.conrio.org.br
São Paulo – SP
Tel: (11) 3663-7800
Fax: (11) 3825-6443
www.italconsul.org.br

JAPAN
Belém – PA
Tel: (91) 249-3344
Fax: (91) 249-1016
Belo Horizonte – MG
Tel: (31) 3499-9620
Fax: (31) 3499-8475
Brasília – DF
Tel: (61) 442-4200
Fax: (61) 242-0738
Curitiba – PR
Tel: (41) 322-4919
Fax: (41) 222-0499
Manaus – AM
Tel: (92) 232-2000
Fax (92) 232-6073
Porto Alegre – RS
Tel: (51) 3334-1299
Fax: (51) 3334-1742
Recife – PE
Tel: (81) 3465-9115
Fax: (81) 3465-9140
Rio de Janeiro – RJ
Tel: (21) 3461-9595
Fax: (21) 3235-2241
www.rio.br.emb-japan.go.jp
Salvador – BA
Tel: (71) 3266-0527
Fax: (71) 3356-5292
São Paulo – SP
Tel: (11) 3254-0100
Fax: (11) 3254-0110
www.sp.br.emb-japan.go.jp

LEBANON
São Paulo – SP
Tel: (11) 3262-0604/0534

LIBYA
Brasília – DF
Tel: (61) 248-6710
Fax: (61) 248-0598

MALTA
Rio de Janeiro – RJ
Tel: (21) 2533-7274
Fax (21) 2533-7250

MEXICO
Belém – PA
Tel: (91) 223-8967/241-7407
Fax (91) 241-7407
Brasília – DF
Tel: (61) 244-1011/6866
Fax: (61) 244-755
Manaus – AM
Tel: (92) 663-5050
Fax: (92) 663-5077
Olinda – PE
Tel: (81) 3429-2088
Fax (81) 3429-2818
Rio de Janeiro – RJ
Tel: (21) 2553-2059/2552-9496
Fax: (21) 2551-3247
www.mexico.org.br
São Luís – MA
Tel: (98) 3232-6732/6232
Fax (98) 3232-6732
São Paulo – SP
Tel: (11) 3081-4144
Fax (11) 3082-4319

NETHERLANDS
São Paulo – SP
Tel: (11) 3811-3300
Fax: (11) 3814-0802

NEW ZEALAND
São Paulo – SP
Tel: (11) 3148-0616
Fax: (11) 3148-2521

NICARAGUA
Brasília – DF
Tel: (61) 248-1115/7902
Fax: (61) 248-1120

NORWAY
Brasília – DF
Tel: (61) 443-8720/8722
Fax: (61) 443-2942

PANAMA
São Paulo-SP
Tel: (11) 3129-4748
Fax: (11) 3120-5482

PARAGUAY
Belo Horizonte – MG
Tel: (31) 3344-6349
Fax (31) 3344-6349
Brasília – DF
Tel: (61) 242-3732
Fax (61) 242-4605
Campo Grande – MS
Tel: (67) 384-6610
Fax (67) 384-6610
Curitiba – PR
Tel: (41) 222-9226
Fax (41) 222-9226
Porto Alegre – RS
Tel: (51) 3241-9576
Fax (51) 3241-9576
Recife – PE
Tel: (81) 3459-1277
Fax: (81) 3459-1277
Rio de Janeiro – RJ
Tel: (21) 2553-2294
Fax (21) 2553-2512

São Paulo – SP
Tel: (11) 3167-7793
Fax (11) 3167-0412
www.paraguaisp.com.br

PERU
São Paulo – SP
Tel: (11) 3819-1793
Fax (11) 3819-1795

POLAND
São Paulo – SP
Tel: (11) 3672-3778
Fax: (11) 3672-8224

PORTUGAL
Belém – PA
Tel: (91) 241-6666/9994
Fax: (91) 241-1181
www.consportbelem.org.br
Belo Horizonte – MG
Tel: (31) 3291-8192
Fax: (31) 3291-8064
Brasília – DF
Tel: (61) 3032-9600
Fax: (61) 3032-9627
Curitiba – PR
Tel: (41) 233-4211
Fax: (41) 222-1190
Fortaleza – CE
Tel: (85) 3261-7420
Fax: (85) 3261-7421
www.consulportugalfortaleza.org.br
João Pessoa – PB
Tel: (83) 226-2120
Fax: (83) 247-1438
Maceió - AL
Tel: (82) 336-4564
Manaus – AM
Tel: (92) 633-1577
Fax: (92) 234-6474
Porto Alegre – RS
Tel: (51) 3224-5767
Fax: (51) 3228-0087
Recife – PE
Tel: (81) 3327-2073/1514
Fax: (81) 3467-8487
Rio de Janeiro – RJ
Tel: (21) 2544-2444/2523
Fax: (21) 2544-3382
www.consuladorj.org.br
Salvador – BA
Tel: (71) 3241-1633
Fax: (71) 3241-1756
São Paulo – SP
Tel: (11) 3084-1800
Fax: (11) 3085-5633
www.consuladoportugalsp.org.br

RUSSIA
São Paulo – SP
Tel: (11) 3064-1591
Fax: (11) 3064-1591

SAUDI ARABIA
Brasília – DF
Tel: (61) 248-3525
Fax: (61) 248-2905

SLOVAKIA
São Paulo – SP
Tel: (11) 3255-9493
Fax: (11) 3255-9493

SOUTH AFRICA
São Paulo – SP
Tel: (11) 3285-0433/3265-0449

Fax: (11) 3284-4862
www.africadosulemb.org.br

SOUTH KOREA
São Paulo – SP
Tel: (11) 3141-1278
Fax: (11) 3141-1279

SPAIN
Belo Horizonte – MG
Tel: (31) 3326-5971
Fax: (31) 3326-5971
Cuiabá - MT
Tel: (65) 682-3840
Fax: (65) 682-3734
Curitiba - PR
Tel: (41) 246-1408
Fax: (41) 346-3377
Natal – RN
Tel: (84) 234-6950
Fax: (84) 2346950
Porto Alegre – RS
Tel: (51) 3338-1300
Fax: (51) 3338-1444
Rio de Janeiro – RJ
Tel: (21) 2543-3200
Fax: (21) 2543-3096
Salvador - BA
Tel: (71) 3336-9055
Fax: (71) 3336-0266
São Luís – MA
Tel: (98) 243-6039
Fax: (98) 232-5081
São Paulo – SP
Tel: (11) 3059-1800
Fax: (11) 3889-8412
Vitória – ES
Tel: (27) 3347-2141
Fax: (27) 3328-2274

SURINAME
Brasília – DF
Tel: (61) 248-3595
Fax (61) 248-3791

SWEDEN
São Paulo – SP
Tel: (11) 3061-1700
Fax (11) 3063-3267

SWITZERLAND
Belo Horizonte – MG
Tel: (31) 3261-7732
Fax (31) 3262-1163
Brasília – DF
Tel: (61) 443-5500
Fax: (61) 443-5711
Fortaleza – CE
Tel: (85) 3226-9444
Fax (85) 3253-1323
Recife – PE
Tel: (81) 3439-4545
Fax (81) 3439-4545
Rio de Janeiro – RJ
Tel: (21) 2221-1867
Fax (21) 2252-3991
Salvador – BA
Tel: (71) 3341-5827
Fax (71) 3341-5826
São Paulo – SP
Tel: (11) 3372-8200
Fax (11) 3253-5716

SYRIA
São Paulo – SP
Tel: (11) 3285-5578
Fax (11) 3253-9290

TURKEY
Belo Horizonte – MG
Tel: (31) 3337-7766
Fax: (31) 3292-9499
Brasília – DF
Tel: (61) 242-1850
Fax (61) 242-1448
Rio de Janeiro – RJ
Tel: (21) 2553-5716
Fax: (21) 2553-5934
Salvador – BA
Tel: (71) 3335-1064
Fax: (71) 3335-1064

UKRAINE
Curitiba - PR
Tel: (41) 222-7773
Fax: (41) 222-7773
Rio de Janeiro – RJ
Tel: (21) 2542-1704
Fax: (21) 2275-1027

UNITED ARAB EMIRATES
Brasília – DF
Tel: (61) 248-0717, extension 212
Fax: (61) 248-7543

UNITED KINGDOM
Belo Horizonte – MG
Tel: (31) 3261-2072
Fax: (31) 3261-0226
www.reinounido.org.br
Brasília - DF
Tel: (61) 329-2300
Fax: (61) 329-2369
Curitiba - PR
Tel: (41) 322-1202
Fax: (41) 322-1202
Recife - PE
Tel: (81) 3465-0230
Fax: (81) 3465-0247
Rio de Janeiro – RJ
Tel: (21) 2555-9600
Fax: (21) 2555-9671
www.gra-bretanha.org.br
São Paulo - SP
Tel: (11) 3094-2700
Fax: (11) 3094-1899

UNITED STATES
Belém - PA
Tel: (91) 223-0800
Fax: (91) 223-0413
Fortaleza - CE
Tel: (85) 3252-1539
Fax: (85) 3252-1539
Manaus -AM
Tel: (92) 611-3333
Fax: (92) 611-3333
Porto Alegre - RS
Tel: (51) 226-3344
Fax: (51) 226-3344
Recife – PE
Tel: (81) 3421-2441
Fax: (81) 3231-1906
Rio de Janeiro – RJ
Tel: (21) 2292-7117
Fax: (21) 2220-0439
www.consuladoseua-rio.org.br
Salvador - BA
Tel: (71) 3113-2091
Fax: (71) 3113-2090
São Paulo – SP
Tel: (11) 5186-7000
Fax: (11) 5186-7159

URUGUAY
Belo Horizonte – MG
Tel: (31) 3296-7527
Fax (31) 3296-7291
Brasília – DF
Tel: (61) 322-1200/4528
Fax (61) 322-6534
Curitiba – PR
Tel: (41) 225-5550
Fax: (41) 232-0436
Florianópolis – SC
Tel: (48) 222-3718
Fax: (48) 222-3718
Porto Alegre – RS
Tel: (51) 3325-6196

Fax (51) 3325-6192
Rio de Janeiro – RJ
Tel: (21) 2553-6015/6030
Fax (21) 2553-6036
Salvador – BA
Tel: (71) 3322-7093
Fax (71) 3322-7096
São Paulo – SP
Tel: (11) 3085-5941
Fax (11) 3088-7874

VENEZUELA
Belém – PA
Tel: (91) 242-7783/241-7574
Fax (91) 242-7783/241-7574

Brasília – DF
Tel: (61) 322-1011/2101-1004/2101-1012
Fax: (61) 226-5633
Rio de Janeiro – RJ
Tel: (21) 2551-5248
Fax (21) 2553-8118
www.consuven.com.br
São Paulo – SP
Tel: (11) 3887-4583
Fax (11) 3887-2535

EMBASSIES

MINISTRY OF FOREIGN RELATIONS
www.mre.gov.br
Tel: (61) 411-6161

EMBASSIES IN BRASÍLIA

Algeria
Tel: (61) 248-4039/248-1949
Fax: (61) 248-4691

Angola
www.angola.org.br
Tel: (61) 248-4489/248-2915
Fax: (61) 248-1567

Argentina
www.embarg.org.br
Tel: (61) 364-7600
Fax: (61) 364-7666

Australia
www.brazil.embassy.gov.au
Tel: (61) 226-3111
Fax: (61) 226-1112

Austria
www.austria.org.br
Tel: (61) 443-3111/443-3373
Fax: (61) 443-5233

Belgium
www.belgica.org.br
Tel: (61) 443-1133
Fax: (61) 443-1219

Bolivia
www.embolivia-brasil.org.br
Tel: (61) 366-3432
Fax: (61) 366-3136

Bulgaria
Tel: (61) 223-6193/223-9849
Fax: (61) 323-3285

Cameroon
www.embcameroun.org.br
Tel: (61) 248-5403/248-2400
Fax: (61) 248-0443

Canada
www.dfait-maeci.gc.ca/brazil
Tel: (61) 424-5400
Fax: (61) 424-5490

Cape Verde
Tel: (61) 248-0543/364-3472
Fax: (61) 364-4059

Chile
www.eta.com.br/chile
Tel: (61) 2103-5151
Fax: (61) 322-0714

China
www.embchina.org.br
Tel: (61) 346-4436/346-1880
Fax: (61) 346-3299

Colombia
www.embcol.org.br
Tel: (61) 226-8997/226-8902
Fax: (61) 224-4732

Costa Rica
Tel: (61) 328-2219/328-2485
Fax: (61) 328-2243

Croatia
Tel: (61) 248-0610/248-7855
Fax: (61) 248-1708

Cuba
www.embaixadacuba.org.br
Tel: (61) 248-4710/248-4130
Fax: (61) 248-6778

Czech Republic
www.mzv.cz/brasilia
Tel: (61) 242-7785/242-7905
Fax: (61) 242-7833

Democratic Republic of Congo
Tel: (61) 552-0335
Fax: (61) 365-4823

Denmark
www.denmark.org.br
Tel: (61) 445-3443
Fax: (61) 445-3509

Dominican Republic
Tel: (61) 248-1405
Fax: (61) 364-3214

Ecuador
www.embequador.org.br
Tel: (61) 248-5560
Fax: (61) 248-1290

Egypt
www.opengate.com.br/embegito
Tel: (61) 323-8800
Fax: (61) 323-1039

El Salvador
Tel: (61) 364-4141
Fax: (61) 364-2459

Finland
www.finlandia.org.br
Tel: (61) 443-7151
Fax: (61) 443-3315

France
www.ambafrance.org.br
Tel: (61) 312-9100
Fax: (61) 312-9108

Gabon
Tel: (61) 248-3536/248-3533
Fax: (61) 248-2241

Germany
www.alemanha.org.br
Tel: (61) 442-7000
Fax: (61) 443-7508

Ghana
Tel: (61) 248-6047/248-6049
Fax: (61) 248-7913

Greece
www.emb-grecia.org.br
Tel: (61) 443-6573
Fax: (61) 443-6902

Guatemala
Tel: (61) 365-1908/365-1909
Fax: (61) 365-1906

Guyana
Tel: (61) 248-0874/248-0875/364-5319
Fax: (61) 248-0886

Haiti
Tel: (61) 248-6860/248-1337
Fax: (61) 248-7472

Honduras
Tel: (61) 366-4082
Fax: (61) 366-4618

Hungary
www.hungria.org.br
Tel: (61) 443-0836/443-0822
Fax: (61) 443-3434

India
www.indianembassy.org.br
Tel: (61) 364-4195/248-4006
Fax: (61) 248-7849

Indonesia
www.indonesia-brasil.org.br
Tel: (61) 443-8800/443-1788
Fax: (61) 443-6732

Iran
www.webiran.org.br
Tel: (61) 242-5733
Fax: (61) 244-9640

Iraq
Tel: (61) 346-2822/346-6612
Fax: (61) 346-7034/346-7442

Ireland
Tel: (61) 248-8800
Fax: (61) 248-8816

Israel
brasilia.mfa.gov.il
Tel: (61) 2105-0500
Fax: (61) 2105-0555

Italy
www.embitalia.org.br
Tel: (61) 442-9900
Fax: (61) 443-1231

Japan
www.japao.org.br
Tel: (61) 442-4200
Fax: (61) 242-0738

Jordan
Tel: (61) 248-5407/248-5414
Fax: (61) 248-1698

Kuwait
www.embaixadadokuwait.org.br
Tel: (61) 248-2323
Fax: (61) 248-0969

Lebanon
www.libano.org.br
Tel: (61) 443-5552/443-3808
Fax: (61) 443-8574

Libya
Tel: (61) 248-6710/248-6716
Fax: (61) 248-0598

Malaysia
Tel: (61) 248-5008/248-6215
Fax: (61) 248-6307

Malta
Tel: (61) 272-0402
Fax: (61) 347-4940

Mexico
www.mexico.org.br
Tel: (61) 244-1011/244-1211
Fax: (61) 244-1755

Morocco
www.embmarrocos.org.br
Tel: (61) 321-4487/321-3994
Fax: (61) 321-0745

Mozambique
Tel: (61) 248-4222/248-5319
Fax: (61) 248-3917

Namibia
Tel: (61) 248-6274/248-7621
Fax: (61) 248-7135

Netherlands
www.embaixada-holanda.org.br
Tel: (61) 321-4769
Fax: (61) 321-1518

New Zealand
Tel: (61) 248-9900
Fax: (61) 248-9916

Nicaragua
Tel: (61) 248-1115/248-7902
Fax: (61) 248-1120

Nigeria
Tel: (61) 226-1717/226-1870
Fax: (61) 226-5192

North Korea
Tel: (61) 244-6544
Fax: (61) 244-6544

Norway
www.noruega.org.br
Tel: (61) 443-8720/443-8722
Fax: (61) 443-2942

Pakistan
Tel: (61) 364-1632/364-1761
Fax: (61) 248-0246

Panama
Tel: (61) 248-7309/248-7423
Fax: (61) 248-2834

Paraguay
Tel: (61) 242-3732/244-8649
Fax: (61) 242-4605

Peru
www.embperu.org.br
Tel: (61) 242-9933/242-9435
Fax: (61) 244-9344

Philippines
Tel: (61) 224-8694/223-5143
Fax: (61) 226-7411

Poland
www.polonia.org.br
Tel: (61) 443-3438/242-9273
Fax: (61) 242-8543

Portugal
www.embaixadadeportugal.org.br
Tel: (61) 3032-9600
Fax: (61) 3032-9642

Romania
www.romenia.org.br
Tel: (61) 226-0746
Fax: (61) 226-6629

Russia
www.brazil.mid.ru
Tel: (61) 223-3094/223-4094
Fax: (61) 226-7319

Saudi Arabia
Tel: (61) 248-3525/248-2201
Fax: (61) 248-2905

Senegal
Tel: (61) 223-6110/321-5866
Fax: (61) 322-7822

Serbia and Montenegro
Tel: (61) 223-7272
Fax: (61) 223-8462

Slovakia
Tel: (61) 443-1263/443-1265
Fax: (61) 443-1267

South Africa
www.africadosulemb.org.br
Tel: (61) 312-9500
Fax: (61) 322-8491

South Korea
www.korea.net
Tel: (61) 321-2500
Fax: (61) 321-2508

Spain
Tel: (61) 244-2776/244-2023/244-2145
Fax: (61) 242-1781

Sri Lanka
Tel:(61) 248-2701
Fax: (61) 364-5430

Syria
Tel: (61) 226-1260/226-0970
Fax: (61) 223-2595

Sudan
www.sudanbrasilia.org
Tel: (61) 248-4834/248-4835
Fax: (61) 248-4833

Suriname
Tel: (61) 248-3595/248-6706
Fax: (61) 248-3791

Sweden
Tel: (61) 443-1444
Fax: (61) 443-1187

Switzerland
www.eda.admin.ch/brasilia_emb
Tel: (61) 443-5500
Fax: (61) 443-5711

Thailand
www.thaiembassy.org/brasilia
Tel: (61) 224-6943/224-6849
Fax: (61) 223-7502

Trinidad and Tobago
Tel: (61) 365-1132/365-3466
Fax: (61) 365-1733

Tunisia
Tel: (61) 248-7277/248-7366
Fax: (61) 248-7355

Turkey
www.turquia.org.br
Tel: (61) 242-1850/244-4840
Fax: (61) 242-1448

Ukraine
www.ucrania.org.br
Tel: (61) 365-1457
Fax: (61) 365- 2127/365-3898

United Arab Emirates
www.uae.org.br
Tel: (61) 248-0717/248-0591
Fax: (61) 248-7543

United Kingdom
www.uk.org.br
Tel: (61) 329-2300
Fax: (61) 329-2369

United States
www.embaixada-americana.org.br
Tel: (61) 312-7000
Fax: (61) 312-7651

Uruguay
www.emburuguai.org.br
Tel: (61) 322-1200
Fax: (61) 322-6534

Vatican
Tel: (61) 223-0794
Fax: (61) 224-9365

Venezuela
Tel: (61) 322-1011/322-9962
Fax: (61) 226-5633

Vietnam
Tel: (61) 364-5876/364-0694
Fax: (61) 364-5836

Zimbabwe
Tel: (61) 365-4801/365-4802
Fax: (61) 365-4803

INDEX

Acknowledgments: Alexandra Vianna, Ana Lúcia Ribeiro, Antonio Moreira Salles, Antonio Pires Monteiro, Bia Fonseca Corrêa do Lago, Carla Joner, Carlos Martins, Carlos Souza, Claudia Moreira Salles, Cristiano Mascaro, Daniela Aslan, Edu Simões, Eduardo Brazão, Gabriela Monteiro, Gilberto P. de Freitas Sá, Helena Margarida Duque Estrada Lopes, Hélio de Almeida, João Gabriel de Lima, João Moreira Salles, José Mindlin, Juan Pablo Queiroz, Joaquim Francisco da Cunha Francisco, Juca Martins, Jun Sakamoto, Lélia Wanick Salgado, Leonor Alvim Brazão, Lúcia Moreira Salles, Luiz Sandler, Marcelo Ferraz, Marcos Moraes, Maria Beatriz Oliveira Valle, Maria Helena Carneiro da Cunha, Maurício Botelho, Mauro Teixeira Leite, Nancy Colina de Bernabó, Randy Charles Epping, Rogério Braga, Rogério Scofano, Rui Alvim, Tomas de Elias, Valentina Violante, Zélia Judith Loss and Zuenir Ventura

Photo Credits